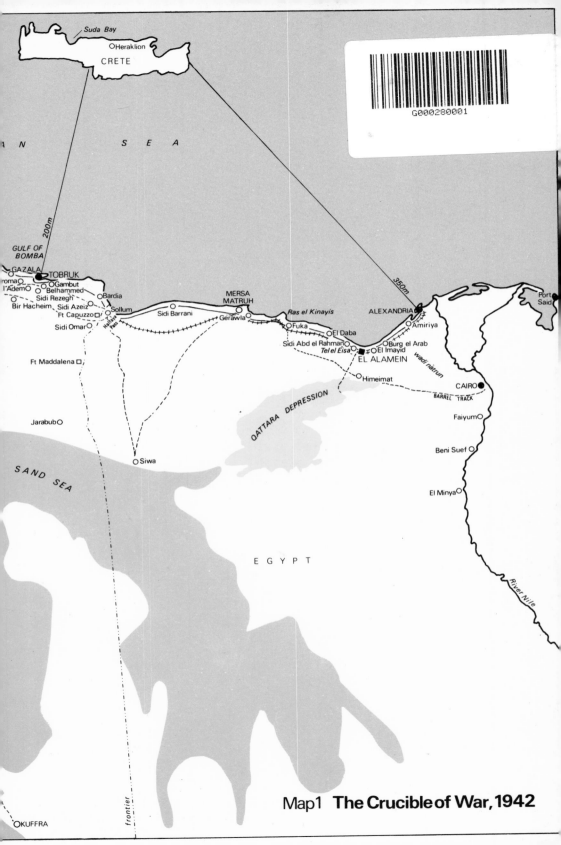

Suda Bay

OHeraklion

CRETE

200m

SEA

A N

GULF OF
BOMBA

GAZALA

roma

l'Adem

TOBRUK

Gambut

Belhammed

Sidi Rezegh

Bardia

Bir Hacheim

Sidi Azeiz

Ft Capuzzo

Sidi Omar

Sollum

Sidi Barrani

MERSA
MATRUH

Gerawla

Ras el Kinayis

Fuka

El Daba

ALEXANDRIA

Amiriya

Sidi Abd el Rahman

Burg el Arab

Tel el Eisa

El Imayid

EL ALAMEIN

350m

Port
Said

Ft Maddalena

wadi natrun

Himeimat

CAIRO

BARREL TRACK

Jarabub

QATTARA DEPRESSION

Faiyum

Siwa

Beni Suef

SAND SEA

El Minya

E G Y P T

River Nile

frontier

OKUFFRA

Map 1 The Crucible of War, 1942

The Crucible of War

YEAR OF ALAMEIN 1942

BARRIE PITT

The Crucible of War

Year of Alamein 1942

JONATHAN CAPE
THIRTY BEDFORD SQUARE LONDON

First published 1982
Copyright © 1982 by Barrie Pitt
Jonathan Cape Ltd, 30 Bedford Square, London WC1

British Library Cataloguing in Publication Data

Pitt, Barrie
The crucible of war.
Year of Alamein 1942.
1 World War, 1939–1945 – Campaigns – Africa,
North
I. Title
940.54′23   D766.82

ISBN 0-224-01827-2

Photoset by Rowland Phototypesetting Ltd
Bury St Edmunds, Suffolk
Printed in Great Britain by
Ebenezer Baylis & Son Ltd
The Trinity Press, Worcester and London

To Frances
with love and gratitude

Contents

Illustrations

FIGURES

The author and publishers wish to thank the following for permission to reproduce photographs: the Imperial War Museum, for plates 2, 7–9, 12–15, 17–18, 20–4, 26–9, and 33; Major-General G. P. B. Roberts for plate 16; the National Archives, Washington, for plates 5, 6 and 19; the Special Air Service Regimental Association for plates 3 and 4; Sado/Opera Mundi for plate 10; Australian War Memorial, Canberra, for plates 25 (neg. no. 129000), 30 (neg. no. 42070) and 31 (neg. no. 14124); Bundesarchiv, Koblenz, for plate 1; and Bibliothek für Zeitgeschichte for plates 11 and 32.

They would also like to thank Mr John Batchelor for permission to use his line drawings, figures 1–7, and also the authors, publishers and copyright holders of quotations used in the text and listed in the Notes.

Author's Note

Once again I must offer my thanks to the librarians, fellow historians, archivists and survivors of the various actions described herein, who have given me so freely of their time, their expertise or their memories. This second volume of the trilogy would have been, as the first one was and the third one undoubtedly will be, impossible to write without them.

In particular I would like to acknowledge my debt to, and also express my affection for, the late Field Marshal Viscount Montgomery of Alamein, K.G., G.C.B., D.S.O., whose kindness to me, albeit peppered with occasional acerbity, remains among my fondest memories. I would also like to thank the late Field Marshal Sir Claude Auchinleck and his erstwhile Chief of Staff the late Major-General Eric Dorman O'Gowan, for the time they spent answering my questions, and, in the case of General O'Gowan, dilating upon their answers.

Happily, there are many more I must thank who are still with us. Both Field Marshal Lord Carver and Major-General Douglas Wimberley were instrumental in correcting an egregiously biased impression I had formed of one of the principal characters in the story which follows, and to them and to both Lady Carver and Mrs Wimberley I must express gratitude for the hospitality they showed me while the operation was in progress. To General Sir John Hackett and Major-General G. P. D. 'Pip' Roberts I must express thanks for answering my questions and allowing me to quote from their answers, and as in the first volume I am again indebted to Generals Walther Nehring and Walter Warlimont. Professor Lucio Ceva has also earned my gratitude for his help in identifying Italian formations in both the main battles described, and also for elucidating the Italian Orders of Battle.

Finally, I must again thank Jane Caunt for retyping the book, Deborah Shepherd for so sympathetically editing it, and this time Frances Mary Moore for drawing the maps and composing the index.

Prologue

It was very cold during the closing days of 1941 along that stretch of the Libyan coast which runs south from Benghasi down to Mersa Brega, and the uncomfortable Indian and British troops of the Eighth Army and the equally uncomfortable Italians and Germans of Panzergruppe Afrika were unanimous in their condemnation of the barren countryside, of the rapacity, vulturine appearance and occasionally murderous activity of the indigenous inhabitants, and especially of the gales which swept eastward across the Gulf of Sirte, drenching them into shivering, sodden immobility or lashing them with sand miraculously dried out and lifted within minutes of the ceasing of the rainstorms. Those who had welcomed their transfer from home with visions of Mediterranean sunshine and subtropical romance cursed their luck and longed for the more moderate climes of Europe.

For the Scots and Coldstream Guardsmen and especially the British tank crews of the 22nd Armoured Brigade down in the south of the area, grouped around the German-held positions at Agedabia, it was an especially bad time. An attack by the Guards during the night of December 26th/27th had gone astray during its approach march and as a result lacked its promised armoured support – which had done nothing to foster the spirit of Christmas good fellowship between infantry and armour in that particular area – while on the following day, some sixty panzers of Rommel's combined armoured divisions had suddenly descended upon 22nd Armoured Brigade and driven it over the Wadi Faregh with a loss of thirty-seven mixed Stuart and Crusader tanks. The survivors had circled around and regrouped at the thoroughly inhospitable cluster of near-hovels which rejoiced in the name of Belandah, but their hopes that they would be given time for recuperation there were in vain; on the penultimate day of the year, another posse of Panzer Mark IVs sought them out and in a sharp and vicious action destroyed yet another twenty-two British tanks before retiring, leaving but seven panzers wrecked and smoking on the field of battle.

It was not only depressing – it was also bewildering, for Panzer-

gruppe Afrika had just been thoroughly beaten, as was demonstrable
by a look at the map. Six weeks before, German and Italian troops
under their redoubtable commander, General Rommel, had stood on
the Egyptian frontier, the rich plunder of the Nile Delta only 250
miles away; now they were back on the borders of Tripolitania and
nearly 600 miles separated them from the fleshpots of Cairo and
Alexandria.

Operation Crusader had been a bitter battle – or series of battles –
with a constant see-sawing at first between the Egyptian frontier and
the desolate wastes lying to the south of Tobruk; but in the end,
Panzergruppe Afrika had been forced to retire, first to Gazala, then
through the green but bedraggled hills of the Cyrenaican bulge, and
finally on Christmas day out of Benghasi to this isolated, cold and
surely God-forsaken spot – en route, so everybody in Eighth Army
hoped, for El Agheila and all stops westward at least as far as Tripoli.

Now, damn it, Afrika Korps were showing every sign of recovery –
the same spirit of aggression that had distinguished their every move
since their arrival in the desert nine months before, the same uncanny
ability to divine exactly where their opponents' weakest spot lay, the
same flair for exploitation, all welded together by a degree of military
efficiency which had impressed all who had witnessed it during the
last six apocalyptical weeks, especially if they had personally suffered
its results. Whatever had caused Afrika Korps's recent retreat, no
one in Eighth Army was under the illusion that it was lack of courage,
determination or military ability (the general opinion was that it was
probably the weakness of the Italian ally or perhaps lack of petrol or
ammunition). In view of the events of the last few days, what other
plans had Afrika Korps for British discomfiture?

There was thus a degree of apprehension among the Guardsmen
and tank crews spread between the Trig el Abd and the coast in the
area to the south of Antelat as the afternoon of December 31st, 1941,
darkened into its early night. Those who were to stand the later
guards ate their meagre rations of hot stew and drank their cocoa
early, then rolled themselves into their blankets in whatever shelter
they could find. Those on first stag carried out the routine evening
jobs and either patrolled their beats or stood together talking quietly
amongst themselves about the past day, the past week, the past
month. And in view of the date, some of them even discussed the past
year . . . and wondered what the new one would bring. But all the
time, they watched towards the south and west, where they knew the
men of the Afrika Korps waited, and wondered what they would do
next.

The answer, when it came, was sudden, spectacular, and totally
unexpected.

As the British sentries changed, the new watch grumbling and shivering after the warmth of their blankets, the old watch bone-chilled and longing for the warmth of theirs, the south-western horizon suddenly exploded in colour and sound. Red, green and white Very lights soared up and down in graceful parabolas, tracer bullets arched up into the sky, searchlights waved their pallid beams to light up the underside of the dank clouds, gun-flashes sparkled, hand-grenades burst – and then the noise came booming across the desert towards the watchers as they dived for their slit-trenches, ran to their posts, woke any comrades still luckily asleep, and prepared for action.

But as they watched and listened, a few became conscious that there was something missing. Among the crash of explosive and the rattle of fire, there was no roar of tank or lorry engine; and neither was there any whine of bullet or scream of shell passing overhead. And then, as suddenly as it had started, the sound and fury ceased . . . and adjutants glancing conscientiously at their watches in order that the event should be accurately recorded, found that it was exactly three minutes past midnight.

The Scots Guards south of Antelat were the first to react – doubt-less their own Hogmanay traditions had occupied their minds all evening – and theirs were the first Eighth Army Very lights to return the salute; but soon the idea spread along the line of British positions, and Brens fired arches of tracer, headlights were switched briefly on, a few grenades were hurled into the empty desert. It was not so spectacular as the *feu de joie* from around Antelat, but then it had not been planned and organised as, obviously, that one had been . . . but it was something.

'Well, well . . . ' remarked one observer. 'Fancy Jerry wishing us a Happy New Year!'

'He'd make it a bloody sight happier if he shoved off back behind Agheila,' one of his more disgruntled fellow officers replied.

So he was quite surprised when, the following day, Afrika Korps began to do just that.*

British troops had begun fighting in the Western Desert on June 11th, 1940 – twenty-four hours after Mussolini, in a hasty attempt to secure a position of advantage when the empires of France and Britain were divided up between the Axis Powers (a process which he thought might begin quite soon), had delivered an impassioned speech from

---

*There follows a résumé of events in North Africa from the outbreak of hostilities there on June 11th, 1940, to the end of Rommel's riposte of January 1942 which pushed the Eighth Army back to Gazala. Readers of *The Crucible of War: Western Desert 1941*, which covers this period in detail, may prefer to turn immediately to page 18.

the balcony of the Palazzo Venezia to a markedly unenthusiastic
crowd, at the end of which he declared war on both of those 'effete
democracies'.

The first troops into action had been those of the 11th Hussars –
the reconnaissance regiment of what later became famous as the 7th
Armoured Division – and during the weeks that followed, their
armoured cars and the cruiser tanks of 4th and 7th Armoured
Brigades had carried out widespread and damaging raids on the
Italian posts along the Egyptian–Cyrenaican border between Sollum
on the coast and Fort Maddalena fifty miles to the south. They had
even carried out one raid down to Jarabub on the edge of the
Kalansho Sand Sea, and been defeated there more by the appalling
heat than by any Italian military ardour.

Then in September 1940, under increasing pressure from Mussolini,
the Italian commander in North Africa, Maresciallo Rodolfo Graziani,
had launched an attack by the Italian Tenth Army across the border
which advanced as far as Sidi Barrani where it halted, apparently
lacking the equipment or fuel – or perhaps the energy or the will – to
proceed further. The armour and infantry of the 7th Armoured
Division had retreated slowly in the face of this advance, maintaining
contact with the Italians and harassing them with minor but irritating
attacks, and when Graziani's forces settled down and began building
a series of what were evidently intended to be semi-permanent camps
stretching in an arc southwestwards from Sidi Barrani, the 11th
Hussars took up close observation positions and all began preparations for reprisal.

The Armoured Division had now been joined by the Sikhs.
Punjabis, Rajputs, Mahrattas and the British battalions of the 4th
Indian Division, the combination taking the name Western Desert
Force and coming under command of one of Britain's most imagin-
ative and competent soldiers, Lieutenant-General Sir Richard
O'Connor. He by then had received orders from General Wavell, the
British Commander-in-Chief, Middle East, to expel the intruders
as expeditiously as possible despite the fact that he would have at
his command but two divisions against the nine enemy divisions
now spread over the desert between Sidi Barrani and the
Egyptian frontier – a complication which apparently caused him little
apprehension.

Sir Richard O'Connor and his men began their attack on the night
of December 9th, 1940, and such was the success which attended
their efforts that by February 7th, 1941, they had not only expelled
Graziani's forces from Egypt, they had also driven them back across
Cyrenaica to the Tripolitanian border at El Agheila, thus completing
the first lap of what later became known by the irreverent as the
Benghasi Handicap. They had advanced five hundred miles in ten

weeks, completely destroyed the Italian Tenth Army and captured in the process 130,000 prisoners including seven generals.

It was an extraordinary feat for so small a force, especially as their own casualties in killed, wounded and missing amounted to fewer than two thousand, but unfortunately for the men who had carried it out (they had been joined shortly after the beginning of the operation by the 6th Australian Division) decisions taken in London, Cairo and Berlin were to rob them of the fruits of their victory. In the face of the imminent invasion of Greece by twelve German divisions, Whitehall and Cairo headquarters now ordered all available trained and equipped forces across the Mediterranean, so the Australians and a New Zealand division (which O'Connor had hoped would be available to speed his force onwards to Tripoli; but not, fortunately, the 7th Armoured Division whose tanks were worn out or the 4th Indian Division which had been sent to Ethiopia to help reduce the Italian Empire there) were transported to the Balkans, and their unhappy destruction as fighting units followed quite quickly. Meanwhile, in Berlin, Hitler, unwilling to allow the further military humiliation of his Italian ally, sent what he called a *Sperrverband* – a 'Blocking Force' – to North Africa, commanded by one of his favourite generals, Generalleutnant Erwin Johannes Eugen Rommel, who thereupon stepped on to the stage he was to dominate for many months.

It quickly became obvious that it was not in General Rommel's nature to hold defensive positions or even to fight defensive battles, especially when he had reason to believe that the enemy forces ranged against him were neither aggressively intentioned nor particularly well organised for their own protection. And of this he became more and more convinced.

Despite total lack of encouragement from his Italian allies in Tripolitania, and in blatant disobedience of orders from the *Oberkommando des Heeres* (High Command of the Army) in Berlin, he launched the armour of his own 5th Light Division and the armour and infantry of the Italian Ariete Division through the El Agheila defile on the morning of March 31st, 1941, and twenty-eight days later was occupying the old Italian positions on the Egyptian border at Fort Capuzzo and Sidi Omar, with a forward outpost at Halfaya Pass, ten miles inside Egypt. The second lap of the Benghasi Handicap had been even more spectacular than the first, and like the British advance westward of three months before, his own to the east had been achieved with remarkably few casualties. Moreover, although his forces had captured only three British generals, these had constituted an even more significant 'bag' than his opponents', for one of them had been Sir Richard O'Connor himself, for whom General Wavell immediately expressed his willingness to offer six

Italian generals in exchange. (The British Government quashed the idea on egalitarian grounds.)

The only circumstance which marred this lightning success was the failure to capture Tobruk, now some eighty miles behind Rommel's own front line, and held in large part by the 9th Australian Division, determined not to lose the port captured by their brothers in 6th Division. It was to prove a continual distraction to Rommel's further ambition and his attempts to storm its defences were to cause him serious losses in both men and material during the months which followed, though these to some extent were offset by the British losses in their own attempts to supply or relieve the garrison.

Of the first there were many by sea, and of the second two unsuccessful attempts by land. In May, the aptly named *Operation Brevity* was launched, to be easily repelled by Rommel's Afrika Korps using for the first time in the Desert War the remarkable 88mm. anti-aircraft gun in an anti-tank role; and then in June, Wavell ordered Lieutenant-General Sir Noel Beresford-Peirse, now commanding XIII Corps (as Western Desert Force had been renamed) to attack again across the frontier, his force strengthened by over a hundred new tanks which Prime Minister Churchill had insisted be rushed out to him across the Mediterranean, despite warnings from the Naval Staff of the risks of such a journey, despite also the shortage of arms in England for the Home Defences.

Operation Battleaxe was a disastrous failure. The new tanks were unfitted for work in desert conditions and their crews were unused to their machines and untrained in co-operation with accompanying infantry, with the result that during the first twelve hours over 50 per cent of the newly provided armour had been knocked out. After but three days' battle, Wavell called off the operation, his mauled forces retiring to their original positions while in Britain a distraught Churchill roamed the corridors of his abandoned house at Chartwell, seeking a solution to intractable problems. He decided that the time had come for a change in the Middle East High Command.

His choice to replace Wavell was General Sir Claude Auchinleck, until then Commander-in-Chief, India, and the new general's brief was to assemble as quickly as possible a force powerful enough to expel Rommel and his army from Egypt, and indeed from North Africa – and to do it soon. An extra degree of urgency was added to the brief by the fact that Hitler had signified his approval of Rommel's achievements by reinforcing the Deutsche Afrika Korps until it consisted of two panzer divisions and one infantry division, and Mussolini had also increased the Italian contingent.

Greatly to the Prime Minister's disappointment, General Auchinleck refused steadfastly to be hurried. His first cable back to Whitehall after taking up his appointment argued that no further offensive in the Western Desert should be contemplated until the main base was secure, and he then stated that in order to expel Rommel and Panzergruppe Afrika from their positions, he would need two and preferably three armoured divisions and one motorised division, and at least a 50 per cent reserve of armour before the first attack.

'Generals only enjoy such comforts in heaven,' wrote Churchill much later, when his blood-pressure had returned to normal. 'And those that demand them do not always get there.'[1] But after more goading from Whitehall, plus the arrival of many reinforcing units including two brigades of South African troops, and also the accumulation of considerable reserves of armour, ammunition, petrol and all the other essentials for war in an environment which provided nothing but an arena, *Operation Crusader* was launched on November 18th, 1941, and the third lap of the Benghasi Handicap began.

It was a soldier's battle, in which the best generalship – Rommel's – was at second-best level. Twice he led spectacular thrusts by his panzer divisions which he thought would end the battle and perhaps take him as far as the Nile Delta, but on both occasions the moves proved in the end to be more to his opponents' advantage than his own, and only the superb competence of his staff and a great deal of personal good luck saved him from catastrophe.

As for the British command, Eighth Army (as it was now called for the first time) had advanced originally under command of Lieutenant-General Sir Alan Cunningham who had recently led a highly successful campaign in East Africa, but whose experience in bush and mountain warfare proved of doubtful value in the desert where armour and mobility were at a premium. Five days after the outset of the battle it seemed to observers that he was losing control, and Auchinleck himself flew up to the battle area to reassure him; for a few days the atmosphere at Cunningham's headquarters steadied. But then a spirited dash by Rommel's panzer divisions combined with ever-rising figures of British tank losses again shook the nerve of the Eighth Army commander, and Auchinleck decided to replace him.

His choice fell upon a member of his own Cairo Headquarter Staff, Major-General Neil Ritchie – who certainly brought calmness to Battle Headquarters for he was a big, cheerful man of conventional military looks, but his last responsibility in battle conditions had been as a major in Palestine in 1918, and many of the senior officers in his new command lacked confidence in his judgment. Only during the periods when Auchinleck was at the headquarters to help and advise had there been a feeling of firm control.

As for the battles themselves, the horrendous clashes of armour and artillery around the Tomb of Sidi Rezegh, the destruction of the 5th South African Brigade on *Totensonntag*, the long ordeal of the

New Zealanders below Belhammed and the chaos and confusion (on both sides) which followed Rommel's 'Dash to the Wire' all left their permanent imprints on the minds of the men who took part in them, as well as adding battle honours to many famous regiments. Respect for the enemy grew on both sides, and although there were inevitably unfortunate incidents such as the machine-gunning of ambulances before their purpose was realised, and the occasional shooting of prisoners, these were almost invariably the results of the haste and confusion of battle and were regretted by both sides. The war in the desert was generally fought with a chivalry unknown on other Second World War battlefields, and this rule held throughout *Operation Crusader*.

In the end, the battle was won more by forces away from the battlefield than upon it. Out of sight and out of mind, the Royal Navy and the Royal Air Force had been doing just as much to defeat Rommel at and over the sea as Eighth Army had been doing on land – and in their tasks these two services had been receiving increasingly valuable aid from a secret and rapidly developing intelligence organisation in England which had often been able to give them the destinations and routes of Axis supply convoys even before they left Italian ports. As a result, whereas Eighth Army were continually receiving supplies of new tanks, new guns and being fed from a seemingly unlimited arsenal, Rommel had already received warning from his Q Branch that stocks of practically everything from shells for the guns to boots for the infantry were down to an alarming level.

The result was that on the evening of December 5th, 1941, an Italian Staff Officer, Tenente-Colonello Montezemolo, arrived at Rommel's headquarters from the Operations Branch of Comando Supremo, and proceeded to paint so gloomy a picture of Rommel's supply position that he was forced to reconsider his prospects for victory.

The most revelatory fact of Montezemolo's résumé – and the one he produced at the outset of his argument – was that of the twenty-one ships of over 500 tons despatched from Italian ports to North Africa during November, fourteen had been sent to the bottom, taking with them 62 per cent – nearly 60,000 tons – of Rommel's supplies. Tankers had been particularly badly hit and only 2,500 tons of aviation or motor spirit had arrived. But it was the loss in Italian shipping which was proving the most damaging factor, and it had now reached such a level that although Comando Supremo would do everything possible to send such essential supplies as rations, medical equipment and perhaps ammunition, Rommel must understand that shipping of reinforcements in anything but derisory numbers was totally out of the question – at least until the end of December. By that time extra German air protection over convoys might be available, but until then Rommel must not expect more men, more tanks, more aircraft, much more ammunition, and he would be lucky to get enough fuel to retreat, let alone to advance further from his bases.

This was a stunning blow to Rommel, whose attitude towards supply problems had been until then somewhat cavalier, for he had always relied upon his highly competent staff and his own good fortune to solve such problems; but now that this combination was apparently failing him, he reacted with cold realism. Time was spent assessing the true picture on the battlefield from the somewhat confused reports, and then slowly and methodically disengaging and withdrawing the troops. (One difficulty was that vehicles captured by both sides had been pressed into the captors' service, and as everything was covered by now with a liberal coating of dust, recognition of units had become increasingly uncertain especially as the very mobility of the battles had thoroughly mixed them up.)

There were arguments with the Italian commanders, Generali Bastico and Gambara, who felt they should do everything to halt the retreat at Gazala and thus try to retain the bulge containing Barce, Benghasi and the Jebel Akhdar, but Rommel was anxious to shorten his own supply lines (and by the same token lengthen his enemy's) and insisted upon withdrawal to the edge of the Gulf of Sirte at El Agheila.

The operation was carried out with exemplary coolness and efficiency by the German element of his command, and most of the Italian units were also successfully extricated, to a great extent because of the lethargy – or perhaps caution – with which the retreat was followed up by the advance elements of Eighth Army. By Christmas Day, these consisted of two brigades of the 4th Indian Division in and around Benghasi, the two battalions of the Scots and Coldstream Guards and ancillary troops of the 22nd Guards Brigade at Antelat, and thirty-five Stuart tanks and fifty-five Crusaders of the 22nd Armoured Brigade at Chor es Sultan; but in the meantime and despite Montezemolo's forecast, Rommel had received twenty-two new panzers through Benghasi (and another twenty-three into Tripoli) with results that have been recounted.

Despite, however, the bloody nose administered to the British armour – and Afrika Korps's high morale as demonstrated by the *feu de joie* – Rommel's chosen stopping place was still behind the salt marshes, the soft sand and the 'camel-humps' between Mersa el Brega and El Agheila, to which locality the panzers duly retired during the opening days of 1942, in rain, mist and depressing cold.

Operation Crusader – the third lap of the Benghasi Handicap – was over by January 5th, 1942, fizzling out in bad weather and worse temper in the desolate sands from which, nine months before,

Rommel had launched the first spectacular advance of the Afrika Korps.

He was very annoyed. In his opinion his army had been defeated, not by superior military conception, training or even prowess, but by logistic inadequacy on the part of his own government and their allies. He had undoubtedly himself made mistakes (and a more expert adversary might well have taken advantage of them to his own irretrievable undoing) but at the end, he felt, only the inadequacy of his logistic support had robbed him of victory. He would pay more attention himself to that side of affairs in future, for it was obviously courting disaster to leave such matters in other hands but his own.

As for the British, although Auchinleck and Ritchie had good cause for satisfaction, the troops themselves were disillusioned. The promises which had been made to them before the battle by Churchill, by their own press and by many of their senior commanders regarding the superiority of their arms and equipment and the pre-eminence of their leaders, had proved empty; and they had in fact developed a dangerous admiration for the leadership of the Afrika Korps and an envy, some of it unfounded, for the enemy's weapons. Though they had been provided with nothing to equal the German 88mm. anti-aircraft and anti-tank gun, their tanks had not in fact been so greatly inferior in power or armour to the panzers, and what had really been missing was adequate training and perhaps a better understanding of the need for co-operation between all arms. Despite the opportunity for mobility offered by the wide, empty spaces of the North African desert, armour still needed the protection of artillery and both could be rendered impotent without accompanying infantry – and all must work together as a cohesive force.

British losses in killed and wounded exceeded the Axis losses by about 1,800, though the Italians lost nearly 20,000 men as prisoners and some posts at the Egyptian frontier garrisoned by Germans had eventually to capitulate, adding another 10,000 to the population of British prison-camps. British losses in tanks, lorries and guns were much greater than the Axis losses mainly because they had so much more to lose, but if the desert behind them was littered with the debris of smashed British armour, the sea-bed between Sicily and North Africa was dotted with torn ships vomiting panzers and unused artillery through gaps in their plates. The Royal Navy, the Royal Air Force and the diverse elements which made up the Army had, in this theatre at least, realised that they were all fighting the same war and close co-operation between them had welded them into a formidable fighting team. Moreover, they had all learned from their experience of the last few weeks something of the grim business of war, and no longer regarded it – as some of them had before – quite so much as an adventurous game for gifted amateurs.

But the war in the desert – or indeed, anywhere else – was never to be the same again. While Rommel had been issuing his instructions for the first stage of the withdrawal to El Agheila, Japanese aircraft on the other side of the world had been approaching Pearl Harbor. A new dimension was being added to the war and as 1942 began, it became a truly global conflict – a development recognised with some significant activity, but surprisingly little ceremony, in Washington, on the first day of the New Year.

1 · Embattled Spring

On January 1st, 1942 the United Nations Declaration was signed in Washington, by which twenty-six nations agreed that only by defeat of the Axis Powers – Germany, Italy and Japan – could life, liberty, independence, religious freedom, justice and ordinary human rights be preserved, and in pursuance of this cause the signatory nations pledged themselves to devote their full military and economic resources to defeat of the Axis, and to the agreement that none of them would entertain a separate armistice or make a separate peace with the enemy.

But the drawing up and signing of this declaration was attended by none of the pomp that such an event might be expected to provoke – indeed only four signatories were present at its first inscription, the remainder being canvassed in their own embassies by comparatively junior officials from the State Department who in some cases had carefully to explain the contents of the declaration to the respective ambassadors, and to argue its merits.

It was thus not surprising that the occasion hardly justified the description 'momentous', and indeed of the signing countries, nine – Costa Rica, Cuba, the Dominican Republic, El Salvador, Guatemala, Haiti, Honduras, Nicaragua and Panama – were not deeply or irretrievably concerned in the defeat of the Axis Powers and were never to become so, while eight – Belgium, Czechoslovakia, Greece, Luxembourg, the Netherlands, Norway, Poland and Yugoslavia – although deeply concerned could in the circumstances contribute but little to the Allied cause, for they were all occupied by Axis forces, their attempts at resistance severely limited by the varying degrees of brutality the S.S. and Gestapo were prepared to use in its suppression.

Of the remaining signatories, Russia and China were both defending themselves desperately from deep invasions into their own heartlands, India was watching with considerable anxiety her own eastern border and the behaviour of the millions of supporters of Mahatma Gandhi who were apparently quite willing to accept Japanese domination if it rid them of the British, while Britain herself and the countries of the Commonwealth, having spent the eighteen months since the Fall of France fighting German, Italian and now Japanese forces with varying degrees of success, were wondering when the tide of war would turn in their favour, and if it would do so before exhaustion weakened them beyond recovery.

Although the Royal Air Force had in 1940 beaten back the attempts of the Luftwaffe to secure command of the air over the British Isles, thus defeating Hitler's plans for an invasion of Britain herself, their own bombing campaign over Germany since then seemed to be scoring little but propaganda successes, while at sea the U-boat campaign was still gravely threatening the island's very source of life, let alone her ability to wage war. And America's recent entry into the conflict, however welcome, seemed for the moment only to add victims to the U-boat tally, for the sinkings off the eastern seaboard between Miami and Cape Hatteras were already assuming alarming proportions.

There were also several other causes of concern for Britain and the Commonwealth, one of which was the general attitude of the people of the United States to the war, which bore understandable but alarming resemblances to that in Britain during the 'Phoney War' period of late 1939. This had been typified by the then Prime Minister Chamberlain's announcement to his family – just before that first war-time Christmas – that he had 'a hunch that the war will be over next spring . . . [not] by defeat in the field but by German realisation that they *can't* win and it isn't worth their while to go on . . . '

This was a prophecy which looked peculiarly unfounded on New Year's Day, 1942, yet it now seemed to be undergoing revivification, for a large proportion of the American people apparently believed that the defeat of Germany and Japan would be achieved quite soon and with but the minimal disturbance of ordinary life. President Roosevelt's New Year message might promise an abundance of war materials undreamed of before in Allied circles – a target for American industry in 1942 of eight million tons of shipping, 45,000 aircraft, 45,000 tanks and half a million machine-guns – but this production on its own would not win the war and its sudden necessity was in itself an admission of grave weakness. Even Field Marshal Sir John Dill, recently sent to Washington to establish close liaison between British and American staffs (and who by the end of the war was to become so beloved and admired by Americans that upon his death a statue to him was erected in Arlington Cemetery), was shaken by the attitude there, to such effect that he wrote that day to the Chief of the Imperial General Staff in London, 'Never have I seen a country so unprepared for war, or so soft.' If his judgment was perhaps a little hasty, it nevertheless gave justifiable warning of the time which must elapse before American military strength could come to the relief of the British and Commonwealth forces already in the field.

And since the Japanese attack on Pearl Harbor and the associated assaults of that epochal day, these had been stretched to – and indeed well beyond – their limits. Within days of the crippling of the United States Pacific Fleet, the Royal Navy was reeling under the losses of the battleship *Prince of Wales* and the battle-cruiser *Repulse* off the Malayan coast, while the British military command in Malaya watched helplessly as Japanese invasion forces poured ashore into Thailand and then into Malaya itself, pushing aside the single Indian brigade holding the northern airfield at Kota Bahru and beginning their swift and seemingly irresistible advance down the peninsula. By the end of 1941 Singapore was under threat and Japanese forces massing in Thailand were obviously about to debouch into Burma, while Borneo, Sarawak, the Dutch East Indies and the Philippines had all been invaded and, worst of all from the point of view of British prestige, Hong Kong had surrendered to the Japanese on Christmas Day after a defence lasting less than two weeks.

Only on the one front in North Africa was there any sign of success for the forces of the Allied Powers – and in view of the exploits of the Afrika Korps during those wet and depressing days at the very end of 1941, even here there was room only for the most cautious optimism. Obviously, in order to push Panzergruppe Afrika back further, Eighth Army would now need time to regroup, to recoup its losses of recent weeks, to rest its exhausted men and replace their battered arms and equipment, and to increase their striking force with fresh reinforcements.

But where would they come from? For in the face of the Japanese onslaught taking place further east, all uncommitted troops and material must be sent there. So even for the one currently victorious force at the disposal of the newly formed United Nations, the prospects as 1942 opened looked bleak, and in the area itself memories stirred of the previous arrival of the British there, when their successes had been negated and their victories thrown away by the decision to send aid to Greece.

Not that higher authority at any level intended to repeat those mistakes. The lessons of that early débâcle were declared properly learned and this time no vital military strength in men or material was to be stripped away from the crucial area in order to bolster inadequate defences elsewhere, however deserving or even critical. Tripoli was still to be the main objective for Eighth Army; plans for the advance through Tripolitania, code-named *Acrobat*, already existed and there were plans for a complementary invasion, code-named *Gymnast* and intended to put an army ashore in Morocco and Algeria, which would open up the back door and help sweep the Axis forces from North Africa once and for all. This plan received support and was indeed extended within days of America's entry into the war, when Mr Churchill visited Washington in order to co-ordinate American and British war efforts, and so interested the American Chiefs of Staff that they agreed to examine the possibilities of expanding *Gymnast* to *Super-Gymnast* by the inclusion of American divisions.

But although nothing should be done to *decrease* Eighth Army strength, in these new circumstances little or nothing could be done immediately to *increase* it, and the Commanders-in-Chief, Middle East, would appreciate that divisions and equipment en route to them must, alas, now be diverted to the Far East. Anti-tank and anti-aircraft regiments, several fighter and some light bomber squadrons, and the entire 18th Division at that moment rounding the Cape must be diverted to India, while the 17th Indian Division which had been intended for duty in Iraq would now remain at home; and in fact, although the intention was that nothing vital should be taken from Auchinleck's strength, could he please release some of his light tanks? – a request to which he had generously reacted by allowing the despatch to Burma of a reconstituted armoured brigade with Stuart light tanks, a 25-pounder battery and an anti-tank battery.

Such had been the pace of events immediately after Pearl Harbor that most of these decisions had been made before the Afrika Korps had retired behind El Agheila – before, indeed, they had so robustly handled 22nd Armoured Brigade as to cause Auchinleck to wonder if he had been wise in his generosity. It was then far too late for him to reconsider his position or to withdraw his offer, and as a result he found himself in early January 1942 examining the condition of his forces facing Rommel's across the Tripolitanian border with some anxiety.

To a letter from Ritchie, still commanding Eighth Army, reporting that last brush between German and British armour, he replied on January 1st, saying amongst other things:

> I agree that our tanks are outgunned by the German tanks, but surely superiority in numbers should counter-balance this to some extent, and the number of German tanks with the heavier gun in them cannot be so great?
>
> I agree too, about the cruiser being too complicated, and delicate a machine for the rough conditions of the Near and Middle East, and that the American M3s [Stuarts], though mechanically excellent, are not comparable to our cruisers or the German medium tanks as fighting vehicles. Still we have got to make do with what we have got, and the Boche has got to be beaten! . . . If we add to our inferiority in material an apparent inferiority in leadership, then we shall be in a bad way and will not deserve to win . . . I have a most uncomfortable feeling that the Germans outwit and outmanoeuvre us as well as outshooting us . . .
>
> If it is true, then we must find new leaders at once . . . No personal

considerations must be allowed to stand in the way. Commanders who consistently have their brigades shot away from under them, even against a numerically inferior enemy, are expensive luxuries, much too expensive in present circumstances.[1]

This opinion was also held by at least one other commander in the area.

Lieutenant-General A. R. Godwin-Austen who had commanded XIII Corps during *Crusader* (XXX Corps had been added to make up Eighth Army and had contained most of the armour) now commanded the troops in Cyrenaica and already considered the 22nd Armoured Brigade unfit for further action. He therefore replaced it at the frontier by the Support Group from the 7th Armoured Division, with orders to hold the line with the Guards Brigade on their right and use their experience to continue harassing Rommel; but the Support Group had been in almost continuous action since mid-November, its men were tired and its vehicles and artillery badly worn.

Thus, despite the intentions in both Whitehall and the Cairo Headquarters, the formations expected to hold the lately won gains were quickly in some disarray, on this occasion because of the need to reorganise fighting units for the next leap forward, and, just as importantly, to accumulate supplies to support it. Moreover, Auchinleck was deeply concerned about the northern flank of his huge command area (which stretched now from Tripolitania to Afghanistan) and the ever-present threat of a German advance down through the Caucasus and on through Turkey or Persia towards the vital oilfields at the head of the Persian Gulf, so he had ordered that once the 7th Armoured Division had recovered from its *Crusader* losses, it should be given a change of scene in Palestine and Syria. The newly arrived 1st Armoured Division should take its place – but even in this substitution, there were extra complications.

The commander of the 1st Armoured Division, Major-General Herbert Lumsden, had been wounded in an air attack within a few days of the completion of *Crusader*, and his place was taken by Major-General Frank Messervy who now found himself with a division which for nearly a year had suffered frustration and fragmentation, and was in a highly unsatisfactory state as a result.

It had been reorganised after Dunkirk, re-equipped with a positively bizarre assortment of tanks of which the most modern had been almost immediately stripped away to make up numbers in the convoy for *Battleaxe*, after which it had again been re-equipped, this time entirely with Crusaders. The division had then been ordered to the Middle East, but as a result of complaints about the mechanical state of tanks arriving in the Delta, the Crusaders had been withdrawn for the necessary modifications to be carried out in England – so little if

any training had been done on them. Shortly after that, the 22nd
Armoured Brigade was removed and despatched for immediate
attachment to 7th Armoured Division as *Crusader* began, and in mid-
September the remaining brigade – the 2nd – and the division's
Support Group, had set out on the long haul around the Cape.

The experiences and condition of 22nd Brigade around Antelat at
the beginning of 1942 have already been described, and it must be
said that those of 2nd Armoured Brigade were unlikely to render it
much more effective. It was sent forward into Cyrenaica at first as a
brigade group, with an infantry battalion, a Royal Horse Artillery
regiment and an anti-tank regiment from its own Support Group
incorporated and training en route with it, but as soon as it arrived in
the area it lost these units, which rejoined the division's Support
Group as this took the place of 7th Support Group at the frontier.
Moreover, 2nd Brigade's tanks had made the journey from the Delta
by rail only as far as Mersa Matruh, and had driven the remaining 450
miles on their own tracks – which as a result were already in need of
replacement; though not quite immediately, as the brigade had used
all its petrol allocation on the way up and for some days there was no
more with which even to drive to the frontier positions, let alone
carry out advanced training there.

By mid-January, therefore, Godwin-Austen's XIII Corps, occupying Cyrenaica and facing Panzergruppe Afrika (about to be re-
christened Panzerarmee Afrika), consisted of two brigades of the
4th Indian Division at Benghasi and Barce respectively (the third was
still back at Tobruk where it had been joined by the remnants of 22nd
Armoured), the 2nd Armoured Brigade hastily training around
Antelat, and the Guards Brigade at Mersa Brega with the 1st Support
Group to their left in the ground leading down to the Wadi Faregh –
the last-named also endeavouring to gain experience, but in ground
so broken and hummocky that wheeled vehicles were slower than
tracked ones, and suffered so much from burst tyres and broken axles
as to be almost useless.

It was extremely fortunate, in Auchinleck's view, that Rommel's
forces could still be considered far too weak and disorganised to be
able even to consider taking the offensive. This opinion – shared by
Ritchie – he communicated to Churchill in a letter dated January
12th:

> I do not think it can be said that the bulk of the enemy divisions have
> evaded us. It is true that he still speaks in terms of divisions but they are
> divisions only in name. For instance, we know that the strength of the 90th
> German Light Division originally 9,000, now 3,500, and has only one field
> gun left.
>   . . . These are much disorganised, short of senior officers, short of
> material and due to our continuous pressure are tired and certainly not as

strong as their total strength of 35,000 might be thought to indicate.

I have reason to believe that six ships recently reached Tripoli averaging 7,200 tons.

I am convinced that we should press forward . . . in view of the heartening news from the Russian front I feel that we should do all we can to maintain the pressure in Libya. We have very full and interesting records of daily conversations between our prisoners Generals von Ravenstein and Schmidt [taken at Bardia]. Making all allowances for mental depression natural in prisoners of war there is no doubt that German morale is beginning to feel the strain not only in Libya but in Germany. They speak freely also of great losses in the recent fighting, mismanagement and disorganisation and above all of dissatisfaction with Rommel's leadership. I am convinced the enemy is hard-pressed more than we dared think perhaps.[2]

It was unfortunate for Auchinleck that his intelligence staff had not been able to listen to conversations between other German officers. Even while Auchinleck was writing his letter, Rommel's chief of intelligence, Major F. W. von Mellenthin, was predicting that at least for the next two weeks, Panzergruppe forces in the area would be more powerful and much better supplied – that is, in much better shape for battle – than the British forces facing them, and that now would be the best time to attack. What is very strange about the situation is that von Mellenthin had little more information at his disposal than had Auchinleck.

Rommel's fortunes had improved remarkably during the four weeks following the diatribe delivered to him by Montezemolo, as a result of several disparate but converging factors. Perhaps the most important was the recovery in energy and morale of the Afrika Korps, which had carried out one of the most difficult of military manoeuvres – retreat in the face of the enemy – without losing cohesion, without losing vast quantities of stores such as the British had abandoned in their retreats, without showing the slightest signs of panic, moving always at their own pace, and with such confidence that at the end they could still turn and deliver those two numbing blows upon the pursuing British armour. They had every justification for regarding themselves as a first-class fighting force still capable of giving an excellent account of themselves.

A second and more immediately apparent factor could be seen on the map – the shortening of Axis supply lines and the consequent easing of their logistic problems. Moreover, not only had the distance from their main supply port – Tripoli – to the front lessened, but the difficulties of the sea passage had eased immensely of late, as had been demonstrated by the arrival of the ships bearing panzers at Benghasi and Tripoli just before Christmas and of the even larger and more important convoy, to which Auchinleck referred, on January 5th.

This had brought Rommel a further fifty-five panzers, twenty armoured cars and a large consignment of fuel and was, as the Chief of Staff to the Afrika Korps, Oberst Fritz Bayerlein, remarked, 'as good as a victory in battle'; but its real significance lay simply in its safe arrival. Montezemolo's predictions, though not entirely inaccurate with regard to timing, had been too pessimistic in tone, for the onset of the Russian winter had released enough German aircraft for Kesselring's Luftflotte 2 to begin operations, and to make an immediate impact.

Moreover, Rommel's forces were for the time being secure from the more serious attentions of the Royal Navy, for whom the closing months of 1941 had proved one of the most disastrous periods in their long history. Of the five capital ships in the Mediterranean at the beginning of November, only one was still afloat at the end of the year, the aircraft-carrier *Ark Royal* and the battleship *Barham* having been torpedoed by U-boats (the latter blowing up with enormous loss of life) and two more battleships, *Valiant* and *Queen Elizabeth*, falling victim to Italian 'human torpedo' crews in Alexandria harbour.

In addition, two cruisers had been sunk by torpedo, two badly damaged in minefields and one withdrawn by the Australian Government for service nearer home. As a result, command of the waters of the mid-Mediterranean and, even more importantly, of the air above had passed into Axis hands. Panzergruppe Afrika was the most immediate beneficiary, and von Mellenthin's prognosis only too accurate.

Rommel struck early on the morning of January 21st – just sixteen days after the last of his rearguards, cautiously pursued by patrols from the Guards Brigade, had retired to El Agheila. He had deliberately omitted to inform both his own High Command and his allies of his intentions, and was thus not very surprised when angry messages arrived from Bastico, or when the Italian Chief of Staff, Generale Cavallero, arrived on January 23rd in a state of high excitement to order that the advance must be nothing more than a sortie to be recalled at the earliest opportunity.

But it had already gone too far for that, and Rommel was glimpsing victory again. To Cavallero's expostulations he replied that only the Führer could order a retirement as it was mainly German troops who were so far engaged, and when his own immediate superior, Generalfeldmarschall Kesselring, voiced opinions which could have been interpreted as backing for Cavallero, Rommel went so far as to hint that Kesselring's expertise as an airman was not totally relevant at that moment and invited him to look at the map.

Already, it revealed a remarkable picture.

Bad going had held up the advance during the first day, for 15th Panzer on the right flank had become bogged in the dunes at the mouth of the Wadi Faregh, and on the left the combined Ariete and Trieste were content to keep pace; but the bad going which held up the panzers also bedevilled the British 1st Support Group, who by the end of the day had left behind sixteen of their 25-pounders, a number of their lorries and nearly a hundred of their soldiers. And as the main road back to Agedabia and the line of the Wadi Faregh diverged, there was by the evening a gap between the Guards Brigade and the Support Group.

Into this gap, Rommel quite reasonably assumed, the British would send what they could of the 2nd Armoured Brigade in the belief that he would lunge for it at dawn the next day – so with a dislocating shift of weight to his left he instead sent two lorried infantry battalions from 21st Panzer and 90th Light, augmented by German and Italian artillery and under command of a first-class tactician, Oberst Werner Marcks, straight up through the Italian divisions on the main road to push aside the right flank of the Guards Brigade and reach Agedabia by 1100 on second day (January 22nd, 1942), then to forge straight on to Antelat and swing east to Saunnu.

General Messervy had acted almost as Rommel had foreseen (although not exactly, for he had directed 2nd Armoured Brigade down to Giof el Matar, behind the 1st Support Group, and not into the gap), so, by the evening of January 22nd, Marcks Group and the Italians held the line of the road from Agedabia up to Antelat and across to Saunnu, with all Messervy's command contained in the hook and cut off from its main supplies at Msus. Meanwhile, to the south of the British, the Afrika Korps armour had crossed their front to reach Agedabia and follow the main advance.

Rommel's idea for January 23rd was for a further extension of the hook by Marcks Group down to Maaten el Grara, the strengthening of the main shaft as the panzer regiments came up towards Antelat, from which position they should be able to block the British armour's attempt to reach their stores, and perhaps even drive them south-wards into the desert. From the anxious inquiries his intercept services were overhearing from British tank commanders desperately short of petrol, it seemed likely they would never reach Tengeder, let alone Mechili – and in any case, the Luftwaffe dominated the air above the battlefield this time as the R.A.F. was too busy evacuating its forward airfields, and was itself short of fuel.

This, then, was the picture with which Rommel faced Cavallero and Kesselring, and it is easy to see why, at the end of the argument, the former went off growling doubtfully, the latter silent and thought-

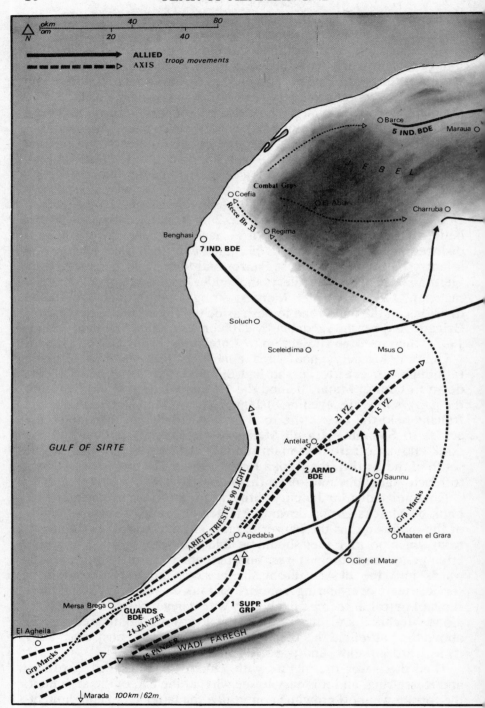

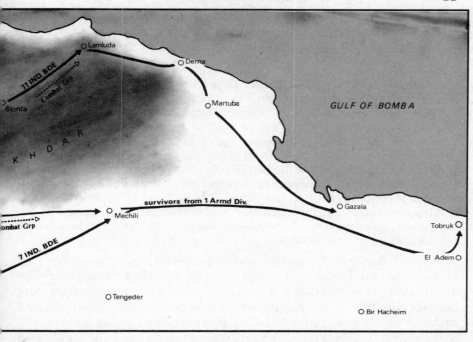

Map 2   Rommel's riposte, January 21st–February 4th

ful. And except for two slight misjudgments, it might all have come off.

The first misjudgment was the move forward by the Marcks Group from Saunnu to Maaten el Grara which took place too early, with the result that when one of the tank regiments of 2nd Armoured Brigade, ordered back to guard the approaches to Msus, arrived at Saunnu they found the place empty, and the second was that a direction to 21st Panzer to get across to Saunnu to take Marcks's place was delayed so the gap in the net remained open. Through it, after a day of confused actions fought out in the barren country south of the Antelat–Saunnu track, most of 2nd Armoured Brigade, the whole of the Guards Brigade and the survivors of 1st Support Group made their uncertain way, congregating at dawn on January 24th about ten miles north of Antelat in positions from which, in theory, they should be able successfully to block Rommel's route to the stores dump at Msus.

They were even given extra time in which to prepare for this, for Rommel had not realised the facts of their escape and Afrika Korps spent most of that day (24th) sweeping south-east and finding nothing but abandoned tanks and lorries (many of which their recovery units were to put back into service); but early on the 25th, the combined panzer divisions moved north on to Messervy's division and literally drove it from the field. According to von Mellenthin who watched the first onslaught and amassed the details of the battle at the end of the day:

> On the right flank, 21st Panzer Division met little opposition, but six miles north-west of Saunnu 15th Panzer ran into very superior tank forces. These were overwhelmed by Panzer Regiment 8, closely supported by anti-tank guns and artillery; it soon became apparent that the British tank units had no battle experience and they were completely demoralised by the onslaught of 15th Panzer. At times the pursuit attained a speed of fifteen miles an hour, and the British columns fled madly over the desert in one of the most extraordinary routs in the war. After covering fifty miles in under four hours 15th Panzer reached Msus airfield at 1100, overwhelming numerous supply columns, and capturing twelve aircraft ready to take off. Further exploitation was impossible as the division was out of fuel, but 96 tanks, 38 guns, and 190 lorries were the booty of the day.[3]

As 2nd Armoured Brigade had already lost nearly seventy of its tanks between January 21st and 23rd, it had thus been effectively eliminated as a fighting force within ninety-six hours of its first contact with the Afrika Korps, which now occupied the road junction at Msus and was happily filling its lockers with English food, drink and cigarettes. Rommel, however, was not so happy as he had hoped to be, for there was very little fuel found there, and he could certainly not achieve his greatest immediate ambition of driving straight to Mechili and then to Derna, thus cutting off the entire British force in Cyrenaica.

In his appreciation of this one fact, General Ritchie was right for the first time since Rommel's advance had begun. He had been in Cairo on January 21st, but arrived in the area the following afternoon (by which time Marcks was driving up to Antelat) announcing among other things that Rommel's latest exploit provided a 'God-sent opportunity to hit him really hard when he puts out his neck, as it seems possible that he may be already doing.'

This was, as the *Official History* points out, a robust reading of the situation, but not an accurate one, for if anyone's neck was stuck out, it was the Eighth Army's.

Not all British opinion in the area was so mistaken, however, for Godwin-Austen's opinion of the fighting ability of the 2nd Armoured Brigade had been conditioned by that demonstrated by the 22nd, and within thirty-six hours he was pointing out that the defences of Benghasi consisted of but one infantry brigade, to which the British armour could hardly come to the rescue if it was also expected to defend Msus as well as 'cover the eastern flank' – which were Ritchie's latest orders. In the circumstances, he requested permission to order a general withdrawal from Benghasi and eastern Cyrenaica as far as Mechili at least, with administrative units going back to Gazala – a request at which Ritchie baulked on the grounds that Rommel must by now be near the end of his resources and that very soon would come the opportunity to turn and strike him. In this Ritchie was supported by both Auchinleck and Air Marshal Tedder, both of whom had come forward to Ritchie's headquarters.

But by the evening of the 25th, what little remained of 1st Armoured Division was back at Charruba, and so far as Godwin-Austen could see there was nothing to prevent Afrika Korps driving on to Benghasi and capturing at least one Indian brigade, plus the ships, port installations and accumulated supplies there. He saw no reason to believe that the resistance so far offered to Rommel's advance would have done much to blunt its edge, and in the circumstances he thought it right to use his own discretionary powers to order total evacuation – of the Indians to Derna, of the shipping to Alexandria, and of the remnants of 1st Armoured Division to Mechili. He was thus somewhat incensed to learn that Ritchie, divining correctly that Rommel was short of petrol but also leaping over-eagerly to the conclusion that the Afrika Korps must now be at the limits of its strength, cancelled the move, instructing 7th Indian Brigade instead to send raiding columns down to attack Rommel's communications south of Antelat, and 1st Armoured Division to stand and defend Charruba and the approaches to El Abiar. Ritchie also took 4th Indian Division under his own direct command, which, in view of the fact that Godwin-Austen had held the rank of acting Lieutenant-General rather longer than he had himself, was tactless, even though the Commander-in-Chief was present at the time and made no attempt to countermand the move.

There now followed almost two days of military hiatus, while the divisional commanders endeavoured to deploy their forces in accordance with Ritchie's instructions, and then, in the face of military reality, to try to persuade him that they were impractical – and all the time, Rommel was reading the intercept reports of the squabbling between his opponents while he scavenged the field for booty, gradually accumulated supplies and decided what he would do next.

As severe sandstorms blanketed the area during January 26th, nobody there was much concerned by the general immobility, least of all the troops themselves among whom were the 1st Armoured newcomers, 'getting their knees brown', as the saying went, and learning the bitter truth about the desert in which they were to fight their war.

The sandstorms that day had not been dense enough however to prevent two reconnaissance aircraft of the 250th South African Squadron from spotting a move by some panzers south-eastwards from Msus and reporting them to Ritchie, who delightedly interpreted it as a splitting of Rommel's forces – one half moving on Mechili and the other on Benghasi. He promptly ordered 1st Armoured Division to move south and fall on the rear of the reported panzers, and 7th Indian Brigade down to block frontally whatever forces Rommel was sending up towards Benghasi, encouraging them with the statement that 'The enemy has divided his forces, and is weaker than we are in both areas. The keyword is offensive action everywhere.'

But the movement of the panzers had been a feint (and only Rommel's luck had put the South African aircraft over it at the crucial moment) and, hearing that the main British moves were planned for the 29th, he ordered the Marcks Group out on the 28th to sweep up around to the north of Benghasi while the Italian divisions and the 90th Light came up from the south. The panzer regiments, after decoying the British armour out into the desert, would remain in the Msus–Charruba area as flank guard to the attack.

In pouring rain he led the Marcks Group himself across the broken country towards Regima, and by dark his Reconnaissance Battalion 33 were blocking the raised causeway at Coefia along which 7th Indian Brigade were endeavouring to escape to join their brother brigade at Barce. There was a frantic confusion of reversing and overturning lorries, a retreat by the Indians back into Benghasi and a well-judged decision by the brigade commander that their best way out of a fast-closing trap would be across the front of the Italians approaching from the south, through Sceleidima and flat out for the Trig el Abd and Mechili. Aided by appalling weather and a great deal of luck, the three columns got through with but few encounters with enemy forces – or at any rate enemy forces willing to prove obstructive – but they had perforce to jettison a great deal of equipment and to travel light. They all reached Mechili where they found the remains of 1st Armoured Division and then went back further, first to El Adem and then into Tobruk, while to the north of them 5th Indian Brigade and 11th (which had been rushed up from Tobruk to Maraua when danger first threatened) made their joint way back along the northern roads through Slonta, Lamluda, Derna and Martuba. They were all back into or behind the Gazala defences by February 4th, though during the last sprint home a number of 11th Brigade guns and vehicles blew up on the mines left on one of the *Crusader* battlefields where XIII Corps's attempt to cut off the Afrika Korps retreat had been roughly handled only seven weeks before.

For many reasons, Afrika Korps did not follow up the British retreat much more closely than they had themselves been followed on their way back to El Agheila. First there was the chronic shortage of petrol, then there was the riveting attraction of the enormous bulk of supplies captured when they entered Benghasi, enough to distract the attention of the most ascetic warrior. The last action of one of the British quartermasters had been to put a match to seven million cigarettes and to organise the evacuation of twelve lorry-loads of rum – but the fire went out and some of the lorries broke down long before they were clear of the hills.

And there were always the constraints of higher command. Mussolini's permission to advance and occupy Benghasi with a small mobile force 'if the British saw fit to withdraw voluntarily' arrived shortly after Rommel's headquarters had actually taken up residence there, but both Il Duce and Bastico insisted that the forward positions for Panzerarmee Afrika could be no further east than Maraua, in front of which only small mobile forces were to operate; and although Rommel briefly considered incorporating Ariete, Trieste, 90th Light and 15th and 21st Panzer Divisions into what he was quite prepared to announce was just such 'a small mobile force' in order to drive the British even further back, he reluctantly concluded that there was not enough petrol to make the project feasible.

None the less, his reconnaissance units, some anti-tank batteries and enough infantry to form them into two combat groups had followed on the heels of the British retreat and were watching the formation of the Gazala positions as the last fugitives slipped into them, and soon afterwards the bulk of Afrika Korps and 90th Light were close behind in the Jebel. Italian divisions stayed in Benghasi and around Antelat while a blocking force came out again from Tripoli to hold the border positions from Mersa Brega down to Marada.

Weary, weatherworn, thirsty but triumphant, Panzerarmee Afrika under their remarkable leader were well back into Marmarica, with Tobruk – for so long their apparently unobtainable objective – again only thirty-five miles beyond their grasp.

On February 2nd, when it was evident that the situation had stabilised, Lieutenant-General A. R. Godwin-Austen formally requested that he be relieved of his command in view of the lack of confidence shown in him by the Eighth Army commander, demonstrated by the abrupt reversal of his decision to evacuate Cyrenaica on the evening of January 25th, and by Ritchie's assumption of direct command of one of his divisions at the same time. General Auchinleck saw fit to accede to this request and, according to the *Official History*, 'this, in the circumstances, was understandable.'

But as the *History* then goes on to admit that Godwin-Austen's reading of the situation during the retreat had been on the whole more realistic than Ritchie's, the question arises as to *how* Auchinleck's agreement had been 'understandable'. Godwin-Austen had been senior to Ritchie at the time of the changeover of commander during *Crusader* – and although the substance of that changeover had been acceptable in the circumstances which prevailed at the time, every account written since stresses the fact that Ritchie's appointment was to be subject to review when the operation ended, and some justification demonstrated for the continuation of Ritchie's command if it were not to be transferred to another, more senior corps commander.

And what justification was there? Ritchie's performance as Eighth Army commander during the second half of *Crusader* had certainly not been as much at fault as Cunningham's, but on the other hand it had not been so outstanding as to obscure Godwin-Austen's right to consideration for the higher post, especially as it had been New Zealanders from Godwin-Austen's corps who had made the junction with the Tobruk garrison during *Crusader*, Indians from his corps who had masked the frontier garrisons, and it had certainly not been Godwin-Austen's fault that the British armour had been so severely handled.

Presumably the immediate justification at the end of *Crusader* was that the Eighth Army under Ritchie's command had won a demonstrable victory, and certainly between the arrival at Mersa Brega and Rommel's riposte there had been little enough time for a cool and just review of the situation; but the lull when the Gazala Line was reached should have provided one – and in view of the validity of Godwin-Austen's prognosis compared with the lack of realism in some of Ritchie's pronouncements, one would have thought the outcome foregone. But perhaps Auchinleck was prompted by one of those qualities which made him so admirable a person – loyalty to his friends and to his personal staff – in which case, he should have omitted that phrase in his letter to Ritchie of January 1st, regarding 'personal considerations'. Perhaps, also, he felt some responsibility for Ritchie's decisions taken during those crucial days when he himself had been present.

Needless to say, the disappointment felt throughout Eighth Army at the sudden reverse was echoed in the British Isles, and cables from 10 Downing Street alternated astonishment with reproof, sympathy with regret. In his replies, Auchinleck made some crucial aspects of the war in the Middle East abundantly clear to Mr Churchill – the 2-pounder gun and the cruiser tanks were both of inferior quality to those in the enemy's service, he claimed, and went on to observe sombrely that these defects were causing Royal Armoured Corps personnel to lose confidence in their equipment.

He did not, however, add that they were also losing confidence in their leadership – perhaps because he was not aware of it; but the fact remains that the troops were beginning to look askance at their officers at many levels and were assessing their abilities with growing scepticism. Cunningham had promised Eighth Army a speedy and complete victory at the beginning of *Crusader*; if Ritchie had not promised them anything it could have been because he had been too busy to visit any formation lower than Corps Headquarters, but as a result the troops felt that not only did they not know him, but he did not know them either. Unfortunately, this set of conditions applied equally to the Commander-in-Chief, who had also not found time to make himself known to a very high proportion of the men under his command. It is difficult for men to believe that the authority under which they serve cares much for them if it remains shrouded in Olympian mystery, especially if its promises prove empty and its directives impracticable.

Their admiration was therefore being increasingly given to the enemy commander, Rommel, who not only won victories but did so by leading from the front where his men could see him – a fact which quickly became well known throughout North Africa. The fact that he led an army with better guns was obvious, that it had better tanks was believed – and it was becoming generally accepted that it was also better trained and operated on a more realistic doctrine. In this the men of Eighth Army were undoubtedly correct, for German appreciation of the interdependence of all arms was fundamental; but the Afrika Korps had another advantage which was not yet evident to all.

The Eighth Army was being enlarged by the arrival from Britain of new formations – the intention was to send out whole divisions but as had happened in *Crusader* sometimes just brigades came out, and these went into action as such, and on occasion found themselves alone. As a result, although the officers and men may have known each other well through training together, when they went into action they were all equally inexperienced, at least in local conditions, and in 1942 often in any form of battle at all.

But Rommel's reinforcements at this time arrived invariably as individual soldiers for his existing formations and were fed into them piecemeal – and when they went into action they were accompanied and most often led by men who had just come out of it. When the inexperienced men of the 1st Support Group retired in front of the first probes of 15th and 21st Panzer Division on January 21st, they were pursued by formations each with a core of battle-hardened veterans who could not only shrug off the discomforts of desert fighting with accustomed ease, but recognise danger immediately it appeared, ignore empty sound and irrelevant fury in concentration on the purpose in hand – and thus teach the newcomers to do the same.

Panzerarmee Afrika Headquarters sent reports on the battles to Berlin, and these contained cool and realistic appraisals of their enemy's performance. As far as *Crusader* was concerned, they had praised the general preparation and the manner in which the approach to battle had been concealed, but they were highly critical of the fragmentation of force and the inability ever to concentrate it all at one decisive point. They also praised the steadiness and reliability of the troops, especially the N.C.O.s. But one paragraph directed a criticism which – if the British public could have brought itself to accept it – would have come as a devastating shock:

> British troops fought well on the whole, though they never attained the same impetus as the Germans when attacking. Officers were courageous and self-sacrificing, *but rather timid if they had to act on their own initiative*.[4] (author's italics)

Too many of those who had spent months in the ranks could still hear ringing in their ears, from their days as raw recruits, the British drill sergeant's basic precept: 'In the army, you're not paid to think, you're paid to DO AS YOU'RE BLOODY WELL TOLD!' – and at first when there was no one to tell them, many of them were lost.

But not all; some of those whose individuality was strong enough to withstand the onslaught of clumsy training (it had improved throughout 1941) began to look for spheres in which their energies and enthusiasms might be more profitably used.

There had grown up in the desert a number of what had become known as 'Private Armies', and in the early days a few of them – notably the Jock Columns formed first to harass the Italians – had been spectacularly effective. However, during the latter days of Wavell's command and the beginning of Auchinleck's too many of them had been conceived and often commanded by men with imagination, but not enough realism and very little professionalism, and many of the quite bizarre adventures upon which these had set out had ended in ludicrous failure. As a result a large number of brave but rather amateur soldiers were now passing their days in German prison-camps wondering what had gone wrong, but their very failure had brought home to those groups which had not suffered disaster the necessity for hard training, and considerable success was now attending some of their efforts. And after the grim disappointments of the early months of 1942, the ranks of these Private Armies were swelled by men who, although they were prepared to risk and even give their lives for their country, were not prepared to have them thrown away by incompetence at the top.

The Long Range Desert Group was by far the most professional of these Private Armies, operating a 'taxi-run' between Cairo and the Jebel Akhdar or points even further west, keeping a regular watch on the roadways along the Gulf of Sirte or in the Jebel itself, and, during the closing stages of *Crusader*, shooting up German and Italian convoys at night and wrecking Axis communications.

Lately, they had been operating from Jalo, but with the Eighth Army withdrawal to Gazala they too came back to set up a forward headquarters at Siwa. This was a much more congenial spot, where Cleopatra was reputed to have bathed in 'Cleopatra's Pool'; now a mixed bag of British, Rhodesians, New Zealanders and Free French disported themselves after their journeys across the desert in the same pool, in the 'Island Pool', the 'Sheikh's Pool', the 'Figure of Eight' and the 'Bubbly Pool' where warm, clear, sparkling artesian water bubbled up from a twenty-foot-deep spring to their infinite refreshment.

Siwa is the nearest approach to the story-book oasis between the Red Sea and Tunisia, and in the early months of 1942 it became a veritable traffic centre through which all who had business behind Axis lines must pass, for all of them had to use the L.R.D.G. service. Every day the patrols went out – taking Arabs to spy on the garrisons at Jalo or Agedabia, taking agents of various nationalities to live with their wireless sets and circle of contacts in the wadis of the Jebel, sending off their survey section under Captain Lazarus to plot yet another piece of unmapped desert; and occasionally aircraft would come in to bear away to hospital the men shot up on the patrols and fortunate enough to get back, aircrew picked up after a crash during one of the Benghasi 'milk run' raids, or escaped prisoners suffering from exhaustion and dehydration after a heroic struggle first against the prison-camp organisations, then against the often crueller forces of nature.

The agents who went up into the Jebel were an extraordinary breed of men – men, as one authority describes them, 'with that cold, two-o'clock-in-the-morning courage' – though rarely of professional agent status and most often of early middle age and retiring nature. One was a marine engineer who had made a great success of his hobby, Egyptology, in the pre-war years, and was now using his knowledge of the dialects of the region to collect particulars of garrison strengths from Benghasi to Derna; another had been a schoolmaster in Cairo where his wife and three children still lived while he organised a circle of Arab agents whose friends and relations worked for the Germans and the Italians and reported the gossip in the messes and canteens to him for onward transmission to Cairo.

One of the most remarkable was the Russo-Belgian Vladimir Peniakoff, who had fought through the First World War as a private in the French Army, between the wars had worked as an engineer in an Egyptian sugar-factory and in 1940 obtained for himself a commission in the British Army. Middle-aged officers on the General List are normally employed at headquarters, but Peniakoff had spent most of his time since enrolling with a battalion of Libyan Arabs raised for patrol and garrison duties, though during the recent retreat he had seen some action with the 4th Indian Division.

By the end of March 1942, he had managed to disengage himself from this service, recruit a small body of Arabs with a deep-seated dislike of the Italians who had driven them from their homeland, and a young British subaltern whom he had known as a schoolboy in Egypt. He then had himself and his diminutive command transported by the L.R.D.G. to the eastern part of the Jebel, in order to 'spread alarm and despondency' – a phrase just coming into fashion.

The first few weeks had perforce been spent assuring the sheikhs of the Obeidat in whose tribal district he wished to operate that the recent reverse suffered by the British was purely temporary, and arranging for them to receive supplies of food, arms and equipment in order that they would be able to play some part in the return of the Eighth Army which, he hoped to convince them, was inevitable.

But once he had gained their confidence and established a rightful presence in the area, his party could commence more destructive operations. These were not spectacular at first – sugar poured into the petrol tanks of unguarded lorries, sand down the oil-intake; an Italian despatch-rider caught at night by a rope across the track, a German sentry knifed. But one evening an Arab came into the camp with a story of a cache of petrol-drums which calculation later revealed to hold 100,000 gallons.

The detailed story of its destruction has been told many times – in fact and in fiction – but the account of the party's retreat from the scene, and of that curious mixture of triumph and reaction, of the dull, stupefied exhaustion of mind and body which typifies such withdrawals, is best told in Peniakoff's own words.

They had spent the day in a nearby cistern, been fed by the brother of the man who was to be their guide in the evening, left their refuge soon after dark and by nine o'clock were at the dump. At one end, three Italian lorries were being loaded with petrol, and the glare from their headlights was a help to the party as they began laying their charges at the other. By eleven o'clock, all charges had been laid, enough prepared evidence left lying around to give the impression that the operation had been carried out by British Commandos (thus providing helpful alibis for the local Arabs, who would undoubtedly be taken in for questioning the following day) and the party had arrived back at the cistern to collect their kit for the long march to safety.

An hour after they had started out, a dull boom behind revealed the premature explosion of one of the charges and as there was no immediate repeat, Peniakoff became convinced that the operation had failed – especially when the scheduled time for the charges to go off came and went. An hour of sweating despair followed as the party toiled on over the scrubby hills, wondering what could have gone wrong, *how* it could have gone wrong, and what could be said to the Arabs who had helped them at so much danger to themselves?

At five minutes to two the skyline behind us exploded. A broad curtain of yellow flame lifted to the sky and stayed there, lighting the bare landscape around us. Rumbling thunderous explosions followed one another, throwing up more flames. Drums of petrol, projected upwards, burst in mid-air, blazing globes of fire that floated slowly down. A moment later a rolling wall of heavy, billowing smoke, lit to a fierce red by the fires burning on the ground, had taken possession of half the horizon and reached to the sky. It seemed incredible that the petty manipulations we had done so quietly in the dark could result in such a glorious catastrophe. It was more than we expected; our reward was ten times what had been promised. Such a munificence made us wonder; we felt slightly awed and very powerful.

For a whole hour the blaze increased in intensity. Our men kept falling out to gaze back at the wonder and then caught up again at a trot. The glare of the burning dump lit our way and made the going easier. Then, as we increased our distance and intervening hills threw longer shadows, I found myself once more stumbling in the dark and hard put to it to keep up with our indefatigable guide. On we walked. Overcome with exhaustion, I renounced my self-respect and asked Mohammed el Obeidi how far we were now from Kaf el Kefra. 'Not far,' he replied laconically and we plodded on.

The first light of dawn came. The fire behind us shone with undiminished fierceness. We plodded on. The sun rose: we were in a barren wilderness of sandy hills and scrub. My head swam with fatigue; to keep awake I tried working out a sum: *The Germans have 200 tanks – they do five miles to the gallon – in battle they run fifty miles a day. How many days' supply are 100,000 gallons of petrol?* I kept losing the thread of my argument and starting again from the beginning – then I got a surprising answer – *sixty-two days*. This was too good; it couldn't be correct.

Patiently I began again. This time the answer came: *a third of a day, eight hours.* As a period as short as that was rather disappointing, back I went to my premises. Mohammed el Obeidi came up to me and said: 'Kaf el Kefra is now near.' We were all well tired out by now, but we went on under the warmer sun. I worked once more on my problem and got as an answer *twelve days.* It seemed satisfactory and I lost interest. We walked . . . Our guide said 'Beyond that hill is Kaf el Kefra.' I laughed out aloud because of a joke of ours: 'When you start on a trip the guide says the objective is *far* – after four hours' walk he says it is *not far* – four hours later he says it is near – four hours' walk again and he says it is *beyond that hill* – then you walk another four hours before getting there.' With dragging feet and an aching body I tramped along for another eternity, then I looked up again: the sun was hardly higher in the sky, which was surprising. Someone said in Arabic: 'There comes Musa riding a camel.' And indeed I saw a rider approaching across the yellow plain – one of our own men, mounted on one of our camels. We had arrived. Musa slid off his camel and shook my hand with fervour – he patted me on the shoulder and pointed to the eastern horizon, where a solid black cloud of smoke stretched from north to south.[5]

If the logistic facts upon which Peniakoff's mind had been working had been correct, his answer to his sum would have been fifty days – but panzers in desert conditions rarely averaged two miles to the gallon, and in battle conditions could easily use up twenty gallons in a morning. With all the back-up and supply vehicles necessary to keep it in action, the Afrika Korps needed a minimum of 150,000 gallons a day – so Peniakoff's second answer was the nearest to the truth. But a battle could easily be lost for want of eight hours' petrol.

It was the partnership between the Long Range Desert Group and the fast-growing Special Air Service which was showing most promise and attaining some unexpectedly good results.

After an initial catastrophe at the onset of *Crusader*, the founder of the organisation Captain David Stirling and his chief aide Lieutenant 'Paddy' Mayne, ably assisted by two other young officers who had realised the necessity of military professionalism, Lieutenants Lewes and Fraser, worked out a system of hard and realistic training which quickly weeded out those volunteers whose motivation in joining had been either search for glamour or escape from discipline, and moulded those who remained into tightly knit units of self-reliant and expert raiders of extremely high morale. Early successes increased that morale, the occasional and inevitable failure did little to dampen it.

As the first parachute drop to be attempted had proved prohibitively expensive in men – and as the R.A.F. were in any case loth to use their machines for such purposes when they thought they could be better used bombing Benghasi – Stirling approached the L.R.D.G. with a proposition: first, the L.R.D.G. should take them to their objectives and collect them after they had carried out their missions; secondly, the L.R.D.G. should train S.A.S. men in the techniques of desert driving and navigation so that in due course their 'taxi-service' would not be required. The response was enthusiastic and a most profitable partnership began.

Four parties had set off from Jalo while *Crusader* was still at its height, and on the night of December 14th they attacked airfields at Tamit, Sirte, El Agheila and Agedabia, and of the four, only one proved unfruitful. Mayne's party at Tamit destroyed a petrol dump and twenty-four planes in fifteen minutes of concentrated action, then broke into a building in which it was evident that some sort of party was being held and sprayed the unfortunate celebrators with Tommy-gun fire. This raid was distinguished by Paddy Mayne's extraordinary feat of destroying one of the planes with his bare hands – tearing out the instrument panel and all the equipment behind it, as, he afterwards claimed, a souvenir. He had, before the war, played Rugby football for Ireland, and his physical strength had always been remarkable.

At Sirte, David Stirling's party was disappointed to watch the planes which had been their objective take off while they were hiding close by, and at El Agheila Lewes's party also found the airfield empty – but they then broke into a transport park and left their 'sticky bombs' on a large collection of transport, and on their way out shot up a roadhouse where Italian drivers were eating.

Fraser's party at Agedabia met with the greatest success, breaking through a well-lit perimeter fence, eluding all the guards and destroy-ing altogether thirty-seven aircraft, then getting clear away in the confusion which flared as soon as their bombs began exploding. It was a notable 'bag' for only four men – and indeed the total strength of the S.A.S. party to leave Jalo had been only thirteen (four officers and nine N.C.O.s and privates) and between them they destroyed sixty-one aircraft and an unknown but considerable number of vehicles, in addition to killing and wounding a number of enemy soldiers.

Another raid was organised almost as soon as the party had returned to base, but this time Fortune did not favour them so highly, for Lewes was killed and Fraser and his party missed the pick-up rendezvous and eventually added to the growing legend of desert marches by walking home – two hundred miles in eight days on half a pint of water each per day.

Reports of some of the early operations, as dictated shortly after they had taken place by the laconic Lieutenant Mayne, make fascinating reading.

5th Operation
Objective: Tamit aerodrome
Method: LRDG S Patrol
Date: 24 December 1941

Operation: Party consisting of Lieutenant Mayne, Sgt McDonald, Ptes Bennet, White, Chesworth and Hawkins. Left Jalo with Sirte party and broke off at Wadi Timet. Motored to within 3 miles of drome and then walked in. Destroyed 27 aircraft but were fired on by MGs etc. and had to run for it. Sergeant McDonald and Private White were cut off but were picked up later. Contacted patrol and returned to Jalo. Both parties celebrated Xmas on the way back. Plenty of beer, Xmas pudding, gazelle etc.

10th Operation
Objective: Derna Aerodrome
Method: LRDG
8 March 1942

Operation: Party consisting of Captain Mayne, Bennet, Rose, and Burns. Walked in to drome 30 miles and arrived at 0400 hours. Walked round drome and split up. Captain Mayne and Pte Bennet destroyed 15 planes. Cpl Rose and Burns destroyed 15 torpedo bombs, petrol and equipment. On subsequent walk back Burns fell out. We met but failed to find rendezvous but were picked up next day. Searched for Burns but without success. Whole party returned to Siwa and subsequently to Kabrit.[6]

One of the perpetual hazards of such operations was the prospect of being left behind, lost, exhausted or wounded, and another was of being shot up by your own aircraft; but as one of the survivors was to remark many years later, it was a better bet than taking part in a bayonet charge.

By this time, the S.A.S. had won recognition and support from the High Command, and had been given permission to increase their strength by another six officers and forty men – though as most regular units were understandably reluctant to release men good enough to meet Stirling's requirements, this increase was only met by the incorporation of fifty Free French parachutists who had come down from Syria. The S.A.S. had also adopted its own cap-badge and motto, 'Who Dares, Wins', and designed and had produced its own parachute emblem based upon a symbolic Ibis with outstretched wings, which the men could wear on their right shoulders when they had qualified as parachutists, and above their left tunic-pocket if and when Stirling considered that they had done well enough on operations. This latter was to become a highly-prized distinction.

On January 17th, 1942, a joint L.R.D.G. and S.A.S. operation was mounted against a different type of objective – the port installations at Buerat – for which purpose a canvas canoe was included, with crew from what was already known as the Special Boat Section; but the expedition was shot up on the way in and lost their wireless truck, the canoe did not stand up to the rigours of desert travel and the shipping in the harbour thus remained unscathed. However the local radio station was blown up (by the S.B.S. crew), bombs were left on several of the port installations and eighteen petrol carriers were destroyed; and a sandstorm protected them all from aerial attack during their journey home.

There then followed a series of unsuccessful attempts to reach Benghasi and attack shipping in the harbour there, but although S.A.S. parties wandered around the port during several nights, bad luck attended these operations and they achieved little. In one of them Randolph Churchill took part, but even his presence was not enough to excite violence, though the party was very nearly discovered by an Italian sailor – too drunk, however, to realise the importance of the occasion. On the way back, fortunately after they had reached their own lines, their car, which was being driven with great élan but rather less skill by David Stirling, overturned – and Churchill's back was so badly injured that he had to be invalided home. It is interesting to reflect upon the opposing emotions which would have been raised throughout Europe and the Mediterranean basin, had it become known at the time how closely the son of the British Prime Minister had escaped capture – and indeed, death.

During May, it became obvious that Malta was in danger of starvation and possible collapse as a result of the blockade which the Luftwaffe and the Italian Navy had been able to mount of late, and that somehow a supply convoy must succeed in getting through. In order to assist such a convoy, it was decided to attempt to weaken the air attack which might be mounted against it by a series of co-ordinated raids against airfields in both Cyrenaica and Crete.

For these raids the entire strength of the S.A.S. was mobilised, including the Free French who had by now completed their specialist training. Eight five-men patrols were briefed, three for Benghasi, three for Derna, one for Barce and one for Heraklion on the north coast of Crete. The raids in Cyrenaica met with varying success; Stirling's personal attack wreaked extraordinary damage but the one made by fifteen Free French ran into total disaster, for in order to help them through an area believed to be swarming with German troops, they had taken with them members of the group known as S.I.G. – Special Interrogation Group – composed of Germans with strong anti-Nazi opinions. Many of the group were Jewish refugees from Nazi Germany, whose courage in undertaking such a mission was extraordinary, but on this occasion they also included two German prisoners-of-war who had persuasively professed sympathy with their views, but who in fact broke away at the first opportunity and reported the presence of the party to their own side. In the resultant battle, fourteen of the Frenchmen were killed or taken prisoner.

But it was the raid on Heraklion in Crete which won the greatest success.

Under command of the Free French Commandant Bergé, the party consisted of three Free French privates, a Greek guide, Lieutenant Costi, and as second-in-command, Captain the Earl Jellicoe, son of the admiral who had commanded the British Grand Fleet at the Battle of Jutland.

After a voyage of four days aboard H.M. Submarine *Triton* the party paddled ashore in rubber boats to land some miles east of Heraklion, whereupon, after unloading, Jellicoe swam back out to sea towing the boats behind him and sank them, for the party was to be picked up from the island's southern shore. They then faced a long and arduous approach march, for the country was very broken, and their confidence was not improved by the fact that the Cretans they encountered on the way invariably greeted them in fractured but enthusiastic English.

They sheltered the first night in a convenient cave, and from nearby spent the next day observing their target, Heraklion airfield, upon which at one time they counted over sixty aircraft, mostly Junkers 88s. Attempts during the next day to move closer in order to mount the attack that night were foiled by the number and depth of defence positions, but by the following evening, after a third cold night and a fourth hungry and thirsty day, the party was close enough for Jellicoe and two of the men to work their way along the side of a German barrack block and reach the inner defences. It was satisfactorily dark, but as the others closed up and Jellicoe moved in to cut his way through the inner perimeter wire, a German patrol came along and the torch carried by one of them illuminated Jellicoe's large and curly head. Incipient disaster was only avoided by quick thinking on the part of one of the Free French privates, who emitted a drunken and ghastly snore which resulted in the patrol moving away with rather Puritan disgust, and by the time they had thought the episode over and returned for closer examination, the raiding party had cut their way through and were concealed in a bomb dump.

As it happened, the effects of the revelation of the gap in the wire were lost in the confusion occasioned by the landing of a flight of eight Junkers 88s, followed immediately by an enterprising R.A.F. Blenheim, which zoomed in at low level and dropped a string of bombs along the edge of the field. Within minutes, the S.A.S. party were running into the darkness which fringed the airfield and laying charges on the aircraft dispersed there in the bomb-proof shelters. They then worked their way back towards the entrance to the camp, still laying charges on any aircraft they came across, and as they reached the area of the main gate they saw in front of them a party being assembled, obviously in order to move out and patrol the roads.

They followed this party through the gates, laid the remainder of their charges on various lorries just outside, and escaped into the darkness; and three days later, having climbed two mountain ranges and walked 120 miles, they were waiting near the rendezvous to be picked up. Unfortunately, their hiding place was accidentally discovered by some Cretans who most uncharacteristically gave them away to the Germans, and after a brisk battle Commandant Bergé and two of the Frenchmen were taken prisoner and the other Frenchman killed.

Jellicoe and the Greek guide Costi, however, had been away reconnoitring a nearby village at the time and so escaped – and they were picked up that night by a caique manned by Royal Naval personnel, which also evacuated a number of Greek refugees and some New Zealanders who had escaped capture when the island fell.

The S.A.S. raid was undoubtedly a success and the idea of co-ordinated operations seemed to promise well for the future. Although the convoy for which the raids had been intended as support still lost fifteen of its seventeen ships, the other two might also have been hit by one or more of the forty-odd aircraft destroyed in those raids. As it was, the stores they carried proved just enough to sustain Malta until the next convoy arrived.

But all such operations were only peripheral to the main conflict. They might occasionally affect its course, but the decisive battles would still have to be fought out by massed armies, such as those which by the end of May had formed in the country to the south of Gazala inlet – poised for yet another clash of arms in which both sides hoped to decide who would dominate the North African theatre and the vital sea-lanes to the north of it.

2 · No Drums, No Trumpets

During the period between the end of Rommel's counterstroke in February and the beginning of the next great desert battle at the end of May, the strategic significance and plight of the island of Malta dominated discussions in both the Axis and the Allied camps.

Malta was, as one authority put it, 'the windlass of the Allied tourniquet' on Rommel's supply lines, its continued existence as a base for submarine and aerial attacks on Axis convoys an ever-present hazard to all his plans, its elimination a boon for which he had frequently clamoured. But for many months, Hitler and the German High Command had turned a deaf ear to all such entreaties, for their attention was fixed on the Russian front and Hitler at least, ever suspicious of naval arguments, was still smarting at the cost to the Wehrmacht of the airborne assault on that other pestiferous Mediterranean island, Crete. So far as the High Command of the German Army were concerned, the entire Italian theatre of war was a 'side-show' in which victories were unsolicited gifts from heaven but which no one was prepared to take seriously – certainly not if added interest was likely to increase the overblown attentions already paid to the upstart Rommel, who was extremely unpopular with most of them, especially with Oberstgeneral Franz Halder, the Chief of Staff.

Until February 13th, 1942.

Upon that date, Grossadmiral Erich Raeder in his capacity of Commander-in-Chief of the Kriegsmarine had an audience with Hitler during which he pointed out to an unusually receptive Führer that Britain's purpose in waging war in Libya and Egypt had little to do with colonial ambitions, but was to protect her main oil supplies in the Middle East. If these could be captured, then not only might Britain be knocked out of the war, but German and Japanese hands might link on the shores of the Indian Ocean.

This was by no means the first occasion when Hitler's mind had dwelt upon that strategic interpretation of affairs, but now it made a deeper impression than before and he ordered Raeder to examine the possibilities of what later became briefly known as 'The Great Plan' – the strategic nightmare which had haunted both Wavell and Auchin-

leck, of an advance down from the Caucasus into Persia meeting a
greatly reinforced drive by the Afrika Korps across the Nile and into
Palestine.

Obviously, supplies to Rommel would loom large in any such
examination, and as a result the reduction of Malta as the principal
block to such supplies quickly assumed a high priority. But as
responsibility for operations in the Mediterranean still lay with the
Comando Supremo in Rome, Generale Cavallero soon became
embroiled in the discussions, and an interesting circle of argument
was revealed. No drive to the Nile could be launched until a sizeable
reserve of supplies had been built up in Tripoli and Panzerarmee
Afrika itself considerably strengthened; no supplies or reinforcements could reach Tripoli in the required numbers or at the necessary
rate while Malta remained active as a British submarine base or
'unsinkable aircraft carrier'; no major assault could be launched
against Malta until R.A.F. bases from which counter-attacks could be
delivered had been pushed much further east than those now lying
behind the Gazala positions.

This hardly presented an unbreakable impasse, but the solutions to
the problems involved served to focus attention in Berlin on the
Mediterranean to an unusual extent. Two plans were evolved –
Operation Herkules for the invasion of Malta for which Cavallero
obtained the promise of a German parachute division, and *Operation
Aida* for the drive to the Nile; and in the meantime, in order to soften
up the Malta defences, Kesselring was ordered to use his Luftflotte 2
to carry out a series of heavy attacks on the island. As this direction
was hardly in conflict with the original instructions to Luftflotte 2 to
safeguard convoys to North Africa it was carried out with formidable
determination, and during April alone Malta suffered two hundred
raids – an average of six per day. Some 6,700 tons of bombs fell on
the island that month and over 11,000 buildings were destroyed,
though fortunately the shelters built in the rock of which the island
consisted saved all but 1,000 lives.

This fierce bombardment had two immediate effects. It enabled a
much higher percentage of Rommel's supplies to reach him, and it so
affected Churchill that he insisted upon an Eighth Army offensive at
an early date – and when it became obvious to Rommel that that
offensive was due, he easily obtained Hitler's agreement that the
Afrika Korps should strike first.

On May 1st, a meeting took place at Berchtesgaden between
Führer and Duce and the decisions were made: the first half of
Operation Aida would begin at the end of May to forestall the British
offensive and would consist of the defeat of the Eighth Army in the
Gazala Line, the capture of Tobruk and possibly the clearance of the
desert as far forward as the Egyptian border. There the Afrika Korps

would stand while *Operation Herkules* took place during the second half of July. And with Malta eliminated and Benghasi and Tobruk open as supply ports, fuel, ammunition and reinforcements could be rushed forward during August for the drive to the Delta, where quite possibly enough loot would be captured to enable immediate further penetration beyond the Nile. By December 1942, therefore, British power in the Middle East could be at an end.

To Rommel, the prospects opened to him were entrancing and the situation novel. Not only were supplies reaching him at an unprecedented rate, but he was being positively encouraged instead of flatly forbidden to develop and carry out his plans. For this attack he need fear no anxious eyes peering over his shoulder, no curbing hand at his elbow, and although he had no intention of revealing all his intentions to anyone but his own personal staff, at least he was not obliged to throw a heavy cloak of secrecy over even the decision to move forward.

As for the enemy opposite, recent experiences and the present euphoric atmosphere of aid and encouragement combined to give him a feeling almost of contempt for them. There had apparently been no change in the command structure which had so signally failed to organise effective resistance to his latest offensive, and as far as enemy troops were concerned, those who in the past had proved the

Map 3   Rommel's view of Gazala defences

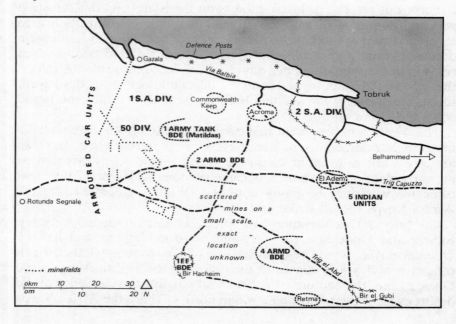

most obdurate – the Australians and the New Zealanders – were conspicuously absent. South Africans held the 'bastion' at the northern end by the coast, a new British division – the 50th, brought across from Cyprus and entirely inexperienced in desert warfare – held the stretch of the line down to just north of the Trig Capuzzo, while well away to the south a Free French brigade held a heavily fortified position at Bir Hacheim.

Undoubtedly, the fortifications themselves were deeply dug and stoutly constructed, the minefields surrounding and connecting them being laid so thickly and in such wide belts as to merit in places the description of 'mine-marsh' – but to Rommel the entire concept of a strongly held line was wrong:

> The basic British plan for the defence of the Marmarica was shaped by a desire to impose on the attacker a form of warfare more to the liking of their own command than manoeuvring in the open desert. The technical execution of the plan was first-rate.
>
> But the premises from which they approached the problem were false. In any North African desert position with an open southern flank, a rigid system of defence is bound to lead to disaster. The defence must be conducted offensively for it to be successful. Naturally, fortified lines can be of great value in preventing the enemy from undertaking particular operational moves. But the manning of such lines must not, under any circumstances, be at the expense of the forces required for the mobile defence.[1]

Even behind the main line, the British seemed wedded to a policy of static defence. Strongpoints, or 'boxes' as they came to be called, had been formed from units of the 5th Indian Division at Point 209, known as Commonwealth Keep, at Acroma on the western flank of Tobruk and at El Adem guarding the port's southern approaches; and there were apparently other, smaller defence posts along the northern coast as a natural precaution against a sea-borne attack – for which, indeed, Rommel had plans. Later he was to write:

> All these fortified points were provided with powerful artillery, infantry and armoured car units, and abundant supplies. The entire line was remarkable for the extraordinary degree of technical skill which had gone into its construction. All defence positions and strongpoints conformed to the most modern requirements of warfare. Countless numbers of mines had been laid – over a million in the Marmarica positions.[2]

But as far as mobile defences were concerned – the armoured units with which Rommel associated the only chances for victory in either defence or offence in the desert – these, as usual, seemed to have been split up into penny packets and distributed about the area, more with the idea that they would be available to go to the help of the static infantry defences than that they might be concentrated to form a striking force of sufficient power to cause a serious check to his own intentions.

According to information reaching him, there was a brigade of heavy infantry Matilda tanks up behind the junction of the South African and 50th Divisions, a brigade identified as 2nd Armoured from 1st Armoured Division lying just west of the junction of the Acroma–Bir Hacheim track with the Trig Capuzzo, and another – 4th Armoured Brigade – well away to the south, level with Bir Hacheim but nearly ten miles east of the fortress and lying across the Trig el Abd. There had, Rommel knew, been some reorganisation inside the British armoured divisions, the Support Groups having been dropped and replaced by what were called Motor Brigades, each consisting of three motorised infantry battalions and a regiment of field and anti-tank guns. One of these – the 7th (presumably part of the 7th Armoured Division) – was loose even further to the south and east, though this unit too appeared irretrievably bound to yet another defence box at a remote location known as Retma.

There had been talk of the British re-arming with a more powerful tank, but Rommel had taken little notice of this as he was of the ever-strengthening opinion that even the best weapons were valueless in the hands of troops not properly trained to use them, especially when the troops themselves were commanded by men who had little understanding of the basic doctrines of armoured, mobile warfare. This was undoubtedly a tenable theory, and his attitude to other information to the effect that heavier anti-tank guns were now arriving in the enemy front line area was conditioned by the same reasoning. In the end, he felt, it would be the experience and training of the men behind the guns which would count.

The only orthodox Allied formations which still commanded Rommel's respect were the armoured car units holding his own reconnaissance battalions well away from the main British and South African positions and, he was well aware, keeping a close eye on every movement of the forces under his command. The highly experienced 11th Hussars were unaccountably absent, but the 4th and the 6th South African Armoured Car units, the King's Dragoon Guards and the 12th Lancers seemed to have inherited some of the 11th's expertise, and certainly did not lack their daring.

However, so far as concealment of intent was concerned, Rommel had a few tricks of his own which might baffle even the shrewd observation of these men when the crucial moment came and his great offensive got under way.

His plans for the opening moves were simple, and herein, he felt, lay their great virtue. He would close up to the South African and 50th Division positions in the north with four Italian divisions – Sabratha, Trento, Brescia and Pavia – strengthened by two regimental groups from 90th Light along the coast, while Group Hecker, consisting of a battalion of Italian marines strengthened by German gunners and engineers, demonstrated at sea and thus drew all enemy attention to the north. In order to add to this deception, two panzer regiments, one from Ariete and one from Afrika Korps, would accompany the first daylight moves towards the enemy in the north, making as much dust as possible to exaggerate their size and to add an extra verisimilitude to the pretence that here lay the axis of the main attack.

But as soon as darkness fell, these panzers would return to their parent formations concentrated around the Rotunda Segnale, for the main thrust. This was to be a hook around the southern end of the Gazala Line, delivered by his massed armour – Ariete Armoured and Trieste Motorised Divisions on the left, 21st and 15th Panzer in the centre, while the bulk of 90th Light, their apparent hitting power augmented by aero-engines mounted in lorries which would churn up so much dust that the appearance of yet another panzer division would be created, would swing even wider out to the right, well down past Bir Hacheim.

Bir Hacheim itself, Rommel considered, would be virtually stamped into the ground in less than an hour by the combined weight of 21st and 15th Panzer Divisions, after which the main panzer force would stream on northwards, defeat the British armour as it came against it in its spread-eagled, isolated positions, smash through the Acroma box and reach the sea. Meanwhile, 90th Light on the outer rim of the wheel would have driven north-east, either by-passed or eliminated the box at El Adem and gone on to reach the edge of the main British supply dump laid out to the east of Belhammed.

All this should happen within the first twenty-four hours, after which the panzer divisions aided by the Italian armour (if they had kept up) would turn *west* and attack the South Africans and 50th Division from the rear, and as these would now be neatly sandwiched between the original Italian attacking force and his own armour, they would probably be eliminated quite quickly despite the strength of their defences. The combined Axis forces then would turn their attention to the final reduction of Tobruk, in which endeavour they would be sustained by the food, water, fuel and ammunition from that enormous British supply dump east of Belhammed, which 90th Light would have captured. In the light of this virtually guaranteed windfall, Panzerarmee Afrika would need to organise re-supply for only three days and fuel for 300 miles, to be brought up behind them by fast convoy.

Euphoria would seem to have been affecting judgment.

As a student of Napoleon's maxims, Rommel was a great – and indeed sustained – believer in the doctrine that, in war, it is not the men who count; it is the *man*. Well, he would, of course, lead Afrika Korps himself; but even with far better communications than the great

Corsican ever had at his command, it was necessary for him to be certain of other important men. Gambara – lately Italian Chief of Staff and commander of XX Corps – had gone; he had been heard to remark, perhaps in pique as a result of his astringent treatment during *Crusader* or possibly even because of more deeply felt emotions, that he hoped 'to live twenty years longer in order to command an army which will then fight the Germans' – and an association which had been abrasive for some time was abruptly terminated.

His place had been taken by Generale Count Emilio Barbasetti, a soldier whose name is engraved but lightly on the pages of military history.

Afrika Korps was no longer commanded by General Cruewell, for he had been overdue for leave and during the latter stages of *Crusader* had suffered acutely from jaundice – a complaint rife among both armies in the desert, generally as a result of drinking inadequately treated water drawn from old, native wells. However, Cruewell returned to Africa just before the offensive began and took command of the infantry movements in the north.

His place as Afrika Korps commander was taken by General-leutnant Walther Nehring, a soldier of cool judgment, quiet wit and great administrative competence, and for the situation in hand he was probably the perfect choice. If *Operation Aida* developed as planned he would never move far out from under Rommel's shadow.

All three German divisions had new commanders – General-leutnant Georg von Bismarck took over 21st Panzer Division from Böttcher, Generalleutnant Gustav von Vaerst replaced Neumann-Sylkow as 15th Panzer commander and Generalleutnant Ulrich Kleeman took von Sümmermann's place in command of 90th Light; and although only von Bismarck was at all well known to Rommel, the homogeneity of training throughout the German Army was enough to ensure that the newcomers would still understand the orders they received, and be well aware of the manner in which Rommel expected them to be obeyed.

Despite Rommel's belief to the contrary, there had also been changes at the top in Auchinleck's command, as a result of his acceptance of Godwin-Austen's request for relief. One of the great figures of the desert fighting, 'Strafer' Gott, who had commanded the Support Group during the O'Connor offensive and the 7th Armoured Division since then, was now promoted lieutenant-general and given command of XIII Corps which contained the infantry divisions, while Willoughby Norrie retained command of the armour of XXX Corps which he had held throughout *Crusader*. Within Norrie's XXX Corps, Major-General Lumsden had recovered from his wounds and resumed command of 1st Armoured Division, so Major-General Messervy took Gott's old appointment commanding 7th Armoured Division.

There were other aspects in which Rommel's information was at fault, too, for there were *three* divisions in Gott's XIII Corps, though Rommel's belief that only two were in the front line was correct. The 1st South African Division held the bastion at the northern end of the Gazala Line, its three brigade groups manning the fifteen miles running down from the coast in descending numerical order – 3rd, 2nd, 1st. Its original commander, General Brink, had returned to the Union after the end of *Crusader*, and in his place had been promoted the commander of the 1st Brigade, Dan Pienaar. This had not been a popular promotion among other troops serving in Eighth Army, especially the New Zealanders who believed with some reason that their ordeal below Belhammed during *Crusader* could have been alleviated had 1st South African Brigade shown a little more willingness to come to their aid; but by May 1942 the South Africans had been in position for four months and, as they were already thoroughly experienced in fortification work, their defences were deep indeed, each brigade group almost boxed in with minefields.

Behind them, garrisoning Tobruk, were the two remaining brigades of 2nd South African Division (one had been totally destroyed during *Crusader*), their divisional strength made up by 9th Indian Infantry Brigade Group from 5th Indian Division, whose two other brigades were held in reserve back in Egypt. This 2nd South African Division and the ancillary troops in the Tobruk garrison were commanded by Major-General H. B. Klopper.

The 50th (Tyne and Tees) Division which had been brought over from Cyprus was commanded by Major-General W. H. C. Ramsden and two of its three brigade groups were where Rommel expected them to be – continuing the line southwards from Pienaar's brigades towards the Trig Capuzzo; but the South African Armoured Car units had been particularly successful in masking the middle part of the line from Axis eyes and the third brigade group – 150th – was well dug in behind minefields south of the Trig Capuzzo, filling the gap between it and the Trig el Abd where it in turn crossed the defence line. Thirteen miles of thickly sewn mine-marsh separated the Trig el Abd position from the Free French brigade at Bir Hacheim, commanded by Brigadier-General Pierre Koenig and united in its determination to re-establish their country's military reputation after the sorry events at home and in the Middle East of the last months. As they too had been in position for some time and had laboured long and hard at their defences, it seemed likely that Rommel's estimate of an hour's possible resistance from them would prove inaccurate.

It was certainly inaccurate with regard to the amount of armour dispersed behind the Gazala Line to meet his own in the drive north. There were, for instance, *two* Army Tank Brigades – the 1st and the 32nd – instead of the one of which he knew, lying up behind the infantry divisions in the north, and between them they could put 116 Valentines and 110 Matildas into the field against him. There was also an extra Armoured Brigade Group (22nd, under a new commander, Brigadier W. H. Carr), the 29th Indian Brigade Group back at Bir el Gubi, and by the time the battle opened another Motor Brigade Group just south of Bir Hacheim – of all of which he knew nothing. Even more important from both offensive and defensive points of view, the Guards Brigade had now been motorised (and renumbered 201st) and stationed in yet another defensive box at the junction of the Trig Capuzzo and the Acroma–Bir Hacheim tracks, quickly and appropriately known to all as 'Knightsbridge'. The Household Brigade always does its best to feel at home.

There were thus five more brigade groups facing Rommel than he was bargaining for – one infantry, two motorised, two armoured – and he had placed one infantry brigade group in the wrong position. Where he was right, however, was in his belief that the men of the army facing him were inadequately trained to meet the kind of assault which the Afrika Korps could mount, and that the co-ordination of all arms which was the key to his own success was still lacking in the Eighth Army.

This condition was exacerbated by differences of opinion at the topmost command level, and disagreement of principle at levels only just below which showed itself on occasion in downright personal antagonism.

There is no doubt that by this time Ritchie's position had become so awkward as to be invidious. Auchinleck's confidence in him had declined since the retreat from El Agheila and the C.-in-C. later told one of his staff, Brigadier Dorman-Smith, that he had had 'to hold his [Ritchie's] hand' the entire time. It seems that he was determined to continue holding it now, especially as there was a fundamental difference of opinion between them as to probable future developments.

The highly secret source of intelligence in England – the Ultra Organisation which by enormous intellectual activity and use of reconstructed Enigma encyphering machines was by now reading Wehrmacht cables almost as soon as the intended recipients – had been able to warn Auchinleck of Rommel's intentions to attack, and to give an accurate forecast of the date. What Ultra had not been able to do, however, was to give him any idea of Rommel's tactical plans for the battle (for these had obviously not been the subject of cables between Tripoli and Berlin) and Auchinleck's personal opinion was that the main attack would come as a smashing blow in the north – at the junction of the South African Division and 50th Division – with an auxiliary attack in the south against Bir Hacheim which, though doubtless serious for the defenders, would still be in the nature of a feint.

On May 20th, therefore, Auchinleck wrote a long letter to Ritchie, setting out the situation as he saw it and urging him to keep the two armoured divisions of XXX Corps together and within supporting distance. After suggesting that 'both your armoured divisions complete should be positioned astride the Trig Capuzzo' he went on:

> I consider it to be of the highest importance that you should not break up the organisation of either of the armoured divisions. They have been trained to fight as divisions, I hope, and fight as divisions they should. Norrie must handle them as a corps commander, and thus be able to take advantage of the flexibility which the fact of having two formations gives him. Moreover, you will be getting the 1st Armoured Brigade before long, and it should join the 7th Armd. Div. . . . [3]

But Ritchie strongly believed that Rommel's main thrust would come around the south of the line – either around or through Bir Hacheim – and replied three days later with a long letter which included the following paragraph:

> I still feel that if his maintenance makes this possible he will try to go round our southern flank. In any case there will be a diversion there and this will probably be the Italian Mobile Corps . . . Anyhow whatever course he may adopt, our main strength is the counter with our armour to destroy him. We are ready for this . . . the ground carefully studied, and I feel confident that our armed forces are prepared to operate either to the south or to the north-west. [4]

However, whether from an excess of politeness or from a feeling of subordination to higher authority, the whole tone of the rest of the letter glossed over this important, indeed fundamental difference of opinion between them, and such was the note of accord struck that Auchinleck replied the same day, saying, among other encouraging phrases, 'I am quite happy about the positioning of the armoured divisions, and I am glad we are thinking on the same lines; this is always comforting!'

It seems likely, however, that had a comparison been made between the battle maps at Ritchie's and Auchinleck's headquarters it would have become evident that they were *not* thinking on quite the same lines. Ritchie had *not* positioned both armoured divisions 'astride the Trig Capuzzo', but deployed 1st Armoured Division to the south of it, and 7th Armoured Division even further south with its armour – as Rommel had divined – more disposed to go to the

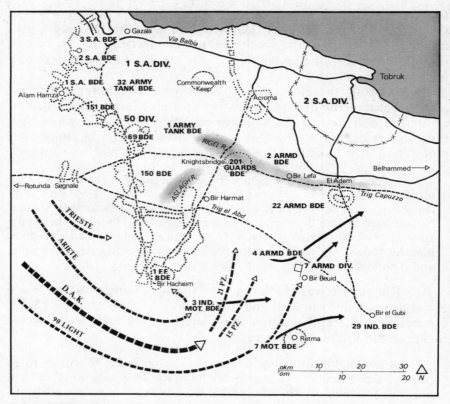

Map 4   May 27th, dawn

support of the isolated infantry boxes than to coalesce with 1st
Armoured Division into a massive armoured force.

Ironically, Auchinleck himself contributed even more to this
potential wide dispersion of the armour when, right at the last
moment, he sent up the two further infantry brigades to hold static
positions along the southern flank of the battle area – 29th Indian
Brigade to Bir el Gubi and the 3rd Indian Motor Brigade to a position
just a few miles south-east of Bir Hacheim. Had they only to act as
blocks to a feint operation (and had the Motor Brigade near Bir
Hacheim been given rather more time to prepare defences) it is
possible that they would have amply fulfilled their purpose, but in the
face of Ritchie's belief that they might lie in the path of Rommel's
main offensive, they acted instead in Ritchie's mind as magnets for
more armoured protection.

Auchinleck was also greatly responsible for the constitution of the
forces holding these isolated positions.

'It was not only the enemy', says the *Official History*, encouragingly, 'who had noticed that the British armour, artillery and infantry had often been unsuccessful in concerting their action on the battle-field.' When some of the lessons of *Crusader* had been studied, Auchinleck had issued directives intended to bring about a closer integration of the various arms essential to any modern battlegroup, and one of the immediate results was the emergence of the concept of the 'Brigade Group'.

Instead of divisions consisting of brigades composed entirely of armour or of infantry, with 'divisional' anti-tank, anti-aircraft, field artillery, engineers and administrative units held separately, these latter units would now be incorporated into each brigade so that, for instance, an infantry brigade group would consist of its three infantry battalions *plus* a regiment of field and anti-tank guns and its own anti-aircraft and engineer units, all trained together. An armoured brigade group would contain three tank regiments, a motor battalion (vehicle-borne infantry) and a regiment of field and anti-tank guns, while a motor brigade group would consist of three motorised infantry battalions and a similar allocation of artillery and engineers. Infantry divisions would consist of three infantry brigade groups, armoured divisions eventually of one armoured brigade group and one motorised brigade group – though for the coming battle both armoured divisions would be stronger than that.

One obvious and beneficial effect of this integration of all arms within a brigade would be to give it a degree of independence which could prove extremely useful should it become isolated; but on the other hand that very independence, unless carefully controlled, could weaken cohesion inside a division. Ironically, this divisive factor was perhaps exacerbated by the fact that the brigades were also being substantially strengthened as new weapons arrived in the Delta – a point to which Rommel might have been advised to give rather closer attention, despite the justification of his attitude to their use or misuse by untrained troops.

Over a hundred new 6-pounder anti-tank guns had arrived in the Delta to begin the replacement of the unpopular 2-pounders, and nearly 250 General Grant tanks had also arrived from America. These, in addition to the reliability of engine and general robustness which had so endeared the American Stuarts to their crews, carried a 75mm. gun firing both anti-tank and high explosive shells together with a 37mm. high velocity turret gun similar to the main armament of the Stuarts. The arrival of these tanks, with more Stuarts (known to their British crews as Honeys) from America and more Crusaders from Britain had not only given Auchinleck a substantial reserve stock (though not the third armoured division which he had stated was necessary) but also the material with which to carry out the 'brigade group' reorganisation.

Obviously, it would take time for the physical side of such reorganisation and re-equipment to take place; how long it would take for the philosophical acceptance of a doctrine which tended to break down the age-old barriers between cavalry and infantry, and to a lesser extent between both of these and the gunners and engineers, remained to be seen. But one extra disrupting factor was already in evidence which made it unlikely that that co-ordination which Auchinleck so rightly desired would be achieved.

Ritchie's problems did not all come from above. As has been related, Godwin-Austen's place had been taken by Strafer Gott – promoted from command of the 7th Armoured Division – and although this meant that at least one of the corps commanders was junior in appointment to Ritchie, the fact remained that Gott had been serving in the desert for longer, and his prestige throughout the entire desert theatre was far higher. He was, moreover, a close personal friend of the other corps commander, Norrie, who consulted him on frequent occasions – hardly an unreasonable course of action, but one which sometimes appeared to exclude the Army Commander from discussions in which he should have played the dominant role.

Further down the scale matters were, if anything, worse. The South African commander, Major-General Dan Pienaar, had already gained for himself a reputation for what has been described as 'sheer bloodymindedness' and his relations with Gott were already strained. As for those between the armoured divisional commanders in XXX Corps, Lumsden and Messervy, since the retreat from El Agheila these had deteriorated to such an extent that they hardly spoke to one another. Herbert Lumsden was a man who combined an intense loyalty to those who served with – and especially under – him, with a hasty temper and a somewhat unforgiving nature, and during the period after he had been wounded, command of his 1st Armoured Division had been given to Messervy, whom – rightly or wrongly – Lumsden blamed for the disasters which followed. Never again, he felt, should any of his own beloved units be entrusted to such inexpert hands, and he made little attempt to disguise his conviction that Messervy was unfit to command armour of any description.

The conferences held by Ritchie before the battle, therefore, were by no means congenial occasions, and little attempt was made by any of those present to adjust their preconceived views. And one of the views held by at least three of them was that if their revered Commander-in-Chief, General Auchinleck, felt that the enemy would attack in the centre or the north, that was where the attack should be expected – whatever the opinions of this comparative newcomer to desert fighting, the Eighth Army Commander.

However, in the face of Ritchie's continued insistence that Rommel *might* come around the south of the line, Norrie did agree in principle that, in that event, the main armour of 7th Armoured Division – the 4th Armoured Brigade – should move to protect those isolated infantry boxes out in the blue, and that 22nd Armoured Brigade should go to their support despite the icy disfavour with which their divisional commander received this suggestion.

Not, Norrie thought, that the situation was particularly likely to arise.

Incredibly – and all the irony of history is reflected here – there was now a combination of circumstances by which Britain might, in theory, have benefited from that discrepancy between Ritchie's apparent agreement with Auchinleck, and his deployment of forces in the field.

Although the Ultra Organisation was undoubtedly the greatest intelligence coup of the Second World War, the Axis Powers were not without their own triumphs in the field, and one of these was the breaking of the American State Department cypher by which its military agents communicated with Washington. Since early 1941, an American 'observer', Colonel Bonner Fellers, had been in Cairo, and such had been his interest and sympathy with the British cause that he had been attached to Eighth Army during the whole of the *Crusader* operation and been given, moreover, a free hand to roam the battlefield. After the attack on Pearl Harbor, his credentials and standing were of course greatly increased, and he was invited to attend General Auchinleck's conferences with the chief British staff officers and their naval and air force colleagues which, as the time for the battle at Gazala came nearer, were held every day.

And every night, Colonel Fellers cabled Washington with their details, and busy interceptors in Bari recorded them, busier interpreters translated them more or less efficiently into Italian and German army jargon, and their superiors then forwarded what information they considered desirable (for like intelligence experts the world over, they felt that it was necessary to guard their sources and often that short-term military advantage was not necessarily the right price to pay for loss of their own long-term omniscience) to Rommel.

So in the last hours before the opening moves of the Battle of Gazala, the German Commander-in-Chief of Panzerarmee Afrika learned – more or less – what the British Commander-in-Chief, Middle East, believed that he and his commander in the field had decided was the best deployment of the Eighth Army troops behind the Gazala Line; and Rommel was to be just as surprised as Auchinleck when he discovered that Auchinleck's intentions and Ritchie's reality were some way apart.

To Rommel, all the auguries on May 26th seemed to beckon him on to swift and convincing victory. A stifling *khamsin* blanketed the area during the afternoon, effectively cloaking both the first stage of the movement of the Cruewell Group towards the enemy defence lines and also the first concentration of armour around Segnale. In the northern half of the line heavy Stuka attacks on the South African and 50th Division positions, followed immediately by concentrated artillery bombardments (and the Italian gunners had lost none of their skill or enterprise) must undoubtedly be focusing enemy attention there, and in the early evening the dust and cloud died away just enough for the armoured feint eastward from Segnale to be seen – and seen to be seen – by South African reconnaissance air-craft.

By the time dusk had fallen the *khamsin* had died and the massed armour of Panzerarmee Afrika could move away to the south-east – and with Rommel in the lead, the first exhilarating stage of the march into Egypt began:

> At 2030 I ordered Operation 'Venezia' and the 10,000 vehicles of the striking force began to move. My staff and I, in our place in the Afrika Korps column, drove through the moonlit night towards the great armoured battle. Occasional flares lit up the sky far in the distance – probably the Luftwaffe trying to locate Bir Hakeim. I was tense and keyed up, impatiently awaiting the coming day. What would the enemy do? What had he already done? These questions pounded my brain, and only morning would bring the answers. Our formations rolled forward without a halt.[5]

One late amendment to his orders had been made, for within the last few hours details of the unexpected density and width of the mine-marsh south of the Trig el Abd and down to Bir Hacheim had come in, and as a result the whole axis of the advance had been side-stepped to the right. It would now be the Ariete Division who would roll over Bir Hacheim on the drive to the north, with Trieste on their left, 21st Panzer on their right and 15th Panzer and 90th Light Division even further out on the rim of the wheel. As the night wore on, the Luftwaffe found Bir Hacheim, bombed it briefly and then pin-pointed the turning-point for Rommel's force out in the desert to the south.

Onward clanked and rolled the vast force – well on schedule – and having executed with admirable competence the massive wheel through over one hundred and twenty degrees, it refuelled and settled down to await the morning. By daybreak 332 panzers (practically all with additional armour at the front) and the 228 Italian M13s and 14s were poised – breakfasted and rested – for the lunge up behind the enemy lines. So far as Rommel could tell, their move had been entirely unobserved, and his optimism was sufficient to dispel any doubts that so gigantic a movement could escape the attention of the vigilant enemy armoured cars. The only apparent check to his plans was the mysterious disappearance of the entire Trieste Motorised Division, unaccountably absent from their position on the left of Ariete.

But there was no time to spare for search or even questioning, for the sky was a clear translucent blue and enemy aircraft must be expected soon to rob him of that vital element of surprise. Orders were shouted, the panzer engines roared and the whole vast cavalcade rumbled forward, creating a huge trident of dust as the three prongs of the advance separated out.

Ariete were first into action, against Indian infantry and gunners of the 3rd Indian Motor Brigade of whose presence they had had no warning but whom they wiped out in half an hour of intense action, overrunning the flimsy infantry positions and the hastily dug-in guns, killing or taking prisoner nearly four hundred and fifty officers and men, and chasing the survivors away to the east. By the end of this short action the Italian tank crews realised that this was not their main objective – the Free French at Bir Hacheim – but that first taste of battle increased their morale and they forged ahead towards the fort now visible on the horizon. Already, Stukas were flying in towards it from the west. It was not quite 0700 on May 27th.

Ten miles away to the east, the artillery and motorised infantry of 90th Light were enjoying a similar success. They had bumped into patrols of the 7th Motor Brigade, pursued them as far as the Retma box and isolated them there, after which they proceeded methodically to break into the defences. These had obviously been hastily prepared and were quickly destroyed – sangars crushed, rifle and machine-gun pits overrun, a few thin-skinned lorries shot up or overturned – and it was only a matter of minutes before the bulk of the defenders were seen streaming off to the east, presumably seeking the shelter of whatever force held Bir el Gubi.

By 0900 the Retma box had been eliminated and 90th Light Division were plunging onwards, to arrive at Bir Beuid where they rounded up a group of astonished British officers and administrative personnel who proved upon investigation to be none other than the Advanced Headquarters of 7th Armoured Division! (In their excitement the captors failed to attach any importance to the greying hair of one of the privates, with the result that General Messervy and two of his senior staff officers, who had taken the precaution of removing their badges of rank as soon as danger threatened, managed later to escape; but 7th Armoured Division were without a command structure and were to remain so for many vital hours.)

But it was in the centre that the most significant successes were scored. The panzer divisions caught the Grants and Crusaders of 4th

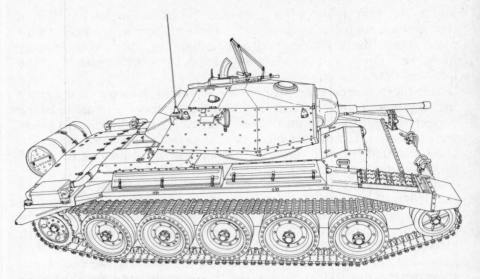

Figure 1   Cruiser tank Mark VI (Crusader): weight 14 tons; armour 7mm.–39mm.;
engine 340 h.p.; maximum speed 30 m.p.h.; armament one 2-pdr, two 7·92mm.
Besa machine-guns; crew 4

Armoured Brigade not only still on their way towards their battle
positions (they had completed a leisurely breakfast before moving)
but in two separate halves. This enabled 15th Panzer to destroy 8th
Hussars as a fighting unit in half an hour of swift but violent action,
then to crash on into two squadrons of 3rd Royal Tank Regiment
which they quickly reduced to ten tanks (out of ammunition by this
time, and three of them with smashed guns) and these they chased off
to the east – where they were promptly seen by the exuberant men of
90th Light, who picked up the scent and drove the quarry away past
El Adem and on towards Belhammed.

All this constituted a spectacular morning's work and behind the
spearheads the desert was already littered with wrecked tanks
belching flame and towering clouds of black smoke, smashed lorries
and trucks, groups of dejected prisoners searching through wreckage,
helping the ambulance crews as the wounded were tended and
moving out towards the periphery of the action in the hope of getting
away. But it had not been achieved without loss, and Rommel,
annoyed by some unnecessary risks run by his over-enthusiastic
assault troops, was already concerned by the cost of the battle so far.

Unfortunately our panzer units attacked without support, although I
had constantly been at pains to impress them not to do so until our
artillery had opened fire. There was also a British surprise awaiting us
here, one which was not to our advantage – the new Grant tank, which

was used in this battle for the first time on African soil. Tank after tank, German and British, was shattered in the fire of the tank-guns. Finally, we succeeded in throwing the British back to the Trig el Abd, although at the cost of heavy casualties.[6]

Ariete had by this time lost over forty M13s (for Bir Hacheim was proving a much tougher nut to crack than anyone on the Axis side had thought probable) and 15th and 21st between them as many panzers, though these of course still lay in the desert behind the advance where the excellent German recovery service was already at work. Nevertheless, at a cost of but one-seventh of their strength, Afrika Korps had already scattered two British motor brigade groups and one armoured brigade group, decapitated 7th Armoured Division and seemed likely to have proved Rommel's assertion that the British armoured command had still to learn the basic arts of their profession.

That this was so was to be demonstrated yet again, some ten miles north of the scene of the destruction of 4th Armoured Brigade Group, when 22nd Armoured Brigade Group moved slowly into view, alone and well out of range of support from its sister brigade group in 1st Armoured Division – the 2nd, then sitting immobile away to the east of the Guards Brigade at Knightsbridge. The resulting slaughter was this time carried out by 21st Panzer Division and within half an hour 22nd Brigade survivors were limping disconsolately back towards the 2nd positions, leaving behind them among the indifferent clumps of camel-thorn the smoking wrecks of thirty of their Grants and Stuarts together with several of their field and anti-tank guns.

But now, the pace of the advance began to slacken. Both panzer divisions had been emptying their ammunition racks and fuel tanks at an alarming rate, and the very success and speed of their victories had dispersed their forward elements even more than had been allowed for in Rommel's original plan. Where Trieste were no one knew, Ariete were still back at Bir Hacheim, the two panzer divisions were more or less together south of Knightsbridge, but 90th Light were away to the east driving up towards El Adem; and between the prongs of the advance was occurring that phenomenon of battles with the British – remarked upon by many frustrated commanders through the ages – the ability of junior ranks from battalion commanders down to troopers to improvise effective action and extricate themselves from the perils in which their generals had left them. Random groups of tank crews, infantry and gunners were coalescing and, out of touch with and thus untrammelled by orders from their superiors, were beginning to fight back effectively. The first intimation of this came to Rommel when he tried to go in search of 90th Light (radio contact had broken down) and found his column blocked by tanks and artillery from the remnants of 4th Armoured Brigade, and some time later he learned that the urgently needed supply columns endeavouring to follow in the wake of the panzer divisions were being fiercely attacked and often completely destroyed by raiding columns of British infantry and artillery from the dispersed motor brigades, materialising apparently out of nowhere.

Moreover, Ariete were suffering ever-mounting losses at the hands of the stubborn French at Bir Hacheim, and in their endeavour to obey orders to 'roll over' the isolated garrison, had already emptied their own ammunition racks and were thus commandeering every shell and every drop of fuel coming up, even when these were brought up by German supply columns trying to get through to their own panzer divisions along the shortest route around the end of the minefields. It was obvious that a crisis was approaching and that if the morning had given Rommel's forces victories with a lavish hand, the afternoon promised nothing but hard fighting.

It began about 1430 as the leading columns of both 15th and 21st Panzer Divisions probed northward towards the area between Acroma and Commonwealth Keep, when they found themselves attacked from the east by ever-increasing forces from the 2nd Armoured Brigade now strengthened by the remnants of 22nd, and then – to their consternation and to Rommel's surprise when he heard about it (he had become separated from his main armour by more of these mysterious small groups) – from the west by Matildas from 1st Army Tank Brigade. It looked as though the British armour was concentrating at last.

Fire and black smoke welled up from the lorries and panzers dotted about the scrub-covered desert, and the battle degenerated into a hundred small but bitter actions fought out on one side by German panzer crews who were still tending to charge forward out of the protective range of their anti-tank guns, and British tank crews finding themselves in action for the first time in toughly armoured vehicles that did not break down, firing guns which could hit their enemies hard at a satisfactory range. Figures for panzer casualties mounted inexorably, and then another near-disaster for the Afrika Korps occurred.

When the combined 2nd and 22nd Armoured Brigades had hit the right flank of the advancing panzer divisions, the tank squadrons on the left had in fact missed the tail of the German armour and found themselves amid the rear echelons and divisional soft-skinned transport where they wreaked considerable havoc, remaining on the field afterwards in order to collect and evaluate some of their booty.

Unknowingly, in so doing they effectively cut off Rommel and his staff from his main striking force, isolating them just north of Bir el Harmat where they were later joined by the harassed and discomfited remains of Ariete, moving north to leave the unquenchable Frenchmen to at least a few more days and nights of undisputed possession of their fortress. Rommel was very angry (but also quite relieved) when nightfall at last brought an end to an astounding day, during which at one moment he had believed the battle won and the British armour destroyed, but which now presented him with a completely different picture.

By the time darkness had fallen, his panzer divisions were 'hedge-hogged' in an area south of the Rigel Ridge not very far west of the intact Guards Brigade, while 90th Light, still out of direct touch, were also hedgehogged just south of El Adem and under attack from recuperated and re-supplied tank formations from 4th Armoured Brigade Group. No supplies were getting through, 15th Panzer were out of fuel and very nearly out of ammunition, and although the recovery teams would undoubtedly have improved the position by the morning, 15th had only twenty-nine 'runners' left. Even 21st Panzer had only eighty runners immediately available, and petrol for only a few more hours of battle.

> I will not deny that I was seriously worried that evening. Our heavy tank losses were no good beginning to the battle (far more than a third of the German tanks had been lost in this one day.) The 90th Light Division under General Kleeman had become separated from the Afrika Korps and was now in a very dangerous position. British motorised groups were streaming through the open gap and hunting down the transport columns which had lost touch with the main body. And on these columns the life of my army depended.[7]

There was, however, one aspect of the situation from which so confirmed an optimist as Rommel could draw comfort while he planned and issued his orders for the morrow. Despite the recent simultaneous attacks on the head of his panzer columns by units from three identifiable armoured brigades – 2nd, 22nd and 1st Army Tank Brigade – Rommel still believed that the British command was fumbling, still lacking both the will to concentrate and co-ordinate, and the technical ability to do so. The overrunning and dispersal of so many separate units during the morning convinced him of this, and he felt that the events of the afternoon had been more coincidental than planned.

In this he was justified, for the reversal of fortunes during the afternoon had been brought about far more by the independent action of British brigade, battalion, company and even platoon commanders than by any co-ordinating action at divisional, corps or army command level, which on May 27th ushered in a period generally agreed to represent the nadir of British generalship during the desert campaign.

From the moment the Afrika Korps had left the Rotunda Segnale the previous afternoon, they had in fact been under close observation by the British and South African Armoured Car units. During the night, one of the South African squadrons had moved so close to the outside flank of the 90th Light that a German motor-cyclist had raced away through their columns, and all the time their signallers were sending out messages giving the movements and locations of Rommel's armoured divisions. These were all picked up by 7th Motor Brigade close to Retma and relayed to 7th Armoured Division on their forward net, and during the hours of darkness alone 7th Motor Brigade H.Q. logged thirteen messages sent out.

They were dismissed at 7th Armoured Division H.Q. as the panic-stricken imaginings of men retiring at night in front of a larger but nevertheless token force, for the majority opinion at that and higher levels was still that Rommel's main assault was coming in the north.

One alert mind at corps level, however, was following the reported movements of Rommel's spearheads with interest and growing anxiety. Major R. M. P. Carver, G.S.O.2 at XXX Corps, was listening in to all these signals, and at 0100 he was sufficiently concerned to telephone the G.S.O.1 at 7th Armoured Division to ask him what he was doing about it all – to be rebuked first for listening in to 7th Armoured Division forward net which the G.S.O.1 regarded somewhat in the light of his own private telephone line, and then for waking him up. The G.S.O.1 certainly had no intention of waking General Messervy on the strength either of the signals which had come in, or of Major Carver's worries – which he suggested could be put to better use in the service of his own formation.

Half an hour later, Carver took the bull by the horns and woke up his own superior, General Norrie, told him of the reports coming in and suggested that he rang Messervy direct – which, somewhat reluctantly, Norrie did. It was, however, to no effect, as Messervy agreed with his own G.S.O.1 that the reports were more likely to be inaccurate than not, and although undoubtedly some force was coming south it was more probably the expected Italian feint than the main German thrust. With this Norrie agreed, and so refused Carver's next suggestion, that he ring Lumsden and order him to put 22nd Armoured Brigade on notice to move south to join 7th Armoured Division some eight miles away. So far as Norrie was concerned, Auchinleck had said the enemy attack would come in the centre or the north, and that was where it should still be expected!

Carver's next move was to ring Lumsden's G.S.O.1 and give him all the information so far to hand and his own interpretation of it – to receive in reply the opinion that even if Carver's information and prediction proved accurate, Lumsden would use every argument he could think of to avoid parting again with 22nd Armoured Brigade, especially to Messervy.

There matters remained while Rommel's armour moved implacably towards their turning-point south of Bir Hacheim, the reports from the armoured cars came in regularly and Major Carver became increasingly worried. At 0400 he felt that he could wait no longer, spoke again to the sceptical and now irritated G.S.O.1 of 7th Armoured Division and, realising that little good was coming of that conversation, woke General Norrie again.

At his instigation, Norrie rang Messervy and suggested that he order his main armour – 4th Armoured Brigade – to battle positions east of Bir Hacheim (to which Messervy eventually agreed) and then rang Lumsden to give him a warning order that 22nd Armoured Brigade should make ready to move south to join Messervy's force. But in the resultant conversation, which went on for some time, Lumsden proved the more passionate advocate, his argument for the moment being that as his tank squadrons were composed mostly in the proportion of one squadron of Grants to two of Crusaders whereas Messervy's regiments were made up of two Grant squadrons to one of Honeys, surely Messervy should come to his aid and not the other way round? What relevance this argument had to the developing tactical situation is now somewhat obscure, but it seems at the time to have convinced Norrie who, to Carver's concern, refrained from giving Lumsden the direct warning order.

Even with Messervy's acceptance of his order, it was nevertheless nearly 0630 before much life was injected into 7th Armoured Division headquarters, and this happened as a result of the startled announcement on the part of the commander of the 3rd Indian Motor Brigade south of Bir Hacheim, Brigadier Filose, that he had 'a whole bloody German armoured division' in front of him; but cool thought on the part of the recipients, despite the conversations between Norrie and Messervy, reasoned that this could not be so (and, indeed, they were right for it was the Ariete) and the brigadier's alarm was adjudged the result of the late arrival of his brigade at the front, as it had only come up the previous day and was still missing many of its anti-tank gunners and support units. Auchinleck's opinion at divisional level at 0645 on the morning of May 27th was still sacrosanct.

It was not to remain so for much longer. Shortly afterwards a report arrived at XXX Corps from an air reconnaissance which Carver had requested, which confirmed all his fears – over four hundred enemy panzers were refuelling south of Bir Hacheim and there was now no doubt as to where Rommel's main attack was aimed. At last all was clear and certain, and it should now be just a matter of following agreed plans and moving brigades to their allotted battle stations, none of the movements across more than twelve miles of known ground, none taking more than half or at most three-quarters of an hour. All should be well.

But it was not to be as easy as that. Messervy when rung a second time by Norrie agreed that 7th Armoured Division had issued a warning order at 0430 as instructed, that 4th Armoured Brigade had 'stood to' at 0545 – and Messervy would now order them to battle positions as soon as possible; but an account written later by the commander of one of 4th Armoured Brigade's tank regiments, Lieutenant-Colonel 'Pip' Roberts, casts an illuminating light on the degree of urgency with which events and orders were at that moment being regarded.

> 'Stand-to' at about 0545 hrs passed off without incident, so we repaired to breakfast. At about 0700 hrs, Brigade HQ, having been disturbed for some hours and now apparently without much on hand, rang up to request that we should furnish a full report as to why tanks numbered so-and-so and so-and-so were returned to Ordnance in a dirty condition.[8]

Colonel Roberts managed only the first two or three sentences on this crucial matter before the phone rang again, and his tanks were on the move by 0720 – by which time Norrie was again deep in argument with Lumsden, endeavouring to persuade him that now it really was time for 22nd Armoured Brigade to go to the support of 4th Armoured Brigade as had been agreed if Rommel's attack came around the south – and again listening to the arguments and pleas which Lumsden had employed before to shield his precious formations from Messervy's control. Surely it was still not 100 per cent certain that the attack was coming around the south? Surely if Auchinleck had said it would come in the centre, more weight should be given to his opinion than to the perhaps muddled and hurried reconnaissance reports of less experienced soldiers? Anyway, as Lumsden had said before, 22nd Brigade regiments had only one squadron of Grants, etc., etc., etc. . . . and when Norrie proved impervious to argument and insisted upon obedience, Lumsden rather sulkily agreed but pointed out that 22nd Armoured Brigade would be unable to move until 0830 at the earliest because, as Norrie would remember, they had not as yet received even a warning order!

By the time 22nd did move, of course, 4th Armoured Brigade had been overrun, two of its regiments annihilated, 7th Armoured Division Advanced H.Q. captured – and within an hour 22nd Armoured Brigade would themselves be facing the weight and ferocity of a triumphant 21st Panzer Division on their own. It was certainly a bad morning for the British, yet the recovery during the afternoon combined with the lack of communications with 7th Armoured Division (Norrie was sure this was purely a technical matter) seems to have given everyone great confidence and according to the battle reports Auchinleck received that evening, to quote from the *Official History*, 'the day ended with the British higher command more satisfied with the day's fighting than was General Rommel.'

On the face of it, there was good reason for this. Except for the 3rd Indian Motor Brigade which had been very roughly handled, the other brigades of 7th Armoured seemed merely to have been scattered, and as both XXX Corps and Eighth Army were still refusing to believe that Messervy and his staff had been captured, no news from them was assumed to be good news. Lumsden's armour had certainly taken a knock and O'Carroll's 1st Army Tank Brigade had lost eighteen Matildas – but the smoking hulks of innumerable panzers dotting the desert demonstrated the effectiveness of the Grants' main armament, and the evening situation maps revealed Rommel's mobile forces apparently contained in an area bounded on the west by the South African, British and Free French positions and minefields, to the north and north-east by the 1st Army Tank Brigade and the brigades of 1st Armoured Division respectively, and in the area along and below the Trig el Abd by the recuperating armour and motorised infantry of the 7th Armoured Division.

Moreover, the vast dump of materials east of Belhammed was still inviolate and even unthreatened, and the reserve 1st Armoured Brigade still unused – though it had lost a few of its Grants (to the fury of the crews) to make up losses in 4th Armoured Brigade Group. Assuredly, there was room for some satisfaction in the Allied camp on the evening of May 27th.

Unfortunately for the British, satisfaction in the evening would seem to have bred inaction in the morning, for during the 28th, Lumsden's armour did little but watch 15th Panzer lying west of Knightsbridge awaiting petrol, while 4th Armoured half-heartedly chivvied 90th Light back towards Bir el Harmat (to which place Rommel had already ordered them) and the British and Indian motorised infantry in the south, still without any firm controlling hand, grouped together and occasionally raided any supply columns they saw. On one occasion they did this to such effect that the unfortunate Oberleutnant in charge burst into tears and declared that Germany had lost North Africa, so perhaps they felt that they were all doing rather well.

But in the meantime, Rommel was busily gathering information, visiting his formations with a total disregard for his own personal safety, and preparing to reassert his dominance of the battlefield. He had ordered a continuation of the drive of the panzer divisions northwards towards the Via Balbia before fully appreciating the state of 15th Panzer, so 21st Panzer went on alone. They reached the edge of the escarpment and shelled movements below, but then could not get down themselves so they turned and attacked Commonwealth Keep, where a mixed garrison of less than a hundred and fifty South African and Yorkshire infantrymen put up a redoubtable resistance with nothing but their small-arms, six old Italian 47mm. guns and some mortars, before they were overwhelmed.

By this time Rommel had found a way through from the south to 15th Panzer positions, ordered 90th Light back towards Bir el Harmat and Ariete to close up, and thus set in train a concentration of his armour in the centre of the Allied positions. Moreover, the mystery of the disappearance of Trieste had been solved, to his unexpected advantage; they had not received the late amendment to his orders and so instead of sweeping to the south of Bir Hacheim, had hit the mine-marsh half-way between the Trig el Abd and the Free French – and as it was undefended, had spent the intervening time 'gapping' a way through it. Not only, therefore, were Rommel's forces now receiving some additional strength as Trieste came through, but a safer and shorter way had been found, albeit tenuous for the moment, along which urgently needed supplies could be brought.

Of course, not everything had gone quite so smoothly for him. Ariete had been attacked first from the west by Matildas of 1st Army Tank Brigade and suffered some losses in M13s, and then by Crusaders of 22nd Armoured Brigade – but these they had fought off with the 88mms which Rommel had given them with instructions to form an anti-tank screen, and which they handled very adeptly. Rommel himself came under what he called 'a wild fire' from an Italian column, and when he eventually returned to Bir el Harmat after his visit to 15th Panzer, he found that his own headquarters had been overrun by British armour and dispersed over the desert.

But the following day, May 29th, started in splendid form for the Afrika Korps, with what was to become a famous piece of *Rommelei*. He had found the head of a large supply column fumbling its way up to the east of Bir el Harmat and personally led it up to 15th Panzer Division positions through an area thickly infested with British tanks, artillery and mobile infantry, at times under heavy fire and all the way in considerable personal danger. Having refuelled 15th Panzer and given them fresh orders, he then took the rest of the convoy across towards the concentration area he had chosen, between the Trig Capuzzo and the Trig el Abd, and to which he had already ordered 21st Panzer to return. Soon all his armour would be together, with full fuel tanks and ammunition racks.

As one of the fiercest tank battles of the desert campaign was about to be fought, this was as well for the Afrika Korps.

Early that morning (May 29th) 90th Light had moved off westward to make the rest of their way back to Bir el Harmat (undisturbed, as

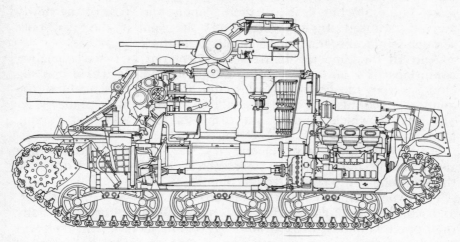

Figure 2   Medium tank M3 (General Grant): weight 28·5 tons: armour
35mm.–55mm.; engine 370 h.p.; maximum speed 26 m.p.h.; armament one
75mm., one 37mm., three ·30 in. machine-guns; crew 6

4th Armoured had just been ordered back to El Adem in reserve),
and Ariete moved north from Bir el Harmat to join the two panzer
divisions. Just before 1100, Ariete saw in front of them the Grant
squadrons of 2nd Armoured Brigade, followed by the Crusader
squadrons, advancing westwards from Knightsbridge against the last
known positions of 15th Panzer. There was a brisk exchange of fire
but the Grants ploughed stolidly forward until they caught up with
the retiring 15th Panzer, who immediately turned and gave battle –
protected at first by their invariable anti-tank rearguard screen and
then reinforced, to their own surprise and 2nd Armoured's discomfort, by the leading columns of 21st Panzer as these came back
down from the north.

For a short time, 2nd Armoured were thus fighting by themselves
on three fronts, and it was midday before 22nd Armoured – sent off
in the morning on their own to attack Bir el Harmat – returned to the
aid of their sister brigade, by which time the battle was reaching its
crisis-point. The Grant crews shot accurately and confidently but
suffered losses because their main armament – their 75mm. guns –
were housed in side sponsons and were thus too low for the crews to
adopt 'hull down' positions; but the Crusaders brewed up with
dreadful regularity, slewing aside with tracks ripped off to litter the
desert like sloughed crocodile skins, their crews burning to agonised
deaths or scurrying desperately among the gouts of sand and the
smoking hulls. The panzers were being hit harder than ever before,
too, and at longer range, and their crews were learning some of the
more bitter lessons of armoured warfare; but for them there was at

least the comforting crack of their 88mms, the bark of the newly arrived captured Russian 76mm. and the sight of their anti-tank screens implacably holding off the British attacks.

And all the time the battle was fought out in the excruciating conditions of a hot and blinding dust-storm which drifted choking clouds across the field with infuriating inconsequence to blind the gunners, to confuse the drivers, to add to the suffocation of the black, oily smoke which plumed out from smitten tanks and flaming ammunition boxes.

'Tanks and lorries', wrote one observer, 'huddled together like sheep: men cowered behind their vehicles panting for breath while the scorching wind swept around them.'[9]

Heat was killing men in that cauldron as surely as shell or bullet, and scorched and blistered flesh was a more frequent cause of agony than open wound or broken limb. At one moment a light tank was holed and set alight while moving up, but its engine had escaped damage and for some time it waltzed around in the dust of no-man's-land, belching smoke from its turret, a mobile crematorium.

> All day long the battle raged and by evening nothing had been won. As the sun sank, blood-orange and huge behind the minuscule silhouettes of the Panzer Divisions, the firing began to die down, and soon in the twilight the last rounds of the day traced like comets across the battlefield and bounced, high above the haze, into a sky of darkening purple.[10]

The British drew back eastwards towards Knightsbridge, the Germans and Italians closer together in their chosen area. During the night the wind died and the dust filtered back to the desert floor; but the fires still burned, the gutted steel hulls glowed with fearful promise for the morrow, and the stench of oil, of death, of anguish lay over the whole area.

This had not been the only battle to be fought on May 29th. On the previous day, Oberstleutnant Westphal, the Operations Chief at Panzerarmee Headquarters, found himself in a situation with which he had become all too familiar during Operation Crusader or The Winter Battle as the Germans called it. With Rommel both absent and out of touch, he was forced to act as de facto commander of Panzerarmee and, trusting that Rommel would eventually approve, he requested Cruewell to bring heavier pressure to bear on the South African and British infantry in the northern sector, possibly to break through them, but at least to ensure that they could not interfere in the crucial battles being fought to the south. This had had results which would have been ludicrous had they not held the element of tragedy. An officer of the Transvaal Scottish, in the line just north of Alam Hamza, described what happened to the Italian soldiers on the morning of the 29th:

In the dawn a great murmur of talking and shouting arose from the enemy positions, which in the dim light were revealed as within 400 yards of our own. We were aghast at such folly. Transport and gun limbers stood well dispersed between the Battalion and the Cape Town Highlanders. The red scars of freshly turned earth and the white blur of rocks in regular lines marked the enemy positions up the entire length of the depression.

A mortar opened fire. The bomb burst under the nose of a troop carrier. Then as one man, hundreds of Italians rose to their feet and, clear and obvious in the morning sun, began to advance down the valley. Through my glasses I watched them approach us and saw the sun flash on their steel. The ground in front and around them began to flick up in clouds of dust; the rattle of machine-guns broke the amazed silence in which we stood. The artillery and mortars opened fire. Gaps appeared in the ranks but still they came on. Of a sudden the ranks wavered and broke, weapons were dropped and the valley was filled with panic-stricken men running for their lives. Hundreds of them wheeled in ragged formation and made up the hillside towards the Cape Town Highlanders, where they halted and broke again before withering fire. Those in front came towards us, racing like hares between the shell bursts, weaving and dodging, running and falling; then in blind panic turning away and fleeing towards the western mouth of the depression, where furious shelling between them and safety turned them back towards us again.

The whole depression shook and echoed to the crash of high explosive and smoke drifted in thick clouds over the face of the battlefield. It was fascinating to watch the enemy rushing in mad fear up and down, too crazed to know where to run. Scores of them running uphill would disappear into the smoke of previous salvos and appear again through the smoke only to run into the yellow dust and black clouds of fresh explosions. The action could not have lasted more than a quarter of an hour before the order was given to cease fire. Scores of men in their yellowish Italian khaki came towards us waving scraps of white cloth and holding their hands high above their heads . . . [11]

Over 400 men and 13 Italian officers were taken prisoner, and one of the officers had with him their operational map – a sketch of the country between Tmimi and Tobruk with hardly a sign of the Gazala positions anywhere. Their feelings of bewilderment and surprise must have been akin to those of the British and South African 2nd Echelon troops caught in Rommel's first Dash to the Wire during the *Crusader* battles, but at least these had had lorries and trucks to take them away from the danger area.

But not all of Group Cruewell's efforts had been so ill-fated, and although none of the South African or 50th Division defences had been breached, Italian engineers had managed to gap quite deeply into the minefields along the line of the Trig Capuzzo, and so by the evening of the 29th, Rommel had two narrow paths through which supplies could be brought for his concentrating armour and of which, because of the battle they had fought that afternoon, they were already again in need.

By this time he had of course abandoned the first *Venezia* objective of reaching the coast and then turning to obliterate the enemy infantry in their defence lines. Despite its dispersion the British armour had proved too strong for this to be achieved, so for the moment he intended to mass all his strength in the middle of the enemy positions with its back to the enemy minefields, and to complete the iron ring around it with an impenetrable anti-tank screen along its northern, eastern and southern flanks, using the massed artillery and anti-tank guns of all his armoured and motorised divisions. He would then employ his infantry and engineers to open wide gaps in the minefields immediately to the west, around Got el Ualeb, and through these gaps he could order forward the fuel, ammunition, food and water for the next stage of his offensive which, with his armour rested and reorganised, would be a break-out either to the north to deal with the enemy infantry in the defence lines or to the south to deal with the Free French at Bir Hacheim. After which, the main thrust would be mounted – due east to shoulder aside the British armour and break into Tobruk.

During the night of May 29th/30th, therefore, the orders were drafted, the men briefed, the remaining petrol and ammunition allocated in accordance with immediate needs, and at dawn the formations began the final moves towards their operational positions; and it was during this process that Rommel learned for the first time

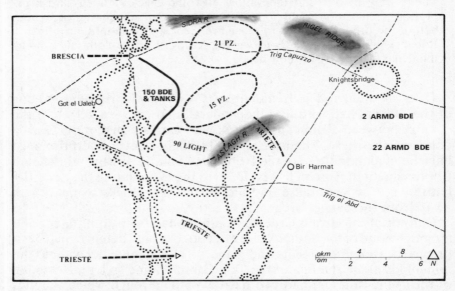

Map 5   May 29th, evening

of the existence of the 150th Brigade Group box between the Trig
Capuzzo and the Trig el Abd, reinforced by thirty infantry tanks from
1st Army Tank Brigade, sitting solidly across his proposed supply
route and presenting an immovable obstruction to any attempts to
reach the minefield or break through to the west.

As it happened, Cruewell had found out about the 150th Brigade
on the previous afternoon. Flying across the area in a Storch in an
attempt to find Rommel, he had been shot down and taken prisoner.
Early summer 1942 had been a bad time for him; his young wife had
died while he had been on leave and his last memory of his homeland
for many years would be her funeral.

Brigadier C. W. Haydon, commanding 150th Brigade, had been
aware of the potential danger in which his command lay ever since
the arrival of the German panzers in the area just behind him, and
since the evening of May 28th, he had watched that danger develop.
He had therefore drawn back the battalion holding the southern
section of the position during that evening (it had been harassing the
Trieste engineers working in the minefield) and set his entire force to
work on slit-trenches and gun-pits from which they could defend
themselves from the coming storm. Fortunately, the brigade's
regiment of Field Artillery – the 72nd – had recently become adept
at resiting its 25-pounders and new 6-pounder anti-tank guns at short
notice (for it had been obvious from the start that all-round defence
would be needed) and as 150th Brigade consisted almost entirely of
men from the mining and ship-building towns of the Tyne and Tees,
the digging was done quickly and efficiently and the defences would
be manned with a spirit of dogged determination unlikely to waver
whatever the odds.

But of course, no infantry brigade armed as they then were could
be expected to hold static positions for long against a heavy armoured
attack – especially when the main minefield defences were behind
instead of in front – and it was evident that Haydon's men could not
stem the onslaught alone; reinforcements must be sent in and
diversionary attacks mounted against Rommel's armour from the
flank or rear as soon as possible. One earnest of the first was the
welcome arrival of the Matildas of 44th R.T.R. the following
afternoon (29th), though the expected return to the brigade of a store
of 25-pounder ammunition – removed from them by a censorious
Tobruk quartermaster before the battle on the grounds that they had
accumulated more than their allocation – did not materialise. The
ration per gun thus remained at twenty-five rounds per day.

As for the second – the diversionary attacks – General Lumsden
sent in words of encouragement and even announced to his staff that
with Rommel's armour penned against the 150th Brigade box, Eighth

Army 'had him boiled' – and indeed it was obvious that if continuous and concentric attacks could now be mounted against the Afrika Korps, its fate would be sealed as soon as its fuel and ammunition ran out. With this in mind the officers and men of 4th East Yorkshire Battalion and the 4th and 5th Green Howards of 150th Brigade settled down to what they knew would be a tough fight, but one in which they were sure that the High Command would see that they were adequately supported.

The first probing attacks against them began during the morning of May 30th as Afrika Korps engineers moved up and began lifting the hastily sewn mines. There was a brisk skirmish between the opposing groups of sappers followed by a rush by German infantry, and then the rest of the morning was occupied by a battle between the Matildas and the German artillery, as the former tried to regain the ground lost. It was only partially successful, but all positions were held during the afternoon against growing but sporadic pressure, and as soon as darkness fell aggressive patrolling began in order to prevent night-time intrusion by the Afrika Korps across the new minefields.

General Ritchie's evening message of 'Well done!' was received impassively by the troops, who had begun to wonder if he knew they were there. So far as they could see, there had been little sign of further reinforcement that day, or of diversionary activity to take the pressure off their hard-pressed front.

In this they were uncharitable. Under the personal direction of General Lumsden, the 9th Lancers had attacked the Afrika Korps positions along the Bir Aslagh Ridge in both morning and afternoon, and in the later attack they had been supported by a squadron of the 3rd County of London Yeomanry and a heavy artillery bombardment by nearly sixty guns, including a number of 25-pounders. Unfortunately, after the first attack the Lancers had only eleven Grants and four cruisers left and the C.L.Y. squadron was not up to strength – so the total armoured strength flung against Rommel's anti-tank screen could hardly be called massive; and the artillery shoot for the second attack had been mistimed, the guns running out of smoke before the tanks reached the ridge from which their close assault was due to be launched, and as a result they were shot to pieces long before they closed. As they were facing an anti-tank screen consisting of ninety guns and including several 88mms the result was hardly surprising; but according to their regimental history, General Lumsden, who had been present for most of the time, thought they had done jolly well.

As for the rest of XXX Corps armour, one regiment of 4th Armoured Brigade Group spent the day attacking unidentified enemy units in the Bir Harmat area, while the rest went down towards Bir Hacheim where thirty panzers and a German repair workshop had been reported. They found neither, but during that day and the next rounded up nearly sixty vehicles and two hundred prisoners from supply columns still down in the area and presumably lost. Doubtless Eighth Army would be glad to receive the extra transport, but the energy used in capturing it was doing little to relieve the plight of 150th Brigade.

But they were not forgotten elsewhere. About 2045 that evening, a column left the Knightsbridge box consisting of a battery of R.H.A., a company of infantry and two troops of 6-pounder anti-tank guns – with what specific object it is difficult to ascertain at this remove – and drove westwards along the Trig Capuzzo until they bumped into the section of the anti-tank screen held by 21st Panzer Division. The survivors returned to Knightsbridge in the early hours, leaving behind them 157 of their companions, five 25-pounders and seven 6-pounders; but at least some of the Green Howards in the northern section of the pocket must have heard the noise of battle and had their hopes lifted, however briefly.

As for activity on their behalf at command level, Ritchie had spent many hours that day consulting with his corps commanders in order to arrive at the best decision, and had almost come to the conclusion that the right course to follow would be a break-out south-westwards by infantry from Gott's XIII Corps in conjunction with a drive around Bir Hacheim by the mobile elements of Norrie's XXX Corps, to put them all astride Rommel's communications and also in an excellent position from which to exploit towards Benghasi and Tripoli once the Afrika Korps had been liquidated. Of course, most of XXX Corps's armour would also have to stay east of the 'Cauldron' for the moment, just in case Rommel broke out towards Tobruk.

But by the evening of May 30th the extent of the casualties suffered by his armour during the day had convinced Lumsden that the only hope of mounting a worthwhile attack on the Afrika Korps by XXX Corps armour lay in infantry attacks against the anti-tank screens followed by mine-lifting by the engineers, after which the tanks could go through. With this analysis both Norrie and Ritchie agreed, and it was felt that such an attack should take place during the next night – that of May 31st/June 1st – by infantry from 69th Brigade attacking Sidra Ridge from the north where they had been lying in the line next to 150th Brigade, and by 10th Indian Infantry Brigade (held so far in Eighth Army reserve) from the east, heading for the Aslagh Ridge and the scene of 9th Lancers' recent set-back. Briefings and movement orders should be prepared as early as possibly the next morning, and issued to the formations concerned before noon. What might be happening to the men of 150th Brigade in the meantime seems hardly to have been mentioned.

Dawn on May 31st had in fact brought them stand-to in their rifle and
machine-gun pits, then, astonishingly, a formal summons to surrender
from Rommel which was equally formally rejected by Brigadier
Haydon. There followed a sharp but heavy artillery bombardment
and an attack by 90th Light infantry who had moved up under the
barrage to just within bombing range. The next hour was one of
tough small-arms fighting which never reached actual hand-to-hand
combat as the attackers were held back from the line of skilfully
camouflaged slit-trenches, and at about 0800 the two sides briefly
drew apart and watched each other for the next moves.

These came an hour later with mixed German infantry and panzer
attacks which finally lost momentum in the face of fire from the new
6-pounders and some Bofors anti-aircraft guns, but not until they had
overrun some of the forward positions held by the East Yorkshire
companies; and from then on the fighting never really stopped until
darkness came and the two sides fell away from each other in sheer
exhaustion.

By this time the East Yorkshire positions had all gone and the
survivors were back in the two main defence lines held by the Green
Howard battalions, some of the 25-pounders and Bofors had been
captured or put out of action, and those left were desperately short of
ammunition. There was no message from Ritchie that evening,
perhaps because he felt that the only real news he had for the troops
was that the projected night infantry attack on the Sidra and Aslagh
Ridges had had to be postponed yet a further twenty-four hours, as
neither of the corps commanders felt capable of mounting and following up such a radical departure from previous plans in so short a time.

But if Ritchie felt unable to do more about the situation in which
150th Brigade now found themselves, Rommel was about to take
very drastic action. During the afternoon he had been approached by
one of Afrika Korps's prisoners, Major Archer-Shee of 10th Hussars,
with the complaint that the water-ration for those captured so far had
been half a cup per day, and Rommel replied that this was all
anybody in the Cauldron – German, Italian or British – was getting.
'But', he added, 'I quite agree that we cannot go on like this. If we
don't get a convoy through tonight I shall have to ask General Ritchie
for terms. You can take a letter to him for me . . .'[12]

But some supplies did get through along the narrow passages, and
Rommel knew that June 1st would be the decisive day. He ordered
the mounting at first light of the heaviest possible Stuka attack on the
150th Brigade positions followed immediately by massed panzer and
infantry onslaughts, and at one crucial moment took personal command of the leading infantry platoon – possibly the first time a
military formation of so small a size was taken into action by so high-
ranking an officer.

'The encircled enemy,' says the Battle Report of the Panzerarmee, 'supported by numerous infantry tanks, resisted stubbornly . . . Each separate point within the fortress-like, strengthened defences had to be fought for. The positions had to be taken in a hand-to-hand fight for each individual bunker . . . The enemy suffered extraordinarily heavy bloody losses.'[13]

So did the Afrika Korps, and even Rommel's personal staff, for both his Chief of Staff Generalleutnant Gause and his Operations Chief Oberst Westphal were wounded that morning, as had been the new 15th Panzer Division commander, General von Vaerst. *Operation Venezia* was proving almost as expensive of senior officers in its early stages as *Crusader* had towards its conclusion. But the end of 150th Brigade was inevitable in the face of the force thrown against them, and shortly after 1400 the weary gunners fired their last remaining rounds, the infantry smashed their rifles, and three thousand survivors of the brigade group climbed bitterly out of their shelters and raised their hands into the air.

Rommel, still close behind his assault troops, went forward quickly to find and congratulate Brigadier Haydon upon the fight he and his men had put up, but alas, the brigadier was dead, killed by a shell-burst during the morning; and Rommel's sincere regret was only equalled by the scorn he expressed for an organisation which could place brave men in such a position, and then do so little to help them. The fact that it could nevertheless spare time and thought to evacuate Cruewell from the area before the battle developed, did nothing to change his opinion.

But in fact Ritchie had not been idle and was expecting the full burgeoning of his plans that very night. With the brigade group from XIII Corps attacking the northern Sidra Ridge and the one from 5th Indian Division attacking the eastern Aslagh Ridge, a concentric attack on Rommel's forces in the Cauldron could begin about midnight, to which 150th Brigade's contribution should be a break-out to the east – and as it was not until the following morning that he became aware of the flaws in his planning, he was able to spend the rest of June 1st exuding an air of calm confidence.

'Ritchie', according to General Messervy writing at a later date and perhaps with some of the inestimable benefits of hindsight, 'was rather stupidly optimistic in remarks and demeanour, though uncertain beneath it all. He was always saying "Ah, now we've got him!" when it was quite clear we hadn't.'[14]

On the afternoon of June 1st Ritchie was unaware not only of the destruction of 150th Brigade, but also that it had been decided at divisional level that 69th Brigade would not after all supply the force for the northern assault; that would come instead from 151st Brigade

Group further to the north, who in the event could only supply one
battalion for the operation, instead of the brigade which Ritchie
expected. As for the attack on Aslagh Ridge, the allotted Indian
brigade left Tobruk so late that they could not concentrate in time so
General Messervy cancelled that part of the scheme, only informing
Norrie after he had done it, a significant indication of the lack of firm
control – or even good communications – which existed now in the
higher echelons of Eighth Army command.

The single battalion which went into action on the night of June
1st/2nd failed, not surprisingly, to reach even its first objectives.

But General Ritchie gave no sign of being much cast down by these
developments, and spent the morning of June 2nd, after the reports
had come in, making yet more plans for the destruction of the Afrika
Korps, still to his mind penned against the British minefields by the
massed guns and armour of XXX Corps, with XIII Corps's infantry
poised to the north awaiting the signal from him to sweep down to the
south-west and wreck Rommel's entire supply and communications
system. Nevertheless, the loss of 150th Brigade could obviously not
pass without comment.

'I am much distressed over the loss of 150th Brigade after so
gallant a fight,' he assured Auchinleck that afternoon, 'but still
consider the situation favourable to us and getting better daily.'[15]

As Auchinleck could see that the situation had now changed
dramatically from one in which Eighth Army was surrounding an
enemy force in its midst and was strangling it, to one in which it had a
wedge driven into its guts by that same enemy force now with open
access to its supplies, he was not happy about Ritchie's appreciation
and his reply expressed misgiving. He gave Ritchie the benefit of
some doubt by suggesting that he must have information not then
available to the Commander-in-Chief, but warned his commander in
the field against the danger of losing the initiative; and it is some
indication of the quality of information reaching Cairo that Auchinleck believed that Ritchie was still in a position to exercise very
much.

Ritchie's method of doing so during the days which followed was to
hold a long series of committee meetings with his corps and divisional
commanders, soliciting their advice and then endeavouring to get
them to act upon it before they changed their minds. Dan Pienaar's
reception of his idea of an advance south-westward out of their
bastion by the South Africans had been, not altogether surprisingly,
so irredeemably negative that, on the morning of June 3rd, the
commander of the reserve 5th Indian Division, Major-General
Briggs, was called forward and asked if he could carry out the attack
instead at short notice, through the South African positions.

'My answer was in shape of an alternative,' wrote Briggs later. 'I suggested a desert move around the south of Bir Hacheim on to Tmimi and Rommel's L. of C. . . . This was agreed to by both Ritchie and Gott.'[16]

So Briggs went away to draw up the necessary orders, but while he was away the logistic difficulties of the idea became apparent and when he came back the whole plan had been changed, on Messervy's suggestion, to a frontal attack on Rommel's positions in the Cauldron on the assumption that, with more time available for planning and preparation, the original scheme of pincer attacks from Sidra and Aslagh Ridges was more feasible. As this solution had the advantage of not leaving Tobruk uncovered, Ritchie preferred it – but Gott considered it too reminiscent of the catastrophic infantry advances of the First World War and actually refused to participate; and such was the atmosphere now reigning at Eighth Army Headquarters that Ritchie accepted Gott's refusal and handed responsibility for the operation to Norrie – who in turn passed it on to Briggs and Messervy, only one of whom had any faith at all in the plan.

It is thus hardly surprising that *Operation Aberdeen*, launched during the night of June 4th/5th, 1942, proved one of the more lamentable fiascos to attend British arms during the North African Campaign – a campaign which between the end of the O'Connor offensive and the Second Battle of Alamein was hardly distinguished by any high, or even acceptable, degree of generalship.

The opening artillery bombardment intended to clear the way for the first stage of the infantry advance towards the Aslagh Ridge crashed down on empty ground as, to quote the *Official History*, 'the enemy's defensive positions lay further to the west than had been thought,' with the result that when the Grants, Stuarts and Crusaders of 22nd Armoured Brigade moved up through the advancing infantry, they ran into the concentrated fire of the waiting (and watching, for no attempt at deception or surprise had been made) German artillery and anti-tank screen, which exacted its usual toll of casualties and caused the survivors to sheer off to the north. A German panzer assault then struck up towards Bir et Tamar, and having shouldered the armour aside went on to attack dispersed infantry positions beyond, and the armour – *believing themselves to have been absolved by divisional orders from all responsibility for the infantry* – made no attempt to help. Needless to say, the infantry positions were lost and those men not killed or captured retired in disarray behind the start lines. Meanwhile, in the northern attack down towards Sidra, 32nd Army Tank Brigade had run on to an unexpected minefield under the guns of the anti-tank screen along the ridge, losing fifty of its seventy Matildas before extricating itself. In the words of von Mellenthin who watched it, 'From the tactical point of view this was one of the most ridiculous attacks of the campaign.'

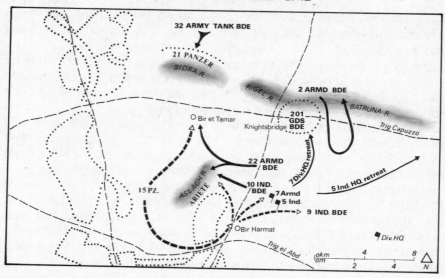

Map 6   June 5th

The situation resulting from all this is cogently epitomised in the *Official History*:

> The unpleasant turn taken by the battle was soon realised at the Tactical Headquarters of the 7th Armoured and the 5th Indian Divisions, but each was occupied by its own problems and there was nobody in sole command to concert their actions. [17]

So much for Auchinleck's directive that co-ordination should be assured at all levels. Even the concept of the 'brigade group' had gone by the board now, as old habits and attitudes surfaced under pressures of a battle fought without firm control at any level, and confusion at the top.

At this point, Rommel took a hand. He led 15th Panzer Division down through a gap in the minefields south-west of Bir Harmat, hooked up to the north, scattered two battalions of the 9th Indian Brigade which were being held in reserve together with those members of 10th Indian Brigade who had managed to extricate themselves from the Cauldron, then overran the headquarters of both brigades and the Tactical Headquarters of 7th Armoured and 5th Indian Divisions, driving Messervy into the Knightsbridge box and Briggs back to El Adem. Still trapped inside the Cauldron were three Indian battalions and four artillery regiments, who with dwindling hope settled down to one of those 'last round, last man' battles now fast becoming an accepted hazard of desert fighting for Eighth Army infantry.

And all the time the Grants and Stuarts of 2nd Armoured Brigade were assembled east of Knightsbridge, moving backwards and forwards in response to a number of orders which eventually cancelled each other out:

> No help reached the doomed units in the Cauldron, for although the 2nd and 4th Armoured Brigades had been placed under General Messervy, who was now in sole command, he was unable in the prevailing confusion to bring them to action.[18]

Beneath this chilly pronouncement by the Official Historian lies another unavoidable conclusion. In the hollow aridity of command at the higher levels of Eighth Army during the opening days of June 1942, even men of the calibre of Gott and Norrie were being emasculated, and losing not only their determination but also confidence in themselves.

This was to have highly significant effects everywhere. One young Hussar officer who had been partly responsible for the accidental death of Brigadier 'Jock' Campbell, one of the heroes of the early desert fighting, was now endeavouring to get himself killed in order to expiate his misfortune (he failed, but in doing so won for himself as a junior officer the Distinguished Service Order, three Military Crosses, the French Croix de Guerre and the American Legion of Merit) and was commanding a small composite force during *Aberdeen*. Many years later, he wrote of those days:

> Then began certain miscalculations by the Generals, which turned victory into defeat. I do not know what other facts have come to light, but no soldier who fought in that battle can ever excuse those highranking officers who at the time were damned but have since been resurrected.[19]

If a regular officer of a famous cavalry regiment could feel like this, the effect of the uncertainty of command upon the ranks of enrolled civilians, unaffected by bonds of professional loyalty and sceptical anyway of military competence at any level, was likely to be profound. And lack of confidence in June was unlikely to be cured in July or in August; and would be very difficult to restore even by November.

Needless to say, one person who was not losing confidence was Rommel, who, with his centre now free, was concentrating on clearing the French from his southern flank:

> As I had foreseen, the British command had decided against committing any major force from the two divisions in the Gazala line to form a second point of pressure on the 21st Panzer Division. Nor had any units of the 2nd South African Division been committed. In a moment so decisive they should have thrown in all the strength they could muster. What is the use

of having overall superiority if one allows one's formations to be smashed piece by piece by an enemy who, in each separate action, is able to concentrate superior strength at the decisive point?

After this British defeat we no longer expected any major relieving attack on our forces around Bir Hacheim, and hoped to get on with our assault undisturbed.[20]

His hopes were justified. Except for columns raiding his supplies up in the north (where Sergeant Quentin Smythe won South Africa's first Victoria Cross of the Second World War), and harassing tactics by the recovered 7th Motor Brigade Group down in the south, the only efforts made by Eighth Army to hinder Rommel's attacks on the besieged Frenchmen were to be the organisation of some supplies (which 7th Motor Brigade took in) and a stream of exhortatory messages sent from Ritchie to Koenig.

Since June 2nd, Bir Hacheim had been subjected to increasingly heavy Stuka attacks, though these had at least been fought off to good effect by the R.A.F., presented at last with an area in which friendly positions were clearly demarcated from those of the enemy, and in which they could thus attack ground forces as well. Moreover, so deeply and skilfully had the French worked on their defences that they were at first almost invulnerable to Stuka bombing, for the ground was so hard that anything but a direct hit on a slit-trench or dug-in position wasted its energy on the desert air.

But at daybreak on June 3rd, it became evident that both Italian and German forces (Trieste and 90th Light) were closing in and shelling began from German 105mm. guns which the French could not reach with their 75mms. Shortly afterwards a message was brought from Rommel by two English soldiers who had been taken prisoner, requesting the surrender of the fort in order to save blood, and pointing out the fate of 150th Brigade; but Koenig refrained from answering this, instead warning his men that their time of ordeal was approaching and reminding them that the eyes of the world were on them – as, indeed, they were.

The event had a fitting sequel. Early on the morning of June 5th after forty-eight hours of heavy and continuous bombardment, a German truck drove up under a white flag to one of the outposts held by the 2nd Battalion of the Foreign Legion, and the officer demanded a parley. As luck would have it, the sentry he approached was a German himself, and was thus able to express the garrison's opinion of the suggestion with considerable force; at which the officer drove off in high dudgeon, only to have his vehicle blown up on a mine within a few yards. To derisive shouts from the onlookers, he and his driver leapt clear of their blazing truck and retired rapidly on foot, and for a few more days the garrison was subjected only to more bombing and shelling.

But the ring around Bir Hacheim was now closing, and with *Operation Aberdeen* so clearly a German victory Rommel could move heavier forces down to deal with this thorn in his southern flank. Elements from 15th Panzer came down, together with the whole of the Hecker Group which had been intended to carry out the sea-borne attack behind Pienaar's positions but had never been used. Through the thick fog which blanketed the area at dawn on June 8th, the French could hear the rattle of tank tracks and the shouts of infantry moving up for attack.

It came at 0800 with German heavy artillery – still well outside the range of any counterbattery fire the French could bring to bear – putting down a heavy concentration on one sector in the north-west, while Stukas screamed in overhead and Me 109s swept in at low level, machine-gunning batteries and observation posts. Then just before 1000, a combined panzer and infantry attack drove in upon the dazed and shaken defenders, aiming for one of the low rises along the perimeter from which, in such uniform surroundings, they would hold a dominant position.

All through the midday period under the scorching June sun, the battle was fought out between the German panzers and the infantry from Chad and the Congo of the Bataillon de marche de l'Oubanghi, with the French Colonial losses mounting all the time, although just behind them the Bren carriers of the Legion waited to rush reinforcements forward if the line broke. Sixty Stukas delivered another concentrated attack in the early afternoon, Kleeman's infantry rushing forward before the last plane had gone or the dust settled; and by now the whole of the northern front was under attack, a dense cloud shrouding the entire fort, and as the signal lines had been ripped apart, Koenig was unable either to communicate with his forward positions or even to see them. Many of the anti-tank guns were hit or captured, at least one 25-pounder had been smashed to shapeless metal and its crew killed, and then a chance German shell landed on an ammunition dump and the resulting flash and roar obliterated all other impressions for several vital minutes. By the time night fell, the line, though not broken, had been pushed back and was badly bent.

By now, medical services were breaking down as the casualties mounted and supplies of everything from drugs and anaesthetics to water for washing the wounds ran out; and an attempt by the R.A.F. to drop supplies was unsuccessful as the parachute failed to open and the precious contents of the pack smashed to pieces on the rock-hard ground.

Yet the morale of the garrison remained high – perhaps because of the severity of their ordeal, and because of the fame they knew their efforts were garnering. London, Berlin, New York and Paris –

especially Paris – were watching this epic in the desert, which had become far more than just a fight for the junction of a few meandering desert tracks. A nation whose military tradition had been the main bulwark of her self-esteem was praying for a miracle which would refurbish her badly tarnished reputation.

Tuesday, June 9th, was another day of scorching sun and mounting thirst. Throughout the previous night the attacking forces had kept up the chatter of machine-guns, the thump of mortar fire and the wide, white glare of Very lights and parachute flares; the defenders were now very tired. Red-rimmed eyes peered from sunken eye-sockets over lined and unshaven cheeks, watching for the assault which would come, almost automatically, as soon as the light grew and the mist thinned.

High explosive first – bomb and shell to blast the gun-pits, to cut again the communication lines, to bury the infantry in choking dust; and then the clanking panzers with the racing, dodging, chunky figures of panzergrenadiers close behind. By midday the line was bending again, more 75mms and another 25-pounder had been smashed, and the Bofors guns manned by British gunners were almost out of ammunition. In one particularly vicious bout of hand-to-hand fighting, the attackers were shot down only yards from a battery.

In the southern sector, too, the pressure was growing all the while as more 90th Light infantry moved around after relief by 15th Panzer; and Rommel was himself on the scene now, urging his troops forward, watching for signs of weakness – but not finding any.

> Continuously exposed to the fire of the French, who fought grimly to the end, our storming parties suffered grievous casualties. However, by eight o'clock that night they worked their way forward to within about 220 yards of the Ridotta Bir Hacheim. During the day, Ritchie made a weak diversionary attack against the 90th Light Division's covering units south of Bir Hacheim . . . We had no difficulty in beating it off.[21]

As night fell, a massive Stuka attack came in, hitting the main dressing station and killing some of the wounded, setting fire to a bunch of lorries and destroying practically all the remaining rations. It was obvious that time for the Free French at Bir Hacheim was running out, and the only decision to be made was whether the end was to be total annihilation or an attempt to save something from the holocaust to fight another day.

That afternoon, in contradiction to Ritchie's continual exhortations to hold out, Messervy had signalled asking if Koenig did not now deem it advisable to pull out – to which Koenig replied that if transport could be brought close enough to evacuate his wounded, he was in favour of withdrawal that night – so much in favour, indeed, that that evening he handed over command of the garrison to the colonel of the Foreign Legion detachment, Colonel Amilakvari – and had himself driven out in his staff car by his British girl driver, presumably to press his arguments more closely.

Unfortunately, Messervy could not organise so complicated a manoeuvre in less than twenty-four hours, and the ordeal of the Frenchmen, Poles, Russians, Germans, Africans – and British – thus continued throughout June 10th, with, in Rommel's own words, 'the French desperately defending every single nest of resistance and suffering terrible casualties as a result.' A break-in along the hard-pressed northern·sector was contained again by the Legionnaires, in the early afternoon the heaviest air attack of the siege dropped 130 tons of bombs upon the shrunken circle of the fortress, and by evening the last rounds of mortar-bombs had been fired off, the last issue of shells made, and men were going from body to body collecting all that remained of the garrison's small-arms ammunition.

As darkness closed in, a small group of French engineers worked their way out towards the western minefield and began clearing a narrow passage on this, the most unlikely side for a break-out to be attempted. All equipment which could not be moved was prepared for destruction, the most important and secret papers collected into a briefcase and taken in charge by a senior officer who knew exactly what to do to them if danger threatened their capture; and two companies of infantry were detailed to remain behind to maintain the appearance and noise of defence while the rest of the garrison crept away.

As always, there were difficulties and mistakes. With the men so exhausted, it took longer than expected to load up, and in the dark trucks went astray and at least one gun and limber fell into a trench and had to be left. But at 2030, the head of the procession – the ambulances and trucks full of wounded, with walking wounded staggering along between them – felt its way through the narrow lane, and turned south to where the guns, trucks and additional ambulances brought up by the faithful 7th Motor Brigade were waiting. Behind them German artillery had set fire to other trucks, and the flames lit the arid desert scene with garish light.

Then things began to go wrong. The besiegers realised what was happening and machine-gun fire chattered on all sides; heavy artillery opened up and shells crashed on the abandoned defences while parachute flares floated down to add whiteness to the nightmare scene.

The guide for the headquarter column missed his way and was blown up three times on unexpected minefields (and lived to tell the tale!) and when Amilakvari eventually caught up with the main body he found it held up by a strong group of 90th Light infantry. As there was nothing for it now but to smash a way through, he gave the necessary orders and two promising officers, Capitaine de Lamaze and Lieutenant Dewey, led and were killed during the desperate foray which ensued.

But they won through. By 0500, the wounded were well on their way, first to Bir el Gubi and then to Gasr el Arid, and by 0700 on June 11th, 1,500 of the garrison had been brought to safety – a number considered disappointing at the time, especially as Koenig himself was unaccountably absent. But by nightfall he had arrived and so had another thousand of his men, and they were still coming in. In the end even some members of the two companies left in the fortress managed to escape and walk back to British lines, and the final count came to nearly 2,700 of the 3,600 who had fought off the first attack by the Ariete on the morning of May 27th, though a large proportion of them were wounded and many would never fight again.

They had left behind them a great deal of equipment – Rommel later claimed the capture of twenty-five guns and several hundred vehicles – and also a reputation. As von Mellenthin put it, 'In the whole course of the desert war, we never encountered a more heroic and well-sustained defence.'

France's honour, so bedraggled after the events of 1940 in the homeland and in 1941 in Syria, had begun its long slow march towards redemption.

It has been said that the French stand at Bir Hacheim 'won valuable time for Ritchie'.

It cannot be claimed that he put it to much use. He had spent a great deal of time visiting and talking to his corps commanders, and on June 4th had written a long memorandum to Auchinleck setting out his appreciation of the situation and his plans for the future, but despite the fact that by then three days had elapsed since the destruction of 150th Brigade opened the wide gap through which Rommel's supplies and reinforcements were pouring, he could still write, 'We must regard the Gazala–Hacheim line as our "Frontier Defences" – the firm base for all future operations until Cyrenaica is secured.'[22]

The fact that Auchinleck replied to it in all seriousness on June 9th (by which time *Operation Aberdeen* had been seen by those on the spot for the fiasco it was and Bir Hacheim was under strong siege) again reveals the quality of information being retailed to Cairo – all of it, even when accurate, first filtered through Ritchie's mind – still so irredeemably optimistic that after Bir Hacheim had fallen he claimed 'our withdrawal from Hacheim releases enemy forces but I think it releases more of ours.'

It was, of course, true that Eighth Army strength in men and

1–2 The commanders: *right*, General der Panzertruppe Erwin Rommel issues orders, with von Mellenthin on the right and Luftwaffe-General Hoffmann von Waldau in the centre; *below*, General Sir Claude Auchinleck and Lieutenant-General Neil Ritchie

3–4 Birth of a legend: *above*, Captain David Stirling
(left) plans a raid with Lieutenant 'Jock' Lewes;
right, Lieutenant 'Paddy' Mayne waits
to carry it out

5 Generalleutnant Walter K. Nehring and his staff

armour on June 11th was still, on paper, greater than Rommel's. Of
the seven infantry brigades in the line when the battle had opened,
five had hardly been engaged, two South African brigades in Tobruk
were still intact and two new Indian infantry brigades – the 11th from
4th Indian Division in Egypt, and the 20th from 10th Indian Division
in Iraq – had moved up into the battle area. As for armoured
strength, Ritchie's estimate of what was left to him was high, but
nevertheless Lumsden and Messervy between them did still command 185 cruiser tanks including quite a large number of Grants, and
Willison's 32nd Army Tank Brigade still disposed of 63 Matildas and
Valentines. Rommel after Bir Hacheim had just over 200 panzers,
but of these 85 were either Italian M13s or Panzer 11s, and it is
evident that in Grants and infantry tanks Eighth Army equalled or
outnumbered their battlefield equivalents – the Panzer Marks III and
IV – and in Crusaders and Stuarts well outnumbered the Axis light
tanks.

Endeavours made by Ritchie, however, to urge XXX Corps into
more offensive action foundered amid the doubts and dislikes
which plagued the armoured command, and all that had been
accomplished while the Fighting French were enduring their martyr-
dom was the disposal of Allied strength in more defensive boxes and
lines in which to await Rommel's next attack whenever he cared to
make it. The comparison with a flock of sheep awaiting their fate at
the fangs of marauding wolves is unavoidable, despite the protestations of aggressive intentions at high levels.

Gott, whose relations with Pienaar had by this time deteriorated to
a level below even those between Lumsden and Messervy, had
nevertheless been able to prise away from the South Africans two
companies of infantry to form a strongpoint at Point 154, east of the
69th Brigade and on the line leading back towards Acroma, and
another force to hold Elwet et Tamar three miles further east. The
positions held by 69th Brigade itself had also been extended eastwards to Bir Heleisi, while a battalion of British infantry (1st
Worcesters) held Point 187 just south-west of Acroma. The Guards
Brigade Group still held Knightsbridge but had detached 2nd Scots
Guards to the north to hold the pass down the Rigel Ridge, while
fifteen miles away to the east lay 29th Indian Brigade Group at El
Adem, also with one battalion detached to the north, in this case to
guard the pass down the Batruna Escarpment where the Tobruk
by-pass crossed it.

The gap between Knightsbridge and El Adem was to be guarded
by 22nd and 2nd Armoured Brigades under Lumsden and 4th
Armoured Brigade under Messervy, all grouped for the moment
around Knightsbridge. Their strength and condition is best described
in the *Official History*:

On 10th June General Ritchie estimated that he had about 250 cruiser and 80 'I' tanks fit to fight, though an analysis of unit records suggests that the true figures were: in the three armoured brigades 77 Grants, 52 Crusaders and 56 Stuarts, and in the 32nd Army Tank Brigade 63 'I' Tanks. Attempts to bring the armour up to strength had been most complicated and not very successful, the basic cause being the differences between the three sorts of cruiser tanks. To get the required tank with a suitable crew to the unit that wanted it was not easy. It led to sub-units being combined, or sometimes lent to other units. Even single tanks and crews had to be sent here and there. Regimental organization was disrupted, and the 1st Armoured Brigade, much to its disgust, had been used as a pool of immediate requirements. In fact expediency ruled, and any fairly well-filled till was raided for the benefit of empty ones. Units disliked this policy intensely. They complained also of many defects in their replacement tanks – of missing wireless equipment and of guns arriving rusted or in grease.[23]

The men complained of other matters, too, and very bitterly. Perhaps because of some realisation of the inadequacy of previous methods of replacing strength lost during the battle, some of the survivors of smashed or brewed-up tanks were now gathered together and formed into crews, then sent to 1st Armoured Brigade, where they were ordered back into action with Grants, Stuarts or Crusaders taken from the Greys, whose crews had manned and cared for them for many months during training and who now regarded them with proprietorial affection.

This system ingeniously combined the worst aspects of any method of replacement. The survivors were often suffering from battle shock, needing rest and hoping for escape from a battle in which they had already experienced set-back and were now sensing ultimate defeat. Now they were to go back in, leaving to the comparative safety and ease of the rear areas entire tank crews who were fresh and unscathed. These in their turn were infuriated to see their own tanks upon which they had often lavished great care being driven off to battle by others, with so evident a reflection upon either their own courage or their own ability.

'Why the hell can't you take your own bloody tanks up yourselves?' was a bitter question being asked by exhausted men of angry ones who had just asked their officers the same question but with more personal pronouns – and as their officers could not answer and felt the same way, the anger which men feel in defeat against authority grew rapidly into hatred and contempt.

There was indeed nothing to be said in favour of this system, for in addition to the fury it aroused it did little to solve the main problem of getting inexperienced men into battle under cool and experienced leadership.

Rommel wasted little time at Bir Hacheim. He and Bayerlein spent the early morning of June 11th examining with some interest and admiration the defence system, and issuing instructions for the disposal of the prisoners and all the captured material. They then planned and put into operation the next moves for the advance to the frontier.

These bore strong resemblances to the original *Operation Venezia*, for 90th Light and the Reconnaissance Battalions were ordered east to pass south of El Adem and make for the Escarpment at Ed Duda and the stores dump beyond at Belhammed, while 15th Panzer with Trieste on their left flank were to move north-east through the gap, making for the airfield just to the north of El Adem. Meanwhile, 21st Panzer, who had remained along the Sidra Ridge on the northern flank of the Cauldron, were to demonstrate against the new line of defences in order to nail the Allied infantry firmly into their positions, while Ariete remained on the eastern flank of the Cauldron, guarding the main Axis supply route and facing the Guards Brigade and the British armour concentrated around Knightsbridge.

These moves began in the middle of the afternoon, and by evening had been reported to Norrie by the R.A.F., who had been over the area covering the last stages of the Free French withdrawal. By this time, the 7th Motor Brigade and two columns of Indian infantry were attempting harassing tactics on the outside flank of 90th Light, and 4th Armoured Brigade were moving rather ponderously south-east from Knightsbridge upon an interception course which, however, ended on high ground in an area known as Naduret el Ghesceuasc. It was a location well known to 4th Armoured, and its commander, Brigadier Richards, felt that it gave him a certain dominance over his old opponents of 15th Panzer, who by nightfall had formed a hedgehog a few miles to the south-east, just within long-range shelling distance.

By the following morning, Norrie had studied the maps and, adding up the estimated armoured strengths available to each side, had come to the conclusion that if the 17 Grants and 28 light tanks of 2nd Armoured Brigade from Lumsden's division were added to the 39 Grants and 56 Stuarts from Messervy's division with Richards at Ghesceuasc, they should be able to inflict considerable damage upon the 64 mixed Panzers III and IV reported opposite them, especially if they attacked in flank and from higher ground. The 27 Grants and 39 light tanks with 22nd Armoured Brigade, reinforced by Willison's 63 mixed Matildas and Valentines, should be ample to keep 21st Panzer and Ariete in check.

This not unreasonable plan was defeated by the ever-present personal antagonisms at the top, and by something akin to churlish disobedience at lower levels, which had of course been affected by

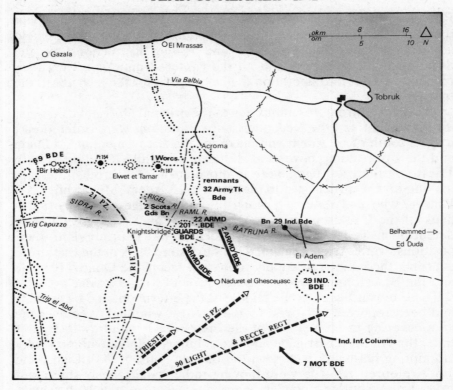

Map 7   June 11th, evening

the attitudes of the divisional commanders. Lumsden as usual was loth to hand over one of his brigades to Messervy, who in turn wished to concentrate his division – now split in half by Rommel's move – by sending 4th Armoured Brigade around behind 15th Panzer, 'regaining the open desert' and joining 7th Motor Brigade well away to the south, from which position they could harry any further advances towards the frontier. But neither the commander of his own brigade nor the one commanding the brigade reluctantly released to him by Lumsden were in agreement with this, the first because he had no wish to leave the Ghesceuasc area for which he seems to have formed a strong attachment, and the second because he wished to return to 1st Armoured command; so after a certain amount of acrimony, Messervy left to find Norrie and discuss the whole matter further.

En route he was nearly caught by flank patrols of one of Rommel's reconnaissance battalions, and was forced to spend the rest of the day hiding in a disused well while both 2nd and 4th Armoured Brigade commanders waited in chilly disagreement for further orders.

But not for long. At least one person concerned had broadcast details of the developing row, either in clear or in so ingenuous a code that it could quite easily be broken, and Rommel's intercept service had reported that '4th Armoured Brigade has refused to carry out an attack to the south-east' early enough for him to plan accordingly. Just before noon, 15th Panzer faced north and moved towards the waiting British tanks – but so hesitantly (for fatigue was affecting the German panzer crews and neither Rommel nor Nehring was present) that the attack was held off by the Grants of both 2nd and 4th Armoured, who then remained on their eminence gloomily watching the enemy manoeuvring below and still awaiting orders from either Messervy or Norrie.

These came at noon, by which time Norrie had realised that Messervy was again missing and had placed all the armour in the area under Lumsden. He now ordered 22nd Armoured Brigade down from Knightsbridge to join the others and thus for the first time concentrate all the cruiser tanks in XXX Corps together, but unfortunately for the British, both Rommel and Nehring had moved fast to correct the enervation in the Afrika Korps. With both men driving hard, 21st Panzer came across from the west to hit 4th Armoured in the flank at about the same time that Lumsden was ordering 22nd down from Knightsbridge, and Rommel himself galvanised 15th Panzer into delivering a devastating attack northwards against both 4th and 2nd Armoured.

According to the *Official History*, it is difficult to establish exactly what happened then, as 'The scanty and conflicting records make it impossible to disentangle the details of the ensuing fighting.' But this is surely an official gloss over a lamentable episode in the history of British arms.

Everybody, from the most junior members of the latest tank crews to join 2nd or 4th Armoured Brigades to the brigade commanders themselves, was affected by the atmosphere and situation in which they found themselves. Those of the tank crews who had fought in the battle beforehand were already cynical about the competence of the men directing it, and their unease was quickly transmitted to newcomers; and however ardently the regimental officers might attempt to stem the tide of disillusion, they were themselves only too well aware of the antagonisms and disagreements at brigade and divisional levels, and of the creeping paralysis caused by lack of confidence up in the more exalted spheres of division, corps and army. Sour discontent seethed throughout the two formations and boiled up into hatred, only a portion of which was directed against the enemy.

This was no frame of mind in which to win a battle against or even withstand attack from troops who, however tired they might be, had lately won two tactical victories and whose morale was high. When von

Bismarck's 21st Panzer crashed into 4th Armoured's right flank they knocked out twenty cruisers in less than half that number of minutes, while 15th Panzer's attack from the south met a line of British tanks whose commanders were watching over their shoulders for the moment when those behind might begin falling back, probably without bothering to inform them beforehand.

At first there was not much chance of this, for both brigades soon found themselves surrounded by panzers and – more dangerous still – by their accompanying anti-tank guns, and as no one fights more fiercely than the trapped, the Ghesceuasc area for over an hour was the scene of desperation, flame and fury in which men performed deeds of enormous bravery under the spur of even greater fear. But when Lumsden at last brought 22nd Armoured down from the north these drew off elements of 21st Panzer, thus opening a gap through which the remains of 4th Armoured promptly fled, leaving a large number of their tanks smouldering on the field, and eventually abandoning even the ones in tow. They drove headlong down the steep Raml Escarpment and did not halt until they reached the Tobruk by-pass not far short of the perimeter, by which time they had been reduced to fifteen runners, medium and light.

Meanwhile, both 2nd and 22nd Brigades had also suffered severely, but were at least back together again and under their own commander, Lumsden. He now drew them close and anchored the right flank of 22nd on Knightsbridge, extending the defence line for both brigades back north-east to reach the Raml Ridge, thus forming a shield parallel to the Knightsbridge–Acroma track along which the inhabitants of the box could escape – for it was evident to all that the Guards now held a salient which might easily be flanked on both sides and then pinched out.

Moreover, although it was impossible then to obtain an exact figure for the day's losses, it was evident by nightfall on June 12th that the balance of forces engaged in the Gazala battles had changed irrevocably. Not only would the British and South Africans continue the battle with lowered morale and an ever-decreasing confidence in their leadership at all except the lowest levels, but from now on they would fight with a numerical inferiority in both armour and artillery. Only in infantry would they possess superior numbers, and as five brigades of these were still penned in fixed positions thirty miles to the west and in obvious danger of being cut off, even this advantage might in the end prove an embarrassment.

One final episode on the evening of June 12th pin-pointed the main cause of the British inadequacy. Auchinleck had become increasingly disquieted by apparent contradictions in some of Ritchie's reports, and so had travelled up to Eighth Army Headquarters that day to investigate them. He found the atmosphere there, however, detached and tranquil, and no hint of disaster or even undue emergency reached him during the whole of that traumatic day; reassured, he flew back to Cairo, but before doing so signalled London, in all sincerity and innocence, saying, 'Atmosphere here good. No undue optimism and realities of situation are being faced calmly and resolutely. Morale of troops appears excellent.'[24]

But within a few hours he was facing the possibility of Eighth Army being thrown back to the Egyptian frontier.

On the morning of June 13th, both the British and German forces in and around Knightsbridge were desperately tired. Although the Guards Brigade had not been so fiercely engaged as the British armour, their position had been the focus of a battle which had swirled about them for nearly seventeen days, they had spent the previous night listening to 21st Panzer move back westwards across their southern flank in order to face up towards Rigel Ridge on the west, and they knew that 15th Panzer were already closed up to their north-east on Raml Ridge. Unless the Scots Guards at the Rigel Pass and the remains of Lumsden's and Willison's armour could hold the narrow corridor up to Acroma, the Guards would therefore very soon be facing exactly the same situation as had faced both 150th Brigade and the Free French, and might share the same fate.

An even greater strain, of course, was imposed on those holding the sides of the corridor, and although the first moves by 15th Panzer were those of men just as exhausted as those who watched them, they were unnerving just the same. One of the watchers was an artillery officer who later wrote:

> About a mile away a column was breaking leaguer. As we watched we saw about thirty tanks open out and begin to move towards us, behind them a long column of guns and lorries stretched down to the Trig Capuzzo. It was a horrible sight to see on an empty stomach at such an early hour.[25]

This attack and the first moves by 21st Panzer towards Rigel Ridge were both held off, but in the afternoon the attacks were pressed home more fiercely (as a result, though the men facing them did not know this, of the presence of both Rommel and Nehring). The Scots Guards supported by South African artillery fought grimly to hold the western flank – so grimly indeed that when the last South African gun had been silenced and the survivors taken prisoner, 'The German commander admonished Major Newman for continuing the fight so long, as needless loss of life had been involved' – which was a compliment in itself. On the eastern wing the battle was so severe that by the end of the day 32nd Army Tank Brigade had been

reduced to twenty Matildas and Valentines, while the estimated
cruiser strength in the three armoured brigades was now down to
fewer than fifty; and Lieutenant-Colonel H. R. B. Foote had won the
Victoria Cross for continually leading tank charges against heavy
odds in a manner reminiscent of Jock Campbell at Sidi Rezegh.

But the end was inevitable, and during the night of June 13th/14th,
Knightsbridge was evacuated and the Guards retired to Acroma, an
event which gave rise to an unexpected comment by Rommel much
later. Although the battle had raged around Knightsbridge for so
long, the box had not been directly attacked except during the last
twenty-four hours, yet despite this Rommel was to write: 'This
brigade was almost the living embodiment of the virtues and faults of
the British soldier – tremendous courage and tenacity combined with
a rigid lack of mobility.'[26]

Either something had impressed him of which no detailed record
was made at the time, or his later experiences with Guards formations coloured his memory.

With the removal of the Knightsbridge salient and the subsequent
closing up by the Panzerarmee to the new defence line to the north,
it was evident that the infantry still in the Gazala Line must get out –
and as the Via Balbia was already within shelling distance of
Rommel's guns, the move must be made quickly. As such a withdrawal would signal the beginning of retreat for the Eighth Army, the
decision had suddenly to be faced as to where the retreat should stop
– a decision within which was bound inextricably the fate of Tobruk.

This was not a matter which had received of late a great deal of
thought, though it had received attention and study some time
previously. Four and a half months before, Auchinleck had issued to
Ritchie as his commander in the field a detailed survey of the overall
situation in the area west of the Nile. In the shape of Operational
Instruction No. 110, this began with the words, 'My present intention
is to continue the offensive in Libya and the objective remains
Tripoli' but in its final passages quite rightly considered the course of
action to be followed should Rommel prove able to launch a large-
scale and subsequently successful offensive.

In the preparation of this section Auchinleck had consulted both Air
Marshal Tedder, who felt that his aircraft would be better used over a
battlefield than as an umbrella for a besieged port, and Admiral
Cunningham, who had stated categorically that with his greatly
reduced forces in the eastern Mediterranean, a repetition of the
supply problems of Tobruk under another siege would prove so grave
an embarrassment for the Royal Navy that the situation might
become untenable. As a result two paragraphs in that directive were
now about to become highly relevant:

(6) It is not my intention to try to hold permanently Tobruk or any other locality west of the Frontier.

(10) Work will be continued in accordance with the original plans on the El Alamein position as opportunity offers, until it is completed.[27]

Although a copy of this directive went, as a matter of course, to the C.I.G.S. in Whitehall, it seems unlikely that it came to Mr Churchill's attention at that time, for after the nine-month siege of the port in 1941, Tobruk had assumed a symbolic importance in his mind which would have produced violent reaction at any suggestion of future abandonment.

And it should be borne in mind that, whatever the military realities of the local situation, Mr Churchill was not alone in his attitude. The British public at home felt much the same way as their Prime Minister, and so did much larger publics in both Europe and America. Tobruk's fame after 1941 ranked with that of Troy, Gibraltar, the Pekin Legation and Mafeking in the past, and was Britain's pledge to Leningrad in the present. Its defence was irretrievably linked in the public mind with defiance and ultimate Allied victory, and its fall would strike the cracked note of disaster ominously enough to raise a spectre of final defeat.

The fact that its fall was also not seriously considered even on the spot is borne out – paradoxically – by the state of its defences; in June 1942 it was in no condition to withstand a resolute attack. On the eastern side, where O'Connor's original attack had gone in, the anti-tank ditch had been allowed to fill, and many thousands of the mines now sewn in the Gazala defences had originally been buried along the Tobruk perimeter – and removed from that perimeter in the confidence that Tobruk would never again be threatened.

Now, suddenly, the impossibility became a probability, especially in the mind of the commander in the field, buoyantly confident of victory until evidence of heavy defeat stared him in the face, and then – no matter what temporary resurgences of hope might come as the result of conference with his corps commanders – rapidly becoming convinced of the necessity of retreat back into Egypt.

As early as the afternoon of June 13th, Ritchie was suggesting the withdrawal of all the infantry in the Gazala Line, which in turn, in his view, would entail the withdrawal of the whole of Eighth Army to the frontier; but to this, Auchinleck, still with the picture of overall success gathered during his visit to headquarters in his mind, would not agree, instructing him instead to hold the defence positions as they stood – Gazala Line facing westward against the Italian divisions, Alam Hamza to Acroma line facing south against Rommel's armoured divisions, with Norrie's remaining armour shielding the Tobruk south-western perimeter around to El Adem and armoured car units and 29th Indian Infantry Brigade continuing the line down to Bir el Gubi. With the information at Auchinleck's disposal, this was not an entirely untenable position, and having instructed Ritchie to adopt it, he cabled the Prime Minister telling him of the decision – a message to which Mr Churchill replied, 'Your decision to fight it out to the end most cordially endorsed. We shall sustain you whatever the result. Retreat would be fatal. This is a business not only of armour but of will-power. God bless you all.'[28]

There are many accounts of what took place during the following days, mostly written from an objective point of view in which the outlooks from Whitehall, Cairo and the battlefront are all presented, generally at the same time. It is an illuminating exercise to follow the events solely from one point of view, that of the battlefront.

Despite Auchinleck's specific instruction to hold on to all present positions, at 0700 on June 14th Ritchie decided to withdraw the South Africans and 50th Division right back to the Egyptian frontier and told Gott to put the matter in train. At 0900, Ritchie telephoned Auchinleck from Tobruk and during a conversation which the South African historians describe as 'guarded and obscure' told him that the state of the army was such that the Gazala Line could no longer be held – an announcement which Auchinleck again countered by urging him to hang on if humanly possible, saying that he would send one of his staff up immediately to review the situation and report back to him that afternoon.

Nevertheless, at 1020 Ritchie issued not only formal orders to Gott to evacuate the infantry from the Gazala Line, but also to Lumsden to take his own headquarters and the remains of 2nd Armoured and 22nd Armoured Brigades back to the frontier after XIII Corps had withdrawn. He then sent a memorandum to Auchinleck, stating that he had ordered Gott to withdraw the forward infantry 'into Army Reserve' (but not stating where he considered this to be located) and that it was his intention to occupy frontier positions and at the same time build up a strong armoured and infantry force in the desert west of the frontier. He hoped, he said, to hold a line from the western perimeter of Tobruk through El Adem to Belhammed and would rely upon the mobile forces to the south to hold back Rommel's armour, thus keeping open lines of communication to Tobruk. As far as Tobruk itself was concerned, he said that the port had supplies for a month, that he was clearing out inessential services and that he might either have to accept temporary investment of the port or, alterna-tively, he could 'go the whole hog, give up Tobruk and withdraw to the Frontier. But surely investment would be the better alternative?'

Ritchie then went forward and visited both Gott and Norrie to discuss with them the details for the withdrawals to take place that night, and when he returned to his headquarters at 1600, found a long message from Auchinleck giving him at least one specific and incontrovertible order:

General Auchinleck to General Ritchie   14th June 1942
                                                        11.30 hrs

1. If in your opinion situation has so deteriorated that you can no longer leave 1st S.A. and 50th Divs in main Gazala positions without certain risk of their being cut off and isolated, then I agree to their withdrawal, undesirable though this is in view of tactical advantage this bastion gives us.
2. While I realise that our armoured forces have been defeated and are now weaker in quantity as well as in quality than those of the enemy, I must stress in my opinion that the enemy, who so far has won all his successes with two German armd and one German motor divs, helped to some extent by one Italian motor div., cannot really be in position to carry out large-scale offensive operations for indefinite period at pace he is doing. He must, I feel, have lost heavily, and we know his ammunition is short. Moreover, we are definitely superior to him in the air.
3. This being so, Tobruk must be held and the enemy must not be allowed to invest it. This means that Eighth Army must hold the line Acroma–El Adem and southwards and all enemy attempts to pass it. Having reduced your front by evacuating Gazala and reorganized your forces, this should be feasible and I order you to do it.
4. If you feel you cannot accept responsibility of holding this position you must say so.[29]

It was perhaps this last paragraph which caused Ritchie the most embarrassment, for having as a result of his past confidence inspired in his superior far too bland a view of the progress of the battle, he was now finding it impossible to bring home the gravity of the situation as he now saw it. Auchinleck's directive to keep Rommel away to the west and south of Tobruk was all very well – but Ritchie had already ordered five infantry brigades and the remnants of two armoured brigades back to the frontier, and he doubted the possibility of altering those orders without engendering the chaos that order and counter-order so often bring about; and he would seem to have been somewhat reluctant about admitting to Auchinleck what he had done.

In this impasse, he reacted in his normal fashion and sought advice from his more experienced subordinates, in this case Gott – and Gott's advice in this instance was coloured by two, and perhaps three, unfortunate disadvantages. First, he was unaware of the deterioration of Tobruk's defences along the south-eastern and eastern flanks of the perimeter and thus still considered it possible for the port to withstand a siege; and secondly, his mind was fully engaged with the problems of extricating the two divisions of his corps from the Gazala Line and getting them back to the Egyptian frontier in accordance with the orders he had been given some ten hours before. Thirdly –

although this is a matter which must remain in the realms of pure conjecture – it is possible that Ritchie did not make it clear to Gott that the Commander-in-Chief was expecting the withdrawal of XIII Corps to stop at Tobruk, so that the two infantry divisions, plus the whole of the remaining XXX Corps armour, would thenceforth be available to hold Rommel's advance along the Acroma–Bir el Gubi line.

Gott's advice was therefore that with the bulk of XIII and XXX Corps back on the frontier, Tobruk's investment was inevitable – but that there was no reason why it should not withstand a siege for at least one and possibly two months. During this time Eighth Army could be thoroughly reorganised in the frontier area with, undoubtedly, considerable reinforcement from such formations as the New Zealand and Australian Divisions, 4th, 5th and 10th Indian Divisions, and 10th Armoured Division now training in the Delta. There was, in Gott's opinion, not the slightest reason to abandon all the permanent installations in Tobruk, or even to set about withdrawing or destroying the huge dumps of supplies stockpiled there for the advance into Cyrenaica. Another siege of Tobruk was inevitable – but the certainty of its successful defence was equally undisputable.

Ritchie's confidence now revived by such forthright encouragement, he returned to his own headquarters and endeavoured to telephone Auchinleck again to obtain permission to allow Tobruk to be invested, but could only speak to one of the Commander-in-Chief's staff officers with whom he left his request. Auchinleck, however, remained adamant, and during the night which followed Ritchie received another directive ordering him to hold the Acroma–El Gubi line and containing this sentence: 'The defences of Tobruk and other strong places will be used as pivots of manoeuvre but on NO account will any part of Eighth Army be allowed to be surrounded in Tobruk and invested there.' It then went on to assure Ritchie that strong reserve forces were being accumulated for him in the Sollum–Maddalena area, and concluded:

> To sum up:
> (a) The general line Acroma–El Adem–El Gubi is to be denied to the enemy.
> (b) Our forces will NOT be invested in Tobruk and your army is to remain a mobile field army.
> (c) The enemy's forces are to be attacked and destroyed as soon as we have collected adequate forces for an offensive.[30]

It would be interesting to know how General Ritchie spent the remainder of the night after receipt of this signal, for he had done nothing to change his original orders to XIII Corps and 1st Armoured Division to withdraw to the frontier, and he did nothing now.

3 · 'A progression of avoidable disasters'

In their superb history of the Sidi Rezegh battles, the South African historians J. A. I. Agar-Hamilton and L. C. F. Turner say about the commander of the 1st South African Brigade at that time, 'It was not Brigadier Pienaar's habit to allow the orders of any superior to pass without thorough examination and discussion . . . '[1] and it was now evident that the recent promotion to major-general had done nothing to modify Dan Pienaar's attitude in such matters. The detailed orders from Eighth Army Headquarters regarding the evacuation of the South African Division from what had been a bastion but had now become an exposed salient were examined – and immediately rejected; and it comes as no surprise to discover that the rejection was thoroughly justified.

According to the staff officer who telephoned General Pienaar early on June 14th (just as coffee was being served to the general and his G.S.O.I.) Ramsden's 50th Division would begin leaving the Gazala Line that evening with a break-out *westwards* through the Italian lines opposite them, while his own South Africans waited throughout the night to lend support as and if 50th Division might need it. Pienaar's men would then evacuate their positions at first light the following morning, June 15th – withdrawing in broad daylight along the narrow coastal strip (indeed, for most of its transport, along the black ribbon of the Via Balbia) unprotected from enemy attack until they reached the Tobruk perimeter twenty-nine miles to the east.

As the events of the night would have warned Rommel that evacuation was in progress, it needed little imagination to foresee the activities of the Luftwaffe and the Afrika Korps (already within shelling distance of the Via Balbia) once the first South African movements had been reported; and if Gott's and Ritchie's staff officers seemed to lack that imagination, Pienaar's own made up for it. Within a very short time the orders were changed and permission given for the South Africans to pull out at the same time as their

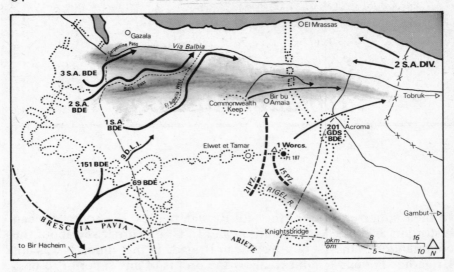

Map 8   Retreat from Gazala, June 14th–15th

neighbours – and so complete was the change of mind at corps headquarters that Pienaar was then instructed that 1st South African's tail must be through the entrance to Tobruk by 0700 the following morning. Moreover, units from 2nd South African Division, assisted by the remnants of 1st Armoured Division, would come out towards them and hold the line of minefields from Mrassas to Acroma, thus covering them for at least the last ten miles of their journey.

Pienaar and his staff wasted no time. From 0930 onwards on June 14th a stream of non-essential vehicles made their way down through the three escarpment passes just behind them – Serpentine Pass, Bill's Pass and El Agheila West Pass – and in the salient itself the dispiriting tasks of destruction began.

> It was heartbreaking to see men picking holes in invaluable 2-gallon water tins, sticking bayonets through tins of bully-beef, cheese and canned fruits, and throwing them down the wadis. Two things, however, the men were determined to take – the Fortress ration of milk and sugar – which stood them in good stead later on. They hurried to where the Fortress reserve of water was kept and filled waterbottles and every available container and then as the sun sank, the Commanding Officer gave the word. The guard peppered the 44-gallon drums with bursts of tommy-gun fire, and the water, that most precious liquid of the desert, ran out over the sand . . . [2]

Speed was obviously essential, but equally obvious was the logistic impossibility of moving the transport of three infantry brigades twenty-nine miles in single file along a narrow road, at regulation speed and with the specified intervals between each vehicle, in the time between sunset on June 14th and 0700 the next day. 1st South African Brigade therefore started moving out early that afternoon, but even so traffic blocks built up at such bottlenecks as the top of Agheila West Pass, and when drivers reached the open road below they tended to stamp on their accelerators and race off in bunches towards their destination. It was not long before enemy eyes were watching the developing chaos and taking steps to increase it.

Some of the Battalion are down the pass, others still jammed in the bottleneck at the top, when the first Stukas arrive. The trucks at the foot of the pass stop. The men run for cover. At the top, the men fling themselves down beside their trucks. The Stukas scream down . . . into the path of the Bofors fire, up and off. The gun at the foot follows their flight through the murk of explosive smoke. The gun at the top ceases to chatter: dead men hang over it and lie among torn sandbags . . .

The column jerks forward . . . Stragglers from other units cut in among the Battalion transport and force the pace. As the Battalion vehicles try to regain their places, convoy discipline begins to go; a panicking few are breaking up the disciplined many: each small group of trucks is becoming an isolated unit. On the Tobruk road a continuous stream of traffic heads for the fortress or is directed around it at the junction of the Tobruk and Acroma roads. This road from Gazala to the Acroma Monument is relentlessly machine-gunned and bombed. Trucks blaze. Men run: ambulances howl towards the hospital in Tobruk: dead men lie in blood and oil and broken glass.[3]

East of the passes, Rommel had spent June 14th spurring on the exhausted men of his two panzer divisions in a heroic effort to reach and cut the Via Balbia and thus add the destruction of more South African brigades to his tally of victories. From late morning the panzers and their attached grenadiers had been probing northwards from the Rigel Ridge trying to break through between the South Africans holding Elwet et Tamar and the Worcestershire Regiment at Point 187 and finding themselves held back at first by unexpected and deep minefields and then, as they tried to lift them, by heavy and concentrated shell-fire.

In this they were unfortunate, for the highly effective system of defence they now encountered was only provided in view of the weakness of British armour in the area; had 1st Armoured Division not suffered such heavy losses during the previous few days, they would have been thrown into the battle in a 'tank versus panzer' action and doubtless brushed aside by Rommel's properly co-ordinated armour and artillery – in which case Dan Pienaar's entire division might well have found themselves in dire circumstances. As it happened, in the absence of strong tank formations all the artillery in the area, including that of the Guards Brigade still concentrated around Acroma, was rushed forward and for many hours held the bulk of both 15th and 21st Panzer Divisions back south of the minefield.

During the morning battles the panzers thus made very little headway, but when news of the start of the Gazala evacuation in the afternoon reached Rommel and Nehring, the two began again to flog the Afrika Korps into yet greater efforts, and 21st Panzer were bleakly ordered by Nehring to take the position at Elwet et Tamar by nightfall in such terms that both divisional and regimental commanders knew that their future careers were at stake. Five miles to the east, 15th Panzer had broken into the Worcestershire positions by 1500 but were still being held by the British infantry and their supporting anti-tank guns when the essential weakness of the British position suddenly became evident.

The Worcestershires were under command of 2nd South African Division in Tobruk, the defenders of Elwet et Tamar under Dan Pienaar at Gazala, the Guards artillery were still under their own brigade commander, and what armour there was in the area (and by evening it had been reduced to two Grants and eight Crusaders) was under Lumsden, who, however, had no means of communication with either of the infantry strongpoints. A decision had in fact been taken shortly after noon that the commander of 2nd Armoured Brigade should take charge of all troops in the area, but no one affected by the order learned of it until days afterwards, and it is not surprising therefore that eventually a critical error was made.

Shortly after 1630 a message arrived at the Worcestershire's headquarters which seemed plain enough, though it was, in fact, corrupt. As there was no overriding authority to which to refer, the battalion began a withdrawal in accordance with its apparent instructions, but under such difficult conditions that they lost over two hundred killed, wounded and missing and it was twenty-four hours before the remnants managed to make their way into Tobruk; and in the meantime, 15th Panzer had overrun Point 187 and pushed on towards Acroma, while on their left 21st Panzer were coming through the gap and aiming for the main objective for the day – Commonwealth Keep.

By nightfall, they were at Bir bu Amaia on the Escarpment just to the east of the Keep, the entire British and South African defence line had been outflanked, the Via Balbia was just below and well within sight and striking distance, and the escape of Pienaar's division and all other troops still between Gazala and the Afrika Korps apparently cut off.

But even Afrika Korps flesh and blood could only stand so much.

That night the exhausted crews of the Panzer Divisions lay in the desert outside Acroma, with nothing between them and the crowded Via Balbia, but they did not stir for all the urgent signals of their Commander-in-Chief, who saw clearly enough that the prize of the Gazala garrison was slipping out of his grasp. When the little force at Commonwealth Keep (Point 209) scrambled down the escarpment in retreat their transport had perforce to make for Acroma direct and trundled past a mass of sleeping Germans on the way. The South Africans politely refrained from disturbing the strangers and were allowed to pass without even a challenge.[4]

While the Afrika Korps slept, XIII Corps escaped. Ramsden had instructed the commanders of his two remaining 50th Division brigades to begin the break-out to the west as soon as darkness allowed, and by 2000 one battalion from each brigade supported by artillery and engineers had gone forward to open the passages through the minefields opposite them, and then through any fixed positions the Italians might decide to hold against them. The actions fought that night by 5th Battalion East Yorks and by the 8th Durham Light Infantry, cloaked at first by dust-storms and then by nightfall, were brisk, violent, and entirely successful – and through the gaps they tore in lines held mainly by the Brescia Division, the bulk of 151st and 69th Brigades then poured and were through the Italian positions and driving down towards Bir Hacheim well before dawn. During the next two days they fought sporadic actions with some of Rommel's supply trains, but as they had had to abandon much of their heavy equipment at Gazala, they were so short of essentials such as wireless sets, anti-tank guns and water-carriers when they reached the Egyptian border on June 16th that they could not be regarded as battleworthy or fit to play much further part for the moment in the defence of the Delta.

They were also under strength, for the third battalion of 151st Brigade – 9th Durham Light Infantry – had been delegated as the last formation to leave the defence line, and when they did so they found the Italian opposition so thoroughly awakened and aware of their plans that their commander, Lieutenant-Colonel J. E. S. Percy, decided that their safest course would be to turn back. They therefore followed the trail of 1st South African Brigade, who by midnight were down El Agheila West and making their way through Tobruk and on towards Gambut and Egypt. Unfortunately, 2nd South African Brigade had missed the top of Bill's Pass and were not down on the Via Balbia in bulk until nearly 0600 on the 15th, and by this time 3rd South African were only just clearing Serpentine Pass even further west. There was thus a very great deal of fast-moving traffic racing along the road towards Tobruk as dawn broke, and as a result, Percy's battalion and the South African rearguards found themselves in increasing danger as the Afrika Korps awoke – to a new day and an infuriated Commander-in-Chief.

By 0800 15th Panzer were on top of the Escarpment shelling the traffic below them, and by noon – by which time only Percy's Durhams and the South African rearguards were still west of Tobruk – they had put one battalion from Rifle Regiment 115 across the road, supported by half a dozen Panzer Mark IIIs and a captured 25-pounder. It looked briefly as though 50th Division would after all pay a heavy price for their escape, but Percy and his dour Geordies had no intention of giving up so near to Tobruk and a semblance of safety. They collected what random guns they could find in the neighbour-hood, some South African carriers and armoured cars and smashed their way through the enemy screen during the afternoon. Unfortunately, few of the South African rearguards elected to follow them and the remainder were taken prisoner during that afternoon.

By nightfall on June 15th there were no Allied formations west of Tobruk or the Acroma–Bir el Gubi line, and Rommel could write that evening in his daily letter to his wife, 'The battle has been won and the enemy is breaking up. We're now mopping up the encircled remnants of their army.' Even Rommel's habitual optimism was hardly exaggerating the situation now, and those two sentences were very close indeed to the truth.

Not that Rommel had exhibited much optimism earlier in the day.

Some time later he was to remark to one of his aides, 'It's a great thing to be a Field Marshal and still remember how to talk to them like a sergeant-major!' and when that morning he had discovered that Afrika Korps had slept while the South Africans had escaped, his anger had been intense and his language violent, picturesque and to the point.

But the outburst was brief, and having vented his feelings in a manner which reminded all present of their days of recruit training, he switched off his anger and began issuing his orders for the day. For the moment, 15th Panzer must stay on the western edge of the Tobruk perimeter and clear up the position there, but 21st Panzer were to undertake the first stage of the encirclement of Tobruk and would move immediately to Bir Lefa. Away to the south, Ariete and the three reconnaissance battalions would form a screen to keep at bay the 7th Motor Brigade and any raiding columns which Eighth Army might send up towards the crucial areas, while closer in 90th Light would again attack 29th Indian Brigade at El Adem.

'*Es kommt darauf an*,' Rommel announced, '*den Kessel um Tobruk zuzumachen*,'[5] which can be roughly translated as, 'the time has come to put the lid on Tobruk!'

There were, as he saw it, three 'cornerstones' outside the main defences of Tobruk – the box at El Adem, the one between Ed Duda and Sidi Rezegh, and the main position at Belhammed – and these

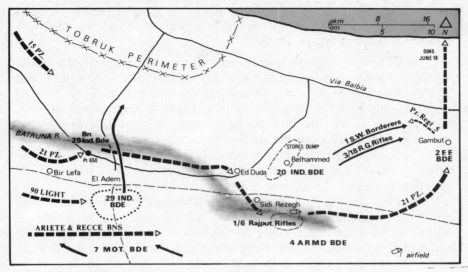

Map 9   Investment of Tobruk, June 16th–18th

must be knocked away before the main assault on the fortress began. By noon he was at the first one south of El Adem watching 90th Light mount yet another attack in the face of heavy and well co-ordinated Indian artillery, and waiting for the bulk of 21st Panzer to arrive just to the north-west – and as they came up he sent them on further. One of 29th Indian Brigade's battalions had been detached and was holding Point 650 at the top of the pass leading down the Batruna Escarpment, and 21st Panzer were told to obliterate them and then carry on towards Ed Duda – aiming at Gambut as their final objective for the day.

Speed, speed and more speed was the criterion and Rommel's driving urgency vitalised everyone; though the Indians at El Adem threw back this latest assault by 90th Light, Rifle Regiment 115 backed up by extra artillery and some of Panzer Regiment 5's Mark IIIs smashed into the hapless 3rd/12th Frontier Force Rifles at Point 650, and in three hours of fierce action wiped them out taking some seven hundred prisoners, many of them wounded – and 21st Panzer were then free to roll on towards Ed Duda where they arrived soon after midnight to find the place practically unoccupied.

The first day of the sweep around Tobruk had therefore gone well, and early the following morning Rommel went back to the Via Balbia at the western end of the perimeter to urge 15th Panzer after 21st. He found them still rounding up prisoners and collecting booty:

> Another six thousand British troops had found their way into our prison camps. Evidence of the British defeat could be seen all along the road and

verges. Vast quantities of material lay on all sides, burnt-out vehicles stood black and empty in the sand. Whole convoys of undamaged British lorries had fallen into our hands . . . [6]

They were very quickly put to use, and as the leading units of the Italian infantry divisions were arriving from Gazala, Rommel sent 15th Panzer off to follow 21st around the perimeter. Then he was himself again at El Adem, urging 90th Light to renew their assault, hurrying up more artillery to help them against the apparently immovable Indians. Overhead the Luftwaffe were occasionally engaged by Bostons and Kittyhawks, but R.A.F. energies for the moment were engaged on ground support for the army in the intervals between evacuating their own landing-strips.

By noon, the news had come to Rommel that Ed Duda was occupied by 21st Panzer and that they were forming up for an attack up the well-remembered slope to the Sidi Rezegh box, now held by more Indian troops (1st/6th Rajputana Rifles). But here the R.A.F. were attacking in force with fighter-bombers and some new tank-destroying Hurricanes, and the division was suffering losses and delay; moreover, isolated groups of British tanks were appearing to the south of the box, apparently from a reorganised 4th Armoured Brigade.

But nothing was to stand in the way of Rommel's determination, and by 1600 the 21st Panzer were grinding up the slope towards the box with one detached anti-tank screen fanning away towards the British tanks – and as darkness fell these dropped back south towards their leaguer area, leaving the Rajputana Rifles to their fate. This was sealed when their artillery ran out of ammunition and by 2030 21st Panzer had taken the airfield, most of the defenders were captured, a small remnant dropping back towards Belhammed.

And half an hour before, Rommel had been told by 90th Light that all the signs pointed to the evacuation of El Adem by the remaining battalions of 29th Indian Brigade, after a resistance which the Afrika Korps War Diary described as 'extraordinarily stubborn'. Tuesday, June 16th, had been a day of significant accomplishment and even Rommel slept a few hours that night. The War Diary entry for that night reads:

> Our next task is to clean up the outlying area of Tobruk and to carry through the encirclement of the Fortress while preventing interference from the south and from the east . . . Army intends to thrust with D.A.K. in the afternoon of 17.6 first to the south-east, then, wheeling to the north, to Gambut and the Via Balbia north of it. Thereby the enemy in Tobruk, and to the east of it, is to be locked in. The encircling ring will be narrowed in the days following so as to create the requirements for the attack on Tobruk itself. [7]

Now there seemed only two obstacles to the encirclement of Tobruk – the remains of the 20th Indian Brigade at Belhammed (it had been one of their battalions that was lost at Sidi Rezegh the previous afternoon), and the apparently recuperated 4th Armoured Brigade – and there was no doubt in Rommel's mind which had to be dealt with first. Not only was the mobile armour the greater threat, but a move towards it would create an impression he required – that he was more interested in sweeping on towards the frontier than in capturing Tobruk.

But in view of the recent expert use by the British of their artillery south of Elwet et Tamar, it would be as well to proceed carefully. Some time was therefore spent regrouping and a few provocative feints were made, but it was not until 1114 (on June 17th) that Rommel received the news he wanted – the British tanks were massing for an advance towards Sidi Rezegh, apparently unaware that the place was already in Rommel's hands. Panzer Regiment 5 moved off to the right wing and waited, the anti-tank screens moved out cautiously and watched for the opening moves.

They came at 1550, in conditions which could hardly have been more advantageous for the panzers – the British tanks advancing slowly and somewhat raggedly straight into the sun, which effectively blinded the gunners, most of whom had had no opportunity before-hand even to fire their new weapons, let alone correct or adjust their sights. Such a dire improvisation of machines and manpower had in fact been necessary to put this force together that even though the tank strength of 4th Armoured Brigade had been raised to ninety, in at least two cases the crews consisted entirely of officers; and – as so often in the past – the three composite regiments which now came into action did so separately.

Yet the two panzer divisions had quite a stiff battle. At one time 21st Panzer was calling for extra artillery support and then somewhat indignantly complaining that much of it was dropping on themselves instead of their opponents – but in the end training and co-ordination paid. By dark the panzers commanded the field of battle upon which the broken, smoking carcasses of yet another thirty-two British tanks remained, while the battered remnants of 4th Armoured Brigade (in truth, the remnants of the two armoured divisions which had faced Rommel when he first attacked the Gazala Line three weeks before) limped away to the south and then back behind the frontier. As a battleworthy formation, XXX Corps had ceased to exist.

But in Rommel's mind this was no time to pursue the vision of a local victory of annihilation, for his most earnestly desired prizes waited to the north. At 1930, he swung 21st Panzer around to face up towards the Via Balbia and the coast, and with his own *Kampfstaffel* some two miles in the lead, drove straight for the area between

Belhammed and the airfield at Gambut, still in use by the R.A.F.

They overran a small but spiteful defence post just south of Gambut and took some Free French prisoners, then ran into extensive minefields which, however, Rommel and his advanced units were able to skirt – and by 2200 they were driving on to the airfield, capturing as they did so fifteen serviceable aircraft and considerable quantities of oil and petrol; and now, stretching away to the west as far as Belhammed, lay the vast stores dump which Auchinleck and Ritchie had accumulated for what they had thought would be their own advance into the Jebel Akhdar and beyond.

Half an hour after midnight came the news that the Via Balbia had been cut to the east of Tobruk, and within another fifteen minutes German troops were on the coast. Tobruk was invested again, the area to the immediate south was clear for the regrouping which would be necessary before the attack on the perimeter could begin, and already reports were coming in from the delighted and revitalised Afrika Korps troops of the enormous haul of loot which had fallen into their hands. And not only loot; two battalions of 20th Indian Brigade – 1st South Wales Borderers and the 3rd/18th Royal Garwhal Rifles – had been ordered by Norrie to break out eastwards from Belhammed during the night and, making uncoordinated attempts to run the gauntlet just before dawn, had run into Panzer Regiment 5 and been captured almost to a man.

The rest of Thursday, June 18th, was spent by Rommel's troops clearing out the remaining pockets of resistance outside the perimeter. One extraordinary defence was encountered at Acroma Keep dominating the Axis By-pass just to the north of the old Acroma box positions, put up by a single company of Transvaal Scottish who had sited and learned to use a captured German 88mm. and four Italian 47mm. guns, all without their proper sights. The position was only eliminated that night after a curt written instruction had been issued by Rommel to the Italian XXI Corps commander, and even then all but one of the valiant South Africans retired successfully into Tobruk.

Meanwhile, Panzerarmee Headquarters were revising plans and issuing orders for the forthcoming assault of the port, while the quartermasters were resupplying units from the Aladdin's Cave which had fallen into their hands. Enormous quantities of food, water and fuel were available for the troops and their equally voracious vehicles, together with clothing to replace tattered uniforms – 'beautiful English leather boots' for the troops and, to their astonishment, 'soft, elegant suede shoes with thick rubber soles' for those officers who did not consider them too effeminate. Ammunition was there in abundance, too, and one of Rommel's chief worries was eliminated when huge stocks of 25-pounder shells were found for the captured British guns which now made up quite a sizeable proportion of his artillery – but this beneficence was rendered almost unnecessary when an astonished but excited gunner officer came in with the news that their own artillery and ammunition dumps, laid down eight months before in preparation for the November attack (which *Crusader* had upset) had just been discovered exactly where they had been left, undisturbed and intact. As Rommel intended to use the same plan of attack as had been drawn up for that occasion – a powerful thrust on a narrow frontage – it seemed that everything was working out in his favour.

Certainly he would have the fullest co-operation for the assault from all his allies and supporting arms. Kesselring, mindful especially of the timetable by which, once Tobruk had fallen, his air fleets would be switched westward for the *Herkules* attack on Malta (after which they would be free to rejoin the massive struggle in Russia), promised the greatest concentration he could organise, and was preparing to bring over every available bomber from Greece and Crete to add to those already in Africa. The Italians were just as enthusiastic, Pavia and Trieste Divisions of XX Corps anxious to play their part on the left flank of the attack, Ariete as eager as the men of the panzer divisions to take part in the armoured breakthrough.

Never before had Rommel been supported by such enthusiasm at every level of the Axis Command in Africa, never before had he directed so eager, so well-equipped, and so experienced a force as that which now grouped together along the Tobruk perimeter. Already they were staging diversionary attacks on the western flanks to distract the attention of the besieged, but the main force was concentrating to the south-east. The only areas of disappointment were to the south of El Adem where the newly arrived Littorio Armoured Division was spread in a wide fan to guard against any attempt to interfere by the remnants of 7th Motor Brigade, reputed still to be away to the south, and to the east where the men of 90th Light Division were deployed south of the Trig Capuzzo between Gambut and Bardia – which they entered and occupied on the afternoon of June 19th. Their shielding role would undoubtedly be important, but was likely to be neither so spectacular nor so profitable as those of the assault troops.

By dusk on June 19th, all was ready. During the morning patrols had ventured as near to the Tobruk perimeter as they dared and on two occasions skirmished briefly with Indian and South African troops holding the bunker line; during the afternoon armoured cars had driven along the outer perimeter exchanging machine-gun fire with static posts. As darkness fell, the panzers left the positions around Gambut and moved up to start lines less than six kilometres from the anti-tank ditch, and among the troops from 15th Panzer

Division was the battalion commanded by Oberleutnant Schmidt:

> Groups of crouching figures huddled in woollen blankets in a little wadi
> at Ed Duda. There was almost no conversation, and that in whispers, as
> though the enemy, who was, perhaps, miles away, might hear us. What
> chatter there was seemed flippant and irrelevant: it was characteristic of
> talk before a battle.
> Next to each group – combat engineers and infantry storm-troops – lay
> the arms and other paraphernalia gathered during the day: explosives,
> grenades, mine-detectors, wire-cutters, flamethrowers, smoke-screen
> candles, machine-guns, ammunition.
> A few minutes to zero hour.
> A few minutes for thought – especially for those of us who had taken
> part, during April and May of the year before, in the futile assaults on
> this almost hated fortress.[8]

But like so many of the attacking troops as they waited that night,
Schmidt could console himself with one thought; at least he knew the
terrain over which he and his men would advance, and had many
times during 1941 watched skirmishes being fought there between his
own men and the Australians. He had thus accumulated a great deal
of valuable local knowledge – far more, for instance, than the Indian
troops opposite, similarly gazing out over the darkened waste,
similarly whispering between themselves, similarly waiting in concealed trepidation for what the dawn would bring.

It brought the most concentrated bombardment the Western Desert
had ever seen. Rommel and von Mellenthin were standing together
outside the battle headquarters on the escarpment north-east of El
Adem and the latter described what happened:

> Promptly at 0520 [on June 20th] the Stukas flew over. Kesselring had
> been as good as his word and sent hundreds of bombers in dense for-
> mations; they dived on to the perimeter in one of the most spectacular
> attacks I have ever seen. A great cloud of smoke and dust arose from the
> sector under attack, and while our bombs crashed on to the defences, the
> entire German and Italian army artillery joined in with a tremendous and
> well co-ordinated fire. The combined weight of the artillery and bombing
> was terrific.[9]

Schmidt was now waiting with his assault group only a hundred
yards back from the edge of the first minefield, and in front of them
lay engineers, some of whom had already lifted a few mines and even
reached the wire fence and cut some small gaps.

But the main destruction was still to come, and one duty unexpectedly allocated to the Stukas was to blast through the minefields; flight after flight plunged down just in front of the waiting men,

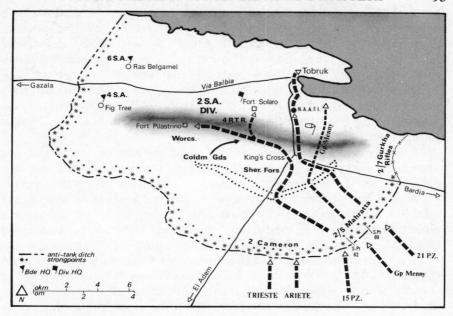

Map 10   Tobruk, June 20th

and the crash of one bomb would be followed by another as the first mine went off, and then more and more in a series, 'like some atomic fission continuing on beyond the first explosive shock'. Then the Stukas would turn and whine back over their heads to El Adem and be back over again within minutes with another bomb load.

As the bombardment started, Schmidt had seen a few isolated defenders race back from the wire and disappear into the ground, but after that little human movement was visible through the fog and murk of the explosions – just the flash of bomb-blast, the gouts of dust and smoke, and once, dimly seen, the hoped-for spectacle of metal uprights trailing strands of wire entanglement whirling high in the air. Every nerve tense, the group waited in their small wadi for the next phase of the attack; a brief pause, a shout and engineers in front rose and raced forward under covering fire from chattering machine-guns on each side. More explosions, wide yellow flashes low to the ground, a few coloured Very lights soaring inexplicably into the air and then suddenly, from points spaced equidistantly along the assault fronts, jets of thick orange smoke which joined together and blanked off the entire scene.

At this, the gunfire ceased abruptly, the assault teams raced forward into the fog, and as they jumped, stumbled, tripped, fell, rose and raced onwards again, choking in the acrid, tarnish-flavoured reek, they heard more shells scream over as the guns opened fire on a new range. Then they were clear of the fog and through the torn and flattened wire, to see in front of them the first of the defenders' trenches – empty and only partly blown-in. As they tumbled down into safety, they heard the sounds of Spandaus opening up on each side and knew that their neighbouring teams were level and their own flanks secure. Somewhere in front British artillery was coming into action, firing over their heads, presumably in search of the lorried infantry and armour still behind.

More assault teams came racing up from the rear, machine-gun fire increased everywhere, men were working along the trench line and grouping for the next overland rush towards the nearest strongpoint. Already a few stunned and totally bewildered Mahrattas were being winkled out from the solidly constructed Italian underground posts – which had certainly helped to save their lives but had also concealed from them everything that had been happening on the surface.

Less than an hour after the bombardment had opened, Strongpoint 69 was taken; by 0630 those on each side had fallen, others were coming under attack and as more and more of the defenders – deafened and shocked by the violence of the assault and blinded by their retreat into spurious safety – gave themselves up, the gap widened while behind it the ubiquitous support engineers were rapidly clamping into position the prefabricated bridges across the anti-tank ditch, or levelling up where silting had taken place. By 0745, ten strongpoints had been taken, the leading infantry were two miles inside the perimeter, the centre company of the defending 2nd/5th Mahrattas had ceased to exist (happily, most of them were prisoners) and to the rear, the leading Mark IIIs of 21st Panzer were arriving at their crossing-points.

By 0830, 21st Panzer's leading squadrons were across and into the bridgehead and 15th Panzer were coming through on the left flank, the first led into action by their divisional commander von Bismarck (in a motor-cycle side-car careering between his files of panzers), the second by General Nehring taking the place of the wounded von Vaerst, all urged onwards towards the vital position of King's Cross at the junction of the El Adem and Bardia roads by the chunky, excited, inspiring figure of their Commander-in-Chief, who had personally supervised the first crossings of the anti-tank ditch in order to ensure smooth passage, and was inside the bridgehead by 0800. Only occasionally did anyone in the bridgehead have time to wonder why the British artillery was so sparse and ineffective, or why there was so little sign of anything which could be interpreted as a well-organised counter-attack – though carrier-borne Gurkha infantry did appear briefly on the right flank, and pin down some of the assault troops there until driven off by panzers. On the left flank of the breakthrough a hard battle was being fought as Ariete tried but failed to smash their way through positions held by the 2nd Camerons, who had not been subjected to so violent a bombardment as had crashed down on the Mahrattas.

Just before 0900 heavy calibre shells began to rumble overhead as South African batteries beyond Pilastrino came into action, but as the bulk of the panzers were through the gap now (over a hundred of them) the fire would not affect the momentum of attack. Just before 1000, 15th Panzer met two British tanks which scuttled rapidly away once the crews saw the mass against them – and on the right 21st Panzer came up against one of the inner minefields which held them up briefly until von Bismarck in his motor-cycle side-car threaded a way through and, with some trepidation, his panzers followed. By 1030, with Nehring and von Bismarck leading one on each flank and Rommel amid the bulk of his armour in the centre, the whole superbly co-ordinated mass of asault troops and artillery, panzers and support infantry, drove inexorably northwards, rolling over defence posts in their path, machine-gunning batteries which tried to harass them on either flank, or sending assault infantry and engineer groups out to obliterate them. Nothing could stop them now.

By 1100 they were approaching the main inner minefield which they knew protected King's Cross, and here they met for the first time something like a serious attempt to check them – by Matildas which came out through gaps in the minefield to try to get within range with their puny 2-pounders; but the anti-tank screen soon stopped them and when the leading Mark IIIs opened up as well, the Matilda crews could be seen jumping from their turrets and racing back towards some form of safety. By 1145, the panzers were at the edge of the inner minefield and the engineers were out in front with their mine-detectors – and a lull fell across the main battlefield. Behind them on the left the panzer crews and assault infantry could hear Ariete still battling in vain with the 2nd Camerons, in front Stukas were howling down on to some unfortunate objective just out of sight while further off flights of bombers cruised unmolested over the port and harbour, their bombs falling away in apparent slow motion, their explosions muted by the escarpment in front, and the cliffs.

Then the engineers signalled clear passage, 21st Panzer struck slightly away to the right and reached the Bardia road to turn westwards along it, 15th Panzer's left flank hit the El Adem road and turned due north, while in the centre a group of over forty mixed Mark IIIs and IVs drove straight over the gapped minefield towards the vital road junction. Here, almost for the first time, they encountered serious opposition – nearly thirty 25-pounders and a few anti-tank guns deployed in a wide fan against them, their crews still working frantically to give themselves some shelter in the form of sangar or sandbag wall. It was obvious that most of them had only just arrived.

The panzers slowed and where necessary reloaded with high explosive instead of anti-tank ammunition; the protective artillery screens moved forward, the infantry dropped from their vehicles and, as machine-gunners began covering fire, moved up to attack. Soon each British or South African troop and battery position was pock-marked with exploding shell and streams of tracer laced above and between the advancing German infantry, each bead of light with seven unseen bullets behind it – while in front the British 25-pounders barked, coughing their heavy shells overhead towards the jostling panzers behind. As the infantry teams closed with each gun, fire concentrated upon it for a few more vital seconds, then lifted abruptly on to the next until, one by one, they all fell silent, smoking and impotent, their crews sprawled bleeding, unconscious or dead behind the riddled screens, around the disordered heaps of empty cartridge cases or unused shells. In the distance, some towing vehicles were limping away, carrying a few lucky wounded to hospital.

By 1230 the gun-line had been destroyed or chased away (one troop from 12th/25th Battery escaped westwards across the El Adem road and 15th Panzer let them go) and the massed strength of D.A.K. moved forward again, to be briefly hindered on the left flank by a brave but ineffectual attack by some Valentines – baulked and the tanks destroyed by the anti-tank screen. And by about 1330, the leading squadrons of both divisions had passed King's Cross, 21st driving on northwards towards the airfield and the port beyond, 15th Panzer veering westwards along the line of the Pilastrino Ridge towards Fort Solaro.

By 1400, Rommel was at King's Cross, standing up in the turret of his command truck to look down at the port and harbour which had been so long denied him. Along each side of his vehicle trudged the dejected, bewildered files of prisoners, few of them – if any – realising who he was.

They had certainly never seen any of their own senior commanders as close to the battle as this.

The main reason for the lack of serious reaction by General Klopper to the events of the morning was that both he and his brigadiers had long assumed that Rommel's attack when it came (and none of them had expected it quite so soon) would be directed against the south-western flank of the perimeter instead of the south-eastern, and as a result the whole of the 2nd South African Division plus the reconstituted Guards Brigade, all the tanks in the fortress and most of the artillery, were deployed west of the El Adem road and the road leading from King's Cross down to the port, while only the 11th

Indian Brigade with a derisory artillery support occupied the eastern half of the garrison area.

Despite the tremendous din of the opening bombardment, Klopper and his senior advisers at H.Q. were united in their belief that the attack on the Indians was nothing but a feint, and that their main attention must be focused on the arc of the perimeter sweeping westwards from El Adem. In this they were sustained by early optimism on the part of Brigadier Anderson commanding 11th Indian Brigade whose first reports had been quite reassuring as only his Mahratta battalion had been penetrated, and as the morning wore on by the dearth of further information on events in the south-east sector. This they chose to interpret as good news; in fact, it was due to a basically inadequate communications system which had totally broken down under the first shock of battle. But behind all the early complacency was the unshakeable conviction that the perimeter defences were still just as strong as when the Australians had held the fortress, despite the fact that not one of Klopper's H.Q. staff had ever bothered to go out and investigate the situation for himself.

The atmosphere in Fortress Headquarters can best be sensed in the Situation Reports (sitreps) sent out at regular intervals to Ritchie at Army Headquarters. The first was sent at 0810 recording 'shelling at 0645 and dive-bombing at 0700', plus a few details of the patrols carried out along the western perimeter during the night. At 0915 a second sitrep reported two enemy companies held and counter-attacked near Strongpoint 67, and a third at 1000 admitted enemy penetration of one mile, this penetration also being counter-attacked.

At 1033, 'Main. S.A. Div.' sent out a sitrep announcing the presence of '20 tanks outside R 48. 15 tanks and infantry in vehicles coming through Gap at 418 420 [*between R 63 and R 65*]. 7 tanks advancing on R 72. 40 tanks and battalion of infantry coming through R 62.'

This situation was at last enough to cause Fortress H.Q. 'some uneasiness' and half an hour later General Klopper admitted that he was 'completely in the dark about what was happening' and proposed to go over himself to King's Cross to investigate. He was, however, persuaded by his staff that his duty was to remain where he was and bear the obscurity with fortitude. Another sitrep was despatched about noon which reported withdrawal by British tanks from a position which it is extremely doubtful that they ever reached, but the signal which most devastatingly depicts the dream world in which the Tobruk Command were living was sent off at 1345 – by which time Rommel was about to arrive at King's Cross and both his panzer divisions were fanning out towards even more vital objectives. '40 tanks now inside perimeter,' it stated, adding that the information was three hours in arrears, but not suggesting that much import should be attached to this condition.

But now at least some awareness of danger began to penetrate the honey haze in the 'Pink Palace' (as the headquarters building west of Fort Solaro had been dubbed) and at about 1400 General Klopper issued orders to the Guards Brigade to face about eastwards and take up positions which would deny the Pilastrino Ridge to the enemy. Then Brigadier Willison rang up and announced that 4th Royal Tank Regiment would seem to have been destroyed in a scrappy and thoroughly ill-organised attempt at counter-attack, and just before 1500 a sitrep was sent out to Eighth Army revealing that panzers were through the last line of defences before King's Cross – information then only an hour out of date.

From then on, news of ever-growing disaster flooded in to Klopper's H.Q. Willison rang in to say that his entire command had now been destroyed, Anderson himself arrived at the Pink Palace with details of the destruction of the Mahrattas, pointing out also the isolation of the Gurkhas east of them and the increasing risk of the destruction of the Camerons; and it was at about this time that someone poring over a map realised that the lorry park in which had been accumulated transport for use in any putative break-out was to the east of the King's Cross–Tobruk road, and that if Rommel drove for the port he would effectively cut the garrison off from their means of escape and win himself a handsome bonus in the process.

Rommel, of course, was intent on doing just that. By 1445, 21st Panzer were down the escarpment to the east of King's Cross, aiming for the N.A.A.F.I. stores building and the eastern airfield – itself given over to supply and transport services, covered with dumps and guarded only by administrative personnel. Further out to the east, 21st Panzer's infantry component, known for the moment as 'Group Menny', were marching almost unhindered for the cliffs overlooking Tobruk harbour.

Driving a covey of British lorries in front of them, the panzers manoeuvred with ever-growing efficiency and confidence. When South African artillery was encountered near the N.A.A.F.I. building, the leading files split into two, adopted hull-down positions and opened up with their machine-guns on the gun crews, whose 25-pounders were unable to wreak much damage on concealed panzers at so short a range. Soon one gun was out of action, and after half an hour's firing ammunition was running low for the others because the main artillery dumps were away to the west behind the South African defences. The battery commander therefore withdrew behind a smoke-screen – and the panzers were free to drive on down towards the airfield and Tobruk beyond.

At 1600, 21st Panzer reported possession of the airfield, and suggested that if 15th Panzer would protect their left flank they could push on down the last escarpment – from the top of which Group Menny were already looking down on small craft attempting to escape from the harbour. However, both 15th and 21st Panzer now ran into unexpected trouble.

The British had long been in possession of a gun which at least equalled the German 88mm. – the 3.7-inch anti-aircraft gun – but unfortunately all suggestions put forward to higher command that a leaf be taken out of the enemy's book and this gun used to administer the kind of punishment to the panzers that the armoured brigades had suffered ever since the arrival of the Afrika Korps, had fallen on deaf ears. The suggestions had in fact been rejected upon grounds which seem to have been based solely upon theory and principle, by staff officers who had never had to face the reality. Field Marshal Lord Carver has recounted one early attempt to use the gun in an anti-tank role in the Knightsbridge box, dubbed a failure by one of the staff officers present because it stood so high off the ground, was provided with inadequate sights and blew a pillar of sand high into the air whenever it was fired. 'One wonders', he commented sadly, 'if German gunners made the same sort of complaints, when the first 88-mms were used as anti-tank guns.'[10]

But now there were three 3.7-inch guns at Fort Solaro and no staff officers present – in fact no officers at all above the rank of captain – and the crews could set to work with enthusiasm and efficiency to offer a resistance which Rommel later described as of 'extraordinary stubbornness'. They had already dug their guns into emplacements, and although they had no specific anti-tank ammunition to fire through their now horizontal barrels, the range was short enough for

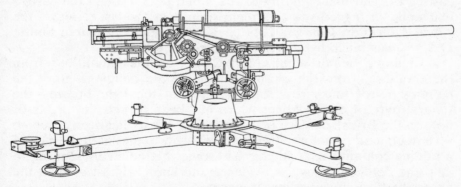

Figure 3   88mm. Flak 18: overall length 25 ft; weight in action 5 tons; horizontal range 16,200 yards; weight of projectile H.E. 20 lbs, A.P. 21 lbs; rate of fire 15/20 per min.; crew 6

them to wreck two panzers with their anti-aircraft shells and stop three more. They caused severe casualties among the panzer crews, replied with 'hellish fire' to a demand for surrender, and in the end were only put out of action by a storming party led with enormous gallantry by Rommel's own driver, which stole up under cover and then rushed the emplacements amid a shower of hand grenades. A single platoon of protective British infantry there might have made history.

But with this last serious obstacle removed, Rommel could order 21st Panzer forward from the airfield and down into Tobruk. There was a brief flurry of signals when it seemed that Group Menny would have to advance into the artillery bombardment which was crashing down on to the port, and then the final thrust was under way. Lumbering forward with self-propelled guns in close attendance, the Mark IIIs and IVs crashed through hastily erected roadblocks or swept them aside, machine-gunned strongpoints into surrender or shelled them into obliteration, reached the road leading down to the port and turned along it. From all sides came the sounds of explosions as the garrison troops strove valiantly to destroy huge dumps of rations, ammunition, fuel and general stores, while from the harbour itself came intermittent fire from ships attempting to hold off for a little longer the moment when they must either abandon the rest of the refugees flooding down in hope of escape, or accept the strong possibility of capture or sinking themselves.

The headquarters of the area administration was overrun by 1720, its commander Brigadier Thompson taken prisoner firing a machine-gun from the roof of a nearby house, as were several naval ratings gamely endeavouring to hold the panzers back from Navy House with rifles issued to them but minutes before. By 1800, a hail of fire was pouring down into the harbour area, the few vessels still there were casting off and manoeuvring to reach and pass through the narrow exit under a ragged smoke-screen; on one of the last to leave, the Naval Officer in Charge, Tobruk, Captain Frank Montem Smith, D.S.O., was killed by a shell fired from the quayside.

And above the port a huge black cloud from the demolitions, from the shell-fire, from the crushed rubble of the buildings, from the flaming petrol tanks rose and wavered in the light breeze – the funeral pyre of all the hopes which had been pinned, justifiably or not, on the British defence of Tobruk since it had first been occupied seventeen months before. Twenty miles away to the south the men of a raiding column which Ritchie had somewhat belatedly sent out to help the defenders saw the evidence and knew, almost without the necessity of discussion, what it meant.

6–7 *Operation Venezia: above*, M13s of the Ariete drive up towards Bir Hacheim; *below*, some of the Frenchmen awaiting them there

8 One of the Grant tanks which seriously worried Rommel at the start of the Battle of Gazala

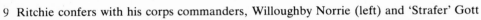

9 Ritchie confers with his corps commanders, Willoughby Norrie (left) and 'Strafer' Gott

But there were still the main bulk of the 2nd South African Division in their positions in the western half of the area, the majority of whom had so far been untouched by the land battle, however much they may have been harassed from the air; though not all infantry formations were still intact.

The Guards Brigade had by now been forced to surrender to 15th Panzer, for when Klopper had ordered them to face about eastwards and move to protect the Pilastrino Ridge from the east, they had found themselves suddenly stripped of all prepared positions, in open ground so rock-hard that it was impossible to dig even fox-holes without explosive. Their only defence against the panzer line which by 1530 was moving against them now rested with twelve 6-pounder anti-tank guns, standing on their portées in the open desert, and these did not last long. Blinded by a heat-haze which cut visibility to less than half a mile, the crews were suddenly confronted by about forty panzers lurching towards them with both main armament and machine-guns blazing; one 6-pounder and its portée were hit immediately and simply disintegrated in an explosion of steel, ammunition and torn bodies, and the others were hardly into action before the panzers were among them, machine-gunning the crews and in two cases simply barging the guns and overturning them.

The panzers ignored the infantrymen, who were totally powerless against them; indeed, such was their impotence that during the whole of their stay in Tobruk, losses for the Coldstream Guards amounted only to six killed and three wounded – but most of them were to spend the remainder of the war in prison-camps, for when the panzers moved on, German armoured cars and lorried infantry arrived and rounded them up. Some of the Sherwood Foresters holding positions south of the ridge were by-passed by the main panzer thrust, but when their commander made contact with Brigade Headquarters just before 1900, he was told that resistance was to cease and that the brigade had surrendered – so hopeless was the position considered.

It is pleasant to be able to record that some at least were not prepared to accept the situation. Major H. M. Sainthill and his reserve company of Coldstream Guards withdrew westwards along the ridge and at some time during the débâcle which ensued, assembled their transport and broke out to the south, made contact with South African armoured cars and escaped across the frontier to fight again. But such feats were the exception, for Klopper had by now lost all control of the situation. In the bickering and argument which occupied the command levels for the next few hours no firm guidance was available to the troops – who were more than willing to fight if given the chance – except orders to stay where they were and not bother their betters.

Klopper's position was now invidious and had, in fact, never been anything but unfortunate. He had been promoted major-general only a month previously and although he had commanded a brigade for the previous four months, his only operational experience had been as Chief of Staff to the commander of 2nd South African Division when they took Bardia six months before. He thus had several brigadiers serving under him in Tobruk who were senior to him in years and in service, and were considerably more experienced, though it cannot be said that advice received from them during the vital hours was of great value or prescience.

As for advice and direction from above, General Gott's views of the defence potentialities in Tobruk have already been outlined, and some flavour of the guidance Klopper was receiving from Eighth Army is indicated by an order received from Ritchie the previous morning, instructing him to relieve the box formed at Point 650 on the Batruna Ridge by the battalion from 29th Indian Brigade. 'If necessary,' the order read, 'you must stage an operation to achieve this.' Such were the relations between the two staffs that Klopper's G.2, in the words of the South African official history, was 'perhaps too polite to point out to the Army Commander that the place had been in enemy hands for four days'.[11] Ritchie's habit of sheltering his superior from grim reality had proved infectious and was now hoisting him with his own petard.

This morning there had come to Klopper from Ritchie a long signal labelled MOST SECRET but which in its wording was so convoluted as to make it almost incomprehensible and its label thus redundant; but from one part of it Klopper gained the impression that a large striking force comprising twelve separate columns with 116 guns and 66 tanks was already poised to fall upon the rear of Afrika Korps immediately it attacked his perimeter. The columns had in fact never even been formed, let alone despatched, but as the long day wore on it seemed to Klopper that any hour must bring this promised relief.

After the series of events which had caused him (at about 1400) to order the redeployment of the Guards Brigade, disasters crowded in upon him at such a rate that a far more experienced man could be forgiven for losing touch with reality. And out of touch with reality was what he and many headquarter and administrative units undoubtedly were! The South African history tells of the annoyance of the staff of one South African brigade when a heavy bomb fell but failed to explode near their mess tent, so their lunch was delayed until sappers could be fetched to destroy it – this at a time when Rommel was already at King's Cross! – and of the officers of a supply company who were taken prisoner by infantrymen from Group Menny while enjoying their post-prandial nap!

But by 1550, Klopper at least was sufficiently alarmed to signal

Ritchie news – only two hours out of date – to the effect that sixty enemy tanks were at King's Cross, and it was a pity that neither Ritchie nor his Chief of Staff, Brigadier Whiteley, were at Eighth Army Headquarters to receive it; not that by now there was much they could have done to help. Then at 1600 (and it is possible to pin-point the time because one of Klopper's staff officers was celebrating his birthday, and the kettle had just been put on for tea) enemy tanks were seen approaching the headquarters area, shell-fire upon it increased rapidly, a flood of refugees streamed past, and with danger apparently so near and immediate Klopper gave the orders for the destruction of all documents, codes, ciphers and even orderly room files – an instruction carried out with such enthusiasm that in the holocaust which followed the telephone exchange and several wireless sets were also put out of action, so from that moment all communication between Fortress Headquarters and the remainder of the Tobruk Garrison ceased. Some signal vans remained to keep Eighth Army in dubious contact with events, but for the next several hours there was no way in which Klopper could have redeployed the still considerable military force under his command, even had he conceived some practical objective for them.

Almost as soon as the destruction of these vital communication systems was complete it became obvious that the exercise had been, for the moment at least, unnecessary. The panzers observed approaching the area had been from 21st Panzer and these now veered north towards Tobruk, while 15th Panzer were still busy dealing with the Guards Brigade and unaware of the proximity of the garrison command – which as a result was now to remain undisturbed for some time to come. Klopper used this period for further discussions with his staff, but finally concluded that he must move from the area anyway, deciding at first to join 4th South African Brigade H.Q. at a location known as Fig Tree, just to the south of the Via Balbia as it approached the western perimeter. At 1700 he sent off a message to Ritchie reading, 'Holding the line El Adem Road. Perimeter almost intact but eastern sector badly mauled. Can you give any information re columns?'[12] but he received no reply to this, perhaps because there was no one at Eighth Army H.Q. sufficiently aware of the situation to concoct a useful answer. In fact Eighth Army's silence was not to be broken until Ritchie returned from his day's peregrinations at 1815 – by which time the last Royal Naval units were endeavouring to escape from Tobruk harbour – when he despatched a personal signal to Klopper. It began, 'Well done, Acroma Keep has made history,' and after some abstruse but optimistic comment, went on:

You are having a very tough fight today and I see this afternoon some enemy tanks have got through the outer perimeter. But I feel quite confident of your ability to put them out after destroying as many as possible . . . All good fortune to you personally and the whole of your grand command.[13]

But by the time Ritchie had delivered himself of this piece of cheerful banality, Klopper had left the Pink Palace and was in the process of re-establishing his headquarters elsewhere. His original choice of Fig Tree had been changed by a rumour of threats to 4th Brigade H.Q. by panzer attack, so he went instead to Ras Belgamel, the H.Q. of 6th South African Brigade to the north of the Via Balbia, though it was perhaps unfortunate that the decision to change destination was only revealed to a part of his staff, and operations and intelligence sections still went to Fig Tree.

It was dusk before Klopper and the last of the signallers left the Pink Palace, and on the road they were caught by the last heavy Stuka attack of the day, fortunately suffering no casualties; but on the journey Klopper decided that the position of the troops in Tobruk had become hopeless and that brigade commanders should now prepare their troops for a mass break-out, to be launched as soon as possible and with 2200 as the zero hour to be aimed for. After a nightmare journey across a westward flood of refugees – angry, disorientated, often wounded and battle-shocked, without arms, rations, water or any idea but to escape from the chaos and danger they had just experienced – he was greeted with considerable surprise at Ras Belgamel, as 6th South African Brigade had been out of touch for some time and had no warning of his arrival. But to its commander he quickly gave the orders for the break-out, instructing him to pass them on to the other brigadiers.

He then embarked upon a frustrating attempt to communicate his decision to Ritchie, which eventually culminated in a reply from Whiteley (as Ritchie was out of touch again) reading 'BGS to GOC. Come out tomorrow night preferably if not tonight Centre Line Meduuar–Knightsbridge–Maddalena. I will keep open gap Harmat– El Adem. Inform me time selected and route. Tomorrow night preferred. Destruction petrol vital.'[14]

Here at least was some note of agreement and signs of possible outside co-operation, though the preference for a delay of twenty-four hours was obviously unacceptable; but as Klopper and the 6th Brigade commander planned the launching of the break-out, the 4th Brigade commander and his staff arrived from Fig Tree, announcing unanimously that it would be quite impossible for 4th Brigade to get out of Tobruk 'on their flat feet!' The whole South African Division was used to being transported by vehicle wherever they went, and Brigadier Hayton and his staff saw no way in which the habit could be broken, even in these circumstances. It was, after all, a hell of a long way back to Egypt and safety, and a formation of brigade or larger size could hardly expect to escape notice while marching across the desert in broad daylight – even if such a feat were practicable – from an enemy of Afrika Korps's efficiency and sense of purpose. Caught on the march by Rommel's armour, the South African infantry would undoubtedly be annihilated – and a far better solution to all their problems would be to form a defensive line running parallel to the western face of the perimeter and facing eastwards, organise the considerable force now concentrated behind it and fight it out until Eighth Army sent in relief.

The best description of the atmosphere at Ras Belgamel as the rest of the night wore on is given, as usual, by J. A. I. Agar-Hamilton and L. C. F. Turner:

> Other officers objected to 4th Brigade plan, chief among them the C.R.A. arguing that the position in Tobruk was hopeless; the guns could fire only until they had exhausted the ammunition in their limbers, and the infantry had no defence against attack from within the perimeter. They recommended that the artillery and such troops as were mobile should be got out at once to strengthen the Eighth Army. Some officers actually worked out a plan by which the two or three surviving tanks would lead a break-out, followed by the armoured cars and the artillery. Another officer is reported to have pleaded tearfully and emphatically for im-mediate surrender, urging on the General that his was the responsibility for preserving 'the cream of South African manhood.'
>
> There followed what has sometimes been described as a Conference, but which was in fact a series of desultory and disconnected conversations during which the arguments for and against breaking out were wearily traversed again and again. Suggestions were thrown out, as for collecting the ammunition for the field-guns from the Supply Depot at the cross-roads, or for attacking the German leaguers, or for laying an additional minefield to cover a 'western box', but they were no more than suggestions, not pressed home. Officers drifted in and out. Someone called in Lieut-Colonel Chadwick, the A. and Q., who was asked about the ammunition supply, but Colonel Bastin, who alone knew the details, was well on his way back to Egypt by sea and Lieut-Colonel Chadwick could not help. Brigadier Anderson, who was anxious to get back to the Camerons at the perimeter, sat dourly outside with a Staff Officer, awaiting instructions.[15]

It was not an atmosphere in which major decisions were likely to be made, or, if made, carried through with much resolution.

Klopper, however, did arrive at one conclusion. Just before 0200 on June 21st he signalled to Eighth Army, 'Am sending mobile troops out tonight. Not possible to hold tomorrow. Mobile troops nearly nought. Enemy captured vehicles. Will resist to last man and last round,'[16] and then he despatched his brigadiers back to their head-quarters with the first firm directive they had been given since noon. It was unfortunate, but perhaps predictable, that during their journeys any resolution which Klopper had managed to infuse into his subordinate commanders evaporated, and by the time they arrived back at their various headquarters there were already dark mutterings about 'the size of the butcher's bill'. At 4th Brigade H.Q., according to the brigade major, when Brigadier Hayton told his battalion commanders that the C.R.A. could only guarantee ammunition for two hours, they all expressed the opinion that wholly useless slaughter would result from further resistance, and it was not long before Hayton was on the line to Klopper, drearily repeating all the arguments which had already been well rehearsed.

Yet all this time, the bulk of the men of the South African Division were waiting with some eagerness for orders for action, coping with the floods of refugees and bullying them back into some degree of confidence, and in a large number of cases working hard for tomorrow's battle (or tonight's if the orders came in time). Without any direction at all from above, gunners had resited their batteries and dug them in, support infantry had already begun digging defence positions facing eastwards, the Worcestershires and the remainder of the Coldstreams had dug in around Pilastrino and a Crusader tank had been sited and dug in as a pillbox up in the northern sector of the line, where a battalion formed from South African police had abjured their proscriptive duties and were preparing to fight like more ordinary men. One company of 2nd Transvaal Scottish had armed itself with all the sticky bombs they could lay their hands on and were impatiently awaiting permission to raid forward into the Afrika Korps leaguers and blow the panzers to smithereens.

As the panzer crews were by this time sleeping that same sleep of exhaustion which had overcome them six nights before on the ridge outside Acroma (to such an extent that one South African party visited a nearby supply depot and drove away a truckload of mines while two other parties made their way westward out of Tobruk port, all picking their route between the forms of German soldiers sleeping so profoundly that they could not be woken) it is tempting to wonder what would have happened had the junior officers and men of the garrison – and there were some 20,000 of them at least – been roughly organised and told to fight their way eastwards, destroying as many of the enemy as they could as they went. It is not inconceivable that they would have so seriously weakened the Afrika Korps that many subsequent battles need not have been fought.

But the garrison's fate was not in their own hands, and as the night wore on the hands in which it did rest became more and more uncertain. The arguments continued, every order passed down from Command was disputed, not even a token gesture of obedience was offered and false information of impending panzer attacks was even fed to Klopper, though perhaps by mistake. His dejected figure was seen, dimly shadowed in the blackness before dawn, alone, weighed down by his responsibilities and deserted by those from whom he should have been given, especially at such a time, unqualified support. He had had one more exchange of signals with Eighth Army, this time with Ritchie himself, which revealed only too clearly the weak grasp of the realities of the situation held at headquarters.

> Ritchie [in answer to Klopper's 0200 signal]: Noted about mobile elements. In respect remainder every day and hour of resistance materially assists our cause. I cannot tell tactical situation and must therefore leave you to act on your own judgement regarding capitulation. Report if you can extent to which destruction P.O.L. effected.

> Klopper: Situation shambles. Terrible casualties would result. Am doing the worst. Petrol destroyed.

> Ritchie: Whole of Eighth Army has watched with admiration your gallant fight. You are an example to us all and I know South Africa will be proud of you. God bless you and may fortune favour your efforts wherever you be . . . [17]

What Klopper meant by his announcement, 'Am doing the worst,' remains something of an enigma, for shortly after the above exchange was concluded, he sent out emissaries to the German forces lying nearest to him with an offer to surrender. A huge white flag was hoisted above 6th Brigade headquarters by some native drivers, and as it flapped open in the first morning breeze, a great moan of disappointment, anguish and misery welled up from all over the western half of the garrison area.

Defeat is bitter in any circumstances, but now in the minds of thousands who were experiencing it, it was compounded by disgrace.

An expression which, albeit colloquial, accurately portrays the feeling throughout the Afrika Korps on the morning of June 21st, 1942, is 'cock-a-hoop'. Certainly there was still some clearing up to be done for in the eastern sector of the fortress the Camerons were still keeping Ariete and Pavia Divisions at bay, while the Gurkhas across the road to Bardia were showing not the slightest signs of surrender, holding as they did no belief in the validity of such a course of action; in any case they were still largely unaware of what had been happening further westward. But to the men of 21st and 15th Panzer Divisions, the proclamation the previous evening of the 'proud victory' of the capture of Tobruk, supplemented within the hour by the news that 15th Panzer had occupied both Fort Solaro and Pilastrino, had been followed for the majority of them by a comparatively uninterrupted night's sleep, and at dawn on the 21st they were well-rested, satisfactorily breakfasted (largely upon captured rations) and eager to consolidate and enjoy their success.

Evidence of the solidity of the victory surrounded them on all sides. Large assemblies of downcast British and South African prisoners were collecting, while from the as yet untaken areas came the sights and sounds of destruction as guns, fuel and ammunition dumps were blown up with a grim efficiency which was itself an expression of the frustration felt by the bulk of the garrison. Lorries were burning on all sides (to the regret and added fury of those who later found that in the chaos of mass surrender they might have escaped had they held on to some form of transport), armoured cars were being pushed over the cliffs into the sea, and infantrymen were smashing their rifles – often with a strange reluctance, considering how violently most of them had cursed the things previously. Major Sainthill, already organising his company's break-out – by far the most successful of those attempted – watched the scene from the high ground west of Pilastrino: 'To the north-west, west, and south, a hundred fires – soon to become a thousand – dotted the landscape: burning guns and vehicles glaring like beacons in the half-light of early morning.'[18]

But few of the panzer crews or their gunner or infantry comrades were much concerned with this destruction; they had their eyes firmly fixed on the huge stores dumps and warehouses wherein their quartermasters were already taking inventories, and the early-comers were already replenishing their stocks of food and comforts:

> There were stacks of tinned beer; huts bursting with pure white flour, cigarettes, tobacco and jam; gallons of whisky; priceless tinned food of all kinds; and tons of khaki clothing – that magnificent clothing, which looked so heavy and was so light and cool to wear.[19]

In addition to travelling for the most part in British vehicles, the Afrika Korps would soon be doing so in British uniforms.

Such bounty and such a feeling of triumph engendered a spirit of euphoria which showed in the Afrika Korps treatment of their new prisoners – already regarded with a degree of fellow-feeling because of the known and shared experiences of desert life. One of the British infantrymen remarked upon it in his account of being captured:

> We scrambled out of our trenches and were soon marched off after being allowed hurriedly to collect a few things together. However, the Germans – Rommel's Afrika Korps – treated us with reasonable consideration and I saw several signs of compassion and nothing of the snarling Nazi we had been led to expect – let's hope it stays that way. As we marched by, a German officer, smiling triumphantly, leant down from the turret of his tank and said to me 'For you, the war is finish. Thank God you have got away alive!'[20]

On another occasion, some South Africans were giving themselves up under the protection of a somewhat bedraggled white towel, when they were horrified by a burst of machine-gun fire directed from behind them on the panzers to whom they were surrendering. In a number of previous instances such an episode had been interpreted (on both sides) as a deliberate violation of the White Flag and indiscriminate slaughter had ensued, but on this occasion the panzers merely returned the machine-gun fire, one of the crew waved the South Africans into cover and later came back to take them prisoner. Occasionally a captor would relieve his captive of a few cigarettes, but generally they were not only allowed to keep any comforts they had with them, but positively encouraged to find themselves some more.

There was, however, one dissident from this mood of happy triumph in which Afrika Korps bathed, and unfortunately for almost everyone inside the fortress area, irrespective of nationality, this exception was Rommel himself. Despite the fact that he was greeted wherever he went by his officers and men as the hero of the hour; that congratulations were pouring in from every headquarter organisation from Tobruk back to Tripoli and would assuredly continue to do so for many hours, from ever more remote but ever more puissant areas of command – and that Tobruk was at last firmly in his hands – Rommel on the morning of June 21st was almost beside himself with fury. His men might view the burning lorries with some indifference, but their Commander-in-Chief's eyes were already fixed on horizons further to the east (despite what may or may not have been agreed before the onslaught on the Gazala Line) and he knew that the destruction which surrounded him was well devised to thwart his plans. Clean shirts and whisky would not take him or his men a kilometre closer to the Nile; what he needed was more transport, a secure source of water (and the Navy had wrecked the water supply and both the refrigeration and distillation plants by the harbour) and, most important of all, petrol; a perpetual goad to his anger during the hours he spent in Tobruk was the towering black cloud drifting back across the fortress from the flaming fuel tanks.

One early result of his exasperation was a violent and uncharacteristic outburst at his meeting with General Klopper at 0940 when, to the astonishment of his captives and the embarrassment of his own staff, he indulged in a spasm of fury which robbed him of all the dignity which might have been expected at such a triumphant hour; and another, even more uncharacteristic, was his proclamation that the prisoners would be made to rue their own destructive activity. Many of those who had added to his difficulties by wrecking subsidiary fuel tanks and in so doing soaked their boots and lower garments in petrol so that they rotted, were not allowed to replace them, and everyone was very thirsty until Rommel himself had moved up to the frontier and less irate tempers were controlling their destinies.

Perhaps fortunately for the prisoners, Rommel wasted no time. Five minutes after the conclusion of the stormy interview with Klopper, he issued an order to Afrika Korps which cut short many a developing celebration by ending, 'All units will reassemble and prepare for further advance,' and by the afternoon, 21st Panzer were making their way with some reluctance eastwards towards Gambut, while 15th Panzer were closing down on the Camerons and marshalling almost the entire heavy artillery under Rommel's command in order to obliterate the recalcitrant Scots if they continued to behave so unreasonably.

In the event, an agreement was reached under a white flag that the Camerons would surrender the next morning – having now held out twenty-four hours longer than the rest of the fortress – and that they would be allowed the honours of war, marching out under arms and headed by their pipers. Lieutenant-Colonel Duncan, the Camerons' commanding officer, also took advantage of the occasion to deliver a sharp lecture to the German officer who came to accept the surrender upon the latter's untidy, unkempt and generally unsoldierly appearance, after which Duncan then drew his revolver and flung it at the astonished man's feet.

On the far side of the break-in gap, the Gurkhas had been dispersed into the precipitous wadis by an onslaught from the rear by Rommel's own *Kampfstaffel*, followed by a hunting-down operation carried out by the whole of the Italian X Corps which occupied them for several days. The last Gurkhas were eventually rounded up between Bardia and Sollum, having walked along the coast, occasionally wading across wadi-mouths and around enemy bathing or search parties, and across the Egyptian frontier.

The frontier, of course, was Rommel's next immediate target, with 90th Light already at Bardia and 21st on their way to join them. But there was always the matter of that agreed timetable by which Afrika Korps would stand on the frontier while the Luftwaffe, a considerable force from the Italian Fleet, and one Italian and one German parachute division with sea-landing brigades in attendance would all descend upon Malta and remove that island once and for all from the chessboard of Mediterranean strategy. And it was to further the implementation of those arrangements that Kesselring arrived at Tobruk that afternoon, determined – after offering his sincere congratulations to his brilliant associate – to begin the withdrawal of Luftwaffe units from North Africa to Sicily.

He found himself faced by no associate, but by an adversary buoyed up with victory, stimulated by anger, and totally committed to a new policy of ruthless pursuit of a beaten enemy however far he might retire, regardless of any agreements entered into with allies or even with the commanders of supporting arms who had recently given him such close and ardent co-operation; and any use of superior rank which Kesselring might have considered bringing to bear was negated by the news that evening that an enthusiastic Führer had rewarded his favourite general by promotion to Generalfeld-marschall!

Even this news was scarcely enough to cause a moment's distraction from Rommel's now dominant purpose. The Eighth Army was for the moment in a state of such all-embracing disarray that it must be caught and finally broken; Afrika Korps had now enough captured transport, enough fuel, enough vehicles, arms and ammunition to take them to Cairo – and a delay of a few weeks, perhaps even only a few days, might allow Auchinleck time to regroup and augment the forces between the frontier and the Nile and perhaps thereby to block Afrika Korps once and for all. This must not be allowed to happen.

To Kesselring's remonstrances that Malta was recovering from the Luftwaffe onslaught of April and early May and would soon be throttling Rommel's supply lines again, Rommel replied that with Benghasi already out of range of British aircraft from Egypt and Tobruk soon in the same happy condition as a result of his own intended rapid advance, the supply problems could be overcome – though this would, of course, make demands upon the gentlemen of the administrative departments in Rome and Sicily almost as great as those given freely every day by the tank crews and infantrymen of the Afrika Korps!

At this, the discussion became, in von Mellenthin's words (he was present all the time) 'exceedingly lively' and ended when Kesselring left, proclaiming his intention to withdraw all his Luftwaffe units to Sicily – a move countered by Rommel who promptly sent off a liaison officer to Hitler's headquarters to argue his case, and a cable to von Rintelen in Rome, which read:

> The first objective of the Panzerarmee Afrika viz. to defeat the enemy field army and to take Tobruk has been attained. Elements of the enemy are still holding out at Sollum–Halfaya–Sidi Omar. The intention is to destroy this enemy, thus opening the road into the heart of Egypt. The state and morale of the troops, the present supply situation thanks to captured dumps, and the present weakness of the enemy, permit our pursuing him into the depths of the Egyptian area. I request you therefore, to induce the Duce to lift the present restrictions on freedom of movement and to put all the troops at present under my command at my disposal so that I can continue the battle.[21]

Needless to say, he had not the slightest intention of awaiting reaction to either of these strokes, and, pausing only to issue an Order of the Day to his troops which though it paid full tribute to

their recent achievements, exhorted them to even greater effort, he
took a few brief hours of rest and at dawn next morning went forward
to Bardia. From here he and his staff organised the closing up of the
15th Panzer Division and the Ariete to the frontier, received with
some relief the news that 90th Light had seized yet another huge
supply dump at Capuzzo which contained 'particularly large quantities of fuel', and prepared to do verbal battle with the Italian
commanders who now came racing up to register their protests.

To Generale Count Barbasetti Rommel announced that he intended to go straight through the Delta, across the Nile, the Canal
and the Sinai Desert, not pausing until he reached the Persian Gulf;
and Generale Bastico's orders to halt where he was he brushed aside
as 'unacceptable advice', adding undoubtedly intentional irritation to
this cavalier treatment of someone who was still his chief with an
invitation to dine with him in Cairo! As both Italian generals had now
learned by bitter experience that Rommel was more likely to get his
own way than not, they merely registered their disapproval and did
not insist very hard upon obedience.

In this they were wise. Rommel's message to von Rintelen had by
this time arrived in Berlin, von Rintelen having felt that so important
a change in plan should go straight to the real focus of decision,
without unnecessary delays at interim and ineffective stations; and to
the surprise of a number of people, Rommel's suggestions received
the immediate and unqualified support of Oberstgeneral Alfred Jodl,
Operations Chief of the Supreme Command. There were protests
from Raeder and the naval staff in Berlin but Jodl was well aware of
Hitler's reluctance to engage upon maritime adventures, especially
after the costly assault on Crete, and guessed how the decision would
go. During June 22nd, the Führer cabled the Duce to the effect that
'it is only once in a lifetime that the Goddess of Victory smiles,' and
such was the inspiring effect of this Delphic inducement that that
night Mussolini sent his full approval to Rommel for the pursuit into
Egypt. The following day he replied to Hitler that he fully agreed
' . . . that the historic moment has now come to conquer Egypt' and
energetically set about the really important aspects of so momentous
an event.

Cavallero was despatched to North Africa to discover how soon
Rommel expected to be in Alexandria and Cairo, and once Mussolini
received this vital piece of information (June 30th) he issued further
orders to the new Generalfeldmarschall to press on immediately to
Suez and there to block the Canal. Il Duce himself would take over
command in the Delta, to which end he flew to Derna on June 29th,
piloting his own aircraft, accompanied by a large transport plane
carrying all the necessary equipment for his triumphant entry into
Cairo, including a white charger.

It is not known whether he intended Auchinleck and Ritchie to drag a carriage full of wreaths behind him.

But much happened on the battlefield during the eight days between the time Il Duce agreed to Rommel's advance, and his own journey to North Africa.

By the evening of June 23rd, Afrika Korps spearheads were crossing the frontier some forty-five miles south of the Sidi Omar box and skirting around the other defensive positions in which Ritchie had reposed the safety of Egypt, prettily named 'The Stables', 'The Kennels', 'The Nursery' and 'The Playground', with the passes down the Escarpment protected by positions known as 'Lovers' Lane', 'The Pub', and 'The Cradle'. However, as there was now no worthwhile armoured force to give support to the unfortunate infantry held in these boxes ('The Kennels' was designed, stocked and equipped to accommodate a complete division for three months, and indeed Pienaar's 1st South African occupied it for four days) Ritchie had decided as early as June 21st that these defensive positions were after all untenable and that 'we can only gain time with distance, repeat distance'. In other words he intended for the moment to put as much space between the Eighth Army and Rommel's forces as possible.

Map 11   Into Egypt, June 24th–25th

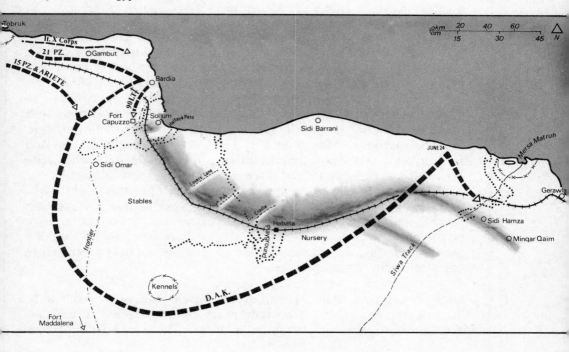

As a result, the triumphant German forces surged almost un-opposed into Egypt and by the evening of the following day (June 24th) had made an astonishing advance of well over a hundred miles to reach the coast nearly fifty miles east of Sidi Barrani – and this with only forty-four panzers, the others having broken down as a result of the wear and tear of the battles fought over the last twenty-seven days and two hundred miles. By the following evening both panzer divisions were deploying south-west of Mersa Matruh, their Commander-in-Chief well aware of Fortune's favour which had given him yet another timely windfall of petrol at the railroad at Habata, salvaged from a store which had been inefficiently set ablaze. According to what intelligence reports his staff could draw up from extremely meagre sources, the British and South African forces were intending to stand on the Mersa Matruh–Siwa line, and if he were to maintain the momentum of the advance, Afrika Korps must break that line tomorrow.

All that day (25th) they had been subject to increasingly heavy air attacks, and they now knew that they would have to do the job on their own for Ariete and Trieste had been reduced by battle and exhaustion to fourteen M13s, thirty guns and less than two thousand infantrymen between them! These, however, were factors which would not affect by one whit the morale of Rommel's men, for by now they felt themselves to be invincible.

This was not an opinion – remarkably enough – shared by the men opposite. These were tired and disorganised – one observer who watched them coming back remarked that in the entire flood of men he did not see one single formed fighting unit of infantry, armour or artillery – and they were very angry; and this anger bolstered their morale. They were not in any way angry at their opponents – to whom, in fact, they gave little thought – but they were furious with those who had sent them into battle with what they believed were inferior weapons, with what they knew to be inferior training and techniques – and, most important of all, under leaders who quite obviously were incapable of discharging their responsibilities.

Their morale therefore received an added fillip that night when news filtered through their ranks that the 'Auk' had at last relieved Ritchie and taken command himself. Perhaps matters might improve now, they thought, exhibiting yet again the propensity of troubled humanity to find a single source for all their ills, a single scapegoat to carry all their communal sins.

Luck plays an enormous part in every phase of life, of course, and in the military profession, especially in its higher reaches, perhaps an even more significant part than in most. There is no doubt that

Ritchie had been extremely unfortunate. His promotion from major-general on Auchinleck's staff to lieutenant-general commanding the Eighth Army in the field – on the face of it a God-sent opportunity – was in fact a trap from which only the high regard in which he was held in important places allowed him eventually to escape.

Command of an army in 1942 would seem to have been above his ceiling, even had the army been already well trained with corps and divisional commanders working in harmony. As it was, those very qualities which caused the Chief of Staff of the Army, General Sir Alan Brooke, to write of him, 'I am devoted to Neil,' and everybody who knew him to refer to him as 'an awfully nice chap', acted to his own – and the Eighth Army's – undoing. What was needed to command the Allied forces after the retreat from El Agheila in 1942 was ruthlessness not charm, leadership not chairmanship of a committee – especially of a committee whose members did not particularly care whether their decisions were unanimous as each was determined to go his own way anyway.

Sandwiched as he was between Auchinleck's determination to 'hold his hand' at almost every stage of the operation, and indifference to his opinion by his corps commanders and almost contempt for them from lower levels, it is not surprising that Ritchie's grip on the battle as it developed was at first weak and in the end non-existent. In the circumstances he is probably to be admired for his sustained optimism, despite its emptiness, for in similar conditions seven months before his predecessor, Cunningham, had lost heart and recommended total abandonment of gains already won.

Ultimate responsibility for the disasters of Gazala and the following weeks lies, not only formally but also actually, with the Commander-in-Chief, General Auchinleck. He appointed Ritchie, and then retained him there despite evidence that his nominee had as yet neither the experience nor the toughness of character or intellect to bear such heavy responsibilities.

Even now, Auchinleck was not relieving Ritchie because of past errors, but for what he rightly perceived to be an even more dangerous mistake that he was about to make. Having first intended to stand on the frontier in positions which could easily be outflanked on the south and only blocked there by the Kennels position (described caustically by one observer as 'like its infamous counterpart Bir Hacheim, it protected nothing but sand and it too hung like a rather less ripe pear on a rather longer stalk'),[22] Ritchie, having at last perceived his danger, proposed to stand instead at the Matruh positions – which without an adequate armoured force were equally indefensible tactically, and as the defence lines had been allowed to deteriorate to the same extent and for the same reasons as those at Tobruk, indefensible even as a static position.

The overall theory for the conduct of the next stage of the defence of Egypt had been that X Corps under Lieutenant-General W. G. Holmes (who had been rushed forward from Syria) should occupy and hold Mersa Matruh, XIII Corps under Gott the area to the south around Sidi Hamza, while Norrie back at El Alamein organised the defences there and held them with XXX Corps. This looked very well on paper, but examination revealed that between them the three corps held hardly enough complete formations to form three divisions.

General Holmes's corps consisted of the remains of 10th Indian Division (which had been flung piecemeal into the battles of the last few days and been knocked about and thoroughly disorganised as a result) inside Matruh, the two remaining brigades of 50th Division, still without replacements for much of the equipment they had left behind in the Gazala Line, some ten miles back at Gerawla and, briefly, two brigades of the 2nd New Zealand Division. General Freyberg, however, had taken one look at the Matruh defences, uttered a few brusquely condemnatory remarks about the chaos in which he and his men were now expected to operate, and roundly declared that he would not allow them to be locked up and almost certainly extinguished as a fighting force in so palpable a trap. He and his command were promptly transferred to XIII Corps and ordered to move out to take position on the southern escarpment around Minqar Qaim.

Needless to say, Freyberg's expostulation had been equalled and even exceeded in caustic criticism by Dan Pienaar's, and when he had at last been given permission to withdraw his division from the Kennels, he had taken them right back to El Alamein and XXX Corps.

As for Gott's XIII Corps, circumstances had combined to rob it of all semblance of cohesion and it consisted of a number of isolated units scattered about the desert. Its only infantry, apart from Freyberg's New Zealanders, were the 29th Indian Brigade after their escape from El Adem and the loss of one battalion at Point 650, and its remaining two battalions had been split into six small groups, of which two – named Gleecol and Leathercol, each consisting of one battery of field artillery and one of anti-tank guns with two infantry platoons in support – covered the entire nine-mile gap between the two escarpments. The others lined the southern escarpment west of the New Zealanders.

The armour was deployed further to the south – 99 assorted Crusaders, Stuarts and Valentines and 60 Grants in the two brigades of 1st Armoured Division (4th and 22nd), while the 7th Motor Brigade, the 3rd Indian Motor Brigade and the armoured cars of 4th South Africans and the Royals, making up the entire remaining complement of 7th Armoured Division, were deployed further to the west along and beyond the Siwa track as outpost and shield.

The intention behind this deployment of tatterdemalion formations was that Afrika Korps should be held in front of Matruh and Sidi Hamza by the infantry stationed there, but if the Germans broke through either between the escarpments or around to the south, they should be struck in flank by Gott's armour. There was enough of it, properly handled, to annihilate every formation in Rommel's command at the moment – though this of course was not known at the time.

But as Auchinleck flew up to Maaten Baggush to relieve Ritchie in the early evening of June 25th, he had already decided that this plan was unacceptable. He had taken with him Eric Dorman-Smith (lately promoted major-general), informing Whitehall that he intended to use him as 'my Chief of Staff' and thereby instigating an academic and occasionally vitriolic argument which was to rage for many a year, as such an appointment was not officially recognised in the British Army. The two men analysed the situation with which they expected to be faced, and planned in accordance with three basic principles which Auchinleck was to stress time and time again during the weeks that followed.

All troops were to be kept mobile and armour was not to be committed except on very favourable terms:

> At all costs and even if ground has to be given up, I intend to keep Eighth Army in being and to give no hostage to fortune in the shape of immobile troops holding localities which can easily be isolated.[23]

This was, of course, rather easier said than done in the existing circumstances, but Auchinleck and Dorman-Smith were encouraged by the thought that Ritchie had at least promised to put space between himself and his antagonists, thereby gaining time; and they had not yet discovered that this last suggestion of the recent Eighth Army commander was as unfulfilled as many of his previous ones had been. On the trip up, they therefore decided that immobile infantry were not to be retained at the front, and that only men for whom transport existed in the form of carriers, limbers, tanks or other vehicles *integral to their units* would stay, the remainder being sent back immediately either to the El Alamein positions or even further back to help man the Delta defences.

This design, when propounded that evening to the various divisional and brigade commanders, gave many present the impression that the era of the independent Jock Column had come again, for in practice at that moment it meant that every infantry brigade would be split into battlegroups, the number and size of which would be dictated solely by the amount of artillery available, further restricted by the amount of transport to hand for protective infantry. This was the only interpretation which those immediate circumstances would allow –

and it served to disguise for a long time that Auchinleck and Dorman-Smith were, ironically, both devoted to the principle that battles are best fought by divisions fighting as divisions or, better still, corps fighting as corps; but *mobile* divisions and corps.

But on the night of June 25th, it brought immediately from Freyberg a declaration that he would appeal over Auchinleck's head to his own Government against the splitting up of the New Zealanders into penny packets, and an air of some uncertainty throughout both X and XIII Corps which was to have unfortunate results in the immediate future.

Additionally, for the moment time was working against Auchinleck. To quote the South African historians again, during the twenty-four hours following his assumption of command:

> 10th Indian Division and 50th Division were trying to establish themselves in the static defences of Matruh and simultaneously to 'make themselves mobile' in the new style, and all this was being done under the threat, implemented forthwith, of an enemy attack. It came perilously near to changing horses in mid-stream.[24]

The New Zealanders began their move to Minqar Qaim that night but suffered some irritating delays, and the bulk did not reach their destination until the following afternoon – by which time XIII Corps in an endeavour to create some sort of cohesion in their ranks had discovered that their entire signals and communications network was – to put it mildly – a shambles; and Rommel had ordered Afrika Korps forward to battle!

His plan for the reduction of Matruh was indistinguishable from that against Tobruk; the panzer divisions were to push the British armour away to the south-east, 90th Light were to encircle the port and reach the coast to the east, the Italians to attract all attention to the west and south; and in the words of von Mellenthin's later account, 'Our advance began on the afternoon of the 26th, and purely by chance it struck the British at their weakest point.'

Massed for a battle against strong armoured and infantry forces which Rommel expected to find concentrated south of Matruh, 21st Panzer and 90th Light advanced due east between the two escarpments, tore aside the thin defences behind the minefield as though they were paper, annihilated both Gleecol and Leathercol and took four hundred prisoners, then leaguered for the night thankful that the attention of the R.A.F., who had been bombing and strafing them all day with powerful effect, had at last ceased.

This move produced a truly ironic situation. Good fortune may have given Rommel access to the heart of the British positions but further advance would, on paper, sandwich the essential striking force of 90th Light and 21st Panzer – together less than one full

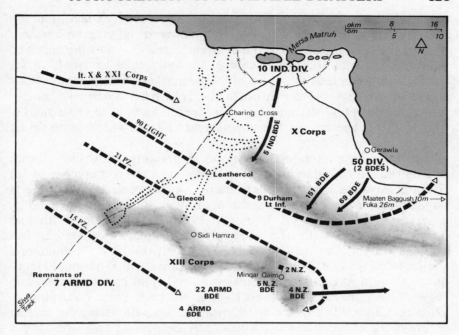

Map 12   Mersa Matruh, June 25th–28th

division in strength and with only sixteen Mark IIIs to face sixty Grants – between two British corps, of which the one containing the most coherent division, the New Zealanders, occupied a ridge overlooking their proposed route.

Meanwhile 15th Panzer had reached the Siwa track above the southern escarpment, and on the northern flank of the advance the remains of the Italian X and XXI Corps were limping up along the coast road to the western defences of the objective.

It all added up in theory to a recipe for disaster; but not in practice. The destruction of Leathercol and Gleecol had been enough to cause the hurried despatch that night of parts of two of 29th Indian Brigade's other formations 'out of danger' into reserve, thus reducing Gott's infantry even further, followed by a report to Auchinleck that the gap below had been penetrated by a force of 'over a hundred' panzers. Already too many people were looking over their shoulders.

Even when daylight on the 27th brought the possibilities of a clearer view, early misfortune thickened the haze of fear and distrust through which the British and New Zealand commanders were peering. During the night Percy's gallant 9th Durhams had moved out from Gerawla into the gap behind Leathercol, found the rock almost impossible to dig and with no mines allocated to give them some kind of protection, found themselves directly in the path of 90th

Light when these moved off at dawn. In the resulting catastrophe 9th Durham Light Infantry were totally destroyed; only three hundred men of the four thousand who had stood in the Gazala Line survived to march off into the prison-camps, the only small consolation for the British being that the noise of their resistance had brought such a storm of artillery fire down on to the area from north-east, north-west and south that their captors were forced away to the east and lay immobile for the rest of the morning until 21st Panzer came up on their right.

But when this happened it caused thoroughly unjustified alarm, among the New Zealanders of all people, even the commander of 5th Brigade Howard Kippenberger describing the scene as containing 'a huge column of transport . . . shimmering in the haze and headed by a group of fifteen tanks. It moved slowly, growing in width and depth.' It also – with the luck of the winners – caused critical damage; in the first artillery exchanges with the New Zealanders a shell landed amid a group of senior staff officers at Divisional Head-quarters, and in the early afternoon a shell splinter tore a deep and ragged gash in Freyberg's neck – the thirtieth scar, according to Winston Churchill, that he bore from war wounds, though of course as Freyberg had explained, 'You nearly always get two wounds for every bullet or splinter, because mostly they have to come out as well as go in.'

By this time, 21st Panzer had become only too aware of the enemy presence on the Minqar Qaim Ridge, and with quite notable initiative curved south around its eastern extremity, thus giving the paper impression that it had cut off the retreat of the entire division, if not of the entire XIII Corps. Unfortunately for the New Zealanders, this move did result in the scattering of their transport echelons which had been parked to the rear for 'safety' – and even more unfortunately for British fortunes as a whole, the move was seen by Gott, charac-teristically patrolling the battlefield alone but for his driver, and interpreted by him as the overrunning of the entire division.

There is no doubt that Gott was very tired by now. He had been fighting in the desert since 1940 with ever-increasing responsibilities, and although his promotions had been well received throughout the Eighth Army – for he was brave, attractive in appearance and manner, and friendly to everybody he met irrespective of rank – it is possible that he was now being asked to act above his ceiling of competence. He was not an intellectual soldier; he had probably been happiest commanding the 7th Armoured's Support Group and un-doubtedly his brief command of that famous division had given him great satisfaction. But he seems to have been overburdened by command of XIII Corps – especially during Ritchie's reign over Eighth Army when he had had to act as a mentor to his chief – and his interpretation of what was happening around him on June 26th shows signs of nerviness and exhaustion.

He had been with the New Zealanders during the first artillery exchange shortly after 0900 and been forced to conduct his conversations with Freyberg in a slit-trench; he knew of the losses among the New Zealand staff and, concerned about 29th Indian Brigade's account of 'over a hundred panzers, had told Freyberg that he 'should side-step if necessary' and not regard the ground around Minqar Qaim as inviolable.

He had then received, just before noon, a signal from Auchinleck to the effect that if withdrawal became necessary, the two corps should fall back into a defensive area south of Fuka upon receipt of the codeword 'Pike' – which was in fact a perfectly normal administrative arrangement for Auchinleck to have made, but perhaps on Gott's overwrought mind left an impression that withdrawal was already being seriously contemplated. He had managed to put Lumsden (whose 1st Armoured Division had been holding 15th Panzer back quite successfully all morning) into touch with Freyberg, and Lumsden had detached one tank regiment to go to Freyberg's aid – and was just contemplating moving his headquarters back closer to Freyberg's in order to give further co-operation, when he received a message from Gott himself saying, 'It's all over. The New Zealand Division doesn't exist.'[25]

At 1655 XIII Corps commanders received directives from Gott to withdraw, and to Freyberg's intense fury (although his head and neck were swathed in bandages and Brigadier Inglis had taken over formal command of the division, Freyberg was still dominant) just as it seemed that he had sufficient armoured support to deal with the panzers to the east, it withdrew and left him and his men to fend for themselves. It was all too reminiscent of Sidi Rezegh, and the New Zealanders' position was made even more critical – though they did not know it at the time – by another action of Gott's. Still out in the desert to the south by himself, he had intercepted a New Zealand supply column bringing up ammunition and water, and deeming its arrival too late, had sent it back to Fuka.

In the meantime, General Holmes's troops in Matruh itself had not been greatly concerned with events so far, their main problem stemming from the appalling quality of communications throughout the entire army. But by mid-afternoon Holmes had gathered that all was not well with XIII Corps, and he was organising attacks southward across the escarpments in order to aid them. In the west, 5th Indian Brigade would drive across the gap towards Sidi Hamza, while further east the two 50th Division brigades would drive down parallel towards Minqar Qaim and the New Zealanders.

By nightfall, therefore, a highly complicated situation existed. The whole of Afrika Korps was strung out between the coast (which 90th Light had reached some ten miles east of Gerawla about 2000) and a point on the Siwa track sixty miles away to the south-west, with 90th Light wedged up in a corner east of Matruh, 21st Panzer isolated fifteen miles to the south with the two New Zealand brigades just to the west, cutting them off from 15th Panzer, who were themselves pressing on the heels of 1st Armoured and being harried by the Motor Brigades of 7th Armoured.

To Auchinleck, who at dusk had no idea that Gott had ordered XIII Corps to withdraw, the situation appeared satisfactory – for even accepting reports which put Afrika Korps strength at between 100 and 150 panzers, the maps showed that the panzer divisions were both isolated and cut off from each other. He was therefore disappointed when during the night he received Gott's interpretation of the situation but, accepting his corps commander's appreciation he duly issued the code-word 'Pike' by which he intended X and XIII Corps to withdraw *in co-ordination* to the Fuka positions – probably beginning the following morning.

But there was no co-ordination, for XIII Corps were already streaming back – not only independently of X Corps, but with their own internal formations acting independently of each other. As in Gott's opinion the New Zealand brigades had ceased to exist no one made any attempt to co-ordinate with them, and the brigades of 1st Armoured Division apparently considered the Motor Brigades of 7th Armoured quite capable of looking after themselves (correctly, as it happened) and left them to do so. No one had actually uttered the words '*sauve qui peut*' but the atmosphere south of the escarpment during those hours was distinctly flavoured with the attitude 'I'm all right, Jack.' It was perhaps appropriate that most were retiring towards positions around a place named Fuka.

But not the New Zealanders. Their break-out from Minqar Qaim has won an epic place in the annals of desert warfare, for with their trucks and carriers scattered and out of touch (one of the officers had left the charging sets with the transport so the signals batteries with the fighting troops quickly ran down) it was decided that the 4th Brigade should cut a way through the enemy force to the east with bayonet and bomb. The 5th Brigade and a Reserve Group, packed on to whatever transport they had with them, would then follow them through the gap:

> All vehicles, including guns, were to form up after dark, head to tail in nine columns ten yards apart, with 5 Brigade in the rear. Zero hour for the attack was 10.30 p.m. and we would move on the success signal from 4 Brigade.

The trucks were packed to the limit and the hundreds of men whom they could not carry were crammed on to the fighting vehicles. Men were hanging on wherever there was standing room, squeezed inside the gun quads, on the guns themselves, on carriers and anti-tank portées, everywhere imaginable.[26]

The bayonet attack by 4th Brigade was entirely successful and practically eliminated the first battalion of Rifle Regiment 104; unfortunately it would seem that German wounded were also killed in the close, fierce, unrelenting violence which encompasses this most searing of all types of battle. But it was soon over and the massed transport behind moved off, picking up speed as it did so.

This was not, however, the end of the action for the leading vehicles veered slightly south and bumped into what General Kippenberger described as 'a laager of about a dozen tanks lying so closely that there was no room to break through between them'. As 21st Panzer had approximately that number left, it looks as though 5th Brigade had run headlong into the entire enemy armoured force between themselves and freedom, and a small but spectacular battle resulted, with tank and anti-tank shells raining down on them, liberally laced with machine-gun fire containing tracer. In the middle of the charge down upon the panzers, Freyberg's head, swathed in bandages until it resembled a football, was seen emerging from the front of his truck as he stood up, and his rather high voice was heard floating back over the mass of vehicles remarking 'By God! Another Balaclava!'

For a few moments we ran on amid pandemonium, overtaking and being overtaken by other frantic vehicles, dodging slit-trenches, passing or crashing into running men, amid an uproar of shouts and screams. I recognised the men as Germans, pulled out my revolver and was eagerly looking for a target when suddenly there was silence and we were out running smoothly on level desert. We were through.[27]

Although Auchinleck's plans had been for the first stage of retreat from Matruh to end around Fuka, there seems to have been yet another misinterpretation of orders at corps level and the New Zealanders went right back to the neighbourhood of Bab el Qattara to join their 6th Brigade south of Alamein where, not unnaturally, they spent the next few days sorting themselves out and counting heads as the rearguards and stragglers came in.

As 1st Armoured Division and the Motor Brigades of 7th Armoured were still withdrawing eastwards in the open desert to the south, and the remains of 29th Indian Brigade were limping into the positions along the Fuka Escarpment, it can be seen that when X Corps received the code-word 'Pike' at 0430 on June 28th (X Corps communications were no better than anyone else's), the possibilities of co-ordination with XIII Corps were by that time minimal. The plan for withdrawal had entailed XIII Corps holding the crests of the escarpments, especially at Fuka, while X Corps columns passed through below, so the hazards which General Holmes and his men had been left to face as a result of General Gott's misreading of the situation were hardly inconsiderable. They were in no way lessened by the fact that neither Auchinleck nor Holmes was aware of XIII Corps's withdrawal until much later the following day (June 28th) – by which time yet another infantry divison were bitterly asking themselves whether any trust should ever be placed in armoured formations.

Ten weeks later, the findings of a board of inquiry set up to examine the causes of the collapse at Matruh were quite clear, and were laconically summed up in the remark by the chairman, 'XIII Corps just disappeared and left X Corps up the pole.'

Ironically enough, of course, during that first stage of XIII Corps's retreat to the east on the evening of June 27th, three brigades from X Corps had been driving south to bring them aid! On the western flank, the assault group from 5th Indian Brigade attempted to cross the Afrika Korps's entry gap, and one company of 1st/4th Essex actually reached Sidi Hamza to find no one there and be heavily shelled before withdrawing the following morning; and further east, 69th Brigade bumped into a part of 90th Light and retired after a brisk action, while 151st Brigade 'hit air' in their search for the New Zealanders, and also returned to their positions east of Matruh. An account by one of the gunner officers who took part reflects the caustic attitude increasingly adopted by the troops to such unprofitable enterprises.

> We marched due south in Brigade groups, exposing our soft skins to every machine-gun and A/Tk gun that cared to fire at us across the moonlit flats. The whole desert seemed to be full of criss-crossing tracer through which we had to march. And then before the moon was down we had to march back through the hole we had punched so that the enemy, now thoroughly aroused, could have more practice.[28]

By the time they had all returned to their positions, General Holmes had received the 'Pike' order, but as what inadequate signals system had been available earlier had by now disintegrated entirely, the general and his chief staff officer had perforce to set out themselves in different directions to find and inform the unit commanders of the plans for break-out. As daylight had come before this chore was completed, it was evident that the men in Matruh would have to remain where they were for at least one more day – by which time (though neither Holmes nor Auchinleck would be aware of it)

XIII Corps would have disappeared totally from the scene, the New Zealanders having arrived back at the Bab el Qattara defences and the armoured and motor brigades to positions some fifteen miles south of Fuka from which it would seem they later refused point-blank to move. Even the battered remains of the 29th Indian Infantry columns – the only troops to find their way to their designated objectives on the Fuka Escarpment – were no longer there by the evening of the break-out, for they had been swept away by the spear-heads of 21st Panzer who, under Rommel's insistent spur, had forced themselves further eastward during the afternoon of the 28th, reached the escarpment, overrun the Indians capturing 20 officers and about 200 other ranks, cut the coast road below, occupied the airfield and captured more transport and general stores. By the evening of June 28th, Matruh was well and truly cut off.

In the event, it is surprising that so large a proportion of X Corps managed to get through, though this is possibly due to the fact that, as one recent writer so cogently put it, 'During 29th June the desert between Matruh and El Alamein was covered with small columns of British and Axis vehicles all moving eastwards, trying to avoid each other'[29] – a problem rendered more complex by the fact that so much of the Axis transport was British in origin, and when collisions took place and their cargoes spilled out on to the ground to join action, they appeared in the moonlight all to be dressed in the same uniforms.

Holmes's break-out plan was simple and on a Homeric scale. All the brigade groups, leaving at 2100, were to drive southwards for twenty miles, then to turn east and make for the Fuka Rendezvous along the level ground between the two escarpments. Unfortunately, this plan was somewhat upset by Rommel's intention to attack Mersa Matruh at the same time, but commencing a little earlier, at 1700.

As a result, the Italians on the west found themselves being unexpectedly overrun by the retreating British, although these wasted little time looking for prisoners but pressed on leaving the Italians to enter Matruh as they pleased – while to the east there developed some fierce fighting in the tangled wadis leading up the first escarpment, with German infantry trying to get down and into Matruh and Gerawla and British and Indian infantry trying to get up and out.

This phase occupied most of the time up to midnight, but when the top of the escarpment was reached by the British and Indians, many Axis headquarters found themselves suddenly caught up, unex-pectedly and violently, in a battle. One such headquarters was that of Colonel Menton, commanding one of the 90th Light Division's battlegroups, and in the frantic mêlée which followed staff officers found themselves fighting with pistols in hand-to-hand conflict; and when the Corps column eventually shook itself free it left behind one brigadier, 20 junior officers and 450 other ranks with the somewhat shaken Colonel Menton.

Even Rommel himself became involved in action far too close for a Commander-in-Chief, even of his ardent temperament. He was under the impression that his attackers were the New Zealanders whom he still believed to be in Matruh, but his account presents an otherwise vivid and colourful picture of the night's action:

> A wild mêlée ensued, in which my own headquarters, which lay south of the fortress, became involved. *Kampfstaffel* Kiehl and units of the Littorio joined in the fighting. The firing between my forces and the New Zealanders (*sic*) grew to an extraordinary pitch of violence and my headquarters was soon ringed by burning vehicles, making it a target for continuous enemy fire. I soon had enough of this and ordered the headquarters and the staff to withdraw to the south-east. One can scarcely conceive the confusion which reigned that night. It was pitch dark and impossible to see one's hand before one's eyes. The R.A.F. bombed their own troops, and, with tracer flying in all directions, German units fired on each other.[30]

One of Rommel's staff who received the order to retire with considerable relief was von Mellenthin, who at one time had found himself firing a sub-machine gun against a 'British column . . . unkind enough to choose a route through Panzerarmee battle headquarters.'

Against this account should be read that of the British gunner officer who had taken part the night before in the abortive raid south of Matruh:

> I gave the signal and went forward at carrier pace, compass set at 180° in one hand, revolver in the other and shouting blue murder at the top of my voice. At once we seemed to be among them. Tracer flew in all directions from a score of flashes of light, AP rushed past our ears or kicked up the sand, the Brens from the carriers on either side clattered and flashed. Boche rose from the ground and scattered from our path. We ran them down – and over. I took pot-shots at Huns; my driver ducked to dashboard level; I glanced at my compass and over the open truck back to my guns. Bullets seemed to pour through the quads or bounce at angles from the wheels. One was fired; it blazed and men jumped on to the next one; the mass came on. The carriers creaked steadily forward firing burst after burst and magazine after magazine. I was never so excited in my life.
>
> We ran our two miles and pulled up in the first clear space while the others came in. Our order of march was gone. We recced round our area, found a Boche column in leaguer on our flank, raked it with fire and withdrew to our bridgehead. Slowly our nerves relaxed; we began to laugh. We were alive again.[31]

So felt many members of those columns as they broke through the encircling 90th Light formations that night, and they pressed on with eager hearts to Fuka where, they had been assured, the armour and infantry of XIII Corps were awaiting them – only to find, as they drew up in the early morning mist alongside British three-tonners and trucks waiting at the rendezvous, that these were occupied by Afrika Korps troops, who at the beginning were just as surprised as they were at the encounter.

But Rommel's men soon appreciated the position in which they found themselves and extracted considerable amusement from the events of the next few hours. Their final count of prisoners delivered so easily into their hands amounted to 60 officers and 1,522 other ranks, together with a large haul of lorries, carriers and trucks and quite a few more guns to add to their now extensive collection of British artillery.

Nevertheless, General Holmes and his headquarters got through after some close shaves; at one time during the night, according to the South African historians,

> They had picked their way through hostile forces, across desert sand in which the deep tracks of enemy armour showed black in the moonlight, escorted for some time by unwitting German armoured cars, past a furnace fire where the clink of beating hammers told that fitters were hard at work on a German tank, standing back politely to allow an unidentified motorised column to pass, which in turn politely refrained from vulgar curiosity, and so into the mist an hour before dawn.[32]

Fellow-feeling makes us wondrous kind, and no doubt many of that 60 per cent of X Corps who, in General Holmes's opinion, reached the haven of the El Alamein defences, did so because at some time German observers thought it best not to enquire too deeply into the identity of those passing in the night. Their thoughts as they watched or listened to the rumbling columns probably echoed those of the British driver during *Operation Crusader*, who found himself approached by the adjutant of Rommel's reconnaissance battalion.[33]

Rommel had three of these reconnaissance battalions now (though like all other formations which had been fighting since May 28th they were by this time well under strength): 580th Battalion were with 90th Light, engaged on the morning of the 29th in penetrating and occupying Matruh and rounding up more prisoners and assessing the loot, while the 3rd and 33rd Battalions were with the Panzer divisions; but it cannot be said that they were providing him with much accurate information about enemy defences in front, for obvious reasons. Their Commander-in-Chief was pressing the advance so fast that not even the British commander knew where all his own forces were, and in any case, there had been no time for Axis reconnaissance in any depth – and now they were both operating and probing forward into areas of which no one, however long they had been with the Afrika Korps, had the slightest experience.

On the morning of June 29th, therefore, as Rommel hustled his exhausted men on again without rest – without even, as 90th Light War Diary sorrowfully records, 'a swim in the sea' or a chance 'to sleep its fill after the heavy fighting for Mersa Matruh and all the hardships of the previous days' – his staff were unable to supply him with a very accurate picture of what lay ahead in the El Alamein defences. To fill this lacuna in his armoury, it seems that Rommel might have fallen into the trap of 'making pictures'.

It was well known that defences had been built around the railway station of El Alamein, making it, in effect, a half-sized Tobruk – and presumably into this must be flooding the survivors of X Corps, perhaps now grouped into one division, say 50th Division. He had received intelligence to the effect that a fresh Indian brigade had been brought up from the rear, and it would seem that they were constructing a defensive box in one of the shallow depressions lying about ten miles south-west of El Alamein station, probably the outer one, Deir el Abyad; away to the south occupying the inland half of the defensive line would be the New Zealanders who had escaped his clutches at Matruh.

British dispositions at El Alamein therefore looked to Rommel remarkably similar to those at Matruh, and it was not unreasonable to suppose that whatever was left of the British armour when it reached the El Alamein positions (for on the 29th it was still strewn over the desert to the south of Fuka) would take up the same position relative to the New Zealanders as it had occupied there, that is, just to the west. In short, in Rommel's opinion, X Corps held the northern sector of the line, XIII Corps the southern sector, and a repeat of his favourite 'bomb-burst manoeuvre' – break in along the junction-line between the corps, fan out north and south behind them – should again be enough to spread panic throughout Eighth Army and cause them to stream off eastwards yet again, not stopping this time until the whole of the Delta lay between them and his pursuing hordes.

Not that the forces under his command really justified the term 'hordes' any longer – or, come to that, even 'horde' – but what they lacked in numbers they must make up in energy and enthusiasm despite their exhaustion. He looked forward to the time when he would be able to give them their well-deserved rest and reward, but that time was still ahead; perhaps in Cairo or in Alexandria. But until then they must keep on the move.

The morning of June 29th he therefore spent chivvying 90th Light out of Matruh and along the coast road towards El Daba and beyond, with the Italian XXI Corps and Littorio wearily dragging themselves along after. The panzer divisions, once they had been relieved of the prisoners who had fallen into their hands at Fuka, were diverted south-eastwards across the desert towards El Quseir, some twenty-five miles south of Daba, the diversion intended to catch some of the stray British groups, columns or isolated vehicles still littering that irregular patch of desert stretching from between Fuka and El Daba on the coast, down to the edge of the Qattara Depression.

Having set them on their way, he then had time to assess the strength at his command, and to plan to utilise it to its best advantage within his overall scheme.

As a result of heroic efforts by recovery teams, it seemed that the panzer divisions would by the following morning have 55 panzers between them, of which 15 were Mark IV Specials with the new long 75mm. gun; in artillery, his own German troops would have over 300 guns of various calibres, of which 29 would be the invaluable 88mms and 39 were captured British 25-pounders – in their own way, almost as effective when used correctly. Even the Italian artillery included eleven 88mms and five 25-pounders among their 200-odd pieces, and they also had 30 of their own 'mobile coffins' as the M13s were by now universally called, for what they were worth.

The problem was manpower, for although the panzer and gun crews were enough to handle their weapons, there was a woeful lack of infantry. There could hardly be 500 grenadiers left to the panzer divisions, or many more than 1,000 infantry to 90th Light – while the total strength in the three Italian Corps – X, XX and XXI – came to but 5,500 rifles. Quality must make up for quantity. It had happened before.

Map 13   Towards El Alamein, June 29th, morning

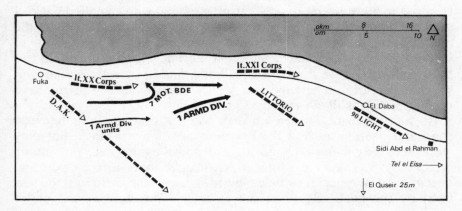

29 June 1942

Dearest Lu,

Now the battle of Mersa Matruh has been won and our leading units are only 125 miles from Alexandria. There'll be a few more battles to fight before we reach our goal, but I think the worst is well behind us. I'm fine.

Some actions make demands on one's strength to the point of bodily exhaustion, but there are quieter periods when one gets a chance to recover. We're already 300 miles east of Tobruk.[34]

The evening reports were mixed. The panzer divisions had struck appalling terrain on the journey to the south-east, which had taken toll of the vehicles and used up a disproportionate amount of fuel; and in the late afternoon they had had a brush with British armour intent on forcing a way through from the rear, probably units of 1st Armoured on their way back to the Alamein positions. On the other hand, 90th Light had not only reached El Daba, but had pushed some South African rearguards out through a cluster of burning supply dumps, and then gone on further to hedgehog for the night about five miles west of a spot marked on the map as Sidi Abd el Rahman. Tomorrow would be the day for briefing and deployment.

Dawn on June 30th brought another series of half-desperate, half-ludicrous confrontations between groups awakening to find their neighbours enemies instead of friends; the panzer crews at El Quseir watched armoured cars just behind them draw rather casually away to the south before racing eastwards at full speed, and breakfast-time at Panzerarmee Headquarters was suddenly disturbed by frantic calls for help from XX Italian Corps, still well to the rear, who had found themselves unexpectedly attacked from behind by 7th Motor Brigade. These, with sublime impertinence, having overrun the Italian corps headquarters and the major part of one division, then halted, about-faced and prepared to hold XX Corps in place until further notice, and the ensuing complaints and calls for help from XX Corps resulted in an outburst of anger from Rommel who signalled back, 'I demand that your Corps should carry out the attack, destroy the enemy and reach its objective. The enemy is under orders to withdraw.' An hour later he added somewhat gratuitous insult to this by signalling, 'Trust your Corps will now find itself able to cope with so contemptible an enemy' – an epithet which history might have warned him was ill-starred.

By 1000, 90th Light were on their way, closing up along the coast road and probing to find the first hint of solid resistance, but they were seriously hampered during the morning by heavy bombing attacks by S.A.A.F. Bostons which caught them in the open and destroyed a number of vehicles, besides dispersing them into the soft sand by the road. By noon they were at Tel el Eisa, and under artillery fire which increased whenever they showed signs of further advance; but so far, so good.

The hapless Italians, however, lacking sufficient transport, equipped with inadequate armour and with their only effective arm, the artillery, on the move, were soon in trouble again. XX Corps managed at last to push the 7th Motor Brigade out of their way, but these indomitable infantrymen then caught up with the bulk of 1st Armoured Division still rumbling back towards the Alamein positions, and both fell upon the rear of the Littorio Division and its accompanying infantry, en route to fill the gap between 90th Light and the panzer divisions. There was a brisk action as the British armour ploughed its way through, and although no attempt was made by 1st Armoured to annihilate its unexpected prey, Littorio later reported that all its tanks had been hit and two-thirds of them were wrecked. Moreover, their artillery was down to six guns, and a hundred men had been killed.

While this had been going on, Rommel was briefing his commanders. His plan was simple, and would on past experience promise the highest chances of success that men in battle could expect. Late that afternoon the panzer divisions at El Quseir would move southwards, making as much dust and noise as possible, thus attracting enemy attention and giving them the impression that they were contemplating a hook around the El Alamein Line – for this was how Rommel insisted on referring to the British position, despite its actual structure of four defensive boxes with minefields scattered between. After dark, they would double back and concentrate around Tel el Aqqaqir in the north, at the western end of the derisory slope known as Miteiriya Ridge and immediately on the right of the 90th Light positions. The Italians would provide flank cover to this concentration of striking power, and during the movements would manoeuvre to the east, thus providing a screen.

At 0300 the next morning (July 1st) the German forces would breach the enemy defences along the line of the Miteiriya Ridge, 90th Light passing along its northern edge, driving through the gap and skirting around the El Alamein box until they reached the coast road and the sea, probably near the place named on the map Alam el Dakar. The panzer divisions on the right would drive along the southern edge of the ridge, passing north of the Indian brigade at Deir el Abyad and leaving them to be masked by one of the Italian XX Corps divisions. The panzers would then swing south, cut down through the British lines of communication and supply until they were behind the New Zealanders and the remnants of the 5th Indian Division next to the Qattara Depression, when they would face west and endeavour to stem the retreat which would undoubtedly follow.

In the meantime, Italian XXI Corps would attack the western face

of the El Alamein box and thus hold the attention of 50th Division
inside, XX Corps (Ariete and Trieste) would accompany the panzer
divisions and attack the New Zealanders from the north, while
Littorio, their artillery augmented by two batteries of 88mms, would
hold 1st Armoured Division in their place immediately west of the
New Zealanders until such time as confusion and chaos had overtaken the Colonials, and the British armour began their retreat
through them to the Delta.

It should all be over in a matter of days, if not hours, for there was
no reason to expect the task to be any more difficult than that at
Matruh, and Rommel wished to be in Alexandria by the weekend –
and it was now Tuesday. Although the news that Mussolini and his
entourage had arrived at Derna the previous day left Rommel
singularly unmoved, the timetable was nevertheless running a little
late, and the utmost efforts must be made to correct this; and such
was the atmosphere of cool confidence at the briefings that not even
the most experienced staff officers seem to have expressed doubts as
to whether the tired and understrength panzer divisions could be
expected to carry out, at night, a march of thirty-five miles through
enemy lines and across unknown country, probably having to overcome at least some opposition on the way.

As a token of which, at about 1600 the panzer divisions, who had
spent the day resting (though severely tried by the stifling heat) were
suddenly shocked into action as the tail of the British armour swung
through them; but their attempts to bring them to decisive battle

Map 14   Rommel's plan for July 1st

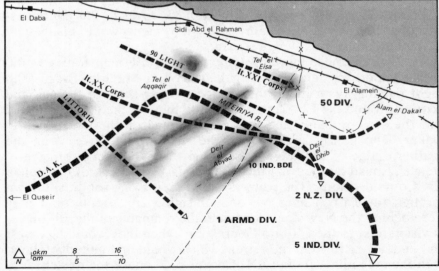

were foiled by the sudden thickening of the sandstorm which had been threatening all day, and the British tanks drew off and disappeared sluggishly eastwards into the choking yellow murk.

Soon it was time to move off. It was late afternoon on June 30th, 1942.

The diversionary move to the south was made by only one panzer division so as to save fuel, but after darkness fell and the two divisions had combined again, something very near to chaos descended upon them both. The going up towards Tel el Aqqaqir proved appallingly rough, an escarpment had to be descended and only one way down was found with the result that 15th Panzer drove straight through 21st and collected one of the latter's rifle battalions by mistake while doing so; and in an attempt to shed (literally) some light on the confusion, both divisions put up such a Brock's Benefit of flares and Very lights that even the Korps War Diary commented on it. 'German Afrika Korps betrays its advance by an uninterrupted pyrotechnic display,' it notes dourly, yet despite the illumination, by 0130 it was evident that they would all be late at their assembly point. Nehring therefore signalled Rommel to the effect that the armoured assault on the El Alamein Line would be delayed by at least three hours, and in the resultant atmosphere of disapproval D.A.K. floundered unhappily northwards.

Their condition was not improved by the sight, as dawn broke, of thirty British tanks congregated exactly on their assembly point at Tel el Aqqaqir (they were 4th Armoured Brigade in their last leaguer before reaching their battle positions) but these moved off as the German panzers arrived. Exhaustion, confusion and delay had depressed everyone present, and, as one of them is reported to have mentioned, it only needed a heavy bombing raid to make their misery complete. This was delivered at 0615 by eighteen Wellingtons, and had the paradoxical effect of getting the armour moving rather quicker than it would otherwise have attempted, for it was soon evident that in mobility lay their only safety.

In the meantime, 90th Light had moved off at 0300 on its task 'to shatter the front line of the enemy, reach the sea in an outflanking attack and thus cause the fall of the enemy's northern Strong Point'.[35] Rommel was there to see them off and all seemed to be going well (but slowly, for no reconnaissance had been possible) when, just after dawn, the leading files saw some British tanks leading away in front and were drawn after them.

These were, in fact, the 4th Armoured Brigade vacating Tel el Aqqaqir and, making too far north, the British tanks bumped into the western face of the El Alamein box and were lightly shelled by South African artillery as a result. Attached armoured cars managed to

persuade the box defenders that they were firing at friends instead of
enemies but the defenders were now wide awake and when they saw
90th Light coming into view on the heels of 4th Armoured, they
poured into them such a concentration of machine-gun, anti-tank and
artillery fire that, for the moment, the northern flank of Rommel's
advance was brought to an abrupt halt.

To the south, however, beyond the Miteiriya Ridge, it seemed at
first as though the panzer divisions were going to have as easy a ride
as 21st had had at Matruh, for when they reached the area to the
north of Deir el Abyad, it became quite obvious that the position was
empty. They could therefore begin their swing to the south as soon as
they liked, and it was during the first stage of this manoeuvre that
they realised that their information had been at fault. The Indian
brigade that should have been at Deir el Abyad was found three miles
to the east – at Deir el Shein at the western end of Ruweisat Ridge –
and when 21st Panzer circled around to the north in an attempt to
by-pass it and then cross Ruweisat itself in their drive to the south,

Map 15   First Battle of Alamein, July 1st

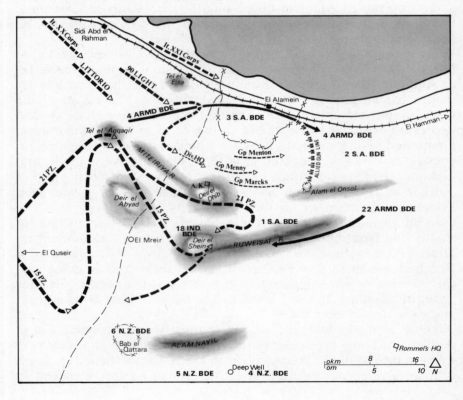

they ran into another strong defence at the base of the northern slope.

At this point, Nehring decided that the Indians at Deir el Shein must be eliminated and a halt was called for reconnaissance and refuelling. During it, both panzer divisions received further unwelcome attentions from the Desert Air Force, together with shelling from the strongpoint and the ridge behind, and it was noon before they were ready to move again – noon on a day made more atrocious than ever by an appalling *khamsin* which produced a fierce, oven-like wind and a thickening sandstorm.

But the sandstorm at least allowed 90th Light to the north to get moving again. Pinned down by the Alamein box artillery for the whole of the morning but conscious of their Commander-in-Chief's presence close behind, they then managed to draw back as visibility worsened and were by 1300 feeling their way carefully along the northern side of Miteiriya – to Rommel's relief and delight. Such was his enthusiasm as he saw the columns disappearing eastwards, that he signalled the Italian XXI Corps to the effect that the breakthrough was almost complete, that they and 90th Light could expect very soon to be able to clean up the Alamein box entirely and reach the coast road, and that XX Corps and Littorio should be ready to move in two hours, straight through the gap opened by the leaders on and past El Hamman towards a point on the coast road only twenty kilometres from Alexandria, named Amiriya! He was not to know that one realistic Italian colonel pencilled on the signal form 'Littorio has fuel for 20 km. To Alexandria – 150 km.'

The attack on Deir el Shein began just before noon with a bombardment under which 21st Panzer's 104 Rifle Regiment worked their way through the sandstorm up to the wire on the north-east corner. Machine-gun fire swept the approaches, some of their vehicles blew up on newly laid minefields, shells and mortar bombs crashed and thumped down on them from every direction, in particular from the ridge behind.

But they reached the wire, slid their Bangalore torpedoes under it and just before 1300 they blew them – and through the gap thus torn the panzers could begin their slow, inexorable creep forward. They were not to have an easy victory, however, for they soon came within close range of 25-pounders whose crews had refrained from wasting their ammunition by firing blind into the murk of the sandstorm, and who now made good practice. One by one the first panzers slewed out of line or brewed up, and only the second wave seemed to be making much progress towards the centre of the box – when suddenly out of the still dense fog they saw the unmistakable outlines of nine British Matildas.

It was fortunate for the panzers that their attendant anti-tank batteries, including three 88mms, had escorted them closely, for the next stage of the battle was intense though not long prolonged. But when it was over, the smoking wrecks of a dozen panzers lay alongside the equally shattered hulls of the nine Matildas, and 21st Panzer Division's striking power had been reduced by nearly a third.

By 1730 the Deir el Shein box was in their hands amid scenes of spectacular desolation. In the break-in section, the bodies of almost an entire British battalion – the 2nd/5th Essex whose first experience of battle this had been – littered the ground and slumped in the rifle-pits, only a dozen survivors remaining. Sikh and Gurkha prisoners watched every move of the panzer crews with impassive, unfriendly gaze, flickering into interest only when the victors, to their enormous relief, came across a bountiful supply of canned beer and could slake their ravening thirst. And when the Germans turned from this engrossing pursuit, they found the ranks of their prisoners considerably thinned as nearly a thousand of them had taken advantage of their preoccupation and slipped away to fight again.

On the south-east sector of the box, 15th Panzer had failed to break in, but as they waited for the final resistance beyond the wire to fade (and this was slackening mostly because of lack of ammunition) they were suddenly threatened by Stuarts and Grants (of 22nd Armoured Brigade), come somewhat laggardly along the Ruweisat Ridge to the rescue of the Indian brigade. In the face of obviously superior force, 15th Panzer retired westwards, but then found themselves under fire from the New Zealanders in the south . . . but dusk was thickening, the British armour were following their normal course and retiring from the scene of action, the shelling ceased, and D.A.K. hedge-hogged for the night where they were, hopeful of peace and quiet – but still fifteen miles short of their objective. They wondered what their Commander-in-Chief would feel about this.

In fact, Rommel was less displeased with the day's fighting than might have been expected, perhaps because he had had such a thoroughly uncomfortable day himself that he recognised that he was lucky still to be alive.

Once the plans for the attack on Deir el Shein had been laid, Rommel had established his Battle Headquarters at Deir el Dhib at the eastern end of Miteiriya Ridge in order more closely to follow the fortunes of 90th Light – but this proved by no means easy for wherever his headquarters moved during this crucial day, the Desert Air Force seemed inevitably to find them and subject them to concentrated attack. His *Kampfstaffel* lost many men and several vehicles, and Gause, his Chief of Staff, had been blown off his feet so many times that eventually he had to be evacuated with severe concussion.

But on the afternoon of July 1st, it was not Rommel's personal entourage which suffered the heaviest concentration of fire but the unfortunate 90th Light infantrymen attempting to encircle the El Alamein box.

After they had disentangled themselves from the western face, they had split into four battlegroups – Groups Menton and Marcks leading on the left and right respectively, Group Menny immediately behind with Divisional Headquarters at the rear – and in this formation they had worked their way slowly eastwards for nearly five miles until they were just short of Alam el Onsol.

And here they ran into a storm of fire from a crescent of gun positions extending from Alam el Onsol just in front around to the north where it reached the edge of the El Alamein box itself. Nothing was missing from it – heavy guns, howitzers, light and medium field guns, mortars, anti-tank guns, all contributing to a *Trommelfeuer* which shook even Rommel, who came hurrying up in an armoured car immediately the extent of the opposition to 90th Light's advance became obvious.

> Furious fire again struck into our ranks. British shells came screaming in from three directions, north, east and south; anti-aircraft tracer streaked through our force. Under this tremendous weight of fire, our attack came to a standstill. Hastily we scattered our vehicles and took cover, as shell after shell crashed into the area we were holding. For two hours Bayerlein and I had to lie out in the open. Suddenly, to add to our troubles, a powerful British bomber force came flying up towards us.[36]

But in his account, Rommel does not mention the most significant fact of all. For the first time in any account of the battles of the Afrika Korps, the word 'panic' appears – in the War Diary of the 90th Light itself.

> A panic breaks out in the Division which is stopped just in time by the energetic action of the Divisional Commander and the Chief of Staff. Supply columns and even parts of fighting units rush back under the ever-increasing enemy artillery fire. The Commanders of Battle Groups, however, succeed in keeping the majority of their units facing the enemy and bring back the troops which have taken to flight.[37]

A rout was in fact prevented and 90th Light dug in along the lines it had reached; but notice was being served that even flesh and blood formed in the Prussian mould can stand only so much.

But gradually, as the German infantrymen dug desperately into the rocky ground to give themselves some form of shelter, the encircling fire slackened and as light began to fade from the sky it ceased altogether – though there was again cause for alarm just before dusk when German fighters swooped above trailing lilac flares – the signal of imminent tank attack, which, however, did not develop. With relief, the exhausted and shaken infantrymen settled down praying for a quiet night despite the fact that they had received an order from Rommel to continue their advance in the moonlight. Nothing, it seemed, would blunt their taskmaster's determination.

Despite the set-backs during the day, Rommel was still confident that victory was at hand. His communiqué that night stated that Panzerarmee had broken through the enemy's defensive front south of El Alamein and that operations were still continuing – an announcement which was translated by the German Supreme Command into the stirring *Sondermeldung*, 'In Egypt, German and Italian divisions supported by strong formations of dive-bombers have broken through the El Alamein positions after bitter fighting. They are now pursuing the beaten British forces which are retreating towards the Nile Delta.'[38]

Shortly afterwards Rommel heard that the British Fleet had evacuated Alexandria and sailed away to the Canal Zone and beyond, and this did nothing to dampen his optimism and helped reconcile him to the flamboyant interpretation of his report in Berlin; but he had nevertheless to think deeply and to make some fundamental adjustments to his plans, for it was now quite evident that the premises upon which he had based them had been far from accurate.

For instance, the defenders in the El Alamein box had proved to be South Africans, not the battered remnants of 50th Division (which had, in fact, gone back to the Delta). Moreover, the formations holding the base of the Ruweisat Ridge were also South Africans, and so were those holding the position at Alam el Onsol – and fresh and rested men at that, thus proving that XXX Corps was holding the northern end of the line and not X Corps as he had believed. Moreover, whether or not there was British armour where he had presumed it to be, west of the New Zealanders, there was certainly a large force of it north of Ruweisat Ridge – including several of the redoubtable Grants – and if these were still exhibiting their habitual distaste for engaging themselves in infantry battles, this did not affect the fact of their presence or the power of their armament if ever it was brought into effective action.

In which respect, that night brought another piece of information to Rommel which gave him pause, and also explained a degree of skill behind the British defence which had already struck him as unusual. Ritchie had gone, and Auchinleck had taken over. He had a new opponent; he must certainly rethink his plans.

But until he had made his final decisions the battle must continue along the agreed lines and 90th Light must press forward, however exhausted they might be, taking advantage of the moonlight and the fact that the men opposite them would be just as tired as themselves, and not quite so experienced. So at 0400 on July 2nd, having enjoyed a 'completely quiet night', the faithful German infantry gathered themselves together, their anti-tank guns and artillery moved to their allotted places, and the whole cavalcade of over six hundred vehicles formed up and began once more their drive to reach the coast; and within fifteen minutes of moving off and less than half a mile of progress, they ran into exactly the same unending, concentrated bombardment that had stopped them in their tracks the previous day. However rapidly the South Africans may have retired from Gazala, they were certainly prepared to stand and fight now.

In the face of such stubborn resistance, Rommel brought new ideas quickly into play. Concentration of force against determined defence must be the keyword, the 'bomb-burst manoeuvre' must for the moment be abandoned, and the panzer divisions go to the aid of 90th Light and take part in the drive to the coast themselves. By 1000 General Nehring had been told that the axis of his advance was to be completely changed, and that XXX Corps and not XIII Corps were to be his opponents; as soon as the panzer divisions had been re-deployed, they were to advance eastward abreast of the Ruweisat Ridge, 21st Panzer on the northern slope and 15th on the southern, crush the South Africans and any other opposition in their path, swing around to the east of Alam el Onsol and then drive up to the coast. On their left, 90th Light would be conforming to their own advance.

As for the southern portion of the attack against XIII Corps, the Italians must now deal with this. The Brescia and Pavia Divisions would take up position at El Mreir just to the north of Bab el Qattara and keep an eye on the northernmost New Zealand positions, while Ariete Armoured and Trieste Motorised Divisions drove south along the route previously allocated to the panzer divisions as far as the spot marked on the map 'Deep Well'. There they would watch for XIII Corps reactions and attempt to block them if a general with-drawal developed.

But it was not to be quite as easy as that. For one thing, if 90th Light had passed a quiet night, the panzer divisions around Deir el Shein had suffered continuous and heavy bombing throughout most of the hours of darkness, and although the panzers themselves had not suffered much damage, their supply columns had been badly hit and totally disorganized. It would take a considerable time to gather them in, and only then could the tasks of refuelling the panzers and restocking the ammunition racks – usually carried out at night – begin. D.A.K. would not be ready to move off until mid-afternoon at the earliest, and not even Rommel's insistence, his mounting anger, his attempts at cajolery, and eventually his tight-lipped, eagle-eyed surveillance could make the slightest improvement in the timings.

It was 1500 by the time the two divisions set off along the sandy, scrub-covered slopes of Ruweisat Ridge, the twenty panzers of 21st Division on the left and the seventeen of 15th Division on the right; and within an hour they were in trouble. Heavy artillery fire from the south disrupted 15th Panzer's movement almost from the start, and the British and South African squadrons of the Desert Air Force occupied the skies above them almost without interval, bombing and strafing – with, admittedly, little practical effect but adding considerably to the nerve-strain, the desperation and longing for rest of men already stretched to the limits of physical endurance.

Then at 1623, 21st Panzer on the northern flank reported the advance towards them of at least a brigade of British tanks containing in their opinion thirty Grants and another twenty mixed Stuarts and Valentines, and moreover – to some consternation at Battle Headquarters – they stated that the British tanks, instead of charging towards them with customary amateur hunting-field élan, were holding off at the extreme effective range of the Grants' 75mm. guns. In addition, at least four batteries of artillery were efficiently co-ordinating their fire with that of the tanks from a position well to the south at Alam Nayil.

In some ways this section of the panzer divisions' reports was the most sobering news to reach Rommel's headquarters that day, although later reports indicating a rigid refusal of either panzer division to go to the other's help or to that of 90th Light to the north – also under merciless air attack while endeavouring to make some headway against the nearest of the South African positions – added to the worries of an already deeply concerned staff.

As for the effect of the day's fighting on the troops themselves, the War Diary of the 90th Light strikes a most unhappy note:

> The German forces, badly exhausted by the heavy fighting and the hardships endured (moving day and night) during the preceding days and weeks, seem unable to take this last English fortress before the Nile Delta with the forces available. The enemy throws the whole of his available air force into the battle against the attack of the Afrika Army. Every twenty or thirty minutes, 15, 18 and sometimes even 20 bombers, with adequate fighter protection, launch their attacks. Although the material achievements of these heavy and continuous bombing and low-flying attacks is negligible, owing to the dispositions of the fighting and supply units, the moral effect on the troops is much more important. Everyone prays for German fighter protection . . . Sometimes German fighters appear singly, greeted by the roaring applause of the troops, but naturally they are not in a position to attack such large bomber formations. The last hope that remains is the Italian Divisions (X and XXI Italian Infantry Corps and XX Italian Motor Corps) which have seen but little action so far and are, therefore, more fit. However, from such comrades there is little to be hoped.[39]

By nightfall on July 2nd, the Afrika Korps had thus hardly shifted forward from their positions held at daybreak, and there was that much less ammunition in their supply trains, that much less petrol for their fuel tanks . . . and that much less energy and resolution for the battle. According to his memoirs, Rommel that night decided that the offensive could only continue for one more day at such a pitch and only a successful breakthrough tomorrow would justify the continuation of the battle.

Not that he revealed those thoughts to anyone else at the time. His orders to Panzerarmee Afrika for July 3rd were that the offensive was to continue, the axes of the drives remain unaltered and that one more grand effort by everybody would almost certainly shatter the opposition and open the way to the Delta, to Cairo and Alexandria, to rest and due reward. The panzer divisions would again drive eastwards and then up to the coast, 90th Light would hold the South Africans in front until the panzers were past them and then join the advance on the left flank; XXI Corps would keep up the pressure on the west side of the El Alamein box, XX Corps hold their position at El Mreir while Ariete and Trieste continue their drive down to the south to cut off the New Zealanders.

But it was no good. On the previous afternoon the later attacks eastward by the panzer divisions had been growing weaker and weaker, and on the morning of July 3rd they showed no recrudescence of strength or purpose. They now had only twenty-six panzers between them and when they moved off from their night hedgehog south of Deir el Shein, they found awaiting them on the southern slopes of Ruweisat the bulk of both 4th and 22nd Armoured Brigades, who between them deployed thirty-eight Grants, over sixty Stuarts and a dozen Valentines. The result was hesitancy and delay, and most of the morning was spent by the panzer commanders in requests to each other for more support, and rather unpleasant recriminations when this was not forthcoming. Tired men become waspish.

As for 90th Light, during the previous evening some of their forward troops, their curiosity aroused by unexpected sounds from in front, had gone forward to find that the nearest South African position had been evacuated – so they settled down there for the night; but dawn brought the advance of a British column which drove them out and took twenty of them prisoner, and 90th Light did little for the rest of the morning but shell the newly arrived column until it, too, pulled back.

No matter how Rommel railed, or what orders he issued, his faithful but exhausted men could do no more against what was obviously becoming a more solid and better-conducted defence with every hour that passed. And then came news of a further set-back which visibly stirred the Commander-in-Chief.

Ariete, the one Italian formation in whom he felt some confidence, had set off just after 0900 on their drive down to Deep Well, but unescorted by Trieste who claimed to be pinned down by 'incessant aerial bombing attacks'. Just short of Alam Nayil, Ariete came under heavy shell-fire from the same batteries which the previous day had co-operated so efficiently in halting the panzer divisions, and while the Italian gunners were endeavouring both to answer the fire and dig themselves in, they were suddenly struck in flank first by mortar, anti-tank and machine-gun fire, and then by a storming bayonet charge by a complete battalion of New Zealanders (19th Battalion, 4th Brigade) which overran them, captured forty-four of their guns, took three hundred and fifty prisoners and large numbers of soft-skinned vehicles . . . and as the rest of the Ariete Division drew back, it was caught again in flank by 4th Armoured Brigade. By noon Generale di Divisione Balotta was despondently reporting to Rommel that his command had been reduced to five M13 medium tanks and two guns.

The cold fact of this catastrophe was that an armoured division – and the best formation his Italian allies could supply – had been virtually destroyed by one infantry battalion and attached artillery; and with this news, Rommel knew that the operation which had begun at Gazala five weeks before was now at an end.

Map 16   July 3rd

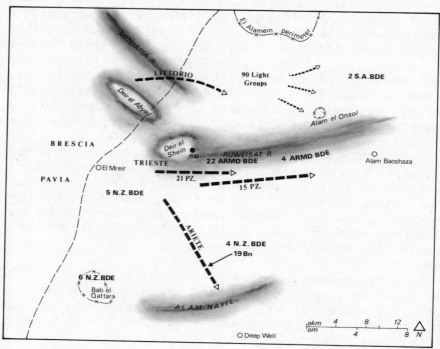

But there were still the closing rites to perform, the last benefits to extract from an operation which had, after all, administered a resounding defeat on superior enemy forces, and advanced his own army three hundred and fifty miles to bring them from the edge of the Jebel Akhdar deep into Egypt.

All was not yet finished, and at 1250 he signalled to the whole of the Panzerarmee, 'I demand energetic action by the whole of D.A.K.' He sent 90th Light forward once more and ordered Littorio to move up close in support, detached his reconnaissance battalions to cover the gap left by Ariete, and drove over to lead the panzer divisions forward himself on this last, dying spasm.

It reaped a small but worthwhile reward. The northern wing made little progress, but along the Ruweisat Ridge where Rommel was present, the two panzer divisions went in together under a co-ordinated bombardment, found a weak spot south of Alam el Onsol and drove through it to reach Alam Baoshaza, beyond the eastern end of Ruweisat Ridge. It would leave the forward troops penned in along a narrow salient, and 21st Panzer were quickly to complain that they were under fire from all sides – but a salient resolutely held can be a telling embarrassment to an enemy who wants freedom to manoeuvre.

At 2256, D.A.K. were ordered to dig in and await the British counter-attack, and that evening Rommel signalled Kesselring that for the moment he was halting the offensive:

> With the present fighting strength and supply situation an attack on a large scale is not possible for the time being. It is hardly possible to supply the army by night, as the roads are almost completely denied by enemy air activity . . . the intention [now] is in the first place to hold the front and regroup in such a manner that 2nd New Zealand Division can be encircled and destroyed.[40]

For this purpose he would need immediately more artillery, especially 88mms, more ammunition, more men, more fuel. But the first stage of *Operation Aida* had now come to an end. How soon the second stage could be launched and the triumphal march to the Nile resumed would depend upon support and encouragement from Rome and Berlin, and reinforcement and supply for the great-hearted, valiant but exhausted men of the Afrika Korps.

4 · *First Alamein*

It is generally agreed that the day upon which the British position in the Middle East lay in greatest danger was Wednesday, July 1st, 1942, and although the immediate cause of that danger lay on the battlefields to the south of El Alamein, there was also grave cause for concern throughout the entire area of the Delta where in some quarters something close to wide-scale panic existed.

What later became known as 'The Flap' was triggered by the evacuation of the Royal Navy from Alexandria during the last days of June. Faced with the possibility of attacks on the harbour by bomber fleets escorted by fighters from nearby airfields, Admiral Harwood (who had taken over from Admiral Cunningham when the latter was sent to Washington to head the Royal Naval delegation there) had dispersed his main force to Haifa, Beirut and Port Said, sent merchant ships and naval auxiliaries through the Canal to the Red Sea and even managed to expedite the repairs on H.M.S. *Queen Elizabeth* so that she could be floated up off the harbour bed and sent to Port Sudan, from which haven she made her way in due course to the United States for complete refitting.

These were, in the circumstances, undoubtedly prudent steps to take, but the speed at which they had been carried out, coupled with inadequate organisation, created an impression of panic which did nothing to cool the already febrile Alexandrian atmosphere, notoriously unstable since before the days of the Roman Empire and now rendered almost incandescent with nervous excitement. Rumours of the imminent arrival of the Afrika Korps fluttered the cosmopolitan hearts of the Levantine populace, for these immediately to be chilled by details of a 'scorched earth' policy to be put into effect by the retreating British as they fled back into the doubtful security of the Sinai Desert – both rumours being unfounded but assiduously cultivated by agents of the Axis Powers, with whom the Delta had long been well seeded.

But if the rich Levantines in Alexandria and Cairo could intrigue avidly to switch the emblems of their sympathies at the appropriate moment from Lion and Unicorn to Swastika, there was a considerable section of the Delta populace whose hopes of successfully executing such a volte-face were non-existent. Since the outbreak of war, Egypt had become a collecting area for refugees from all over Europe and especially from the areas bordering Russia – Poles who had refused to accept the tragic fate of their country, Greeks and Cretans who had fought against the invaders and then fled to fight again, Serbs, Croats and Montenegrins who had escaped the mesh of politics at home to begin weaving another abroad but with so anti-fascist a vein that their fate would be most unpleasant once the shadow of the Gestapo fell upon them. Above all, Jews from all over Europe, whose lives had already been clouded and often shattered by personal loss and tragedy, had flocked to the Delta in the hope that eventually a homeland for them would be set up in nearby Palestine – and to these this sudden close reappearance of danger assumed the menace of an apparently implacable fate. Not surprisingly, among them a degree of justifiable panic arose, first with the news of the fall of Matruh and then with the Berlin announcement of the defeat of the Eighth Army at Alamein; the embassies of any nation which might be able to offer the remotest chance of further escape were besieged, and the railway stations and exit roads from both Cairo and Alexandria were flooded and inevitably choked.

Among the ordinary Egyptian traders and shopkeepers, uninterested in who won the war but eager to make a profit from whatever circumstances ruled, a cruel dilemma existed. Torn between a desire to keep open and sell high to a public uncertain how long the piastre would hold, and a cautious instinct to board up their shop-fronts against the attentions of a possibly panic-stricken mob, they oscillated between the two attitudes with each changing rumour and thus added considerably to the general uncertainty. There was a run on the Bourse, the Egyptian Cabinet was said to be in continuous session, the cotton market closed, and a rumour spread that the students at the University, considered a hotbed of political agitation, were planning action of an unspecified but probably violent nature.

The one note of brightness in this gloomy picture was provided, oddly enough, by that indestructible element on the Egyptian scene, the *fellahin*, who behaved with a sardonic impartiality which compelled admiration and increased the abrasive affection which existed between them and the ordinary British troops. They might scream and shout at each other, and 'black bastard' was the ordinary term of both address and reference of the latter to the former, but they frequently found themselves laughing at the same things together – generally the antics or predicaments of their respective superiors – and had remarkably little difficulty in communication.

At this juncture, once any immediate opportunity for loot had been seized (and at Sidi Bish, one of the Royal Navy camps outside Alexandria, the 'wogs' were into the area rummaging through the tents and store-huts even before the White Ensign had been lowered), the grinning, white-clad natives assisted with relish the efforts to escape of those who but recently had regarded and treated them with disdain. They carried the enormous trunks and suitcases along the streets to the railway stations, fought for places for their clients on the grossly overcrowded trains leaving for Palestine or Luxor, roped unwieldy packages and crates on to overloaded and dishevelled trucks and cars – all with gusto and high spirits and in an atmosphere of amused tolerance which was one of the few redeeming features of an otherwise unseemly interlude.

It cannot be said that officialdom did much to help. The Egyptian Army and Gendarmerie disappeared from the streets which were patrolled instead by English officers self-consciously wearing their revolvers, and groups of other ranks equally self-conscious because they were headquarter clerks and orderlies suddenly enrolled into emergency units to keep order, and with but little idea of how to set about it. Other groups of soldiers on the Cairo streets were also self-conscious – and worried too, for they were from fighting units which had been at Gazala or one of the intervening battle-areas, had during the retreat overshot the stop-lines at the frontier, Matruh or El Alamein, and were now anxiously avoiding the eyes of Authority – especially those of the Military Police – as they had for the moment no wish or intention to return 'up the Blue'.

And above both cities during that epochal day, especially over the centre of Cairo where the main Allied Military Headquarters lay, towered a black cloud from which drifted down into the streets a perpetual rain of charred paper, from the bonfires of official and confidential documents which a worried Command had ordered to be destroyed. As had happened in Tobruk during the last hours before capitulation, office staffs interpreted the order with widespread enthusiasm, and masses of ordinary administrative files went up in smoke in addition to the documents which might genuinely have been of use to an occupying enemy force. For months afterwards chaos existed at such ordinary levels of military life as pay, equipment returns, and acting, unpaid promotions, and one South African officer was able to boast afterwards that during the holocaust he had put all the documents relating to nineteen Courts of Inquiry to the flame, thus bringing relief to a few doubtless undeserving wrong-doers.

'Ash Wednesday', as the day inevitably became known, was to live for many a day in the memories of those who were present, and time has done little to diminish a remarkable legend. But even more remarkable was the speed with which the panic died. By the evening of July 3rd the packed exits had emptied, the crowds of refugees

returned – shamefacedly in many cases – and the somewhat mere-
tricious life of the Delta was resumed, the only physical reminder for
the civilians being the soot waiting to be washed away by the next rain,
for the headquarter personnel the empty files and the destroyed equipment, and for the Royal Navy when they returned the looted and
gutted establishments which they had so hastily abandoned.

It is very difficult to explain this sudden cooling of the emotional
climate except in terms of Mediterranean volatility, for it had not yet
become evident, even at the front, that the scales of war were tilting
back in favour of the Allies.

There are several descriptions of the condition of the Eighth Army and
the situation it faced during those critical days of July 1942, ranging
from Churchill's 'brave but baffled' to John Connell's more extended
delineation in his biography of Auchinleck:

> Some great, decisive battles have been fought at a campaign's be-
> ginning, and in history's light there is about them a strange morning
> freshness, an air of innocence and youthful ardour . . . But there are
> other battles, even more far-reaching in their consequences, which are
> fought at the latter end of long campaigns, in a wintry, grey Arthurian
> dusk, or in some stony pass beneath a torrid, unsparing sun that knows
> no romance and no illusion. The soldiers in such battles are trained
> fighters, lean and sinewy men, toughened by many hardships, disappoint-
> ments and losses . . .
> The first Battle of Alamein was of this latter kind . . . [1]

It would seem that John Connell was rather nearer the truth of the
matter than the Prime Minister (certainly in speaking of the 'disappointments and losses'), for although the men of the Eighth Army
were as brave as any soldiers were likely to be after such a run of
defeat, they were not particularly baffled in the sense of being
puzzled as to the reasons for their plight.

From their ranks when they had stood at Gazala nearly 70,000
were now missing, mostly as prisoners (33,000 at Tobruk alone), and
they had been forced to witness with ever-increasing frustration the
destruction or abandonment of tanks, guns, trucks, ammunition,
food, petrol and water – all having been brought to the battlefield at
enormous cost and expense of energy (much of it their own) – upon a
scale which appalled them. The vast majority of them had led lives of
narrow circumstance, and the sight of waste upon such a mammoth
scale both shocked and infuriated them. And they put the blame for
this colossal waste of valuable resources – of both men and material
– squarely upon the shoulders of their commanders.

It is often forgotten that there had been compulsory education in
the United Kingdom for over a hundred years which at the very least

had taught a large number of the commonalty how to think. Even more often overlooked by those who considered themselves well educated was the possibility that those who had not had the benefit of their own advantages might compensate for their lack with a basis of sound common sense. It did not need a course at a Staff College to perceive that matters had gone sadly amiss for the Eighth Army during the recent desert battles, and although the precise targets of the criticisms by those who had suffered most may not have been identified with total accuracy, the general direction in which they were aimed was not greatly off course.

The men knew that they were as tough physically as their opponents; they believed (rightly) that their adaptation to desert conditions was better than that of the Germans for they both knew of and believed in their national inheritance; and they knew that their own native intelligence and shrewdness were enough to withstand enemy onslaught, if they were not shackled by impracticable precepts imposed from above.

And this they had seen happening at every turn of the battle. Even at the most immediate levels they were commanded by eager and enthusiastic young men who, though undoubtedly brave and idealistic, quoted to them and were guided in their first (and often fatal) actions by unrealistic concepts of battle; and if their company and battalion commanders were adapting themselves to the realities of desert warfare in 1942, it seemed that any new expertise these were acquiring was not percolating very far upwards; the most reasonable explanation of the recent unbroken run of defeats was that the High Command were as out of touch with the realities of battle as were the subalterns they had recently trained.

In contrast to their own defeats of the last few months and the inadequacies of the men who commanded them stood the successes attending the efficiency and co-ordination of the Afrika Korps under their now-legendary commander, Rommel – all of which the fighting troops of the Eighth Army had closely observed, and with which they had been only too closely involved. And they wished that they were commanded by such as Rommel, and controlled by as efficient an organisation as that under which the Afrika Korps had won such conspicuous success. 'Organisation' had long been associated – often disparagingly – with the German temperament and with a supposedly Teutonic rigidity of mind and practice; but men of the Eighth Army could in July 1942 see that it had given to their opponents advantages which had proved superior to the individuality and initiative which, according to their instructors, were their own birthright – which in any case had not been much in evidence of late. Less slack 'jolly good show' amateurism and more tightly controlled professionalism was needed if the tide of war was to be turned.

'Rommel thinks it all out and takes whatever he needs with him,' stated one hard-faced infantry sergeant at this time. 'Our lot! Christ, they couldn't organise a piss-up in a brewery!'

This criticism undoubtedly constituted a gross slander against the faithful supply and administration services which saw that the troops were properly fed, that weapons and ammunition reached at least the forward supply dumps, that mail from and to home was safely delivered, that medical and dental services, hot baths, music and entertainment were all available in the rear areas for those who could get there. But the sergeant's complaint reflected a feeling throughout the entire army that this efficiency did not extend to where it was most needed – on to the field of battle. Infantry facing attack without adequate artillery support and whose promised shield of armour had failed to appear, found little consolation in the fact that their pay and cigarette rations were safely waiting for them ten miles to the rear, especially when it seemed most likely that they would eventually be enjoyed by the enemy.

The spirit of disaffection was by no means confined to the lower ranks. On July 4th, the day following Rommel's decision to dig in and concentrate on holding the ground won, Auchinleck ordered XIII Corps to drive north-westwards through the El Mreir positions across Rommel's communications; but the only formation to make the slightest effort to obey was 5th New Zealand Brigade, who came up against the Italian X Corps, were heavily dive-bombed and in due course fell back to their start line. Commanding officers of other formations seem hardly to have given this instruction serious consideration.

However, Rommel had seen the movement and moved 21st Panzer back and down towards El Mreir leaving 15th Panzer and 90th Light to fill the gap on Ruweisat Ridge, and these movements were in turn seen and reported by 1st Armoured Division – now in XXX Corps. In the hope that the Afrika Korps might be withdrawing, Auchinleck ordered both XXX and XIII Corps forward in the early afternoon, and the 1st Armoured Division with two squadrons of Grants overran 15th Panzer's Rifle Regiment and were in the process of taking nearly two hundred exhausted men prisoner when some of the leading Grants blew up on mines and a single 88mm. gun opened up on them – at which they hastily retreated, leaving the Germans to be captured later by a weak marauding column.

That day's fighting had several unlooked-for sequels. It reinforced Auchinleck's opinion that, despite his reputation, Gott had lost both confidence and energy; and that night in Norrie's caravan, the commander of 1st Armoured Division, General Lumsden, argued with Norrie for the immediate relief of his division in terms, according to one witness, 'almost insultingly insubordinate', on the grounds that they were exhausted. How they could have been considered more drained by battle than the infantry they had so often failed to support is difficult to understand, and they certainly had less valid claims for relief than the men against whom they were fighting.

Norrie, himself a cavalryman (11th Hussars), calmed Lumsden down and persuaded him that his division must remain where it was – but two days later he was himself relieved by Auchinleck of his command at his own request as he felt that, like Gott, he was over-tired. His place as XXX Corps commander was taken by Ramsden, but so many changes at top level exacerbated the confusion and genuine exhaustion throughout Eighth Army, and little happened actively to wrest the initiative from Rommel for a few more vital days – during which time he built up his defences largely in the form of interlinking minefields filled with British mines brought forward from Matruh.

Two days later an attempt was made to repeat the XIII Corps attack north-westwards from El Mreir but it met the same fate as the one on July 4th, though on this occasion 7th Armoured Division scored one notable success. It was being reorganised as a 'Light Armoured Division', its 7th Motor Brigade being joined by 4th Light Armoured Brigade consisting solely of armoured car regiments, and these cut through behind the German and Italian lines to reach Fuka on the evening of July 7th where they shelled the airfield and fuel tanks before withdrawing. At the same time, David Stirling and Paddy Mayne were out raiding with their S.A.S. patrols, and the Long Range Desert Group were running their usual highly effective taxi-runs back towards the frontier and Cyrenaica beyond.

And now, gradually, plans discussed between Auchinleck and Dorman-Smith began to show signs of fruition. Two further principles of action had been decided between them – first that the bulk of the artillery would be grouped together and operate directly under Auchinleck's control, and secondly that instead of attempting as in the past to destroy the most *powerful* enemy formations opposite – Rommel's panzer divisions – the opening attacks of the next offensive would be directed at his *weakest* link, the tired, static, under-equipped and not over-enthusiastic Italian infantry.

Rommel had already withdrawn his Afrika Korps formations to the neighbourhood of Deir el Shein and Deir el Abyad in order to rest them, leaving the line from the coast west of El Alamein down to and across Ruweisat to be held by the Sabratha and Trento Divisions of XXI Corps, with the Brescia and Pavia Divisions on their right; opposite them and into the El Alamein positions were now arriving, from Syria and Palestine where they had been training, Morshead's 9th Australians – lean, fit, bored and quite confident of their ability to deal with Rommel's Germans, let alone the Italians.

On the night of July 7th/8th a raid was mounted along the southern
flank of Ruweisat by men of the Australian 24th Brigade, which hit
15th Panzer Division in leaguer and so worried Rommel that the next
morning he replaced 15th Panzer's commander with Colonel Menny –
and under cover of the raid and with purely deceptive intentions, the
New Zealanders evacuated both El Mreir and the Bab el Qattara box
to take up position some three miles to the south-east, releasing the
bulk of their artillery to go further north. Little happened the
following day, for apparently no one reported the move to Rommel for
over twenty-four hours, but during July 9th the New Zealanders were
able to watch appreciatively as a full-scale attack preceded by a heavy
bombardment was mounted on their recent positions, 90th Light
coming down and occupying El Mreir while the tanks, guns and lorries
of the Littorio Division rumbled into Bab el Qattara. There was thus
even less German or armoured support now for the Italians in the
north.

Moreover, it seemed that Rommel had swallowed the bait completely and believed that his long-hoped-for breakthrough south of El
Alamein was imminent; that night he gave orders for the panzer

Map 17   July 10th

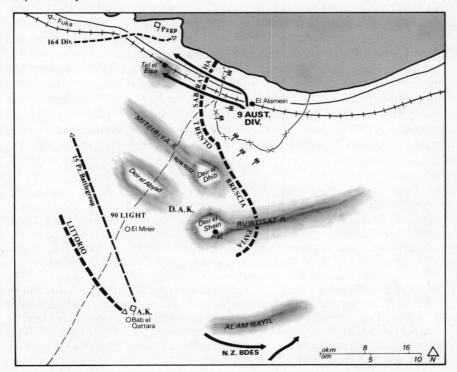

divisions to be ready the next day to sweep south-eastwards behind the Littorio and 90th Light, while he himself spent the night in one of the concrete shelters at Bab el Qattara recently occupied by the New Zealanders. His armour was now all in the southern half of the Alamein gap, as were all his German troops, while north of Ruweisat and totally unprepared for their fate, waited the hapless Italians of XXI Corps.

At 0330 on the morning of July 10th, Rommel was woken by the sounds of a bombardment which even at the distance of fifteen miles reminded some of his older companions of the dreadful First World War barrages, and he suddenly realised that he had been out-manoeuvred. By 1000, the Australians of 26th Brigade supported by thirty-two Valentines had attacked westwards out of the Alamein defences, advanced abreast the road and railway and captured the commanding feature of Tel el Eisa, having en route virtually destroyed two battalions of the Sabratha Division who, unfortunately for themselves, had been in the process of taking over part of the northern sector from the 7th Bersaglieri Regiment.

Panzerarmee headquarters were only three miles further back along the coast road and von Mellenthin, having also been woken by the bombardment, was soon shaken by the sight of hundreds of Italians fleeing past in panic and rout, having discarded their weapons and in some cases their boots in order to run faster. Fortunately, the leading formations of the first reinforcements to be sent to Rommel from Crete (164th Division) had just arrived in the neighbourhood, and from these von Mellenthin managed to form a defensive front to guard the headquarters, but by this time Rommel had abandoned all his plans for a sweep to the south-east and the Delta beyond, and come hurrying north with a battlegroup from 15th Panzer which he picked up on the way – to run immediately into 'terrific artillery fire from El Alamein' which effectively brought them all to a halt:

Next day, the 11th July, the British continued their attack south of the coast road, using powerful artillery and air support, and several more Italian units, this time of the Trieste, were overpowered and taken prisoner. Increasing numbers of troops had to be drawn off from the southern front and thrown into the fighting south of the coast road. Soon the whole of the Army artillery was brought into action, after which the British attack slowly petered out.

The British drive along the coast had brought about the destruction of the bulk of the Sabratha and a large part of the Trieste, and important sectors of the country had fallen into enemy hands. We were forced to the conclusion that the Italians were no longer capable of holding their line. Far too much had already been demanded of them by Italian standards and now the strain had become too great.[2]

More important, for the first time for many months, Rommel had been forced to dance to his enemy's tune. He made an immediate attempt to regain the initiative with an attack by 21st Panzer on the Alamein box but this failed in the face of blanket bombing of the assembly area by the R.A.F. followed by the shattering power of Auchinleck's massed artillery as the panzers tried to move forward, and in the evening Rommel broke off the attack 'in an extremely bad humour'. Next day he threw 21st Panzer in against the Australians with similarly depressing results, and by evening of July 14th he was facing the facts that the better part of two Italian divisions had been destroyed and that his precious armour was even further worn down – all to no avail.

Then during the night of July 14th/15th the second phase of Auchinleck's plan was launched – another attack on the Italian front-line infantry, this time aimed at sweeping them from Ruweisat Ridge and attacking the vital Deir el Shein area behind, in which 15th Panzer were then assembled together with the bulk of Panzerarmee's reserve artillery, several supply dumps, a strong concentration of anti-aircraft guns and the headquarters of D.A.K. and the Italian X Corps. Auchinleck was in fact repeating Foch's tactics of 1918 – a tattoo of hammer-blows on different parts of the enemy line designed not only to bludgeon the point of impact, but gradually to wear down the reserves both by casualties and exhaustion.

Unfortunately for Auchinleck, his immediately junior commanders had not attained the expertise or control of the British or French under Foch so many years before, and his plans went sadly awry because of this. Although XXX Corps were intended to exert some pressure in the north, the main attack on the western end of Ruweisat and Deir el Shein was to be carried out by the New Zealanders of XIII Corps and it does not seem that the corps commander, Strafer Gott, concerned himself very much with their plans of attack. Perhaps this was because Dominion troops always had the right of appeal over the heads of their British commanders to their own governments if they felt a lack of confidence in their orders, and after recent events many were threatening to use this right; but on this occasion Gott seems to have left everything to the New Zealand brigade commanders without question (Freyberg was still in hospital) and afterwards at least one of them, Howard Kippenberger, admitted to some poor planning.

Their 4th Brigade on the left was aimed at the western end of Ruweisat and had an approach march of six miles, of which the last three would be through enemy positions. If all went well the advance would put them on their objective (Point 63) at daylight, but by that time they would be out of range of their own supporting artillery and totally dependent for flank protection upon whatever heavy armament they had been able to carry or drag forward themselves. The obvious remedy was for armoured support to accompany the attack or at least to follow it closely, and General Lumsden ordered 22nd Armoured Brigade with its thirty-one Grants and forty-four mixed Stuarts and Crusaders to rendezvous with the New Zealanders at Point 63 by dawn – and with this agreement, the infantry went forward with great courage and considerable expertise on a silent night attack.

By daybreak, the New Zealanders had reached all their objectives, the ridge was in their hands, some companies had fought their way into Deir el Shein, over a thousand prisoners had already been taken and in Deir el Shein itself the Italian headquarters (including four generals) were about to surrender; but then 15th Panzer appeared behind the New Zealanders, having circled around them, and abruptly reversed the situation. As 15th Panzer's total strength amounted to fewer than twenty-five mixed Mark IIs and IIIs and their rifle regiment was down to fewer than three hundred men, the presence of 22nd Armoured Brigade at that moment would have made an appreciable difference – but they had not moved from their leaguer at Alam Nayil. In desperation, Kippenberger went back to fetch them:

> After ages, perhaps twenty minutes, we reached a mass of tanks. In every turret someone was standing gazing through glasses at the smoke rising from Ruweisat Ridge four miles away. I found and spoke to a regimental commander, who referred me to his brigadier. The Brigadier received me coolly. I did my best not to appear agitated, said that I was commander of 5 New Zealand Infantry Brigade, that we were on Ruweisat Ridge and were being attacked in the rear by tanks when I left an hour before. Would he move up and help? He said he would send a reconnaissance tank. I said there was no time. Would he move his whole brigade?
>
> While he was patiently explaining some difficulty, General Lumsden drove up. I gave him exactly the same explanation. Without answering he walked around to the back of his car, unfastened a shovel and with it killed a scorpion with several blows. Then he climbed up beside the Brigadier, who was sitting on the turret of his tank . . . The General asked where we were and the Brigadier pointed out the place on the map. 'But I told you to be there at first light,' General Lumsden then said, placing his finger on Point 63.
>
> I jumped down and did not hear the rest of the conversation but in a few minutes the General got down and in a soothing manner which I resented said that the Brigade would move as soon as possible.[3]

But by the time they did move, it was much too late. The New Zealanders had lost 1,500 officers and men before the situation stabilised, and in nobody's eyes were the 1,600 Italian prisoners they had taken a worthwhile exchange. Nevertheless, Ruweisat Ridge remained in the hands of the New Zealander survivors and the two brigades of the reconstituted 5th Indian Division which had attacked on their right, for the counter-attacks insisted upon by Rommel failed in the face of concentrated XXX Corps artillery which, with Auchinleck close by, was again being used in mass.

The material captured and the commanding positions won by Eighth Army between July 5th and 17th were sufficient to drive home to Rommel the fact that the forces now under his command were not strong enough to attempt any further advance towards the Nile, and that they would be extremely fortunate if in the near future they were not driven back to the frontier:

> On that day [17th July] every last German reserve had to be thrown in to beat off the British attacks. Our forces were now so small in comparison with the steadily growing strength of the British, that we were going to have to count ourselves lucky if we managed to go on holding our line at all.[4]

Kesselring and Cavallero arrived at Rommel's headquarters that afternoon and a long wrangle ensued which made very clear again just how near the bottom of the barrel they were . . . 'It can't go on like this for long, otherwise the front will crack!'[5]

It seemed that at last Rommel's fortunes were on the decline.

Unfortunately for the British, very few people in the Eighth Army possessed Wellington's intuition of affairs 'on the other side of the hill' and so to many among them matters still looked much more serious on their own side. Undoubtedly the grip which Auchinleck had taken on the army was much firmer than that to which it had been lately accustomed, but it seemed to some observers that the very stuff of which the army was composed had become so friable and denatured by disappointment that it was crumbling in his hands.

That week Auchinleck had been forced to signal Whitehall asking that the death penalty be reintroduced for desertion, in order to stem the flow to the rear of men who had decided to soldier no more – at least under the reigning authorities. In the event Whitehall refused Auchinleck's request, knowing that only Parliament could grant it and that the revelation there of the circumstances in which the request had been made would cause such a public outcry that chaos and confusion would result. They also knew that the correct cure for the condition was not death for those at the bottom but professional competence at the top and time for confidence in it to be restored.

In fact, the discontent which was causing such malaise throughout the British and Commonwealth fighting troops in the Middle East was not now so much attributable to the High Command, for already that one small victory – albeit defensive – had raised morale. But there were other factors which caused dissatisfaction, not least among them the contempt felt by the infantry for the armour, rising according to Kippenberger almost to hatred in the case of the New Zealanders. It had begun after Sidi Rezegh, increased during the retreat from El Agheila, was by no means assuaged by events during the Gazala battles, and by July had reached such a pitch that, to quote one embittered rifleman, even the cavalry were beginning to notice it.

And in itself, this situation aggravated another almost fortuitous cause for malcontent throughout Eighth Army. For what had seemed excellent industrial reasons at the time, it had been decided many months before that the Dominions and Commonwealth would contribute only infantry divisions to the war effort, and that Great Britain would provide armour. Thus the opprobrium which fell upon the armoured divisions from the ranks of the Australians, the New Zealanders and the South Africans tended to spill over on to the British infantry formations as well, even though their own attitude to the armour coincided with that of the Dominion troops. 'Pommie bastards' was a common term of reference to any troops from the United Kingdom, and it reflected a dislike and distrust which did not make for confidence at any stage of a battle.

Not that the Dominion troops had all that much confidence in each other, the relations between the Australians (in particular those of the 9th Australian Division) and the South Africans being especially strained. Many months later a group of the former were sitting in a well-known establishment in Cairo when a party of the latter entered. As the leading South African came abreast of their table, one of the Australians stood up and offered him a chair.

'Sit down, cobber, and take a drink,' the Australian said. 'You look all in. What's the matter – just run all the way from Tobruk?'

The resulting fracas was one of the more spectacular bar-fights the Middle East has seen (even taking into account the destruction of Shepheard's Hotel many years and one war previously) from which the author, who had been incautious enough to start laughing, was fortunate to escape with nothing worse than a split lip and two badly cracked ribs.

Even among United Kingdom troops there were 'tribal' dissensions. The Scots and Welsh have always had their differences with the English, among whom there was anyway an inherent coolness between southerners and those born north of the Wash; the Irish had an outlook entirely their own as had the Guards battalions, while men of the Rifle Brigade had a tendency to talk only to other Green Jackets. There were differences between the regular infantrymen and the 'hostilities only' troops, each blaming the other for recent defeats and united only in their detestation of tanks and all who rode in them – and neither were they particularly enamoured of the artillery whom they were only just getting to know. What *esprit de corps* there was therefore stopped short at battalion, battery or squadron level except among the Dominion troops, and even here it was restricted to their own formations.

None of these differences, of course, would have mattered or given rise to anything more than competitive ribaldry in a victorious army, or even one that knew clearly and throughout its entire being the direction in which its immediate aim and purpose lay. But in addition to the dreary history of the last few months, the Eighth Army was now suffering from a lack of clear guidance and especially of a clarion call to action which it would have positively welcomed, even had it been a 'Backs to the Wall' declaration calling upon it to stay where it was and either win or die.

Unfortunately, Auchinleck was in a painful dilemma and could not provide this, for although he undoubtedly sensed the benefits to morale which would follow such a call, he also knew that his prime duty must be to keep the Eighth Army in being.

For some time after he took command, Eighth Army intelligence continued to overestimate Rommel's strength, and according to the papers on Auchinleck's desk in early July his own uncoordinated and dishevelled forces could still be outmanoeuvred, and if trapped as at Tobruk or as had nearly happened at Matruh, it would be destroyed. In such a case England's only army in the field would be gone and the Middle East – perhaps even the war – would be lost. Auchinleck's situation at this time strongly resembled Jellicoe's at Jutland in 1916 where, although the best he could do would be to damage the Kaiser's High Seas Fleet severely, if he made a mistake he could lose the war in an afternoon.

Auchinleck had therefore to be very careful and to lay adequate plans for the further escape of Eighth Army by yet another retreat should this prove necessary – and there was no way of taking the essential precautions and keeping the troops at El Alamein in ignorance of them. This had been quickly demonstrated during the latter days of June, when Howard Kippenberger had been called back to take temporary command of the New Zealand Division in the absence of Inglis (the senior brigadier who was in command in Freyberg's absence) who had gone back to Cairo.

In search of information, Kippenberger had called upon his immediate superior, Gott, whose command post was nearby and whose reaction was to walk with Kippenberger out of earshot of others in the post and hand him a communication from G.H.Q. This began, 'The Chief has decided to save Eighth Army,' and went on to detail the precautions taken in the Delta – the defences being dug west of Alexandria, those at Wadi Natrun and Mena to shield Cairo, the building of boat bridges across the Nile – and also the routes to be taken by the various formations should the worst occur and a general retreat be ordered. The South Africans, for instance, were to retire through Alexandria, the New Zealanders down the 'Barrel Track' to Cairo, then up the Nile and eventually – according to Gott – back to New Zealand. According to the corps commander, Inglis had gone back to arrange the immediate evacuation of the New Zealand rear echelons and hospitals down to the Sudan – and to Kippenberger's protests that his countrymen at least were ready and fit to fight and that it would be criminal to abandon Egypt and a quarter of a million base troops in the face of 25,000 Germans and a hundred panzers (*sic*), Gott sadly replied that only the New Zealanders remained battleworthy, and that the real situation was as bad – if not worse – as that indicated by the letter.[6]

This was not only a gross exaggeration, a repetition of the tragic misinterpretation of affairs made by Gott at Matruh, but a fearful example of the state to which even a man of Gott's integrity and courage could be reduced by the strains of two years' continuous conflict. And it was to have serious repercussions throughout the army, for although Kippenberger determined not to mention the matter to anyone except his closest colleague (who also agreed to keep silent) it would seem that there were others who shared Gott's pessimism – among them Dan Pienaar who proclaimed quite openly that the only possible line of defence against Rommel was the Suez Canal.

And there were other reasons, deeper and on a strategic level, which prevented Auchinleck from committing Eighth Army to a 'win or die' posture at Alamein.

On June 28th, Hitler had launched his great summer offensive, splitting the Russian front on either side of Kursk, driving east towards Voronezh and eventually Stalingrad, and, even more dangerously from Auchinleck's point of view, south-east towards Rostov and the Caucasus. This offensive was one of the causes of Rommel's critical shortage of reinforcements and supplies, for Hitler's attention was now riveted upon Russia and not Africa; but this advantage for Auchinleck was outweighed in a signal from the British Military Attaché in Moscow with the information that the Caucasus was expected to fall within a month, which would put German armies on the borders of Persia – still contained in the area of Auchinleck's command.

And whatever Mr Churchill and the British people might think, Auchinleck was well aware that in the opinion of the Chiefs of Staff, the oil-fields of the Middle East were in the final analysis more vital to the Allied cause than any other asset in his charge.

Even if Rommel and the Afrika Korps were now held at Alamein or even beaten back to the frontier, events in Southern Russia might still necessitate the abandonment of Egypt, of the Suez Canal, perhaps even of Palestine and the Eastern Mediterranean ports, in order to protect the oil-fields at the head of the Persian gulf and the ports through which they could fuel the Allied war effort. In such circumstances, the defence of Egypt would become an irrelevance and the commitment to it of the only effective armed force in the area a perhaps fatal irresponsibility.

Whatever the advantages to morale of a 'Win or Die' call to the Eighth Army in July 1942, there was no way in which the Chief of the British Middle East Command, as it was then constituted, could make it and preserve his integrity.

The best solution to the problems posed by both Eighth Army's morale and the defence of the oil-fields would of course be the destruction of the Afrika Korps – a course of action being pressed with increasing fervour upon Auchinleck by Mr Churchill, whose reactions to the events of the last few weeks had varied between violent anger and brooding melancholy. In a signal to Auchinleck which was originally couched in such critical tones that the C.I.G.S. Sir Alan Brooke tried to persuade the Prime Minister not to send it (it was, in the end, modified) he wrote:

> The only way in which a sufficient army can be gathered in the northern theatre is by your defeating or destroying General Rommel and driving him at least to a safe distance. If this were accomplished before the middle of September, the Australian and New Zealand Divisions could return to their stations in Palestine and Syria and the 41st Division could be sent to the northern theatre direct.[7]

It then went on to detail other troop movements which were in train to help Middle East Command, but the plain fact emerged that the fate of the area lay in no one's hands but Auchinleck's and that if he wished to avoid an attack on both fronts, the one nearest to him must be eliminated as quickly as possible. He must, in fact, launch another attack against Panzerarmee Afrika.

By the time the fighting on Ruweisat Ridge had died down on the evening of July 17th, all Eighth Army's infantry divisions were closed up along the front and in contact with the Italians, while both 1st Armoured Division and 7th Light Armoured were held in reserve at the rear or on the flank. A second Indian Motor Brigade (161st) had arrived from Iraq and joined 5th Indian Division which had now become very weak, and there was in the neighbourhood an extra reinforcement for the armour. The 23rd Armoured Brigade had arrived at Suez on July 6th as the first instalment of the 8th Armoured Division, and by July 11th its 156 Valentines (still armed with 2-pounders) had been fitted with desert filters and judged adequate for action. Their crews, however, were obviously still unacclimatised to a Middle East mid-summer, and no one knew how much of their training in England would stand up to the realities of a desert battle.

None the less, their addition to 1st Armoured Division would raise the tank strength at Auchinleck's disposal to 323 of which 61 would be Grants and over half the still useful Valentines. On the face of it the possibilities of dealing the Afrika Korps a heavy and possibly lethal blow were thus not as low as might have been expected, though it was a pity that time did not allow Eighth Army to be built up to even greater strength, while Rommel was left to languish at the end of his extended supply lines.

The plan now adopted was basically similar to Auchinleck's earlier attacks – left- and right-handed blows delivered in quick succession – though better co-ordination between them was hoped for and this time XIII Corps would strike first in the south and XXX Corps second in the north. Operational orders were issued on July 17th, instructions for pursuit on the 20th, and for army/air co-operation the following day, just a few hours before the first attack was to go in.

The original plan was for XIII Corps with 1st Armoured Division

Map 18   Auchinleck's final plan for July 22nd–25th

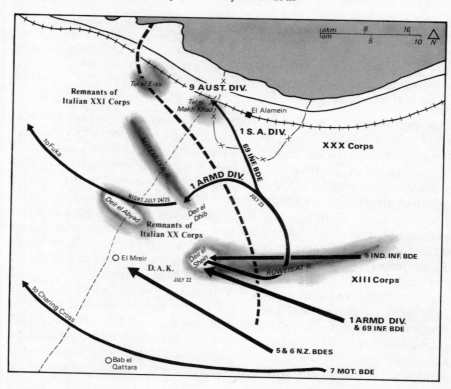

to drive north-westwards into Deir el Shein, Deir el Abyad and El Mreir and thus either scatter the German core of the defence or, more likely, draw in all Rommel's reserves. The timetable called for the New Zealanders and the Indians to be at El Mreir and Deir el Shein respectively by dawn on July 22nd, and in such firm control by the end of the day that the armour could then be released to go north to join XXX Corps on the 23rd, who would attack on the 24th/25th across the south-eastern end of Miteiriya Ridge, break open the rear defences of Rommel's army and allow the 1st Armoured Division to race through for the Fuka bottle-neck. The Motor Brigade of 7th Armoured would converge with it from the south while the armoured cars of the 4th Light Armoured Brigade sped towards Mersa Matruh. Thus even if part of Afrika Korps fought their way back out of the trap, the entire Italian element should be captured.

The whole plan of attack depended upon the close co-operation of the XIII Corps infantry with the armour from the moment the battle began, on the efficient disengagement of the armour immediately that stage was fulfilled (and it would be on a very tight schedule), and on its rapid transfer to the north followed by its equally close co-operation with XXX Corps infantry, some of whom would have opened wide gaps in Rommel's minefields to let the armour through.

In this regard, the *Official History* comments that the opening phase had at least the advantage that it would be under the control of one corps commander, but Kippenberger, whose brigade would provide support for the 6th New Zealanders attacking towards El Mreir, reveals a significant difference between theory and practice:

> I was very unhappy at the divisional conference. Again there was no Corps conference although this was a Corps battle, and we knew only at second hand what the other formations concerned were to do . . . It is essential, and elementary, that such details as starting-time and start-line, axes of advance, objectives, boundaries, lateral communications, artillery support, siting of headquarters, should be co-ordinated, if commanders are to help one another and do the best for their own troops. We knew very little indeed on these points.[8]

The brigadier commanding the supporting armour – newly arrived from Britain – was present at this conference, and although he promised that his armour would be at the right place to protect the infantry at their most perilous time – dawn – he resolutely refused to consider moving his tanks during the hours of darkness. No matter what might have been claimed for the performances of Rommel's panzers (and he gave the impression that he believed all those stories to be gross exaggerations) armour just could not move at night; but the infantry should not worry, for he was quite sure that his tanks would cover the necessary distance before the Germans would be able to mount any worthwhile attack upon them. And nothing that

Kippenberger or Brigadier George Clifton, 6th Brigade, could do or say would make him change his mind. As Gott was not present the New Zealanders had to accept the position, but when Kippenberger returned to his headquarters, he told everybody but his senior staff officer to leave and then dictated the following memo: 'The Brigadier has returned from the divisional conference and says there will be another bloody disaster.'[9]

As an omen to support this sad prognostication, both General Lumsden and Brigadier Briggs of 2nd Armoured Brigade had been wounded on July 18th in a Stuka attack, and Major-General Alec Gatehouse – a veteran of the early desert fighting – brought forward from the Delta where he had been training 10th Armoured Division, did not arrive to take Lumsden's place until the evening of July 20th, far too late for him to make any adjustments to the plans even had he considered them necessary.

And the following day brought yet another set-back to Auchinleck's plans. Ramsden, commanding XXX Corps's sector, had long felt that the South Africans now lacked the necessary aggressiveness and enthusiasm for so strenuous a task as breakthrough and pursuit, in addition to which his relationship with Pienaar left much to be desired. From the first he had therefore suggested and counted upon the Australians for the main burden of the fighting in the north when the XXX Corps break-out commenced, and to this Auchinleck had willingly agreed.

The Commander-in-Chief was therefore considerably dismayed and angered to be met at XXX Corps H.Q. on the afternoon of July 21st by a white-faced Ramsden announcing that General Morshead was objecting to the part his men were expected to undertake on the grounds that they had already played the stormtroops' role in too many actions, and that the plans showed too wide a dispersal of his troops for them to have much chance of success. Morshead had also stated that in his opinion there had already been so many changes in the timings of the attacks as to sow seeds of doubt in his mind as to the clear-sightedness of the planners themselves, and Ramsden added the gratuitous information that he thought Morshead's real reasons for objecting were that the Australians had no faith in the British armour, of whose reputation they had learned from the New Zealanders. He concluded with the announcement that Morshead was insisting upon reference to his Government before further action.

After the months of strain to which Auchinleck had been subjected it is hardly surprising that his first reactions were violent and extreme – he 'went through the roof' according to Ramsden – but he quickly calmed down with the realisation that he could not fight this battle without everybody's co-operation, that Morshead was fully entitled to what he was claiming, and after the events of the last few months could hardly be blamed for doubting assurances from corps or Army commanders with regard to armoured support.

Morshead was invited to 'come for tea' that afternoon, and a polite but tough session of bargaining took place at which it was finally agreed that only one Australian brigade should be employed, that the South Africans would operate on their inner, left flank clearing minefields, and that the British 69th Brigade, which was temporarily under command of 7th Armoured Division, would be brought up from the south at the same time as the armour came up from XIII Corps, and this would precede the armour through the gap and join the Australians for the break-out and pursuit. The three generals then parted, leaving Auchinleck with Dorman-Smith who had been taking notes throughout, and who now announced quite clearly that in his opinion the whole operation was unsound and should be called off.

It would take, in Dorman-Smith's opinion, at least forty-eight hours for 69th Brigade to move from their positions after the XIII Corps attack, up into the Alamein box in order to play their part in the vital break-out – and during that time Rommel would have been able to regroup his forces to meet it; and at this stage there was no time left to put in train elaborate deceptive measures to disguise from Rommel that Auchinleck was shifting his weight.

But military plans seem often to possess a momentum of their own. Perhaps Mr Churchill's exigence was weighing heavily on Auchinleck's mind, while far away to the north Rostov was already under heavy attack, and with its loss the Caucasus would be open to a flood of German armies. After but the slightest pause, Auchinleck shook his head. The operation must go on as now planned.

Just before dusk on the evening of July 21st, a brisk bombardment opened up along the whole length of the front (for the Australians were creating a diversion in the north so as to give XIII Corps as much advantage as possible) and the two XIII Corps infantry divisions – 5th Indian on the right along Ruweisat Ridge aimed at Point 63 and Deir el Shein, New Zealanders on the left coming up first from the south and then swinging left and into El Mreir – began their advance. The flank formations along the inter-divisional boundary would concentrate on gapping the minefields so as to let the supporting armour follow through – 23rd Armoured Brigade with their Valentines supporting the Indians in the north, 2nd Armoured Brigade with their mixed Grants, Stuarts and Crusaders following the New Zealanders. It was a close, moonless night and the thunder of the guns drowned out the crunch of gravel under trucks and carriers, the crash of grenades, the shouts of anger and fear, and the continuous muffled tramp of marching feet.

Then the bombardment ended, the attacking infantry ran clear of the shell-bursts and charged on towards their dawn objectives, taking them both after hard but valiant fighting. By 0500, the three New Zealand battalions and Brigade Headquarters were at their turning-point 2,000 yards east of the El Mreir depression, while 3rd/7th Rajputs were fighting furiously in Deir el Shein and 1st/2nd Punjabs had taken Point 63. Now was the time for the armour to come up, especially as General Nehring – despite the opinion of the new Royal Armoured Corps brigadier – had not thought it necessary to wait until daylight before sending in his panzers and the New Zealanders were under heavy attack by both 5th and 8th Panzer Regiments less than a quarter of an hour after they arrived. Many of their anti-tank guns had been blown up on the minefields as they came through, as had a lorry-load of sticky bombs which might have been of some use in the hands of men as desperate as the New Zealanders then became.

Kippenberger was back at his own Brigade Headquarters, waiting for news of his compatriots:

> Soon after daylight, from wounded and a few stragglers who had got in, it had become clear that there had been another disaster . . . There had been no appearance of the tanks. The German tanks moving in the darkness, and some of them actually following the brigade through gaps in the minefield, had attacked at first light and the survivors, quite helpless, had surrendered . . . There was nothing left of the rifle companies of the Twenty-fourth and Twenty-fifth except one company of the Twenty-fifth which had lost direction and had not reached the depression; little was left of the anti-tank battery and there were heavy losses in transport. Most of Brigade Headquarters was missing with the Brigadier . . . Worst of all, we had again relied in vain on the support of our tanks and bitterness was extreme.[10]

According to the *Official History*, two regiments of the 2nd Armoured Brigade did try to get forward to give aid to the New Zealanders, but one was held up by anti-tank fire and the other ran on to the minefields which had not been properly gapped by the infantry as they went through, for the techniques of minefield gapping had been forgotten since the days of O'Connor.

But one armoured brigade at least was determined to keep its promise of support. At 0800 – three hours after they had been required and without, apparently, a word of warning from anybody watching – the Valentines of 23rd Brigade with their young and unblooded crews formed up, with 40th Royal Tank Regiment on the right and 46th on the left, and attended by a total breakdown of its wireless communications charged forward with all the exultant courage and lack of tactical wisdom of the innocent and unrealistically trained.

10 Bridge across the anti-tank ditch, June 20th, 1942

11 Into Tobruk at last, June 21st, 1942

12 Major-General Bernard Freyberg, V.C., who brought his New Zealanders safely back to El Alamein

13 Auchinleck takes over; behind him his newly appointed Chief of Staff, Major-General 'Chink' Dorman-Smith

For about a mile and a half, they swept forward not unlike a flotilla of destroyers at sea and certainly impelled by the panache of a cavalry charge; but then they came within killing range of the German anti-tank screen whose crews had by then had time to recover from their astonishment at such a scene after three years of war. There was a crash of gunfire, the leading tanks disappeared under a cloud of smoke and sand, the ones immediately following swung around past them and ran straight on to a minefield. Nevertheless, fifteen tanks from 40th Royal Tank Regiment broke through and reached their first objective – to find themselves flanked by anti-tank guns which unhurriedly picked them off; five eventually pulled back into safety. Of 46th Royal Tank Regiment's Valentines, thirteen were lost in the minefield, a few fell back but some pressed onwards after fanning out, disappeared to the west of El Mreir and were never seen again. Within two hours of setting out on its first action, 23rd Armoured Brigade had lost 93 of the 104 Valentines with which it had begun its advance (many had broken down on the way up from the Delta) and over 150 of its officers and men.

In the meantime, 22nd Armoured Brigade, whose task had been to protect the southern flank of the New Zealanders, had been sitting about in front of Howard Kippenberger's 5th Brigade positions, and out in no-man's-land beyond:

> They had several tanks hit and after a while realized they were doing no good and departed. One angry regimental commander saw me and stopped to apologize about the affair. He said that he felt bitterly humiliated but I am afraid that I did not answer very graciously. When they had gone, the charred skeletons of about forty of 6 Brigade's vehicles remained on the sky-line.[11]

The fighting on XIII Corps's front went on for the rest of the day, 5th Indian Division fighting back and forth along Ruweisat Ridge (for with the destruction of 23rd Armoured Brigade they too found themselves attacked by both German armour and Italian artillery) and in the end they were forced back almost to the positions from which they had set out in the morning. And below them along the inter-divisional boundary, the 9th Lancers and the 7th R.T.R. of 2nd Armoured Brigade tried to reach any New Zealanders who might have still been holding out at El Mreir (it seems unlikely there were by that time), lost five more tanks and had to reverse the others back out through the narrow lane in the minefield which was all they had been able to find. Kippenberger's closing comment on the action is understandably bitter, and not wholly unjustified:

> Two infantry and two armoured brigades had been employed. They had made three unrelated attacks from different directions at different times. A single small Panzer division of some twenty or thirty tanks and a fifth-

rate Italian infantry division easily dealt with all three attacks in succession and inflicted crippling losses.[12]

And yet, in one way, the object of this action had been achieved; Rommel's attention had been refocused in the south, his armour had been brought down there and although he had undoubtedly scored a success he would now be off balance for an immediate heavy and determined attack in the north. Although Auchinleck was shaken by the evidence of the inefficiency, the lack of co-ordination and the plain amateurism displayed throughout his army, probably wondering like Wellington whether there was anybody holding a position of responsibility in it who was both willing and professionally competent to carry out his orders, it nevertheless looked as though there was nothing to prevent the overall plan of battle from being carried through.

The Australians had not only leaned hard on the defences (mainly Italian but well 'corseted' by units of 90th Light) around Tel el Eisa, but they had broken out across Tel el Makh Khad in very tough fighting indeed during which one of the private soldiers won a posthumous Victoria Cross, and by nightfall were pushing towards Ruin Ridge on the southern side of Miteiriya. As the defences had been unexpectedly stubborn the advance was running late, and it was early evening before fifty-two Valentines from 1st Army Tank Brigade, which had been waiting in close attendance for most of the day, were on their start line ready to go forward on the last stage, carrying infantry and engineers to deal with mines on the way.

It was thus nearly 1900 before they set off, to run very quickly on to an unknown minefield in which some twenty tanks were put out of action, after which they became lost in the dark, found a ridge with a ruin on it which they quite understandably believed to be their objective, decanted their infantry, waited to give support to the next battalion to come through, after which they withdrew leaving the infantry to dig in on the reverse slope. It was not until the following morning that it became obvious that in the darkness they had stopped some 2,500 to 3,000 yards short of their objective, and that beyond the Australian infantry now lay a line of well-sited German positions with at least twenty guns well dug in amongst them. There was nothing they could do now but wait until the reinforcements arrived from the south.

This was the position at dawn on July 23rd; no further large-scale attack would be launched until midnight July 26th/27th and thus for eighty-four hours the defenders, already strongly positioned in front of the Australians, were able to sow more mines, dig in more guns and fill the gaps in their ranks from replacement units which, although not 'fit for tropical service' yet, were all thoroughly imbued

with basic German Army doctrine, and had been trickling into the
lines over the past few days at an ever-quickening pace.

The only misjudgment in Dorman-Smith's warning had been an
under-estimate of the time the armour and extra infantry would take
to come up.

The sad story of the last July attack is quickly told.

All through July 26th a heavy sandstorm cloaked the battle area
but despite this the South Africans did not begin gapping the
minefield south-east of Miteiriya until darkness, and by midnight
there was still no clear way through. Soon after midnight, 24th
Australian Brigade launched their attack towards Ruin Ridge and by
0300 had at last taken the south-eastern end of Miteiriya Ridge, at
which they swung right towards the break-out area expecting the
Durhams and East Yorks of 69th Brigade to come up on the left and
drive towards Deir el Dhib. These had been delayed by the uncleared
minefields behind and arrived late, and were then further delayed by
the necessity to clear more mines themselves as they fought their way
forward – and their technique was faulty. Carriers, trucks and men
were blown up in a chaos of explosion and disorder, but by 0800 the
bulk of the men of 69th Brigade were at Deir el Dhib, with the
Australians slightly ahead of them on their right.

But missing from the 69th Brigade's ranks were the anti-tank gun
flank screens who had all lost their way in the darkness, some being
blown up and only one arriving at dawn within a mile of the men they
were intended to protect. Needless to say, their predicament was
quickly appreciated by 90th Light, who moved in, first of all by
themselves and then supported by one of the reconnaissance
battalions whose heavy armoured cars and light panzers, unopposed
by either anti-tank guns or tanks, easily overran the unprotected
British infantry and began rounding them up.

On this occasion at least, the British armour cannot be accused of
not trying to help. Enough obloquy had been poured on the men of
2nd Armoured Brigade – and indeed on all those who wore the black
beret – during the preceding weeks for them to be very eager to
recover their reputations; but tanks which run on to uncleared
minefields blow up, and there is nothing the crews can do but bale out
as quickly as possible. The minefields in those crucial gaps had been
immeasurably thickened during the eighty-four hours' grace given to
the defenders, and neither the South Africans nor the British had the
time, the men or the expertise to lift them.

Three Grants blew up within a few minutes of 6th R.T.R. starting
through, while behind the Australians the faithful Valentines of 50th
R.T.R. pressed on despite much greater losses, for they were
endeavouring to take the Australians' heavier supporting weapons up

with them. But they lost thirteen Valentines before they eventually fought their way through to the last known positions of the 2nd/28th Battalion in front – to find that these had been completely overrun and even the prisoners had been marched away.

The same fate had by noon overtaken the two 69th Brigade battalions – 6th Durham Light Infantry and 5th East Yorks – whose casualties were even higher than the Australians, with the result that the brigade was taken out of the line. By the time Ramsden, with Auchinleck's agreement, called the battle off, the Eighth Army had lost yet another thousand men and over thirty tanks – and if such figures seemed small compared with the losses during *Crusader* and the Gazala battles, the trouble was that Eighth Army could no longer afford them.

By July 28th, the Alamein front was quiescent – on Rommel's side, so it afterwards became clear, because he was short of ammunition; on Auchinleck's side, because he was short of men. The July fighting had produced one success and one failure for each of them. Auchinleck had halted Rommel's drive to the Nile – but the Afrika Korps was still in existence and Auchinleck dared not transfer any of his men to the northern front.

During the following twenty-four hours, Dorman-Smith completed an analysis of the situation throughout the Middle East with re-commendations for a thorough reorganisation of the Army, and having read it through and agreed to it, Auchinleck sent off his regular report to Whitehall, containing the sentence, 'We must therefore remain temporarily on the defensive and recruit our strength for a new and decisive effort.'

This, he added, was not likely to become possible before the middle of September. It was not a forecast to find much favour with the Prime Minister.

5 · *Churchill Intervenes*

It had seemed at the immediate moment an especially cruel stroke of Fate that Mr Churchill should have been with Mr Roosevelt when the news came through that Tobruk had fallen. They had been drawing up a programme of talks and discussions in Washington when General Marshall, American Chief of Army Staff, had entered the President's office with a telegram which, after glancing at it, Roosevelt handed without a word to the Prime Minister.

'Tobruk has surrendered', it read, 'with twenty-five thousand men taken prisoner.'

It was, Churchill later wrote, one of the heaviest blows he was to receive during the war, not only because it exposed the emptiness of the assurances he had lately received from Auchinleck that there was no intention of allowing Tobruk to be isolated, let alone captured, but by its reflection upon the fighting capabilities of the British forces. Only four months before, eighty-five thousand men had surrendered to an inferior Japanese force at Singapore and this melancholy repetition seemed to cast doubt upon the British will to fight; it was indeed a bitter moment, and he was not to know then that thousands of miles away the men being marched towards their prison-camps were feeling the disgrace as keenly as he was.

The kindness now extended to him by Mr Roosevelt and his advisers stands as a landmark in human generosity and compassion. 'What can we do to help?' was the first question the President asked, and with its answer put in train movements which were to send three hundred Sherman tanks and a hundred self-propelled 105mm. guns in six fast American ships to the Suez Canal. This extraordinary gesture of faith was even more remarkable in that the tanks had just been issued to American armoured divisions who had until then been training on obsolete equipment, and they had now to be withdrawn . . . and an argument that they would better serve the Allied cause by being left where they were would have been hard to counter.

But there are, incredibly, advantages to be drawn even from so unpromising a situation as that in which Churchill now found himself.

He had flown to Washington in order to accomplish two tasks. (This was the first time so important a personage had ever flown the Atlantic; it had taken nearly twenty-seven hours and before he had left, Mr Churchill had advised the King that in the event of his death on the journey, His Majesty should entrust the formation of a new government to Anthony Eden.) The first task had been to agree joint United States and British co-operation in the development of an atomic bomb, and the second was to try to persuade both the President and his advisers that an attempt to invade France across the English Channel was an impracticability in 1942, perhaps even in 1943, and that a more advantageous project would be a joint Anglo-American invasion of North Africa. This would be just possible in the time and with the shipping available, and it would also threaten Rommel from the rear and thus help to make not only Egypt but also the essential Middle East oil safe – at least from attack from the west.

American opinion at this time was focused on the need to help Russia which they felt overrode any possible requirements of the Eighth Army, and the most direct way to do that – and incidentally to finish the war rather more quickly than the British seemed to think possible – would be by a direct strike through France aimed at the heart of Hitler's Reich; and American optimism and confidence would brook no arguments that at least the first part of that programme, *Operation Sledgehammer*, to put a force of six divisions across the Channel, could not be achieved by the end of 1942. They were unimpressed by British warnings that the English Channel was most unlikely to provide weather calm enough for a large-scale operation at any time after September, unwilling to accept that even American technology and industry could not produce in time the necessary shipping and landing-craft for such a task, and frankly disbelieving when it was suggested that the defenders of Hitler's *Festung Europa* were both brave and competent enough to fling an American assault force back into the sea within hours of its attempt to land.

Now the fall of Tobruk focused all attention on the Middle East, simply by the apparent scale of the catastrophe. Military opinion in Cairo and perhaps elsewhere might argue the unimportance of the fortress from a tactical point of view, but public opinion throughout the world from Berlin to Washington was solid in its belief that the fall of Tobruk constituted the most telling blow to British and Allied prestige in three years of war, and in Washington they knew something must be done quickly to retrieve it. And logistic calculations would probably demonstrate that if shipping were used to take men and weapons to the Middle East in worthwhile numbers, there would be too little left to build up American forces in Britain for an early cross-Channel operation. It says a great deal for the good nature of George

Marshall, who was firmly set upon *Operation Sledgehammer*, that he did not allow this development in any way to sour his relations with the British.

To Mr Churchill, therefore, the last days of June 1942 were packed with contradictory emotions – humiliation at the military débâcle, flooding gratitude for American generosity, relief that an operation which in his own opinion and that of his advisers would be doomed to disaster was now less likely to be pressed.

But there were, of course, other dangers. If the events in the desert had weakened General Marshall's case for a cross-Channel operation, it had strengthened the hand of Admiral Ernest J. King, Chief of the Naval Staff and Commander-in-Chief of the U.S. Navy, who felt that the right strategy for his country was to turn its back for the moment on Europe and concentrate all available forces in the Pacific. For him, the Japanese were the chief enemy and Hitler could wait . . . even if this entailed the subjugation of Great Britain and the destruction of the British Empire. Fortunately, Roosevelt had little or no sympathy with this attitude, and wished – especially in view of forthcoming Congressional elections – that American troops should be in combat with German forces before the end of the year. Events seemed to indicate North Africa as the only possible theatre – but all Churchill's persuasiveness would be needed before it was certain and he had to return home before a decision was reached.

There were, of course, even more problems at home for him to face. In democracies, the position of a war-time leader is obviously affected by military events, and the run of desert defeats had brought a ground-swell of political dissatisfaction to the surface, resulting in a by-election defeat for his Government, and the proposal of a motion in the House of Commons, reading, 'That this House, while paying tribute to the heroism and endurance of the Armed Forces of the Crown in circumstances of exceptional difficulty, has no confidence in the central direction of the war.'[1]

This was the political situation which confronted Mr Churchill upon his return to England on June 27th, the problem which had to be resolved first.

'This is Tobruk,' he had said glumly when told of the by-election defeat, but doleful prognostications from Sir Stafford Cripps about the vote of No Confidence he would face in the House were dismissed with some contempt.

'You can't run a war as if you were in a laboratory,' Churchill growled at some of the complaints which Cripps suggested would be brought against him, and his faith, not only in public support but in his own powers to persuade and control Parliament, were fully justified when after a superb speech at the end of the two-day debate the motion was defeated by 475 votes to 25.

But it had all taken up valuable time and energy, and would not have occurred had Eighth Army held Rommel at Gazala; if, in Mr Churchill's opinion, Auchinleck had either been in command from the beginning or had taken command much earlier than he did.

Even after his parliamentary success there were other large matters to divert the Prime Minister's attention temporarily from events in Egypt. As the figures for shipping losses in the Battle of the Atlantic ('The only thing which really frightened me during the war,' as he was afterwards to write) came in, they revealed that over 400,000 tons had been lost in the early days of July and that of one 35-ship convoy to Murmansk, U-boats had sunk 24; and in Russia itself, the great German drive towards the Don and the Caucasus had begun. Stalin's demands for a Second Front grew every day more strident and abusive, and soon their effect upon Washington became only too evident. On July 18th, General Marshall, Admiral King and the President's friend and close adviser Mr Harry Hopkins arrived in London, and after a brief colloquy with the American Service Chiefs there (Generals Eisenhower, Clark and Spaatz, and Admiral Stark) took up again with the British the arguments for *Operation Sledgehammer*.

Their instructions from Mr Roosevelt (although of course Churchill did not know this at the time) were to fight as hard as they could for *Sledgehammer* in 1942, for in the case of a Russian collapse Mr Roosevelt considered the operation imperative, but if they could make no headway against British opposition, then they were to 'determine upon another place for U.S. troops to fight in 1942'.

In this regard, they were to consider such factors as the effect upon the Allied War Effort of the loss of Egypt and the Suez Canal, the loss of Syria and the Mosul oil-wells, the loss of the Persian Gulf and access to Persian oil – and the concomitant risks of German occupation of the whole of the northern coast of Africa and much of its western coastline as well.

You will determine the best methods of holding the Middle East. These methods include definitely either or both of the following:
(a) Sending aid and ground forces to the Persian Gulf, to Syria and to Egypt.
(b) a new operation in Morocco and Algeria intended to drive in against the back door of Rommel's armies. The attitude of French colonial troops is still in doubt.

And the President's directive ended:

Please remember three cardinal principles – speed of decision on plans, unity of plans, attack combined with defence but not defence alone. This

affects the immediate objective of U.S. ground forces against Germans in
1942.

I hope for total agreement within one week of your arrival.

FRANKLIN D. ROOSEVELT
Commander-in-Chief[2]

In support of Mr Churchill in the arguments which then ensued
were his own Chiefs of Staff of whom Sir Alan Brooke as Chief of the
Imperial General Staff was spokesman, and for three days the
arguments for and against *Sledgehammer* were wearily repeated.
Against the American statement that an immediate cross-Channel
operation would be the best way of helping Russia by drawing
westward a large part of the Luftwaffe, the British argued its impracticability.

Even if the minimum required force of six divisions was ready and
waiting to go at that moment (and everybody agreed that this was not
so) it was doubtful if the landing-craft would be ready by September
which was the latest date at which reasonable sea conditions might
still be expected. And in the extremely unlikely event of American
optimism in the matter proving justified – how would the six divisions
be fed and supplied throughout a winter when they would be under
attack by German troops still confident of eventual victory?

In the British view, even if six divisions could be put afloat on the
Channel before the end of the year, they would inevitably be lost,
perhaps at sea, and if not, then either during the landing operations
themselves or at some time during the following winter; and as hour
followed hour, it became evident to the Americans that nothing they
could say would change that opinion. There was an exchange of
cables with Washington on July 22nd and 23rd, and then to Churchill's
enormous relief, an acceptance by Roosevelt that there could be no
Sledgehammer that autumn, followed by instructions to his rep-
resentatives to plan for an 'expanded *Gymnast*' – a series of landings
in North Africa which would include British troops as well as
Americans, with the British taking the greater risk of landing inside
the Mediterranean at Algiers and accepting the danger of the Axis
closing the Straits of Gibraltar behind them.

Overjoyed, Churchill christened the expanded operation *Torch*
and set about agreeing details of the composition of the ground, air
and naval forces to be engaged. General Eisenhower would be
Supreme Commander with a combined Anglo-American Staff, and
Churchill suggested that the Deputy Commander should be the
British General Sir Harold Alexander. Commanding the British
task force should be Lieutenant-General Sir Bernard Law Montgomery, who at that moment was commanding troops in south-east
England.

With all these vital matters at last agreed and in train, the Prime Minister could turn his mind to what was still the only active theatre in which the armies of the Western Allies were engaged, the desert.

As has already been related, the Prime Minister's high and romantic hopes for sweeping victories once Auchinleck had replaced Wavell in June 1941 had been quickly dashed, and within but a few weeks Churchill had been wondering if the change he had insisted upon had been the right one. His admiration for his new nominee consequently plummeted, and was not increased by Auchinleck's steadfast rejection of his own recommendation for command of the Eighth Army during *Crusader*, Maitland Wilson, and the appointment of Cunningham instead. (Churchill seemed to have a prejudice in favour of Green Jackets or, as they have lately become known, the 'Black Mafia' – as had Anthony Eden who had served with the 60th Rifles during the First World War; Wilson's original regiment had been the Rifle Brigade.) And Cunningham's performance during *Crusader* had done nothing to increase Churchill's confidence in Auchinleck's judgment.

But at least *Crusader* had been a victory (once Cunningham had been replaced) and had eventually moved the flags on Mr Churchill's War Map a satisfactory distance in the right direction; and Mr Churchill was sufficiently realistic and magnanimous to repress his disappointment when Rommel's riposte swept the desert army back so soon to Gazala.

But by March his impatience had been proving stronger than his sympathy, and cables flew between Whitehall and Cairo opening further a rift between the two men, despite the fact that each was to retain a high regard for the other. This regard, however, did not curb Churchill's language, and Sir Alan Brooke had had on many occasions to use all his cajolery to persuade the Prime Minister to remove such phrases as 'Soldiers are meant to fight!' and 'Armies are not intended to stand about doing nothing!' and clothe his vehemence in more diplomatic words.

Auchinleck's blank refusal during March and April to consider an early attempt to retake at least the nearer airfields in Cyrenaica had especially infuriated Churchill, whose historic terms of office at the Admiralty had given him a particular affection for the Royal Navy and its associations.

'The bloody man doesn't seem to care about the fate of Malta,' he exploded. 'Anyway, we can't settle this by writing letters'[3] – and he had requested Auchinleck to come to London for further discussion.

This invitation, for what he doubtless considered adequate reasons, Auchinleck declined – and the Prime Minister's first reaction was to suggest Auchinleck's immediate replacement by the general then serving as Governor-General of Gibraltar; and when Brooke and the other senior military advisers stood firm against this, Churchill relapsed into a state of bottled anger which found vent many years later in his memoirs, when he accused Auchinleck of refusing to come to London because it would be easier for him to reject Churchill's reasonable demands from Cairo than in Whitehall.

Matters between them had thus become increasingly strained during April, and by early May Churchill's eagerness for offensive action having at last been matched by Brooke's and that of the other Chiefs of Staff, Auchinleck had been sent a cable which was in effect a demand upon him either to attack Rommel at Gazala in the near future or to resign his command. A few days then passed while Whitehall awaited the reply, and when Auchinleck's agreement came to attack in early June, Churchill's relieved response contained the sentence, 'I should personally feel even greater confidence if you took over direct command yourself as in fact you had to do at Sidi Rezegh.'[4]

The outcome of this seemingly reasonable request reveals the wide divergence in view between the impulsive, romantic Prime Minister in London and the professional Commander-in-Chief in the Middle East.

Churchill looked upon the desert as a battleground upon which military glory was to be won by the defeat of a famous corps under a brilliant general – the victory then to provide Eighth Army with a springboard from which to seize North Africa, reunite Great Britain with at least a part of that world of France which he so passionately admired, and then from the Tunisian coastline to threaten Sicily, to invade Italy and thus to attack the main enemy 'up through the soft underbelly of Europe'.

But to Auchinleck (and to Wavell before him) the desert was nothing but the western flank of a theatre of war extending from Afghanistan, via Persia and Iraq (which had reverted to Middle East Command in January 1942), Syria, Palestine, Egypt and Libya as far as Cyrenaica, to which the greatest menace lay on the north-western flank through which might break German armies driving down through the Caucasus towards the essential Persian oil-fields. To both Commanders-in-Chief, the conflict in Libya was a tangential affair to be conducted by subordinates, while they themselves kept their eyes firmly on the main area of threat between the Black Sea and the Caspian. As a result, Auchinleck's reply to the Prime Minister's request contained the paragraph:

Much as I would like to take command personally in Libya I feel that it would not be the right course to pursue. I have considered the possibility most carefully and have concluded that it would be most difficult for me to keep a right sense of proportion if I became immersed in tactical problems in Libya.[5]

It was this last phrase which particularly stuck in Churchill's gullet. He did not regard the conflict with the Afrika Korps as a 'tactical problem in Libya' and according to his physician, Sir Charles Wilson, he twice spat the phrase out with great scorn.

'Rommel! Rommel!' he had raved. 'What matters but beating Rommel?'

And the events of June and July, once they had occurred, had seemed to justify his more narrow perspective. Now, at the end of the month which had seen the halting of Rommel's offensive, the decision for *Torch* and his political victory in the House of Commons, he felt he had time to review the whole situation in the Middle East and make any necessary adjustments to guard against further defeat and disaster.

He had already agreed that Sir Alan Brooke should go out to Cairo at the end of July in order to carry out his own investigation as to what had gone wrong, and with the news of another developing stalemate and the suspicion that soon he would be presented with arguments to the effect that several more weeks must elapse before another offensive against Rommel could be launched, Churchill decided that he would go out too. He felt in any case that it was now his own unpleasant duty personally to inform Stalin that there would be no Second Front in Europe that year to lift pressure off the Russian armies, and to try to convince him that an October invasion of North Africa, especially if preceded by a resounding victory in Egypt to sway the loyalties of the French and thus give the Americans a perhaps rapid and bloodless route through Algeria and Tunisia towards Sicily and Italy, would go far to rectify the omission.

Cairo would be a half-way stop en route to Moscow.

Churchill and the C.I.G.S. travelled by separate routes to Cairo – Brooke via Gibraltar and Malta, Churchill in an American Liberator which also called at Gibraltar but then made a long sweep south across the Sahara to reach the Nile at Beni Suef, and then fly north to land at one of the Cairo airfields. Nevertheless, they arrived within half an hour of each other just after dawn on Monday, August 3rd, and a few hours later Churchill was installed in an air-conditioned room in the British Embassy in Cairo, exhilarated by movement, travel and the sense of being 'the man on the spot'. He knew he was right to be there; at Gibraltar he had learned of Auchinleck's latest report containing the declaration that no further offensive action could be taken in the desert until mid-September, which would not suit at all. Even were such action spectacularly successful, time would be required for its impact on the French in North Africa to affect their attitude to *Torch* – more time than that between mid-September and the end of October, which was the present target date for the Anglo-American invasion.

The Middle East Command must be spurred to greater efforts, and if necessary sweeping changes made; and in this respect he was greatly heartened by the arrival in time for lunch of his old enemy and now great friend, the South African Prime Minister Jan Smuts, who had flown up from Pretoria. Churchill hated sacking people however much they might have deserved it; Smuts had a quality of ruthlessness which would support him if and when the knife had to be wielded. He had also a sharp tongue and an abrasive wit which added to the gaiety of lunch and left everyone in fine fettle for the labours of the evening – for Mr Churchill was a great believer in the benefits of afternoon sleep, and would not be available again before five o'clock.

It was in fact six o'clock before work commenced, when Sir Alan Brooke arrived at the Embassy from G.H.Q. with Auchinleck who had come back from the front for the meeting. It was the first time Prime Minister and Commander-in-Chief had met since the latter's appointment just over a year before and many differences had occurred between them since; but each could still appreciate the other's great qualities. It was not, however, a meeting to please Churchill for it was quickly evident that nothing he could say would change Auchinleck's opinion that the Eighth Army could not be ready to launch a major attack for at least six weeks; and for the moment Churchill did not feel inclined to reveal the plans for operations at the other end of the Mediterranean and the resultant political factors which made an earlier desert victory so desirable. In any case, he doubted whether Auchinleck would be swayed much by such considerations.

But when the meeting broke up and during the dinner which followed, Mr Churchill pondered the next moves; and at midnight he sent again for the C.I.G.S. Upon one point Brooke and Churchill were now in agreement – that Auchinleck's place was in Cairo and not at the front, and that a competent and energetic general must quickly be appointed to command the army in the field. It would seem, from everything Mr Churchill had heard, that the most distinguished, most highly thought of general in the area was Strafer Gott who, as Mr Churchill pointed out, 'had not earned the title "Strafer" by nothing'. Gott was also, though this does not seem to have been mentioned at the time, a Green Jacket, his original regiment being the King's Royal Rifle Corps (60th Rifles).

Mr Churchill, however, had never met General Gott, and from what Brooke had heard it seemed likely that Gott, after so long in the desert, might be rather tired. Brooke suggested instead that General Montgomery should be transferred from the *Torch* Task Force to take over Eighth Army, but to this Mr Churchill objected on the grounds that instant action was required and Gott was already in Egypt whereas Montgomery was back in England; perhaps a better solution would be for Sir Alan Brooke himself to take over Eighth Army – a suggestion which tempted the C.I.G.S. most damnably, but which upon deep reflection he forced himself to refuse. During eight months of often excoriating nervous strain he had managed to learn some of the techniques by which his turbulent master could most easily be handled, and he felt that he would thus serve both the army and his country best by staying where he was. It was nearly two o'clock in the morning, after a long and eventful day, before either of them got to bed.

Not surprisingly the Prime Minister, never an early riser by choice, was not seen during the following morning; lunch was again spent in relaxed but invigorating company (they were joined by General Wavell who had flown over from India) but at six o'clock Churchill presided at a meeting of the most authoritative British and Commonwealth personalities in the area – Brooke, Auchinleck, Wavell, Smuts, Admiral Harwood and Air Marshal Tedder, and the Minister of State for the Middle East, Mr Richard Casey. For nearly three hours they discussed the situation throughout the entire Middle East Command, but even when Churchill revealed the Anglo-American plans and explained the political necessity for an early and spectacular desert victory, Auchinleck remained obstinate in his declaration that the Eighth Army could not launch a major attack for at least six weeks. Mr Churchill was very ill content.

The meeting broke up in time for dinner, but afterwards Churchill talked again into the night with Brooke. The C.I.G.S. still pressed Montgomery as the preferred choice for Eighth Army commander, reinforcing his argument with evidence he had collected that Gott really was tired, and adding another of his day's discoveries – that despite some old antagonisms between Auchinleck and Montgomery, Auchinleck was nevertheless prepared to accept Montgomery as his commander in the field.

But Churchill would not agree and became a trifle testy. Gott was on the spot and could take over within days, Montgomery was three thousand miles away – and while such matters as changes in command were being discussed, why was no more important task being found for Maitland Wilson than command of a virtually unemployed army up in Syria, and occasional chairmanship of Boards of Inquiry?

Fortunately for Brooke, visits to the front were scheduled for the following day and even Mr Churchill would have to rise by 0445 – so argument did not continue long and they were in bed by one o'clock in the morning; though the unfortunate C.I.G.S. did note that as a 59-year-old professional soldier he was already feeling the strain of four days and nights of incessant travel and argument in hot, humid and thoroughly unfamiliar conditions, whereas the 68-year-old Prime Minister seemed to be more and more in his element.

They flew up to Burg el Arab at first light the following morning, and Sir Charles Wilson who accompanied them wrote in his diary:

> Very early this morning the P.M. drove with Auchinleck to his head-quarters behind the Ruweisat Ridge. There, in a kind of wire cage, we breakfasted with some men burnt brown by the desert sun. There were flies everywhere. When they were disturbed they rose in a cloud with a buzzing sound.[6]

However admirable Auchinleck's determination to endure the same discomforts as his troops, these conditions were not such as to recommend him to Churchill, and the subsequent session of argument with Auchinleck and his equally unyielding Chief of Staff, the enigmatic and (as Churchill discovered) unpopular Dorman-Smith, in a hot, cramped caravan, with desks and maps covered with sand and no air-conditioning or even an efficient fan to clear away his cigar-smoke, did nothing to ease the discontent. Nothing Churchill could say seemed to make the slightest impression upon these two determined, self-contained, assured professional soldiers who kept him stiffly at a distance, replied to his exhortations with cold facts and figures, and remained unmoved by his pleas. Coolly (despite the conditions in the caravan) and politely (though once or twice there was a gleam in Dorman-Smith's eyes which may have betokened a sardonic reply trembling on his tongue), they rebutted every argument with logistics, every call to action with lists of ration strengths and reinforcement tables.

And in the end, thoroughly displeased, he had to leave.

However, he did cause them some slight inconvenience, for Auchinleck had called a Corps Commanders' Conference for later that morning but Churchill upset this by insisting that Gott accompany him on the journey back to Burg el Arab for lunch with the R.A.F., as he wished to talk with the famous desert warrior.

He arrived in somewhat better mood. Gott had impressed him, and had himself been affected by the Prime Minister's enthusiasms. He had admitted that after so many years away from home he was looking forward to leave – about three months would be very acceptable – but in the circumstances he knew that this was impossible, and if Mr Churchill felt that he was capable of fulfilling satisfactorily the onerous duties required of the Commander of the Eighth Army, then he would willingly accept them. To both Mr Churchill and Sir Charles Wilson, Gott appeared to possess both the physical attributes and also the reserves of mental and spiritual strength to carry out the job.

The reception at Burg el Arab improved the occasion. Here was no wire cage filled with flies, no imprisonment in heat and sand; here was an open beach cooled by Mediterranean breezes, white napery, gleaming silver, brandy in goblets, and in due course (it had been delayed by mechanical breakdown en route) an excellent luncheon sent out from Shepheard's Hotel. Here also from the Air Force officers, all of group captain's rank and above, was confirmation of many of Churchill's beliefs. Here, as Sir Charles Wilson wrote that night:

> It is a new atmosphere. These men have not taken a bad knock; they are on top and know that they are on top. In an impersonal war of millions they remain individuals. These fellows were not groomed in a mess before the war. Their thoughts are not borrowed from others and their speech is forthright. They are critical of the Army, they say what is in their minds without batting an eyelid . . . Certainly the Army's shortcomings were set forth succinctly. It is not to them that one will look for a recommendation for mercy when the Commander-in-Chief stands in the dock . . . As we retraced our steps towards Cairo at the end of the day, the P.M. remained sunk in his own thoughts. He did not speak once, but I have a feeling that it is all settled.[7]

There seems to be no record of what exactly the R.A.F. officers said at that undoubtedly portentous lunch-time session, but some indication was provided many years later when Lord Tedder's memoirs were published. In a letter written at that time to his superior at home, Air Marshal Portal, he had written:

> The difference between those Army meetings and [our own] meetings is the difference between a funeral breakfast and a wedding breakfast. There's no life about them. Too many old men and 'nice chaps'. As Auck. remarked to me, the Army is suffering from 'good fellows'.
> Some commander should have been shot after the bolt from Agedabia. I wish he [Auchinleck] was a better judge of character and more ruthless in judging people solely by results. I also wish he had the ability to inspire the Army here. I am afraid he hasn't.[8]

Undoubtedly, Mr Churchill had a great deal to ponder on his way back to Cairo on the evening of August 5th, 1942.

That evening was spent quietly, and to the surprise of some people, Mr Churchill, although he had obviously been excited by the day's travel and sight-seeing, was not particularly talkative and wished to retire quite early to bed. But the following morning he burst into Sir Alan Brooke's bedroom while the latter was still dressing with the announcement that his thoughts had taken shape during the night, and that after breakfast he and Brooke would thrash them out.

The Desert Army needed a new commander, and a change in Commander-in-Chief would also bring in new ideas and new blood –

a point which Auchinleck had himself suggested over a month before when, at the nadir of British fortunes immediately after the fall of Tobruk, he had offered his resignation should Whitehall have lost confidence in him. But Churchill had not wished to remove Auchinleck then, and did not wish to do so now – but he had thought of a new solution to all their problems which would keep the best men in responsible positions, and side-step the failures. This solution he now explained to the C.I.G.S.

The chief complaint Churchill had against Auchinleck was his preoccupation with the northern front at the expense of the war in the desert – and he accepted that this was a preoccupation which, in Brooke's opinion and those of the other Chiefs of Staff, was thoroughly justified. Very well, perhaps the oil at the head of the Persian Gulf was more important than Egypt, but nevertheless Rommel must be beaten – and beaten sooner than Auchinleck thought possible.

Therefore Auchinleck must be allowed to concentrate wholly upon the front which he considered most important, and another Commander-in-Chief appointed to take over the area in which the battle against Rommel was being fought. In effect, Churchill proposed to split the present Middle East Command into two – Near East and Middle East. The new Near East Command, extending only as far east as the Canal, would have a new Commander-in-Chief and a new Army Commander under him, while Auchinleck would command the new Middle East theatre consisting of Syria, Palestine, Persia and Iraq, with whoever could be agreed by mutual consent commanding the forces there.

As for personalities, why shouldn't Brooke stay in Cairo as Commander-in-Chief, and as he seemed to favour Montgomery as Eighth Army commander, very well, Montgomery could be sent out as quickly as possible and someone else be found for Force Commander for *Torch*? To the Prime Minister, elated by success and inspiration, it all looked perfect.

It did not look so good to Brooke, and a long day's tactful manoeuvring to change some of the Prime Minister's ideas ensued. Much though he would have liked to accept the post of Commander-in-Chief, Brooke still felt the best service he could render his country was to stay at Churchill's side; moreover, he would not like Auchinleck to think that he had come out to Egypt to supersede him. And another point at issue was the detail of the division of the commands, for in Brooke's opinion the Suez Canal would make a very poor inter-command boundary.

Mr Churchill did not take too kindly to these blocks to his flow of inspiration, and his temper was thus somewhat uncertain at a morning meeting with some of the G.H.Q. staff; he was especially short with one of Auchinleck's favourite staff officers, Lieutenant-General Corbett, who a few days previously had been undiplomatic enough to inform Churchill that he himself had already been briefed to take over command of Eighth Army. He was soon to regret his temerity for when at the end of a day's discussions and bargaining a long telegram was sent to the War Cabinet in London, the suggested changes in command were as follows:

1 General Auchinleck to be offered the post of C-in-C of the new Middle East command.
2 General Alexander to relinquish the appointment of Deputy Commander, *Torch* and become C-in-C. of the new Near East Command.
3 General Montgomery to succeed General Alexander as Deputy Commander, *Torch*.
4 General Gott to command Eighth Army under Alexander.
5 General Corbett to be relieved of his appointment.
6 General Ramsden to be relieved of his command of XXX Corps.
7 General Dorman-Smith to be relieved of his appointment.[9]

Eighth Army would require two more corps commanders, but these choices could be made when the more senior appointments had been agreed.

The following morning (August 7th) was spent quietly, recovering to some extent from the previous day's travails and awaiting the War Cabinet's reply which arrived about noon. They agreed the changes in personnel but questioned, as had Brooke, the dividing line between the two new commands; and they were quite firmly of the opinion that the term Middle East Command must be retained for Egypt and the Western Desert. Whatever else the new command should be called, in the public mind 'Middle East' included the area of the present battleground and it would be unwise to change this.

But these were minor points, and were quickly dealt with. Confirmatory telegrams were despatched, key personnel sent for and for a few hours it seemed that all would now progress smoothly and Mr Churchill's plans for a new command structure, with the key positions held by the men in whom he felt most confidence, would be fulfilled. But then fate took a hand.

That afternoon, as Gott was flying back from the front to take up the reins of his new command, the Bombay aircraft in which he was travelling was attacked by German fighters and forced down. Despite the fact that it was on the ground and burning, the fighters attacked again and again and only three members of the crew, a medical orderly and one passenger – already wounded – escaped. General Gott and sixteen other passengers all perished in the flames, and by eleven o-clock that evening Churchill had been informed that he must choose again.

Whether or not his tiredness would have prevented Gott from making a first-class commander for Eighth Army, whether or not he possessed the intellectual abilities for such a post, his death affected the army – and indeed the personnel of the whole Middle East Command – in the same way as had that of Jock Campbell. He was the last of the legendary figures from the early days of the desert war, the days of 'Wavell's Thirty Thousand'. Those days were now gone and a new era was heralded.

That night a cable was sent to Whitehall asking that General Montgomery be sent out by special aircraft at the earliest possible moment to take command, under General Alexander, of the Eighth Army. As he was to play so vital a part in the remainder of the Middle East campaign and the eventual defeat of Afrika Korps it will be as well to try to find out what kind of man, and soldier, he was.

Lientenant-General Sir Bernard Law Montgomery was at the time of his appointment to command Eighth Army some three months short of his fifty-fifth birthday, and had spent most of his time on earth as a non-conformist.

This would seem at first sight somewhat unexpected, for he came of unblemished 'establishment' stock, his paternal grandfather being Sir Robert Montgomery, Commissioner of Lahore at the outbreak of the Indian Mutiny and as a result of the absence in Kashmir of the Chief Commissioner, Sir John Lawrence, virtually in command of the Punjab throughout those early, crucial days. His immediate disarming of the Native Infantry Regiments in the vicinity undoubtedly saved great bloodshed, for they were later proved to have been deeply involved in the planning of the rebellion; this example of swift thought and direct action would be echoed in some of his grandson's more ebullient achievements.

His mother's father was the celebrated Dean Farrar whose best known work was the novel *Eric, or Little by Little*, which in its Victorian heyday rivalled *Tom Brown's Schooldays* as a popular call to manliness, cold baths, the straight bat and a spirit of collaboration with the Almighty made easier by the unassailable tenet that He was an Englishman. One of Dean Farrar's curates was Henry Montgomery, Bernard's father, who later became Bishop of Tasmania (Bernard spent the years between his second and fourteenth birthdays there), ending his service to the Church as Secretary for the Propagation of the Gospel in Foreign Parts, Prelate of the Order of St Michael and St George (of which he wore the insignia of the Knight's Grand Cross), Prebendary of St Paul's Cathedral and a favoured preacher to the Royal Family.

From such a stock one would have expected orthodox attitudes, acceptance of one's place in the hierarchy and unquestioning obedience to authority, all contained in an ethical macedoine with muscular Christianity, strenuous physical activity and not a great deal of mental concentration.

But Montgomery's mother was a remarkable woman who had become engaged to her father's curate at the age of fourteen (Henry was then thirty-two), married at sixteen and had borne her husband five children by the time she was twenty-five, with four more still to come. Photographs of her at the time show a remarkably good-looking young woman with dark hair, high forehead and straight features, but with a strong jaw and a mouth which would be a recommendation for a commanding officer. During the family's stay in Tasmania she had had to cope with entirely strange surroundings, bring up a growing family, and perform the many pastoral duties expected of a bishop's wife, for long periods entirely on her own as her husband's duties frequently took him away on protracted and arduous journeys.

It all made for an undoubtedly hard life for her, and like many another parent before and since she took it out on the children; in particular, she seems to have taken it out on her fourth child, Bernard, whom, in the opinion of one of his sisters, 'she did not love.'

Cause and effect in these circumstances is impossible to establish (and anyway an unfair and irrelevant exercise), and whether or not Bernard was a more than usually unpleasant and bloody-minded small boy, such a sorry station in the family pecking order was bound to produce a reaction of disturbing violence. If he could not secure his mother's love and attention by being dutiful and good, Bernard would, and did, secure it by other means – and was as a result in a continual state of bondage and disgrace.

'My early life was a series of fierce battles,' he was later to say, 'from which my mother invariably emerged the victor.'[10] And it does not seem that he received any support from his elder brothers (his older sister died at the age of nine in Tasmania), who both accepted their mother's iron rule with more docility than he did, and tended to exclude their naughty brother from their company with all the ruthless beastliness of the very young and immature. His only friend and companion in those early years was his young sister Una who thus, though an extremely attractive child, drew upon herself her mother's dislike and her brother's fiercely protective spirit.

Bernard adored his father, but the bishop was present only rarely and with perhaps an inadequate knowledge or insight into the family condition (and anyway a typically Victorian attitude to authority) tended to support his wife against his unruly son. Despite therefore the undoubtedly satisfactory social standing of being a member of the bishop's family, despite also the carefree Tasmanian background in which he grew up, Montgomery's statement that he had an unhappy, indeed miserable, childhood, is unlikely to be much of an exaggeration.

It was certainly to form ineradicable impressions upon his mind, and thereafter to influence his attitudes to life and its problems. One such impression would seem to have been that authority near at hand was evil and to be resisted at all times, though authority at a distance (with occasional closer visitations) was not only acceptable but often to be welcomed. Another was that the unfortunate ones in life could only depend upon each other.

The Montgomery family returned to England in 1902 and Bernard and one of his brothers were immediately sent to St Paul's School, Hammersmith, where, on the first day, Bernard was asked if he wished to go into the 'Army Class'. This was, in fact, not so much a class exclusively for boys who had already made up their minds to follow a military career, as one for boys to whom practical as opposed to academic pursuits were more attractive; but it is doubtful if Bernard or his brother fully appreciated this and quite certain that their parents did not. It is also doubtful if Bernard had given the matter a great deal of thought beforehand, but quite certain that his immediate decision on the matter – without the slightest consultation with either of his parents or indeed anyone else – would provoke a scene of almost Apocalyptic fervour when he returned home that evening. And so it proved.

His mother had apparently intended that he should follow his father into the Church – as uncomfortable and thoroughly unsuitable a profession as she could choose for him, one suspects – and although the bishop, once he had expressed surprise and initial disagreement, made no attempt to change his son's mind, this was not a matter upon which she was disposed to agree without violent protest.

But there was a great deal of her own intransigence in her son, and her treatment of him had done much to give it a positively adamantine quality. 'I want to be a soldier,' he announced flatly, and no remonstrances, no threats, no arguments, no cold vituperation (she would not stoop to tears or cajolery) would weaken his determination. He remained in the Army Class and, after five years at St Paul's, entered the Royal Military College at Sandhurst in January 1907.

This at last removed him from his mother's immediate thraldom, and although much later in life he would claim that at this point he broke almost completely with her, it seems in fact that relations between them improved. Certainly his letters home for many years were mostly addressed to 'My Darling Mother', though whether she replied so affectionately is doubtful; even when fame crowned his efforts to attract her attention, it seems that he was never anything but the least favourite child.

Such a relationship between mother and son was unlikely to produce in the latter a relaxed, stable individuality, imbued with natural courtesy, an abundance of charm, or inexhaustible good nature.

Montgomery passed into Sandhurst 72nd in an intake of 170 and at first did well, so that after six weeks he was among the selections for promotion to the rank of lance-corporal – an honour which normally indicated bright prospects and further advancement.

It went, however, to his head, possibly because to obtain it he had had to overcome disadvantages other than those of personality. Judged by today's standards Sandhurst at that time was a focus of the most appalling snobbery, the majority of its intake being sons of serving army officers and often from old-established military families whose sons had provided senior army officers for decades. They came mostly from the public schools of Eton, Harrow, Wellington, Cheltenham, Clifton or Bedford, and thus formed close coteries which regarded those suffering the paralysing inconvenience of having been educated at other centres of learning as 'outsiders' if not actually 'bounders'; and they were generally in receipt of greater financial allowances than Bishop Montgomery could afford, for everyone entering the British Army would need a private income of at least £100 per annum, and in the case of those destined for the fashionable regiments of the Household Brigade of £400 or more.

Montgomery's allowance of £2 per month was derisory in comparison and he has recorded how jealous he was of most of his fellows at Sandhurst, for they possessed wristwatches; but his prowess at games, combined with the undoubted acuteness of brain when he cared to use it, was enough at first to override these quite significant disadvantages. At St Paul's he had been captain of both the School cricket XI and the rugby XV and would probably have captained the swimming team had not that position already been held by his brother – and during his first term at Sandhurst he was not only picked to play rugger for the College, but was a member of the team which then inflicted a notable defeat upon their traditional rivals from the Royal Military Academy at Woolwich.

He was thus at first accepted, albeit with some scepticism, into the upper hierarchy at Sandhurst. In a society in those days as robust and philistine as any in a robust and philistine age, his promotion and indeed notoriety then led to his becoming, in his second term, the leader of a gang of young thugs, who, had their ancestors been more plebeian and their circumstances more commonplace, would certainly have ended in front of the Bench of Magistrates and quite possibly in prison.

The culminating episode in a brief career of undiluted ruffianism reminiscent of Flashman, Westward Ho! or the gun-room in a ship of the line during the Napoleonic Wars, concerned the pinioning of an unpopular cadet by five of Montgomery's associates while Montgomery himself set fire to his shirt-tails. This resulted in severe burns and hospitalisation for the victim, and although the latter was to behave impeccably and refuse to divulge the names of his attackers, the authorities easily guessed their identities and Montgomery was reduced to the rank of 'Gentleman-cadet' and, one imagines, lost whatever credit he had won from the College élite.

It taught him a severe lesson. It also removed him from the company of the unambitious hell-raisers who were quite content to waste their time at Sandhurst, and as he had no money with which to pursue a social life outside the Academy, he was faced with the alternatives of either being idle on his own or occupying his time by working hard.

He worked – perhaps because of his Victorian upbringing and Irish-Scots ancestry (the family home set up by his great-great-grand-father was at Moville on the Inishowen peninsula north of London-derry) among whom the 'work ethic' played so large a part; certainly because of his realisation that only by passing high enough in the final examinations could he hope to secure a commission in the Indian Army, the only force in which as a young subaltern he would be able to live on his pay.

But he had left it just too late. His final passing-out place was 36th (out of 150) and only those who passed out among the first thirty were accepted for the Indian Army; but at least his comparatively high placing allowed him choice of such English regiments as would accept an officer with the minimal private income of £100 per annum, which his father was prepared to find. He chose the Royal Warwickshire Regiment ('because I liked the cap-badge'), a sound county regiment with an excellent reputation but into whose officers' mess he hardly fitted.

He had no social, family or even local connections with the Warwickshires; he lacked any form of social or military polish, Sandhurst having failed completely to impart the slightest gloss to his abrasive personality; he was too slight in build, too unremarkable in feature (except for a pair of level grey eyes often so cool as to be frigid) to cut a dashing figure, and his performance on horseback was mediocre; and he had no conversation outside the military world (which had by this time already become his overmastering interest), failing completely to understand why 'shop' was not talked in the mess. Keenness is not a quality which has ever provoked much admiration in officers' messes, but the advantages of having one member who possessed it are obvious. Montgomery soon found himself Sports Officer, posted to the first battalion in India (which did not, however, put his pay up to parity with that of Indian Army officers) and appointed assistant adjutant with the rank of lieutenant.

He seemed to enjoy the minutiae of military life – the drills, the parades, the eternal weapons training and marches – and he certainly enjoyed the sport, excelling still at cricket, taking up hockey and proving a more than capable performer, even buying a cheap horse and winning a race on it, though falling off at both the beginning and the end. He was undoubtedly a hard-working, capable and probably happy young officer, and if his unshakeable conviction that he knew better than anyone else the best way of getting anything done upset many of his fellows, there were quite a number who were prepared to let him get on and do it. Three years passed very rapidly in Peshawar and Bombay, and in 1913 the whole battalion returned to England where Montgomery not only passed out top of the musketry course at Shorncliffe, but also, under the spur of a new acquaintance, a Captain Lefroy, nourished his capacity for hard work with a study of Clausewitz and long talks upon the almost forbidden (for junior officers) subjects of strategy and military theory.

He was soon to see whether they bore any relationship to practice, for in August 1914 the battalion were mobilised for war and within four weeks he was in action in France.

His experiences between 1914 and 1918 were to leave an ineradicable mark upon his entire personality – as happened, of course, to hundreds of thousands of other young men. But whereas so many of those who survived spent the rest of their lives imbued with a deep hatred of war and all its beastliness, Montgomery's repugnance was directed almost solely towards the waste of men and material which had occurred through incompetence at the top. So many men had died as a result of poor planning – or unnecessary deviation from a good plan – that for the rest of his life his first question upon being faced with any problem would be, 'What's the plan? Must have a good plan!'

His first experience of action was during the Battle of Le Cateau, and his own description is as revealing as any:

Our battalion was deployed in two lines; my company and one other were forward, with the remaining two companies out of sight some hundred yards to the rear. The C.O. [Commanding Officer] galloped up to us forward companies and shouted to us to attack the enemy on the forward hill at once. This was the only order; there was no reconnaissance, no plan, no covering fire. We rushed up the hill, came under heavy fire, my Company Commander was wounded and there were many casualties. Nobody knew what to do, so we returned to the original position from which we had begun to attack. If this was real war it struck me as most curious and did not seem to make any sense against the background of what I had been reading.[11]

Montgomery took two men out to try to bring in the wounded company commander, but there were no stretchers and eventually the unfortunate officer had to be left to be taken prisoner and spend the rest of the war in a prison-camp.

Meanwhile, the rest of the battalion took part in the retreat to the Marne, followed by the subsequent formation of the trench-line up to the Channel coast and the first sanguinary battles around Ypres. It was here that Montgomery's military career, and indeed his life, were very nearly abruptly terminated.

During one of the many futile attempts to break through the opposing lines, Montgomery was ordered to take his platoon forward to occupy a group of buildings on the outskirts of Meteren. Drawing his sword (recently sharpened) he shouted, 'Follow me!' in the approved fashion and ran forward, very quickly to be confronted by a trench full of German soldiers, one of whom brought his rifle around and pointed it at the sword-waving subaltern. As the only exercise with the sword he had ever been taught was saluting-drill and having, as he later wrote, 'read much about the value of surprise in war', Montgomery uttered a loud yell, launched himself through the air and kicked the unfortunate man in a very tender spot 'in the lower part of his stomach'. He had taken his first prisoner.

But later during the day when he was reorganising his men for another advance and standing up to do it, he was hit in the chest by a German rifle bullet which passed completely through him. One of his men bent over to put on a wound dressing, was himself hit and fell across his officer's body, thus protecting it throughout the rest of the daylight hours and against several more rifle and machine-gun bullets. The soldier was killed and Montgomery was hit again in the knee, and when eventually stretcher-bearers found them both (some five hours after he had first been hit) he was judged so far gone that a grave was dug for him; but with a lack of co-operation which some would call typical, he refused to die, was eventually transported back to a hospital in England where he recovered to find that he had been promoted captain and awarded the Distinguished Service Order.

This was a most unusual award for any officer below the rank of major to win, and for a lieutenant to win it has become generally accepted as a 'near miss' for a Victoria Cross; no one during either war was ever to suggest that Montgomery possessed anything but a high degree of physical courage.

Upon recovery, his organising talents were recognised and he spent the remainder of the war 'on the staff' – as brigade major, as General Staff Officer Grade 2 first to a division and then to a corps, and in

1918 G.S.O.1 to another division. But he was a most unusual staff officer for those days, bringing to his duties a philosophy from earlier times.

Many survivors of the First World War have written about the hatred induced by the sight of the red tabs of a staff officer among fighting troops, generally caused by the staff's lack of understanding of front line conditions, exacerbated by an attitude of superiority and condescension especially among the temporary officers, springing from their conscious belief that they were the elite of the army. Many in the higher formations gave the impression – often a true one – that they regarded the brigades, divisions, corps and armies as in the line simply to carry out their own grand designs, irrespective of any ideas the troops or their officers may have had themselves, and certainly unquestioning of such instructions as they received, especially when they demanded that an attack must be 'pressed home regardless of loss'. In the opinion of many of the staff, the regimental officers and men were simply there to do as they were told – and certainly not to reason why.

Montgomery's view was that the staff were the servants of the troops, and that it was the staff's job to see that whatever objective was given to fighting troops, it was within their capability and that they were provided with everything necessary to achieve it. Today this is accepted doctrine, but during the First World War such an attitude in some circles was enough to mark its holder as a maverick of unsound and possibly revolutionary views to be rigorously excluded from the cosiness of the staff coterie. As this was not an exclusion which gave Montgomery a moment's regret or even discomfort, his unpopularity increased and the suspicion with which he was generally regarded by his fellow-officers on the staff deepened.

But fortunately there were some General Officers who could appreciate efficiency and use a capacity for concentration and hard work, however abrasive the personality of its owner. At the end of the war Montgomery became a staff officer with the British Army of Occupation, already dedicated to his profession to a degree which allowed him no distractions – social, idiosyncratic or even sexual. He had no time for cocktails and his only conversation was professional; any facet of his personality which did not contribute to increasing professionalism – laziness, love of physical comfort, enjoyment of food or drink – was already being ruthlessly eradicated; and as for women, at worst they could be as tyrannical as his mother and at best they were a waste of time. Very soon he would be announcing to younger officers with the finality of a diktat that 'You cannot be both a good officer and a good husband.'

His progress up through the military hierarchy between the wars was slow – it could hardly be otherwise in a contracting army after a war fought 'to end wars' – but it was steady, though punctuated by episodes vividly illustrating his unorthodoxy and sometimes gravely threatening his career.

He spent 1920 undergoing the Staff Course at Camberley (the students between them had won seven V.C.s and 170 D.S.O.s and all had a tendency to argue with their instructors, so Montgomery's rumbustiousness was not particularly noticeable at that time) and was afterwards sent to Southern Ireland as brigade major to 17th Infantry Brigade at Cork, engaged upon that depressing duty of 'giving aid to the civil power'. This was followed by another stint as brigade major, this time to 3rd Division where he had the good fortune to serve with a Brigadier Holland who was prepared to let him take over the running of the entire brigade; after which he was given a Grade 2 appointment with 49th West Riding Division. Here he organised a series of lectures for young officers at which he was the sole instructor, and continued the process of teaching junior officers his theories of warfare – and, one suspects, looking for promising youngsters to support him when, as he was sure it would, his hour came. One of the young officers during that spell was a Lieutenant Francis de Guingand.

He then returned as company commander to the Royal Warwick-shires (not a popular appointment with some as he had been away from his regiment for over ten years) but in 1926 was sent back to the Staff College for three years as an instructor, and it was at this point that his true bent was revealed, for it was as a teacher and trainer of troops that Montgomery would always shine. The time passed quickly – and in the end profitably for among his confrères there were Alan Brooke and the Hon. Harold Alexander (as a student), both of whom were to support him in difficult times ahead, and Oliver Leese, John Harding and Miles Dempsey who were to hold critical positions under his command.

Then in 1930 came the most important appointment in the life of any infantry officer – command in his own regiment. Montgomery became a lieutenant-colonel commanding 1st Battalion, Royal Warwickshire Regiment, and was almost immediately involved in his first major conflict with Authority. In addition to his duties as battalion commander, he was appointed secretary of a committee of distinguished senior officers whose task was to rewrite the *Infantry Training Manual* – an appointment which Montgomery interpreted as an instruction for him to do the rewriting while the committee rubber-stamped his work without argument.

'I was', he wrote, 'selected by the War Office to rewrite the Manual of infantry training' – which was not exactly what the War Office had in mind, but what he proceeded to do. 'In it', he later concluded with Olympian simplicity, 'I dealt with the whole art of war.' When the distinguished officers on the committee presumed to question some of his pronouncements he ignored them until their protests became too vociferous, then listed their amendments, suggested the disbandment of the committee and completion of the book by himself working alone, and when by some mysterious means as yet unchronicled all this came about, he arranged the publication of the book without including a single suggested amendment, later recording that the book was considered excellent 'especially by the author'.

He then took his battalion to Palestine (at the beginning of 1932) and later in the year to Alexandria, where it was expected to fulfil the usual standards of smartness and barrack-room drill required of garrison troops. This it notably failed to do. It was reported scruffy in appearance and offhand in manner, and to the shock and dismay of the authorities Montgomery went so far as to abandon official church parades on the grounds that if the men really wanted to go to church on Sundays there was nothing to stop them, but if they did not they might as well have a day's rest and relaxation. They got little enough otherwise for he worked them very hard, and as a result on exercises out in the desert the Royal Warwickshires revealed a standard of infantry training that no other formation had envisaged, let alone achieved. On one occasion, encouraged by a far-sighted superior, Montgomery was given command of a brigade (with de Guingand, now a major, as his chief staff officer) and with his own battalion in the van, executed a complicated manoeuvre at night which not only thoroughly defeated the other side but also silenced those pundits who had long claimed that movement of troops during darkness was an impossibility. As Montgomery himself had been by no means certain of this point but thereafter became thoroughly converted, that was undoubtedly a significant night's work.

After Alexandria he was posted back to India for a three-year appointment to the Staff College at Quetta, this time as Senior Instructor (he was there during the dreadful Quetta earthquake of May 1935) and then at last in the summer of 1937 came his first senior promotion, to brigadier commanding 9th Infantry Brigade at Portsmouth.

Again followed that same pattern of impeccable performance in training and on manoeuvres (9th Brigade became one of the 'star' brigades in the British Army, chosen for many experiments in new equipment and fresh ideas) punctuated by incidents of almost grotesque provocation. The most spectacular of these was brought about when Montgomery decided that the Brigade Funds for providing his soldiers and their families with extra comforts and amenities was in need of replenishment, and hit upon an unusual method of achieving this.

On Southsea Common near Clarence Pier were some football

fields owned by the War Department and upon one Bank Holiday when they would not be in use Montgomery offered to rent them to a circus proprietor, despite the fact that he had not the slightest authority to lease W.D. land. The man offered a £1,000 fee and was somewhat surprised to find himself then engaged in a tough bargaining session with this most unusual army officer, who eventually settled for £1,500. At this stage, the Portsmouth City Council heard of the matter and, not particularly wanting a circus on their sea-front during the Bank Holiday, forbade the deal – whereupon Montgomery approached the mayor, who he knew was promoting some charitable project of his own, and offered to donate £500 of the £1,500 to it if he could persuade the council to change their minds.

This was all satisfactorily concluded, the fair took place, the brigade's funds were replenished and quickly spent; but then the War Office learned the details of the episode and were shocked to the cores of their amalgamated orthodox souls. That a senior officer should have the commercial acumen even to conceive the scheme was bad enough – that he should then bargain with a circus proprietor as though he were a Levantine merchant (and win!) and follow this with something perilously close to bribery of a civil functionary, was not to be borne. Or at least, not *quite* to be borne; if Montgomery were to hand over the £1,000 to the War Office, then the matter might be overlooked – though probably never forgotten – to which their bête noire replied with impeccable logic that such a course was no longer possible as the money had already been spent. He would, however, be quite willing to send them the receipts.

On this occasion, Montgomery was saved from the wrath of outraged authority by Wavell, who was commanding the whole area and had greatly appreciated the presence of so hard and efficient a worker within his bailiwick – and was himself blessed with a sense of humour. Shortly afterwards, wafted onwards by sighs of relief from certain quarters in Whitehall, Major-General B. L. Montgomery sailed again for Palestine to take command of 8th Infantry Division garrisoning the northern half of that strife-torn country; the division in the south was commanded by Major-General Richard O'Connor. It was the time of the Arab Revolt against ever-increasing Jewish immigration into the country (as a result of Nazi persecution), and the role of British troops was to attempt to keep the peace. They were thoroughly hated by both sides.

It was not, however, long before Montgomery and O'Connor between them had the area under control, Montgomery's methods being, as usual, often unconventional. Jewish shopkeepers on one occasion disapproved of one of his ordinances and closed their shops for twenty-four hours, so Montgomery sent for their senior representative and informed him that the shops would now remain closed for the whole week; and that method of exhibiting displeasure waned sharply in popularity from then on. But with the end of the Arab Revolt in 1939, and danger so obviously looming on another front, Montgomery indulged in some determined, single-minded lobbying and as a result was given command of 3rd Division, part of Southern Command in England and earmarked to go to France upon the outbreak of war. By the end of September 1939, he and his division were in France, training hard and digging that line of defences which almost everybody knew would be abandoned the moment Hitler's troops made the slightest signs of an advance and the British Expeditionary Force moved forward into Belgium to meet them.

That period was distinguished by two personal performances of almost unexampled but unconscious iconoclasm, sandwiching between them a piece of military bravura which went some way towards extricating II Corps – and indeed the entire B.E.F. – from sudden disaster.

His first *faux pas* was brought about, typically, by his concern both for the well-being of his men and, more importantly, for their efficiency as soldiers. Not surprisingly in an area populated by thousands of soldiers aware of the fact that they might soon be fighting for their lives in a foreign country, the local brothels were well patronised and the incidence of venereal disease rose. The view at the top of the British Army hierarchy was that such a situation really should not arise and should be strenuously ignored if it did, but Montgomery put the cat among the pigeons by issuing an ordinance above his own signature which admitted the facts, did nothing to impute guilt to those immediately concerned, and ordered that those soldiers who felt themselves in need of what he called 'horizontal refreshment' should be fully instructed of what safeguards to take and provided by the army with the means of doing so.

Inevitably, a copy of this document fell into the hands of the Royal Army chaplains' Department, who *en masse* reacted with the fatuous unreality to be expected of them at that time. Unfortunately, the Commander-in-Chief, Gort (who afterwards became the Governor-General of Gibraltar), belonged to the school of military thought which considered a smart turn-out, good drill and gentlemanly conduct the only real essentials, so the padres found a receptive ear, and Montgomery's corps commander (Sir Alan Brooke) felt compelled to take corrective action and administer a severe rebuke. This Montgomery accepted with surprising humility, the Church Militant was assured that the disreputable officer's career would be suitably affected, and venereal disease remained unnecessarily high throughout the British Expeditionary Force.

Later, when the German armies were pouring through the Low

Countries, Alan Brooke had cause to thank the gods that he had stood firm against more drastic action being taken against his unruly subordinate.

At midnight on May 27th/28th, the Belgian Army capitulated and a gap suddenly opened between II Corps's left flank and a French division to the north, through which the Germans could easily penetrate and thus cut off the retreat of the B.E.F. to Dunkirk. In this dilemma, Brooke turned to Montgomery and ordered him to execute a move which in the words of one of Montgomery's biographers, Lord Chalfont,

> will be recognised at once by any soldier as one of the most difficult and dangerous manoeuvres in the whole science of war – a movement to a flank by night across the front of an enemy position. Montgomery's task was to disengage from his position at Roubaix, get his division into transport and move in the dark, without lights, over twenty-five miles of minor roads and then get his troops dug in by dawn in an unfamiliar new sector, to meet the overwhelming German attack which was now inevitable.
>
> It was an operation which could at any moment collapse into a comprehensive shambles – it needed only one false move to have the whole division wandering aimlessly about the Belgian and French countryside . . . It needed a high standard of training, impeccable staff work and a commander with nerves of steel.[12]

Fortunately, 3rd Division had them all and Brooke's diary entry the following night, referring to Montgomery, stated, 'Found he had, as usual, accomplished almost the impossible.' Trust and co-operation were beginning to work both ways.

But shock tactics in dealing with uncomprehending superiors were still part of the Montgomery technique. Gort as Commander-in-Chief had been instructed by the Government to appoint a corps commander to control the final, most dangerous stages of the Dunkirk evacuation, and had chosen for the job the commander of I Corps, Lieutenant-General Michael Barker – to be confronted very quickly by a cold-eyed Montgomery informing him that Barker was in no mental or physical state to undertake so responsible and intricate a task, and that it should be given instead to Major-General the Hon. Harold Alexander.

Whether persuaded by Montgomery's logic or stunned into acquiescence by his presumption, Gort agreed and Alexander took control – and an unexpectedly large number of Allied soldiers got away to fight again; but Gort was never heard to express any gratitude to Montgomery for his advice, or indeed any great admiration for him.

Back in England, Montgomery was at first engaged in preparing defences along the southern coast in which his division were to immolate themselves if and when the German invasion occurred, and he did this with his customary efficiency, though continuing his harassment of authority with his repeated pronouncements that Dunkirk had not been a glorious victory for British arms but a defeat and a disgrace. He was also pointing out at the same time that every Englishman killed on the beaches or on the landing-grounds would be one fewer to help in mobile defence, which was the only kind likely to be of any effect against a blitzkrieg of the type which had brought about the collapse of France.

Eventually, some of that summer's panic and confusion died, Montgomery was given command of V Corps in Hampshire and Dorset, then in April 1941 of XII Corps in the vital area of Kent, and at the end of that year of the entire South-eastern Command. The realities of the military situation during these months of danger had been such that however many people and institutions Montgomery had alienated on his way up, his military competence was so patent and so necessary that his employment and promotion were more vital to the nation than the smoothing of bruised feelings or ruffled feathers.

Not that he ceased increasing animosity against him at all levels.

His immediate superior during the first few months after Dunkirk was Auchinleck, and after his insubordination during that period it says much for the Auk's generosity of spirit (and acceptance of the military reality after the fall of Tobruk) that he would ever have Montgomery in his theatre of command. During the short time Montgomery served in 1940 as one of Auchinleck's divisional commanders he treated the orders he received with scant attention, and whenever he wanted anything of note he rejected the normal channels of military communication and went over Auchinleck's head – on two occasions directly to the Adjutant-General. It was something of a relief to all when Auchinleck went back to India as Commander-in-Chief, and one factor of an increasingly embarrassing conflict – albeit the innocent one – was removed.

Montgomery at this period did not restrict his alienating policies entirely to those above him.

Many officers had been taking advantage of the fact that they were stationed now in England to have their wives and families living close by – some, by coincidence, were serving quite close to their homes anyway – but Montgomery brought this cosy situation to an abrupt close by decreeing that no wives or families of serving soldiers were to be allowed to live within thirty miles of the Channel coast, or within the operational area in which their husbands were serving.

This was misconstrued by many of the sufferers as a piece of overbearing misogamy on the part of an arrogant and deprived general,

14 The Cairo Conference, August 5th, 1942: (front row) Field Marshal Smuts, Winston Churchill, General Sir Claude Auchinleck, General Sir Archibald Wavell; (back row) Air Chief Marshal Sir Arthur Tedder, General Sir Alan Brooke, Admiral Sir Henry Harwood, the Rt Hon. Richard Casey

15 Revitalised command: Winston Churchill with Generals Alexander and Montgomery in the desert, August 23rd, 1942

16 After Alam Halfa: Brigadier 'Pip' Roberts introduces an Italian prisoner (far left) to an unimpressed General Montgomery. Wearing the topee is Mr Wendell Wilkie, President Roosevelt's personal representative.

but Montgomery's argument that if the invader did come those
officers would be, not unnaturally, over-concerned with the fate of
their nearest and dearest and thus would not concentrate exclusively
on their duties, is by no means groundless. And there was another
justification for his edict.

The vast majority of the men serving under Montgomery's command at that time had been used – whether in the regular army or
not – to fairly regular hours. If they had not followed 'nine to five'
professions they had had 'eight to six' jobs – and with their families in
the neighbourhood they tended to spend the day looking forward to
'knocking-off time', followed by an evening with their wives and
children.

This was not a schedule likely to increase the efficiency and
dedication of an army which might soon be fighting for its life and
that of the nation, for not only did it detract from individual
concentration, it also militated against the formation of communal
spirit and that co-ordination and understanding which it is one of the
chief purposes of officers', sergeants' and corporals' messes to
inculcate and develop. An officers' mess which is sparsely attended
upon anything but a temporary basis is the sign of an uncoordinated
formation – and co-ordination was what Montgomery was aiming at
throughout his command.

Another thing he was aiming at was physical fitness, so he insisted
not only that the fighting troops were kept hard at work whatever the
weather, but that even headquarters administrative staff were to do a
seven-mile run every week – and one pear-shaped colonel who
complained that such an effort would kill him was coldly informed
that his death now in training would be less damaging to the army
than his death after action had been joined. 'If you are going to die –
die now and let us find a replacement.'

This then was the military career of the man who in August 1942
was to fly out to Egypt to take command of Eighth Army. But the
picture would not be complete without mention of the few years
during which love and some semblance of a family life had brought a
new and unexpected factor into Montgomery's life.

Despite his repeated affirmations to young officers, he had apparently succeeded for ten years in being both a good soldier and a
good husband.

He met the woman who was to bring – briefly – happiness and a
softer approach to life in 1926, though whether this was accidental or
the result of a deliberate decision on his part that it was time he
married has often been argued. She was Betty Carver, a widow with
two young sons whose first husband had been killed at Gallipoli –
and she was also sister to that other irascible military genius, Major-
General Patrick Hobart, the founder and original trainer of the 7th

Armoured Division, with whom Montgomery's relations were never to be much more than civil.

They were married in July 1927, and Betty introduced Montgomery into a world of which he had before had no experience at all – a world of books and music, of amusing and friendly conversation ranging over wide horizons, of men such as the humorous poet A. P. Herbert and the painter Augustus John. It was a world which Montgomery could make no attempt to join, but which he appeared quite happy to sit in a corner and watch – and especially watch the woman he so obviously adored being happy and content.

She on her part was more than willing to re-enter the military social world in which she had to a great extent grown up, to play her part as a rising officer's wife, treating his more outré performances with a degree of gentle mockery and understanding affection, and bringing about for him what was undoubtedly an unexpected and recurringly delightful revelation – that life with a woman could produce not only friendship and happiness, but also understanding, loyalty and, incredibly, approval. Very few people beforehand, and certainly no women, had ever admitted to Montgomery that occasionally he might be right about something.

She bore him a son in 1928, went abroad with him to Palestine, Alexandria and India, travelled on leave with him through the Holy Lands and afterwards to Japan, and in 1937 came home with him to England when he was posted to command the brigade at Portsmouth. Then, because she was feeling rather run down, she went to Burnham-on-Sea for a holiday while her husband was concerned with manoeuvres on Salisbury Plain, and one morning while sitting on the beach was bitten by an insect on the leg. A few days later she felt weak and was admitted to the local hospital; and by the time Montgomery had been sent for and arrived, it was obvious that something was badly wrong.

The infection spread and in those days before antibiotics, multiplied with frightening rapidity until gangrene set in and the leg had to be amputated; and in her run-down state she was in no condition to withstand the shock. On October 19th, 1937, with her husband's voice reading from the 23rd Psalm the last sounds she would hear on earth, she died – and Montgomery's ten brief years of marital happiness were at an end.

The shock to Montgomery was traumatic. It marked the end of a period in which some of his attention had been directed away from military matters, and the beginning of another in which it was totally redirected into its old, habitual narrow arc. He drowned his tragedy in work, he numbed his sorrow with mental fatigue and, as mind and body recovered, his concentration on his profession brought its due reward of increasing technical expertise and understanding.

But he never forgot his experience, and almost certainly never lost a feeling that something important had been ripped brutally away from the pattern of his life. Even the success which later came to him seems not to have compensated for this, and he was on one occasion to say (forgetting perhaps his earlier comments on Life with Mother) – 'I have never lost. Except when my wife died.'
Other things he said were:

I went through the whole war on the Western Front, except during the period I was in England after being wounded; I never once saw the British Commander-in-Chief, neither French nor Haig, and only twice did I see an Army Commander. The higher staffs were out of touch with the regimental officers and with the troops. The former lived in comfort, which became greater as the distance of their headquarters behind the lines increased.[13]

By the time the 1914–18 war was over it had become very clear to me that the profession of arms was a life-study.[14]

There are only two answers to most military problems. One of them is wrong.[15]

An army is a most sensitive instrument and can easily become damaged; its basic ingredient is men and, to handle an army well, it is essential to understand human nature.[16]

It is important to remember that all men are different . . . If a commander thinks that all men are the same and he treats the great mass of human material accordingly, he will fail.[17]

Every man who is worth his salt should have ambition.[18]

Study the individual soldier. Create the atmosphere of success. Morale means everything.[19]

You must learn to pick a good team of subordinates, and once you have got them stick to them and trust them. All men are different and all generals are different; so are brigades and divisions.[20]

You must have the will to win; it is much more important to fight well when things are going badly than when things are going well.[21]

If you worry you merely go mad.[22]

The discipline demanded of the soldier must become loyalty in the officer.[23]

There are no bad soldiers; only bad officers. [He was aware that this was not a Montgomery original.]

Of equal significance, of course, were some of the things said about him:

He is clever, energetic, ambitious and a very gifted instructor. But to do himself justice he must cultivate tact, tolerance and discretion . . . very refreshing to meet. He revels in independence and responsibility.[24]

An officer of great military ability who delights in responsibility. He is very quick. He writes very clear memoranda . . . definitely above the average and should attain high rank in the army. He can only fail to do so if a certain high-handedness, which occasionally overtakes him, becomes too pronounced . . . He is really popular with his men whom he regards and treats as if they were his children.[25]

Brigadier Montgomery is one of the cleverest brains we have in the higher ranks, an excellent trainer of troops and an enthusiast in all he does. His work this year in the gas trials was of a very high order. He has some of the defects of the enthusiast, in an occasional impatience and intolerance when things cannot be done as quickly as he would like, or when he meets brains less quick and clear than his own.[26]

He could describe a complex situation with amazing lucidity and sum up a long exercise without the use of a single note. He had a remarkable flair for picking out the essence of a problem, and for indicating its solution with startling clarity. It was almost impossible to misunderstand his meaning, however unpalatable it may be. In an argument he was formidable and ruthless.[27]

Quick as a ferret; and about as likeable.

Nobody in those days ever said of him that he was a 'nice chap'.

6 · 'A cool and refreshing breeze'

With both armies relatively quiescent after the July battles, the fighting at Alamein was largely lifted in early August into the third dimension, where the Royal Air Force, augmented by sixteen South African Air Force squadrons and eight from the Royal Australian Air Force, dominated the skies.

During the retreat from Gazala they had at first been unable to offer the armies much protection as their fighter squadrons had been busily skipping backwards out of danger from desert airstrip to desert airstrip, while the bombers could give little help in the face of the inextricable entanglement of the Army units with each other and the similarity of their appearance to that of the Axis formations. But with the stabilising of the line south of Alamein, the rapid development of bases for fighters and light bombers around Amiriya and for mediums and heavies back in the Levant, the Desert Air Force began to play an increasingly crucial role in the conflict.

During the latter part of the retreat they had already caused Rommel considerable trouble by bombing concentrations of Panzer-armee vehicles, and had won the everlasting gratitude of the Eighth Army by keeping dive-bombers away from the long columns of slow-moving trucks and lorries; 'Thank God you didn't let the Huns Stuka us,' Freyberg had said to Tedder when he got back from hospital, ' . . . we were an appalling target.' Now as Eighth Army reorganised and Rommel awaited supplies and planned his next stroke, the Wellingtons, Albacores and Bostons were out all night and often all day, bombing the harbour installations at Sollum, Matruh, Derna and Tobruk, searching for tankers bringing Rommel his vital fuel, or coasters creeping up with his ammunition, and strafing and bombing the Axis convoys making their increasingly perilous way along the narrow ribbon of the coastal road.

Above the battlefield itself, Hurricanes, Kittyhawks, Spitfires and Tomahawks ranged continuously, machine-gunning every movement they saw, chasing away the occasional Stuka or Me 109, and carrying out the essential reconnaissance which the armoured cars, blocked at one end of the line by the sea, at the other end by the Qattara Depression and along its length by the ever thickening belts of minefields, were finding increasingly difficult to carry out.

Plain statistics can in this instance give a clear indication of the growing Allied air strength and activity. During the twenty-two days following the opening of the Gazala battle on May 26th, the Desert Air Force had flown 5,732 sorties; between July 1st and 27th over 15,400 sorties were flown, all in direct support of Eighth Army or of attempts by the Royal Navy to help the Army. Inter-Service co-operation had become the vital factor under the pressure of immediate danger, and four times during July, cruisers and destroyers based on Haifa or Port Said had bombarded the port at Matruh with the aid of flares dropped by Albacores, sinking two merchant ships, wrecking port installations and thus further aggravating Rommel's already precarious supply situation.

Obviously all this had been carried out at some cost – the Allies lost 113 aircraft in the area during July, in most cases complete with pilots and crews for they had been operating either over the sea or over parts of the desert in hostile hands; but Air Marshal Tedder's greatest need at this time was for machines, not men. As a result of the Empire Air Training scheme he often found himself with crews for several squadrons standing by awaiting aircraft (to their great disgust) while many promised Hurricanes and Tomahawks had been diverted to India in the face of the Japanese onslaught, and now more aircraft were being held back in America to equip the rapidly growing U.S.A.A.F.

Even the announcement that Major-General L. H. Brereton was coming out to the Middle East in order to establish complete American formations to take part in the coming battles was not unalloyed good news, for such formations would not be ready for action for some time to come whereas their aircraft were needed now.

So what machines there were in the area had to fly all the time – often with alternating crews. Engines and airframes were subjected to enormous strain as the machines flew out on seven or eight sorties every day, the pilots and crews making half that number – which was almost as great a strain on the men as on the machines in the conditions in which they had to live and fly. Intense heat, continual dust and grit, sweat and sand caking every exposed part of the body, flies everywhere; and in the air, sandstorms blocking out the targets, choking the gun-barrels, turning the cockpits into individual furnaces.

But at least the Desert Air Force was spared one horror to be continually endured by the troops on the ground – the sight of the dead lying among the minefields, obscene and swollen in the blazing sun until they burst, to drench the neighbourhood with the reek of putrefying flesh.

During the early days of August, Eighth Army had drawn wearily back from immediate contact with the enemy, thankful that for the moment it seemed unlikely that they would be called upon for much more active duty than patrolling and occasional raids, bitter at the waste of life and effort of the last few weeks, and sceptical of promises of better times to come. Hopes raised by the news that Auchinleck had replaced Ritchie had fallen again in the face of the evident failure of the attacks mounted in July, and the fact that the advance of the Afrika Korps had at least been ended was a negative benefit which did little to improve morale or to lift any but the most volatile spirits.

Dour dissatisfaction was the mood of the mass of the army, cynical in its attitude to authority, doubtful of the ability of any formation other than the individual soldier's own to perform well in either attack or defence, over-ready to blame other units or arms for every failure. This mood of pessimism had reached such a stage that despite the disappointments of July, the information that Auchinleck was himself to be replaced was greeted with even more bitterness by some; few had ever heard of the new general from Britain who in Eighth Army opinion would be unlikely to possess desert experience, would have to be carried by Eighth Army until his 'knees were brown' and until then could be expected to make the same mistakes that all the other commanders had made in the past – at the cost of Eighth Army sweat and blood.

Even the news of Churchill's presence caused only the slightest alleviation of discontent, for comparatively few of the fighting troops saw him and most of his time had been spent talking to senior officers. So the men observed the comings and goings of the staff cars bearing newcomers forward and taking old hands away with cynical detachment, and one of the first observations made by their new Commander-in-Chief, General the Hon. Sir Harold Alexander, was that although the men looked tough and fit, they showed little sign of cheerfulness, many of them turning their backs on his car as it went by, and very few making the slightest attempt to salute it.

Realising, however, that it was more important for him to inspire a proper respect in the future than to attempt to enforce its outward signs in the present, he concentrated for the moment upon the terse but extremely comprehensive directive he had just been given, written in the Prime Minister's own handwriting upon Embassy notepaper, for his future conduct of the Middle Eastern conflict:

1. Your prime and main duty will be to take or destroy at the earliest opportunity the German–Italian Army commanded by Field-Marshal Rommel together with all its supplies and establishments in Egypt and Libya.

2. You will discharge or cause to be discharged such other duties as pertain to your Command without prejudice to the task described in paragraph 1 which must be considered paramount in His Majesty's interests.[1]

Well, at least it was not clouded by ambiguity.

The changeover in command was to take place officially on August 15th, and there would inevitably be a certain measure of upheaval and disjuncture which not even the studiously polite and civilised behaviour of all but one of the participants could disguise.

On August 8th, with the final changes as a result of Gott's death agreed with the War Cabinet, Mr Churchill had written to Auchinleck:

Cairo
8th August 1942

Dear General Auchinleck,

1   On June 23 you raised in your telegram to the C.I.G.S. the question of your being relieved in this Command, and you mentioned the name of General Alexander as a possible successor. At that time of crisis to the Army His Majesty's Government did not wish to avail themselves of your high-minded offer. At the same time you had taken over effective command of the battle, as I had long desired and suggested to you in my telegram of May 20. You stemmed the adverse tide and at the present time the front is stabilized.

2   The War Cabinet have now decided, for the reasons which you yourself had used, that the moment has come for a change. It is proposed to detach Iraq and Persia from the present Middle Eastern theatre. Alexander will be appointed to command the Middle East, Montgomery to command the Eighth Army, and I offer you the command of Iraq and Persia including the Tenth Army, with headquarters at Basra or Baghdad. It is true that this sphere is today smaller than the Middle East, but it may in a few months become the scene of decisive operations and reinforcements to the Tenth Army are already on the way. In this theatre, of which you have special experience, you will preserve your associations with India. I hope therefore that you will comply with my wish and directions with the same disinterested public spirit that you have shown on all occasions. Alexander will arrive almost immediately, and I hope that early next week, subject of course to the movements of the enemy, it may be possible to effect the transfer of responsibility on the Western battlefront with the utmost smoothness and efficiency.

3   I shall be very glad to see you at any convenient time if you should so desire.

Believe me,
Yours sincerely,
Winston S. Churchill[2]

This epistle was conveyed to Auchinleck that same morning by one of Churchill's staff, feeling 'as if I were just going to murder an unsuspecting friend,' and after Auchinleck had read it with typical impassivity, he asked a few questions and indicated that he doubted whether he could accept command of the new theatre, for a number of reasons.

These reasons he detailed during a 'bleak and impeccable' interview with Churchill the following day, Sunday, August 9th. Although he accepted the grounds given for a change in command, Auchinleck felt that the reduction of his responsibilities to such a small proportion of those he had lately been shouldering would look to the public too much like the appointment of an unsuccessful general to an operational sinecure – a policy of which he would thoroughly disapprove had it happened to anyone else and which he could therefore not accept himself. He also voiced strongly the opinion that such a division of the Middle East Command would prove impracticable, as the new zone would rely for its supplies and reinforcement upon passage through either the new Middle East theatre or through India and a crisis in either of those areas would affect delivery, however crucial the situation in Iraq or Persia might be.

In the circumstances he asked to be allowed to retire into oblivion (in the event he was to become Commander-in-Chief in India within a year) though at Mr Churchill's urgent bidding he agreed to give the matter a few more days' thought; but he warned the Prime Minister that he would be unlikely to change his mind between then and Churchill's return from Moscow in ten days' time. In the meantime, he would return to the desert to hand over his command.

That day Alexander arrived and the interview between the interchanging Commanders-in-Chief was as polite and friendly as the inevitable embarrassment would allow; but on August 12th Montgomery arrived and the atmosphere became much less cordial. As neither Alexander nor Montgomery was due to take up his respective command for another three days, Montgomery's superior at that moment was Auchinleck and to him he must first report.

It was a prickly, thoroughly uncomfortable interview in which Montgomery made little attempt to ease the situation either by trying to gloss over the past and pretend that his recent insubordination to Auchinleck had been mere misunderstanding, or even doing much to disguise his attitude of thinly veiled contempt for all military command as it had been exercised to date in the Middle East. It is doubtful whether he took in much information from the War Map he was shown or from the situation outline as given by Auchinleck, and he got out of the room as quickly as he decently could. But within a matter of hours, it became evident that he was again paying scant attention to any instructions Auchinleck had given him, and also that

an entirely new set of conditions would henceforth apply in the
Desert War.

John Harding was then Deputy Chief of General Staff at the Cairo
H.Q. and has given an illuminating account of the immediate effect
of Montgomery's arrival in the establishment, and of his own first
meeting with his two new superior officers on that portentous
afternoon.

> The first I knew of the changes in command was one afternoon (August
> 12th) when my orderly came in and said,
> 'The Commander-in-Chief wants to see you.'
> So I said, 'Who is the Commander-in-Chief?'
> I went along to the C-in-C's room, and there, sitting at the desk, was
> Monty: and sitting on the desk, drumming his heels against it, was Alex.
> I didn't know what their respective appointments were. Nobody had told
> me. Monty introduced me to Alex:
> 'You know General Alexander?'
> It was the first time I had ever met him, but I knew all about him of
> course. Monty said,
> 'Well John, you've been out here a long time. Tell me everything.' And
> then he put me through a catechism for about an hour, with Alex not
> taking any real part in the discussion, and I was quizzed on all the
> formation commanders down to brigades. At the end he said,
> 'From all this muckage, can you organise for me two desert-trained
> armoured divisions and a mobile infantry division?'
> I asked, 'And hold the front too, presumably?'
> 'Yes, of course.'
> 'Yes, I think I can.'[3]

According to Montgomery, the formation of this *corps de chasse* as
an equal opponent to the Afrika Korps and a means of exploitation of
the breakthrough at Alamein he was already planning, was a result of
deep thought on his part during his journey out from England, and
the agreement by Harding that its formation was a practicability
became the basis upon which many plans for the future were to rest.
But having given a significant glimpse of how he saw the relationship
between himself and his eventual Commander-in-Chief, Montgomery
then travelled up into the desert the following day to visit Eighth
Army advanced headquarters. On his way he picked up his old
acquaintance Freddie de Guingand who had been acting since the
beginning of July as Auchinleck's B.G.S. at the front, and questioned
him closely on recent events there and again on the performance of
various commanders and their formations.

As de Guingand and Montgomery had worked together successfully before, it was not surprising that there was great similarity in
their points of view, and as the former expressed the doubts he had
already begun to feel for the methods and intentions of the present
command, he found his sentiments echoed with redoubled fervour by

the newcomer. De Guingand's account of what followed sparkles with an enthusiasm noticeably absent from his narrative of previous events:

> He [Montgomery] then went through his proposals for the future. It was extraordinary how he had spotted most of the weaknesses even before his arrival. And he gave out his ideas to a gathering of all the Headquarters Staff officers that very evening as the sun was setting below the Ruweisat Ridge . . .
>
> That address by Montgomery will remain one of my most vivid recollections . . . We all felt that a cool and refreshing breeze had come to relieve the oppressive and stagnant atmosphere.
>
> He was going to create a new atmosphere . . . The bad old days were over, and nothing but good was in store for us. A new era had dawned.

Above all,

> Any further retreat or withdrawal was quite out of the question. Forget about it. 'If we cannot stay here alive, then let us stay here dead!'[4]

This was unquestionably what everyone present wanted to hear – as did the rest of Eighth Army, and Montgomery was determined that they should indeed all hear it during the next few days. But in the meantime there was an opportunity for another blatant swipe at that particular manifestation of authority of which his mother had been the primal fount, and of which Auchinleck was now the most immediate representative.

Dismissing Ramsden (who had been appointed temporary Eighth Army commander until the time of Montgomery's official assumption of command) back to his corps, Montgomery had as early as two o'clock that afternoon sent a signal back to Cairo H.Q. ordering the immediate destruction of all plans within Eighth Army for withdrawal, and then announced that he was not waiting for the elapse of two more days before taking up his command, but was doing so immediately. He then left for an inspection of XIII Corps and a talk with their temporary commander Freyberg (in whom he found a sympathetic ear, especially when he laid it down as an ineluctable principle that from now on divisions would fight as divisions and that the day of the Jock Column or even battlegroup was over), trusting that any violent reaction to this latest piece of discourtesy would be expended by the time of his return.

There seems, in fact, to have been no immediate or obvious riposte by Auchinleck, however bitter that moment may have been for him, so Montgomery could later write of that night, 'It was with an insubordinate smile that I fell asleep: I was issuing orders to an Army which someone else reckoned he commanded!'[5]

There was undoubtedly an element of gratuitous arrogance, perhaps even of brutality, in the method adopted by Montgomery in taking command of the Eighth Army when he did, but those who criticise him for not waiting that extra forty-eight hours should remember the part time can play in warfare. Had Auchinleck taken over first from Cunningham and then from Ritchie two days earlier than in fact he did, who can say what benefits might have accrued or losses been avoided? Even more important is a lesson to be drawn from the whole catalogue of war, that a general driven always by a desire to get things done quickly is more likely to be granted victory than one whose habit of mind allows him to accept the passage of time with easy acquiescence.

Montgomery, as has been suggested, was not the model of the 'nice chap' so popular at all levels of the British regular army – charming to his equals, authoritative to his subordinates and especially to 'the men', preferably big, handsome and splendidly filling his immaculate uniform; vested, except to his staff, with a degree of Olympian remoteness.

Montgomery was none of those things; indeed, had he possessed any of these attributes he would possibly have attempted to discard them because he sensed that, at that moment, those very qualities which the British were supposed traditionally to admire were stained in the eyes of Eighth Army with defeat – and in some cases with disgrace. His very physical insignificance would be an asset now, and he would make the men of the desert accept him quickly by his own identification with them – by adopting their own style of informal dress, by being seen by them all, by talking to them in the language they understood, above all by saying the things they wanted to hear even though some of them might not stand up to strict examination.

In this last category came, then and later, many statements or inferences with regard to the past in which, according to him, everything had always been done wrongly whereas from now on-wards everything would be right. All the past, according to Montgomery, had been a dismal catalogue of weakness, muddle, bad training, bad planning and low morale, with leadership mediocre at best and abysmal in general; and if such a simplification was unfair to Auchinleck and to many of the other officers who were soon to find themselves sent back to England under the cloud of Montgomery's stinging disfavour, these could presumably hardly have arrived at their various stations in life without having recognised that life itself is not a condition in which justice or fairness plays an appreciable part.

It had been, after all, not very fair that so many brave young men had lost their lives, their limbs or their freedom as the result of mistakes made, time and time again, by some of the men now gloomily complaining of Montgomery's lack of good breeding as they made their way back to a civilian comfort and security denied, sometimes for ever, to the victims of their own professional incompetence.

The first to feel the impact of the new man's personality were of course the corps and divisional commanders and the staff, and to these Montgomery made his intentions crystal clear in a very short time. As he had told Freyberg, the expressions 'Jock Column' and 'battlegroup' were to disappear from the lexicon of the Eighth Army as henceforward they would fight as they had been organised and trained – in divisions and corps. Another expression to go must be the term 'box', which so far as their new commander was aware was a contraption with a lid on it to hold the occupants down; this would be replaced by the term 'defended area' – and as 'consolidation' had in the past been a term often interpreted as an excuse for sitting down and doing nothing, the new expression would be 'reorganising', with its emphasis on gathering strength for future action.

If some well-used terms were to be replaced by others, certain practices – one above all – were to disappear completely. A total embargo was placed upon what the new Army Commander called 'bellyaching' and in case any present were not aware of his own interpretation of that expression he spelled it out for them. 'Bellyaching' meant arguing about orders and would cease forthwith; in future, orders issued from Army Headquarters – almost invariably through Freddie de Guingand who was quickly confirmed as Montgomery's Chief of Staff – would be obeyed without question, and would certainly not be regarded, as seemed to have happened in the past, as little more than a basis for discussion. And when Major-General Callum Renton, who since the first desert victory in 1940 had worked his way up from command of the 2nd Rifle Brigade to command of 7th Armoured Division, made the mistake of believing that the new man did not mean what he said and argued about the employment of armour during the forthcoming battle, he found himself the recipient of a tongue-lashing from his new corps commander which left him white-faced and shaken, and when the battle was over was relieved of his cherished command.

For preparations for the forthcoming battle – and everyone was quite certain that Rommel must either strike soon or abandon any hope of reaching Cairo – were obviously Montgomery's first preoccupation. There was general agreement that Rommel would try to break through during the moonlit period at the end of August, probably in an attempted repeat of his success at Gazala with a right hook through the bottom half of the opposing line, followed by a drive up to the coast in order to cut off the infantry of XXX Corps around and in the Alamein defences, and then the final triumphant advance to Alexandria and Cairo.

These potential dangers had already been foreseen by Auchinleck and Dorman-Smith, and their plans to deal with them had entailed the consolidation of the defences from Tel el Eisa past the El Alamein box down to Ruweisat Ridge (held from north to south respectively by 9th Australian, 1st South African and 5th Indian Divisions) with an extension by 5th and 6th New Zealand Brigades of XIII Corps further southwards down to Bare Ridge on Alam Nayil. Behind the XXX Corps positions were held the Valentines of 23rd Armoured Brigade, while further south on a ridge named Alam Halfa leading back north-eastwards from behind the New Zealanders was ensconced the 21st Indian Infantry Brigade, taking the place under Freyberg's command of 4th New Zealand Brigade, recuperating in the Delta from their recent heavy losses and undergoing training as the first Commonwealth armoured brigade.

Also under XIII Corps command were the two armoured brigades and one motor brigade of 7th Armoured Division, 22nd Armoured Brigade in the wide gap between the New Zealanders and Alam

Map 19   Auchinleck's dispositions for Alam Halfa

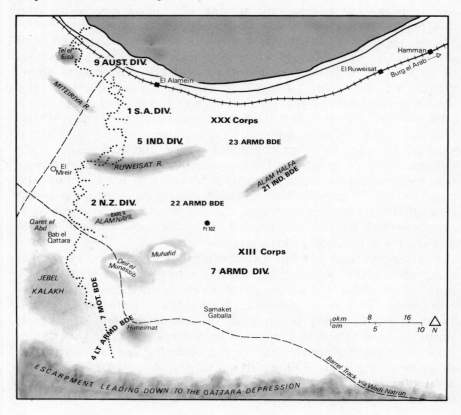

Halfa, 7th Motor Brigade patrolling from the southern edge of the New Zealand positions down to Himeimat, and the armoured cars and light tanks of 4th Light Armoured Brigade operating west of the minefields and around Himeimat itself.

In accordance with Auchinleck's plan to keep Eighth Army mobile and capable of manoeuvre, transport was held available close to every defensive position, with the general philosophy that Rommel's forces should be contained and channelled during a fluid battle, revolving around the fulcrum of the Alam Halfa position. Whether 7th Armoured Division would close up into the gaps to the east of the New Zealanders or instead stay out to the south and threaten the outer flank of Rommel's advance was a matter which had apparently not been thrashed out before Montgomery arrived and was, as has been mentioned, the subject of some initial disagreement.

Montgomery did not think much of these plans for a mobile battle. On past form Rommel's men were likely to be better at it than his own, and he was well aware that yet another disaster which could be blamed upon armoured incompetence or upon lack of co-operation between infantry and armour would wreck his own future just as surely as it had wrecked Ritchie's and Auchinleck's. Moreover, in this particular battle he did not want his men to be mobile; he wanted them to stay where they were and fight, thus bringing into full play that one quality of British troops which had compelled even Rommel's admiration – their tenacity.

Montgomery had already declared that there would be no further withdrawal, and to underline this assertion he now ordered all second echelon transport back from the front, the stockpiling of food and ammunition in the forward areas, the further thickening of the minefields and the formation of one solid front from the coast to Alam Nayil, no longer fragmented 'by all this "box" business'.

Instead of an open system into which Rommel could penetrate, he would form a fortress against which Rommel must hurl himself and in so doing perhaps dash the famous Afrika Korps to pieces; but to do this Montgomery needed more infantry and more armour. During the evening after he had so brusquely taken command of Eighth Army he instructed de Guingand to ring up Cairo H.Q. and request the immediate despatch forward of 44th (Home Counties) Division, and when the staff replied that the division was still unacclimatised and could not move up until the end of the month, Montgomery rang Harding who in due course passed on the request first to Auchinleck and then to Alexander.

'If that's what Monty wants, let him have it,' replied Alexander when the request reached him, setting a precedent he was to follow for many months.

The bulk of the division arrived on Alam Halfa ridge two days later, its third brigade coming up the following day; and quite soon afterwards, Major-General Gatehouse was instructed to bring up the H.Q. of his 10th Armoured Division, together with the seventy-two Grants and twelve Crusaders of 8th Armoured Brigade to take positions along and to the south of the ridge.

Now the fortress could take shape – a solid defence stretching down from Tel el Eisa on the coast as far as Alam Nayil (with thick minefields going further on down to Himeimat) and an equally solid flank stretching back from Alam Nayil along the Alam Halfa Ridge. And to give added toughness to the defence and added striking power to the artillery, the orders to the troops were quite unequivocal – in itself a factor to boost morale considerably. All Corps positions were to be fought to the last man and the last bullet, as were the New Zealand and 44th Divisional positions of XIII Corps, while the Valentines, Grants and Crusaders of 22nd Armoured, 23rd Armoured and 8th Armoured Brigades were to be regarded for the most part as mobile artillery fighting alongside the infantry from hull-down positions. They were only to move forward in charge or counter-

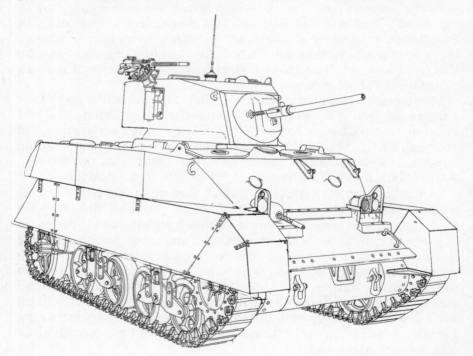

Figure 4   Light tank M3 (Stuart): weight 12·3 tons; armour 25mm.–40mm.; engine 250 h.p.; maximum speed 35 m.p.h.; armament one 37mm., three ·30 in. machine-guns; crew 4

attack if specifically ordered to do so by their new corps commander, Lieutenant-General Brian Horrocks, a protégé of Montgomery's who had been especially flown out at the Army Commander's request to take over Gott's old command.

As for the 7th Armoured Division, despite recent pronouncements 22nd Armoured Brigade was to be detached for the battle and placed under Gatehouse in 10th Armoured Division, while the Stuarts, Crusaders and armoured cars of 7th Motor Brigade and 4th Light Armoured Brigade would endeavour to stop Rommel on the mine-fields south of the New Zealanders, and if this proved impossible then to harass the southern flanks of any breakthrough to the greatest possible extent. To give an impression of greater strength down in that area and thus perhaps to impose an extra degree of hesitation upon the Afrika Korps, two dummy tank battalions were moved down to the east of Himeimat, dummy infantry positions were dug around Samaket Gaballa and some stretches of dummy minefield laid; and with memories of Allenby's device before the third battle of Gaza in 1918, a false map of the terrain showing a hard level surface below the Alam Halfa Ridge where there was in fact a patch of soft sand was planted in an old scout car which then 'accidentally' blew up on a mine just east of Himeimat and was abandoned by its crew.

By August 25th all formations were moving into position, and somewhat to the surprise of a number of the troops, they all knew what was expected of them. Much more had happened to Eighth Army than just the reinforcement and redisposition of its constituent corps, for Montgomery had begun reshaping it to his own specifi-cations.

He had also begun – rather unexpectedly in view of his strong puritanical strain – by easing the lives of his immediate staff.

'What's this, a meat safe?' he had asked as soon as he saw the wire mesh cage which had so offended Churchill. 'You don't expect me to live in a meat safe, do you? Take it down and let the poor flies out!'[6]

And very soon his headquarters had moved to Burg el Arab, close – to Air Marshal Tedder's great relief – to the R.A.F. head-quarters, and alongside the sea in which all could wash away the sweat and grime of desert living. A large mess tent arrived, white tablecloths and shining cutlery appeared, a good cook was found and competent servants to help lift everyone's morale and capacity for work.

'Let us be at least as comfortable as we can,' Montgomery said, and saw to it that this precept was obeyed not only at his own head-quarters. Every soldier in his command was soon to learn, often to his surprise, that the new general considered him worth looking after and likely to fight better after a good night's sleep.

Montgomery never pretended that he did not thoroughly enjoy the methods by which he both made himself known to his troops and excited their enthusiasm; and the fact of his enjoyment should not obscure the necessity for the process. For too long the men of Eighth Army had been expected to endure the hardship of desert life, the heat, the thirst and the boredom, then to walk forward into appalling danger, towards death, wounds or captivity, all at the behest of remote Olympian figures whose names they hardly knew, who were rarely seen except as shadowy figures on the back seats of large cars rolling past swathed in dust, who never spoke to them except in reproof for some military solecism such as appearing before them with their shirts unbuttoned, and whose ignorance of military reality they felt had been so often demonstrated by themselves, and paid for in their own blood.

Now the most senior officer in their army, the man who most closely controlled their own personal destinies, was suddenly coming out to see as many of them as possible – not only to talk but apparently also to listen to them; to tell them not only that they each had an important part to play in his plans, but what that part was; to tell them what they had long believed was true – that they were as good soldiers as their opponents in the Afrika Korps – and what they now hoped to be true – that in the next battle he was going to prove himself to be as good a general as Rommel.

'We are going to hit Rommel for six out of Egypt!' he said, in his high, slightly lisping voice – stressing, however, that this was to be the long-term aim and that the immediate prospect was for a purely defensive, stone-walling battle – and when he walked along the ranks inspecting them, he looked deliberately and coolly into every man's eyes so that all felt, in that sudden, surprising moment, the creation of a personal bond. It might not be a bond which everyone welcomed, but whoever found himself looking back into those clear, grey-blue eyes felt irrevocably that military authority could never again lie elsewhere. Here, undoubtedly, was the man in command; whether he was competent to fulfil his promises would remain to be seen but of one thing all felt immediately certain. If he failed, he would fall with them himself. There would be no buck-passing with Montgomery.

The fact that he was prepared not only to be known but also instantly recognised was unusual enough among British regular officers who, once they had been promoted beyond regimental service, seemed generally to prefer a cult of anonymity except among themselves; but the methods he used to advertise his presence caused amusement throughout the bulk of the army at first, and shocked disgust followed by glum acceptance in some of the more exalted circles. From the beginning in the desert he adopted the woollen pullover, the corduroy or khaki drill trousers, the desert boots of the old Eighth Army hands, not bothering to display his badges of rank and relying at first instead upon warning and expectation to establish his identity. By the time the staff car or truck bringing Montgomery to visit a new formation drew up in its cloud of dust, everyone in the area knew who was arriving.

And then, of course, there was the matter of his headgear. His first unorthodoxy in this respect was to accept an Australian slouch hat while visiting their 9th Division, and to claim that in view of his childhood in Tasmania he was entitled to wear the Australian sunburst badge in addition to his own General Officer's insignia; but as the hat was so large and as he had so many units to visit, it soon became covered with the badges of almost every formation under his command and the result was slightly ridiculous. Eventually he changed it for the headgear which was soon to become indissolubly linked with his name – a black beret with the badges of the Royal Tank Corps and the General Staff – in itself a perhaps subconsciously significant combination, holding out as it did the promise of co-ordination between infantry and armour under a command knowledgeable of both.

Inevitably, as more and more men saw him and heard what he had to say, the stories began to circulate, the myths accumulate; and as Montgomery was in fact satisfying what de Guingand has described as a 'craving throughout the army for guidance and inspiration', they were all, whatever element of ridicule or mockery they may seem to contain, favourable. Rommel was reputed to be anxiously scouring the Afrika Korps for someone with knowledge of the rules of cricket in order to explain which six he was to be hit for, and after one of Montgomery's addresses at which he had mentioned – as he frequently did – 'the Lord, Mighty in Battle,' one young officer blandly inquired whether He could be presumed to be actually under command, or merely in support.

But Montgomery's sincerity, his clarity of vision (and few were then to question its width) and the total lack of ambiguity with which he expressed himself won enormous loyalty and enthusiasm.

'He told us everything:' one hard-bitten Regimental Sergeant Major told Vladimir Peniakoff, 'what his plan was for the battle, what he wanted the regiments to do, what he wanted *me* to do. And we will do it, sir. What a man!'[7]

It was not long, either, before he was being talked about on the opposite side of the front, among the German and Italian commanders planning for the next attack. But not much was known about him then, and certainly no one suspected that within eight months one of them would deliver himself of one very striking judgment: 'The war in the desert ceased to be a game when Montgomery took over.'[8]

For Rommel, the war in the desert had ceased to be a game well before July and by mid-August it had become something of a nightmare.

For one thing, he was himself very ill. He had now spent nineteen months on active service in Africa, which for a man of over fifty was a remarkable feat, even taking into consideration the care lavished upon him by his devoted staff. The elation of victory and advance had sustained him until July (as it had done a large proportion of his army) but with the development of the stalemate his spirits drooped and he began to be subject to fainting fits which he tried to hide from his staff, and especially from his medical adviser.

But with no improvement during August in the military situation (in fact, an exacerbation of problems of all kinds) there came no relaxation of tension for him and his physical deterioration became so evident that Professor Hörster insisted upon a complete examination. This revealed circulation and blood pressure problems, chronic stomach and intestinal catarrh and, of all incapacitating complaints in such circumstances, nasal diphtheria. The blocking of the nose and sinuses and consequent irritation of the throat which this infection causes in a cool and temperate climate is sufficiently debilitating to put most people to bed for several days; in the heat, dust, grime and general lack of sanitation of the war-time desert in August the resulting discomfort must have been excruciating – and the effort of will required to keep going at all, let alone to retain command of an army in the field, extraordinary.

Moreover, ill health was rife throughout his entire army, for however adaptable German Army training and doctrine were for the actual fighting of battles, it had not often been called upon to deal with tropical or sub-tropical conditions and the medical problems they bring. Panzerarmee Afrika lacked the historical experience of fighting in such intemperate climes as those of the North-West Frontier of India, for instance, which sustained the British Army, and German standards of hygiene were insufficiently rigorous while the diet was in general lacking in both variety and balance. Jaundice was widespread, desert sores universal (as they were in all armies, for no one found a complete cure for them), trachoma and amoebic dysentery commonplace; and with the halt after the sweep forward from Gazala and the gradual fading before their eyes of the enticing vision of delights ahead for them in Cairo and Alexandria, the Afrika Korps were beginning to show on their faces and in their bearing the strain of the last months.

And for the old hands of 90th Light, and 15th and 21st Panzer Divisions, the relative calm on the battlefield brought little or no alleviation of their discomforts for the supply situation seemed to become, if anything, worse as day followed day. At first they had welcomed the arrival at last of more German comrades to share the rigours of the desert war – units of 164th Division were now in the line with them, as were the Ramcke Parachute Brigade – and they were even prepared to welcome the Italian Folgore Parachute Division who had a good reputation and appeared to bear themselves well; but then it transpired that all these formations had come out to North Africa by air, so they possessed almost no lorries or other forms of transport of their own. Their rations, fuel, ammunition and everything else they would need to live and fight in the desert would therefore have to come forward on the existing supply mechanisms, already grossly overburdened by the tasks of supplying just the original Afrika Korps.

Now it became evident that there had been a serious incipient disadvantage in those large hauls of British supplies which had seemed so heaven-sent a few weeks before – in the sequestered batteries of 25-pounders so quickly put to efficient use by German artillerymen, in the capture of the massed parks of British lorries; for when the dumps emptied there were no factories behind German lines to manufacture British ammunition, or spare parts for the British trucks and lorries – and these by the end of July made up 85 per cent of Afrika Korps transport.

Most crucial of all, with the battle line now static there were no more reservoirs of British petrol to be gathered into their hands, and every drop to reach their fuel tanks must first cross the Mediterranean, then survive the unloading operation, often under heavy R.A.F. attack, then make the long and arduous journey forward from Tobruk, Benghasi or even Tripoli – journeys which themselves used up as much of the precious fluid as actually arrived.

As always happens in conditions of strain unrelieved by action or immediate danger, relations between the two Axis partners now worsened rapidly. To German eyes the weight of supplies arriving in North Africa for Italian formations appeared grossly out of proportion, not only in relation to military worth, but even out of proportion to plain numbers. Rommel was to claim to the German representative in Rome, von Rintelen, that Panzerarmee Afrika contained 82,000 Germans and but 42,000 Italians – yet during August only 8,200 tons of supplies arrived for the German element while 25,700 tons came in for the Italians; and in view of the dominance of the skies above Panzerarmee by the R.A.F., Rommel found it an additional annoyance that 8,500 tons had arrived safely for the Luftwaffe.

There were thus several matters of disagreement to upset even further the Generalfeldmarschall's uncertain blood pressure, perhaps the most serious being the arrival in Libya of two-thirds of the Italian Pistoia Division with over two hundred of their vehicles but with orders that they were not to cross the frontier into Egypt – while his own 164th division, already in the line, had to bring their supplies forward with a total of sixty vehicles, many of them already showing signs of the battering they were taking as they rolled and shuddered under excessive loads over disintegrating desert roads and tracks.

Cavallero on his occasional visits to the front would make promises to have such matters put right. 'But it just as frequently happened that on his next visit he would say with a laugh that he had made many a promise in his time and not all of them could be kept.'[9]

But it was not all the fault of the Italians, two of whom had specifically warned Rommel after the fall of Tobruk that to attempt the advance to the Delta while Malta remained to threaten his communications was to court disaster; and Malta during July and August was again justifying its description as the 'windlass of the Allied tourniquet' on Rommel's supply lines. R.A.F. reconnaissance aircraft based on the island kept the Allied Command fully informed about the movements of supply convoys, and these were attacked by submarines and by surface craft during their voyages and by R.A.F. Wellingtons and R.N.A.S. Albacores as soon as they arrived at their destinations.

In this activity both the R.A.F. and the Navy were now being aided to a significant extent by another service; the Ultra Intelligence was at last 'coming on stream' in an astonishingly effective manner.

A study of Military Intelligence in the First World War and the opening months of the Second can draw cynical reflections from even the most eager student of such recondite affairs. In the majority of cases its products always seemed to be either inaccurate or too late to be of use: and on the rare occasions when they were both correct and delivered in time, then they were ignored by the generals commanding the battles either because they did not believe them, or because the armies were already committed to a plan of battle and for one reason or another the generals were unwilling to modify it.

There were, of course, other reasons why the full benefit of the remarkable breakthrough achieved by the Bletchley organisation could not be reaped during the early months of the war. The knowledge in April 1941 that twelve panzer divisions were about to sweep down through the Balkans, and the routes they were to take, was in the hands of Maitland Wilson's headquarters in Greece by the end of March – but with the forces and equipment available to the Allies at that time, there was nothing they could do but skip out of the way when the panzers came through. You cannot stop military force with just the knowledge of its strength and intention.

Moreover, it was vitally important that nothing should reveal to the German authorities that their Enigma codes were being broken, for in German belief in their inviolability lay one of Britain's best hopes for eventual victory; and the shielding of this Enigma-breaking capability imposed delay and sometimes total embargo on the use of the information it gathered until organisations could be devised and set up to ensure that the dissemination of that information did not reveal the secret of its origin.

By the end of 1941 such an organisation was in being in the Middle East, and had, in fact, foreseen the arrival of the German merchant-ship *Ankara* at Benghasi in mid-December, with her cargo of twenty-two panzers. Unfortunately, consultations between the head of the relevant Intelligence section, Brigadier John Shearer, and his naval advisers convinced him that the *Ankara* would never be able to reach the Benghasi quays through the wrecks and debris with which the waters of the harbour were now choked, in order to unload her cargo.

He reckoned without the luck, the determination and the sheer expertise of the master of the *Ankara*; he was also ignorant of the fact that, to quote the words of Mr Ronald Lewin who first revealed the story in his book *Ultra Goes to War*, 'A current working into the blocked channel at Benghazi had gouged out enough space for *Ankara* to reach the quayside and get her tanks ashore. It was a feat characteristic of so indomitable a ship.'

The whole episode was itself characteristic of something else – the misfortune which dogs inexperience, especially of a new weapon or technique; but such episodes tend in themselves to provoke intense activity towards their correction, and so it proved in this case. One of the officers in the Intelligence section at Middle East Headquarters concerned with the analysis of the Afrika Korps logistics, and who was also one of the few in receipt of Ultra intelligence, was Major Enoch Powell, who after the *Ankara* affair brought to bear on the problem that cold, incisive and totally logical brain which has since brought him political notoriety together with considerable un-popularity among those not so intellectually endowed.

At his suggestion and with his participation, a small and secret inter-service committee was set up which met early every morning and analysed all the previous twenty-four hours' information, mostly from Ultra but also from other sources, regarding the Panzerarmee's supplies crossing the Mediterranean either by sea or by air. Time and systematisation inexorably built up a picture of Rommel's logistic service from which not only could the size of the supply convoys and the dates and ports of departure be provided, but also the names, specifications and past record of achievement of individual ships – and from this information the cargoes they were most likely to be carrying were deduced.

This knowledge was comparable to that provided by radar to R.A.F. Fighter Command during the Battle of Britain, for it meant that instead of flotillas of submarine or surface craft patrolling the wide seas in the hope of finding a convoy and perhaps sinking some of the more valuable cargoes, a single submarine or a flight of aircraft could now be directed to an exact destination, certain that they would find there a convoy amongst which would be the specified ships they were to attack and sink. As a result, the still exiguous forces at the disposal of Admiral Sir Henry Harwood and Air Marshal Sir Arthur Tedder were able to obtain results far out of proportion to their size, so that of thirty ships, fourteen barges and six supply submarines to leave Italy for North Africa during August, seven of the largest ships were lost taking with them to the bottom 1,660 tons of ammunition, 2,120 tons of general supplies, 43 guns, 367 assorted vehicles and, most crucial of all, 2,700 tons of petrol and oil – and although 12,800 tons of fuel did arrive, this was hardly enough to sustain the Panzerarmee in its positions, let alone to build up reserves for a battle.

The most crippling disadvantage under which Rommel now laboured was the abrupt switch after the fall of Tobruk of Hitler's attention from the North African to the Russian front. The massive drive through Southern Russia was gathering strength – Maikop fell on August 9th, Piatigorsk on the 10th, Mosdok was under threat by the 15th, and already just beyond the tips of the arrows marking the direction of advance for von Paulus's Sixth Army there beckoned the irresistible lure of Stalingrad – and the Afrika Korps was now a minor formation fighting an unimportant campaign against a secondary enemy. Rommel might still attract favourable comment whenever the Führer could spare a thought for him, but his requirements did not at that moment warrant even the momentary distraction of the High Command's attention from the Russian Front, and when Professor Hörster reported to O.K.W. that Rommel was 'not in a fit condition to command the forthcoming offensive' and his message was accompanied by the suggestion that Guderian should be sent out to command Panzerarmee Afrika on an acting basis until Rommel was fit again, the curt response 'Guderian unacceptable' arrived that night and no other replacement was suggested.

The message was quite clear; Rommel must make do with what he had in the area, bearing in mind all the time of course that under no circumstances would Hitler countenance a retreat – even as far as the Egyptian frontier.

But Rommel could see quite clearly that the longer he stayed where he was, the greater would be the strength built up against him (he already knew that a 100,000-ton convoy bringing every sort of supply for Eighth Army would arrive in the Suez Canal at or before the beginning of September) until a point would be reached after which it would be totally impossible for him to advance and his army would be able only to wait where it was until the British decided that their strength was so overwhelming that they could just move forward and crush it.

He must, therefore, advance – and soon, or the British minefields now growing thicker every day between Qaret el Abd and Himeimat would become as impassable as the defences the British had already formed from the coast down past Ruweisat Ridge.

The plan for battle he therefore evolved during the second half of August would rely for its success upon secrecy and, above all, on speed of execution. During one of the moonlit nights at the end of August, the two Afrika Korps panzer divisions, with Ariete and Littorio on the left flank and the combined German and Italian reconnaissance battalions on the right, would smash through the southern half of the British line, throw back the armoured cars and tanks of the 7th Armoured Division, and drive flat out for the area just south-west of El Hamman, arriving there before dawn. On the left of the Italian armoured division, 90th Light would move forward through the Munassib and Muhafid Depressions towards the gap between the rear of the New Zealanders and the new British division on the Alam Halfa Ridge. In the northern section of the line, the attention of the Australians, South Africans and Indians would be held to their front by pressure from the Italian divisions, plus local attacks by the 164th on the coast and the Ramcke Parachute Brigade in the centre.

By dawn the Afrika Korps divisions must be in position facing north for the breakthrough to the coast near Ruweisat Station and once this was reached von Bismarck's 21st Panzer were to turn east and race for Alexandria while 15th Panzer, back under command of von Vaerst and accompanied by 90th Light as soon as it had scattered the forces holding the Alam Halfa Ridge, were to drive south-east for Wadi Natrun and Cairo. Behind them the Italians would afford protection against any attempts the British might make to fall on the rear of the panzer divisions, and once these had turned east they would be able to wreak their usual havoc among the British supply depots, thus drawing off the British motorised forces who could then be defeated piece by piece as had so often happened before:

We placed particular reliance in this plan on the slow reaction of the British command and troops, for experience had shown us that it always took them some time to reach decisions and put them into effect. We hoped, therefore, to be in a position to present the operation to the British as an accomplished fact.

Things were then to move fast. The decisive battle was on no account to become static. With large British forces pinned down by repeated minor attacks by the German–Italian infantry left in the Alamein line, the decisive battle was to be fought out behind the British front in a form in which the greater aptitude of our troops for mobile warfare and the high tactical skill of our commanders could compensate for our lack of material strength. Separated from their supply depots, the British would be left with the option of either fighting it out to the end in their line or breaking out and falling back to the east, thus relinquishing their hold on Egypt.

Summing up, the success of the operation depended – the supply question apart – on the following factors:

(a) The effectiveness with which our move into the assembly area was concealed.
(b) The speed with which the breakthrough of the British line and the thrust into their rear could be achieved – in other words on the accuracy of the reconnaissance.[10]

But of course the supply question was not one which could ever be 'apart' or anything but vitally important. Given that the German gunners were so accurate that very little ammunition would be wasted, given that with an overwhelming victory in sight they would be willing to go hungry for a few days – even so, with all the willingness in the world they could not move without petrol. The plan relied totally upon the timely delivery of at least four days' supply before the attack was launched, and a continuous supply coming up every day at least equalling the amount burnt the day before – and nothing which had happened since Panzerarmee's arrival at El Alamein evoked the slightest confidence that such a supply would be maintained.

Yet Rommel could not wait, for time was so evidently not on his side. Even had the Italians blandly announced that they could not provide what were obviously his minimum requirements, he could not remain where he was without courting disaster – a disaster which began to loom even more ominously when on August 21st the R.A.F. began 'round the clock' bombing, which shook the nerves of even the toughest Afrika Korps units, depriving them of sleep, gradually wearing down their numbers and reducing even further the amount of transport available to feed them.

He *must* attack – and on August 27th both Kesselring and Cavallero visited him and were forced to agree. Kesselring thereupon promised to fly out to him a minimum of 500 tons of fuel a day while Cavallero assured him that 6,000 tons would immediately be despatched from Italy; and on August 30th Rommel received 1,500 tons taken from the Luftwaffe by Kesselring which together with the amount already with the panzer divisions was considered enough for a week's battle. As for the main bulk, he received another message from Cavallero: 'You can begin the battle now, Herr Feldmarschall. The petrol is already under way.'[11]

The die was cast; that night the moon, five days past full, would rise just before midnight and by that time the panzer divisions must be waiting at the edge of the British minefields between Alam Nayil and Himeimat, ready to sweep forward through them as soon as the engineers pronounced it safe to do so. They had already moved forward to their assembly areas during the four previous nights – a quarter at a time, the places from which each quarter had moved being then occupied by supply vehicles to confuse the R.A.F. while the panzers themselves were hastily camouflaged in their new positions in the broken ground around Jebel Kalakh. On August 29th the wheeled vehicles had gone up in one bound.

Assembled and ready to move forward were 200 panzers including 26 of the new Mark IV Specials with the long 75mm. gun, and 243 Italian mediums – for what they were worth. If they could only break through the minefields quickly, then skirt the Alam Halfa Ridge and reach the coast, they should prove enough to create the required panic amid the British ranks and enable Afrika Korps to crash through to the Delta and the rich loot of the supply depots there. So long as the petrol arrived regularly and on time.

As darkness fell on the evening of August 30th the leading panzers moved off towards the western edge of the minefields, engineers in front with infantry to guard them and lead the way through the lanes as soon as these were clear. All seemed to go well for the first half hour, but above the rumble of the panzer engines could be heard the high whine of aircraft, and although the more optimistic proclaimed them to be Me 109s the older hands recognised them for what they were – Hurricanes on reconnaissance. They wondered how long it would be before the bombers arrived.

Not long. Even as the first troops reached the British minefields, Wellingtons droned in above the massed panzers still in the assembly areas, parachute flares lit up the scene like daylight and the bombs came down; and from then on the night was a calvary of exploding H.E., of burning lorries and panzers – and of even more ominous events at the front. The minefields were much more extensive and sewn much more thickly than had been expected or previously experienced, and it was taking more time than had been allowed to get through them. The artillery was making things worse by shelling the passages through which British armoured cars had been observed passing, and this brought immediate reaction from anti-tank guns and artillery of the British motor brigade opposite; as parachute flares floated down behind the attacking infantry and engineers, these were silhouetted and subjected to a remorseless hail of rifle and machine-gun bullets. There had certainly been no surprise . . . and by daylight it was only too evident that speed was lacking too, and the programme well behind schedule.

There was other bad news for Rommel when he arrived at the

advanced H.Q. at Jebel Kalakh at 0800 on the morning of August 31st; General von Bismarck, the gallant and enterprising commander of 21st Panzer Division, had been killed when his motor-cycle combination blew up on a mine, and General Nehring, commander of the Afrika Korps, had been badly wounded in an air attack. Already, the basic provisions for success seemed to be lacking and the portents ominous; but knowing – like every successful general – that matters are never as bad or as good as they first appear, Rommel decided to wait and see what progress Afrika Korps made that morning. Temporary command had been taken over by the Chief of Staff, Oberst Bayerlein, and Rommel and he had worked closely enough together already for each to know and trust the other's judgment; when Rommel went forward to find Bayerlein he was greeted with the first good news of the day – that Afrika Korps were at last through the minebelt and could now deploy.

However, adjustments must be made. With the British now thoroughly alerted, there was little or no chance of the panzer

Map 20   The Battle of Alam Halfa, August 31st

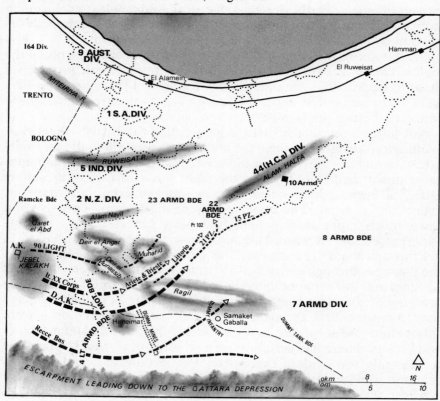

spearheads reaching that first objective south-west of El Hamman unassailed – probably from both north and south by 10th Armoured and 7th Armoured Divisions respectively – so the turn north must take place earlier. The best axis for the advance of the Afrika Korps would now be the line of telegraph poles which led up from Himeimat towards the centre of the Alam Halfa Ridge, while Littorio and Ariete could swing up on their left towards Point 102 in the gap between the New Zealanders' rear and whoever was on Alam Halfa, while 90th Light in their turn guarded the Italians' left flank.

There would undoubtedly be a tough battle for the ridge, but so long as the Grants of 10th Armoured Division were properly lured forward on to the 88mm. anti-tank screen and there destroyed in the usual manner, then the experience and expertise of 21st and 15th Panzer should be enough to deal with the holders of the ridge, who had just been identified by Intelligence as a new and unfledged division straight out from England. In the meantime, the reconnaissance battalions were successfully pushing back armoured cars south and east of Himeimat and would soon be free to cover the right flank of 15th Panzer. Things were not so bad, after all.

News from the north was quite satisfactory, too. Ramcke's parachutists had attacked the infantry opposite and destroyed one company before retiring, 164th Infantry Division had attacked the Australians and kept their attention firmly away from the main battle area and although the Italians opposite the South Africans and the Indian troops had scored no notable successes, they had at least held their positions. The greatest menace on that front, as here in the south, was from the R.A.F. who were still omnipresent, and if allowed to keep up their continual attacks would undoubtedly prove an embarrassment when the time came – as it shortly would – for refuelling the panzers and refilling the ammunition racks.

Fortune, briefly, was again on Rommel's side. Just as the fuel gauges in panzers and lorries were dropping to dangerous levels a dust storm blew up, thickening quickly into the choking yellow fog which made everyone's life miserable except those quick-witted enough to appreciate the protection it gave from the enemy aircraft, now impotently returning to base. By 1300, the panzer divisions were ready to move forward again with Littorio close alongside, though Ariete and Trieste were lagging behind – delayed, so they said, by more British minefields which had apparently been laid even thicker in the northern sector of the defences. It was thus 1500 before XX Corps were moving, well behind on the left flank of the advance.

But by this time, puzzlement and some frustration was nagging the commands of both panzer divisions. Soft sand had bedevilled them since shortly after their first move and already the petrol gauges were again dropping alarmingly; and where was the British armour? Two hours' sweat and slog through the sandstorm had brought the leading panzers (Mark IIIs with some of the Mark IV Specials) to the point where the line of telegraph posts veered east and some of them followed it, leading along almost parallel to the ridge, their commanders cursing the fog, their eyes sore from the grit and the perpetual strain of watching for the enemy.

Then at last from their rear came the sounds of battle; away to the north-west, from the foothills around Point 102 had suddenly appeared some Grants and some Crusaders, evidently about to attack the van of the panzer advance. The Mark IIIs swung left and moved out, the anti-tank screens formed up with their usual precision and waited for their prey to be lured forward. It all promised a repeat of the classical baited trap which had succeeded so often before – though it did seem that the panzers were having to move rather far forward and the Grants were strangely hesitant.

But the range closed, the Grants opened fire, the panzers halted and fired back and quite soon twelve of the Grants were burning furiously although anti-tank fire from out of the setting sun had knocked out some of the panzers too. But as the sun went down further, the wind dropped, visibility improved and the panzer crews could see that the destruction of the Grants had left a sizeable gap in the British defences. Gingerly, they moved towards it, waiting for the next wave of British tanks to appear, cursing the sun which, as it dropped, effectively blinded them; to such an extent that they were but three hundred yards from the waiting Rifle Brigade anti-tank screen before they saw it, and they thus caught the full blast of highly accurate and concentrated firing, augmented immediately by heavier artillery fire from behind the near foothills which screamed overhead and fell among the following waves and the waiting 88mms.

Instinctively, the panzers charged forward at the anti-tank screens and overran the forward platoons, but then at last saw what they had been waiting for; over the rise in front of them came the leading waves of a squadron of Grants, with more waves following, all exhibiting the usual panache of British armour, the speed, the waving pennons, the clouds of dust, the élan of the hunting field. Waiting only to fire off one hasty salvo, the panzers turned and sped for the protection of the 88mms, confident that behind them the field would soon be littered with the burning hulks of yet more British tanks. As the light was fading fast, this would be the last action of the day.

As far as ground action was concerned this was so – but it did not end quite as the panzer crews expected. As they reached their anti-tank screens, the only noise of battle they heard above the roar of their own engines was the crash of 25-pounder shells landing amongst them, and when they turned they saw that the British armour had only pursued them as far as the edge of the gap into which they had penetrated, and were now waiting there in defensive positions out of effective range of the 88mms. And very soon afterwards came news that an attempt by the leading panzers of 15th to attack the British infantry on the middle of the Alam Halfa Ridge had had the same unsatisfactory result, running first into minefields and then into such a concentration of artillery fire that they too had been forced back into the soft sand below the ridge, where they expended even more of their precious petrol retiring into the leaguer area.

By this time darkness had fallen, and precedent demanded that a decent silence should now fall upon the battlefield, the British withdrawing into remote leaguers, the Afrika Korps refilling their fuel tanks and replenishing their ammunition racks.

But somebody was making new rules. There was to be no respite for the Afrika Korps now, for all night long the British artillery on the ridge poured shells into the area just below while the R.A.F. carried out a long session of pattern bombing on the eastern flank, which caught the hapless reconnaissance battalions in the open desert, banished all hope of sleep for the entire Panzerarmee, wrecked several of their vehicles and killed and wounded a large number of their most experienced men.

And there was no petrol coming up. The lanes through the minefields were choked, attacked by marauding armoured cars and occasionally menaced by artillery fire, and moreover it would seem that the supply echelons were lacking in the enthusiasm necessary to get the supplies forward. This lack of initiative was noticeable elsewhere too, for many observers that day felt that Afrika Korps were not attacking with their usual fire, and Rommel was later to make a significant comment upon the new factor which had entered the desert war against him:

> Anyone who has to fight, even with the most modern weapons, against an enemy in complete command of the air, fights like a savage against modern European troops, under the same handicaps and with the same chance of success.[12]

So when the morning of September 1st came, only 15th Panzer had sufficient petrol to mount an attack – against the western end of Alam Halfa Ridge – and this was to prove as inconclusive and as puzzling as had been the attacks of the day before. The division moved off shortly after first light, probing between the scene of the previous day's fighting and the most western infantry positions on the ridge, to find themselves caught in yet another devastating artillery bombardment and then attacked from the east by a force of mixed Grants and Crusaders which again refrained from chasing the panzers as they fell back to the protection of the 88mms; the British tanks thus escaped their planned annihilation although the panzers themselves did manage to knock out seven of the Grants at a cost of a couple of their own Mark IIIs. By early afternoon, 15th Panzer were back to the positions from which they had started, but with rather less petrol and ammunition with which to face the immediate future.

And behind them, Rommel and his staff were becoming increasingly worried – and indeed, severely persecuted. The R.A.F. had hardly paused in their attacks all day, concentrating especially on the area around Ragil where one bomb had killed seven of the staff of 15th Panzer Division, whose commander von Vaerst had now as senior officer taken over command of the Afrika Korps from Oberst Bayerlein. All that night it was the same as the night before – a continuous thunder of artillery from the ridge and the crash of shells amid the dispersed lorries and panzers, the whole scene lit by parachute flares and the garish light of burning vehicles as Wellingtons and Albacores flew overhead in such perfect formations that the more cynical among the Afrika Korps men christened the attacks 'Party Rally raids', their high explosive bombs bursting with shattering effect on the hard desert floor, cutting down anything standing two feet above it with whining scythe-blades of steel. Besides the actual physical destruction, the effect on the officers and men of the Afrika Korps was becoming grave as lack of sleep, the strain of waiting for the next bomb, the consciousness of how helpless they were under skies so completely dominated by the enemy, all began to take their toll. By the following morning (September 2nd) Rommel was coming to the conclusion that he must abandon the operation.

The last three days had been for him a deeply disturbing experience. Excitement and the anticipation of battle had brought about a brief improvement in his health for a day or so before the advance began, but now the gnawing symptoms of stomach trouble were back, the nausea and the blocked nasal passages all adding to the problems with which he must wrestle. As he went forward to seek out von Vaerst for the morning conference, the signs of incipient defeat and demoralisation were all around him. Not only were the panzers unable to move forward because of empty fuel tanks, but the men were unwilling to come out of their slit-trenches because of the continual air attack – a condition vividly illustrated to Rommel when he was himself forced to dive into one, whereupon a huge shell splinter ripped through the blade of a shovel lying on the lip of the trench and a piece of red hot metal fell in beside him.

There was another ominous factor about the air attacks on this day, too. Amid the perfect formations of aircraft wearing the R.A.F. roundels were now appearing Mitchells and Liberators with the white star of the U.S.A.F. – a token of the force which would be thrown against Germany once the full industrial strength and manpower of America was mobilised.

But the most immediate problem for Rommel was still the shortage of petrol; and one piece of news brought to him that afternoon was that a supply convoy of nearly three hundred lorries had been caught just east of Himeimat by some marauding light tanks of 7th Armoured Division, which scattered them and destroyed fifty-seven of their number. This meant that there now remained in the advanced areas only one petrol issue for the depleted panzer and soft-skinned vehicles left to him – enough for a move of about one hundred kilometres over good going, perhaps half that distance over the kind of surface with which they were now surrounded. Would they, in fact, have enough fuel even to retreat to safety . . . wherever that might now lie?

That evening he went back to Jebel Kalakh and there found Kesselring awaiting him – sympathetic to his problems and willing to throw every aircraft at his disposal into the task of protecting the army on the ground, but nevertheless the bearer of bad news. The R.A.F. had been active over other places than the battlefield, and two of the tankers bringing petrol across from Italy had already been sunk; as for the five hundred tons per day promised by Kesselring himself, although this was being despatched from the various dumps in which it had been stored, it was 'consuming itself' on the way forward in the tanks of the vehicles bringing it up over the appalling roads and tracks.

The searching analysis of the supply situation which this provoked then unearthed more unpleasant facts. Of the 5,000 tons of petrol which Cavallero had promised would be in Rommel's hands by the following day, 2,600 tons had already been sunk, 1,500 tons was still in Italy (despite Cavallero's message on the eve of the attack) and the prospect of the remaining 1,000 tons arriving in time to be of use was limited indeed.

That night Rommel sent off a report to O.K.W. telling them of his decision to call off the operation, to withdraw his divisions gradually along their own tracks to the starting line, there to await either the necessary reinforcement and supplies to begin again . . . or whatever fate the Gods of Battle and the new British general had in store for them. As the report went off the R.A.F. arrived punctually over the battle area, the hapless troops around Ragil being especially sub-jected to relentless bombing, brilliantly illuminated by flares which they could not extinguish and which seemed never to die. A new terror was let loose upon them that night when down from the noisy darkness above came hurtling two 4,000-pound bombs which shook the floor of the desert and flung into the air huge lumps of stone to add to the death and destruction from bomb splinters.

The night of September 2nd/3rd was the bitterest to date in the history of the Afrika Korps and in the military career of their general.

From the new British general's point of view, of course, matters looked very different.

By noon of the first day of the battle, Montgomery had concluded that all the forecasts made by his intelligence staff had been correct, that the main Afrika Korps drive was in the south and that the attacks in the north were merely holding operations which could easily be beaten off. He thereupon ordered 23rd Armoured Brigade to move their Valentines down behind the New Zealanders to plug any gap which might exist there, and told Ramsden to start thinning out the forward troops of XXX Corps in order to form a reserve in case opportunity arose for unexpected exploitation.

He then checked that his staff were efficiently collecting all necessary information, and began himself a series of regular visits to his chief subordinates. Horrocks had been dissatisfied with the defence put up both by the 7th Motor Brigade and the 4th Light Armoured Brigade in the south, telling Renton that the 7th Armoured Division appeared more concerned to save their own skins than to fight the enemy – a comment which outraged all who heard of it and which in view of the comparative fragility of the vehicles then with both brigades was certainly unfair; but it ensured that from that moment on, every unit in the division hit as hard as it could whenever the opportunity presented itself.

But this attitude in itself had to be watched, for Montgomery's total embargo on piecemeal armoured forays remained and indeed he was at pains to emphasise it wherever he went. When by the morning of September 3rd the R.A.F. reported that all the enemy vehicles in the area were now pointing westwards and that over a thousand of them were driving in that direction just north of Ragil, the instructions issued to Horrocks were that XIII Corps could close up behind them but that offensive moves should be limited to patrol activity aimed at harrying enemy soft-skinned transport and supply columns.

Not only did Montgomery want as much of his armour as possible preserved for his future plans but, whether he had read it or not, he was in agreement with that part of Dorman-Smith's appreciation of July 27th which read, 'None of the formations in Eighth Army is now sufficiently well trained for offensive operations. The Army badly needs either a reinforcement of well-trained formations or a quiet period in which to train.'[13]

No such well-trained formations had arrived, and as for the 'quiet period in which to train' – both Dorman-Smith and Auchinleck had declared that no offensive could possibly be launched before mid-September even under ideal conditions, and this was another point with which Montgomery would have agreed. There would thus be no launching of armoured brigades into battle, however enticing the prospect might look, for there was too great a chance that the enticement might be deliberate, the prospect deceiving.

However, if the armour was judged lacking in the training and efficiency to carry out an assault, the same was not true of all of the infantry – and as it happened, some of the most experienced were exactly poised to deliver a perhaps lethal blow at what might still be Rommel's weakest point. If the New Zealanders could drive south as far as Himeimat, they might so choke the escape route of the Panzerarmee that an appreciable part of it might not get back. Freyberg was therefore instructed to mount such an attack during the night of September 3rd/4th, though as his men had already borne so much of the campaign in the desert, he was given 132nd Brigade of 44th Division to accompany his own 5th Brigade, still commanded by the redoubtable Howard Kippenberger.

Operation Beresford was a failure for a number of reasons, the chief being that however ill Rommel might be, he was not so distracted as to attempt to withdraw his main forces through a narrow gap without first ensuring that the sides of the gap were adequately stiffened. Defences had been prepared along the northern edge of both the Muhafid and Munassib Depressions and also of Deir el Angar further out to the west, and during September 2nd these defences had been occupied by elements of both the Ramcke Brigade and the Folgore Division, both in their first desert battle and both eager to prove their superiority as parachutists over ordinary infantry.

It was into these defences that the men of the 4th and 5th Battalions of the Royal West Kents (132nd Brigade) ran headlong, after a badly delayed start, a thoroughly confused advance garishly illuminated most of the way by a burning truck, and a complete breakdown of communications. Although the brigade commander, Brigadier C. B. Robertson, had taken the trouble to ask Kippenberger's advice upon some details of the attack, he then took little notice of it, advanced too quickly himself, was badly wounded and had to be evacuated, leaving his already disintegrating brigade without a commander.

On the eastern flank of the attack, the New Zealanders did rather better, though their two leading battalions lost touch and diverged leaving between them a gap into which trundled some supporting Valentines whose crews, under the impression that the infantry were still in front, drove unexpectedly into the German defences and lost twelve of their number before they could extricate themselves. Meanwhile, the Maoris on the left flank had charged rather over-enthusiastically out towards Muhafid and the morning found them in the open desert, while on their right the other New Zealand battalion was also unpleasantly exposed.

In all, *Operation Beresford* had that night advanced rather less than two miles into empty desert and Allied forces were now occupying exposed positions in front of defences manned by determined and enterprising troops – at a cost already of 700 casualties from 132nd Brigade and 124 from 5th New Zealand. Moreover, 6th New Zealand Brigade had mounted a diversionary attack on 132nd Brigade's right, and lost another 159 men including their commander, the ebullient and irrepressible George Clifton, who was taken prisoner. (He escaped a day or so later, was recaptured and sent to Italy where he then escaped four times, being recaptured close to the Swiss border on the last; after which he was sent to Germany where he broke out another four times, was badly wounded on his eighth attempt but finally made it on his ninth.)

By the evening of September 4th, it was thus evident that the attempt to close the gap had failed, and Montgomery ordered the exposed formations to withdraw out of danger during the night. The only offensive measures from then on were to be by the armoured cars and light tanks in the south which should continue their harrying activities; under no circumstances should the heavier armour be engaged.

Hindered only by continual shelling and the gradually subsiding attentions of the R.A.F., the remains of Panzerarmee were thus allowed to withdraw during the next day until they reached the edge of the British minefields, where their rearguards halted, 15th Panzer going back to Jebel Kalakh, 21st Panzer remaining further forward with some of its units occupying the edge of Munassib and others the only visibly worthwhile gains the battle had made for Rommel – the twin peaks of Himeimat from which good observation of the southern part of what became known as the Alamein Line was available. However, as Montgomery had already decided to mislead Rommel into a belief that when he at last attacked, he would do so in the south, this vantage point was later to provide nothing but bogus information, but quite a lot of that.

On the evening of September 5th Montgomery issued an Order of the Day which announced:

> The Battle of Alamein [sic] has now lasted for six days, and the enemy has slowly but surely been driven from 8 Army area. Tonight, 5th September, his rearguards are being driven west, through the minefield area north of Himeimat. All formations and units, both armoured and unarmoured, have contributed towards this striking victory, and have been magnificently supported by the R.A.F. I congratulate all ranks of 8 Army on the devotion to duty and good fighting qualities which have resulted in such a heavy defeat of the enemy and which will have far-reaching results.[14]

Like quite a number of war-time announcements by both sides, this one attained its purpose but does not stand up well to close examination. The main bulk of the infantry of XXX Corps had hardly seen action at all, and although the armour of XIII Corps had played some part in the battle, it had not been in the mobile role for which armour is intended. The gunners had done well, the R.A.F. magnificently; but it was petrol shortage which had contributed as much as any other factor to the defeat of the Afrika Korps, so perhaps Montgomery should have included the Royal Navy (and, privately, the Ultra Organisation) in his congratulations.

British losses in killed, wounded and missing amounted to 1,750, German losses to 1,859 and Italian to 1,051 – so from the point of view of the 'butcher's bill' it would seem that the British had done better. But the Germans had left the wrecks of only 38 panzers behind and the Italians had lost only eleven of their tanks, while despite Montgomery's caution, 67 British tanks had been so badly damaged that even with the ease of recovery after the battle they had to be written off. The difference in aircraft losses – 41 German and Italian against 68 British – was a reflection of far greater activity by the R.A.F. than by their opponents.

But these comparisons could not be made by the men on the battlefield, and they were busy making others. They were remembering the proclamation made to them before the *Crusader* operation and the Gazala Battles, and what validity those promises had afterwards proved to contain; and they reflected now that even if Rommel had not yet been 'hit for six', he had at least been adequately stonewalled, which was all that Montgomery had said would happen this time. The little man with the funny hats had been as good as his word on this occasion, and would thus certainly deserve a second chance; if he delivered as well next time, Eighth Army would begin to believe that he knew his job, and might then be prepared to follow him with some of the enthusiasm and confidence which they had given to some of his precedessors – and lost in a welter of incompetence and mismanagement.

There were now certainly grounds for hope – hope that in future their lives would not be sacrificed uselessly, hope that the machinery of the army would not break down as soon as it was exposed to the realities of battle, hope that they would be told the truth about their equipment and leadership before they had to trust their lives to either, and that in the future any exhortations to battle would not be so empty and meaningless as in the past.

Above all, there was hope that Rommel and his Afrika Korps were not, after all, invincible, and that in time Eighth Army could and would beat them.

In the circumstances, they were even prepared to believe their new commander when he said they needed more – and radically different – training.

7 · Daffodil, Hyacinth, Snowdrop and Tulip

There were some units in Montgomery's new command – or at any rate operating in the Eighth Army theatre – which were already committed to action and thus beyond reach of new training methods, which for some at least was to prove unfortunate and for many fatal.

During the early summer, Lieutenant-Colonel John Haselden (who had acted as guide for the famous Keyes Raid on Rommel's headquarters at Beda Littoria just before *Crusader*) had spent a great deal of time behind Axis lines disguised as an Arab, collecting and sending back much valuable information. He had come back to Cairo at the end of July and early in August had suggested, to a newly constituted command for raiding forces in Alexandria, that he return to Tobruk with a few picked saboteurs and there blow up the bulk fuel storage tanks which were so heavily concreted as to be virtually immune from air attack, his party then escaping south into the desert to a rendezvous with the Long Range Desert Group.

In the circumstances of August 1942, any suggestions for the destruction of more of Rommel's petrol supplies were welcomed with enthusiasm – but on this occasion with perhaps a little too much. Before many days had elapsed, a slightly bemused John Haselden found himself commanding a much larger force than he had ever contemplated, taking part in a combined operation of ever-increasing complexity.

The final plan for *Operation Daffodil*, as this attack on Tobruk was called, envisaged the penetration of the Tobruk defences along the El Adem–Tobruk road by a party of commandos with sappers and signallers attached, travelling in three lorries with Afrika Korps markings, the men disguised as prisoners-of-war, with members of the highly secret Special Interrogation Group (S.I.G.) dressed in German uniforms acting the part of lorry drivers and guards. The men from S.I.G. were mostly Jews who had escaped from Germany and were thus fluent German speakers, and their fate if taken prisoner was certain death, quick if they were fortunate.

Having entered Tobruk, this force (Force B) would seize the easternmost inlet at Mersa Sciausc under cover of the heaviest air raid the port had experienced up to that time, capture the coastal guns in the neighbourhood, and hold the inlet while a company of Argyll and Sutherland Highlanders with machine-gunners from the Royal Northumberland Fusiliers (Force C) came ashore from a flotilla of sixteen motor torpedo boats and three Fairmile motor launches which would have made the journey from Alexandria. The joint forces would then fight their way westwards, capturing the coastal and defence guns along the southern shore of the harbour, while in the meantime Force A, consisting of a battalion of Royal Marines with attached gunners and sappers, would be landed at Mersa Mreira to the north of Tobruk itself. This force would fight its way into the town, join hands with Forces B and C, and then capture the guns on the northern side of the harbour. With all the harbour protection guns then affectively silenced, the destroyers upon which the marines had travelled, H.M.S. *Sikh* and H.M.S. *Zulu*, would then enter the harbour and land specialist demolition parties to destroy the fuel tanks, harbour installations, any enemy shipping present and a tank repair shop. The destroyers would then evacuate the wounded and part of the attacking force, while the rest moved out into the area around the port, wrecking all Axis installations they could find, releasing British and South African prisoners-of-war believed still to be there, and sequestering all enemy transport, in which they would escape out into the desert.

Both the journey in and the escape out would be led by L.R.D.G. patrols who would be in complete control of timing and movement to and from the area, and these, while the main actions were being fought, would themselves wreck the radio direction-finding station along the El Adem road, destroy aircraft on the adjacent landing grounds, help release some of the prisoners, hold the main exits for the escaping forces and then lead them back to Kuffra when they had emerged.

According to the latest intelligence reports (gathered, according to one account, from a South African soldier who had been taken prisoner in Tobruk, put to work in a German officers' mess and had subsequently escaped), Tobruk was weakly held by only two battalions of Italian second-line troops, with a possible stiffening of not more than a thousand German technicians. Given complete surprise and the luck which normally attends youth and daring, it was by no means impossible that the operation would attain many of its objectives, and thus create enormous confusion behind the Axis lines in addition to destroying yet more of Rommel's precious petrol and his equally essential unloading facilities.

And this was not the sole operation to be mounted that same night, as a pattern of simultaneous raids had been planned. David Stirling was to take a large party of his S.A.S. mounted in forty heavily armed jeeps into Benghasi, which they were to take and hold for as long as necessary in order to sink all ships in the port, block the inner harbour and destroy oil storage and pumping plants; and the L.R.D.G. patrols which led them were at the same time to attack the airfield at Benina. This was *Operation Snowdrop*; *Operation Hyacinth* was a wholly L.R.D.G. affair at Barce where two patrols would attack the landing-ground and destroy all aircraft there, causing as much chaos and confusion among the Italian garrison as possible.

All parties would then endeavour to escape south to Kuffra (a distance of some 500 miles from Barce and Benghasi, be it said) and as they must all therefore pass close to the Jalo oasis, it would obviously be best if the oasis were in friendly hands. *Operation Tulip*, would therefore take place on the night after the main raids in the north, whereby Force Z – a detachment of the Sudan Defence Force, guided of course by another L.R.D.G. patrol – attacked the fort at Jalo and held it until all raiding forces had withdrawn through the gap and were well on their way to the south. The Sudan Defence Force would also send one motorised battalion from Baharia towards Siwa as a demonstration which might distract Axis attention – and especially Axis aircraft – away from the more vulnerable areas to the west.

John Haselden's original idea had therefore ballooned from a single operation carried out by a maximum of ten men, into four operations engaging a total strength of nearly seven hundred in the raids themselves, and at least as many in administration. Moreover, a considerable naval force would be engaged, as in addition to the two destroyers and the M.T.B.s and M.L.s mentioned it was obviously necessary to put heavier ships to sea to afford protection against both air and sea attack, especially during the withdrawal. The cruiser H.M.S. *Coventry* and eight Hunt class destroyers would accompany the forces attacking Tobruk, and another cruiser with five more destroyers would bombard Daba during the night of the raids in order to provide some form of diversion,. This deployment of naval strength was by no means popular with Admiral Harwood and his staff, for they were all well aware that the Royal Navy would shortly have an important part to play in a large-scale battle, and that losses which they could ill afford must inevitably occur during this previous – and comparatively unimportant – series of operations.

Other commanders were also worried. For instance, the successes which had attended S.A.S. operations to date had mostly been won by small groups of men, rarely of more than ten and usually of four or five; now David Stirling was required to take nearly two hundred men into action, quite a high proportion of whom were inexperienced in

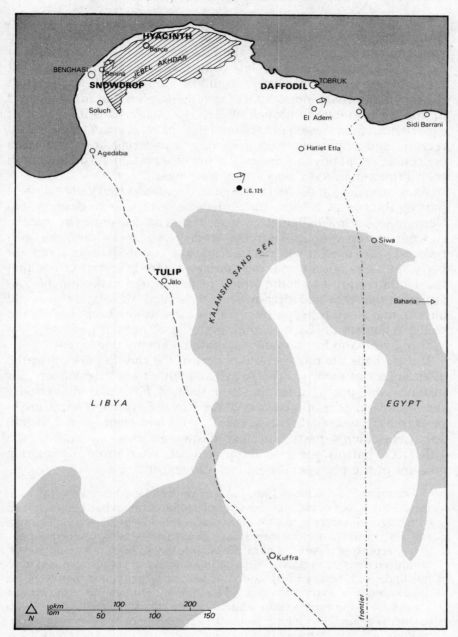

Map 21   The raids of September 13th

raiding, and some hastily – and thus perhaps inadequately – trained. Both the inexperience and the size of the force would rob it of the vital element of flexibility, for the first necessitated close control of every individual unit and vehicle, which with the second meant that the only approach to the target could be along a road, and through the inevitable roadblocks. Shock, speed and bluff had often sufficed in the past to burst through these, but many of Stirling's most experienced men viewed the accumulation of vehicles and equipment, recruits and armament with misgiving, wondering how so large a concourse could possibly escape enemy observation at some point in their fifteen-hundred-mile journey from base.

As for the naval officers in charge of the always tricky operation of putting the troops ashore, some of these were near to desperation. Neither *Sikh* nor *Zulu* had been spared from normal duties in order to concentrate on rehearsal for the landing operations, and not long before D-day itself it was realised that the two destroyers could not carry sufficient boats to put the marines ashore in one wave and that the landing-craft – so rudimentary in design and makeshift in construction that they had already been christened 'shoe-boxes' – would have to make two trips, putting half the force ashore each time. In the single rehearsal on Cyprus, the operation of putting just one wave ashore had taken far too long . . . with no enemy interference.

But perhaps the most serious aspect of the run-up period was the evident lack of security. The Argyll and Sutherland Highlanders, for instance, had practised landing from their M.T.B.s and M.L.s under the interested gaze of members of the Royal Egyptian Yacht Club in Alexandria, and Vladimir Peniakoff, who had been invited to join John Haselden's party but had hastily attached himself to the L.R.D.G. patrols going to Barce instead, later wrote a withering account of the pre-operational lack of control:

The night of September 13th, 1942, might well have been a nightmare to the enemy if, out of the blue, his lines of communication had been attacked by mysterious forces in five different places spread over 250 miles. German and Italian headquarters would have been flooded with conflicting messages, reporting a party of parachutists on Benina landing-ground and an armoured division in Barce, and a certain amount of confusion might have resulted. As it was, unfortunately for us, our bright young men were far too excited to hold their tongues: when they were turned out of the Middle East H.Q. in the evening they gathered in the bars and night clubs of Cairo to discuss again their childish plans: their friends joined in with suggestions picked from boyish books that they had pored over in earnest only a few years before, Drake and Sir Walter Raleigh, Morgan and the Buccaneers were outbidden, new stratagems poured out in a stream of inventiveness, while circles of admiring Levantines formed round the excited youths, and the barmen's ears visibly stretched while they mixed their drinks in feigned aloofness.

Later at night lovely dark Syrian heads on crumpled pillows listened carefully to their blond bed-fellows: military plans mingled with the raw pleadings of inexperienced passion. Early next morning the telephones in Gezirah and Qasr el Dubara buzzed with shrill Levantine voices exchanging notes in French, Italian and Greek, mixed with English military expressions and names of units. The Cairenes loved to impress their friends with a knowledge of our future operations, and wasted no time in spreading around any scrap of information they had managed to collect: amongst them, indistinguishable, just another bridge-playing Levantine, was the Italian agent, sitting pretty with an easy job indeed. No romantic disguises for him, no purloining of secret documents, no treacherous accomplices to be kept in order – no risks at all, in fact, no expenses and no trouble: he just stayed at home and answered the telephone. A host of enthusiastic voluntary helpers, unwitting and unbidden, provided him with solid material for daily reports, which, enciphered, went on the air from a discreet wireless set in a villa off the Pyramids Road.[1]

There is, undoubtedly, a degree of imaginative fictionalisation about that picture, for many of the colourful details are unprovable; but in its essence it would seem to be accurate, bearing out the sentence in a letter written later by one of the more senior officers concerned: 'Security in these operations was quite appalling.'[2]

Nevertheless, the first stage of the main operations went quite smoothly. The commandos under John Haselden completed the trip down to Kuffra with ample time to spare and then, guided by two L.R.D.G. patrols under Captain David Lloyd Owen, travelled north along the western edge of the Kalansho Sand Sea, slipped past Jalo during the night of September 8th, and reached Hatiet Etla some ninety miles south of Tobruk by September 10th. There they rested, cleaning and checking their weapons, and Haselden briefed them all again on their individual tasks.

On the morning of Sunday, September 13th, they moved off to a wadi some thirty-five miles south of Tobruk, rested there briefly and were then guided by the L.R.D.G. to within sight of the by-pass, where they packed into three lorries, the men detailed as drivers and guards changed into German uniforms, all arms were hidden but kept ready for instant use, and the nerve-racking opening moves began. They were somewhat delayed by the difficulties of descending the escarpment, but once down drove smoothly along the road amid scattered and only slightly curious Axis traffic and, to their immense relief, were then waved casually through the roadblock at the entrance in the perimeter wire by Italian guards too bored even to bother to look at the papers one of the S.I.G. men had ready.

Inside, matters did not proceed quite so smoothly, as they quickly met a fast-moving convoy coming towards them and their middle lorry was struck a glancing blow by a German staff car carrying, according to another S.I.G. man, a high-ranking officer. None of the lorries stopped – indeed they accelerated away – while behind them the Axis convoy slowed to a halt, various angry voices shouted after them but eventually the convoy started off again, doubtless with someone writing down the lorry numbers for disciplinary action to be taken at some future date. For another uncomfortable period the commandos were accompanied by three motor-cycle combinations bearing German military police who seemed unnecessarily inquisitive, and for a time it seemed that Very lights erupted on every occasion they passed an important Axis installation, giving the impression that their course was being charted; but no attempt was made to stop them, and the most memorable moment in their journey into Tobruk came when Haselden nodded casually towards an impressive rock-face looming out of the near darkness (for it was by now nearly 2100) and said, 'That's the bomb-proof oil-storage depot we must destroy later tonight.'[3]

At least one officer swore bitterly to himself as they drove past for it seemed quite obvious that had the occupants of that one lorry baled

Map 22   The raid on Tobruk

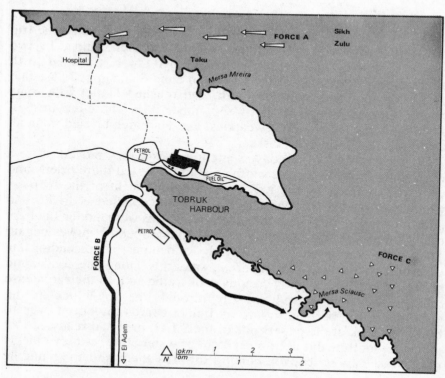

out there and then, the oil which was, after all, the prime target of the
raid could have been destroyed within such a short time that little or
no resistance would have been encountered. Haselden's original plan
would seem to have been eminently feasible – and without such a
large commitment of manpower and equipment.

They skirted Tobruk town, turned east and only a few minutes
after the scheduled time were debussing at the head of the inlet which
was their objective, sorting their weapons, those who had travelled in
German uniforms quickly (and with some relief) changing into their
own. Aircraft were droning in above them, one party moved off in
the dark to the reported positions of two heavy coastal guns on the
east shore of Sciausc Bay, and as the bombers arrived over Tobruk
town and harbour the air raid alarms were given and the port area
sprang to life. Everything was going according to plan.

It continued to do so for a little while longer.

The main commando party moved up through the wadi and had
little difficulty in taking over the crucially important headland overlooking Sciausc Bay, the Italian gunners and support infantry making
the fatal but very natural mistake of believing that they would be
safer if they remained in their billets and did not venture out into the
increasingly noisy night beyond. Many of them were thus killed by
grenades thrown through barrack windows or dropped down ventila-
tors into the underground shelter, and those who ran for it were
hunted down amid the rocks and crannies of the steep-sided wadi and
the majority killed – although a few prisoners were taken. From one
of them, an N.C.O., was elicited the statement that the garrison had
recently been increased to at least a brigade and that there were over
two thousand extra German troops inside the perimeter waiting to go
forward into the line at El Alamein; but little notice was taken of
what a frightened prisoner was saying.

Within an hour the first success signal was fired indicating that the
headland was secure, and once Haselden received a similar signal
from the party looking for the coastal guns, he could raise Base H.Q.,
who would then order in the light craft with the Argylls to join him,
and the destroyers now presumably off the Mreira inlet to send in
their marines. But the second party was having a thoroughly frustrating time.

They had run into an unexpected minefield very shortly after
setting out, and Haselden's success signal went up before they were
even clear of it. But they pressed on, cursing the slowness of the
sappers in front, gradually working down towards the beach until at
last they reached it and could move more quickly in the shadows of
the overhanging cliffs. They found a Spandau nest and a radio
station, both of which they stormed and destroyed in sharp, vicious
actions, and then at last one of a recce party sent out in advance

reported back that they had found the heavy guns' positions –
disused and unmanned. Their success signal went up just in time for
Haselden to send off the code-word which would bring in the M.T.B.s
and the destroyers.

But from then on everything went wrong.

The officer whose job it was to position and flash the light guiding
in the M.T.B.s had also, incredibly, been sent off on a forward
reconnaissance and had left his Aldis lamp behind; so in order to save
time he tried signalling with his torch, which was not only far less
powerful but white instead of red. It was hardly surprising that the
men offshore were puzzled.

They were not only puzzled, but also out of communication with
one another as a direct consequence of lack of training. The two
columns had kept good formation throughout the daylight hours, but
with darkness had been faced not only with the turn in towards
Tobruk, but also with the need to increase speed from eighteen to
thirty knots. One column snatched away into the darkness and lost all
cohesion, and although the other column built up speed gradually and
thus kept more or less together, when they reached the coastline from
which should be shining the essential guiding light, they found
complete blackness complicated by an almost total ignorance of their
exact positions. It had proved impossible to hold a precise course at
such high speeds in the choppy sea, for radar in those days was not
available for such small craft and even their signal sets were so
rudimentary as to be almost useless, especially when close under the
cliffs.

By 0230 on Monday, September 14th, therefore, Force C had been
reduced from an organised force to nineteen individual but blind
units, probing like a small swarm of bees searching for an entry along
the length of a darkened coastline, while ashore waited Haselden and
his commandos, unable to move without the reinforcement the small
boats were carrying. In the event, two M.T.B.s bearing machine-
gunners from the Royal Northumberland Fusiliers eventually found
the inlet at about 0400, discharged their cargoes of men and weapons
with some difficulty but to the enormous relief of those awaiting
them, then turned to leave, whereupon one stuck on the mud and had
eventually to be abandoned. But this was all the reinforcement the
commandos were to receive, and they were already nearly three
hours late in opening their clearing operations along the southern
shore of the harbour.

If anything, matters were even worse with Force A. Captain St J.
A. Micklethwaite aboard H.M.S. *Sikh* had received the 'Proceed'
signal on time, and also one from the submarine *Taku* off Mersa
Mreira to the effect that weather conditions were acceptable for
landing operations. Punctually at 0300 his two destroyers arrived two

miles offshore and the complicated business of putting the 'shoe-boxes' over the side and filling them with the first wave of marines began.

It was an agonising task. Whatever the youthful captain of *Taku* thought, the seas were unruly enough to cause the destroyers to rock, the lifting wires to sway, the 'shoe-boxes' to bump on the decks and crash against the sides – and to buck and heave diabolically when in the water. A shackle broke, a man's hand was caught and crushed – and the marines were still penned out of the way below decks.

But eventually, all the landing-craft were alongside, the first party of marines, slung about with weapons of every sort, climbed perilously down into them, the towing craft carefully shepherded the bucking 'shoe-boxes' into position and the tow ashore could begin. *Sikh* and *Zulu* turned and steamed away into the darkness so as to be less easily detected should enemy suspicions be aroused, intending to turn back to meet the returning landing-craft as soon as the relevant signal was received from the marines' commanding officer in one of the power-boats.

Unfortunately, the signal Captain Micklethwaite received was to the effect that that particular power-boat (the only one carrying a signal set) had broken down, that it and its accompanying train of lurching landing-craft were drifting helplessly away to the west, while the other tows – minus their commanding officer – disappeared into the darkness towards their as yet unidentified landing place.

The landing place was to remain unidentified. Although the captain of the *Taku* had considered conditions good enough for the main landing operations, he then found that they were too rough for the launching from his craft of two folboats bearing specialists, whose job it had been to inspect the beaches for possible obstructions, find the entrance to the inlet and then signal in the landing-craft and the marines. Like the M.T.B.s and M.L.s further to the east, those landing-craft not wallowing helplessly out at sea were now slowly moving inshore, blind and uncertain of their position. Eventually, they drifted into beaches some two miles west of their intended landing place and quickly ran into trouble.

By this time both *Sikh* and *Zulu* had come back to meet the supposedly returning landing-craft, edging much nearer inshore than had been agreed in order to cut down the interval between the landings of the first and second waves; and at 0500 they suddenly saw lights flashing from the coast and heard the unmistakable sounds of battle. The seventy-odd marines who had managed to land were being attacked, while two hundred of their comrades waited at sea, totally unable to get ashore to help them.

Five minutes later, as the crew of *Sikh* were hauling aboard the cold and frustrated marines of two landing-craft and the broken-down power-boat, a searchlight beam shot out from the shore, wavered, touched *Sikh*, moved on, returned and held her. Within minutes coastal defence guns had opened up and among the first salvoes was a shell which smashed through the destroyer's thin side and exploded in the engine-room, wrecking the steering and the lubrication system to the main shaft. *Sikh* could now do nothing but circle slowly, and thus drew upon herself the attentions of every German and Italian gun along that stretch of coast that could be brought to bear. Coastal guns threw 5-inch shells into her, 88mm. anti-aircraft guns lowered their barrels and poured in their shot; by 0545 she was helpless – but *Zulu* was coming in to try to tow her out of danger.

Four times *Zulu* made the delicate manoeuvre to pass a line to *Sikh* – by now both ships were under concentrated enemy fire – and on the fourth was successful. The line brought across a rope, the rope the end of a hawser quickly made fast, and *Zulu* turned away with *Sikh* slowly veering after her. But by now it was daylight and the coastal guns were making very good practice; and just as *Sikh* was pulling clear into line behind her sister-ship, a shell exploded on *Zulu*'s quarterdeck and by the time the smoke and flame had cleared the end of the broken hawser had slipped overboard and *Sikh* was on her own again.

For another hour *Zulu* tried to protect *Sikh* with smoke in the hope that her engineers might get her moving again, but *Zulu* was taking punishment herself all the time and at 0708 Captain Micklethwaite decided that *Sikh* was lost. He ordered *Zulu* to rejoin *Coventry* at sea, gave the order to abandon *Sikh* at about 0800 and half an hour later, surrounded by the survivors of her crew and of the marines she had carried, the destroyer finally sank. She was about three miles offshore by then, and for several hours the survivors clung to pieces of wreckage, the badly wounded dying, all becoming weaker and weaker until, with the sounds of battle ashore subsiding, an Italian landing-barge came out to collect them.

By dawn it was quite clear to everyone in the area that *Operation Daffodil* had failed. For over two hours the M.T.B.s which had not found the entrance of Sciausc Bay had cruised up and down vainly searching for the guiding lights, but after 0530 were blinded by search-lights whose beams had been directed seawards once the diversionary nature of the R.A.F. activities had been realised at the Garrison Command. The M.T.B.s' speed had usually been enough to take them out of trouble even when caught by the searchlights, but their manoeuvring brought them no nearer their objective and their cargoes of Argylls and Northumberland Fusiliers became ever more vociferous in their demands to be put ashore to help their comrades, even if not in the agreed place.

But the M.T.B. commanders were unanimous in their refusal. Either the soldiers would be put ashore at the right place, or not at all; and when daylight began quickly to spread across the scene it was all too evident that little would be gained by throwing yet more men into a lost battle. Moreover, another and even more dangerous threat to the M.T.B.s became apparent; from the direction of El Adem airfield came the whine of engines as Stukas and Me 109s rose in an angry swarm and came hurtling across the bay at them. The Fairmile motor launches drew the first attack because of their size, but the volume of fire which rose from their decks as every automatic weapon aboard and most of the rifles opened up, deterred their attackers for a while, though near-misses rocked them like corks and flooded their decks. One M.T.B. was hit squarely and blew up with a roar which echoed around the bay.

Then, as they circled and their young commanders wondered what next they could do, H.M.S. *Zulu* came slowly towards them. It was evident that she had been hit hard and often and had developed a distinct list, but there was nothing they could do to help her and even less to help her sister ship. Orders were shouted to them from *Zulu*'s bridge and reluctantly the young M.T.B. commanders turned to obey. They were to return on their own to Alexandria – or at least as far along the coast in that direction as the petrol remaining in their tanks would take them – leaving Haselden and his men to their fate.

By dawn the commandos were penned into the bridgehead they had taken so triumphantly four hours before, by an Italian battalion which was swiftly being strengthened by German troops rushed across from the port area. Moreover, as *Sikh* sank and *Zulu* drew away, the guns which had been hammering them could turn their attention to the headland; a hastily constructed sangar, the Italian blockhouse which had served at first as headquarters for Haselden and aid post for the wounded, and the stranded M.T.B. down in the inlet served as nuclei around which the commandos gathered and which became the centres of resistance.

At first Haselden, ever the optimist, declared that although it was quite evident that the Argylls were not to arrive, it was the plain duty of the commandos to continue the fight in order to take pressure off the marines of Force A; but shortly after 0700 came a signal saying that Force A had failed to land, so he gave the orders for every captured gun, emplacement and hut to be destroyed and then for each man to try to make his own way south to the desert and escape.

But of course the second part was much easier said than done. An attempt was made to load the wounded on the last remaining truck, man the sides with heavily armed men and crash out through the ever-tightening ring – but the attempt was seen in preparation, an ambush was prepared for it and Haselden himself, who had spotted the trap, was killed trying to warn the truck of the danger and at the same time to disperse it. Down in the inlet, frantic efforts were made to shift the M.T.B. off its embracing mudbank, but first efforts were defeated by technical ignorance ('I just don't know which bloody buttons to push!' one officer was heard complaining) and when eventually someone did get the engines to start, the commandos were no more successful than the Navy had been in moving the craft. Two of them manned the twin Oerlikons throughout and kept the wadi ridges on each side clear of all but snipers – but these inevitably caused some casualties and in time the ammunition drums were empty.

There was then a short but curious silence (except for the curses of the men still trying to shift the hard-stuck hull), broken after a short while by the sounds of engines from seaward. Then, smoothly but powerfully, an E-Boat slid into the inlet, its decks crowded with German infantry, its deck guns covering the M.T.B. and the forlorn but grim group around it. As it was so obviously the end for them, the commandos laid down their arms and the German soldiers and marines poured ashore to take them prisoner. The wounded were gently and carefully carried aboard, the British weapons collected and piled on one side, the fit commandos congratulated and assembled aboard the E-Boat by Germans, obviously impressed by their performance and, they said, not unamused by the panic and chaos so small a band had sewn among their Italian allies. The commandos by the M.T.B. were among the luckier ones.

On the headland above, the groups fighting in the sangar and the Italian blockhouse were facing the same inevitable surrender and for the same reasons – growing casualties and rapidly decreasing stocks of ammunition; they were also subject to much heavier attack than those down in the inlet – from artillery, from mortars and from heavy machine-guns in addition to the ever-growing infantry strength being brought against them. Eventually, when the guns in the blockhouse fell silent and those in the sangar had an average of but three rounds left apiece, the giant sergeant-major who had been the soul of the defence since Haselden had been killed, rolled over, wriggled out of his by no means white shirt and, holding it above his head, rose slowly to his feet. He had already revealed on several occasions that he led a charmed life, but this latest exhibition astonished everyone who saw it, for despite the cease-fire in the defended area, rifle and machine-gun bullets continued to pour in from every side and they were quite evidently all aimed at him. Yet all that happened was that the off-white shirt between his hands was riddled, and eventually split apart.

But then there was heard above the sounds of firing an ever-increasing volume of German orders and rebukes, a tall Oberleutnant was seen to rise from behind some rocks and run across to them followed by a group of men wearing Afrika Korps insignia, and these, much to the commandos' relief but also to their astonishment, formed a ring around them to protect them from a horde of furious and vociferous Italians, obviously intent upon avenging the deaths of many of their comrades. A few Italians got through but were apparently too incensed to use their heads or their weapons and tried to club the commandos to the ground (one took a swing at the sergeant-major and although he left him with a bloody mouth was himself neatly felled by a colossal clip around the ear) but the Afrika Korps quickly threw them out and then began to steer the commandos away, rather like police escorting a football team off the field after one of today's more tumultuous soccer matches.

Even given the volatility of the Latins, it all seemed unusually ferocious, but as became evident afterwards, they felt they had cause.

Even the marines in the 'shoe-boxes' which remained in tow had had an appalling time. The hastily constructed landing-craft proved so unseaworthy that most of the men were violently sea-sick before they had gone far, and although their power-boats kept going, many of the tow-ropes snapped and had there not been double ties, some 'shoe-boxes' would undoubtedly have gone individually adrift. Even so, the task of finding and retying broken ends of rope between heavy-laden and unmanageable craft, yawing at every twist of a choppy sea in almost complete darkness, had called for enormous reserves of both strength and courage; by the time the power-boats were inshore and casting off, the marines were cold, wet and exhausted.

They were also under fire, but such was the turmoil of the breaking waves that none of the 'shoe-boxes' was hit. Too many of them, however, themselves hit rocks, splintered, rapidly filled and sank, or capsized and threw their living cargoes into the sea, where many of them were crushed between 'shoe-box' and rock, and many others dragged under by their heavy equipment and drowned. By the time Major Hedley, the most senior officer to land, could collect all the survivors together, he had fewer than sixty men including half a dozen officers left and so much time had been lost that darkness had gone, any element of surprise in their attack had long dispersed – as had any chance of reinforcement. Out to sea, *Sikh* was ablaze fore and aft, *Zulu* being repeatedly hit. As there was obviously no hope of succour or rescue from that direction, and equally little chance of attaining any of Force A's objectives, the unanimous decision of all officers present was that they should split up into three groups, fight their way out towards the perimeter and escape into the desert, in the hope that the L.R.D.G. would pick them up.

But first they had to climb up one or more of the wadis which seamed the cliffs, reach the high ground and somehow make their way through the enemy positions which obviously dotted the ridge. Each party found, as soon as it started, that even the wadis held small enemy groups, each of which had to be stormed and eliminated, so by the time the groups reached the ridge their numbers had already been severely reduced.

But then they saw in front of them a small level plain, clustered with palm trees under which were pitched neat lines of tents. As they reached the edge of the area, men broke from the tents and ran away towards a building on the far side and, assuming this to be either a headquarters or an armoury, the marines opened fire and gave chase. As they reached the clumps of trees and tents, they heard movement and shouting from inside, so they riddled them with tommy-gun and pistol fire as they rushed by, and threw grenades into the open flaps.

It was not until they reached the square in front of the building and saw the Red Cross on the door that they realised what they had done – shot up lines of hospital tents filled with sick and wounded. Had they gone much further they would have hit a compound with tents containing sick and wounded British and South African prisoners-of-war.

Clear of the hospital area, the marines now found themselves within sight of the road leading from the west into Tobruk, along which lorry-loads of both Italians and Germans were hurrying towards the main defences. It was quite obvious that they would not be able to cross it in daylight, but behind them, in the wadis they had just climbed, were several caves and dug-outs which had housed the Australians during their epic siege of the previous year; there they went into hiding, and from the mouth of one of the caves, Major Hedley watched the *Sikh* sink, and *Zulu* limp away out to sea.

But the Royal Navy had still not paid the full price for their part in this ill-fated operation.

H.M.S. *Coventry* and her eight Hunt class destroyers had duly trailed their coats along the African coast in order to confuse Axis radar, and by 0630 had returned almost to Alexandria when Captain Dendy aboard *Coventry* received a message reporting the fate of *Sikh*, and ordering him to return as quickly as possible to render what assistance he could to the battered *Zulu*. At least two of his destroyers were short of fuel so he ordered them into harbour, and with the others reversed course towards a given rendezvous.

It was quickly obvious that the night's activities had thoroughly aroused all Axis aircraft in the eastern half of the Mediterranean, and long before the time for sighting *Zulu*, *Coventry*'s somewhat rudimentary radar screen was indicating unidentified groups of aircraft approaching. A hurriedly summoned Beaufighter arrived from Alexandria in response to requests for aid but at best the only help it could give would be observation and advice; which shortly before 1124 it provided.

But hardly had its message been received and *Coventry*'s stern guns swung on to a new bearing, than fifteen Ju 87s broke cloud just behind her and by 1126 *Coventry* was a broken ship. One bomb practically blew off her bows forward of No. 1 gun, two bombs exploded on the forecastle deck just below the bridge demolishing everything under the compass platform and starting a fire below, and a fourth bomb smashed through the upper deck and exploded in a boiler room, destroying the radar equipment at the same time.

After this it was evident that even if *Coventry* could be kept afloat, the operation of towing her back to Alexandria would so hamper the accompanying destroyers that one or more would inevitably be very badly damaged, so the decision was taken that the cruiser must be abandoned and sunk; but an almost unbelievable combination of circumstances complicated this operation out of all reason.

Her scuttling charges had been unprimed as a result of experience on previous convoy work, when it had been discovered that near-misses from enemy aircraft or guns could make them explode, thus completing the enemy's work for them; and the fires below caused by the bombing made it impossible for anyone to approach and re-activate them. Moreover, when Captain Dendy instructed one of the accompanying destroyers to torpedo his stricken ship, he learned to his bitter astonishment that of the flotilla appointed for this operation, only the two destroyers which he had ordered into harbour to refuel carried torpedoes, the others being regarded and armed as anti-aircraft and anti-submarine vessels.

The only destroyer in the vicinity carrying torpedoes was *Zulu*; *Coventry* would therefore have to await her arrival before receiving her death blow, while the other destroyers around picked up survivors and fought off more attacks by Ju 87s and 88s.

And *Zulu* was herself now in great danger. Stukas had found her just before 0900 and by the time she reached the rendezvous point and the stricken *Coventry* she had survived three concentrated attacks, the last by four Ju 88s and five Ju 87s – and even as she reached the circle of protective Hunt class destroyers and slowed to aim her torpedoes at the wallowing but still floating *Coventry*, another swarm of German aircraft dropped out of the clouds.

The next ten minutes produced one of the most concentrated sea-actions of the Second World War, when, in a circle less than three miles in diameter and in the air above it, seven destroyers fought off sixteen aircraft while one of their number sank the crippled cruiser in their midst; and when, at 1505, *Coventry* at last slid under the waves, the battle continued as *Zulu* and her escort set off on the voyage back towards their own air cover based on Alexandria.

Two of the Hunts, loaded with wounded from *Coventry*, raced off at full speed, and the other four remained to help the by now badly hit older ship, whose ordeal was by no means over. At 1600, six Ju 88s and twelve Ju 87s arrived overhead and it was quite obvious that *Zulu* alone was their target. One of their bombs burst in the engine room, and it seemed at last as though the end had come, but Commander White was determined to save his ship if possible (Alexandria was but a hundred miles away now) and the destroyer *Hursley* tried to take her in tow. There were moments similar to those off Tobruk as the ships manoeuvred and the tows parted but at last *Hursley* and *Zulu* were linked and the slow, careful journey could begin, with the remaining three destroyers circling to keep off the now slackening air attack.

They were defeated by time and nature. By dusk *Zulu* was so deep in the water that *Hursley* could barely make ten knots and her captain was genuinely worried that if *Zulu* went suddenly, his own command might be dragged down before the tow broke; and Commander White saw his point. H.M.S. *Croome* was ordered alongside to take the last of *Zulu*'s survivors, and orders were given for the tow to be broken – and hardly had the last order been carried out when *Zulu* suddenly rolled to starboard, her commander and skeleton crew were thrown into the water and the destroyer vanished from sight in a maelstrom of bubbling and spewing turmoil from which, fortunately, all survivors were rescued. The rest of the journey was comparatively uneventful, and all four Hunt class destroyers were back in harbour by the following morning – but three more M.T.B.s and two of the motor launches had been caught and sunk on their trip back along the African coast, and every single craft was hit and damaged in some way. Admiral Harwood and his staff had been right to regard *Operation Daffodil* with scepticism.

So far as the land forces were concerned, the marines hiding in the old Australian dug-outs were rounded up by German infantry during the evening of September 12th, and most of the surviving commandos were under guard by nightfall, though a few were caught trying to make their way out into the desert during the next two days. Five men – including one of the S.I.G. men – eventually walked back eastward sufficiently far to reach the British lines, the last one being picked up, a wasted skeleton, long-haired, bearded but quite composed, on November 18th.

As for the only other formation concerned with *Operation Daffodil*

– the L.R.D.G. patrol under David Lloyd Owen – they had met and shot up an Italian patrol within an hour of despatching the commandos, had run into a number of hastily erected roadblocks on their way towards the perimeter and managed to dodge around them and, somewhat to the astonishment of all concerned, caught a lorry full of German soldiers under an Oberleutnant who had decided, not unreasonably, that Tobruk was becoming too noisy for a section en route to the main battlefront to enjoy a good night's sleep, and were therefore seeking one in the empty and comparatively peaceful desert to the south.

By this time it had become evident that the operation was not going according to plan, no contact with Haselden was possible despite the most expert attempts by the signallers, and David Lloyd Owen knew that his first duty was to keep his patrol intact and available for what promised to be complicated and perhaps desperate rescue operations. He abandoned the attempt to penetrate deep into the Tobruk area, leaving the radio stations and the aircraft unattacked, the prisoners unrescued.

In this he was well advised as his services were going to be urgently needed elsewhere in the near future.

Operation Snowdrop, the S.A.S. raid on Benghasi, had proved just as great a disaster as the raid on Tobruk, the only difference being the instant and spectacular way in which disaster struck.

An advance party under Paddy Mayne had gone up into the Jebel, contacted one of the resident agents there who was already troubled by movements of German and Italian units which seemed to suggest that the Benghasi raid was expected, and who now despatched one of his Arabs into the port to obtain specific information. The Arab returned thirty-six hours later with a report that Benghasi teemed with newly arrived Axis troops, that the whole population was talking about the impending raid, that civilians were being evacuated from danger spots and minefields, roadblocks and ambushes were being set up around the town perimeter – especially at the planned entrance-point for the attackers. The date for the attack – September 14th – was freely talked about, and even some fairly accurate figures discussed for the hour.

When David Stirling arrived with the main body and learned of all this, he signalled Base Headquarters in Alexandria and suggested that, although the raid itself should not be cancelled, at least the time and planned approach should be varied, but he quickly received a curt signal telling him to ignore 'bazaar gossip' and adhere closely to his schedule. The Arab had probably made up all the details of his report, the signal implied, possibly because of relations or property in Benghasi which might be harmed during the raid; perhaps he had not even gone into Benghasi, but had instead lurked in the foothills outside concocting his story.

Just after dusk on September 13th, the main party began the intricate descent of the escarpment above the Soluch–Benghasi road and found it so much more difficult for such a large convoy than had been expected that by the time they had reached the bottom they were well behind schedule and the R.A.F. raid, intended to attract enemy attention up into the air during the close approach, was over and the Wellingtons and Mitchells already on their way back to base. But on the road, speed was picked up and the head of the column made good time until suddenly it ran into a roadblock.

There was no light on the bar across the road and there appeared to be no sentry – circumstances themselves unusual enough to arouse suspicion – but what caused the gravest doubts were the signs of recent digging on each side of the road which seemed to indicate new minefields. Stirling called forward his chief sapper officer, Captain Cumper, who examined the disturbed surfaces, and then turned his attention to the roadblock. Here there was apparently no trouble for with an audible click a catch snapped back, the bar hinged upwards to leave a clear road, Captain Cumper stepped back and with a gracious wave of his hand invited the leading jeeps to go through.

'Let battle commence!' he announced in imitation of a well-known comedian of those days, and hardly were the words out of his mouth when it did, with quite astonishing ferocity.

Breda machine-guns opened up on the head of the column from

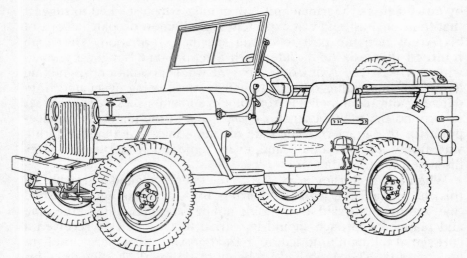

Figure 5   Willys jeep: overall length 131 ins; width 62 ins; weight unloaded 2,750 lbs; payload 800 lbs across country, 1,200 lbs on roads; speed 55 m.p.h.; fuel consumption (loaded) 17·5 m.p.g.

just beyond the roadblock, submachine-gun and rifle fire poured into the flanks while mortar-bombs exploded along its length. The leading jeeps raced forward through the block (there was nowhere else for them to go and to remain stationary would have been suicidal), one was hit by an incendiary bullet in the petrol tank, the resultant flames throwing a fiery, garish light over the whole diabolical scene, and every gun in the column – and each jeep was fitted with twin Vickers – opened up to add its rattle to the din. Many of the jeeps deployed off the road, their comparative lightness saving them from destruction on the new minefields, and as they came up abreast of the head of the column, the sheer weight of fire they were able to bring to bear began to turn the conflict in their favour.

But the overall situation was quite clear; the Arab had been right, their attack had been expected, they had been effectively ambushed and despite their momentary superiority on the field, they would be in severe trouble once reinforcements arrived – and these must assuredly be racing in from other points all along the perimeter. With the element of surprise gone there was no hope for the attainment of any of the raid's objectives and, reluctantly, David Stirling gave the order to withdraw.

It was, inevitably, a case of every man – or at least, vehicle – for himself in a race to reach the comparative safety of the escarpment wadis before daylight; and most of them just managed. But as they hastily camouflaged their vehicles and found what cover they could among the rocks and boulders of the wadi-sides, they could see in the growing light swarms of aircraft rising like angry wasps from the airfields around Benghasi (including Benina which in the light of the night's events had remained unattacked by the L.R.D.G. patrols). For over an hour the S.A.S. men remained unobserved and safe, but then a random burst from one of the searching aircraft hit the truck containing reserves of explosive and ammunition, and the resulting pyrotechnics attracted every Axis pilot in the area; for the rest of the day the wadis were combed, more men were wounded and killed and more trucks destroyed. Surprisingly, no ground force was sent out against them, so by nightfall the survivors could reassemble, assess the damage and begin a further stage of the withdrawal.

It was a nightmare journey back across the Jebel, worst of all for the wounded who were thrown about as the vehicles bucked along unmade tracks or no tracks at all, everyone endeavouring to reach by dawn the base wadi where the doctor waited, and there would be food and drink, more ammunition and good cover. One man had been shot through the lung, one had a badly shattered arm, and the resident agent who had insisted upon taking part in the attack had found himself too close to an exploding hand grenade and now carried several parts of it in his legs and body. There were a number of other minor wounds for the doctor to take care of when eventually they all arrived, and the vehicles were again dispersed and camouflaged, the men settling down for another uncomfortable day under what cover they would find.

Their presence was betrayed to the searching aircraft by what would appear to have been gross negligence or stupidity. Somebody during the morning drove in a jeep and a cloud of dust from one wadi to another, and the bored pilot of one of the CR-42s saw it; from then on the area was continually covered by at least twenty aircraft, combing wadis, shooting up every clump of bushes under which the S.A.S. might be sheltering, bombing the wadi sides to release boulders upon anyone underneath, raking every declivity or shadow which might hold a camouflaged vehicle. By the time the sun went down, 'with sickening deliberation' as Fitzroy Maclean was later to write,[4] there was barely enough transport left to carry the fit men as far as Jalo, let alone any of the badly wounded.

In the end, the resident agent and the corporal with the shattered arm were taken, the other wounded left with a medical orderly and one of the Italian prisoners, who went into Benghasi the following day and brought out an ambulance to take them to hospital. Nothing is known of their fate, for none of them, not even the medical orderly who was unhurt, lived to report upon events after the main body left the area.

Three days later on the evening of September 18th, the leading S.A.S. vehicles were less than thirty miles from Jalo, but as one of the trucks destroyed during the first day had been the signal truck, no one knew if the fort there was in the hands of the Sudan Defence Force or not. Fitzroy Maclean took a jeep to find out – and quickly found himself in the middle of a battle; like the men on Operations Daffodil and Snowdrop, the S.D.F. on Operation Tulip had been expected and were still, after four days, fighting in the area of the oasis for possession of the fort.

But at least contact with the Sudan Defence Force made possible the refilling of the empty S.A.S. petrol tanks and ammunition racks, the men at last had something more than a teaspoonful of bully beef for their day's ration, and their water-bottles could be filled. Moreover, the Sudan Defence Force signal sets were working and from H.Q. they then received news of a column of German armoured cars combing the desert behind them, together with orders that the whole joint force was to retire southwards towards Kuffra as quickly as possible. Although exhausting, the withdrawal was comparatively uneventful for the enemy armoured column was never seen, and by the evening of September 23rd, the survivors of Operation Snowdrop were arriving in Kuffra, many of them wondering whether their journey had been worth while.

The only operation of September 13th which could claim any worthwhile degree of success was *Operation Hyacinth*, the L.R.D.G. raid on Barce.

Three patrols under Major J. R. Easonsmith had left Faiyum on September 2nd and made their way across the Sand Sea to emerge into the open desert south of the Jebel Akhdar on September 10th – a route chosen on the grounds that no one in his senses would try to take twenty-two vehicles across such appalling country in September; the ruse seemed to have worked for no hostile aircraft or units at all were seen. By September 12th, the three patrols – one of New Zealanders, one of Rhodesians and a Guards patrol – were into the southern foothills and by the following morning two of them were but fifteen miles away from Barce, the Rhodesians having joined the S.A.S. in *Operation Snowdrop*. Arabs sent into the town by Peniakoff reported the presence of some Italian tanks, probably M13s, but no apparent expectation of immediate attack, so soon after dusk the patrols moved off.

They cut telephone lines en route, shot up an isolated police post, ran into two M13s just outside Barce and killed the crews, and at the entrance to the town separated into three groups each with a distinct task. The New Zealanders under Captain N. P. Wilder made for the airfield along the Maddalena road which they entered with no trouble, threw grenades into the nearest buildings and set fire with incendiary bullets to a large petrol bowser. In the glare of the towering flames which this produced, the nine trucks and single jeep of the patrol then circled the airfield, methodically shooting up the thirty-two aircraft parked around the edges, while from the last truck one of the sappers planted short-fused bombs on any aircraft not alight by the time he reached it.

Meanwhile, the Guards patrol under Sergeant Dennis (the officer commanding the patrol had been injured in an accident while crossing the Sand Sea) were attacking buildings and barracks at the other end of the town with grenades and machine-gun fire in order to deter the inhabitants from interfering with the New Zealanders, while around the main square of the small town, Easonsmith and Peniakoff were operating in a similar manner between buildings which were either administration blocks or officers' quarters. Neither the Guards nor Easonsmith encountered much opposition, and towards the end of his depredations, Easonsmith and his companion found an empty and unguarded transport park where they wrecked a dozen trucks and cars.

By this time, Wilder's objectives had all been achieved and his patrol were running short of ammunition, so he led them off the airfield and up the long main road towards the railway station – to find that the Italians had at last organised some resistance and two

M13s blocked the way, their shells fortunately aimed too high and screaming away into the darkness.

There was no possibility of retreat, so Wilder in the leading Chevrolet stamped on the accelerator and charged forward, pushing one M13 off the road, crashing into the second and wrecking it – and wrecking his own vehicle at the same time. He and his crew immediately leaped aboard the jeep racing up behind but as they roared off towards the station cross-roads, the driver was blinded by tracer pumped out of their twin machine-guns at an enemy post ahead, hit the curb and overturned the jeep. When it was righted, Captain Wilder was found underneath, unconscious and soaked in petrol, so the next truck behind collected him and the patrol then escaped out of town, except for the last truck with the sapper and his bombs, which had been cut off and was not seen again.

By now all parties were making their way back towards the base wadi where the doctor and spare vehicles and equipment had been left, and before dawn everyone had arrived although Peniakoff and Easonsmith had at one point run into a minor ambush and the former lost the little finger of his left hand. Wilder had recovered consciousness as the petrol in which he was soaked evaporated, and nobody for the moment was badly hurt so they dispersed the vehicles in rolling, scrubby ground, camouflaged the trucks and settled down for a hot but uneventful day's rest.

This they were not to enjoy. A group of Tripolitanian horsemen was seen riding towards the area and Easonsmith went off with a pair of jeeps to scare them away – and on return, decided that as their position might now be reported to the Italians, the group should move. During this operation they were seen and fired upon by two old Italian CR-42s which then hastily alerted the Italian command, and for the rest of the day the L.R.D.G. men were harassed by all the aircraft in the area not similarly engaged over the S.A.S. positions. By nightfall their doctor had six casualties to look after including Peniakoff and Captain Wilder who had been hit in both legs, and one of the men whose stomach had been torn open by a bullet which passed right through his body.

Twenty-seven fit survivors with one undamaged Chevrolet truck, one jeep in sound order and another with a punctured petrol tank and a torn tyre were now all the remaining effectives of Easonsmith's command, with enough petrol and water for about two hundred miles.

Fortunately, this was the kind of situation for which the L.R.D.G. had long made provision, and forty miles away was hidden a truck with water, petrol and rations, while nearly one hundred and fifty miles further south was a disused airfield, L.G. 125, which had been assigned as rallying point for stragglers from the operations and from which, with luck, the wounded might be flown out. The problem (apart from getting there) was communication, for one of the day's casualties had been the wireless truck.

Easonsmith now divided his group into a walking party of twenty-three plus himself, with the damaged jeep accompanying them to carry their gear, and a second party consisting of the six wounded men, the doctor, a navigator and a fitter, to travel as quickly as possible in the truck and the sound jeep first to the reserve truck in order to collect their portion of the rations, then to L.G. 125 and then, if necessary, down through the Jalo gap to Kuffra. In the doctor's opinion, Parker, the man with the stomach wound, would not live to reach that last destination by surface vehicle.

It was a warm, dark, moonless night and the going was so bad that for the first hour both parties kept together. Peniakoff, who had also been hit by splinters in the knee which in consequence was now stiffening up, was with the driving party and left a vivid description of that night's journey:

> Davis, our navigator, tried to keep a straight course and the driver did his best to follow his instructions, but the night was so dark that he could only just see far enough ahead to avoid crashing into trees and boulders. Of the general lie of the land he could see nothing: he drove ahead in a straight line as long as he wasn't stopped by an impassable obstacle. We found ourselves, at one time, driving along the steep side of a hill at such an angle that we could hardly cling to our seats and we expected the truck to topple over, but it righted itself; then some time later, we stopped dead with our front wheels nearly over a cliff, a vertical drop of forty feet or so to a wadi below. We drove round, followed the curving cliff edge for a long time, found a way down, slid and skidded to the wadi bottom and started climbing up the opposite bank. Night was wearing out, there was no time to send a man on foot to reconnoitre ahead: if dawn found us anywhere near our starting point, the planes would soon be on us and our adventures at an end. The climb out of the wadi proved difficult: it was steep and full of screes which had to be rushed, and protruding rocks which should be taken with care. The heavy truck rocked and swayed, the uphill wheels on rock, the downhill ones on shingle in which they spun, digging a hole which slowly brought the truck to a dangerous angle: suddenly the wheels gripped (having reached rock, I suppose) and sent us lurching forward, over boulders and through high bushes with a loud crash. We pulled up on a level keel, and while the fitter got down to inspect the damage, Lawson injected a dose of morphia to Parker, to whom the jolting was agony.[5]

There was no vital damage to the truck and as the ground was not now so broken they made better speed for about twelve miles, halted just after three o'clock for a rest (which by now both navigator and driver needed as badly as the wounded), carried on during the morning and eventually found the reserve truck in the Wadi Jerrari in mid-afternoon. Having helped themselves to food, water and petrol and left a note for the walking party, they continued in the direction of L.G. 125 until darkness fell, then halted and slept for ten hours.

Parker was still alive in the morning but in great pain for the morphia seemed to be losing its power to ease his sufferings. He could not be given anything to eat or – far worse – to drink, and he was conscious always of the limitations which under such circumstances a badly wounded man places on the movements and chances of escape of his comrades; almost the only words he spoke during the journey were in apology for the trouble he was causing them.

By the morning of September 17th, the navigator reckoned they were but thirty-miles from L.G. 125 – marked by the tail of a wrecked Hurricane standing upright – and they found it before noon, carefully reconnoitred to ensure that the area was not in enemy hands and then occupied the disused hangars and dug-outs, searched and found reserves of petrol which they did not need, and water, bully beef and biscuits which they did. But they still lacked means to communicate with base, and Lawson the doctor decided that they should stay at the landing-ground either until someone arrived who could order in aircraft, or until Parker died . . . which would surely be in but a few days.

Fortunately, aid was at hand.

Throughout September 16th, Easonsmith's walking party had trudged on towards the Wadi Jerrari, and on the morning of the 17th they heard the noise of vehicles over the crest of a hill. Judging them to be of another L.R.D.G. patrol, they fired Very lights, but these were not seen so it looked as though the walk was going to be a long one after all. An hour later, however, they reached the top of a rise to see the Rhodesian patrol which had accompanied them up from Faiyum to the Jebel and then joined the S.A.S. approach to Benghasi breakfasting in the hollow below.

Not only did this mean the end of their own immediate tribulations, but also that a situation report could be sent to H.Q. who took swift action to rescue the wounded at L.G. 125. David Lloyd Owen was still at Hatiet Etla and was ordered to the landing-ground where he arrived the evening of the same day as the wounded, and as a result of much radio traffic and some excellent organisation, a Bombay of 216 Squadron put down on the airstrip the following day at 1300. That night the wounded slept in Kuffra and the following day were flown back to Heliopolis, in due course arriving at the New Zealand General Hospital at Helwan. It is pleasant to be able to record that all survived their wounds.

By September 25th, the remaining L.R.D.G. men from *Operation Hyacinth* – including two Guardsmen who had been cut off in Barce and had walked out to L.G. 125 on their own – were back at Kuffra.

The operation had caused the destruction of a dozen Axis vehicles, thirty-two Axis aircraft and had probably killed the same number of Axis soldiers, at a cost of six Allied wounded, ten prisoners of war and fourteen assorted vehicles. Five decorations were shared among the participants – two D.S.O.s, one M.C. and three M.M.s.

Attempts to justify the raids of September 13th, 1942, read a little thin.

The raid on Tobruk alone had caused the loss of a cruiser, two destroyers, four motor torpedo boats, two Fairmiles and, according to the *Official History*, 280 naval officers and men, 300 Royal Marines and 160 soldiers; and the other raids caused losses among the S.A.S. and even more valuable L.R.D.G. men, not to speak of the vehicles and equipment destroyed.

According to Fitzroy Maclean, the signal received by the Sudan Defence Force ordering them to withdraw to Kuffra also claimed that the raids had achieved their main object, causing the diversion from the front or retention behind it of large numbers of enemy troops and aircraft – which was undoubtedly true at the time. But there is no point in causing an opponent to weaken his defences if advantage is not taken of that weakness. Not until the end of the month was any attack mounted on any part of the Alamein Line (by 131st Brigade at Munassib) – a hiatus which gave ample time for any of Rommel's strength which might have been withdrawn or withheld to cope with the raiding forces, to be returned to their original positions.

The stated main object of the raids before they took place had been destruction, not diversion – destruction of Rommel's petrol, of his harbour facilities, of aircraft, transport and key installations – and the proclamation of a different main object in the light of what actually happened smacks of sophistry. Only at Barce had any concrete results been achieved, and if the local profit and loss account there appeared quite reasonable, embodying that account into the overall balance sheet reveals an Allied disaster. The loss of *Coventry* alone outweighed the destruction of the Macchis and Capronis at Barce, and nothing had been achieved to offset the loss of the two destroyers, the commandos, the Royal Marines and the seamen or indeed anyone or anything else.

One lesson which might have been drawn was that in raiding operations, economy of force is essential; and another is that any planned pattern of separate attacks can easily be discerned by an intelligent foe, who can read a map as well as anyone else. Once the objectives of the various raids had been marked around the edge of the Cyrenaican bulge on the map at Panzerarmee H.Q., the escape routes of any raiders not evacuated by sea quite obviously funnelled down towards Jalo and the gap. The L.R.D.G. had pleaded for the

Sudan Defence Force to attack the fort there on the same night as the rest of the raids, but been overruled by the planners who had not yet learned to give their opponents credit for as much intelligence as they had themselves.

Overconfidence and lack of security in military affairs are marks of the amateur; and in Cairo a thorough professional was watching developments with a critical eye. Perhaps Montgomery should have vetoed the raids immediately he arrived in Egypt, but he had many other things to do, his personal experience and knowledge of such formations as L.R.D.G. and S.A.S. was minimal and their reputation so high that he allowed them to proceed despite his conviction that nothing should happen in his area of command which had not been controlled from the outset by himself.

The failures of the operations of September 13th confirmed him in this belief. He was to use raiding forces himself on many later occasions and in time he came to value both L.R.D.G. and S.A.S. very highly, but the brigadier in charge of the Raiding Forces H.Q. at Alexandria in September 1942 received no further promotion during his military career (though he remained in the Middle East until the end of the campaign) and when David Stirling went to see Montgomery to ask for a free hand in recruiting throughout Eighth Army, he received a very cold and firm refusal.

Montgomery had other plans for the best, the bravest, the most imaginative – in short, the most professional – of the men under his command, than allowing them to concentrate in small private armies of whose value he had still to be persuaded.

8 · *Prelude to Battle*

There is no doubt – even discounting General Montgomery's conviction that troops suffering the grievous disability of not having been trained under his personal direction would be unlikely to withstand the rigours of battle – that Eighth Army in August 1942 lacked certain military qualities essential for victory against so skilful a foe as the Afrika Korps, in any area of the desert and especially in the Alamein positions.

Enough examples of the lack of co-ordination between infantry and armour had already occurred for it to be obvious that that facet of battle-winning technique needed polishing, and indeed the whole principle which still to a great extent permeated the Royal Armoured Corps thinking – that their task was to eliminate the enemy panzers and leave the infantry to fight their pedestrian battles on their own – was in need of rectification. Moreover, with the arrival of the three hundred Shermans from America, many of the tank crews – especially those newly arrived from England – had now to learn how best to take advantage of a tank whose armament, power and reliability were well above any they had previously experienced.

There were also both general and particular aspects of infantry training in need of improvement, not least because among the divisions which had been out in the desert for some time there existed a belief that 'the best training is fighting' and as they had seen so much of it, they must already be well trained – a dictum which might have been truer had more of Eighth Army's fighting in recent weeks been successful. As it was, it seemed likely that some of the habits which had contributed to failure in the past might have become ingrained, instead of being eradicated; and in any case, many of the N.C.O.s and company officers now with Eighth Army had only recently been promoted as a result of casualties at Gazala and since, and thus lacked certain proficiencies – for it takes more than just a period of time as a good rifleman to make a satisfactory corporal or as a subaltern to make a good captain.

As for the new infantry divisions arriving in the desert, not only did they need to accustom themselves to the heat and the dust, but also to develop 'desert sense' – a lack of which was demonstrated with blinding clarity one night when Major-General Douglas Wimberley, commanding the newly arrived 51st Highland Division, left his caravan in a dust storm and took two hours to find his way to the mess tent four hundred yards distant. Moreover, like the men of the 44th Division at Alam Halfa, the Highlanders had for the most part never seen action, for their division had been almost totally destroyed in France in 1940, and since been reconstituted.

But there was an even more fundamental reason for retraining the desert army, as a totally new approach to battle was necessary at Alamein. For the first time in the desert fighting, there was no open flank for the attacking force to hook around – no Bir Enba Gap as for 7th Armoured and 4th Indian in 1940, no wide space as for XXX Corps during *Crusader* or Rommel's forces during the Gazala battles. By September 1942 the defences of both armies stretched all the way from the sea just north of Tel el Eisa down to the Qattara Depression south of Himeimat, and every day which passed saw those defences thickened. The mine-marshes between the opposing sides grew ever more extensive (the Germans referred to them picturesquely as 'devil's gardens') and if the shortages of barbed wire did not allow entanglements of the complexity of the Western Front of 1918, the overall situation would nevertheless demand an attack of 1918 style.

The keynote of this – and indeed of all attacks upon the First World War trench system once it had been firmly established – had been massive artillery bombardment followed by direct infantry assault, and the cornerstones of the philosophy which directed them had been the cold, grim facts of attrition. Only in April 1915 when the Germans had used gas at Langemark and in November 1917 when the British attacked the line at Cambrai with massed tanks had surprise alleviated the necessity for an attacking force to be at least three times the strength of a defending force, and to lose lives in a corresponding proportion; and no one was suggesting the use of gas at Alamein. As the use of armour on the field of battle had become commonplace and no other completely new weapon was available, Eighth Army had now to retrain for the type of battle which their fathers had fought, and of which most professional soldiers and every amateur soldier had prayed there would be no repeat. Strafer Gott had refused to allow his men to partake in the assault on the northern flank of the Cauldron at Gazala exactly because it would have borne too strong a resemblance to First World War tactics, and it is interesting to speculate upon how he would have faced up to the realities of the situation at Alamein had he lived.

But however Gott might have reacted, Montgomery was quite

prepared to draw the inevitable conclusions from his analysis of the problem, and with those conclusions the equally inevitable fact that in order to break through the Alamein positions and defeat the Afrika Korps, many brave men – probably the best in Eighth Army – were going to lose their lives. Some warning of this was given in one of his memos:

> This battle will involve hard and prolonged fighting. Our troops must not think that, because we have a good tank and very powerful artillery support, the enemy will all surrender. The enemy will NOT surrender, and there will be bitter fighting.
> The Infantry must be prepared to fight and kill, and to continue doing so over a prolonged period . . . [1]

But if his training directives to the rank and file stressed the toughness of the battle ahead, his directives to senior officers were to ensure that within the overall context of defeating the Afrika Korps, the minimum of lives were to be lost *unnecessarily* – and to those two ends, victory and the most economical expenditure of lives, all training was to be directed. Not every training programme in the annals of the British Army had been based upon such clearly defined principles.

In one important aspect the forthcoming battle would differ fundamentally from those of the closing stages of the First World War. Along the trench lines of the Ypres Salient and the Somme battlefields, barbed wire entanglements had been the chief impediments to attack, and in the great Allied assaults the first task for the lumbering tanks had been to crush paths through them for the infantry to follow. Now the main obstacles were the minefields and the roles must be reversed; infantry and engineers must now make gaps for the armour to pass through and so an essential new element of training for the desert army must be that of mine-lifting on a large scale. During the O'Connor offensive small units from the Royal Engineers had been employed on this task for the assaults on Bardia and Tobruk, but now with mine-marshes several hundred yards wide to be gapped – under fire and at night – it was evident that deep thought and considerable practice would be necessary before the obstacle they represented could be overcome.

Infantry patrols and aerial observation had given quite an accurate picture of the extent and basic pattern of the Axis minefields, but there were obviously some factors about them only known before the attack to the German engineers who had sewn them. These engineers, under command of a Colonel Hecker, had by the end of September sewn nearly half a million 'devil's eggs', as they called them (a large number of them British, collected from Gazala and Tobruk), in a

regular pattern from north to south with variations resulting from the
lie of the land. The front edge of the German defences was both
wired and mined to a width of between 500 and 1,000 yards, and
within this band were dug battle outposts to hold a company of
machine-gunners and riflemen, often accompanied by watch-dogs, for
every 1,500 yards.

Behind this first belt was an empty space between 1,000 and 2,000
yards wide and behind that another mined strip some 2,000 yards
wide, within which were posted the remaining two companies of each
defending infantry battalion, with their heavy machine-guns, mortars,
anti-tank guns and other supporting weapons.

The open space between the two mine-belts was cut into irregular
shapes by lateral belts crossing between the outer and inner fields in
the form of narrow triangles, with their apices to the front and
passages up in the median lines for counter-attacking infantry and
reinforcement for the battle outposts. The main purpose of these
lateral belts was to channel any force breaking through the outer belt
into the enclosed quadrangles where they would run on to smaller,
haphazard minefields, and also find themselves under heavy bombardment from guns previously ranged into the area.

Over 95 per cent of the mines were anti-tank mines which would
not necessarily destroy a tank but would certainly cripple it, probably
by blowing off a track; and would certainly wreck a wheeled vehicle
and kill the majority of its occupants. Many of the mines were interconnected so that a string of them would explode if a tank or lorry
went over one, many were booby-trapped to explode at any but the
most expert attempts to defuse them, and some large British aircraft
bombs and heavy-calibre shells which had fallen into German hands
at Tobruk had been buried in the open spaces and ingeniously
connected to trip-wires with 'push-pull' igniters to explode them at
either an increase or a release of tension on the wire.

Fortunately for the attacking infantry, only some 3 per cent of the
mines available at that time were anti-personnel mines – though even
this known proportion was enough to make the task of walking across
a mine-belt one of particular sensitivity. These S-mines, as they were
called, consisted of metal cylinders from which protruded small wire
horns, almost invisible in the dust even in daylight. When the horns
were trodden on, a charge blew the cylinder into the air to about
waist-height where it exploded in a spreading circle of shrapnel and
ball-bearings. Frequently several of these, too, were interconnected.

Such then was the pattern of the defences through which the
infantry of the attacking divisions would have to walk (not run, for
the impact so generated could set off an anti-tank mine) with tingling
feet and weapons not heavier than a light machine-gun, while behind
them the engineers must clear wide passages before even the infantry

support weapons – heavy mortars, heavy machine-guns or anti-tank guns – could come up to join them.

As for the passage of armour through the minefields, the plan of attack would call for three wide corridors to be opened up for them during the first night, and as along most of the front the mine-marsh net covered an area over three miles deep, it was soon obvious that a very large number of highly trained engineers would be required, every one working to a carefully conceived plan.

The first problem for each team would be to find each separate mine – and although nearly five hundred of the newly invented electronic mine-detectors (called, after the nationality of their inventors, Polish detectors) would arrive in time for the battle, these had been hastily manufactured and many of them were to prove defective. In any case their method of usage – the operator standing upright, wearing earphones to detect the change in tone and sweeping the ground ahead from side to side with the instrument on the end of a pole – seemed likely to lead to an unacceptably high casualty rate.

The alternative method and the one which was mostly to be used, called for the careful prodding of each square foot of ground, generally with a bayonet, the scraping away of the sand when the bayonet point struck metal, the gentle exploration around the base of the mine for booby-traps or trip-wires, and then either the explosion of the mine from a distance or the careful removal of its igniter. Anti-personnel mines could be neutralised by inserting a nail into the hole in which had sat the safety-pin, removed when the mine had been planted.

It would all be a matter of very cool nerves and very steady hands, neither being ruffled or disturbed by the violence of battle raging on all sides. As protective infantry would have aroused the enemy at least in the battle outposts, the violence was likely to be extreme.

By mid-August the Eighth Army School of Mine-clearance had been set up near Burg el Arab under a Regular Royal Engineer, Major Peter Moore, who had already distinguished himself during the first battles on Ruweisat Ridge, was one of the few men who had shot his way out of trouble with a revolver and one of the even fewer who had actually wrestled with an armed antagonist in the dark. Together with a New Zealand engineer, Major A. R. Currie, Moore worked out the requisite composition of teams for mine-clearance and a drill for them to follow – and even in an armchair nearly forty years later without the slightest possibility of personal involvement, reading the drill instructions can evoke feelings of cold discomfort; how it looked and sounded to the men under training and faced with the realisation that theory would become practice in but a few days requires little imagination.

The team would be led into action (after the infantry) by an officer and four men, marching on a compass-bearing and unrolling a white tape which would eventually mark the median line of the gap. Upon reaching the area in which it had been deduced (from foot patrols and aerial photographs) that the forward edge of the minefield lay, a stake would be driven into the ground and a blue light mounted to shine to the rear. The whole leading party would then spread out in line abreast and advance in a stooping position rather like the popular impression of a gorilla on the move, with fingers brushing the ground, backs of hands to the front feeling for trip-wires, eyes anxiously scanning every inch of ground for the treacherous S-mine horns. Direction would still be controlled by the man with the compass who would also unravel the tape.

Behind them would come first a jeep or, more often, a small utility truck, with a heavily sand-bagged floor and steering wheel extended to avoid impaling the driver when the almost inevitable explosion took place. The main purpose of this vehicle was to discover if the forward edge of the minefield really was where it had been suspected, or nearer – and the evidence of the latter would be the truck's destruction.

Behind the vehicle came three teams of nine men, each team to clear a width of eight feet making a twenty-four-foot wide gap in all.

The first three men of each team were the trail-blazers – unrolling more tapes as guides, and the ones on the outside of each twenty-four-foot width planting stakes eventually to hold guiding lights for the heavy vehicles and tanks coming through afterwards. (In all, 88,775 lamps were to be used!) These three teams of three men, working abreast, also dealt if they had time with the trip-wires, booby-traps or S-mines found and marked by the first team to go through if these had not already been defused.

The second trio in each of the three teams were the detectors – sweeping the ground with the electronic brooms if these were available, painstakingly prodding every foot of the ground across and forward if they were not; and upon every mine they found, they planted a white metal cone for the teams behind them.

These teams defused the mines – first scraping away the sand, then beginning the heart-stopping process of feeling for booby-traps under or close by, finding and tracing the connecting wires to other mines, praying that no heavy-footed moron was jumping up and down on another in the string. When eventually the mine was proved isolated, a length of wire was looped around it and with the area cleared of friends, it was pulled out – and if it did not explode during this operation, the job of removing the igniter was undertaken.

Disarmed, the mines could then be piled at the side of the passage to await further clearance and the team moved forward. And as the twenty-four-foot wide passage behind the last trios lengthened, lights could be lit on the cross-bars of the stakes marking the outside edges, green on the inside, orange on the outside, and support weapons for the infantry in front – still trying to force their way forward with nothing heavier than their rifles and light machine-guns – could come through to join them.

During training it was found that 200 yards could be cleared in an hour using the electronic detectors, 100 yards prodding with bayonets. As the main inner and outer mine-belts were known to be respectively 500 and 1,000 yards deep *at least*, and the extent of the minefields inside the quadrangles was not known at all, it can be seen that a very large number of teams would be needed, and that every member of every team would need, in action, a remarkable degree of concentration. As one trainee was heard to remark reflectively at the end of one of Peter Moore's opening lectures, it was quite likely that under certain circumstances, the whole business could become 'bloody hazardous'.

One other method had been devised for clearing the lanes, and the principle behind it was successfully used eighteen months later during the invasion of France – that of Flail Tanks. 'Scorpions', as they were called in the desert, consisted of elderly Matildas with drums fitted forward which would revolve, and in doing so flail the ground with whirling chains; several were manufactured at Abbassia and tested near Wadi Natrun, but the tanks were indeed old, the extra engines fitted to revolve the drums still experimental, and the columns of dust which arose from the operations blinded the operators and choked the filters and tank engines after a very short period. A few Scorpions were to be used by XIII Corps in the south, and had one unexpected gain. According to one badly shaken prisoner, the sight of the slowly advancing pillars of dust from which emerged such dreadful clanking noises and random, violent explosions, was far more frightening than even the preceding barrage, despite the fact that most of the Scorpions ground to a smoking halt long before they reached the Axis lines.

So far as infantry training was concerned, all divisions carried out detailed and rigorous rehearsals, typified by those of two brigades of the New Zealand Division – the 5th and 6th, to which was attached the 9th British Armoured Brigade as the conversion of 4th New Zealand Brigade to armour was progressing too slowly for it to be ready for the forthcoming battle.

General Freyberg had by this time been given some detail of the part his division was intended to play in the forthcoming battle together with particulars of the location, so he was able to have laid out in the desert lines of token weapon pits, and wire and dummy mine-belts in fairly accurate reproduction of the area over which his men would be fighting – taking at the same time, of course, stringent precautions against security leakages.

For a few days the separate units carried out ordinary weapon-training and night marches, then on September 24th the entire division moved ten miles in formation to an assembly area where battle headquarters were set up and communications laid out as for action. At 2030 the division moved off along lines of guide lights – 5th Brigade on the right and 6th on the left with the armour of 9th Brigade waiting for the signal to move – but soft sand delayed many of the lorries, and morning mist and fog blinded some units which thus failed to arrive at their correct destinations; at the afternoon conference Freyberg had several trenchant criticisms to deliver.

But that night the two infantry brigades moved forward in bright moonlight to a lying-up area, dug themselves in and dispersed all transport by dawn, to spend the whole of that day (26th) lying concealed. At 2200, the riflemen rose from their pits and preceded by a token live barrage set off through the dummy minefields, followed closely by engineer teams clearing real but unfused mines. Bofors guns fired tracer along the boundary between the two brigades, 25-pounder tracer marked the outer edges of the divisional area, pre-posted instructional teams and umpires fired live ammunition over the heads of the advancing infantry and detonated carefully sited explosive charges to give extra realism to the exercise; and as the infantry battalions leap-frogged through each other's positions, and the support weapons came up, the Shermans of 9th Brigade moved into the prepared corridors to pass through the infantry and offer them dawn protection.

As dawn broke, the anti-tank gun screens opened up with live ammunition on dummy panzers ahead massed as though for a counter-attack.

It constituted a very realistic exercise and many lessons were learned from it. Traffic jams had occurred as soon as vehicles in any number had reached even the widest bottle-neck, armour had jammed almost solid at the entrance to the corridors and the chaos when one tank had broken down would obviously prove fatal in battle; it had also been realised that British tank crews and signallers used different jargon and expressions from the New Zealanders and the resultant misunderstanding shook everybody, a situation not improved by yet more evidence of cavalry disdain for foot-sloggers.

Perhaps the greatest lesson learned from the exercise, however, was the degree of truth behind Montgomery's maxim that everyone in battle must know what is going on. To some extent because of security, but more because of a human desire to give the impression that they were members of an elite who knew more than the commonalty, junior officers and N.C.O.s had not passed on sufficient information about the purpose of the exercise in general, and the parts each unit had to play in particular, to the men expected to carry it out. As a result, many of them had become bored with marching and counter marching, with lying in fly-infested trenches throughout a long, hot day, with abjuring cigarettes at night and driving vehicles either with wind-shields removed or smeared with wet sand which had frequently to be renewed to avoid reflection of the bright moonlight – and often the inevitable periods of chaos had been extended by practical jokers alleviating monotony. As a result, Freyberg decreed that the armoured brigade and certain other units would remain in the area for further indoctrination, and his instructions for all future operations were very clear indeed upon the necessity for better communication at all levels.

But another weakness noted by one pair of eagle eyes was that too many of the men had shown signs of distress during the approach marches and had been forced to fall out of the exercise through sheer exhaustion. Soon commanding officers throughout Eighth Army were reading a memo from the Army Commander, containing the passages:

> This battle for which we are preparing will be a real rough house and will involve a very great deal of hard fighting . . . There must be no weak links in our mental fitness.
> But mental fitness will not stand up to the stress and strain of battle unless troops are also physically fit.
> This battle may go on for many days, and the final issue may well depend on which side can best last out and stand up to the buffeting, and ups and downs, and the continuous strain, of hard battle fighting.
> There will be no tip and run tactics in this battle; it will be a killing match; the German is a good soldier and the only way to beat him is to kill him in battle.
> I am not convinced that our soldiery are really tough and hard. They are sunburnt and brown, and look very well; but they seldom move anywhere on foot and they have led a static life for many weeks.
> During the next month, therefore, it is necessary to make our officers and men really fit; ordinary fitness is not enough, they must be made tough and hard.[2]

This point received even further emphasis at the end of the month when the new commander of XIII Corps, Lieutenant-General Brian Horrocks, decided to capture an area of ground near Deir el Munassib for extra artillery deployment during the coming battle, and used the unblooded 131st Brigade of 44th Division to obtain it.

On the morning of September 30th the brigade advanced under heavy morning mist and equally heavy artillery cover (which did more to neutralise the advantages of the mist than it was worth) with tanks of 4th Armoured Brigade in support. Two battalions of the Queen's (1st/6th and 1st/7th) met no worthwhile opposition in the north but the unfortunate 1st/5th ran into positions still held by the Italian Folgore and the Ramcke parachutists and were brutally handled, losing in killed, wounded and captured nearly three hundred officers and men before evening.

Attempts to relieve the survivors and renew the assault by the armoured brigade broke down in confusion caused by inexperience and misunderstanding, and on the morning of October 1st Horrocks called off the operation, sending 132nd Brigade in to take over the occupied ground in the north. Here the newcomers found that even though the two Queen's battalions there had had little fighting there were a number of cases of exhaustion and heat-stroke, that although no one had been wounded several men had lost direction and were not seen again, and the ambulances were full for the trip back.

This and other episodes demonstrated only too clearly the evident unfitness for battle of some brigades, and Montgomery's expressed intention that all divisions were to be kept intact and fight together as they had been trained had perforce to be modified – a move made even more complicated by the proclaimed readiness for battle of a Greek infantry brigade and two French infantry brigade groups.

The result during the training period was a bewildering interchange of formations between divisions which continued through the opening days of the battle, and produced such improbabilities as two of 44th Division's brigades joining armoured divisions as support infantry, and at one time 50th (Northumbrian) Division consisted of Percy's brigade of Durham Light Infantry, plus the Greek Brigade and one brigade group of Fighting French.

If this was rather unsettling for the troops themselves it posed acute problems to the command, especially as two of the corps commanders were new to the theatre. Horrocks had joined Eighth Army to take Strafer Gott's place at the head of XIII Corps before Alam Halfa, and on September 10th Lieutenant-General Oliver Leese came out from England (again, at Montgomery's request) to take over XXX Corps from General Ramsden who, it will be remembered, had figured in Churchill's signal to the War Office of August 6th for replacement. A big, solid but quick-witted ex-Guardsman, Leese provided a complete contrast to the mercurial Horrocks, but had at least the advantage that as his corps would consist largely of Dominion troops – Australian, New Zealanders and South Africans, plus the 51st Highland Division – no one was to suggest the transposition of any of their brigades in view of native sensitivities.

Command of X Armoured Corps – the *corps de chasse* which

Montgomery had instructed Harding to form as a riposte to the Afrika Korps – was, however, to present some problems. The senior armoured commander in the theatre was Lieutenant-General Herbert Lumsden, recently promoted, a cavalryman who had at no time been closely involved with Montgomery's previous career and who had voiced strong objection to his superior's decision to wear the black beret of the Armoured Corps.

It is hardly surprising that Montgomery wanted him replaced, but on this occasion Alexander stood firm against his subordinate as he felt that too clean a sweep was being made of the old desert commanders – a stand in which Alexander was supported by his own Chief of Staff, Major-General Richard McCreery, another ex-cavalryman and indeed one from Lumsden's regiment, 12th Lancers. It was not to prove the happiest of Alexander's decisions, possibly because Montgomery resented it and was not prepared to try very hard to make it work.

It is also possible that Lumsden was not prepared to try very hard either, and as a result, Montgomery on October 6th had to make changes in his plans for fighting the battle.

He had announced his original plan for *Operation Lightfoot*, as he chose to call it – with, in view of the extent of the minefields, perhaps rather macabre flippancy – to the corps and divisional commanders and some of their staff on September 15th, and the essence of the tactics to be used was that infantry and engineers would cut passages through the enemy defences in both northern and southern sectors through which the armour should pass *unopposed* (the main bulk, X Corps under Lumsden, in the north), then break clear of all Axis positions and when well behind them, wheel and place themselves across the enemy lines of communication on 'ground of their own choice'. Here they would form a defensive block and fight off Rommel's panzer divisions, who must attack or face swift starvation. In view of the large numerical superiority of the British armour over the panzer strength, it was felt that they could afford if necessary to trade tank for tank – and still have enough left at the end to be able to round up the isolated Axis infantry and thus eliminate at least the German presence on Egyptian soil. There would then be little trouble from the Italians in Tripolitania, especially in view of the imminent Anglo-American invasion at the other end of the Mediterranean.

But during the days which followed it became increasingly evident that among the Commonwealth commanders at least, there was deep scepticism as to whether the armour possessed the ability to carry out their part in the plan or perhaps even the will to try very hard. Freyberg made it his business to have long discussions with both Morshead and Pienaar (whose voice of protest had been curiously muted since Montgomery's arrival) which he followed with other talks with both Lumsden and Gatehouse, whose 10th Armoured Division was the one scheduled to pass through the New Zealand sector of the line. These convinced him that, as in the recent past, the armour was more likely to act with caution than with determination.

As a result, the three Commonwealth commanders requested an interview with Oliver Leese and voiced their disquiet – greatly to Leese's astonishment as, with no previous experience of the desert war, he could not believe that the armour would not obey the Army Commander's orders to the letter. However, a few days later Leese's own B.G.S. attended a X Corps conference and could hardly believe his eyes and ears at the general atmosphere of casual disregard for Montgomery's edicts, amounting almost to insubordination, which ruled there.

He reported this impression to Leese who in due course talked to Montgomery about it, and within a few hours the armoured commanders had been told quite clearly that Montgomery's orders allowed them no latitude whatsoever, and must be obeyed to the letter. The Commonwealth commanders were then told that they need have no further qualms as the armour would do as it was told, and Freyberg's blunt comment, 'They won't!' even at this reassurance, was enough greatly to diminish his popularity at the top of Eighth Army.

It was also enough, however, to prompt Montgomery to examine much more closely the type and state of training now being carried out in the X Corps area, and as a result, to quote the *Official History*, 'He feared that he might be asking too much of his "somewhat untrained troops",' and abruptly reversed the principles behind the original plan.

Instead of breaking clear through all the Axis positions, bursting into open country and thus leaving a gap between British armour and British infantry, X Corps would now deploy as soon as they had passed through the corridors, form a screen to cut the Axis armour off from *their* infantry – and behind this screen the infantry battle would be fought. In other words, instead of first eliminating the panzer divisions so that the Axis infantry would wither, he would now eliminate first the Axis infantry so that, with no front holding, the Axis armour could be isolated; and when, inevitably, the panzers tried to break through the shield to aid their own infantry, X Corps would at least be close enough to XXX Corps for mutual support, and both would be kept tightly under Montgomery's personal control.

Distrust between infantry and armour was not, however, a one-way affair, and Lumsden made no secret of his belief that the passages through the minefields would not be completed during one night, and that dawn would catch his armour penned in narrow, blocked lanes, probably under concentrated anti-tank fire; and he received

Montgomery's instructions upon this point with blank incredulity. Should XXX Corps infantry and engineers fail to clear the passages entirely during that first night, the Army Commander ordered that X Corps would complete the job themselves with their own attached infantry and engineers, and fight their way forward to their designated positions on their own – a proposition so far opposed to Lumsden's thinking and the cavalry traditions requiring mobility, space in which to manoeuvre and a certain freedom to improvise, that even in the face of the Army Commander's specific instructions he still told his brigade and regimental commanders that they were not to try to rush anti-tank guns, and to make sure that the exits from the passages were not under anti-tank fire when they attempted to pass through them. What they were to do instead seems not to have been specified.

There was undoubtedly much to be said for Lumsden's point of view, especially in view of the difficulties which were attending X Corps's training. Originally intended to consist of three armoured divisions – 1st, 8th and 10th – one armoured division – the 8th – had been disbanded as no support infantry could be found for it, and as a result the 10th Armoured Division faced the problem of absorbing two extra brigades – one armoured from the disbanded 8th Division, and 133rd Brigade from 44th Division, which had itself hurriedly to adapt not only to a lorried infantry role but also to attachment to armour – a prospect undreamed of before departure from England only two months earlier.

Moreover, it was common practice throughout the Armoured Corps that new and reconditioned tanks should be concentrated by types in squadrons – a reasonable arrangement in most circumstances, but one which that summer entailed constant transfers of tanks and crews from squadron to squadron – and often transfers back a week later when newer or better reconditioned tanks arrived from the depots. Needless to say, every commander was trying to get the new Shermans, and often these were promised but Grants or even Crusaders turned up in their place; and some Shermans were actually delivered to their squadrons the day the battle began, lacking many important pieces of equipment.

Lumsden thus undoubtedly faced greater problems than Leese with his intact Commonwealth divisions and eager Highlanders, or Horrocks down in the south with only feint operations to organise; but it does not appear that Lumsden grappled with those problems with either the solid faith of the former or the enthusiasm of the latter – indeed the differences in attitude between Lumsden and Montgomery, amounting in the end to mutual antipathy, probably deepened the cavalryman's air of scornful disbelief to contrast with his superior's incisive certainty. This was not the frame of mind in which to weld the main thrust of Eighth Army's attack into a solid, homogeneous force.

That this was evident to others became clear when Leese informed de Guingand that the Commonwealth commanders were still dubious about the armour's intentions, but when de Guingand reported this to Montgomery he was told that there would be no more changes of plan. Bellyaching had to stop; orders would be obeyed, not discussed.

Not that General Montgomery felt that he himself must so slavishly obey directions from above.

It will be remembered that one of the main reasons for Auchinleck's removal from command of the Middle East theatre was his unshakeable conviction that Eighth Army would not be ready to attack the Afrika Korps positions before mid-September, and his refusal to allow the Prime Minister to persuade him otherwise. It was an opinion with which Auchinleck's successor not only agreed, but extended.

As soon as the Battle of Alam Halfa had been won and Montgomery's prestige at home as a result considerably increased, he announced that he needed a full moon for his attack at Alamein, that the army would not be ready in time for the September moon but would instead attack on the night of October 23rd. The response from Whitehall was immediate and expected – that the attack must be made in September in order to synchronise with various Russian attacks and preface *Operation Torch* by sufficient time for real advantages to accrue – but Montgomery, loyally backed by Alexander, declared that it would be suicide to attack so soon, that he would guarantee victory in October and that if Churchill insisted on the previous date then he must get somebody else to command the Army.

It was, as Montgomery was later to agree, pure blackmail . . . but it worked, and Churchill, after some ritual growling, accepted the situation despite the fact that once more Malta was under heavy attack by the Luftwaffe and unless supplies reached the island it would be starved into submission by November. His acceptance was perhaps made easier by a message from Roosevelt to the effect that the American military commanders were experiencing unexpected difficulties and that they now felt that the North African invasion could not take place, after all, until early November.

There was therefore to be a gap of seven weeks between the end of the Battle of Alam Halfa and the beginning of the Battle of Alamein. The time might not have been spent with total efficiency, but no one could say that much of it was wasted.

Very few battles in history have been won unless they included in their preparations and plans an element of surprise – but from neither the strategic nor geographical factors in Egypt in 1942 would it be possible to extract any high degree of this valuable quality. Nothing could hide the enormous build-up of men and material now arriving in the Suez ports, and it was obvious to all that an attack on the Panzerarmee was intended; there was nowhere for this to happen except at Alamein, and no practical alternative to a frontal assault.

Only in timing and local tactics could deception be practised and a degree of surprise thus perhaps achieved, and Montgomery's preparations from the beginning were meant to extract as large an element here as possible.

He had already determined that the main stroke would take place somewhere along the northern half of the line, so from the beginning everything was done to give the impression that it would occur in the south. The twin peaks of Himeimat had been left in German hands after Alam Halfa, and from their heights a great deal of activity could be seen, while in the early days of September at least, Axis observation aircraft found it far easier and safer to penetrate here than nearer the coast.

Dummy administration camps were erected in XIII Corps's area to the south of Ruweisat Ridge, existing dumps were expanded by empty cases and tentage while totally empty ones were erected in between, and a dummy fresh-water pipeline was laid complete with three dummy pumphouses, leading from Bir Sadi in the north and obviously aiming for Gaballa in the south. Each night a trench was dug about five miles long and a dummy pipe made from old petrol cans laid alongside it. During the following night a similar trench was dug and the one dug the night before was filled in (by troops who knew what was happening, otherwise there could have been trouble) and the length of tin piping shifted south; and after a comparatively short time it became evident to the morning Luftwaffe observation plane that the project would not reach its destination until early in November.

But the main deceptive operation was mounted in the north, and such was its scope and size that it even achieved an operational code name – *Bertram* – of its own. Here an early decision had been taken by one of Montgomery's staff officers, Lieutenant-Colonel C. L. Richardson, and followed throughout with admirable consistency – that every evidence of concentration of force would be openly displayed as quickly as possible so that, when no assault immediately developed, the enemy would grow used to its existence and notice no change when fact replaced fiction.

Numerous slit-trenches were dug in advanced positions and then left unused; thousands of dummy vehicles, guns, tanks and dumps were erected during the first weeks of October – enough to give the concentration needed for an attack – but as day followed day they either remained static or were moved around enough by the deception staff to add verisimilitude to their existence, while back around Wadi Natrun the real tanks, guns and lorries arrived, were tested and the crews given at least some training in their use. When eventually these moved into the operational area they did so under cover of darkness, took the place of the dummies and these or others were erected in the training areas to give the impression that no change in concentration had taken place.

This routine was followed when the New Zealand Division had finished their exercise and moved to battle positions, men and vehicles disappearing into the previous concentration while in the dummy camp they left behind, small detachments moved about, lit fires, drove vehicles around and kept up a flow of routine signals. Maintaining a consistent signals density was an essential part of the plan, and this was achieved when the divisions moved forward by imposing wireless silence upon them in their new positions but keeping a nucleus signal section behind sending out bogus messages; when eventually X Corps moved up, the entire signals organisation of the disbanded 8th Armoured Division, which had been retained for just this purpose, continued the wireless traffic.

There was even a special section formed under a hurriedly commissioned world famous illusionist, Jasper Maskelyne, to conceive and execute the more *outré* effects. A dummy railhead was set up with a dummy oil-discharging point nearby, and around these locations were piled inflammatory materials in which were buried remotely controlled igniters; when the Luftwaffe bombed the areas the igniters fired the heaps, and following waves of bombers dumped their loads on what appeared to be worthwhile targets. Alongside a dummy oil-jetty, they erected a convertible tanker which one day presented the picture of a one-funnelled ship to aerial observers, and the next day two funnels and a mast on a lengthened hull or some other variation. The main water pipeline from Alexandria was replaced by one with a larger bore, but all the work was done at night and the old one left apparently undisturbed, and the new water-point thus supplied concealed in El Imayid Station and not used until the opening of the battle.

All the time this activity in the rear areas was taking place – the armour training, the specialists carrying out their own esoteric duties, the supply services building up the dumps – the bulk of Eighth Army infantry had of course, despite brigade training exercises, still to hold the line. They were at times very thinly spread, for not only were the entire New Zealand Division absent but in turn each of the Australian brigades also went back for training exercises, as did brigades from the South African Division. Some relief was provided by substituting individual brigades from the 51st Highland Division for those with-drawn from the front, and indeed the practice not only gave the Jocks some invaluable experience, it also formed a bond between them and the Australians in whose area they did most of their replacement duties which was to prove very valuable in the near future.

But there were times for the men in the foremost positions – patrolling and exploring the minefields in front, fighting off the occasional foray by Afrika Korps or Ariete armoured cars, digging their slit-trenches deeper or building up their sangar walls – when it seemed that they were alone in a hot, dusty, fly-ridden and dangerous world, very much at the sharp end of the war.

During the day along most of the line, they lay in their trenches trying to sleep unless they were on guard, cursing the flies, the dust and the heat, wriggling into whatever shade they could contrive, wondering if they could afford to smoke another cigarette; and when the time came for their own spell of duty, they watched the enemy positions through dancing heat-waves or listened anxiously for ominous sounds beyond the blur of the daily sandstorm. Despite the dangers it could easily bring, everyone longed for nightfall.

Once darkness had fallen, everything began to happen. Picks and shovels rose and fell as everyone – especially in the areas closest to the enemy – tried to deepen his own shelter, with compressors in the rocky areas if he was lucky, sometimes with explosive. Behind the immediate front positions, gun-pits, medical posts, headquarters and supply positions had to be dug out, while in front the barbed wire was strung on pickets driven into rock or sand, with mines somehow concealed among it all. Sweat was being used to save blood.

Above them all, R.A.F. or U.S.A.A.F. bombers either roared close and dropped their bombs ahead on Axis gun-flash or pre-recorded target, or zoomed away high in the sky towards Benghasi, or Tobruk, or Benina or any other of the nodal points behind Rommel's lines; and occasionally the Luftwaffe would come over, and if Junkers or Heinkel was low and slow enough, everyone would pause in their tasks, listening for the faint whisper of a falling bomb before diving into shelter. And all the time the work was punctuated by the staccato rattle of machine-gun and rifle fire as patrols met and fought brief actions amid the minefields, creeping silently about their duties of search and reconnaissance until their own target areas coincided with those of the enemy. Every morning there were new corpses out in no-man's-land, lying unburied, quickly to swell up and blacken in the daytime heat.

Reinforcements came up during the night, units returned from training in the rear areas, men came in from leave or hospital, passing as they did so the ones going back – the lucky ones with just minor injuries, desert sores, 'Gyppo tummy' or even better still a temporary posting; the not so lucky in swaying ambulances en route for base hospitals. Trucks brought up rations and, most welcome of all, water; staff cars brought up an occasional visitor of greater or lesser importance, despatch riders would bump their way through tangles of trenches to find battalion and sometimes company headquarters. The traffic during the night was continuous – but slow and cautious, picking its way through the maze of gun-pits, haphazard dumps and random training areas still infested with unexploded bombs or mines, each vehicle trailing its plume of dust to add to the gloom.

With dawn came a cessation of all this activity. Patrols would by now be back in their own lines, the privates into their slit-trenches, officers or N.C.O.s reporting to the headquarter positions and if they were lucky enjoying an early cup of rather chemical-tasting tea. And as the sun came up behind them, the whole Eighth Army stood to against the possibility of a dawn attack, infantry waiting tensely, gunners already into action as the light grew, for with the sun behind them the first hour of a fine morning gave them the best visibility of the day; and from then on, the artillery would boom and bang away all day at known enemy positions or along tracks known to carry supplies for the Panzerarmee, for by mid-September the big Allied convoys had arrived at Tewfik and there was no shortage of ammunition.

But the infantry were back in their 'slitties' again, cursing the flies.

Yet despite the hardship and monotony of the life, Eighth Army morale was good again, and rising. The sense of purpose and grip which had started with Alam Halfa strengthened every day, many more men were seeing much more of their divisional and corps commanders than ever before in the desert war, and a large number had even seen and been talked to by Montgomery himself. Moreover, there were visible and concrete signs that their new Army Commander really did have their welfare at heart, an instance of this being that despite the fact that he was a non-smoker himself the cigarette ration arrived regularly, and if a platoon, company or battalion did particularly well an extra issue might arrive for them with a message of appreciation.

Even more importantly, the water ration (of at least one water-bottle per day per man) arrived with reassuring regularity, and although it usually tasted of chlorine and was never cold enough, it was always drinkable; and to palates long used to chemical adulterants, sometimes positively 'sweet'. And then there were those eagerly awaited short spells of leave back in the peace and comfort, not to say luxury, of Cairo or Alexandria.

Every division made their own arrangements, but those of the New Zealanders were typical. A 'Four day' leave consisted in fact of six days away from the unit, the first and last days being devoted to travel back and forth, the days between spent as each man chose. There had been little chance of spending accumulated pay for weeks and sometimes months past, so if the men wished they could stay at their own expense in clubs or in selected hotels; or they could stay for nothing at rest camps designed and organised expressly to free them from the usual constraints of army discipline. Meals were available at almost any hour, beer was on sale with little regard for licensing hours, canteens and cinemas were there in the camp, transport into Cairo provided at hourly intervals and for those who wanted them, conducted tours to places of interest.

There were baths, tennis courts, swimming pools, laundries and even friendly quartermasters who would replace torn or sweat- and sand-caked clothing without demur. There were cabarets in the cities in the evening, the vast Pole Nord bar in Cairo and many smaller establishments like it; Groppi's for cakes and ice cream, for officers the cool though musty lounge at Shepheard's with gin slings and servants in white gallabiyas. And for those who wished to take advantage of them and who could avoid the vigilance of the military police, there were also, of course, the forbidden delights of the Burka or Sister Street in Alex; otherwise there was little chance of feminine company, for what there was had long been appropriated by the Base Staff.

One interesting development for the front line infantry was that, having been made up by reinforcements to full strength, some formations by the end of September were finding themselves over-strength. The news of Alam Halfa and the possibility that the new Army Commander might know his job had combined to persuade some absentees that perhaps the time had come for a return to their units, and most commanding officers were content to exact retribution in the form of extra duties without referral to a higher authority which might have felt it encumbent to take more drastic or even penal action. The numbers were not yet great, but the rate of return was increasing.

On October 6th Montgomery issued to the corps and divisional commanders and their immediate staff the bones of the overall final plan. There were five main points:

1 The main attack by XXX Corps in the north would take place on a frontage of four divisions. Two corridors were to be cleared through the minefields, and through these lanes X Corps would pass.
2 XIII Corps in the south were to stage two attacks, one directed past the Himeimat Peaks and on to the Taqa Plateau, the other into the area of Jebel Kalakh, both with the object simply of disguising the main thrust of the assault and thus holding in the south enemy forces

which might otherwise be transferred to the main attack front.

3 On both fronts the enemy forward positions were to be destroyed though heavy casualties in the south, especially among the tanks of 7th Armoured Division, were to be avoided.

4 Once X Corps were through XXX Corps positions and the main enemy defences, they were to deploy so as to prevent interference with XXX Corps operations against the Axis infantry. Offensive action against the enemy armour would only be undertaken when the infantry battles had been won.

5 The battle would commence at night during the full moon period.

As the recipients could read calendars as well as Montgomery himself there was little doubt in any of their minds as to the date of the attack, so few of them were surprised when Montgomery called for an assembly of all XXX and XIII Corps officers down to the rank of lieutenant-colonel on October 19th, with one for X Corps officers the following day. They proved memorable occasions.

Speaking clearly and incisively but with his curiously flat, almost metallic voice, the Army Commander first explained the reorganis-ations which had taken place throughout Eighth Army since the end of August, then outlined his plans in some detail – the break-in, the 'crumbling' process behind the X Corps shield, the break-out. He then went on to specify the almost overwhelming superiority in guns and tanks which Eighth Army held over Rommel's forces, but warned strongly against any belief that the battle would be a walk-over. It would be very tough, he stressed repeatedly, and every man in the army must be prepared to kill the enemy and go on killing until the battle was won – even chaplains, he announced to some amusement, 'one on weekdays and two on Sundays!'

Spectacular results must not be expected too soon, for in the final analysis a battle such as this promised to be would only be won by prolonged and consistent effort, directed from firm bases, maintained with offensive eagerness by men of high morale. The whole affair would last, he told them, for twelve days – and one point of interest is that in the notes from which he delivered these addresses he had originally written '10 days' and that at some time very shortly before beginning to speak, he had crossed out '10' and pencilled '(12)' in the margin.

It would therefore seem that despite his instructions to both XXX and X Corps that they were to force their way through the minefields during the first night, and that X Corps must form the shield by dawn on the first morning, he did not really expect them to do so; Panzerarmee could hardly last eleven days after so decisive a separation of their infantry from their armour.

The officers were then dismissed with instructions that every one of their men was to be told of the overall plan and the part he was to play in it, but not for obvious reasons until October 21st after which all leave would be stopped and Eighth Army virtually sealed off from the outside world. By then, the final moves up to their start lines for the attacking troops would be well under way.

The main tasks for the commanding generals were completed by October 20th (if they were not, as one of them later commented, it was by then too late to do anything about them) but from that time until the opening of the battle the lives of the staff officers were of immense concentration, constant activity and for some of them, nightmarish worry. Theirs was the responsibility of ensuring that by the morning of October 23rd, over 2,000 guns, 1,000 tanks and some 220,000 men were all in their assigned positions, and that all the ammunition, petrol, helmets, ambulances, shell-dressings, shovels, haversacks, full water-bottles, guiding beacons, searchlights, tins of bully beef, matches and mortar-bombs, Very pistols and bagpipes, mine-detectors and paybooks and everything else that the soldiers would need to fight a battle lasting twelve days would be instantly available to them when and where required. And at least 60 per cent of all these men and all this material had to be moved during four successive nights, in such a manner that no trace of its passing would remain on the desert floor to be observed by hostile eyes during the hours of harsh desert light in between.

On October 18th the 450 assorted tanks and 2,000-odd lorries of X Corps moved openly down into positions well south of Alam Halfa behind XIII Corps headquarters, carrying with them canvas replicas of every vehicle on strength. These were carefully erected, and during the next four nights the corps moved north again to its final assembly area around El Imayid, slipping into the dummy positions which had been there since the beginning of the month, carefully obliterating all tracks left by this prodigious move – which had perforce been meticulously dovetailed into another taking place across its axis by the two infantry brigades of the New Zealand Division, with their Divisional Cavalry and the 9th Armoured Brigade which was attached to them and had come up from Wadi Natrun. Both moves had also to be correlated with the moves of isolated brigades of the other XXX Corps infantry divisions, rejoining the line after training exercises in the rear areas.

Parallel tracks led to the last staging areas before the move into the front lines – Diamond, Boomerang, Two-bar and Square leading off the coast road into the northern section of the line and the positions held by the 9th Australian Division, running from the coast to about two miles south of Tel el Eisa. Sun, Moon and Star tracks fed the positions of 51st Highland Division to the south of the Australians, a

short spur off Star plus the Bottle and Boat tracks fed the New
Zealanders on the left of the Highlanders, while the single Hat track
fed the South African Division holding the left flank of the XXX
Corps attack front. It was along these tracks, each identified at night
by their symbols cut into the sides of lamps shining to the rear, that
first the infantry element of Montgomery's striking force must make
their separate and dusty ways to their attack positions; and it was
through the eight-mile front which these comprised that the two lanes
must be cut for the passage of the armoured divisions – 1st and 10th –
of X Corps. To the south of the South African Division stood the 4th
Indian Division holding the left flank of XXX Corps, stretching down
for nearly another twelve miles across Ruweisat Ridge to the junction
with XIII Corps.

Thousands of men laboured day and night in the rear areas, tens of
thousands marched and countermarched, climbing in and out of
vehicles, coughing in the thick, swirling dust-clouds, sweating under
the weight of pack and shovel and rifle or machine-gun – a few not
understanding or even caring what it was all about, but most knowing
full well that they were taking part in as significant a piece of
administrational expertise as the modern world had seen up to that
time, the move of the Eighth Army into position for the Second
Battle of Alamein.

Its successful execution in broad daylight would rank as a feat of
organisation to compare with any; its completion at night is a matter
for perpetual wonder, especially when its successful concealment is
taken into consideration. Every track made by a vehicle was brushed
away before daylight, the military police who had spent the preceding
hours directing the blacked-out convoys in ever-increasingly complicated moves through ever-thickening dust-clouds hastily snatching
up the pickets holding the guiding lamps, while alongside them
engineers replaced the fence lines, the dummy huts and dummy
minefields which they had removed a few hours before, to disguise
once again the very existence of the tracks to the front.

And there was vital work to be done – and disguised – much
further forward. Start and guide-lines were laid out on every
divisional front during the four nights before the attack – nearly nine
miles for every division – accurately surveyed, meticulously plotted,
and laid down first in near-invisible telephone wire, to be covered
during the last hours by white tape. One battalion commander spent
over eighty hours by himself out in no-man's-land on this chore
alone, on occasion narrowly avoiding death at the hands of friendly
patrols; but the work was done, and at least during the opening hours
of the battle the leading troops would know where they were and
where they were going.

If Lieutenant-General Horrocks in the south felt any disappoint-

Map 23   The Alamein Line, October 23rd, 1942

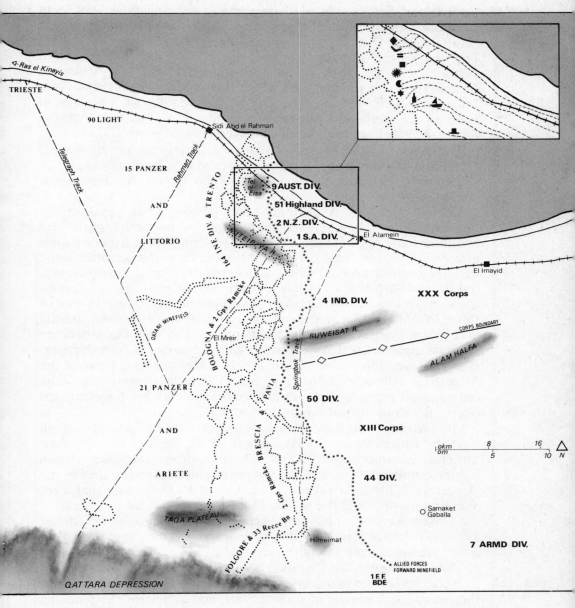

ment about the comparatively minor part his own command was
allotted in the forthcoming battle, it did not in any way affect his
energy or activity. Here in the XIII Corps area was played out the
reverse side of the deception plan. Here, day and night, Axis aircraft

might perceive a constant swarm of activity, Rommel's intercept service could listen to the stream of signals between the various brigade and divisional headquarters, many of them fictional but some from the 50th Division on the right next to the corps boundary, down through 44th Division positions in the centre to those of the 1st Fighting French Brigade near the edge of the Qattara Depression; behind these the units of the old adversary, the 7th Armoured Division, gravely manoeuvred, chattering unceasingly as they did so. Huge and badly camouflaged dumps grew daily, massed parks of vehicles accumulated and occasionally moved a little nearer to the front, the pipeline from the north edged ever closer to Gaballa.

The cloak of deception over the whole enterprise never slipped, *Operation Bertram* was meticulously carried out. Ironically, it may in some part have been unnecessary, for the Desert Air Force now commanded the skies.

Since the end of August they had possessed the capability of 'round-the-clock' bombing for limited periods, but both logistics and common sense had held them back and to some extent dispersed their effort until the last, vital period – at least so far as the activities of the fighters and day-bombers were concerned. Too much attention was not to be drawn to the battlefield itself, though prime targets further afield were continually attacked. Every night there were twenty or thirty Wellingtons over Tobruk, and on most nights Sollum, Bardia and Mersa Matruh received a visitation – as did Suda Bay whenever reconnaissance revealed worthwhile concentrations of Axis shipping. Benghasi was the chosen target for the Liberator squadrons of the Middle East detachment of the U.S.A.F. as theirs were almost the only aircraft capable of the return journey; altogether they dropped over a hundred tons of bombs on the port.

On October 9th there was an exception to the partial ban on daylight attacks when reports came in of the flooding of some Axis airfields. Baltimores of 55th and 223rd Squadrons and South African fighter-bombers of 2nd and 4th Squadrons, all escorted by British and American fighters, attacked the airfields at El Daba, and that night Wellingtons attacked the field at Fuka – but except for that occasion the Desert Air Force held itself in check until the morning of October 19th, its prime activity over the battlefield merely to chase away Axis reconnaissance from the northern section.

Then, during the last four days before zero hour, Air Vice-Marshal Coningham set out to achieve two main aims – to clear the air above the entire battleground of Axis aircraft, and to destroy the potential of both the Luftwaffe and the Regia Aeronautica to interfere with Eighth Army activities or even to contribute very much to those of the Panzerarmee. During the day the Hurricanes and Spitfires ranged the desert strip between El Alamein and Himeimat, while further west Baltimores and Kittyhawks struck again and again at El Daba and Fuka and at night Wellingtons and Bostons continued the attack. To the north Albacores and Seafires of the Fleet Air Arm swept the coastal waters, and the Liberators pounded the areas further west along the Egyptian frontier and beyond – and all the time they kept the eyes of the Axis forces watching upwards, every day more fearfully. An average of over five hundred and fifty sorties were flown every twenty-four hours by the aircraft of the Royal Air Force, the South African Air Force, the Royal Australian Air Force and the United States Army Air Force, and there were few members of the Eighth Army who were not aware of their activities and profoundly grateful for them. The resentment that the soldier had felt for the airman since the desperate days of Dunkirk vanished and never returned; at last it was evident to all that both arms were fighting the same war and the days of the Luftwaffe's domination of the battlefield were gone.

By dawn on Friday, October 23rd, the Eighth Army was in position. All along the front soldiers lay in their slit-trenches, sweating, roasting in the concentration of heat from which they might not escape for any reason at all, plagued the whole day by the flies. Behind them, the artillery banged away occasionally, neither increasing nor decreasing the weight of fire that had been thrown at the Axis positions every day for the past few weeks; occasionally a machine-gun would chatter, a motor-bike would roar off into the distance, trucks would trail dust-clouds back towards the headquarter areas. Above them, the air squadrons cruised and sometimes roared low overhead; and the air shimmered and the sun blazed.

And then, at last, it began to sink. The heat drained from the sky, the air lightened, sometimes shifting slightly to give the first of the cool evening breezes. Suddenly the flies were gone, movement could be sensed all around, a hum of low voices. The stars were out. It was dark.

Out of the ground climbed the Eighth Army, stretching its limbs, coughing, swearing, still keeping voice low. Rifles clunked on the ground, webbing creaked, metal lids on cooking-pots clanked as hot food came up, mugs slurped into the tea dixies; out in front the forward patrols moved cautiously back, passing as they did so the hurrying figures laying out the white tape. And everyone glanced at their watches every few minutes.

Back at his tactical headquarters by the coast into which he had moved that morning, the Army Commander talked briefly with his corps commanders, and satisfied himself among other things that his message to the troops ending with the confident assertion that 'The Lord Mighty in Battle will give us the victory' had reached every one of them. He had a cup of tea with de Guingand at about half past four, then settled down with a book to read until retiring to bed, which he did earlier than usual in the hope of getting solidly to sleep before the barrage began. It seems that he was now quite confident of the readiness for battle of the army under his command.

It is at least likely that he may have wondered briefly about the state of the enemy.

The condition of the Panzerarmee by this time was serious – so serious indeed that a proportion of even the Afrika Korps itself was becoming despondent. With the obvious rebuff to Axis hopes at Alam Halfa, dreams of rest and recuperation amid the fleshpots of the Delta had faded abruptly, and the resultant fall in spirits was accompanied by an inevitable recrudescence of the physical ills which had plagued the army during July. An extra depressant to Afrika Korps morale had been the news that the health of their heroic commander had suffered as much if not more than their own, and on September 23rd he had left for extended leave and treatment at his home near Wiener-Neustadt. It says much for the regard in which he was held that no one doubted that he would return.

His replacement, General der Kavallerie Georg Stumme, had arrived on September 19th and proved to be a large, good-humoured man, lately commander of a panzer division on the eastern front, who announced that after the rigours of a Russian winter he positively relished the climatic conditions in the desert. This hardly recommended him to the men newly under his command, unlikely to view any replacement for Rommel with much favour, and now disgruntled and inclined towards contempt for one so totally unversed in the grim realities of desert warfare. And although Stumme was to find little room for criticism in the disposition of the forces under his command or with the proposals for fighting the battle which so obviously loomed, his position was not made easier by Rommel's announcement just before he left, that he would abandon his cure and return to take command the moment the battle began.

As for Rommel's condition, it was in many ways both physically and mentally worse than that of his army. He was, of course, much older than the majority of the men under his command and had been in the theatre longer than most – but now a totally new factor was added to the psychological burdens he already bore. He was not used to circumstances forcing him to admit that he might have been wrong, but after Alam Halfa he could not disguise from himself the fact that the position of the army under his command would have been far more secure were it back on the Egyptian frontier, with its supplies arriving regularly and unmolested by enemy forces operating from Malta; and many voices would be raised in chorus should he so much as hint at his acceptance of this fact, pointing out that he had only himself to blame for the fact that they were not.

His main battlefield concern was the total dominance of the air above it and above the vital supply lines feeding it, by the enemy. Not only did this curtail his own possibilities for reconnaissance and at the same time reveal every movement of his own troops to hostile eyes, but it wore down the nerves and hopes of his men even further. Perhaps most important of all, by limiting large-scale movement of every kind to the hours of darkness, it wasted a great deal of that essential element in warfare – time.

It was thus with a heavy heart that he set out for home on September 23rd, calling first at Derna where he depressed his spirits even further by undertaking what he knew in his heart to be a pointless exercise. From the Italian headquarters there he obtained promises that 3,000 workmen would be immediately provided to repair the road surfaces, which had by then become so pitted and worn that daily wastage on his already exiguous transport had become unacceptable; that 7,000 tons of rails and sleepers would be brought to the area to aid that condition even further, and that in view of the recent events at Tobruk and in the Jebel, the Italians would immediately assemble and despatch a sufficiently large and aggressive force down to Kuffra to capture the oasis, and thus eliminate it as a base for British commando raids. (He was not surprised to learn, upon his eventual return to Africa, that none of the promises had been kept.)

At Rome, his experiences were in similar vein. Il Duce welcomed him warmly, expressed some surprise at his tale of supply shortages and lack of logistical support and promised to rectify the matter, then sent him on his way with assurances of his continued and complete confidence, expressed in the bland but hardly encouraging exhortation, 'You have done the impossible before, Herr Feldmarschall. We are all sure you will do it again!'[3]

And when eventually he arrived at the Führer's 'Wolf's Lair' in East Prussia, he found a similar atmosphere, the whole place aglow with unfounded optimism. Praise and congratulation were poured upon him, he was surrounded by beaming and sycophantic headquarter personnel (his old enemy Halder had been dismissed the day after Rommel left North Africa for introducing an unwelcome note of cold realism into this febrile climate) but his attempts to get across some understanding of the parlous condition of Panzerarmee Afrika were total failures. Goering, in particular, brushed aside all tales of difficulties present or future, assured Rommel that despite the evidence of his own eyes, the Luftwaffe and not the R.A.F. dominated the skies everywhere, and as for the possibility of significant aid for the Allies from America: 'Quite impossible! Nothing but latrine rumours! All the Americans can make are razor blades and Frigidaires!'[4]

The only note of genuine help or understanding seemed to come – as usual – from the Führer himself, who did spare time to listen without interruption to Rommèl's by now somewhat tired and cautious list of grievances, promising to send to the Mediterranean a large number of Siebel ferries – a type of craft which had proved fairly immune to air and torpedo attacks. Moreover, 'In the near future I'll be sending you in Africa a heavy-mortar brigade, five hundred barrels, as well as forty of the newest Tiger tanks, to be followed by several assault gun units!'[5] And even Rommel's by now engrained scepticism was not proof against promises from so high an authority.

As a result, the next few days spent as guest of the Goebbels family in Berlin passed happily, both his spirits and health improving under the stimulus of good food and continual, indeed lavish, admiration amounting to flattery. On the last day of the month, after a brief ceremony in the Reich Chancellery at which the recently returned Führer presented him with the baton of his new and exalted rank, he was quite able to present to the world the picture of a supremely capable and confident Army Commander.

The occasion was a mass rally at the Berlin Sportpalast Stadium at which Rommel was the guest of honour, Hitler making to the assembled Party and Wehrmacht notables a speech in praise of the new Generalfeldmarschall – all duly recorded and then broadcast throughout the Axis-dominated and much of the neutral world by the whirring press cameras and the German radio networks.

At Goebbels's request, the whole rodomontade was repeated three days later in the Ministry of Propaganda, when, his hand still holding the knob of the door through which he had just made a somewhat theatrical entrance, Rommel delivered himself of the following defiant – and in view of the realities of the situation, surely unwise – announcement: 'Today, we stand just fifty miles from Alexandria and Cairo, and we have the door to all Egypt in our hands . . . We have not gone all that way to be thrown back again . . . what we have, we hold.'[6]

A few hours later, he left at last for home, for rest and re-cuperation, and for Dearest Lu.

For the remainder of Panzerarmee there was, of course, not the faintest hope of leave at home, only at best the relaxation of widely spaced two-day visits to rest camps on the coast where, although their food was prepared by trained army cooks and not just by the appointed member of the platoon, it was basically the same as that available in the line; not for the Afrika Korps the delights of hotel cuisine or even a well-stocked city bar, and they were fortunate if their visit to the rest camp coincided with a delivery of beer. Even the water was becoming more and more unpalatable, for the bulk came from old wells and cisterns along the coast, many of which had been damaged during the various stages of the 'Benghasi Handicap' and again during early October when heavy rainstorms washed sand and dirt into the caverns and further polluted the already murky liquid. But at least there was swimming in the sea, and clothes could be washed in it; though there was very rarely any new linen or drill to replace the now worn and sand-clogged uniforms.

If life was Spartan in the rest camps, it was grim indeed at the front. Hygiene had still not improved even among the German contingent – and with the desperate water shortage, lice infestation was common throughout the whole Panzerarmee – while the ordinary Italian soldier was by now so tired of the war that only such obviously life-preserving measures as the digging of shelters or the thickening of minefields in front were willingly undertaken. Washing, disposal of waste or even of dead bodies was a chore to be avoided, flies and stench being accepted as preferable to physical exertion; in this the Italians at least contributed to the additional discomfort of their enemies wherever the opposing lines were close together.

Not surprisingly in these circumstances the sick rate rose every week, but as all forms of transport were limited both because of petrol shortage and vehicle deterioration the severity of sickness which would justify release to a base hospital rose all the time, and jaundice, dysentery and scabies were rife throughout the divisions in the line. Food for all was dull and unvaried – tinned meat, hard biscuits, a small bread ration of uncertain quality, little margarine, fewer vegetables of any sort and none fresh – and for the Germans it was on occasion so short that battalion commanders had to go cap-in-hand to neighbouring Italian units. The almost offensive magnanimity adopted by the latter on these occasions did nothing to improve relations between the allies, already strained by the events of the last few months.

These relations could not be alleviated by keeping the two nationalities apart either, for Rommel had decreed that the Italian units should be 'corseted' by German units down sometimes to company level. This meant, for instance, that the German 164th Infantry Division and the Italian Trento Division both occupied the whole length of the line from the coast down to the end of the Miteiriya Ridge (and facing Montgomery's XXX Corps's main attack front), their fighting troops thoroughly intermingled, their various headquarters situated close together so that German control, euphemistically designated 'help and advice', would be constantly available, certainly down to battalion level and sometimes lower. To the south of this conglomerate, the Bologna Division with two groups (Heydte and Schweiger) of the stout Ramcke Brigade of German paratroops faced the 4th Indian Division positions down to Ruweisat Ridge – almost exactly opposite the junction of XXX and XIII Corps – while immediately south of this lay two more groups of German paratroops (Burckhardt and Hubner) with the Italian Brescia and Pavia Infantry Divisions holding the line opposite the 50th and 44th Divisions. The Folgore Division held the southern end of the line down to the Qattara Depression, but even these were supported by Rommel's 33rd Reconnaissance Battalion.

The 15th Panzer and the Littorio lay behind the northern sector and the 21st Panzer and the Ariete behind the southern, their respective command units also situated so close as to be practically united; and along the coast back from Sidi Abd el Rahman almost to Ras el Kinayis lay the 90th Light and the Trieste Divisions in reserve. In theory, no one was going to move anywhere without complete agreement between two equal partners; in practice, no one was under any illusions as to who would be in control.

Rommel's original philosophy behind this deployment of his forces was based upon the realisation that British preponderance of men and weapons had now reached such a stage that in any form of mobile battle it would outweigh the superior skills of even the Afrika Korps. The battle therefore must be fought as a static slogging match . . . but this would give an even greater advantage to the enemy, as it would bring out the finest qualities of the British infantry, and especially of the Australians and New Zealanders for whom Rommel had the highest admiration.

As there was no way in which he could defeat the Eighth Army by brawn, they must be beaten by brain. He must out-think the new Army Commander.

In this task, Rommel considered that he possessed certain advantages. While writing what had become the German Army's standard manual of infantry tactics, he had spent much time in deep study of British methods of attack in the First World War, and he now felt that the situation at Alamein would see a repetition of their use. With this in mind he had designed his forward defences to absorb the shock of the artillery barrage and the initial impetus of the infantry assault, keeping his main defensive positions back out of artillery range.

His whole front, he considered, would be subject at the outset of the battle to powerful attacks at many points, which would continue until General Montgomery made up his mind as to which attack looked most promising and began to reinforce it. During the pause for the redeployment which this would necessitate – unduly prolonged by German standards by the almost traditional slowness of thought at British command level – Rommel would have time to move his panzer divisions behind the most threatened areas, and indeed, once he was certain of his antagonist's choice, concentrate his main strength there first to block the danger and then to counter it. He must, however, be correct in his interpretation of Montgomery's decision for with supply conditions as they stood, once he had moved one pair of armoured divisions north or south, there would not be enough petrol to move them back again.

This original plan had, however, been modified in the light of the crippling shortages of petrol and transport. There was just not enough of either adequately to feed the forces in the southern half of the line – and the suspicion grew that this was where the main blow would fall. Every indication seemed to confirm that the British would attempt a massive attack south of Ruweisat Ridge, and by the beginning of October it was evident to all at Panzerarmee Head-quarters that they could not make the defences there impregnable without an enormous increase in logistic support – and in the possi-bility of such support no one any longer believed. The probability of the southern half of the line breaking must therefore be faced, and plans laid to cope with the development.

Although everything must still be done to absorb and slow the impetus of this southern assault, if and when it broke through the infantry defences the panzer divisions behind must be preserved, swinging back to the south and west, while what remained of the southern defences themselves must hinge back along the Ruweisat Ridge–El Mreir line, to find shelter behind the 'Qatani minefield' which would now be thickened and run east–west from the Ramcke Brigade positions in the line back as far as the Rahman Track. In this position, they would block any attempt by the attacking forces to drive northwards, channelling them instead westward into the desert where they would then be attacked from both sides by the combined German and Italian armour, with the reserve divisions deployed down from the coast as necessity dictated.

As for the northern half of the line from Ruweisat up to the coast, this of course would be made as impregnable as German military expertise could make it with the materials available. As there was, in fact, rather more material than Rommel ever admitted in his despatches and reports to Berlin (for obvious reasons), this should prove effective in blocking any British attack north of Ruweisat Ridge, even if Panzerarmee's fears were unfounded and the main attack fell there instead of in the south.

This then was the prospect and these the probabilities facing General Stumme and his immediate subordinates as October passed – and few of them faced the future with much optimism, especially as with only one exception they were all new to the desert. The Afrika

Korps itself was now commanded by Generalleutnant Ritter von Thoma after Nehring's wounding during Alam Halfa; Generalleutnant von Randow commanded 21st Panzer in von Bismarck's place and Generalleutnant Graf von Sponek the 90th Light in Kleeman's. Of the divisional commanders only von Vaerst and Lungershausen of 164th Division were still in Africa (and the latter was hardly an old hand) while of the chief staff officers, Gause and von Mellenthin had both gone back to Europe, the first as a result of wounds and the second with acute amoebic dysentery, Westphal was ill with jaundice and even the indestructible Bayerlein viewed the immediate future with deep foreboding.

One of the psychological reasons for the mood of depression at the top could have been that there were no plans at all for any form of offensive action. Not even a vague date for the possible resumption of the drive to the Nile was discussed – perhaps because no one could conceive of such a prospect under any but Rommel's command, perhaps because of ever-growing conviction of the Panzerarmee's weaknesses. Not enough fuel, not enough transport, shortage of ammunition for a prolonged battle, disheartened allies, even the German element of the Panzerarmee no longer the elite fighting force of earlier days, for the old hands were showing signs of strain and the newcomers were of neither the physique nor standard of training of the original Korps.

Yet the Germans were still the nucleus of the force which must somehow hold back the growing power of the Eighth Army. As such they could not be risked night after night before the main battle in deep patrols probing the enemy defences, and as the Italians were not willing to undertake anything but sporadic and small-scale reconnaissance, and as command of the air had passed so irrevocably to the enemy, this meant that the intelligence section had very little sound material to work on – and with the departure of the brilliant von Mellenthin no intuition or long desert experience to guide them. In this respect the High Command had received yet another blow; Colonel Bonner Fellers had been recalled to Washington and no longer broadcast his nightly messages from which the Rome codebreakers had been able to extract the details of British plans and deployment.

General Stumme and his staff were not therefore in receipt of a continuous stream of accurate information, but he was not himself yet affected by the general air of pessimism and indeed for the moment all felt fairly secure. The minefields were already thick and work was progressing on them all the time – to such an extent that of one aspect of the attack when it came they could be absolutely certain; it must take place in moonlight. As every piece of evidence which came into intelligence hands indicated that neither an increase

17 An L.R.D.G. patrol sets out for the Jebel Akhdar

18 Desert rendezvous

19–20 German minefields formed the first obstacle to be crossed when the attack
came in

in logistical support behind the enemy lines nor a forward movement of troops into attack positions was taking place during the week or so before the October full moon, then at least they had until the end of November to finalise their defensive plans, to hope that Berlin and Rome would at last appreciate their position and do something constructive about it.

They might, for instance, send out some more of the new Mark IV panzers, for although there were a few with both the 15th and 21st Divisions, most of the 220 panzers they held between them were the old Mark IIIs with the 50mm. gun. Ariete and Littorio added between them 340 Italian tanks, but some of these were too light to be counted as much more than armoured cars, and singularly ineffective ones at that. As usual, the most valuable contribution the Italians were making lay with their artillery, over half of the 500-odd field guns in the Panzerarmee being theirs and nearly 300 of the anti-tank guns. This together with the 550 German anti-tank guns – including 86 of the 88mms (although nearly half of these were at the moment assigned to anti-aircraft duties) – should prove effective in blocking if not destroying the British armour, especially if the tanks' cautious tactics at Alam Halfa were just a passing phase and they could be tempted back into their old, amateur, hunting-field follies.

Not, of course, that the Panzerarmee artillery would match that of the Eighth Army in any way. There were no false hopes on that score, for since their arrival at Alamein back in July they had all had ample experience of the British predilection for gun-fire, of their present possession of overwhelming superiority and of their skill in using it.

So, as the October weeks passed and the nights became colder, both the command staffs and the 50,000-odd German and 62,000 Italian soldiers at Alamein, however dolefully they might view their ultimate prospects, were not particularly anxious about the immediate future. The staffs continued to plan and to hope, the troops passed their days lying in the forward trenches watching the minefields in front or, if they were in the armoured divisions, working on their vehicles or practising battle drills – bearing in mind all the time the shortage of fuel and ammunition. October 23rd was exactly the same as every other day, and like the men a few thousand yards away to the east those at the front watched the sun go down and felt the first breaths of the evening breeze with relief.

Then they too, climbed out of their trenches, stretched luxuriously, grumbled among themselves, waited for and then consumed their evening meals and went about their allotted night-time tasks. Picks and shovels rose and fell, relief parties moved up to the forward positions and those who had watched all day moved back, rubbing their eyes and looking forward to a few hours' sleep. Along the front, a few patrols moved out along the known paths through their own minefields.

Occasionally those who possessed watches glanced at them to see how much of their stag had passed, how much remained. Just after the hands registered eight o'clock there were sounds of gun-fire at the northern end of the line, those up there cursed the Australians who were obviously about to launch one of their large-scale raids, those to the south blessed their good fortune and hoped it would last the night. Like the day, it promised to be an ordinary one.

Forty minutes later, the eastern horizon suddenly turned pink and for a few brief seconds an astonished silence gripped the world.

9 · El Alamein: The Onslaught

The opening barrage at Alamein remained or will remain in the memories of those who heard it to the end of their lives. It was not so much the sheer volume of sound – though this was surely great enough – as the impact it made, sweeping over the ranks of waiting men like a solid, moving force, shaking the very foundations of the desert floor.

Eight hundred and eighty-two field and medium guns opened up along the length of the front, raining steel and high explosive on the known enemy artillery positions and their ammunition dumps, and within minutes of the opening of the barrage Wellington bombers were overhead to drop an additional 125 tons of explosive upon them. Every now and then the vast clamour would be marginally increased by a deep roar as bomb or shell found its target, and red flame shot like a violent tropical flower into the sky – to the grunted satisfaction of the XXX Corps artillery commander standing next to de Guingand on a slight rise close to Tactical Headquarters.

Some six miles to the west of them as they stood there, the infantry of XXX Corps were already marching forward through the made gaps in the British minefields – line upon line of steel-helmeted figures, bayoneted rifles held at the high port, Bren-guns at the carry, boots crunching the desert gravel, grenades, shovels, picks or entrenching tools slung from their webbing. Behind the leading companies the engineers were already moving up to begin their intricate tasks as soon as the forward edge of the enemy minefields was reached, while behind them the heavy Valentine infantry support tanks of the 23rd Armoured Brigade waited impatiently for assurance of clear lanes.

Fifteen minutes after the opening rounds had been fired, the guns paused, their crews readjusting the ranges, and then – precisely on the hour (2200 British time; nine o'clock Axis time) – the guns roared out again and this time the barrage fell close in on the line of known enemy forward defence posts. On towards the curtain of exploding shell the leading infantry marched now into hostile ground, cutting their way through enemy wire, tramping with tingling feet over enemy minefields, listening for the crack of enemy bullet, the crash of enemy shell or mortar-bomb.

Every three minutes the line of the barrage lifted forward one hundred yards and the infantry closed up, sometimes to see just in front of them an enemy post to be charged and silenced, sometimes to see the remains of one wrecked by the barrage, sometimes to hear away on their flank the harsh clatter of a Spandau awaiting its fate at the hands of comrades abreast of them, or of the mopping-up parties following close behind. They prayed that their support tanks would be up soon.

The further the infantry advanced, the thicker became the fog of battle, for in addition to the smoke of the explosions every shell which landed flung up clouds of dust, and the whole area of the main advance was quickly shrouded in dense obscuration. Along each brigade boundary coloured tracer from specially sited Bofors guns kept separate the main bodies and at the rear searchlight-beams lanced the sky to intersect above specified orientation points, but within brigade, battalion and especially company areas, direction had to be maintained by lonely navigating officers (generally subalterns) marching unhesitatingly forward with eyes glued to compasses, counting steps and constantly adjusting for stumbles on uneven ground, for occasional lapses of concentration caused by whiplash crack or nearby crash. These men were indeed the very pin-point of the sharp end of battle, and far too many of them were to lose their lives during that first, dramatic night.

The other navigational aid for blinded infantry was, of course, the barrage itself, dropped immaculately on to carefully calculated grid lines lifting regularly and inexorably towards the final objectives as the night wore on. If the infantry could keep close behind it – and live – they should be on those objectives by 0245, giving them three more hours of darkness in which to dig themselves in, for their mortars, heavy machine-guns and anti-tank guns to come up, for the engineers to clear the corridors and for the armour to pass through and form that vital protective screen behind which the infantry would 'crumble' the Axis infantry.

But before that they would have a pause for adjustment and reorganisation. Just over half-way to the final objective was an area variously called the Red Line or the First Objective, to be reached by the barrage and the forward infantry by just before midnight. Here there was an hour's wait while bypassed enemy strongpoints were destroyed, while wounded were tended and evacuated, while platoons and companies sorted themselves out and refilled their ammunition pouches, while second wave battalions came up and prepared to take over the lead; and in many ways most important, while commanding officers tried to find out exactly what had happened and conveyed that vital information to the anxiously waiting divisional commanders at their posts at the rear.

To the Australian General Morshead in the north, to General Wimberley of the Highland Division next to him, to General Freyberg to his left and to the South African commander General Pienaar, these were indeed the most testing moments. How were their men doing? What sort of opposition were they encountering? Had the British artillery done their work? And at first reports seemed

Map 24   *Operation Lightfoot*, northern sector, October 23rd–24th

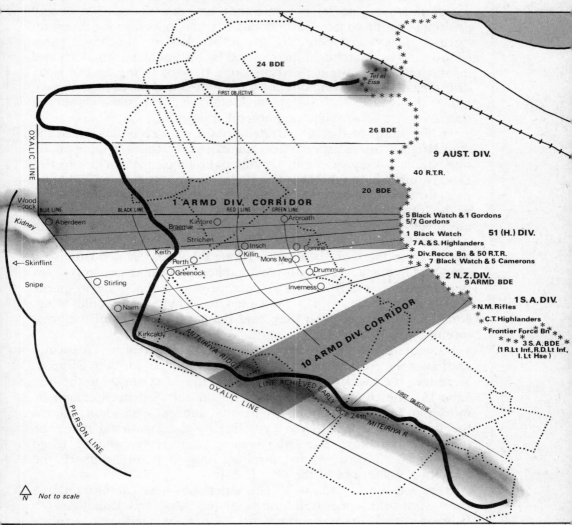

too good to be true for there was little sign or sound of enemy artillery, and the first casualties to come limping back spoke more of accident, of occasional mortar-bomb or random machine-gun fire, as the cause of their wounds. By midnight, it seemed, the Red Line had been reached all along its length, the support companies were moving up to take over the next stage of the advance, the mopping-up companies were clearing the by-passed opposition and the engineers were already at work deep into the minefields.

The Australians, in particular, were making excellent progress. Their 24th Brigade had, in fact, undertaken the raid which had begun at 2100 and might be called the prelude to the battle. In the coastal sector north of the railway line they had attacked known enemy positions, captured five German infantrymen, added to the diversion by use of smoke-screens, by cut-out models of crouching figures silhouetted by searchlight beams, and by continual machine-gun and mortar fire. In addition, Hudson aircraft added to the confusion by dropping self-destroying dummy parachutists and flares further back along the coast, and naval small-craft had run close in under destroyer fire to simulate attempted landings.

To the south of the 24th Brigade positions, two battalions of the 26th Brigade drove expertly and aggressively forward, wiping out all opposition as they went and arriving not only on their first objective exactly on time, but then sending their follow-up battalion (2nd/28th) in a storming rush onwards to the final objective, the northern corner of the 'Oxalic Line' as it was called. During the night the Australians advanced over 7,000 yards from their original start line – but with only the first 3,000 through no-man's-land, that last 4,000 yards thus left an open flank on their right. Along this line, facing north, were now hastily dug a line of anti-tank and heavy machine-gun posts each deeply wired in for all-round defence and manned by a special 'Composite Force', who now waited for what dawn would bring, conscious of the fact that they held the northern hinge of the great 'break-in'.

Immediately to the south of the 26th Brigade sector was the wider section of the Australian front, the responsibility of the 20th Brigade. Here too, the two leading battalions had fought their way to the Red Line in time though the battalion on the left had been caught by mortar and machine-gun fire on the way, and lost some eighty men in the fierce battle which followed. But by the appointed time, the follow-up battalion, 2nd/13th, were in position and waiting to go forward on the last stretch, awaiting only their own support, the forty-two Valentines of the 40th R.T.R.

Here was the first set-back. The Valentines were still blocked in a deep minefield some 1,500 yards to the rear, and with the 26th Brigade attack ready on the north, the whole divisional artillery

opened exactly on time and, *faute de mieux*, the 2nd/13th followed –
but a few minutes late and without their support. Not surprisingly,
this part of the Australian advance proved the most costly for that
few minutes' lag lost much of the protective effect of the barrage, and
there was now an opening flank on their left where the Highlanders
were also falling behind in their time schedule. Machine-gun fire
harassed the 2nd/13th from enemy strongpoints ahead and on the
flank, and as their numbers dropped, the pace inevitably slowed,
despite both expert teamwork and individual gallantry.

With the young subalterns so exposed it was not long before
several platoons were commanded by sergeants, and one of these,
blinded by smoke and dust, adopted the age-old tactic of marching to
the sound of the guns; on the way he found and obliterated one
enemy strongpoint, then set out alone to make contact with the rest
of his company and in doing so captured nine German prisoners on
his own.

But by this time Australian experience had come into force, and
the 2nd/13th battalion commander decided that with dawn approaching he must use the remaining dark period to dig in and prepare for
counter-attack, wherever he might be – so, some 1,000 yards short of
Oxalic, he regrouped his men. To his relief, some of the Valentines
arrived in time, 'looming up like battleships' out of the murk, and
took position among his defences.

Thus by dawn the northern corner of the 'break-in' was achieved,
the upper half of the Australian sector of Oxalic held, the line then
bending back about 1,000 yards to the 2nd/13th positions, in front of
which one strong German post had been attacked and almost
destroyed, the ground 'carpeted with German dead' but then left as
enemy fire poured into it. The first night of Alamein for the
Australians was at least an 80 per cent success.

General Wimberley's Highlanders had been faced with a much more
difficult task than the Australians on their right, and in the event they
came up against tougher opposition. Whereas the flanks of the
Australian attack had been parallel and they fought along the length
of a rectangle, the Highland Division was to move forward from a
start line less than a mile and a half long into an expanding funnel five
miles long towards a final objective line just over three miles long.
Moreover, although many of the Jocks had been briefly attached to
Australians for raids and 'line experience', it was, for all except the
few survivors from the First World War, their first taste of battle.

It was extremely fortunate for them that Douglas Wimberley was
not only a professional soldier of long experience, but one whose
basic military philosophy insisted that in battle the morale of the
infantry soldier was the factor of highest importance. He had

therefore used his not inconsiderable powers of persuasion at all levels to ensure that over 90 per cent of his division were genuine born and bred Scotsmen (thus overriding the tendency of Army Administration to regard all soldiers as 'bodies' and thus interchangeable) and also that too zealous security regulations should not deprive his division of their identity. His men wore the kilt whenever conditions allowed, and every one of them went into action that night with a St Andrew's Cross of white scrim tied across the back of his pack as both a means of identification and a proclamation of nationality. And to underline the point even further, alongside each platoon officer marched his piper, so that throughout that night in the centre section of the main attack the wild skirls of the most eerie, exhilarating and frightening music the battlefield knows would pierce the din of shell and mine exploding and the hoarse racket of gun-fire.

To aid control of the advance Wimberley had inserted extra intermediate objective lines – Green Line some two miles from the start and nearly a mile short of the Red Line, and Black Line half-way between the Red and the final objective Blue Line. He had also given all known enemy strongpoints Scottish names, chosen moreover from the localities from which their designated attackers came. The Gordons and the Black Watch on the right, for instance, would find Arbroath, Montrose and Forfar barring their way to the Green Line, Dufftown and Braemar on the second stretch and Aberdeen their final objective, while the Argyll and Sutherland Highlanders would storm Paisley and Renfrew, Greenock and Stirling.

To demonstrate his complete confidence that his men would take their objectives, General Wimberley had moved his own Battle H.Q. as far forward as possible and in the silence preceding the barrage he had stood in one of the gaps watching his Jocks file past in the moonlight:

> Platoon by platoon they filed past, heavily laden with pick and shovel, sandbags and grenades – the officer at the head, his piper by his side. There was nothing more I could do now to prepare them for the battle, it was only possible to pray for their success, and that the Highland Division would live up to its name and the names of those very famous regiments of which it was composed.[1]

On the outside flanks of the Highland Division sector were two battalions, one to leap-frog through the other at the Red Line – 1st Gordons passing through the 5th Black Watch on the right next to the Australians, 7th Black Watch passing through the 5th Camerons on the left next to the New Zealanders. Between them were four lanes along each of which one battalion would fight the whole way – 5th/7th Gordons on the right, then the 1st Black Watch, then the 7th

Argyll and Sutherland Highlanders while the lane next but one to the New Zealanders was to be taken by the divisional reconnaissance battalion supported by Valentines of the 50th Royal Tank Regiment.

As they moved forward, one of the officers whose job it had been to check the guiding tapes for the last time, turned to watch the barrage and the first advance:

> Through the din we made out other sounds – the whine of shells over-head, the clatter of machine-guns . . . and eventually the pipes. Then we saw a sight that will live for ever in our memories – line upon line of steel-helmeted figures with rifles at the high port, bayonets catching the moon-light, and over all the wailing of the pipes . . . As they passed they gave us the thumbs-up sign, and we watched them plod on towards the enemy lines, which by this time were shrouded in smoke. Our final sight of them was just as they entered the smoke, with the enemy's defensive fire falling among them.[2]

There was not a great deal of enemy fire at the beginning for it seemed that the weight of the British barrage had numbed the faculties of those unfortunates upon whom it had fallen, when it had not killed them. The first enemy posts the Highlanders encountered yielded but a few prisoners, all half-stunned and acquiescent to control – one Italian officer wearing pyjamas. But inevitably, the further the advance penetrated, the more resistance grew and it must be said that the pipe music attracted fire. Piper Duncan McIntyre of the 5th Black Watch was quickly hit twice but hardly faltered in his step, but a third shot brought him to the ground and when later his nineteen-year-old body was found, his fingers were still on the chanter.

But soon the code-words began coming back to Wimberley's head-quarters – Inverness was the first, telling Wimberley that the Camerons, his own regiment, had taken their first objective and were nearly on the Red Line. From then on the names came in regularly – Drummuir and Mons Meg on the left, Killin, Comrie and Insch in the centre, Arbroath on the right; but as the names came in so did the first casualty figures and these mounted inexorably.

Now began the first of many arguments with which the whole period of the battle was plagued, as to which positions had been reached. Not only had shell-fire shrouded the entire area with dust and smoke while enemy mortar and machine-gun fire had taken its toll of navigating officers, but a line drawn on a map can mean very little to men moving across a flat surface almost totally devoid of identifying features. When the 5th Black Watch on the right paused at what they considered to be the Red Line, the Colonel of the 1st Gordons who were to take over the advance from them swore they were still 400 yards short – and that the barrage falling just in front of them was an Italian defence and not British support.

In this it seems possible that the Gordons colonel was right, for when eventually he led his men towards it – after a pause for nine minutes in the hope that it would lift, they disappeared into the curtain of fire and it was morning before news of their exploits came back. Two companies of the Gordons had by-passed a strong enemy post at Kintore and gone on to attack Braemar, and although they captured all but a small corner they had by this time been reduced to three officers and sixty men. Another company supported by Valentines attacked Kintore, but even when dawn broke the position there was still uncertain – though General Wimberley believed that some of his men had reached Aberdeen, despite the fact that the tanks which had gone forward had found themselves blocked by minefields.

The 'Fog of War' was certainly thick on the morning of October 24th on the right flank of the Highland Division – as indeed the Australians had discovered; and to the immediate south of the 1st Gordons, their 5th/7th Battalion had also suffered severely from machine-gun posts in the Keith and Strichen areas short of the Black Line. One company had been cut to pieces while trying to outflank a minefield, and another pinned down by accurate machine-gun and mortar fire so that by dawn the whole of the right flank of the Highland Division was still short of the Black Line and with a serious casualty rate.

On the left flank, however, although casualties had still been high, better fortune had attended the efforts and sacrifices of the attacking battalions. The 1st Black Watch had swept on past the Red Line, cleared all the opposition through the Black Line and were on the way towards the Blue Line when it was realised that their strength had been so reduced that a withdrawal to the Black Line positions would be wise. Only one officer was left of the company which had cleared Perth, and in the confusion of the fighting it had lost touch with the rest of the battalion.

To their left, Lorne Campbell's Argyll and Sutherland Highlanders had run into fierce opposition once they passed the Red Line, one company had lost contact, two in the lead had been reduced to a quarter of their strength and the squadron of Valentines which had been attached to help them storm their final objective, Stirling, had been blocked by an unexpected minefield. Like the Australians to the north, the Argylls dug in short of their main objective, but dawn found them in positions strong enough to hold. Fortunately, both their flanks were secure.

On the left flank of the Highland Division front, 7th Black Watch had passed through the 5th Camerons on the Red Line and at first it seemed that bad luck was haunting them. Within an hour six navigating officers had been killed or wounded, and by the time the

Black Line was reached the two leading companies had been reduced almost to platoon strength. But this lane of the attack had one advantage over the others – their final objective, Kirkaldy, lay on the north-western end of the Miteiriya Ridge and as such was identifiable – and with the fire coming from it, visible. Captain Cathcart led his company and the survivors of one of the other leading companies forward in a probing, cautious advance which developed into a wild charge at the end and the mad confusion of hand-to-hand fighting; and by 0400 the final objective on the left flank of the division had been captured – the only final objective to be won by the Jocks during that first, traumatic night. But only fifty men were left of Cathcart's company, one officer had been killed and all the rest wounded, and there was for a time some doubt as to whether they were out there all on their own. Where were the New Zealanders?

The nearest New Zealanders were, in fact, some way out in front of them and to the left, for their long experience of desert fighting and their undoubted ardour had swept them along close behind the barrage – and in some cases through it.

Like General Wimberley's men, General Freyberg's had advanced into an opening funnel, from a start line barely a mile long to a final objective three miles long – beyond the crest of the Miteiriya Ridge. Unlike the Jocks to the north, however, the New Zealanders' two infantry brigades were supported by the 9th Armoured Brigade actually under Freyberg's command – and their commander, Brigadier John Currie, had no intention of allowing the trust which had been built up during training between his tank crews and the New Zealand infantry to be dissipated.

But the first advances had, of course, to be made by the infantry battalions – 23rd on the right and 24th on the left, both as far as the Red Line with the 28th Maori Battalion mopping up behind them – then 21st and 22nd Battalions following through after 23rd, and 26th and 25th battalions on the left after 24th. Close behind them would come the mine-clearing parties, then the infantry support vehicles bringing up heavy mortars and anti-tank guns, then the Crusaders and finally the Grants and Shermans of the Armoured Brigade.

It was as well that their time fighting together in North Africa had bred in the New Zealanders a spirit of trust and confidence between themselves which in no way hampered their individual independence. On the right flank the commander of the 23rd Battalion, Lieutenant-Colonel Reginald Romans, found himself and the majority of his command on the Red Line so exactly on time and having experienced so little strong opposition that he decided upon Nelsonian tactics despite the fact that he was out of contact with both his left hand company and brigade headquarters (the rear-link signals jeep had run on to a minefield). Announcing that casualties among the pace-counters had confused the extent of the advance and anyway that 'We can't stop here; we haven't fought yet!' he ordered and led a further advance of the three remaining companies through his own barrage, past several well-manned enemy posts, and only admitted that they might all be too far forward when they found themselves on the slope of Miteiriya Ridge.

The fact that he had now to lead the survivors back through his own barrage again and possibly through the ranks of the 21st and 22nd Battalions who might not immediately recognise them as friends in view of the direction in which they were moving, disturbed him not at all; and they were, in fact, safely back on the Red Line by 0300, in contact again with their missing company and with 24th Battalion on their left, but not with the Camerons on their right.

This situation daunted nobody, especially as the Maori companies had already cleared the area behind of all overrun opposition. The Maori company commanders had been slightly puzzled to find no sign of Romans's men on the Red Line but would seem to have accepted the possibility of unorthodox behaviour on the part of 23rd Battalion, and had continued mopping up along their whole front, their left hand company helping the flanking platoons of 24th Battalion clear up some enemy points across in the South African sector, where progress had not been so rapid.

Despite the rather puzzling reports reaching Freyberg's head-quarters at first from the Red Line, the general saw no reason to delay the advance of the second wave, so the four follow-up battalions lined up in the dust and smother shrouding the Red Line positions, with their intelligence and provost sections in front to carry out the tasks of navigation and pace-counting. To the planned second, the infantry rose to their feet and moved forward into the dark haze, and so close did they stay to their barrage that they overran several enemy posts with the defenders still crouching in their trenches; and on the right the men of 21st Battalion also came across the debris of some enemy posts wiped out by Romans's men or mopped up by the Maoris, still hunting across the ground in front.

But as the funnel widened, the battalions separated, within them the gaps between the companies grew and even platoons risked losing touch with their neighbours. Still undaunted, however, they pressed forward and by 0200 the 25th Battalion on the extreme left were on the crest of Miteiriya Ridge, to find in front of them on the forward exposed slope a thick and extensive minefield. Here they dug in, discovered the presence of 26th Battalion some 600 yards to their right and swiftly and efficiently organised the filling of the gap with two companies of the Maori Battalion, happy to be up at the front with their compatriots.

The 21st and 22nd Battalions had been even more successful and by 0230 the New Zealand battalions were all either on the Miteiriya crest or further on down towards the bottom of the forward slope, digging in furiously, their heavy weapons slowly coming through. On the right flank, there had been briefly some concern as the subalterns of the 21st Battalion and the 7th Black Watch who had commanded the outer platoons of their respective divisions, who knew each other and agreed passwords with which to communicate during the crucial times, had both been killed – and so had been the first runner sent out by the New Zealanders to make contact. But he had been seen by one of the Black Watch privates who, although already wounded, went out under fire, found the message, brought it in to Captain Cathcart and then went out again to find and reassure their neighbours of Scottish presence on their flank. From the north-west tip of Miteiriya Ridge, therefore, across the whole of the New Zealand three-mile front, the crest and most of the forward slope were in XXX Corps's hands well before dawn broke. By 0300, the main concern of Brigadier Gentry, commanding the left hand, 6th Brigade, was lack of contact with the South Africans on his left flank.

The South Africans had been delayed by a combination of bad luck and poor communications. On their right flank the Natal Mounted Rifles were given the task of taking the Red Line, and this they achieved with few casualties and deceptive ease, for there had been few enemy posts directly in the path of their advance and no immediately apparent dangers on the flanks. But the dangers nevertheless existed and when the Cape Town Highlanders began moving up to take over the second stage of the advance to the ridge, they immediately ran into concentrated fire which killed the two leading company commanders and pinned down the forward platoons until a reserve company could be brought up. There then followed frantic attempts to reorganise the available men for the advance from the Red Line, and to postpone the artillery cover until they were ready. Such checks to an agreed time-table seem inevitably to expand into lengthy pauses, it was 0200 before an effective creeping barrage began again and nearly 0400 before the men from Cape Town had effectively cleared their original start line.

From then on, they had a fairly clear run – due in some cases to New Zealand raids from the right flank on enemy posts in the path of the South African advance – and they were on the crest of the ridge by dawn and at least in contact with the New Zealanders some 600 yards away on their right.

But on their left, the Frontier Force Battalion had had perhaps the worst time of any of the Commonwealth Divisions; not only had they run on to an uncharted minefield only 1,200 yards from their start line, but a position identified as a 'dump' by their photographic interpreters proved instead to be a well-fortified strongpoint manned by stalwart and unshaken German troops of the 164th Division.

The leading Frontier Force platoons were quickly cut to pieces, and attempts by the survivors of 'A' and 'B' Companies to outflank the post foundered on booby-traps and mines, while machine-gun fire extracted its inevitable price. One platoon appeared at first to be succeeding in working its way along the northern flank, only to find that it was then cut off, subject to merciless mortar and rifle attack and reduced eventually to one corporal and seven men.

In the end, with only some fifty men of the Frontier Force Battalion still effective they were reinforced with a company of the Natal Mounted Rifles, and supported by brigade mortars and heavy machine-guns they stormed the post. In fifteen minutes of desperate close-quarter fighting they overcame a stubborn and courageous resistance, but the battalion suffered 189 casualties that night, capturing only 36 exhausted but defiant German prisoners in exchange. The action undoubtedly constituted the most bitter fighting they had experienced in two years of desert warfare, and even with reinforcements from the Natal Mounted Rifles, they were still a mile short of their objective when they were forced to dig in before dawn.

The left hand half of the South African advance was undertaken by the 3rd South African Brigade, consisting of the 1st Rand Light Infantry, the Royal Durban Light Infantry and the Imperial Light Horse. The task for the R.L.I. was to take the Red Line, and as on the South African right flank, this proved more difficult than expected owing to an unidentified strong post manned by yet more Germans of the 164th Division. In the end, Bangalore torpedoes were used to blow apart the wire defences, and a murderous engagement then followed with three attacking platoons charging in with bayonet and bomb while on the flanks other platoons waited and picked off the few Germans who attempted to escape.

The battalion was well under strength when it eventually reached the Red Line, and the two follow-up battalions had also been delayed by anti-personnel mines and the survivors of by-passed enemy posts; but the delay in the barrage for the second advance gave them time to assemble on their new start line. Here, on the right the Royal Durban Light Infantry quickly became aware of the problems facing the Frontier Force Battalion and were obliged to form a defensive flank, and it was still held in place when the delayed barrage came down again at 0200, and the advance towards the eastern edge of Miteiriya Ridge could be recommenced.

Like the New Zealanders, the South Africans tried to keep as close behind the barrage as possible, and the Imperial Light Horse on the left were especially successful in this, not meeting serious opposition until within 600 yards of their final objective. Here they were delayed by another lone enemy post surrounded by an anti-personnel mine-field, but they were through and on to their objective past the eastern end of Miteiriya Ridge by 0430, with the R.D.L.I. firmly in position on their right – though with nearly a mile of the ridge in 2nd Brigade's sector still in enemy hands and the survivors of the Frontier Force Battalion blocked well short of it.

Thus the marching infantry of XXX Corps had reached their final objectives – the Oxalic Line – at both the northern and southern ends, were dug in about a mile short of it in the southern half of the Australian sector and three-quarters of the Highland Division sector, had captured three-quarters of the crest of the Miteiriya Ridge, and in the New Zealand right hand sector were down at the bottom of the forward slope.

Moreover, in the New Zealand sector the 9th Armoured Brigade had realised some though not all of its ambitions, and at least the New Zealand infantry had not lost their faith in them. Nevertheless,

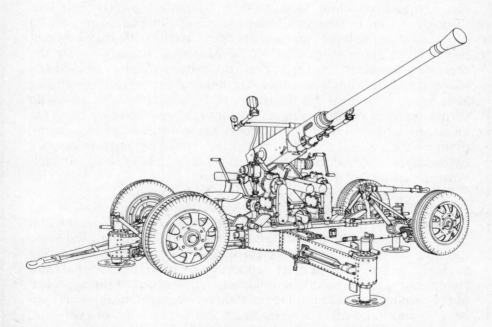

Figure 6　40mm. A-A gun (Bofors): overall length 21ft; weight 2·4 tons; vertical range 12,000 ft; weight of projectile 21 lbs; rate of fire (practical) 60/90 per min.; crew 6

the armour had had a frustrating time, for it was 0300 before word came that gaps had been opened in the first minefield and even these were partially blocked by blown-up Scorpions which, despite all the efforts of their crews and the basic soundness of the idea behind them, had proved too old and decrepit for the tasks which faced them. Many were stuck deep in the minefields, sometimes with the mines they had flailed out of the ground lying on their carapaces, unexploded and threatening.

The 9th Brigade Crusaders had gone forward close behind the infantry (as had the 50th R.T.R. Valentines with the Australians and the Highlanders), but the problems of getting the heavy Grants and Shermans forward in worthwhile numbers were to prove more difficult. On the right behind the 21st and 22nd New Zealand Battalions the heavy squadrons of the Royal Wiltshire Yeomanry pressed forward through the murk following its lighter guiding vehicles, but when these dodged around the dead Scorpions, many of the Grants or Shermans following blew up on uncleared mines and added to the blockages. But they stayed where they were and the gunners engaged enemy posts harassing the mine-lifting parties, and as the gaps widened, more tanks could edge past.

On the left, Shermans of the Warwickshire Yeomanry with their Grant squadrons close behind slowly but surely picked their way through the maze (the small isolated minefields proved more of a problem than the large, foreseeable ones) and by 0400 they began at last to climb the eastern slope of the Miteiriya Ridge. Once on the crest they found the 25th New Zealand Battalion slightly to their left – and the thick minefield which had held up the infantry extending across their own front. Six Shermans of the leading squadron blew up within minutes of attemping to go through, and however hard the engineers laboured (and Major Moore himself was in the area urging them on) it was soon evident that there would be no way through before dawn. Regretfully, the Warwickshires pulled back to hull-down positions behind the 26th Battalion.

But on their right the Wiltshires had had more luck.

By 0400 both the 21st and 22nd New Zealand Battalions were well dug in at the bottom of the forward slope of Miteiriya Ridge, the 21st had received their heavy mortars and anti-tank guns, the 22nd some mortars but only two anti-tank guns, and it was while endeavouring to clear a wider route for more support weapons to come up that their commander, Lieutenant-Colonel Campbell, learned of the approach of the armour behind him. He immediately brought more of his men back to clear and mark a wider route and to the relief of everyone, just after 0600 the leading squadron of the Royal Wiltshire Yeomanry breasted the crest and drove on down towards the New Zealand front line. Nine of them blew up on the left flank where they caught the edge of the thick minefield, but fifteen swept on down the slope, past the New Zealanders and ahead towards the known positions of more enemy posts.

But dawn was breaking and one factor becoming ominously clear. Infantry and artillery might be able to live on the forward slope of the ridge or the broken ground at the bottom, if they had arrived in darkness with sufficient time to dig in; but tanks in daylight must either find 'hull-down' positions from which to act as semi-static artillery – or keep moving.

Soon after the Wiltshires began engaging the enemy posts, they came under fire from leading units of the 15th Panzer Division which were moving up into the battle area – at a time, moreover, when fuel tanks were running low. Prudently, they retired up the face of the ridge and by full daylight the tanks of 9th Armoured Brigade were refuelled, ready to repeal any counter-attack the enemy might mount – but behind the crest and behind the infantry. It would seem that the idea of tanks forming a screen in open country behind which infantry could fight infantry battles – or even just find protection – might be in need of revision.

Nevertheless, to the Royal Wiltshire Yeomanry went the honour of being the first – and only – armoured regiment to break out beyond the infantry's final objective on the first day of the Battle of Alamein.

If the infantrymen of XXX Corps had reason to feel some satisfaction with their performance, the same could not be said of the tank crews of X Corps, who had spent a thoroughly frustrating and unhappy night.

The tasks for the two divisions of X Corps (1st and 10th) in detail were as follows: they were to leave their assembly areas after dark and move forward until their respective leading units reached the Springbok Track at half past midnight, whereupon they would pause to refuel and then begin their main move forward at 0200. The 1st Division – 2nd Armoured Brigade followed by the 7th Motor Brigade – were to make their way along the Sun, Moon and Star tracks and on through their designated main gap straddling the Australian southern and the Highland Division northern flanks, while the 10th Armoured Division – 8th Armoured Brigade, 24th Armoured Brigade and 133rd Lorried Infantry Brigade – would use Bottle, Boat and Hat tracks to reach their own main gap through the New Zealand sector, up to and over the Miteiriya Ridge.

The plan called for the leading tanks of 2nd Armoured Brigade to burst out in the north through the Australian and Scottish positions along the Oxalic Line before dawn, and establish themselves in position about a mile further west. In the south, first the 8th

Armoured Brigade and then the 24th would cross the Miteiriya Ridge, pass through the New Zealand-held portion of the Oxalic Line, swing west and join the 2nd Armoured Brigade to form the 'Pierson Line', 8th Armoured Brigade in the centre and 24th Armoured Brigade anchoring the southern end of the line about three miles south-west of Miteiriya.

In the north the riflemen of the 7th Motor Brigade would form a flank guard with their anti-tank guns and heavy weapons on the right, while the infantry of the 133rd Brigade did the same in the south, the massed armour of the entire corps between them, well concentrated to guard XXX Corps and to annihilate the panzer divisions if they attacked.

In the next stage, the whole corps would move forward into an area known as Skinflint which would lie across the Rahman Track, while the corps's armoured cars ranged forward to the north-west to locate 15th Panzer Division, and to the south in order to give due warning of any northward move of the 21st Panzer Division.

It was undoubtedly a very ambitious programme, especially as it had now been accepted that the responsibility for clearing the wide gaps through which the armoured divisions would move would rest with their own engineers, the mine-clearance by XXX Corps engineers being expressly for the benefit of the infantry and only coincidentally of value to the X Corps armour.

Obviously the tasks of the engineers and leading armour of the 1st Armoured Division were going to be complicated by the fact that both the left flank of the Australians and the right flank of the Highland Division were dug in some way short of the Oxalic Line – but in the event this did not greatly affect the issue, for minefields, misfortune, confusion and the almost indescribable dust-clouds which enshrouded the armour as soon as it moved forward *en masse*, combined to delay them to such an extent that by dawn they had hardly reached the Red Line.

Again, as with the New Zealanders' armoured brigade, it was the scattered, unidentified minefields which caused the most trouble, three Shermans on the extreme right blowing up on them early in the move forward, thus displacing those behind off the marked gaps, causing them either to blow up themselves or often to crush down the flimsy pickets holding the essential signal lamps. Tempers and tank-engines both became overheated, dust-clouds blanketed the heads of the columns and billowed back over those trying desperately to see what was happening ahead . . . and time crept inexorably by.

And whereas the infantry had at least some idea as to how many paces they had marched forward, the armour gauged its progress by a combination of time elapsed, fuel consumed, landmarks recognised and some degree of faith and hope; and under the conditions reigning behind XXX Corps's front after midnight on October 24th, in none of those factors could much reliance be placed. When therefore the leading tanks came under fire from Kintore and Strichen – both of which were presumed to have been reduced by the Jocks – the assumption immediately made was that the fire must be coming from enemy posts much further west – from beyond the infantry final objectives, which they themselves must now be close behind. Soon, therefore, the armour reasoned, once the sappers had cleared whatever mines there were immediately in front, their Grants and Shermans would be able to break out towards the Pierson Line. But until then they must stay where they were.

Armoured opinion in the northern sector when dawn broke was therefore convinced that their spearheads were some 3,000 yards further forward than they actually were, and in the arguments which soon began to rage it would seem that as old desert-worthy veterans they were not going to yield their opinions to those of a lot of newly arrived foot-sloggers from outer space . . . or north of the border, or wherever it was they came from.

It was a difference of opinion which was to cause difficulties and high words for some time to come.

In the south, down in the New Zealand sector, 10th Armoured Division faced problems of a different order. Here they had a comparatively clear run as a result of the successes of the New Zealand infantry, at least as far as the crest of the Miteiriya Ridge for the whole width of the proposed armoured front. Their problems, however, sprang from an *embarras de richesse* – two armoured brigades and a lorried infantry brigade trying to get forward through a comparatively narrow passage in order to reach their positions on the Pierson Line all at more or less the same time.

But in addition to the clear run given them by the New Zealanders, the clearance of the minefield gaps had also been attended by remarkable success. The planned routine worked well, not too many of the Polish detectors broke down, and the teams probing with bayonets worked efficiently and coolly despite the darkness and the danger – and on the left flank under the personal supervision of their chief trainer Peter Moore himself. There were only two occasions when infantry had to be summoned to attack unsubdued enemy posts, and only one serious check to plans when two lorries bearing Military Police with the essential pickets were blown up. Incredibly, the tasks of the entire section were then carried out by the one lone survivor, staggering forward beneath a crushing load of pickets, running backwards and forwards all night and showing a total unconcern for the bullets which hissed by his ears with increasing frequency as the night wore on. Before dawn that particular route was lit all the way through.

Mine-clearance along all the lanes was steady across the width of 10th Armoured Division's front until the crest of the ridge was reached – and on the right where the New Zealand battalions had gone forward, the sappers followed on down the slope. But the same minefield which held up the left hand infantry battalions obviously presented an even greater problem to the sappers who now, if they wished to use their detectors, had to stand upright and ignore the hail of bullets and later of shells which whistled and screamed close by them. But the job had to be done, and a gap cleared for the tanks of the leading armoured brigade (the 8th under Brigadier Custance) to break out into the open and drive for their place in the Pierson Line; so the divisional C.R.E., Lieutenant-Colonel McMeekan, despite having already been blown up and as a result almost completely deafened, collected five more of his sappers and, in the hope of finding a possible German gap through the mines, led the group slowly down the forward slope of Miteiriya Ridge – thus forming, at that moment and in that place, the tiny lead force of the Eighth Army.

They had progressed some 150 yards when they were seen by an enemy machine-gun post which promptly pinned them to the ground until McMeekan decided that time was passing too quickly, whereupon he crawled back through the field to the shelter of the crest. Here he found that his own signals set had been broken by the same blast which had deafened him, and his efforts to contact the leading armour and call them forward were frustrated by bad luck and a degree of bureaucratic incomprehension among those he first came across which it is surprising to find so far forward.

As a result vital minutes were lost and when the leading tanks of the Nottinghamshire Yeomanry, guided now by Peter Moore, came up over the crest of the ridge, they were silhouetted against the greying eastern sky. In five minutes of furious action six of their Crusaders were knocked out, the Grants behind them attempted to deploy and ran on to the minefield and within a short time the survivors were all forced back to hull-down positions behind the ridge, leaving sixteen of their number smoking wrecks on the forward slope. To their right they found their divisional comrades of the Staffordshire Yeomanry similarly sheltered, and these in their turn had the Grants and Shermans of the New Zealand 9th Armoured Brigade on their right.

On the left of the Nottinghamshire Yeomanry the line was eventually extended by the late arrival of the 3rd Royal Tanks – who had been badly held up by unexpectedly thick minefields and did not climb the eastern slope until well after daybreak – but then the whole of 8th Armoured Brigade at least were close up behind the New Zealand infantry.

But behind them, the light was growing to reveal a scene of such confusion as to stun the mind.

Down the reverse slope of Miteiriya Ridge and the flat ground at the bottom were congregated the ammunition and fuel trucks, the water-carriers, the artillery and ambulances, staff cars and pick-ups and all the heterogeneous manpower which made up the 'tail' of an armoured brigade, while behind them the whole of 24th Armoured Brigade under Brigadier Kenchington – 140 tanks of the 41st, 45th and 47th Royal Tank Regiments, plus the vehicles and personnel of *their* tail – were stretched back through the old no-man's-land as far as the original British minefields.

As for divisional headquarters and the three battalions of the 133rd Lorried Infantry Brigade intended to form by morning the protective screen at the southern end of the Pierson Line, these were all still back in the area of the Springbok Track, about three miles south of El Alamein Station. They had hardly moved all night and now accepted their orders to disperse as the light grew, with frustration but phlegmatic resignation.

The same orders given to the men of 24th Armoured Brigade, however, were greeted with a certain degree of incredulity. Not only was there very little room to 'disperse' in, but what there was was pocked with slit-trenches, sewn with as yet unplotted minefields, still shrouded with dust and only too often stained with the blood of wounded men still awaiting evacuation. Moreover, their own dispersal had to be superimposed upon the dispersal of the tail of the New Zealand Division and – more crucially – across the lines of communication and supply along which the New Zealand administration services were frantically trying to get food, water, ammunition and reinforcements to the heroic companies holding the forward and most exposed positions reached by the main assault of the entire army. They were not going to be thwarted in their tasks by the domestic convenience of units from another division – which was not even a member of the same corps – especially when those same units were the ones who should have been forward protecting the very men whose lines of supply they were now blocking!

The scene has been most aptly described by an observer as looking 'like a badly organised car park at an immense race meeting held in a dust bowl'.[3] But few race meetings have been attended by so many men in so impatient a frame of mind.

One of the most impatient, not surprisingly, was Bernard Freyberg – already himself on Miteiriya Ridge – who not only wanted to see the gallantry and success of his men thoroughly exploited, but also to see them protected by rather more than their own Armoured

Brigade, doughty though its performance had been. Soon after 0700 he got word to Leese back at XXX Corps H.Q. that in his opinion the moment had come for a supreme effort to be made by 10th Armoured Division to break out and reach their intended position on the Pierson Line – and three-quarters of an hour later he was inquiring acidly why so little seemed to be happening.

The answer he received was to the effect that everything possible was being done but the armour was held up by the congestion on the eastern flank of Miteiriya Ridge, complicated by the fact that the only completely mine-free lane had been commandeered by the New Zealand supply services; but two hours later there was still no sign of movement, and perhaps with the hope of shaming the 10th Armoured Division forward, Freyberg's Chief of Staff informed Leese's that Currie had been ordered to take his brigade up over the crest again and down through the forward infantry positions. As they would be grossly outnumbered, would Lumsden please order at least 8th Armoured Brigade after them in support?

The answer when it came was that Lumsden considered that the operation was 'not on', that 10th Armoured Division must remain where it was for the moment reorganising itself and clearing wider paths forward, and that any attempt to cross the ridge except at night or perhaps under cover of a sandstorm would be suicidal.

In this opinion the commander of X Corps was undoubtedly correct, for heavy and accurate anti-tank fire met every sign of movement forward by Currie's tanks, and by midday attempts by the Wiltshire Yeomanry to repeat their exploits of a few hours before had reduced their strength to one Sherman and three Grants.

It was time for a reassessment of the situation.

First reports to reach the Army Commander were, not surprisingly, somewhat confused, but by 0845 a fairly clear picture had emerged and half an hour later he had issued orders to the corps commanders. Along XXX Corps's front, the greatest priority was to be given to clearing the 'northern lane' to get 1st Armoured Division through and on to its position on the Pierson Line; on their right, the Australians would strengthen their present positions and be prepared to begin 'crumbling' operations against the enemy infantry that night. In the south, Freyberg's New Zealanders would begin exploiting their success beyond Miteiriya ridge by driving down across the South African front, the reserve brigade from Wimberley's Highland Division coming up to take their place along and in front of the ridge. Wimberley's first job, however, would be to clear the remaining enemy posts in front of his other two brigades, advance up to the Oxalic Line and let the armour in the north through.

So far as Gatehouse's 10th Armoured Division were concerned,

Montgomery would issue orders for their further employment when he had investigated their situation more closely, with which object he left de Guingand in charge of his own H.Q. and went forward through the dust and confusion to find Freyberg's.

By this time both Leese and Freyberg had visited Miteiriya Ridge and satisfied themselves that it was at least safe from counter-attack, although they were still in the dark as to what the armour of X Corps intended. This to a great extent was due to the fact that they had been unable to contact either Lumsden or Gatehouse, but the former now arrived from the northern sector and Montgomery, after listening to what all three had to say, issued his orders.

There would be no change in the plan or the main objectives, despite twenty-four hours' delay. The formations in the northern sector already had their orders, and now he laid it down specifically that Gatehouse's armour must break out as soon as possible through the New Zealand positions and reach the Pierson Line, and in order to assist them Leese must quickly organise the support of every piece of his artillery which could be brought to bear. Montgomery then returned to his headquarters, but immediately rang up Lumsden's Chief of Staff and stressed that the armour must get out through both fronts quickly, and in the southern one in time for the New Zealanders to get on with their southern exploitation. He was quite prepared to accept casualties to ensure that success was achieved.

But it was not to be as easy as that. After the conference, Leese returned to the ridge and at last found Gatehouse, grimly surveying the burnt-out remains of the 9th Brigade tanks and some of his own, watching the immediate response by the waiting German anti-tank guns to the slightest sign of movement above the crest-line. To Leese's explanation of the Army Commander's intentions, Gatehouse replied that his tanks had been trained for a static role, not for charging forward over uncleared minefields at well-entrenched enemy positions – a response which Leese was quickly reporting to Montgomery by telephone from New Zealand headquarters.

He also reported wide expectation of attacks and the steps being taken – especially by Gatehouse – to repel them, together with Freyberg's continued belief that with the support of one of Gatehouse's brigades, the New Zealand Divisional Cavalry and the remains of John Currie's 9th Brigade could break out – perhaps under smoke? – if only somebody would give the word. Freyberg apparently also believed that the barrage of fire which descended on Miteiriya Ridge at the slightest signs of movement was the result of an enemy decision to shoot off all their remaining ammunition before retiring; nobody could ever accuse the New Zealand commander of pessimism.

By this time de Guingand had been able to analyse the first intelligence reports to come in. Neither 21st Panzer Division nor 90th Light seemed to have moved from their positions in the south or in reserve, the latest count gave a total of nearly 1,000 prisoners taken of whom over 300 were German, and it seemed that the whole of one Italian regiment and the larger part of one German regiment had been completely destroyed.

First estimates of the cost gave an overall figure for killed, wounded and missing from XXX Corps of approximately 2,500 – 350 each from the Australians and the South Africans, 600 from the New Zealanders and nearly 1,000 from the Highlanders – which on the face of it did not seem unduly high. However, the vast majority of the killed and badly wounded had obviously come from the rifle companies, for whom among the Commonwealth divisions and especially the New Zealand Division there were very few available reinforcements. And XXX Corps's infantry had still to close up to several critical lengths of the Oxalic Line before the armour could break out – after which the infantry 'crumbling' battle would have to be fought.

It was fortunate that infantry casualties down in XIII Corps's area had been comparatively small.

The basic ambiguity about the tasks given to XIII Corps – to bring such pressure on their portion of the front as to hold 21st Panzer in position, yet not to hazard the Grants, Stuarts and Crusaders of 7th Armoured Division (they had no Shermans) – called for a nicety of judgment difficult to exercise amid the chaos of battle. The situation was also complicated by two other factors, one being the direction that despite the necessity to conserve the armour, every opportunity must be taken to exploit to the fullest extent any weaknesses found in the opposing defences. The wish both to have cake and eat it is apparently as common among Army commanders as it is among more ordinary humans.

The second complicating factor was brought about by the pre-battle phase of the planning, for if opportunities are freely given to the enemy to observe one's own manoeuvres and assembly of force, it becomes exceedingly difficult to obtain at the same time an accurate picture of the defences against which that force must operate. The result had been that the supposition that Panzerarmee's main defence line in the south was still that from which they had advanced at Alam Halfa had not been challenged, and the fact that it instead now lay along the line of the most westerly of the old British minefields, codenamed February, had gone unnoticed. Horrocks's corps thus faced a much tougher task than was realised, especially as Rommel had deliberately stationed there the toughest of the Italian infantry, the Folgore parachutists, together with a strong leavening from the German Ramcke Parachute Brigade.

The basic plan of attack for XIII Corps was for the main strength of 7th Armoured Division – 22nd Armoured Brigade – preceded by a minefield task force and supported by a creeping barrage provided by the combined artillery of 7th Armoured Division and 44th Division, to break through both the January and February minefields south of the Munassib depression and there form a bridgehead into which would follow the armoured cars, Stuarts and Grants of the 4th Light Armoured Brigade and the infantry of 44th Division. Meanwhile, 1st Fighting French Brigade as part of 7th Armoured Division would hook around to the south of the Himeimat peaks and capture the ground to the west and, it was hoped, the peaks themselves. Then, with the bridgehead firmly held, both brigades of 7th Armoured plus the French would drive westwards as far as Jebel Kalakh and the Taqa Plateau, while to the north of the attack area 50th and 44th Divisions acted together to straighten out the line.

All units were faced with a long approach march – in the case of

Map 25   Southern sector, October 23rd–24th

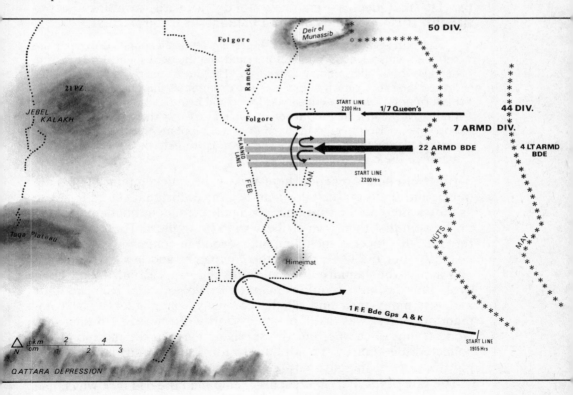

the armour one of over ten miles, for after Alam Halfa two extra protective minefields, Nuts and May, had been laid by Royal Engineers east of January. Four and a half miles separated those two from each other, and another six miles of no-man's-land had to be crossed before the minefield task force arrived at the front edge of January, to begin cutting the four gaps for the tanks to pass through. January was known to be nearly 500 yards wide, two miles separated it from February, which was itself now reputed to be nearly 1,000 yards wide.

It looked like being a long journey, and with this in mind Brigadier Roberts sent off the lead units of 22nd Armoured Brigade at 1845. In brilliant moonlight they made such good time through their own Nuts and May minefields that Roberts called a halt at 2000 to avoid congestion on the start line itself, but the carrier platoons, the reconnaissance regiment from the 44th Division, the sappers and the two companies of protective infantry which made up the minefield task force went on ahead, their six Scorpion flail tanks clanking along with them. Behind them soon stretched the trail of lamps on pickets, alight to guide the following armour, while on their right flank the infantrymen of the lead battalion of 131st Brigade (44th Division) – the 1st/7th Queen's – marched stolidly forward, awaiting the onslaught, trusting in the guns and the armour for protection:

> The barrage began. It was a shattering fantastic sound, drowning the subdued whispering of boots in the sand and the occasional clink of a rifle or bayonet as the infantry moved up. The din of nearly 1,000 field guns firing along the front was like gigantic drum-beats merging into one great blast of noise. As we went forward we could hear the sighing whistle of the shells overhead and the flicker of their bursts on the dark horizon and beyond . . . Bofors guns on fixed lines were lobbing tracer shells in a lazy curve towards the enemy lines ahead of us, to help the Queen's Brigade maintain the correct axis of advance.[4]

But the enemy reaction here was to be quicker than further up north, and shells crashed down among the unfortunate battalion even as they waited on the start line, giving the erroneous but demoralising impression that their own artillery were firing short. Three officers of the 1st/7th Queen's including the second-in-command were killed instantly, but the C.O. rallied the companies and led them forward and across the January minefield into the gap beyond. Here, however, they ran into positions manned by Folgore and Ramcke units and lost many men and all the company commanders. The commanding officer was taken prisoner shortly afterwards and then shot while trying to escape, but the survivors early in the morning were collected together by the adjutant to form small bridgeheads guarding the exits of the gaps now cleared through January.

The fate of the 1st/7th Queen's exemplified the bad luck which had dogged 44th Division since its formation, and would do so until its eventual disbandment.

On the left of the Queen's advance through January, the minefield task force had met with varying fortunes. Soft sand had made the work heavy and the job slow, and at one time and another all the Scorpions broke down through overheating and time was lost while the engines cooled and the crews carried out repairs. Number 1 lane in the north gave the greatest trouble, its location dominated by an enemy post almost immediately opposite. As a result it was not through despite the utmost gallantry until nearly 0430, but number 2 on its left was through nearly three hours before as was the most southerly lane number 4, while number 3 lane was through by 0215 although the sand along its whole length was so soft as to render it unusable by wheeled vehicles. Unfortunately – and ironically – dead Scorpions partially blocked every one of the three lanes which had been opened early, causing delay when the time came for the Grants and Crusaders to edge gingerly around them.

The price paid by the minefield task force had been high, and when their commander, Lieutenant-Colonel Lyon Corbet-Winder, assembled the survivors in the gap between January and February, he quickly concluded that he had only enough men to attempt two gaps through February. Fortunately Brigadier 'Pip' Roberts, bringing 22nd Armoured through as quickly as possible, was not unduly disturbed at the prospect of such limited passage for his tanks through what he still thought to be an unmanned minefield, concentrating as he was for the moment on getting his squadrons together after their passage through January.

They were by no means unscathed. Their ten-minute delay had served to bring them to the start line exactly on time – but their guides had not waited and when the time came for the bulk of the armour to begin passing along the marked gaps, some of the lights had already gone out. Moreover, the alert enemy artillery caught the supply lines and set alight many of the soft-skinned vehicles, all of which caused delay, resultant loss of the protective effect of the barrage, casualties in men and machines among the minefields, and when they eventually cleared January, some of the congestion which was proving so dangerous in XXX Corps's area.

By 0400 most of the 5th Royal Tank Regiment were through January on the right, and with Corbet-Winder's force ahead they cautiously moved westward towards the near edge of February. Soft sand and breakdowns again held up the right hand squadrons, while those on the left reached February but immediately came under heavy fire which not only held them back, but also made it almost impossible for the task force to clear the gaps for them – and by now it was nearly 0500 and the eastern sky was lightening. A bridgehead between January and February was obviously all that was to be achieved during this first night, and with the object of stabilising it, all units drew back from February and began the tasks of consolidation – well aware of the fact that unless the Fighting French had been successful in all their tasks, the bulk of 7th Armoured Division would face the daylight hours penned in a comparatively small area under the direct observation of enemy forces on the Himeimat peaks.

Brigadier-General Koenig had divided his force into two groups – Group A under Colonel Amilakvari consisting of two battalions of the Foreign Legion, and Group K under his own command consisting of a squadron of Moroccan Spahis with Crusader tanks, and a company of anti-tank guns. Soft going and several deep wadis slowed up the entire force but the Foreign Legionnaires reached their forming-up areas to the south-west of Himeimat well on time. At 0230, supported by what little artillery they had been able to bring up with them and under a smoke-screen put down by the R.A.F., the 1st Battalion on the right advanced against strong opposition but forced their way forward until their left flank became exposed. Amilakvari then ordered 2nd Battalion to move up to protect them, but as they did so they were themselves attacked in flank by the German Kiel group in eight captured Stuarts, who had managed to evade (or were not seen by) the Crusaders of Koenig's Group K, also held back by the bad going.

As Amilakvari's force thus lacked even the protection and support of the anti-tank guns in Koenig's command and as darkness was fading, the orders were given for a withdrawal of about three miles to the south-east – but an admirable but unfortunate reluctance to retreat on the part of the Legion caused delay, and when eventually they came back it was in broad daylight and across open desert. All their vehicles were lost together with over a hundred of their men and, most unfortunate of all, the commander was killed; and the loss of the gallant Amilakvari who since Bir Hacheim had seemed to epitomise the very spirit of the Foreign Legion, so deeply affected the regiment's morale that no further French contribution to the fighting was to take place for several days.

Himeimat peaks therefore remained in German hands, and during October 24th no element of 7th Armoured Division could make the slightest move in daylight without immediate observation and response.

To John Harding, at last free of staff duties and with his first divisional command, the situation was so criticial as to call forth every facet of his considerable military talent. General Horrocks visited him shortly after daybreak to discuss whether his 7th Armoured could even now break through the February minefields without incurring the prohibited degree of losses, and they agreed that it probably could, but not until after nightfall – and for the proposed attack the remaining two battalions of the Queen's Brigade from 44th Division would be placed directly under Harding's command.

Harding's day was therefore one of almost feverish activity. Not only had he to ensure that as little damage as possible was suffered by his exposed formations, but they must also be marshalled as far forward as possible without betraying too obviously their plans for further operation – not that they had many alternatives. He held a short conference with his brigade commanders during the morning, crouched in the lee of a tank amid the heat and dust of continual shelling, some of which exploded uncomfortably close, and worked out the details of the night's attack. Warning orders were issued by midday to bring the 1st/5th and the 1st/6th Queen's down from the north, and for them quickly to establish close liaison with the remains of Corbet-Winder's force. Artillery cover for the operation had to be carefully planned, and all the time, despite attempts by the R.A.F. to bomb known or observed enemy gun positions, shells burst among the tanks and supply vehicles of the formations in the bridgehead, while at one time panzers were seen massing as though for a counter-attack in the north – which, however, remained nothing but a threat.

The Queen's battalions had a long march down to their start line, and there would seem to have been some administrative delays on the part of the Queen's Brigade staff – so that it was not until 2230 that the infantry advanced behind their artillery barrage. At first all seemed to go smoothly and they thrust through the width of the February minefield and nearly half a mile beyond it, but then, when they tried to consolidate they found that the ground was rock-like, slit-trenches difficult to dig and sangars almost impossible to build; rifle and machine-gun fire opened on them from the flanks, mortar-bombs exploded amongst them, and their losses rose sharply as they anxiously awaited the arrival of the armour – or at least of some protective artillery.

But some of the enemy guns which had been shelling the gap between January and February during the day concentrated their fire into the area through which the minefield parties were trying to clear gaps, and the northern sector especially erupted continually under shell-burst or mortar-bomb. This gap was nevertheless cleared by 0230, although the pickets bearing the lamps were too far apart and the gaps between them not filled with wire which was the usual practice in such cases. The result was that when the tanks of the 4th County of London Yeomanry began following through, some of them lost their way and wandered off the cleared path, blowing up in the minefield. Others were knocked out by the efficient anti-tank guns opposite the end of the gap, and in all the C.L.Y. lost twenty-six of their tanks together with their colonel and second-in-command. In the confusion the idea spread that the gap had not in fact been properly cleared, and as the exit from the gap cleared in the southern area was covered by an 88mm. firing along the edge of the minefield, catching tanks of the 1st R.T.R. in flank as they came through, a bleak picture began to emerge from the reports as the night wore on.

Harding, who had already narrowly escaped death when a shell landed just in front of his jeep, killing his A.D.C. who would normally have been driving it instead of Harding himself, now intervened personally. Highly conscious of the need to conserve his armour, he stopped their further attempts to pass through February, and in the light of the reports he had received ordered the colonel commanding the sappers personally to ensure the clearance of the gaps. After registering a formal protest, the colonel called for volunteers, took them to the entrance to the northern gap where they were immediately subjected to such heavy fire that he dispersed them. He then commandeered two tanks in which he and one of the engineer squadron-commanders set off, and together they drove through the gap.

The leading tank was hit five times but not penetrated, both tanks reached the far side of February, then turned around and drove back – one of them losing a track and being abandoned when almost home – after which the colonel reported to Harding and told him in no uncertain terms that the gap *was* clear, that the tanks which had been blown up had left it, and that the majority of casualties had been – and undoubtedly would be – caused by the accurate anti-tank fire which dominated the gap exits.

In the circumstances, Harding thus had no choice but to halt the attempts to pass the armour through February, hold the bulk of 22nd Armoured Brigade where it was between January and February, allow the remains of the battered 4th County of London Yeomanry to retire through January and join the still practically immobile 4th Light Armoured Brigade – and leave the unfortunate Queen's battalion alone in their highly exposed bridgehead some two thousand yards in advance of their nearest support. The sacrifice the night before of the 1st/7th Queen's had apparently not been enough to placate whatever gods had decreed the elimination of the 44th (Home Counties) Division.

At the morning conference with Horrocks it was agreed that no daylight attempt either to clear more gaps in the minefield or to pass armour through the existing ones to the closer support of the Queen's was feasible, and that the coming night held only two alternatives. Either 22nd Armoured Brigade should try yet again to get through February, or a totally different action should commence to the north – an attack on the western end of the Munassib Depression by the 50th Division, in which it could be supported by the 4th Light Armoured Brigade which had so far seen practically nothing of the fighting.

These alternatives were put by Horrocks to de Guingand for communication to Montgomery (who at the time of the call was at a meeting with Alexander), and half an hour later de Guingand phoned back to say that the second alternative was preferred. The plight of the Queen's was appreciated but further support for them must be provided by the other 44th Division brigade – 132nd. The tanks of 7th Armoured Division must be preserved, certainly for the pursuit when the break-out took place, perhaps even for transfer to XXX Corps and employment there.

There had been something of a crisis during the night and plans might well have to be changed.

That crises in human affairs are often caused by lack of communication is doubtless a commonplace but is nevertheless true, and during the morning of October 24th in XXX Corps's area, communications in one important aspect had been unnecessarily complicated.

Freyberg's requests that 8th Armoured Brigade should support his own armour in an attempt to 'get the battle moving again' had had first to be passed by his own Tactical Headquarters to XXX Corps headquarters, who then passed them to X Corps and thus down to 10th Armoured Division – who replied by the same channels; and as both Lumsden commanding X Corps and Gatehouse commanding 10th Armoured Division had been out of touch – Lumsden in the northern corridor and Gatehouse on Miteiriya Ridge – delays were inevitable and protracted.

The same lack of communication had also caused a degree of confusion inside X Corps itself.

Gatehouse on Miteiriya Ridge had seen both the losses incurred by 9th Armoured Brigade when they had tried to move down the western face, and also what he considered to be evidence of impending German counter-attacks. In the circumstances it was imperative that his armour should give what defensive support it could to the New Zealanders, and when Freyberg told him that, despite Lumsden's opinion, there *was* a clear gap through which armour could move towards the New Zealand right flank, he ordered 24th Armoured Brigade to make their way as soon as they could across behind 8th Armoured Brigade and up on to the ridge on their right; and in due course 47th Royal Tank Regiment began the move.

But in the meantime, orders had arrived from Lumsden, sent while he was still up in the northern sector and direct to 24th Armoured Brigade as he could make no contact with Gatehouse on the ridge. The brigade were indeed to move across behind 8th Armoured Brigade – but not then to swing west to take position in support of the New Zealanders, but to continue into and across the Highland Division sector in order to help 1st Armoured Division forward along the northern gap, all in accordance with the Army Commander's earlier instructions. In the resultant confusion from these conflicting orders, hesitation grew, time was wasted, what little momentum had been gained was lost, and the tank crews drew back into themselves and took comfort in immobility. There is some attraction in the old soldier's cynical maxim 'Never obey the latest order; it's already been cancelled!' to men who know only too well that one false or unlucky move can result in themselves and their three or four closest companions being burnt to death in a steel box.

It is also arguable that had 24th Armoured Brigade carried out Lumsden's orders, they would have compounded confusion in the Highland Division sector to a disastrous extent.

General Wimberley, anxious to locate his forward units and ensure that they were both supported and supplied to the best possible extent, had set out shortly after first light to visit them himself:

> We had not been out long, when somewhere about the Red Line, on the 1st Black Watch front, I was trying to find Roper Caldbeck. There were some shells and mortar-bombs flying around, and I had just started off in my Jeep to go where I had been told Roper now was, when I felt myself sailing into the air, and then, for a time, knew no more . . . at the time I thought it was a mortar-bomb scoring a direct hit on my Jeep; perhaps more probably it was a mine. Anyhow I lay on the sand, and when I became conscious again, I suppose in a matter of seconds, I could not for a minute or two move hand or foot, in fact for a second or two I thought I was dead and coming to in another world. However, in a few minutes I was up to find myself practically unhurt, I had had some skin removed in various places, and was a bit bruised as I had been blown quite a long way from the remnants of the Jeep.[5]

Two of the other occupants of the jeep had been killed and the other seriously wounded, and although Wimberley had been extremely lucky, he was nevertheless out of action for the rest of the morning, and the separate formations of his division thus without control above brigade level. One of the results was that when he returned to the active area shortly after noon, he found that arguments between his own brigade and battalion commanders and those of the 2nd Armoured Brigade about the positions reached by their respective formations were growing heated, and although attempts had been made during the morning to clear away some of the enemy posts blocking the way to the Oxalic Line, it was obvious

21 Lieutenant-General Montgomery with his corps commanders, Lieutenant-Generals Leese (XXX Corps), Lumsden (X Corps) and Horrocks (XIII Corps)

22 Lieutenant-General Leese (second from right) with his divisional commanders, Major-Generals Morshead (9th Australian), Wimberley (51st Highland) and Pienaar (1st South African)

23 General Montgomery in the Grant tank from which he watched the progress of the battle

24 Montgomery with the two corps commanders whose formations were to advance over the same ground, at night and shrouded in dust; even had they been close friends there would have been difficulties

that a major attack must be organised if the armour in the northern corridor were to have any chance of breaking out.

The mechanics of this attack were comparatively simple to set out. From reserve the 2nd Seaforths were brought up, all remaining Valentines from 50th R.T.R. marshalled in support and as much artillery as was available in the area briefed to supply cover; and it was here that the problems began. The commander of 2nd Armoured Brigade, Brigadier Fisher, was still adamant that his forward units were much further forward than Wimberley's men said they were, but also that Wimberley's 1st Gordons were not on the Blue Line at Aberdeen as Wimberley claimed.

This part of the argument was complicated by the fact that the armour had named that vital area 'Kidney' from its contour shape on the map, believing it, moreover, to be a raised plateau instead of a depression which it in fact proved to be.

Time was short, tempers were brittle, argument reached the pitch when prestige began to assume more importance than fact, to such an extent that when the commander of XXX Corps's artillery offered to carry out a swift survey and settle the matter of exact locations, his offer was brusquely rejected by both sides. Even more importantly, Brigadier Fisher would not allow his own artillery to take part in the cover for the infantry attack as it would, he claimed, be shelling his own formations. Wimberley then suggested that as Fisher would not order his tanks forward to reach the Gordons at Aberdeen (Kidney) on their own, perhaps he would allow them to follow one of Wimberley's battalions which would be sent up to clear the way – but this was also rejected on the grounds that Fisher was not a part of Wimberley's division, not even a part of the same corps. He could only accept orders from his own commanders.

What would have been the position if 24th Armoured Brigade, operating solely under Lumsden's orders and without reference to Leese, Freyberg or Wimberley (or Gatehouse, for that matter) had in fact moved into and across the Highland Division sector during the morning is, of course, now impossible to state; but in view of the reigning confusion and the lack of understanding which still existed between infantry and armour – at least when they were separated into corps – it seems unlikely that the results would have been satisfactory.

Orders for 2nd Armoured Brigade in fact arrived in time for them to act in support of the attempts by the Seaforths to clear two enemy strongpoints just ahead, and although the regimental commanders complained that they had not been given adequate time to prepare, the 9th Lancers and the 10th Hussars did set out behind the Jocks who in a gallant daylight attack took both their objectives at a cost of eighty-five casualties – including all the officers and the sergeant-major of one company, which was led forward on its last charge by the company clerk.

Meanwhile, away to the north the Australians had begun to drive forward on their own left flank in order to reach the Oxalic Line across their whole front. Their supporting Valentines of 40th R.T.R. had closed up during the night and once daylight came drew a great deal of enemy fire, and the position was not helped when a squadron of Mitchells, briefed to attack the suspected location of an enemy headquarters, unloaded their bombs instead on the unfortunate 2nd/13th Battalion. But the 2nd/17th Battalion now came up from the rear in support and drove towards the junction between 20th and 26th Brigades, and when to the south the Seaforths had gone into their attack it would seem that the right hand regiment of the 2nd Armoured Brigade, the Bays, followed along the 2nd/17th's tracks.

But dust and confusion still had a part to play. The 9th Lancers lost contact with the Seaforths quite early and veered north-east towards the Australian sector, the Bays ran into minefields and were shelled by enemy anti-tank guns, some reputedly 88mms, lost six Shermans and promptly pulled back, veered south and ran into the 9th Lancers; together they edged their way carefully forward through the mine-fields, their sappers walking in front, guiding them roughly along the axis between the Highland Division and the Australians. Only the 10th Hussars kept contact with the Seaforths and were thus well away to the south, but nevertheless Brigadier Fisher, still under the impression that his brigade had started out from a position some 3,000 or more yards further west than it actually had, felt that the movements of his squadrons justified an evening report to the effect that two of his regiments were at last on their final objective – the northern hinge of the Pierson Line – with one slightly behind. They were in fact still well short of it and, having lost in all some twenty Shermans between them, they withdrew another 500 yards after dark.

But with his main armoured brigade reputedly out past the Oxalic Line, General Briggs, commanding the 1st Armoured Division, brought forward the riflemen of the 7th Motor Brigade, and by midnight they were closing up behind the forward positions.

The Australians and the Highlanders might have known different, but from the reports reaching General Montgomery during the evening of October 24th, he had every reason to believe that matters were progressing very satisfactorily in the northern corridor.

He did not, however, feel the same confidence in matters further south.

Crises caused by lack of communication will also be magnified by basic misunderstandings on the part of one or other of those concerned, especially if no attempt can be made to clear up that misunderstanding.

General Lumsden was the senior armoured commander in Montgomery's army at that time and, as has been mentioned, relations between them were cold almost to the point of being glacial. Not only were there differences in personality and upbringing to cause misunderstanding between the two men, but the distaste and scorn which Lumsden would seem to have felt for Montgomery at the time of Alam Halfa had undergone a change during the interval – and not a change for the better. According to an officer who saw a lot of both of them,

> Herbert Lumsden had very great abilities, there's no question about it – but the effect on Herbert Lumsden of Monty was like a stoat on a rabbit. He'd freeze up, become . . . not himself; and Monty saw him in this frozen-up state. Herbert was scared stiff of Monty.[6]

This was no condition in which the commander of the Eighth Army's main striking force could explain certain inalienable facts to the Army Commander, especially as the latter's misunderstanding of those facts would seem to have been of long duration.

During the First World War – the last time that Montgomery had been connected in any way with massed armour launched against strong defensive positions – the main and indeed original purpose for armour had been to protect infantry against machine-gun and rifle fire. Against such fire, tanks were invulnerable and apart from mechanical breakdown only the hastily adapted tactics of the German artillery ever stopped them. Throughout the British Army, therefore – with the exception of the armoured units themselves – the belief had been fostered that the role of armour in such a battle as Alamein was to lead and protect the infantry, who would follow up and consolidate ground won. And although the existence of minefields had necessitated an initial reversal of the leading roles, once the XXX Corps infantry reached the Oxalic Line and the sappers had cleared the minefields behind it, it was thought that the armour should have little difficulty in breaking out.

This was the philosophy behind the scheme to launch X Corps out on to the Pierson Line and then further forward towards Skinflint; but it took little account of the development of specialised anti-tank guns and formations, and of the training of both German and Italian field artillery in the same role. Lumsden was well aware of the dangers which would face his armour once they attempted to move out past the front infantry line, and he said so – somewhat elliptically – to Freyberg:

Playing with armour is like playing with fire. You have got to take your time about it. It is like a duel. If you don't take your time you will get run through the guts. It is not for tanks to take on guns.[7]

As it happened this was a conclusion to which Freyberg himself was also coming, as were those other Commonwealth commanders who had seen much of the desert fighting, and during the daylight hours of October 24th considerable doubts grew in the minds of the XXX Corps divisional commanders as to the ability of the X Corps armour to break out, even at this second attempt, unless their own infantry cleared the ground before them of all enemy artillery. And even had there been time to set up such an operation, there were hardly enough infantry left to carry it out, especially in view of the 'crumbling' battles they would then be expected to fight.

There was also far too little co-ordination between the staffs of the New Zealand infantry and its attached armour (of XXX Corps) and of the 8th and 24th Armoured Brigades (of X Corps), both of whom were expected to attack the enemy from adjacent sectors though in different directions.

The plan called for a programme of timed artillery concentrations starting at 2200, dropping at first just in front of the right hand, 5th New Zealand Brigade positions, and then extending in front of the advancing armour until both brigades of X Corps were on the positions along the Pierson Line, running north–south some 3,000 yards to the west. Meanwhile, the New Zealand artillery would fire a creeping barrage from the left hand, 6th New Zealand Brigade area, to the south – and behind this the New Zealand Cavalry and the remains of John Currie's 9th Armoured Brigade would advance and from a protective screen running west–east from the southern end of the Pierson Line back to the infantry positions at the bottom of Miteiriya Ridge. The supporting infantry of 10th Armoured Division – 133rd Lorried Infantry Brigade – would come up and take over the positions held by 5th New Zealand Brigade on the right, who would then be free to follow their own armour southwards in the exploitation role ordered by Montgomery, while the 133rd infantry then followed their own armour out towards the Pierson Line.

It is difficult to believe that even with the state of training to which Montgomery had brought the Eighth Army by that time, so complicated a series of manoeuvres could have been successfully carried out, even with the closest possible co-operation between all brigade and divisional staffs concerned. As it was, both Gatehouse and his tactical headquarters were so mobile that Freyberg was unable to make much more than fleeting contact during the afternoon with his fellow divisional commander in the operation, while Gatehouse's divisional headquarters were so far back that the staff there were often unaware of latest developments and thus unable to make valid decisions even when news of those developments arrived via first XXX Corps and then X Corps H.Q.s.

As the afternoon wore on and doubts as to the viability of the plans for the night's operations grew in Freyberg's mind, he warned his 5th Brigade commander that he expected considerable delays in the programme, and shortly after dusk rang General Leese and, to quote from the *Official History of New Zealand in the Second World War*, 'started an argument that has echoed down the years'.

The operation could not be a success, said Freyberg, because the 10th Armoured Division was not 'properly set up' and was in any case being commanded from too far back – which was perhaps an unfair reflection upon Gatehouse's character but not upon the administration for which he was responsible. Leese, worried by such a report from so highly regarded a source, managed to make contact with Lumsden and tactfully pass on the warning – and was further worried by Lumsden's reaction, which was rather to the effect that as neither he nor anyone else high in the armoured command had much confidence in the plans for the night's operations, he was not surprised at Freyberg's comments. By the time Leese had thought matters over and decided he should report all this to Army Headquarters, Montgomery had retired for the night and de Guingand absorbed the information himself, hoping that news would improve as the night wore on.

If anything, it got worse.

As soon as dusk fell the whole of Miteiriya Ridge became a scene of intense activity and, as command was so divided, soon one of equally intense confusion. On the forward slope, XXX Corps infantrymen and heavy weapons crews emerged both to stretch cramped limbs and, more urgently, to try to improve their defences; from immediately behind them supply parties hurried to and fro across the crest ferrying food, water and ammunition to their comrades in the front line, and soon they found themselves part of a growing, busy throng as X Corps sappers with their own infantry covering parties began clearing more lanes for the armoured advance, due to start shortly after 2200. And the situation of everyone there was soon much complicated as the Axis gunners, having spent the late afternoon and early evening restocking the ammunition dumps and resting their crews, opened fire on the ridge in the confidence that their exertions would not be wasted. Having spent the day in apparent inactivity, what could the British armour do except attempt to come over the top that night?

Time did nothing to improve the situation. The New Zealand sappers had gone forward as early as possible to clear the gaps for their Divisional Cavalry on their drive south, but were delayed by the enemy artillery and were thus still out working when their own guns opened up with the covering barrage, mortally wounding their commander and causing some other casualties. It also fell on some of the most forward infantry positions and thoroughly disorganised one company of the 26th Battalion which, not surprisingly, retired precipitately and was unavailable as a fighting force for some hours.

But two squadrons of the Cavalry did get out and their Bren-gun carriers and light tanks moved slowly through the gaps, out past the minefields and despite small-arms fire, occasional anti-tank fire and the loss of a couple of tanks on scattered mines, one of the squadrons pushed south nearly two miles before halting to await support.

Unfortunately for them, their supporting armour from 9th Armoured Brigade were blocked by the movements of one of the 8th Armoured Brigade regiments – the Staffordshire Yeomanry – who instead of first moving behind the ridge and down through a gap on the right, found the gap through the left-hand 26th Battalion area and used that. Their Crusaders drove across the intended route of the 9th Brigade and reached a spot about 500 yards clear of the minefield, but in a south-westerly, not westerly, direction; and then they too halted to await their fellow squadrons from their own brigade.

But by now, Brigadier Currie, anxious to get his heavier tanks out to support the divisional cavalry, and furious at the blocking of their intended route, had personally reconnoitred a path over the crest and around the edge of a minefield, and sent the Grants and Shermans of the 3rd Hussars off, followed after a short delay by the Warwickshire Yeomanry. The first formation these came across was the Staffordshire Yeomanry, whom they helped to clear up some machine-gun posts and sent off to the west, while they themselves drew away south-westwards and eventually made contact with the cavalry.

Meanwhile, the second regiment of 8th Armoured Brigade, the Nottinghamshire Yeomanry, had been trying to get out and join the Staffordshires, but their soft-skinned supply columns had come up first on the left behind the ridge where they turned to await their heavy squadrons coming up further to the right. Unfortunately, they had hardly pulled to a halt when a random enemy shell or mortar-bomb hit one of the leading vehicles which happened to be carrying petrol. The flames spread rapidly through the columns as the vehicles were packed nose to tail and also double banked, and the resultant inferno attracted the attentions of practically every enemy gun and aircraft in the vicinity. Soon some twenty-five lorries were ablaze, petrol drums and tanks exploding, small-arms ammunition crackling furiously, mortar-bombs and shells erupting in a pyrotechnic display as spectacular as it was disastrous. Valiant attempts were made to drive some of the rear vehicles clear, but as several of these promptly blew up on mines bordering the cleared gaps, most of the vehicles were reduced to smoking wrecks by morning.

Needless to say, the holocaust effectively halted the advance of the tanks of the Notts Yeomanry, who in their turn blocked the advance of the third regiment of 8th Armoured Brigade – the 3rd R.T.R. – and in the circumstances and especially in view of the attention the flames were attracting, Brigadier Custance ordered both formations to disperse as much as they could and await further instructions.

As for the movements of 24th Armoured Brigade, the squadrons of both of their leading regiments – 41st and 47th R.T.R. – had already been dispersed as confusion had overtaken their mine-clearance force. It would seem that these had at first begun clearing a gap through the wrong minefield, then lost contact with their recon-naissance party which, although they had advanced through the correct minefield, had come under heavy fire and promptly retired. As a result the sappers did not commence their appointed task until nearly an hour after they were supposed to have completed it, and even then they soon abandoned it when mistaken warning of an enemy counter-attack through their area reached their commanding officer. As he led his men back up towards the crest, he then lost contact with both his own infantry covering party and also his wireless truck.

It was a most unfortunate chapter of accidents, in view of which it is hardly surprising that at about midnight Freyberg rang Leese to say that as far as he could see 10th Armoured Division were sitting about doing nothing, or that shortly afterwards Custance rang Gatehouse to suggest that in view of the evident disorganisation of his brigade, the advance should be abandoned. Gatehouse passed this message on to Lumsden with the recommendation that it should be accepted, and it seems that Freyberg overheard it and again rang Leese . . . who then reported the whole matter to de Guingand.

In fact de Guingand had already received a call from Lumsden to the effect that as both his divisional and brigade commanders felt that the armoured attack for that night should be called off, he, Lumsden, was inclined to agree; and in the circumstances de Guingand felt that the occasion had arisen when one of the Army Commander's strictest edicts must be disregarded. Telling both Leese and Lumsden that they should report to Army Tactical Headquarters at 0330, he went along to General Montgomery's caravan and woke him up.

Presumably General Leese went along to the conference worried about the situation in general, but confident that little fault would be found with the performance of his own command. General Lumsden, however, must have viewed the immediate prospects with reluctance and his own long-term prospects with foreboding – although possibly by this time he would have welcomed any opportunity to leave Montgomery's command.

They found the Army Commander sitting in front of newly marked-up maps, showing the reported positions of the crucial formations in XXX Corps's sector. On the right, the known Australian positions showed the firm holding of the northern corner of the Oxalic Line – but also the main strength of 1st Armoured Division out through Kidney and thus on to the top end of the Pierson Line. Montgomery's inference that their infantry support from the 7th Motor Brigade was at that moment either out with the armour or was closing up to it – and that both armoured and infantry brigades must be under heavy attack – was thus so reasonable that no one challenged it.

In the extreme south of the sector, according to reports, matters were also going well, with the New Zealand Cavalry and the 9th Armoured Brigade out on their intended objectives, and the New Zealand infantry poised to commence their southward exploitation. Only along the length of the Miteiriya Ridge did the map indicate any difficulties, where 10th Armoured Division were stuck and their commander, General Gatehouse, apparently unable to drive his squadrons out into the battle.

But overall, the situation looked by no means hopeless and both Leese and Lumsden gave their own opinions on the battle's progress without, apparently, contradicting any of the assumptions shown on the map. Inevitably, Lumsden found himself defending Gatehouse and, indeed, repeating his divisional commander's arguments of the morning to Freyberg. Later, Montgomery was to record in his diary:

> Gatehouse had said that he did not care about the operation and that if he did get out he would be in a very unpleasant position on the forward slopes of the Miteriya [sic] Ridge; his Division was untrained and not fit for such difficult operations; he wanted to stay where he was. Lumsden was inclined to agree with Gatehouse.[8]

From Lumsden's previous utterances it seems likely that that last sentence was something of an understatement, but whatever arguments were put up by the X Corps commander they were of no avail. Quietly but firmly Montgomery insisted that the plan would be adhered to, the armour must break out over the ridge, reach the Pierson Line and shield the infantry during their 'crumbling' operations. He then dismissed Leese, and

> spoke very plainly to Lumsden and said I would have no departure of any sort from my original plan and orders; I was determined that the armour would get out from the minefield area and out into the open where it could manoeuvre; any wavering or lack of firmness now might be fatal; if Gatehouse, or any other commander, was not 'for it' and began to weaken, then I would replace him in command at once.[9]

There are different versions of exactly what happened next, but it would seem that while the conference had been going on, Gatehouse, still awaiting a decision from Lumsden regarding his request made some three hours before that the attack across Miteiriya be abandoned, made his way back from the ridge where he had spent most of his time since his armour had reached it, to his Divisional Headquarters still back near the Springbok Track.

Here he at last made contact with Lumsden who told him of the recent meeting and the Army Commander's inflexible demand that Gatehouse's brigades cross the ridge, make their way down through the minefields and out on to their designated positions on the Pierson Line; and this order Gatehouse refused to accept or obey. As he wrote later, Gatehouse then had no course but to report his attitude direct to Montgomery by telephone, which he did, apparently opening the conversation with the unlikely query, 'What the hell's going on here?'

In the tense atmosphere brought about first by the circumstances, secondly by the anger which Gatehouse undoubtedly felt at what he considered to be the misuse of his armour, and thirdly by the annoyance his opening remarks and general lack of deference almost certainly caused Montgomery, there was ample opportunity for misunderstanding – compounded almost immediately by Montgomery's accusation that Gatehouse was fighting his battle from far too far back, and must immediately move himself and his headquarters up closer to the front. To the end of his days, Montgomery insisted that he had ordered Gatehouse to adhere to the original plan and get his armour out on to the Pierson Line; but Gatehouse was equally insistent that the Army Commander had at last seen the danger of sending six armoured regiments clanking downwards through an unlifted minefield at night, to find themselves in open country at dawn – and had agreed that only one regiment should attempt it. This should be the Staffordshires who were already out and could stay there, protecting the right flank of the New Zealand Cavalry and the 9th Armoured Brigade.

Presumably as a result of these misunderstandings, four hours later Montgomery wrote that all was now well, with both 2nd Armoured Brigade and 24th in position on the Pierson Line, one regiment of 8th Armoured Brigade out and on its way to its position on the left of the 24th and the returned flank on the left firmly held by Freyberg's armour.

It was to be some hours before he was disabused of this optimistic impression.

In the absence of General Gatehouse from the area of Miteiriya Ridge it is hardly surprising that the strongest personality in the area became invested with the aura of command over all present . . . and in the circumstances Bernard Freyberg was hardly likely to deny himself any opportunity to push X Corps armour out to assist his own, XXX Corps, infantry.

What influence he brought to bear on Brigadier Custance is impossible now to assess, but the latter, having received no firm reply to his request to be allowed to abandon the advance, was by 0230 reassembling the two regiments of his brigade still behind the ridge, and urging them out in support of the Staffordshires. By 0330 the leading formations of 3rd R.T.R. were feeling their way out through the mine-gaps in the area of the 6th New Zealand Brigade on the left and from then until 0500 both their tanks and those of the Nottinghamshire Yeomanry 'streamed out' to the southwest. By the time greyness was spreading into daylight from the ridge behind them, the 3rd R.T.R. were beginning to fill the gap between the Staffs and the 3rd Hussars of Currie's 9th Armoured Brigade, while the Notts Yeomanry were following through and swinging up to the right as they cleared the minefields.

There was also a lot of movement at the western edge of the ridge. Brigadier Kenchington, commanding the R.T.R. regiments of 24th Armoured Brigade, had remained largely in ignorance of the conference and arguments which had been taking place at high level and, in the absence of any contrary instructions, was still intent upon getting his 83 Shermans and 48 Crusaders out and on to the Pierson Line, however much behind time they might be.

By about 0400 reports came to him that at least one gap was clear through the main minefield on the right, and soon after 0500 his leading squadrons, hastily assembled from their dispersed positions, came over the crest of the ridge and down the forward slope. Their objective was some 3,000 yards in front of them, and they were intended to link with 2nd Armoured Brigade on the right and the Notts Yeomanry of the 8th Armoured Brigade on their left – so when, as the light grew, they saw large numbers of Shermans and Crusaders grouped some two miles away to the north, they assumed, correctly, that these were the tanks of the 2nd Armoured Brigade and, incorrectly, that they were all now on Pierson.

Moreover, less than 1,000 yards to their left they could see the Staffordshires moving out of a hollow in which they had evidently spent the night and, in company with the first Grants of the 3rd R.T.R. to arrive, advancing slowly to the west. Although the tank crews of the 24th Armoured Brigade could not see them, on the extreme left flank of those advancing Grants were some Shermans of the 3rd Hussars, the right hand formation of Currie's 9th Armoured Brigade, the other units of which were facing roughly south. Behind Currie's tanks, the lightly armoured Stuarts and carriers of the New

Zealand Cavalry were prudently retiring to the shelter of the ridge.

But the move of 8th Armoured Brigade to reach their positions at the southern end of Pierson was not to go unchallenged. Random mines claimed three of the Hussars' tanks and accurate anti-tank fire quickly reduced six of the Staffordshires' Crusaders to blazing wrecks . . . and it was while this was happening that Gatehouse's order to Custance that only one regiment of the brigade should be sent forward and the other two retained behind the ridge, at last got through.

By 0615 those orders had reached the regiments themselves and, to quote from the New Zealand *Official History*:

> . . . through some misunderstanding all three obeyed the latter part of the order with such alacrity that by seven o'clock the whole of 8th Armoured Brigade was in cover of the ridge, while several tanks of 3rd Hussars in error conformed with the withdrawal.[10]

They had withdrawn laterally across the rear of the remaining squadrons of the 3rd Hussars and of the other regiment of Currie's command, the Warwickshire Yeomanry (the Royal Wiltshire Yeomanry, after their ordeal during the opening twenty-four hours of battle, had handed over their few remaining tanks to the Warwickshires and retired from the fray), and these were thus to find themselves as the sun came up with their right flank unsupported, and spread out in a long arc facing south-west and south in low ground overlooked by enemy artillery. However, as there did not for the moment seem to be any well-organised opposition immediately ahead, John Currie decided that his safest course would be to assume the offensive and move further forward – an admirable decision foiled only by the fact that he was now short of both fuel and ammunition.

His suggestion to Freyberg that he should send his squadron back behind the ridge for re-supply was accompanied by the revelation (to Freyberg) that 9th Armoured Brigade were once again out front on their own, and as Freyberg's attempts to obtain information about the intentions of 10th Armoured Division were proving unsatisfactory, Currie was ordered to remain where he was for the moment, in order 'to discourage enemy counter-attacks' – a duty at which 9th Armoured Brigade proved successful, as none developed while they were there.

By now it was nearly 0800 on the morning of October 25th, and Montgomery, back in the Army Headquarters and still confident that his orders were being satisfactorily carried out, issued more detailed instructions for the employment of the X Corps armour. Having now reportedly broken out through the minefields and reached the

Pierson Line, it was 'to locate and destroy the enemy's armoured battle groups, and to ensure that the operations of the New Zealand Division south-west of the Miteiriya Ridge were not interfered with by enemy armour from the west'.

Three hours later, still with the assurance from the commander of the 1st Armoured Division, General Briggs, that 2nd Armoured Brigade were actually on the northern end of Pierson and that 24th Armoured Brigade were in contact on their left – and unaware that 8th Armoured Brigade had retired behind the ridge – Montgomery issued the next round of orders.

In the north, Briggs was to take over command of 24th Armoured Brigade which then with his own 2nd Armoured Brigade would 'act offensively against any enemy armoured battle groups' they encountered; in the south, all three regiments of 8th Armoured Brigade were to form a line down to the junction with 9th Armoured Brigade which would continue to face southwards, holding the flank. Gatehouse would command all this southern armour, the 5th New Zealand Brigade would follow down and support 9th Armoured Brigade in their exploitation to the south, and Brigadier Lee was to confirm his 133rd Brigade as present to hold the vacated positions along the ridge.

These orders were issued at 1030, after which Montgomery turned his attention from such purely tactical matters to confer with his superior officer, General Alexander, who had arrived to pay him a visit and collect the next list of Montgomery's requirements – and it was while these talks were in progress that the news arrived from XIII Corps's area that the 7th Armoured Division had been unable to penetrate the February minefield, and the subsequent decision made not to pursue that particular objective.

Other news arrived, too. With daylight Brigadier Fisher had at last been forced to accept that his 2nd Armoured Brigade was not, in fact, on the end of the Pierson Line, and that Kidney was still at least 1,000 yards further on to the west; and in an endeavour to correct the situation he sent both the Bays and the 9th Lancers further forward and at last out beyond the front infantry defences. They had hardly reached the edge of Kidney when they found themselves under 88mm. fire, the Bays lost eight Shermans in as many minutes, the Lancers lost two Crusaders and attempts by the third regiment of the brigade, the 10th Hussars, to outflank the enemy gun positions faded in the face of evidence of enemy counter-attack.

Soon 2nd Armoured Brigade were once again back behind the Oxalic Line . . . and on this occasion accurate reports were quickly in Montgomery's hands. By the time the Army Commander bade farewell to Alexander, he was aware of the fact that some of his plans were not going quite as well as he had believed; and having arrived at

Freyberg's headquarters at 1130 and listened to the latest reports from Lumsden and Leese, who had both been summoned there, he had by noon learned that other parts were also in disarray.

Despite the successes which had attended the infantry, it seemed that the armour were still unable to break out and perform their shielding role. Whether it was a case of 'could not' or 'would not' was for the moment immaterial – what mattered now was that the battle was 'fizzling out', all momentum was dying and unless something was done to enliven it again the enemy would be given time to stiffen what defences were still in their hands and build new ones; in which case the tasks carried out since the evening of October 23rd would all have to be done again.

Those present were agreed that this must not be allowed to happen, and three of the four – Freyberg, despite his junior rank compared with that of Leese, Lumsden and Montgomery, was also in attendance – felt that the correct solution would be a continuation of the battle by the same methods as used so far. The proposed exploitation to the south by the New Zealanders should for the moment be postponed, and instead another massive artillery and infantry attack should be mounted to clear the ground in front of XXX Corps for another 4,000 yards, in the hope that the armour might then be able to break out from there.

But Montgomery disagreed. Such a course would be too obvious, and it almost smacked of dancing to the enemy's tune; it certainly smacked of reinforcing failure instead of success.

An entirely different approach to the battle must be adopted, directed along an entirely different axis. New factors must be introduced.

One new factor was, in fact, already being introduced, but on the other side of the line. Generalfeldmarschall Rommel was returning to take command of the Panzerarmee Afrika.

10 · *Pause for Reflection*

During the first fifteen minutes of the Battle of Alamein, the known German and Italian gun positions opposite the XXX Corps front had each received nearly one hundred 4.5- or 5.5-inch shells or their equivalent weight in 25-pounders, and although this concentration caused relatively few casualties in men, it smashed a large number of the guns and wrecked the main Panzerarmee communications. Moreover, the Wellingtons which soon arrived overhead were equipped to jam the Axis wireless in addition to dropping their bombs and so, once the main barrage preceding the infantry attack began and the thick pall of smoke and sand cloaked the area, the only information to come back was brought by German runners – usually wounded – and this was, obviously, fragmented and extremely limited.

There was no word at all from any of the forward Italian positions, for although many of them had fought bravely, they tended to disintegrate immediately they attempted withdrawal. Those right at the front were all either killed or captured and at least one Italian regiment – the 62nd of the Trento Division – seemed virtually to have disappeared. The German front-line infantry also suffered severely as a large part of the 382nd Regiment of Lungershausen's 164th Division had been overrun, but as the night wore on it became evident that most of the posts back in the main defensive area were not only still in existence, but were defending themselves stoutly.

At Panzerarmee Headquarters on the coast near El Daba, therefore, there was for some hours ignorance as to the extent of the enemy penetration of the minefields, and doubt even as to whether the thrust in the north by the Eighth Army was the main one or, as many thought, only a feint. General Stumme had thus to spend some hours drawing deeply upon his reserves of experience and self-confidence, exhibiting his normal calm to all with whom he came into contact despite the mighty sounds of battle which came thundering in from just a few miles away to the east. He did, however, refuse permission for either German or Italian artillery to reply to the

British bombardment by shelling probable enemy concentration areas, only too well aware of the fact that his slender reserves of ammunition did not allow for wastage should he have been deceived and the areas empty.

It would be time enough to reply in force to the enemy assault when he had gathered evidence of Montgomery's real intentions, and it was with this in mind that he left his main headquarters shortly after dawn to visit 90th Light Division's Tactical H.Q. along the road to Sidi Abd el Rahman. To Westphal's suggestion that he should follow Rommel's example and take with him both an escort and a signals truck, he replied jovially that he would not be long and that he certainly would not venture into danger; his driver and Oberst Buechting from the staff would be all the company he required, and his car adequate to carry them.

But at 90th Light H.Q. Stumme found that the situation was just as obscure as it had been further west, although there was news from 15th Panzer H.Q. away to the south-east. Here, apparently, 115th Panzergrenadiers were heavily engaged – with Scotsmen it was thought – and there was also news of more panzergrenadiers even further south in action against New Zealand troops. However, reports were still somewhat vague and uncertain, so Stumme decided that an investigation further forward was both justified and safe.

In this he was mistaken. Shortly after setting out, the car came suddenly under machine-gun fire so accurate that Oberst Buechting in the back was immediately killed by a burst through the head. The driver, with admirable despatch, swung the car around and headed back at high speed, and it was not until he arrived at 90th Light H.Q. that Obergefreiter Wolf realised that his only passenger was the dead Buechting, and that General Stumme, whom he had last seen standing on the running-board and hanging on to the rear door, was no longer present.

Parties were immediately sent out to find the missing general but they all ran into enemy fire, and soon the message was passed back to Westphal that the Commander-in-Chief had been either killed or taken prisoner. Until such time as his successor was appointed, Westphal was once more *de facto* commander of the Axis armies facing the main enemy in North Africa, and his experience in similar circumstances during the previous year can have done little to console him. As it was, a shadowy picture of the battle was at last emerging from the darkness and confusion, and he could only hope that by the time it became clearer, someone else would have arrived to take the relevant decisions.

According to reports at last coming in from 15th Panzer Division, an Italian and a German battalion had disappeared completely in the northern sector, 'wiped out', according to one report, 'by drunken negroes with tanks', while to the south violent battles were being fought by both Italians and Germans against the Scotsmen. From the Miteiriya Ridge area came confused reports that the ridge itself had been lost, that tanks were already attacking positions in front of it but that positions were still held on the eastern face by some of the 164th Division stalwarts; and that when 15th Panzer units had come up against their first Sherman, they had been impressed by its size and apparent invulnerability, and shaken by its fire-power.

During the late morning came news from the southern front that enemy tanks in large numbers had penetrated the forward minefield and overwhelmed many of the Folgore units, but that other Folgore units nearby with men from the Ramcke Brigade were available for counter-attack. They were awaiting orders but in view of the mass of armour which the British had thrown in in the south, it could still be that here was where Montgomery intended the main breakthrough to take place, so care must be exercised not to waste force in small packets. Certainly 21st Panzer and the Ariete must remain where they were.

This was the picture which had emerged by the time when, to Westphal's relief, General der Panzertruppe Wilhelm Ritter von Thoma arrived during the afternoon from Deutsches Afrika Korps Headquarters to take command in Stumme's absence – and Westphal had some sympathy for the new Commander-in-Chief's explosion of anger when the picture was exhibited. To von Thoma's startled eyes, he appeared to be taking over a static line which had already been breached in several places, with no mobile reserve in hand which could be moved up to seal those breaches – and to a man trained lately in Rommel's tactics and anyway of Rommel's temperament, this was inexplicable.

But for the moment, explanations must wait. Whatever the situation, counter-attack was essential in at least one area, and to ensure that it was carried out speedily and with utmost force, von Thoma immediately left Panzerarmee Headquarters for 15th Panzer, to organise and oversee a thrust by the 8th Panzer Regiment towards the area in the northern sector which all his tactical instincts told him would be crucial.

He was not at that time to know that other eyes had marked that area down, too; one set naming it Kidney and the other Aberdeen.

Rommel had by this time been at a convalescent home at Semmering in the mountains near Vienna for nearly three weeks, and although every comfort had been heaped upon him together with the devotion of the extremely competent medical staff – and the presence of his wife and son – it had been by no means a time of unalloyed relaxation. His mind too often returned to the desert which had occupied it so completely for the last eighteen months, and to the men who had served under his command and who now stood in such danger.

He could read the reality behind the euphoria of the news broadcasts and the daily newspaper headlines, and even more clearly see through the cheerful optimism which bubbled across the surface of the letters he received from Westphal and Stumme, especially when they obviously avoided answering certain specific questions he had asked in his own letters to them. He was, as he later wrote, 'incapable of attaining real peace of mind', and as conscious as everyone else connected with the Panzerarmee of the approach at the end of October of the full moon period.

But perhaps, as most intelligence reports had indicated, another month would go by before Montgomery was ready?

During the afternoon of October 24th he was disabused of this hope. Generalfeldmarschall Keitel, Hitler's chief sycophant on the O.K.W. staff, rang up to inform Rommel that the long-awaited assault had opened the previous evening, that the British were attacking with unprecedented force both on the ground and in the air, and that General Stumme had disappeared. Was Rommel well enough to return to the desert and take up again the reins of command?

No one who knew Rommel could have doubted the answer, but the next few hours were spent in deep anxiety as Keitel would certainly not take the responsibility for such an important order himself. But in the evening the telephone rang again and this time it was the Führer himself on the line: could Rommel start for Africa immediately? He was to ring Führerhauptquartier before taking off in case the situation should have eased, but in the meantime urgency was the note for all action.

Rommel drove immediately to Wiener Neustadt where his airplane had been ordered for 0700 the following day, and before midnight the Führer had called him again to confirm that his presence was obviously vital at El Alamein. He was at Rome by 1100 on October 25th (by which time Montgomery was at Freyberg's headquarters recasting his plans), listening grimly to the latest news from von Rintelin. 'I knew there were no more laurels to be earned in Africa,' he was to write later of his return to the desert, 'for I had been told in the reports from my officers that supplies had fallen far short of my minimum demands.'[1]

He crossed the Mediterranean via Crete to Qasaba, continued the journey in his faithful Storch and arrived at Panzerarmee H.Q. just after dusk – to take up the battle again 'with small hope of success'.

General Stumme's body in the meantime had been found, along-side the track leading forward from 90th Light Division H.Q.

Apparently he had hung on to the side of the car for as long as possible after Wolf had turned it around, but then suffered a heart attack (his blood pressure had really been too high for tropical service) either before or immediately after falling off. It is doubtful whether his sudden death gave the British any great advantage, for it took place so early in the battle that the time had not been reached for vital new decisions; and anyway, German staff efficiency had quickly filled the breach.

But there were, of course, far too many other breaches which even German staff efficiency could not fill. They could do nothing about the fact that there was apparently only three days' petrol issue available instead of the thirty days' supply which in the circumstances would be necessary if defeat were to be averted. They could do nothing about the fact that after a day spent on limited counterattacks 15th Panzer Division had only 31 panzers still fit for action, and that recovery teams were finding it almost impossible to carry out their duties in the face of the storm of fire which swept the operational area at the slightest signs of movement upon it; or the fact that the overwhelming superiority of the enemy artillery, augmented as it was so frequently by air bombardment, was having its effect upon the morale of even the German element.

> I slept only a few hours and was back in my command vehicle at 0500 October 26th, where I learnt that the British had spent the whole night assaulting our front under cover of their artillery, which in some places had fired as many as five hundred rounds for every one of ours. Strong forces of the panzer divisions were already committed in the front line. British night-bombers had been over our units continuously. Shortly before midnight the enemy had succeeded in taking Hill 28, an important position in the northern sector.[2]

Rommel drove first of all out towards the scene of this latest attack – a relatively small and gentle rise which, however, in that flat and desolate landscape gave observation over what was evidently going to be a crucial area in the days to come. Elements of both Littorio and 15th Panzer had attempted piecemeal counter-attacks against the position, but already the enemy were well dug in with their heavy weapons to hand so it would be necessary to launch a concerted attack to regain the position.

Orders were issued, the 90th Light Division and Rommel's own *Kampfstaffel* brought up to help; and under Rommel's personal direction the attack went in at 1500 – immediately to be blanketed under a concentration of fire which reminded Rommel of his days on the Western Front twenty-five years before. Soon all his assault force was halted and taking refuge in whatever cover they could find – at which the guns ceased their thundering and bombers arrived overhead to make the position even more precarious; and from then on at least eighteen bombers arrived once an hour to keep up the pressure. An attempt by Italian and German dive-bombers to attack enemy supply columns and give reassurance to the unhappy Axis troops failed tragically; attacked by some sixty Allied fighters the Italians jettisoned their bombs over their own lines and the Germans were caught over their target by an intensity of anti-aircraft fire never seen before in Africa.

Sick at heart, Rommel returned to his command truck and then to his headquarters where Westphal had been preparing the latest intelligence reports.

From them, Rommel came to one specific conclusion and upon it decided to take a major risk. Despite the previous opinion registered by his intelligence staff, he came to the conclusion that Montgomery's main assault was concentrated in the north; he would now order 21st Panzer Division, part of the Ariete and most of the southern artillery to come northwards to help seal off the enemy drives. If he was wrong, the move would have eaten up much precious petrol – but in this regard Westphal could provide a modicum of good news. The tanker *Proserpina* with 2,500 tons of petrol aboard was due in Tobruk the following day, followed closely by the *Tergesta* with another 1,000 tons of fuel and 1,000 tons of ammunition; this would give him an extra six days' supply under battle conditions, more if he could divine exactly where his panzers should go at any particular time.

The petrol could also give him a little more room to manoeuvre. Surely he could still rely upon slowness of thought at British command level, and upon the inability of British armour to fight a mobile battle? With all his panzer forces in the north, perhaps he should allow the British tanks to come through the minefields and then smash them in a battle of manoeuvre in the area south of El Daba? It would certainly be a better idea than throwing his main force into the battle area *en masse* in an attempt to regain lost ground, for there they would be subject to both British artillery and British bombing.

His evening report to the Führer's H.Q. again stressed the danger to the entire Axis army unless there was an improvement in the supply situation, but his letter to Dearest Lu, though regretting the shortness of their time together, was by no means despairing.

But the night of October 26th/27th was even noisier than the previous one. Relays of British bombers flew along the coast road, circled the battle area, found the 21st Panzer Division on its northward move and seriously delayed it, though casualties were light; and at 0200, yet another furious barrage opened along the northern sector of the front and the sky grew 'bright with the glare of muzzle-flashes and shell-bursts'.

By dawn it became evident that the enemy had improved their

position around Hill 28, and were also attacking again at their
original break-in point to the south-west (around Kidney). During
the morning Rommel drove down the Telegraph Track to behind Tel
el Aqqaqir and watched the unending barrage, the continually
repeated air bombings, anxiously awaiting news of the arrival of his
panzers from the south and considering their best employment.

This proved to be a waste of mental energy. During the morning
had come the dreadful news that both *Proserpina* and *Tergesta* had
been bombed and sunk, the former just outside Tobruk.

> At 1430 I drove to Telegraph Track again, accompanied by Major
> Ziegler. Three times within a quarter of an hour units of the 90th Light
> Division, which had deployed and were standing in the open in prep-
> aration for the attack, were bombed by formations of eighteen aircraft. At
> 1500 our dive-bombers swooped down on the British lines. Every artillery
> and anti-aircraft gun which we had in the northern sector concentrated a
> violent fire on the point of the intended attack. Then the armour moved
> forward. A murderous British fire struck into our ranks and our attack
> was soon brought to a halt by an immensely powerful anti-tank defence,
> mainly from dug-in anti-tank guns and a large number of tanks. We
> suffered considerable losses and were obliged to withdraw. There is, in
> general, little chance of success in a tank attack over country where the
> enemy has been able to take up defensive positions; but there was nothing
> else we could do.[3]

Only seventy tons of petrol arrived that day – flown in by the
Luftwaffe – and this was hardly enough to move the newly arriving
formations into positions from which they might block further enemy
attempts to break out. So far from enticing the British armour
forward into a mobile battle, there was nothing his panzers could do
but act as mobile artillery and help to hold a static line.

> In the evening we again sent S.O.S.s to Rome and to the Führer's H.Q.
> But there was now no longer any hope of an improvement in the situation.
> It was obvious that from now on the British would destroy us bit by bit,
> since we were virtually unable to move on the battlefield. As yet,
> Montgomery had only thrown half his striking force into the battle.[4]

It might perhaps have been truer to say that as yet Montgomery had
been unable to devise a method whereby he could *get* more than half
his striking force into the battle; but since the midday conference at
Freyberg's headquarters on October 25th, he had been giving deep
thought to the problem. Another side of the problem, of course, was
that at the same time as he was reorganising his armour (for by now
he had decided that this would be essential) he must also retain the
initiative and 'make the enemy dance to his own tune'.

For this second purpose, he decided that he must use the best
instrument still left in his armoury, and this was undoubtedly the 9th

Australian Division. Already it had been clearly illustrated that the infantry were more likely to achieve their objectives than the armour, and of these the Australians had suffered the fewest casualties and had more reinforcements available. Moreover, they were in exactly the right position to open a new offensive in an entirely new direction, and one to which the enemy must immediately react.

Instead of continuing the attack westwards, the Australians would now drive north towards the coast from their exposed right flank, cutting both the road and the railway and, in so doing, isolating the Bersaglieri Battalion and the Germans of the 125th Regiment in the 'nose' of the salient. The armour and infantry of 1st Armoured Division (2nd and now 24th Armoured Brigades and the 7th Motor Brigade) would guard the new left flank of the Australians to the west and at the same time help and protect the Highlanders clearing away the last obstacles up to Oxalic, while at the same time the New Zealanders and Gatehouse's 10th Armoured Division (which now consisted only of the 8th Armoured Brigade and the 133rd Lorried Infantry) would consolidate behind Miteiriya Ridge, the infantry patrolling vigorously, the armour preparing to withdraw for re-organisation.

The sooner it could all start, the better, and as it happened General Morshead had already foreseen the necessity for his men to drive at least some way in the new direction. About 2,000 yards due north of the northern corner of XXX Corps's break-in, held by his own 26th Brigade, lay the high point marked on the British maps as Point 29 (and on the German maps, Hill 28) from which observation both of his own positions to the south and the ground to the north past the railway and road as far as the sea could be obtained. For the safety of his own men the position should be quickly taken and as early as the morning of the 24th he had told Brigadier Whitehead to prepare a plan for its capture.

As always, the Australians had begun patrolling in front of their positions as soon as they were established, and early on their first morning they had captured a few prisoners, one of whom still possessed a map of the minefields in the area. Then at dusk on the evening of the 25th, they watched a German reconnaissance party approach their own positions and indeed penetrate well into them before being attacked and captured – to provide amongst the prisoners the commanding officers of both the 125th Regiment and its 2nd Battalion. Both carried important documents and one of them typified a response often met with in German prisoners; whereas the Italians very often knew nothing of value to their captors and were anyway not interested in much besides their immediate evacuation from the battle area, German prisoners, reacting apparently to military discipline, seemed automatically to try to do their best to answer all questions fully and accurately, especially when these were put to them by an obviously senior officer.

As a result of these two episodes, two companies of the 2nd/48th Australian Battalion set out at midnight October 25th/26th, overcame all opposition and reached their first objective 1,000 yards ahead dead on time, their third company racing through in carriers to arrive nine minutes later on Point 29 itself and find that the preceding artillery barrage had so stunned the Germans there that the fight lasted barely two minutes. In view of the fact that the Australian gunners had nearly 16,000 rounds of ammunition, mostly 25-pounder, at their disposal, this was not altogether surprising.

Matters did not go quite so well on the Australians' right flank in the attempt to broaden the drive northwards, for 2nd/24th Battalion met strong opposition from the Germans of the 125th Regiment, and although the leading Australian company did reach the objective, they had then to fall back as their support could not get through. Nevertheless, ground had been won, over 200 Germans captured and the northern edge of XXX Corps's break-in now curved back in a shallow crescent from Point 29 to Tel el Eisa. It also confirmed Montgomery's opinion that the drive to the north would compel the enemy's attention, for as has already been related, during the whole of the next day (26th) Rommel threw his forces against the penetration, always to see them founder against the Australian defences and suffer under the artillery and air bombardments. The 'crumbling' process was undoubtedly working.

To the south of the Australian positions, however, matters were not proceeding smoothly, principally because of argument and confusion. There was still disagreement between the Highlanders and the 2nd Armoured Brigade as to where their respective forward units were, and General Wimberley was anxious to clear the whole way up to the Oxalic Line, still in part tantalisingly just beyond his reach. Moreover, his northern flank was still appallingly congested, with the tanks, trucks, guns and men of the armoured brigade continually milling around amongst his own infantrymen, and it was here that he wished to make his most important advance – to Aberdeen and the still-isolated company of the 1st Gordons of whom nothing had been seen since they advanced through the Red Line barrage on the first night.

But because of the presence of the armour and their insistence that they were in positions which the Scots disputed, no artillery cover for the advance to Aberdeen could be agreed and in some desperation Wimberley sent in a silent attack about an hour before midnight. It ran almost immediately into serious opposition, but at least found the missing company – away to the right of the advance, thirsty, tired, almost out of ammunition but still in being. But at dawn Aberdeen was still not wholly in the Highlanders' hands.

All other Oxalic objectives in the Highlanders' sector had been captured, however, by the morning of October 26th. Stirling had been attacked by the 5th Black Watch with some of the 46th R.T.R. Valentines in support, but they found the defences vacated and, surprisingly, two demolished 88mm. guns and a few small guns still in working order; and further south the 7th Argyll and Sutherland Highlanders at last secured Nairn after a stiff fight. Except for part of Aberdeen, the Scots were therefore closing up along the whole length of their line.

What had been noticeably missing, however, was still co-operation from the armour and as a result some opportunities had been lost.

General Briggs had decided that an attempt should be made to occupy at least in part the vital Kidney feature (still believed by many to be a ridge) and he proposed to send in the reserve battalion from the 7th Motor Brigade, the 2nd Rifle Brigade, but when news of this proposal reached General Wimberley he pointed out that the riflemen would be attacking over the same ground and at the same time as his Gordons. There seemed to be an obvious and advantageous solution to the problems posed – that the Rifle Brigade should follow the Gordons, clearing routes for their own vehicles at the same time so that once the Gordons reached Aberdeen, the riflemen could leap-frog through them and occupy Kidney.

But as the two parties could still not agree as to where either of them were or where their respective objectives lay, the men from 7th Motor Brigade were held back until after dawn when they attempted a daylight advance which, not surprisingly, ran immediately into stiff opposition. Their reports insisted that this was coming from Nairn, but this locality was so far off their intended route that there was from this particular débâcle an advantageous outcome; Army Command at last lost patience with the bickering over map reading and insisted that at a specific time that day, flares should be fired from advanced positions upon which cross-bearings would be taken.

The result was a severe jolt to the self-esteem of the armour, who were nowhere as far west as they claimed and whose navigation was thus demonstrated as inferior to that of the infantry – and even the infantry had not been as accurate as could have been wished.

But before that problem was cleared up, the armour had been attempting to reorganise itself for the next phase of the battle. Gatehouse's division moved out of the New Zealand area during the night of the 25th/26th, both 8th Armoured Brigade and the 133rd Lorried Infantry making their way to the rear, while 24th Armoured Brigade moved specifically over into 1st Armoured Division area. In view of the night's operations on 51st Highland Division front it was not, of course, possible for the R.T.R. regiments of the brigade to move directly north from the positions they had reached in front of the end of Miteiriya – so instead they went back across the ridge, then right back to the Springbok Track and up forward again via Star track. It took them the whole of the night of October 25th/26th – their third without sleep – and they were all exhausted upon arrival.

By the morning of October 26th, then, the Australians had extended the bridgehead northwards as far as Point 29 which they held firmly, the 2nd and 24th Armoured Brigades and the 7th Motor Brigade of 1st Armoured Division were at least on or just behind the Oxalic Line in the Kidney area, and except for Aberdeen, Oxalic itself was held down to the western end of Miteiriya Ridge – which was itself held along its crest. South of the South Africans the 4th Indian Division still held their anchor position at the bottom of XXX Corps's sector, their activities and by now somewhat restive spirits confined to raiding, their chief contribution to the battle so far being the repeated information that whatever else the enemy opposite might be doing, they were certainly showing no signs of withdrawal.

The attack by XIII Corps infantry on Munassib during the night of the 25th/26th (which it will be remembered had been preferred to the continuation of the attempt to punch a hole through the February minefield) had been almost as great a disaster as the previous attempt in the same area at the end of September. Two battalions from 69th Infantry Brigade set off after dark, and although the 6th Green Howards took part of their objective and 45 Folgore prisoners, the 5th East Yorkshires soon found themselves being shelled either by the enemy or by their own supporting artillery, lost over a hundred men and promptly retired to their starting line.

The action did, however, distract attention from further south where the two unfortunate Queen's battalions of 131st Brigade had endured a grim day of heat and exposure, west of February. The survivors quietly withdrew during the night into the bridgehead between February and January where 22nd Armoured Brigade had at least dug some defences, though the infantry were not to have the consolation of armoured protection for very long. The following night one of them awoke

> . . . just in time to see the last squadron of Sherman [*sic*] tanks belonging to the 7th Armoured Division rumbling away down the minefield gap, their wireless aerials whipping in a thin arc against the grey dawn sky as they bucked and lurched down the uneven track. There was not enough room inside the bridgehead which, as I learned later that day, was only about 500 yards deep at its furthest point, for the tanks to deploy. Besides, they were needed to regroup and stand by to reinforce the main attack in the north.

But it was a cheerless moment to face the dawn on an empty stomach and know that the total defence in the extreme south of the sector was two infantry brigades, strung out along some 2,000 yards of front, with the badly knocked-about remnant of the Free French Brigade in reserve somewhere to our left rear.[5]

But by now Rommel had withdrawn 21st Panzer, a major part of the Ariete and most of the artillery from the south, and Montgomery, too, was concentrating all the Eighth Army strength in the north. To all intents and purposes the battle in the original XIII Corps area died away after Munassib, and what troops were left down there spent the days in desultory mortar and small-arms exchanges with the equally unenthusiastic troops opposite, the nights in patrolling and reconnaissance through the minefields, awaiting news from the north.

No one has ever caught the air of irrelevance, of unreality, which can in daylight pervade large sections of a battlefield better than did Tolstoy in his description of Borodino. Fierce conflict might occupy one corner of the field with companies of men locked in combat, anguish and death . . . but within only hundreds of yards wagon trains are being unloaded in haste but no evident peril, squadrons gravely manoeuvre, batteries fire into apparently empty air, men march and countermarch. Even more men stand about waiting for orders, crowd around water-points or ration-trucks or – far more likely and more often – lie down and go to sleep.

This is an aspect of battle not often described and even less often appreciated. Even less appreciated is the difference made to the picture of conflict when later remembered, by a posture of offence instead of defence, of a condition of low instead of high morale, and especially of a final result of failure against that of success.

To Rommel and indeed to many of his men, the events of October 26th left a pattern in their memories of unceasing turmoil – of counter-attacks flung back time and time again, of shattering bombardment and of a long succession of implacable air attacks:

> The British resisted desperately. Rivers of blood were poured out over miserable strips of land which, in normal times, not even the poorest Arab would have bothered his head about. Tremendous British artillery fire pounded the area of the attack.[6]

Reports on the British side, however, especially of the early part of the day, seem to have been about an entirely different set of circumstances, enacted under entirely different conditions. To them, October 26th was a day of comparative peace and quiet. The Australians, certainly, were subjected to some shelling during the day, but compared to the counter-bombardment which they could themselves call up immediately they located the enemy batteries, it was insignificant. The first Axis counter-attacks of the day had come in against the base of the new salient where the Australian 2nd/13th Battalion were still in positions they had occupied and been strengthening ever since they took them in the first night's assault – and even there the M13s and Semoventis of the Littorio Division turned away under the heavy shelling which caught them long before they could wreak much damage.

During the morning, the axes of the counter-attacks edged northwards towards the newly won ground around Point 29, and at first the Australians there found their movements between the still shallow defences somewhat circumscribed by mortar and small-arms fire; but once their own observers had passed the requisite information back to the gunners and these had come into action . . . again, danger passed.

Early in the afternoon, an undoubtedly serious concentration of panzers, infantry carriers and guns appeared to the west and northwest, shell-fire increased, and groups of infantry could be seen deploying; but a few curtly worded sentences into the microphones by the Australian observers brought first the scream and crash of heavy and accurately directed shells, and shortly afterwards the roar of aircraft and the equally shattering explosions of 500-pound bombs. Gradually the enemy groups disintegrated, the shell-fire slackened, trucks and guns were seen withdrawing away to the west, and by late afternoon it was quite evident that the counter-attack had been called off – without, from the Australians' point of view, ever seriously developing.

On the other sectors of XXX Corps's front, the picture was the same. The area held by the newly found Gordons was rather unfairly subjected to random shelling, as was the newly taken Argyll and Sutherland position at Nairn, but Valentines of 40th R.T.R. encountered no problems in moving north to support the Australians, although 2nd Armoured Brigade, also ordered to move north to cover the western flank of the new Australian positions, found themselves still in argument as to their exact positions. When they did move they came under fire either from Aberdeen or from some of the counter-attacking forces further north, at which point they withdrew through the 7th Motor Brigade positions back to their starting point. The tank crews of 24th Armoured Brigade, not surprisingly, were either fast asleep or attempting to replenish their fuel tanks and ammunition racks in such an exhausted state that their presence amid the marching Highlanders, hard-working sappers, disgruntled truckdrivers and infuriated staff and liaison officers threatened to reduce confusion to chaos.

Further south on Miteiriya Ridge, the New Zealanders and their close friends of the 9th Armoured Brigade spent the day under intermittent shell-fire, observing and reporting enemy movements away to the west, occasionally calling down artillery concentrations whenever the panzers approached too close or congregated into worthwhile targets. After their efforts during the opening phase of the battle, the Kiwis were enjoying something of a well-earned rest.

To Montgomery also, October 26th was a day for little movement, but much deep thought and concentration. The basic changes to be made in the original plan were clear in his mind, and it was now necessary to decide upon the details – and in this regard, he had to bear in mind the cost of the battle so far.

According to de Guingand, casualties to date amounted to 4,643 in XXX Corps, 455 in X Corps and 1,037 in XIII Corps. Overall, this was by no means an exorbitant price to have paid for the gains made, but in detail it posed some problems. Infantry were making by far the greatest contribution to victory, and as the most trustworthy arm infantry must provide much of the power in the newly planned operations; unfortunately, infantry had borne the brunt of the battle so far and were critically short of reinforcements. The Australians had lost nearly one thousand men, as had the New Zealanders, while the Scots had lost nearly double that number – and the most realistic attitude to take was that the casualties had been from amongst the best, whose replacement in quantity was evidently difficult and in quality might prove impossible.

Another obviously realistic attitude to take was one of deep scepticism towards intelligence figures regarding Axis losses. According to the latest reports, Rommel's forces had been depleted by the staggering figure of 61,000 men, 530 tanks and 340 field guns, which if true would have left the Panzerarmee in shreds; and those responsible for producing the estimates must have been slightly puzzled as to why Eighth Army were not already well into Cyrenaica.

As they were still barely past the Oxalic Line, however, their Army Commander issued during the morning a general directive to help them along the way.

The Australians would renew their drive to the north during the night of October 28th, and until then the other infantry of XXX Corps would do little but solidify the existing front, facing west, and fight off counter-attacks. The armour left in the area would move to act as shield to the Australians but would not attempt to move out beyond artillery protection, and this would be augmented at all times by the close co-operation of both bomber and fighter squadrons.

The original Australian positions would now be taken by General Wimberley's reserve formation, the 152nd Brigade, while further south the New Zealanders would be withdrawn entirely from the battle, their places along the ridge being taken by the South Africans who would side-step to the right and thin out the line in general, *their* places being taken by the 4th Indian Division following the same procedure.

So far as XIII Corps were concerned, General Horrocks was to ensure that 7th Armoured Division suffered no more losses, and was regrouped to enable it to move north immediately word was received that 21st Panzer was doing the same. All moves should be completed by dawn of October 28th, and all formations should then be standing by to put new plans into operation; but in the meantime only shielding measures were to be taken, and energies conserved for a major offensive in the near future.

It is ironic that during the proposed 'quiet period' when recuperation and reorganisation were the intended order of the day, the fiercest and certainly the most famous action of the Battle of Alamein was to be fought.

It took time, of course, for General Montgomery's detailed orders to be disseminated down to the levels at which many of them would come into operation, and meanwhile there were phases of existing operations to be completed.

The Australians, for instance, on the night of October 26th/27th, were intent upon straightening the line eastwards from Point 29 back towards Tel el Eisa and fighting off the stalwarts of Lungershausen's 125th Regiment, equally intent upon recapturing the ground lost the previous night. This led to some fierce close fighting during the hours before midnight, but after midnight the Australians managed to disengage for long enough and at sufficient distance for their one great superiority to come into action. Shortly after 0200, as Rommel noted, Australian artillery opened fire along the northern sweep of their front to such effect that afterwards their patrols went forward almost without opposition, and by dawn all their objectives were taken together with 41 stunned and shocked German prisoners and one intact 88mm. gun.

To the Australians' south, General Briggs was making strong efforts to get his armour out into that shielding role that the Army Commander was still requiring, but he had decided that even before his armour could disentangle itself from the confusion amongst the Highlanders, he must secure a firm base for them further forward. To achieve this, he would send two rifle battalions of the Motor Brigade forward, one on each side of the Kidney feature, to attack and occupy areas from which they could dominate the enemy anti-tank posts, thus creating a passage through which the armour could pass. Both 2nd and 24th Armoured Brigades would then at last be out in the open and the Motor Brigade units could connect up and follow them, while units of 133rd Lorried Infantry Brigade moved into the vacated positions – 'Woodcock' about a mile north-west of Kidney, 'Snipe' a similar distance to the south-west.

The commanding officers of both rifle battalions – 2nd King's Royal Rifle Corps in the north, and 2nd Rifle Brigade in the south – had had brief opportunities for reconnaissance during the morning, but as the flare-firing exercise had not by then been conducted the doubts as to locations of both start lines and objectives persisted. Even after the experiment there was still some uncertainty because the armoured formations were reluctant to accept the evidence, so when at 2130 the Bren carriers of the K.R.R.C. set off, they were forced after a while merely to follow the artillery barrage, despite the fact that it was not falling in what they considered to be the right direction.

On the way they came across an entirely unexpected post held by the Gordons and some equally unexpected enemy anti-tank posts from which they collected nearly a hundred prisoners, and when daylight came they found themselves in open ground, quite obviously not Woodcock, fully exposed to enemy fire. It seemed to the commanding officer that they could serve no useful purpose there, so he ordered a withdrawal which eventually took them back through the Gordons' outpost to a position east of Kidney, not far from where they had started out.

Lieutenant-Colonel Victor Turner, commanding the 2nd Rifle Brigade, had been so uncertain of the locations of his start line and his objective – and conscious of the differing opinion regarding these of the commander of the 1st Black Watch for whom Turner had considerable respect – that in the evening of the 26th he had reported his anxiety to 7th Motor Brigade H.Q. where, however, he was told that it was too late to change arrangements.

He therefore issued orders that his force was to follow the line of the artillery barrage which in the event proved to be some 45° north of the line as calculated by his own navigating officer. Zero hour was 2300, the barrage opened five minutes before and the change in direction delayed the advance of the infantry and engineers by ten minutes. Little opposition was experienced over the first 1,000 yards at which point they came up against wire, but this, on examination by the engineers, proved only to surround a dummy minefield.

During the next 1,000 yards, the infantry captured some twenty prisoners and saw several other enemy troops scattering in front of them, leading them over the crest of a ridge to an area about 500 yards further forward. Here Colonel Turner halted his force, disposed them for immediate defence and fired the success rocket to bring forward the heavy weapons.

These had been left with the second-in-command of the battalion,

Major Pearson, and had been waiting on the start line for nearly an hour during which time they had been subjected to random shelling and been bombed at 2330 by a lone aircraft. This set fire to two of the vehicles and caused casualties to which the doctor was at that moment attending, and as Pearson immediately gave the order to advance, the convoy started off without their medical officer or the ambulances.

The trucks and guns found the going very bad, with long ridges of soft sand which sucked the wheels down to the hubs and turned the comparatively short journey into a nightmare of sweat and frustration. But by dint of much hard work and considerable determination, 19 of the 27 6-pounder anti-tank guns arrived at the chosen position together with their ammunition trucks, and all were off-loaded by 0345. The empty trucks left, again under Major Pearson, two hours later, by which time Colonel Turner's force were endeavouring to take up their positions, despite a small but confused battle taking place in their midst.

In the dark, Colonel Turner had halted his force in the middle of what later proved to have been a German engineers' dump, about 800 yards to the north-east of a leaguer of enemy tanks and trucks. When C Company's Bren carriers fanned out to take their positions, they had climbed a shallow ridge where they found wire and also some dispirited Italian soldiers who gave themselves up. But there was a gap through the wire, and as there appeared to be a group of about 150 equally dispirited-looking soldiers some 500 yards beyond it, the carriers made their way through – to find themselves in the middle of the leaguer, which promptly sprang into active and hostile life.

The prisoners bolted – to be shot down indiscriminately by both sides – the carriers hastily retreated with the loss of one of their number, but leaving one enemy truck ablaze and sufficient dismay and confusion in the leaguer for its commander to decide to seek further security. It lay, he thought, away to the north, and in order to attain it the entire force formed up and began an advance to the north-east – to run very quickly into the south-west corner of Snipe, where both C and B Companies of Turner's force were just siting their first anti-tank guns. In the ensuing fracas an Italian self-propelled gun was destroyed and a German medium tank set alight, from which one valiant crew member jumped into a convenient trench and sniped at British positions until shortly after dawn when a grenade put an end to his activities.

Dawn also revealed their position to 300 embattled riflemen.

They were dispersed inside an oval of scrub-covered desert whose longer axis ran north-east and south-west for just over 1,000 yards, its shorter axis being half that length. The usual undulations and small dips provided cover for most of the guns, and soft sand at the bottom of most of them scope for improvement. An abandoned German dug-out just west of the centre point provided Turner with head-quarters, around which B Company's five anti-tank guns were deployed in the south-easterly sector covering the angles 90° to 225°, C Company's four guns to the south-west covering 225° to 315° and A Company's four guns in the northern sector facing north-west and north. Alongside A Company's guns were six more from 239th Battery of the 76th Anti-tank Regiment, covering the north and north-east sector, under command of Lieutenant Alan Baer.

This battery had been detached to join Colonel Turner's force late in the evening, with the cryptic valediction from the regiment's second-in-command, 'From all the signs, I should think it highly probable that you are in for a death or glory affair!' – a point of view which gained force as daylight grew.

Although the night's action had died down except for those of the lone sniper, the enemy force from the southern leaguer had drawn only a little way back to the south-west – and now the riflemen could see the security which its commander had been seeking – a solid and menacing-looking German leaguer about 1,000 yards away to the north. As this was coming rapidly to life, all gun crews along the north-west quadrant braced themselves for action and watched closely for the first signs of movement. These when they came, however, provided the riflemen with both surprise and relief, for instead of turning towards them both the German and Italian forces began to move off westwards, thus exposing the vulnerable sides of their armoured vehicles.

This provided a temptation which could not be withstood despite the danger that yielding to it would bring, and fire on the panzers was immediately opened. In return the position itself was heavily shelled and for nearly half an hour the whole northern sector of Snipe was a chaos of smoke, blown sand and explosion – but when the last of the enemy withdrew out of range the reports which came into Turner's headquarters claimed that six German panzers, eight Italian tanks and two Semoventi guns had been destroyed, and two German panzers hit – and moreover, smoking remains of several could still be seen to confirm the tally, while enemy recovery teams were at work towing others away. On the debit side, three of the anti-tank guns had been put out of action, and one had proved to have been sited in such soft sand that it had almost buried itself by its own recoil. But the action had clearly demonstrated that hard-hitting anti-tank guns, well sited and well dug in, could extract an extortionate price from any panzer force which might try to eliminate them.

On the other hand, of course, the action had also revealed, first to the local enemy and soon to Rommel, that there was a powerful

British force apparently isolated some 1,000 yards into their own positions; heavy counter-attacks must be expected shortly.

As it happened, however, the first danger came from behind.

The original plan called for the armoured brigades to come out to the support of Woodcock and Snipe at about dawn – but as the Woodcock force was obviously nowhere near their objective, the 2nd Armoured Brigade remained more or less where they were. But 24th Armoured Brigade received word that 2nd Rifle Brigade were on Snipe and at 0730 they breasted a protective ridge and saw, some 2,000 yards in front of them and surrounded by a zareba of burnt-out Italian and German panzers, a well-sited concentration of guns upon which they promptly opened fire. This was, as the writer of the most detailed account of this action says, with massive understatement, ' . . . galling':

> In an attempt to stop it, Turner sent out his Intelligence Officer, Jack Wintour, on the dangerous mission of making his way to our tanks in a bren-carrier. This Wintour accomplished. He succeeded in abating the fire of the leading squadron, but the remainder of the brigade continued to bombard their friends. The irrepressible Wintour then calmly returned.[7]

Shortly afterwards the tanks of the 24th Armoured Brigade began advancing westwards towards Snipe – but the Rifle Brigade crews along the southern quadrant of the position could see some 25 panzers, all with long-barrelled guns with 'muzzle brakes' – presumably Mark III or IV Specials – moving into hull-down positions behind a ridge about 1,500 yards away, from which to attack the advancing Shermans. The gun crews opened fire at once again into the vulnerable sides of the panzers – to see the nearest three brew up almost immediately, their crews machine-gunned as they jumped clear by the approaching Shermans who at last appreciated the true position.

By 0830 the leading squadrons of the armoured brigade had actually moved into the Snipe position, much to the discomfort of the riflemen and especially the anti-tank gunners of the 239th Battery, for the Shermans attracted devastating shell-fire from the German gunners who seemed to be using a new technique. One of the hull-down panzers would drop a smoke shell as near as possible to one of the tanks, and immediately the 88mm. anti-tank guns and the heavy panzer guns would shell the smoke – larger and much more visible than the camouflaged Shermans. Within a quarter of an hour seven Shermans were blazing, the whole area had become a confusion of smoke, fire and shell-bursts, and that basic fact of armoured warfare was yet again patently obvious: against dug-in guns or hull-down tanks, stationary vehicles in open country – however well armoured – were too vulnerable to live. To everyone's relief the

order was given for the Shermans to withdraw, which they did about
0900 – to cause yet another revelation.

As the Shermans drew away to the east, fire was opened upon them
by panzers and guns some two thousand yards away to the north. The
nearest anti-tank guns to these attackers were those of 239th Battery,
but it was only under pressure from one of the Rifle Brigade officers
that Sergeant Binks was persuaded to open fire at such an extreme
range; but he hit and stopped one of the panzers with his third shot,
and harried another which came out to tow away the casualty. The
British undoubtedly now had an effective anti-tank weapon.

What the men in Snipe lacked, however, were two important
services. Some men had been killed and more had been wounded –
and the medical officer and his ambulances were still back at the start
line, unable in daylight to move forward. Even more important, the
attached gunner observation officer had disappeared during the
night, and in the developing circumstances his presence and expertise
would have been very useful. In the folds and dips of the desert

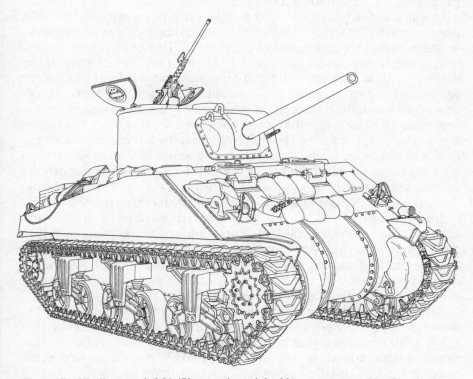

Figure 7   Medium tank M4 (Sherman): weight 32 tons; armour 25mm.–55mm.;
engine 460 h.p.; maximum speed 23 m.p.h.; armament one 75mm., one ·30 in.
machine-gun, one ·50 in. machine-gun; crew 5

surrounding the embattled riflemen, slight though they were, were now congregating enemy units with guns and panzers which neither anti-tank guns nor small-arms could hit – and the crying need was for the kind of dropping artillery blanket protection which was proving so effective elsewhere along XXX Corps's front. A gunner observation officer could moreover have cured another problem which was besetting Turner's force, and at 1036 he sent out a message clarifying it. 'What we most need is artillery support. We have a suspicion that our own artillery is landing on us.'

Moreover, it was quite obvious that if action on the scale so far experienced were to continue all day, another urgent need would be for more ammunition, so in an attempt to solve all their problems at once, three carriers under an officer and a sergeant made a dash for the eastern ridge behind which waited their support, carrying the more severely wounded. Unfortunately, neither they nor the convoy held in readiness by Major Pearson were ever able to get back through the storm of fire which greeted everything which showed itself over the crest, and by mid-morning it was quite evident to the men at Snipe that they were on their own, at least until darkness fell.

It was soon equally evident that this was a point not lost upon the enemy, and by 1000 Italian infantry were moving in groups nearer to the western perimeter and forming up for attack. Turner briskly instructed one of the Scout carrier platoons to 'see them off' (which they did by driving straight at them with Bren-guns and rifles blazing) while some readjustments were taking place within Snipe itself, for more danger was now threatening from the south-west. By enormous effort and at some cost two guns were therefore quickly moved down into the sector, but as Bren carriers were the only vehicles now left in the area and as they had no towing hitches, the guns had to be pulled out of the soft sand with ropes attached to the tracks – and the movement above ground churned up clouds of sand which were promptly shelled by the enemy, causing on this occasion the loss of one officer and three riflemen.

But the movement of the guns proved worthwhile almost immediately for as they settled into their new positions, thirteen Italian M13s came over the western ridge, while away to the south more than twenty panzers moved out of their hull-down positions apparently intent upon attacking the Shermans of the 24th Armoured Brigade, now themselves hull-down behind the eastern ridge opposite.

The Italian tanks were quickly dealt with as all the guns along the western flank opened up together. Four M13s were hit in the first salvo and the remainder scuttled back behind their ridge – a not unreasonable course of action, for the M13s had been vulnerable even to the old British 2-pounders, and for them to advance against the new 6-pounders was suicidal.

But in the meantime, an interesting case of what Colonel Turner was later to refer to as 'cross-trumping' was taking place along the southern perimeter. As the panzers crossed their ridge and came out into the open towards the 24th Armoured Brigade positions, they once again exposed their sides to the watching riflemen, one of whom, Sergeant Calistan, was to prove as accurate a shot with his 6-pounder as had Sergeant York with his rifle in the Argonne twenty-four years before. Within a few minutes of setting out, the panzer commander had been forced to detach half his force to attack the Snipe position from which such dangerous fire was coming, only to find that now the vulnerable sides of this force were exposed to the guns of the hull-down Shermans of 24th Armoured Brigade.

The range was long, but the nerves of the gunners remained steady, neither set switching their fire to the panzers actually attacking them but concentrating instead upon those crossing their sight-lines towards the other target. Soon at least eight of the panzers were alight, others were going to their aid and attempting to tow them out of danger, while others had turned under the weight of fire and were back under cover again. The longed-for co-operation between armour and infantry – admittedly of the same division in this case – seemed at last a reality.

Conditions inside Snipe, however, were by now serious. More men had been killed and many more injured, and as the heat grew the lack of skilled medical attendance, of much more than shell-dressings in the way of medical equipment or of water to spare for washing wounds, added considerably to their sufferings. Flies covered the bodies of the living, and as the heat rose towards noon so did the intensity of enemy fire.

Six of the carriers were hit during a burst of shelling just before midday, their flames adding to the heat and fury, their smoke drifting across the gun positions and confusing the gunners. There were not so many of these now, and many gun crews were made up to strength by officers whenever danger threatened, or by other gunners running over from unthreatened positions. Six guns had now been knocked out, leaving but thirteen to cover a 2,500-yard perimeter – but from all reports written about this action, morale everywhere remained astonishingly high. Many of these men had taken part in previous desert battles and had known the frustration of trying to fight off panzer attacks with inadequate weapons. Now, in their own hands, they had a battlewinner – and few of them would have exchanged their fate with another's; they were professional soldiers of a famous regiment, in the type of action for which they had long trained.

The shortage of ammunition, already a general problem, now tended to become acute in the south-western sector. Two jeeps, driven by one of the company commanders and a corporal whose gun had been put out of action, were used to redistribute what ammunition there was, driving everywhere through thick dust, heavy shelling and a torrent of machine-gun fire.

Then shortly before 1300, the shelling concentrated, the machine-gun fire increased and from over the ridge to the south-west appeared eight Italian M13s and a Semoventi self-propelled gun – doubtless encouraged by the fact that all but one of the defending guns in the southern sector had fallen silent.

Unfortunately for the Italians, the exception was Sergeant Calistan's, although at that moment one of his crew was lying badly wounded and the others were all away from the gun, scrounging ammunition from the nearest wrecks. Realising the danger and the predicament, Colonel Turner and Lieutenant Toms raced to Calistan's assistance, the colonel taking post as loader and observer, Toms as No. 1 to Calistan as layer; together they waited until the M13s were within 600 yards.

Calistan's expertise combined with their own thin armour proved fatal to the Italian tanks. He had picked off five of them and the self-propelled gun before they had closed to 400 yards, and was prevented from making a clean sweep right away by the fact that only two rounds of ammunition were left – a difficult situation as the remaining three M13s, gallantly manned, were still advancing, their machine-guns pouring in fire on the defiant gun-post. Lieutenant Toms turned and raced for a jeep some hundred yards behind him, drove to the nearest wrecked gun and with the strength of desperation threw aboard every round he could find. He arrived back behind Calistan's gun in a storm of machine-gun fire which set the jeep's petrol-tank alight as he pulled up, but with total disregard of the flames, Turner and a corporal who had run across to help lifted the ammunition clear and flung it towards the gun. As he turned for the last time, a shell fragment pierced Turner's helmet and cut deep into his skull causing the blood to pump out over his face and blind him.

But the three remaining tanks were now within 200 yards and their machine-gun bullets were whining close by the sweating men, deeply denting the thin gun-shield. It was now all up to Sergeant Calistan, but he apparently refused to be hurried; with the clarity of movement of a top-class soloist, he took his time and scored a hat-trick – all three tanks bursting into flames as he hit them, the crews perishing to a man inside.

'Hardly miss 'em at that range,' he is reputed to have said much later. 'Poor bastards!'

'After this,' says the Rifle Brigade history, 'there was a comparative lull' – but 'comparative' would seem to have been the significant word.

Random shelling and mortar fire continued all the afternoon, more

men and officers were wounded. Colonel Turner recovered full
consciousness for a time and insisted on visiting the gun positions, but
a combination of pain, loss of blood and the increasing heat began to
give him hallucinations, and towards the end he had to be kept in the
headquarters dug-out by force. As six of the other ten occupants were
also wounded conditions inside were difficult in the extreme,
especially as nearby shelling blew in clouds of sand and the flies were
everywhere. By 1600, the majority of the officers had been killed or
wounded, all gun positions were commanded by N.C.O.s and most of
them had been hit at least once – and now trouble came from yet
another source.

General Briggs, commanding 1st Armoured Division, was faced
with a dreadful dilemma. He was well aware of the situation and the
condition of his men on Snipe and the need to get help to them, but
he also knew that his armour would be needed during the next
offensive stage of Montgomery's plan (and it should be remembered
that the battle being fought by the Rifle Brigade battalion was taking
place during a designated 'quiet' period). He was also aware of what
had happened to the Shermans of 24th Armoured Brigade when they
had reached Snipe during the early morning, and what had happened
since to everything else which showed itself over the protective ridge
behind the position.

He could not send armour out to help – at least not in daylight. But
he would try to grant Turner's repeated request for artillery support,
so 2nd Armoured Brigade were ordered to help supply it and their
attached artillery of the 11th R.H.A. edged up to the crest with their
Priests – 105mm. howitzers mounted in M3 tank chassis – and
opened fire. It was unfortunate that the armour had still not identified
correctly either their own position or that of their forward infantry,
for the heavy shells smashed viciously down into the Snipe area,
adding considerably to the difficulties there.

'During an unpleasant day,' Colonel Turner's narrative records
sadly, 'this was the most unpleasant thing that happened.'

By this time Rommel, who it will be remembered was watching this
action from his place along the Telegraph Track, had put together his
main counter-attack against the whole of the northern front. Units
from the 90th Light Division moved cautiously in from the west
towards the Australian positions just south of Point 29, while parallel
and further south (across the original Woodcock area) a force
estimated at thirty German and ten Italian tanks advanced to attack
the positions held by some of the 2nd Armoured Brigade. Those in
the north immediately disappeared into a storm of artillery fire and
shortly afterwards were thoroughly dispersed by bombing, while

those crossing Woodcock would seem to have been destroyed by their own lack of intelligence.

Presumably they had only just arrived in the area and certainly they had been most inadequately briefed, for they advanced in open phalanx, at least seven of them crossing in front of the remaining four guns of the 239th Battery on Snipe at less than 200 yards' range. The action was as spectacular as had been Sergeant Calistan's in the south, the battery's tally being nine panzers destroyed and several hit, while one of A Company's nearby guns claimed another four destroyed though it is probable that one or two of these were duplicated by the 239th.

But now the second wave of Rommel's counter-attack was launched, and from it fifteen panzers were detached specifically to assault the north-western face of the Snipe position, in which by that time only two guns were left to defy them – those of Sergeant Hine and Sergeant Miles – though frantic attempts were made by Lieutenant Holt-Wilson to turn one of the nearby guns around to help. Between them the three guns had thirty rounds of ammunition left.

Making good use of ground, the panzers crept nearer and nearer, their machine-gunners sweeping the gun positions whenever their turrets gave them a sighting, driving the gun crews first in behind the screens, then as the range closed and the bullets penetrated, into the shelter of nearby trenches. Sergeant Miles was himself hit and his crew pinned down, but when the three leading panzers were about a hundred yards from Miles's gun, Sergeant Swann crawled the fifty yards from Battalion Headquarters under intense machine-gun fire, loaded the gun, aimed and fired it.

In rapid succession he scored two hits on the leading panzer whose crew promptly baled out, while Sergeant Hine waited until another Mark III was within one hundred yards and then hit it with a shot which went clean through and hit the third Mark III about ten yards behind it. This third panzer backed away into a hull-down position and continued to pump machine-gun fire over the Snipe position until it apparently ran out of ammunition, a pursuit in which it was joined by all the other panzers of this particular assault, none of which thereafter exposed itself sufficiently for the gunners to get a shot at it.

A kind of stalemate thus resulted and at 1844 the adjutant, Captain F. W. Marten, sent out a signal to 7th Motor Brigade H.Q. reading 'Twenty tanks lying doggo in valley to the north of us at about one thousand yards. We are being swept by machine-gun fire. Expect attack at any moment.'[8]

Fortunately none developed in strength but in the meantime other signals were being sent to and fro. The Rifle Brigade codes had been burnt earlier in view of the close danger in which the headquarters lay, so clear though somewhat veiled language had to be used, and the first orders to be received were to the effect that 'friends' would come out to take the place of the riflemen 'at dinner time'. The riflemen should wait and see the said 'friends' comfortably in place, after which their own transport would arrive to take them home.

To the reasonable query as to whether it would be an early or late dinner, the reply was 'the fashionable time' – with which the riflemen had to be content despite the possibility of misunderstanding; but in the meantime there was work for the survivors to do. About 1900 the light began at last to drain from the sky, and by 1940 the panzers had all withdrawn to the north-west where a few were incautious enough to remain silhouetted against the pale evening sky. At them were fired the last few rounds of anti-tank ammunition, 'more of a gesture of relief than with any hope of hitting them' – but to everyone's gratification one hit was scored, the last of a remarkable day.

Back towards the headquarters dug-out now began to close the survivors of the outlying posts, all still crawling under a horizontal screen of machine-gun bullets from the static enemy posts around, many dragging wounded comrades between them. Lieutenant Holt-Wilson went around the gun positions to make sure that every gun had been either destroyed by the enemy or had had its breech-block removed, while the wounded were loaded on to the remaining jeeps and Bren-carriers, and sent off into the darkness. The one carrying Colonel Turner and Major Bird eventually made its way to the dressing station of the Highland Division, the others reached their own lines but not before running through a minefield laid that morning across their line of withdrawal, fortunately without further injury to the wounded. And the remaining fit riflemen on Snipe settled down to await 'the fashionable time'.

Eight o'clock came and went, half past eight, nine o'clock. All around them they could hear the sounds of German recovery teams and ambulances at their rescue work, and not surprisingly they did nothing to interfere. By 2130 there was no sign of either the 'friends' or their own transport and someone was heard to remark that it looked as though headquarters were on a bloody diet, at which the decision was taken to commence withdrawal at 2230 if there was still no sign of relief.

The survivors of A and B Companies therefore set out on foot at this time, but shortly afterwards the British artillery opened up on the enemy positions with exactly the kind of barrage for which the riflemen had been praying all day. One of its effects was that the panzers moved out of the leaguers, straight towards Snipe – so rather hastily and still without seeing any of the 'friends', Battalion Headquarters and the remaining men moved out, leaving behind them a scene which daylight would reveal as one of quite astonishing desolation, and also of considerable mystery. A month later a committee of inquiry into the action examined the scene and counted the wrecks of 34 tanks or self-propelled guns – and no one has ever been able to establish how many of both had been towed away.

Immediate losses among Colonel Turner's force amounted to about a hundred killed and wounded but many of the wounded, including both Turner and Major Bird, recovered to fight again. When General Montgomery heard of the action and had time to assess its results he was, of course, delighted. Turner received the Victoria Cross, Sergeant Calistan was recommended for one but received the Distinguished Conduct Medal instead; several D.S.O.s and lesser awards were made, but perhaps the highest accolade came from Rommel himself, for the men on Snipe must have contributed greatly to that 'murderous British fire' which 'struck into our ranks' and brought his heaviest counter-attack against the XXX Corps salient to a halt. It was certainly the Snipe action which caused him to conclude: 'There is, in general, little chance of success in a tank attack over country where the enemy has been able to take up defensive positions.'[9]

The non-arrival of the 'friends' had been due to inexperience and poor navigation, not to neglect.

Despite the events of the previous few hours around Snipe, the opinion was still held at command level that the front in general was 'quiet' for the moment and that nothing much remained to prevent the occupation of the Kidney area which had been so troublesome in the past. Now at last Brigadier Lee's 133rd Lorried Infantry Brigade could prove its value, taking over the positions and duties of 7th Motor Brigade including, of course, Woodcock and Snipe.

But exhaustion among the front-line formations was by now taking its toll, and tempers were very short. When Lee arrived at 7th Motor Brigade H.Q. he could elicit very little useful information, and when some time later he met both Lumsden and Gatehouse (who was coming up to take over this part of the front on Montgomery's latest instructions) Lee was told that he must make his own arrangements, but that all he had to do as far as Woodcock and Snipe were concerned was to 'walk through'.

He was, however, to be given ample artillery support – and it was this which crashed down on the panzers and drove them out towards Snipe. By this time, of course, the arranged relief hour had long passed, Turner and the wounded were already home and the fit Rifle Brigade survivors were walking out. Somewhere they must have passed their relief – the 5th Royal Sussex – but these in any case did not reach as far west as had the riflemen, digging in before dawn some 1,000 yards to the south-east of the recent battlefield.

As for the other battalions of Lee's brigade, the 2nd Royal Sussex in the centre of the advance reached the Kidney feature satisfactorily, but their colonel was killed and as the night wore on and daylight began they found themselves pinned down by small-arms and mortar fire from ridges away to the west.

The fate of the 4th Royal Sussex, however, was more complicated. Theirs had been the task of 'walking through' to Woodcock, but the unending confusion in the minefield gaps held them up twenty minutes behind their barrage, after which they went forward and attacked 'in good order and aggressive spirit' the first opposition they encountered. It was unfortunate that this was a post in Aberdeen held by the Gordons, but the episode had been inevitable ever since the planned axis of the Sussex advance had been laid straight across it.

The advance continued when at last proper identification had been achieved, but the battalion then came under heavy fire from the left flank and the company sent to deal with it was practically annihilated as it had run unexpectedly into an alert panzer leaguer.

Eventually, Lieutenant-Colonel Ronald Murphy considered that he had led what was left of his battalion as far as Woodcock (he had, in fact, reached the eastern edge) so he halted them and deployed them for defence, to find that the ground was rock hard so at dawn the slit-trenches were still far too shallow. Moreover, both German and Italian armoured units were close at hand, the wireless had broken down, and there was little sign of 2nd Armoured Brigade units which, they had been assured by Lumsden, would be up at first light to support them.

Those units were, however, on the move – though too far to the north. The Yorkshire Dragoons were already in action against an unexpectedly strong panzer attack which overran them and then turned south towards Woodcock, while still further north the 9th Lancers were moving towards Point 33, followed closely by the Bays; and from this vantage point both cavalry units in due course watched the panzers sweep across the ground held by the 4th Royal Sussex, knocking out the anti-tank guns easily as they had not yet been dug in, killing about sixty of the Royal Sussex, including Colonel Murphy.

Half an hour later they also watched the melancholy spectacle of 300 disconsolate infantrymen being marched off into captivity. But by then the cavalry were under orders to move back again as part of a general reshuffle of units, for General Montgomery had now completed his detailed plans for the next phase of the battle.

It was the morning of October 28th.

11 · The Crumbling Process

It is clear that we now have the whole of Panzer Army opposite the Northern funnel and that we shall never get the armoured divisions out that way. I have therefore decided to make this a defensive front, to be taken over by XXX Corps. 1 Armd Div. and 24 Armd Brigade to be withdrawn into reserve.[1]

These were the basic conclusions and decisions which General Montgomery communicated to his two northern corps commanders and their chiefs of staff at a meeting held at 0800, October 28th. The Australians would continue their drive northwards to the coast that night, using the occasion also as a means of annihilating any enemy units they could draw into the battle, and for this purpose they would be given as much artillery as could be spared from all other sectors, plus the instant co-operation of British and South African bomber squadrons when required.

Then at a moment to be decided by the Army Commander – probably the night of October 30th/31st – XXX Corps infantry would drive north-westwards from the original Australian west-facing front towards Sidi Abd el Rahman while armoured car regiments would break south-westwards from the flank of the advance to circle around and cut enemy communication and supply routes. The armoured divisions would be held in check until opportunity arose for them to be used either against any unexpected pockets of enemy resistance or, in the event of a clear breakthrough, to race ahead and block an enemy retreat until such time as infantry and artillery could come up and complete his destruction. The only armour to be embroiled in the immediate battles to the north would be the infantry support squadrons of 23rd Armoured Brigade, whose Valentines had already contributed much to the infantry advances.

The Army Commander's main problem at this point, of course, was where the infantry for this crucial drive along the coast would come from and, equally important, who would command it. There were, in fact, two divisional generals who had, in Montgomery's opinion, the experience, the co-ordinating staffs and the aggressive drive for such a task, but one of them was the Australian commander, General Morshead, who was already deeply committed. Fortunately the other one, General Freyberg, was calling for lunch.

Over it, Montgomery told his visitor what would be required of him.

First, Freyberg's own 6th Brigade, who had left Miteiriya Ridge during the previous night and were now to have a few days' rest and recuperation lying in the sun and swimming close to Army H.Q., would be called up to take over the western face of the Australian salient through which the drive to the coast would take place. Then for the advance itself, in view of the casualties already suffered by the New Zealand battalions, Freyberg would be fed with brigades brought up from the south – first the 151st Durham Light Infantry (under the newly promoted Brigadier Percy) from the 50th Division, then the 152nd Brigade from the Highland Division, then the 131st Queen's Brigade from the 44th Division, and then if necessary the Greek Brigade. John Currie's 9th Armoured Brigade would cover the southern flank of the advance and would be given top priority of all tank replacements, and one or other of the armoured divisions would be deployed further to the south either to shield or to exploit as occasion demanded. In which respect, as it was now obvious that 21st Panzer Division were no longer in the south, John Harding had been ordered to bring Roberts's 22nd Armoured Brigade up into the Alamein sector.

General Montgomery, of course, would have the final decision upon the exact timing of the break-out, but in the meantime General Freyberg would have a great deal of work to do as the detailed movements of several brigades of infantry and almost two armoured divisions through an area already severely congested would have to be worked out, and time was short. They parted immediately after lunch and Freyberg in due course made his way to XXX Corps headquarters to discuss his problems further with General Leese.

He found when he got there that events during October 28th on XXX Corps's front had been very similar to those of the previous day. The combined South African and Royal Air Forces had continued to dominate the air above the battlefield, and their contributions to the ground battles had been generous and often conclusive in that they both identified danger of counter-attack as it appeared, and then neutralised it by bombing before it could properly develop. The two surviving Royal Sussex battalions, although neither of them so aggressive or so far forward as had been the 2nd Rifle Brigade the day before, attracted a certain amount of attention from the enemy though not enough to cause them to vacate their positions, which was fortunate as behind them the 8th Armoured Brigade were taking over from the 2nd Armoured Brigade, and neither of them had much time to spare for any troubles in which the infantry might find themselves.

Further north, New Zealand artillery formations were moving into the Australian sector, while the gunners already there, again aided by the combined air forces, broke up Rommel's repeated efforts during the day to mount an effective counter-attack against Point 29.

Altogether October 28th was another day during which the generals planned and their staffs endeavoured to administer, when the infantry dug in and kept their heads down, when the armour argued and exchanged places, and the shell and the bomb arbitrated. And at sea another Axis tanker, the *Louisiano* with 2,000 tons of petrol aboard, was sunk by torpedo, thus adding to Rommel's anger and anxiety when eventually the news reached him – and it was no consolation to him that with 271 fewer armoured vehicles in running order than when the battle had started, Panzerarmee Afrika's daily consumption of petrol was less than had been predicted. It was also on the 28th that the writer of the Panzerarmee narrative recorded that their counter-attacks were continually failing under heavy defensive fire, then developing into tank duels in which the British tanks 'firing from hull-down positions at over 2,000 yards range simply outshot our tanks'.

By midday Rommel had become aware of the concentration of force taking place along the northern flank of the Eighth Army positions, so he had moved 90th Light further along the coast with their head-quarters east of Sidi Abd el Rahman and brought all German formations except the Ramcke Parachute Brigade up from the south. The whole of the Afrika Korps was now in the quadrant curving from north of the Kidney feature to the coast, with the Bersaglieri and the 125th Regiment of Lungershausen's 164th Division still holding the salient pointing forward towards Tel el Eisa; and during the afternoon they all at some time or other shelled the Australian positions which bulged ominously to the north.

The majority of the officers had also had opportunity to read an Order of the Day issued by Rommel early that morning, to the effect that they were now all engaged upon a battle of life and death, that all orders were to be obeyed without question and that any soldier who disobeyed would be court-martialled regardless of his rank – a reminder of their duties which many considered both unnecessary and offensive.

Then at nine o'clock in the evening came the stroke for which they had been waiting all day – a tremendous enemy bombardment of the area around 'Hill 28', eventually concentrating on the positions of the 2nd Battalion, 125th regiment:

> The British launched their assault at about 2200. The weight of this attack was something quite exceptional. However, by concentrating every gun in the area, we managed to break up the British attacks, which were

mainly made from Minefield I. Further to the north, in the gap between Minefields I and H, British tanks and infantry succeeded in making a penetration. The battle raged at this point with tremendous fury for six hours, until finally 11/125th Regiment and the XI Bersaglieri Battalion were overrun by the enemy. Their troops, surrounded and exposed to enemy fire from all sides, fought on desperately.

Army H.Q. had meanwhile been moved farther to the west. I spent the whole of that night with a number of my officers and men on the coast road roughly in line with the old H.Q. site, from where we could see the flash of of bursting shells in the darkness and hear the rolling thunder of the battle. Again and again British bomber formations flew up and tipped their death-dealing loads on my troops, or bathed the country in the brilliant light of parachute flares.

No one can conceive the extent of our anxiety during this period. That night I hardly slept and by 0300 hours [October 29th] was pacing up and down turning over in my mind the likely course of the battle, and the decisions I might have to take. It seemed doubtful if we would be able to stand up much longer to attacks of the weight which the British were now making, and which they were in any case still able to increase. It was obvious to me that I dared not await the decisive breakthrough but would have to pull out to the west before it came. Such a decision, however, could not fail to lead to the loss of a large proportion of my non-motorised infantry, partly because of the low fighting power of my motorised formations and partly because the infantry units themselves were too closely involved in the fighting.[2]

Rommel was beginning to look over his shoulder.

The Australian attack on the night of October 28th/29th had not in fact been as tactically successful as Rommel's account indicated. The 2nd/15th Battalion drove north for some 3,000 yards from the top of the Point 29 salient, overcame several enemy posts and took 130 Italian and German prisoners at comparatively low cost, though among those killed had been their own colonel. Away to the right a somewhat depleted and exhausted battalion, the 2nd/13th which had been in the thick of the recent battles, reached their first objective, the Fig Orchard, on a north-easterly drive from the base of the salient but there they found themselves being heavily mortared in positions anyway strewn with anti-personnel mines.

Two nearby enemy posts were attacked, the first at high cost as a mortar-bomb had exploded right in the middle of the platoon, the second by a patrol of ten men under command of a corporal. First they attacked two machine-gun posts with grenades and bayonets, then rushed across to the mortar post which the machine-guns had been protecting and captured the crew, whom they then took with them to the final objective carrying the three captured weapons.

But an attack by 2nd/23rd Battalion in the ground between those two advances supported by Valentines of 46th R.T.R. developed – to quote from the official Australian history – 'into the type of muddle for which there were several derisive epithets in common army parlance'. One company of infantry advanced riding on the Valentines, but some of these missed the marked gaps and had tracks blown off as a result, others behind tried to dodge around and ran on to other mines, and in the meantime the enemy gunners, alerted by the barrage which had by now gone far ahead of the tanks, pumped fire into the area. Casualties were heavy – and crippling, for the commander of the armour and all his squadron leaders were killed or wounded so communications broke down between infantry and armour at battalion level, and were then further confused when the brigade commanders of both the Australian infantry and the British armour went forward themselves to find out what had happened, and lost touch with their headquarters.

Yet despite these mishaps, 2nd/23rd captured a German position with six guns and 160 men, and the survivors of one company actually reached the railway line but were then forced back. At dawn the battalion were dug in about 1,000 yards in front of their original positions, but it was some hours before they had linked up with the 2nd/15th on their left and the 2nd/13th on the right, and even then contact was tenuous. But if the overall attack had not gained its full objectives, the three battalions had between them taken over 200 prisoners and killed an unknown number of enemy soldiers, and yet another demonstration of Allied air and artillery superiority had been given to a worried Axis command.

The advance had also given the Australians at the tip of the salient a commanding view over the ground leading to the coast, which would allow them accurately to plan the next operation; and it also gave them during that morning a certain amount of amusement. Evidently the exact extent of their success had not been appreciated by the enemy and several Axis vehicles drove unconcernedly into the new Australian lines, some carrying ammunition, some carrying food; none, unfortunately, carrying beer.

The following daylight hours (of October 29th) along the length of the main front passed with the same comparative lack of major action as had the previous two days, though another succession of counter-attacks was launched against the western face of the new salient. This was now held by men of the 2nd/17th and 2nd/15th Australian Battalions, and the assaults on their new positions were so hammered by artillery as they formed up, and then beaten back by anti-tank, mortar, machine-gun and rifle fire as they approached, that when evening fell, to quote from the Australian historian, 'It could be seen that dreadful casualties had been inflicted on the attackers.' Grey and khaki-uniformed bodies dotted the sand, wrecked vehicles burned, their ammunition racks spitting violently in the flames or tearing the vehicles apart with shattering explosions; smoke wreathed up into the short twilight, small stretcher-parties moved between the dark clumps, bearing away their sad burdens.

'Crumbling' was still paying off.

That night the 2nd/23rd Battalion mounted another attack to take some of the ground that had eluded them the night before, to find that the first 1,000 yards had been evacuated – so with no more losses they were level and in contact with their brother battalions on each side. On the morning of October 30th, therefore, the maps showed just that one small advance, the reports told of little but patrol activity, and the men at the front watched carefully not only the occasional enemy movements, but also the comings and goings of their own commanding officers and their adjutants whose activities, they had learned long ago, foreshadowed their own dangerous employment by but a few hours.

In this they were prescient, for on the night of October 30th/31st began an action in the Australian sector to contend in ferocity with that of the 2nd Rifle Brigade on Snipe. It was also, from the point of

Map 26   Australian attack, night of October 30th–31st

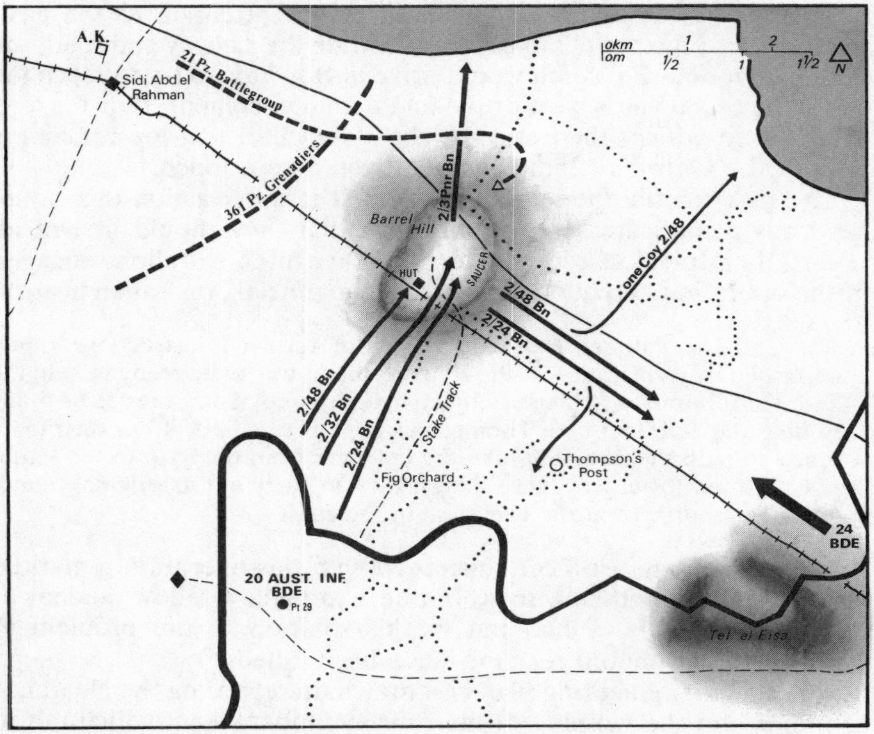

view of sheer planning, one of the most complicated small operations in the history of warfare.

The tactical idea behind it was to eliminate the Axis positions in the salient pointing back towards Tel el Eisa, in particular the strongpoint known as Thompson's Post, but undoubtedly the main purpose was to continue the 'crumbling' process against the Axis troops, and to draw as many of them as possible into a battle of attrition.

From the narrow salient now stretching up past Point 29, the 2nd/32nd Australian Battalion would drive north-eastwards and ensconce themselves across both the railway and the road at a locality known as Barrel Hill, while close behind them would follow the 2nd/48th Battalion on the left and the 2nd/24th on the right. These two battalions, using the 2nd/32nd Barrel Hill position as a base, would then turn sharp right and during the second phase of the operation drive south-east down along and between the railway and the road until they were north of Thompson's Post, at which point 2nd/24th would turn right and attack the post itself, while 2nd/48th sent a detachment out to the left to try to reach the sea.

Meanwhile, the men of the 24th Australian Brigade, who had not moved from their positions north of Tel el Eisa since they had opened the Battle of Alamein with their diversionary raids seven nights before, would drive forward to hold enemy attention to the east, while back at the 2nd/32nd positions astride the railway and road, the 2nd/3rd Pioneer Battalion would drive northwards to try to reach the sea some 5,000 yards west of the 2nd/48th detachment, thus forming a pocket in which, theoretically, the Bersaglieri and the remaining men of the German 125th Regiment would be trapped.

The task for the Pioneers – whose first infantry action this would be – was complicated by the direction that they should first of all regard themselves as reserves for the other three battalions engaged in the operation. To quote again from the official Australian history:

> The 2nd/3rd Pioneer Battalion therefore received instructions (aptly described by its historian as the IF plan) that it was to be ready to help the 2nd/32nd Battalion to take its objective if required; if not, then to be ready to help the 2nd/24th take Thompson's Post, if required; if not then to be ready to help the 2nd/48th take the defences from the road to the sea; if not required for any of these things, then to carry out its original role of advancing north from the firm base to the coast.[3]

As one fairly senior officer concerned with this operation remarked reflectively to another with whom he had been a fellow student at Staff College, 'If we had put in this solution to the problem at Camberley, we should certainly have been failed!'[4]

A detailed engineering plan was drawn up regarding the clearance of mines and the gapping of the railway embankment which ran in places some four feet above the desert level, to allow not only the infantry heavy weapons through, but also supporting Valentines from 23rd Armoured Brigade; and the plan for supporting artillery for the various phases of the operation – one of which at least would require a *receding* barrage with the infantry walking towards it from the far side – was of a complication that only a gunnery genius would fully appreciate. Australian, New Zealand and Highland Division artillery regiments were to take part, augmented by field batteries from the armoured divisions and medium guns from XXX Corps, giving a total of 312 field guns and 48 medium guns scheduled to fire some 64,000 rounds; it would undoubtedly be a noisy night, and was being preceded by an afternoon of swelling uproar as fighter-bombers roamed the coastal area searching for targets, while shortly before dusk three squadrons of Bostons and Baltimores arrived overhead and dropped 85 tons of bombs into what by any reckoning was a restricted area.

They successfully cloaked the sounds of the men of the 2nd/32nd moving up to their start line, but these arrived just a few minutes late and had to race forward to catch up with their supporting fire as it crashed down in front of them. They had nearly 2,000 yards to cover to the railway line, but the air-bombardment and the artillery had left few pockets of resistance on their direct route, so the 2nd/32nd were at the railway line on time, having taken prisoner nearly 175 men of the German 1/361st Battalion. Against rather heavier opposition they then crossed the 400 yards to the road and thus reached the further lip of their base, which now formed a saucer of about 500 yards' diameter in which was contained a concrete hut. This had probably originally been a maintenance store but it now housed some German wounded together with three German medical officers and their orderlies who, with a scrupulous adherence to the rules of war which would undoubtedly have been approved by their commander, worked steadily on through the days which followed alongside Australian counterparts who now moved in with them, ministering to the wounded of both sides without discrimination.

Behind the 2nd/32nd came the men of the 2nd/48th and the 2nd/24th followed eventually by those of the Pioneer Battalion, all of whom lost some men mopping up a few posts on the flanks of the original advance, two platoons of the Pioneers surviving a potentially disastrous attack on one post by but a narrow margin. They had attacked independently and from different directions and were only saved from annihilating each other by what their historian delicately calls 'the inimitable profanity of their language'.

Both 2nd/24th on the right and 2nd/48th on the left had swung to the south-east on time, but as 2nd/48th moved up to their second-phase start line they came under machine-gun fire and had to send out a company to quell the post to the north from which it came – and in the darkness and confusion 2nd/24th found themselves apparently alone; but promptly at 0100 the covering barrage crashed down along the line of the advance, and 2nd/24th set out on their 2,250-yard drive to the first objective north of Thompson's Post. As the guns firing their cover were pointing almost straight at them, the advancing infantry had to keep at least 600 yards back from the curtain of fire, and in doing so they thus lost much of its protection. Before very long, both battalions – for the 2nd/48th soon came up on the left – were fighting vicious actions with diminishing strength against stern and intelligent opposition.

On the right the leading company of the 2nd/24th ran into three posts early in the advance which all had to be stormed with grenade and bayonet, after which the company had to swing left to help the reduction of another post which held an 88mm. These actions left gaps through which the follow-up companies ran into devastating machine-gun fire which killed one company commander and wounded the other, then killed or wounded every subaltern or warrant officer who took over, at the same time reducing the already shrunken platoon strengths even further. On two occasions enemy machine-gun posts were silenced by lone men attacking with grenade and Bren-gun after the rest of the platoon had been put out of action – and when at last Colonel Weir brought his headquarters through to consolidate on that focal point north of Thompson's Post, his battalion had been reduced to 84 men!

The ordeal of the 2nd/48th was no easier. They reached their objective after two hours during which time one of the companies had been reduced to five men, including the sole surviving officer who had himself been wounded. Their right hand company had on occasion crossed to help the left hand companies of 2nd/24th and taken part in their ferocious battles, though these had not been lacking on their own sector, where one of their sergeants had also led an attack which put an 88mm. out of action.

The 2nd/48th reserve companies, too, had come forward through the remnants of the attacking companies, and faced the same devastating fire. One young subaltern led a bayonet charge against successive machine-gun and mortar posts which were holding up the whole company, and in doing so took fifteen prisoners – but when he came to lead them back he found that he had only two men beside himself left from his platoon, and when he arrived he found that he now commanded the whole company – of five men. As for the other assaulting company, there is no point in trying to improve upon the official version:

Hammer had heard no word from Robbins, whose company had pressed on close to the objective, because Robbins had been killed and all his platoon commanders and his headquarters men had either been killed or wounded. The company had been caught in open ground as it approached the end of its advance and 16 men were killed assaulting the objective. When Robbins had been killed and the officers commanding the other two platoons severely wounded, Sergeant Kibby took command and organised an attack on the objective with the survivors, perhaps a dozen men, in converging groups. The attackers were forced to ground within 20 yards of it. Kibby jumped up and charged, hurling grenades which silenced the post, but not before he had been caught by the enemy's fire, which cut off the life of a soldier whose gallantry in this and earlier actions at El Alamein could not have been surpassed.[5]

Shortly after Sergeant Kibby's gallant action (for which he was later awarded a posthumous Victoria Cross) Colonel Hammer came up and discovered that his battalion had been reduced to 41 (including himself), and that all his communications had been wrecked. He therefore decided to cross the railway line to try to find Colonel Weir and decide what to do, and while doing this fought a small action on his own during which he took two prisoners and was shot through the face. And on arrival at the 2nd/24th headquarters, he found that Colonel Weir had departed upon the most desperate venture of the entire operation.

Incredible as it may seem now – though probably not so incredible as it did then – the first message Weir had received once his communications had been re-established with headquarters back behind the original lines, was that it had been reported that Thompson's Post was unoccupied – so the proposed barrage to cover his attack had been cancelled, and would Weir please investigate and verify the report, occupying the Post should it prove to be true! And in response to what has been called 'a fearful mandate' Weir himself had set out with fifteen men to find out.

They reached the outer wire and indeed penetrated it without incident, but with great care as all concerned were deeply sceptical about the grounds upon which the operation was being mounted. Inevitably some heavy foot kicked a stone or a rifle clinked on a buckle, challenges rang out and the next moment the night erupted with all the noise and confusion of a close-quarter battle. But it was one in which at least one side had no wish to linger and Weir and his men were back through the wire at very short notice (leaving one man dead and another wounded but with a medical orderly already bringing him out) and right back on the railway line listening to Hammer's message within an hour.

However proud they all might have been of Australia's fighting reputation – and Heaven knows they had themselves contributed enough to it – there was no point in some 120 men, most of whom had been wounded at least once, attempting to hold a position which warranted the presence of at least one whole battalion, and preferably the best part of two; and within a very short time both groups were making their way back towards the 2nd/32nd positions. The survivors of 2nd/48th went straight away – taking with them some 200 German prisoners – but the trials of 2nd/24th were not yet over. On their way back south of the railway line, they went through a minefield planted with aerial bombs and two of them detonated, killing twelve men and wounding sixteen among whom was Colonel Weir. Most of the wounded were stretcher cases, like the greater proportion of the 264 wounded suffered by the two battalions during those few hours of action.

By now the 2nd/32nd men had been able to carry out a certain measure of consolidation. Engineers had cleared wide gaps through the approaches from the south, but their bulldozer and the truck containing much of their explosive had been blown up on mines and they had to tackle the job of gapping the railway embankment with pick and shovel. In this they had been assisted by some of the Pioneer Battalion so the gap was through in four hours and by 0400 the infantry heavy weapons were up and in position, despite the fact that the locality of the gap had been under enemy fire almost from the moment work was commenced.

Even more valuable than the heavy weapons, however, was the arrival of the 289th Battery of 6-pounder anti-tank guns, manned by Rhodesians, who now joined the three troops of the 9th Battery of the 2nd/3rd Anti-tank Regiment. In the dark, the various troops were disposed to cover every segment of the northern semi-circle, but except for those few guns sited south of the embankment, there was little broken ground to provide any cover, and the crews set to to dig themselves in.

The arrival from the east of the exhausted survivors of the 2nd/48th and 2nd/24th (they took position respectively north and south of the railway on the eastern lip of the saucer) at least clarified one point. None of the IFs now obtained and the Pioneers could therefore set out on their prime task – that of attempting to reach the coast to the north – although in this they could apparently no longer have the support of either the battery of anti-tank guns or the platoon of medium machine-guns which they had originally been promised.

This diminution of strength does not seem to have depressed the Pioneers in any way, for they were typical of their breed and independent to the point of bloody-mindedness. They were also extremely tough physically despite the fact that they were, in general, older men than those usually serving in combat formations. One of their company commanders, Major Rosevear, typified in several ways both the maturity and the outlook of the men he commanded: his biographical note states that he was born in Tasmania on June

6th, 1900, and served as a lance-corporal during the First World War with the Australian infantry; but it then adds with studied neutrality, 'When he enlisted under the name of H. G. Brown in 1916 Rosevear gave his year of birth as 1895.'

Now Rosevear and his companions awaited their orders to move out and the bombardment to give them cover, and both arrived at 0430. There was now so little time left for the leading company to advance the required 3,000 yards and then to dig in before dawn that no attention was paid to strict formation or last-minute briefing, and the platoons were off immediately, very close behind their artillery cover.

Captain Owens's company led through quite heavy fire and reached the first objective 1,500 yards in front on time, having collected 30 prisoners and three machine-guns on the way, and then at 0500 Captain Stevens's company went through them and drove on towards the coast. They were prevented from reaching it by their own barrage, which unaccountably ceased advancing some 1,200 yards short of their objective (some of their shells had been dropping short anyway) but maintained the curtain of fire until dawn was obviously near. Abandoning the idea of reaching the sand-dunes, Stevens thereupon ordered his men to dig in and took stock of his situation. It was not promising; his signals officer had been badly wounded so he had no communications either with his commanding officer or with Captain Owens behind him, and his Artillery Forward Observation Officer's truck had been blown up and the officer himself was missing – and as the light grew it revealed that there was little likelihood of reinforcement or supplies getting through to him while daylight lasted.

Like the infantry they had left behind them, the Pioneers were disposed in various positions at the bottom of a saucer with the enemy around three-quarters of the rim – and it was quickly evident that that enemy objected strongly to their presence. Machine-gun and rifle fire harassed the Pioneers' every movement, occasional mortar-bombs exploded in their midst and there was no doubt that soon heavier weapons would be brought to bear, so Captain Stevens – whose command, it is interesting to note, now constituted the right flank of the Eighth Army – sent out a patrol to enfilade the opposition from the flank.

It was not a success. The lieutenant in charge was badly wounded, all the N.C.O.s were hit and half were killed, and at the end only four men got back unscathed; and after another hour's increasingly heavy attack, the entrenched survivors were interested to see a German officer rise to his feet some 200 yards away and walk towards them carrying a white flag. Their continued resistance was, he suggested, a waste of time and of life. The Pioneers had no hope of

relief or reinforcement, and as an alternative to annihilation surrender was surely no dishonour, no reflection upon their courage;
and as he had tried hard to make both his tone and his suggestion
reasonable and persuasive, the Oberleutnant may well have been
upset by his reception. According to the *Official History*, remarks
'not in the best of taste' were addressed to him, the basic tenet of
which was, 'If you want us, come and get us.'

By noon, Stevens's company was completely invested and shortly
afterwards the Germans sent in an infantry attack accompanied by
some light tanks in front of which they put down a smoke-screen –
and as ammunition stocks in the post were all but exhausted, the
remaining pioneers used the smoke as cover for escape. About half
got away, the others being taken prisoner; Stevens himself lay in the
sun all day apparently dead and covered with someone else's blood,
but after dark he crawled some distance, then rose shakily to his feet
and walked back to the main lines. Owens's company in the meantime
had also been overrun, and by mid-afternoon Rosevear's company
was under attack, as was the whole of the Saucer.

But the 2nd/32nd had now received yet another reinforcement
which would add considerably to their powers of resistance. Since
0300 on October 31st, 32 Valentines of 40th R.T.R. under Lieutenant-
Colonel J. L. Finigan had been groping their way carefully up the
'Stake Track' past the Fig Orchard on the western side of Thompson's
Post, and by first light had reached the railway line. The engineers
preceding them had suffered several casualties, they had themselves
lost some tanks on the way up and as they turned westward along the
line they promptly lost another two; Colonel Finigan thereupon
decided to lead his squadrons forward on foot, and it was while doing
so that he met Colonel Hammer, nursing his very painful face wound,
and learned the details of the situation.

Finigan's original orders had been to support Hammer's battalion,
and although he had hoped to find them more to the east than they
were, he saw no reason to adjust those orders in any way. Bringing
his tanks on across the railway line, he deployed them to the west of
the 2nd/48th positions, his northern flank across the road – and as the
light was growing fast, his men now had time and opportunity to
assess their situation.

This, one of their number had no hesitation in describing as
'distinctly dodgy'. The Valentines were in a salient overlooked on
three sides by enemy forces on higher ground, and if in the immediate
neighbourhood there were many doubtless indomitable friends, these
had the advantage that they were able to dig both themselves and
their guns into some sort of shelter. The tank crews, on the other
hand, had no choice if they wished to defend themselves but to sit in
their thinly armoured vehicles standing some seven and a half feet

above ground, of which the highest nearby rise was the four-foot railway embankment behind them.

By the time it was full daylight it was quite obvious that anyone within 3,000 yards who cared to glance in their direction could not fail to see them, and one person who did so promptly reported the fact to Rommel, adding that in standing where they did the Valentines effectively cut off the German troops in Thompson's Post and their Bersaglieri comrades.

Rommel by this time had long abandoned any faint hope he might once have held of winning the battle outright, and was now even suspecting that his idea of holding the enemy in position until they ran out of energy and determination was also doomed to disappointment. In order to preserve some part of his army and the lives of the devoted men he had led for so long, he had therefore ordered a reconnaissance of the Fuka positions some seventy miles back, and been quite encouraged when reports told of the possibility of strong defences in the north, and ground so broken in the south on the edge of the Qattara Depression that no attacking armoured force could penetrate there.

But this still left him with the almost insuperable problems of the movement back itself, for there was hardly enough fuel to move his armoured divisions that far, let alone for transport to lift the non-motorised formations who might therefore have to be sacrificed. Even before those problems were faced, however, there would be the equally intransigent task of disengaging his most valuable troops from the battle in which they were already deeply committed, without letting enemy forces flood through and overwhelm the entire Panzer-armee, mobile and non-mobile units alike.

Air support in far greater strength than was available at the moment would be required in any circumstances, and especially in the face of the present almost complete domination of the skies by the enemy – but when applied to, Kesselring could hold out little or no hope for even the smallest increase. Already he was being pressed to release some of the Luftwaffe formations for service on the Russian Front in an apparently important battle raging around Stalingrad, and there was even doubt that the morale of the Luftwaffe crews here in the desert could stand much more of the strain of this continual conflict. That Italian pilots sometimes failed to press home attacks had long been accepted, but during the last few days reports had come to him of Stuka pilots jettisoning their bombs indiscriminately over friend and foe alike – and nowhere near their targets – immediately Hurricanes or Tomahawks appeared.

Morale among even his trusty soldiers was sagging, too. Under the devastating artillery barrages which fell upon every assembly of Axis troops, counter-attack after counter-attack had broken up – sometimes before they had even begun to advance – and an ominous account of over a hundred infantrymen of 15th Panzer Division giving themselves up to British patrols in the central area told its own story. Even the 21st Panzer Division under their new commander, Generalleutnant von Randow, were showing signs of depression – not all that surprisingly in view of the fact that every day since their arrival in the north they had been bombed at almost hourly intervals by squadrons of eighteen British or South African bombers, flying in those imperturbable formations already dubbed 'Party Rally raids' by the cynical recipients.

But 21st Panzer Division still constituted the most reliable armoured formation at his disposal, and during the night of October 28th/29th he had ordered their withdrawal from the line to give him some sort of mobile reserve, to be replaced at the front by the now battered and attenuated remains of the Trieste Motorised Division with their 34 outdated M13s. As for the only other Italian division in which he had much faith – the Ariete – they were all back in the south and he only hoped that with the support of the Ramcke Brigade and the Folgores they would be able to hold out if Montgomery decided, after all, to mount a major assault down there.

Not that this was likely. Captured British documents and the obvious concentration of Eighth Army strength in the north supported his growing conviction that their commander intended to drive along the narrow coastal strip of Egypt, in the belief that the use of a properly laid road would compensate for the restricted width of the advance and the lack of space for wide manoeuvre – at which, after all, the British were not particularly adept. His own concentration of 90th Light Division in the north with their headquarters near Sidi Abd el Rahman, together with those units of Lungershausen's 164th Division which were still in their pre-battle positions, was the best counter to that design, and only time would show if the formations were strong enough to withstand the assault when it came, or nimble enough to extricate themselves if and when it became obvious that they were not.

At least there had been no casualties among the topmost commanders – other than Stumme. General Ritter von Thoma still commanded the Afrika Korps with cold efficiency and Bayerlein had returned from leave on the morning of October 29th and been immediately despatched to join him; von Randow with the 21st, von Vaerst with the 15th and Graf von Sponek with the 90th Light were all still alive and active, and instantly responsive to his demands. If only the same could be said of the Italians!

Generale Barbasetti had arrived at Rommel's headquarters on October 29th – in place of Maresciallo Cavallero who had been, fortunately for him, detained in Rome – and received the full blast of Rommel's anger, exacerbated at that particular moment by the arrival of the news of the loss of the *Louisiano*. Where were all the supplies that Rommel had been repeatedly promised? Where was the ammunition, the guns, the trucks and the reinforcements which weeks ago Il Duce had agreed were necessary and which Rommel had been almost pleading for ever since his return?

Above all, where was the fuel? And it was not the slightest good assuring him that it was on its way in heavily armoured Italian cruisers to Benghasi, as it would take too long to reach him from there and too much of it would be burned up by the transport bringing it.

Tobruk was the port to which all supplies must now be directed if they were to be of the slightest use, and if this entailed the Italian Navy's venturing into danger from Royal Air Force or Royal Navy torpedoes, it was no more than that in which the Panzerarmee had stood for months; in any case facing danger was what naval craft were built and bought for!

The tirade went on for some time and it was a discomfited, indeed outraged, Generale Barbasetti who eventually departed with whatever dignity was left to him, unaware that he was, in fact, lucky to get away when he did. Later that day as Rommel was conferring with Westphal and others of his staff, they were all suddenly electrified by a message to the effect that two British divisions had made their way through the Qattara Depression, scaled the sides and were now sixty miles south of Mersa Matruh and moving rapidly north-west! Air patrols were sent out, one of the Fascist reserve divisions alerted and the relief of 21st Panzer Division by Trieste delayed – until the following morning (October 30th) when, to quote Rommel's words, ' . . . we discovered that the whole story, which had come to us from Comando Supremo, was a pure invention.'

Italian popularity suffered even further diminution later that morning, first with the news that Trieste were now apparently too weak in numbers to take over all the 21st Panzer Division positions so that one German infantry battalion must stay where they were, and then that the Littorio Division grouped with the 15th Panzer Division had only 23 tanks to contribute to the mobile reserve which Rommel was endeavouring to put together.

This last exercise in itself was revealing a number of disturbing factors, such as that the entire Afrika Korps could muster fewer than a hundred panzers – including several Mark IIs – and now, as Rommel pointed out to Kesselring who arrived for a visit during the afternoon, those happy, carefree days when recovery teams could scavenge the battlefield for replacements or when numbers could be maintained with captured British tanks were but a dim memory.

The only good news during that day (October 30th) was that 600 tons of fuel had, after all, arrived at Tobruk (enough for twenty-four hours) but even this was dampened by reports that the R.A.F. were shooting up everything that moved along the coast road, so the petrol still might not arrive at the front.

So plans for that withdrawal must at least be drawn up and warning orders issued. Perhaps an opportunity would arise to whip the infantry out of the line under cover of darkness, load them into whatever transport could be found and race them back to the Fuka line with the panzer formations covering them, fighting a delaying action to give the infantry as much time as possible to dig themselves in. It was a slim hope, but perhaps the Gods of War would relent, perhaps the British were more tired than they appeared.

In the meantime, that mobile reserve must be formed – and it was while more attempts were being made to withdraw panzers from the line and replace them with infantry during the night of October 30th/31st that once again the massed British artillery in the north erupted, its opening salvo crashing down on positions held by remnants of the 1st/361st Battalion and almost annihilating them. Shortly afterwards all contact with them was lost as was that with one of the Italian artillery positions nearby, and from then on the night was filled with noise and fire from which very little useful – or even intelligible – information emerged until dawn, when a detached section of the 361st Grenadier Regiment reported not only the presence of enemy infantry patrols right up near the coast, but also a force of thirty heavy tanks between the railway and the road.

Rommel had, of course, been conscious all the time of the exposed position of the troops out in the Tel el Eisa salient, but had considered their presence there a positive check to enemy plans so long as they could be supplied and, if necessary, reinforced. Now it looked as though he might have left them there too long, so driving immediately to Sidi Abd el Rahman he set up a command post from which a relieving operation could be mounted, and sent for von Thoma to come up and form a battlegroup from elements of both 21st Panzer and 90th Light Divisions, augmented by some of Panzer-armee's mobile artillery.

Apparently the Afrika Korps staff found this direction almost incomprehensible, as it meant that von Thoma would be abandoning a central position commanding large forces in order to command small forces on the flank – though not so incomprehensible as did von Thoma himself when he arrived. Rommel had already set up the first attempt to get through to Thompson's Post, and he ignored von Thoma's presence and continued to direct the assault himself; by 1100 the panzers, artillery and infantry were assembling, the battalion commanders issuing their orders – and when at 1105 bombers arrived overhead and the British artillery opened fire yet again, it took the

presence of Rommel to hold the group together and get it moving
down towards its objective.

As they did so, they could see the British tanks also begin moving –
towards them to form a shield between the railway embankment and
the road. Perhaps they were even heavier tanks than they looked.

They were, of course, still the Valentines – now committing themselves to a battle in which their foes could destroy them at anything
up to 1,200 yards whilst their own puny 2-pounders could do little
until the panzers were within four hundred, and then only if they hit
the vulnerable sides.

But the Australian infantry and the Rhodesian anti-tank gunners
were with them and they themselves were, after all, infantry support
tanks; no matter what the odds, they would not desert their friends,
and in any case everyone in the Saucer had faith in both the main
artillery behind them and in the R.A.F. – a faith in which they were
not to be disappointed. The first assault at about 1130 consisted of
fifteen panzers which rolled down upon them between the road and
the railway with an infantry escort north of the road, but before it
approached within hitting distance a flight of Bostons dropped a load
of bombs on the panzers, and artillery had thoroughly dispersed the
infantry.

But some of the panzers swung up to the north and through the
remains of the 2nd/3rd Pioneer positions, then down again against
the main defence, and soon the Valentines were being driven back
towards the embankment. Two of the Rhodesian anti-tank guns were
wrecked, and with the panzers driving implacably down between the
smoking remains, the hard-pressed Valentine crews tried to beat
them by movement – tempting the panzers forward towards one
troop of Valentines while another manoeuvred to catch them from
the flank. They scored some successes that way but at a dreadful
price, and as the afternoon wore on the smoke from burning
Valentines drifted over the confusion to mix with the blown sand and
the heat-haze, to cut visibility drastically.

This could have been a saving factor for the Valentines had they
wished to take advantage of it, but while they had ammunition and
their guns could fire it they had to stay and wreak what damage they
could – and there were other targets besides the seemingly invulnerable panzers. An 88mm. gun and its trailer were wrecked and
at least one half-tracked vehicle set alight – and then somewhat to
the defenders' astonishment, they saw that the attack was faltering,
the panzers drawing back.

Perhaps they had run out of ammunition, perhaps they had been
unprepared for such violent opposition, but as they went the German
battlegroup left behind them in the Saucer four wrecked panzers and

one burning furiously, the 88mm. gun and the remains of several lighter vehicles; but 21 of the Valentines had been knocked out including several which had brewed, and 44 crew members were dead. This was a heavy casualty rate for such a small armoured force, and the survivors were glad to receive orders to withdraw to the south of the railway line as daylight faded, though some of them were unable immediately to move even that far. Radiators and fuel tanks had been ruptured by hits, batteries cracked and the electrolite drained away, so fewer than ten Valentines were in the end to make the journey – but those that did found that they had that day earned the deepest respect and admiration of the Australians who had been watching them. 'The courage of these men', wrote the historian of the 2nd/48th Battalion in a judgment made by men who knew their subject, 'made their action one of the most magnificent of the war.'

The battle in the Saucer, however, was by no means over. Reports reaching General Morshead that day (October 31st) had revealed to him the losses sustained by the battalions of 26th Brigade during the last eighteen hours, and he decided that they must be relieved by the two battalions of the 24th Brigade which had seen so little action since the first night of the battle (the third battalion was the 2nd/32nd which could have been judged lately to have seen enough for the whole brigade). So during the night of October 31st/November 1st, Brigadier Godfrey brought his fresh battalions around and fed them up into the forward positions from which the exhausted survivors of 2nd/24th and 2nd/48th were withdrawn, thus considerably increasing the strength to support their brothers in the 2nd/32nd and their new-found Rhodesian friends.

They were in position by dawn to watch first of all an air battle in which British and American fighters shot down seven Stukas and chased away the remainder of a large group sent over to bomb them, then the regular shelling of yet another battlegroup forming up now under command of von Thoma and Bayerlein to mount the first of the day's attempts to relieve Thompson's Post. It came in just after midday – a battalion attack supported by panzers and sustained artillery cover which included at least eight 88mm. guns firing air-bursts above Australian positions – but was beaten off at the cost of twelve of the anti-tank guns which had been an especial target of the German attack.

Another assault came in at 1525, and this one developed into an almost continuous mêlée which showed no sign of flagging as the afternoon wore on, despite the solid and unyielding defence against which the attackers were hurling themselves. However, some of the panzers swung well north and through the dunes to make contact with Thompson's Post, and many were seen closing down on its northern side just about the time when a major disaster struck the men in the

Saucer. All day long the German artillery had been shelling their positions at intervals, and in the early evening a lucky shell hit the command headquarters, killing Brigadier Godfrey and three of his staff and severely wounding two others.

The brigade major took charge, but pressure from the north had been such that now there were no Australians across the road, and with the loss of the anti-tank guns the safest place for the bulk of the infantry was now obviously south of the embankment – and with their withdrawal there, the German corridor to Tel el Eisa was strengthened and the way opened for the withdrawal of the Axis troops in the salient.

This was still an idea to which Rommel was unresponsive. During October 31st both von Thoma and Bayerlein had suggested that the troops in the salient should be warned to ready themselves for immediate evacuation if and when the enemy blocking force were swept aside, but Rommel had then vetoed the idea, as so hasty a withdrawal would probably mean a loss of invaluable heavy weapons; anyway, a German presence at Thompson's Post could still prove a vexatious thorn in the enemy's side if it could be maintained.

But he had been away from the Sidi Abd el Rahman front checking on the situation further south (where he later recorded that waves of enemy aircraft, each of eighteen or twenty planes, had bombed Axis positions thirty-four times in less than eight hours) and on his return to the north on the afternoon of November 1st he went to see for himself the extent of the carnage wrought on that small battlefield across the road and railway line.

'Seven wrecked tanks lay around "The Hut" alone, and farther on we could see another 30 or 40 destroyed British armoured vehicles,'[6] he wrote, but he nevertheless listened without comment to one piece of von Thoma's report. The colonel of the battalion at Thompson's Post had made his way back to Sidi Abd el Rahman during the preceding night, and the impression he had left with Bayerlein was that although he and his men would stay there if so directed, there were not half so many of them now as there had been when the battle opened and most of the survivors had been wounded at least once; moreover the bulk of the defences had already been smashed by artillery fire.

Rommel at that particular time did not give specific orders regarding withdrawal, but at least he did not repeat his flat rejection of the previous day. In any case, he had other matters to consider. The supply situation was as bad as ever, and if there had been a temporary alleviation regarding fuel, ammunition was now running crucially short especially for the anti-tank guns. Only forty tons had arrived since the opening of the battle and, in contrast to the extravagance shown by the British, both Italian and German gunners had to exercise the shrewdest economy. Concentrated fire was a thing of the past, harassing fire the best which could be afforded.

But if supplies were not getting through, messages were still arriving from Rome:

> For Field Marshal Rommel
>
> The Duce authorises me to convey to you his deep appreciation of the successful counter-attack led personally by you. The Duce also conveys to you his complete confidence that the battle now in progress will be brought to a successful conclusion under your command.
>
> Ugo Cavallero[7]

As there were indications that such easy optimism was just as prevalent at the Führer's headquarters, Il Duce's platitudes did nothing to soothe Rommel's temper or relieve his anxieties. These were mounting in the light of reports and assessments submitted by his intelligence staffs, who were becoming increasingly alarmed by indications that the enemy were grouping for yet another gigantic onslaught upon what had now become an attenuated and threadbare line of defences. British troops were massing again just to the south of the known Australian positions, and it seemed that thorough preparations for a devastating blow there had been taking place for some time.

In this the staffs were correct, though they were not to know of the diplomatic manoeuvrings which had been necessary before Eighth Army plans could take the shape they did, nor the political storm the course of the battle had been causing in the British camp during the last few days.

If Brigadier de Guingand's fortitude had been tested in the early morning of October 25th by the crisis which entailed the awakening of his chief, October 29th had called upon all his reserves of loyalty, imagination, tact and charm. It had been fortunate that he was so well-endowed with all of them.

Quite early in the morning the intelligence staff at Army H.Q. had collected from both field sources and Ultra a significant body of evidence to the effect that Rommel was concentrating 90th Light Division and a considerable proportion of his remaining armour opposite the Australian section of the front. It looked indeed to some of them as though he were abandoning his policy of 'corseting' the Italians with his German troops, and instead was withdrawing the latter and packing them solidly up into the coastal sector – directly in front of the proposed drive by the newly assembled forces under General Freyberg; and it struck several of them that an adjustment of direction would not only increase the chances of success, but also promise greater results.

If Freyberg's drive was directed more to the south than was currently planned, and hit the line of junction between the regrouping Italian and German forces, and especially if its main assault fell most heavily upon the Italians just south of that junction, it might break through completely and thus, if the X Corps armour followed up quickly and strongly enough, open up an opportunity for first pressing the Germans against the coast and then cutting them off with a short northward drive to the sea.

This was the suggestion put by de Guingand to Montgomery at the first morning conference on October 29th, and it was with some disappointment that afterwards he had to report to his colleagues, 'No, he won't have it' – a decision which added to growing worries among some of them that the battle was not going according to plan.

They were not the only ones either, for in both Cairo and Whitehall anxious eyes had been watching every development, and not always with the rocklike confidence of the man in charge. For Mr Churchill especially, the strain of leading his country for two and a half years of perhaps the greatest danger she had ever faced now reached its climax, for he realised quite clearly that if the attack at Alamein should fail his own career would be over and he would be toppled from power – which would then pass to others who would surely prove in the end to be lesser mortals than himself. Not only would his own life be reduced to waste and ashes, but the hardship and perils which his beloved country had faced since 1940 would be extended far into the future. The weight of the world sat on the Prime Minister's shoulders during that first week of Alamein, and on the morning of October 29th seemed likely to crush him, for news had arrived that despite Montgomery's assurance that Eighth Army would break through the enemy defences in less than a fortnight, here he was already *withdrawing whole divisions from the battle*!

The storm burst over Sir Alan Brooke's head early that morning. What was his protégé Montgomery doing, allowing the battle to peter out? Why was he taking troops out of the battle? Why did he say he would break out seven days after the break-in if he only intended to fight in a half-hearted manner?

'Haven't we got a single general who can win even one battle?' Churchill cried, and for a moment Sir Alan thought he was going to hit him.

The storm slackened under Sir Alan's stout defence of Montgomery's actions to date, but it flared up again at a Chiefs of Staff meeting in the afternoon and needed the cool common sense of the South African Field Marshal Smuts to calm the atmosphere; but later Brooke recorded that although during the conference he had maintained an exterior of complete confidence, he was by no means unworried himself. 'I had told them what I thought Monty must be doing . . . but there was just that possibility that I was wrong and Monty was beat.'[8]

If doubts existed at such a level, it was hardly surprising that questions were being raised much nearer the scene of action, where physical danger would be present if the Eighth Army collapsed – and it was in connection with these that de Guingand's resources were again tested.

When General Alexander arrived for the scheduled morning conference and report, he was accompanied this time not only by his own Chief of Staff, Lieutenant-General Richard McCreery, but also by the Minister of State in Egypt, Richard Casey; and the last-named bore with him a cable from Mr Churchill pointing out the imminence of the landings in North Africa, and the desirability of an obvious, overwhelming *and early* victory at Alamein in order to encourage the French in Morocco and Algeria to throw in their lot with the Anglo-Americans.

In response, Montgomery described the situation and his plans, and, according to de Guingand, 'radiated confidence'; but afterwards Casey drew de Guingand aside and asked him if he really was happy about the way things were going. According to the only witness present at that time, the Chief of Intelligence, Colonel Williams, Casey seemed unconvinced by de Guingand's protestations of confidence, and at one point mumbled something about cabling Churchill to warn him that bad news might be on its way – at which de Guingand exploded in a spectacular (and possibly feigned) burst of rage.

'For God's sake don't!' he exclaimed, adding, 'If you do, I'll see you're drummed out of political life!' – although what effect a soldier of de Guingand's standing at that time could have had on the position of a career diplomat – who in any case was not in political life as such – only de Guingand himself could have imagined. But it would seem that his momentary display of conviction had been enough to muzzle Casey for no such cable was ever sent, and after the Minister of State had left de Guingand could once again devote himself to the sphere of his military influence, especially to the matter of the forthcoming operation about which he and his colleagues still retained their early morning opinions.

They had learned shortly before the conference that in these opinions they had the agreement of General McCreery, who announced that he would certainly advocate in the strongest terms that General Freyberg's assault should not be delivered along the coast, but down in the area just north of Kidney Ridge; and de Guingand's diplomacy was once more called into action. Montgomery disliked McCreery (not least, one suspects, as the latter was such a strong supporter and friend of General Lumsden) and de Guingand knew

25 One of the Shermans that tipped the balance

26–7 Some of the men who commanded the tanks (Major-General Alec Gatehouse
on the right) . . . not always to the satisfaction of the Army Commander

28–9 Throughout the battle it was always the infantry who had to take – and
       hold – the ground

that pressure from that particular quarter would thus be immediately counter-productive.

'I will go and talk to Monty about it again – don't you, for goodness' sake!' he pleaded. 'If one can persuade him it's his own idea . . . '

And although the subject was brought up during the conference to be brushed aside once again by Montgomery, de Guingand went back to see his chief after Alexander's party had left. How he put the case, whether or not he did manage to make Montgomery believe that it was all his own idea, it is now impossible to say – but when de Guingand emerged he did so with Montgomery's full agreement that the axis of Freyberg's attack would now lie along an extension of the original Australian sector's northern boundary, and not along the coast road. The sigh of relief which went up at Army H.Q. was echoed later by Bernard Freyberg himself.

'That's what I wanted to do originally,' he grunted; and promptly asked for a lot more tanks to be put under his command. It was a request he was frequently to make and almost as frequently to have refused, but the new scope of this operation undoubtedly entailed much more armoured participation, so much of the rest of the day was occupied by drawing up plans in more detail and to a greater scale than before. It seems that this was done to the Army Commander's satisfaction, for his diary entry for that night ends with the passage:

> The Armd Car Regts will be launched right into open country to operate for four days against the enemy supply routes.
>
> The two Armoured Divisions will engage and destroy the DAK.
>
> This, in effect, is a hard blow with my right, followed the next night with a knock-out blow with my left. The blow on night 31 Oct/1 Nov will be supported by some 350 guns firing about 400 rounds a gun.
>
> I have given the name 'SUPERCHARGE' to the operation.[9]

The assault opened in fact at 0105 on November 2nd, having been postponed for twenty-four hours at General Freyberg's request after he had observed how exhausted the attacking infantry were by the time they had arrived in their assembly areas. The Geordies of 151st Brigade, for instance, had been brought up from south of Ruweisat Ridge but failed to reach their bivouac area at Makh Khad on time, owing first to the difficulties of moving across almost unmapped desert which was nevertheless congested with both traffic and static military units, and secondly by what the New Zealand *Official History* calls 'the inertia of several bodies of 10 Corps who resisted being shifted to other areas'.

In the end, strong measures had to be taken at a high level to get these formations to move at all, for X Corps hubris was undimmed despite the events of the last few days and they still reckoned they were something of a law unto themselves. Even the squadrons of Pip Roberts's 22nd Armoured Brigade had not been made particularly welcome when they came up from XIII Corps's area, and now they waited in isolation around Imayid Station some miles east of El Alamein itself.

But during the extra period, granted somewhat reluctantly by General Montgomery, the units did get themselves sorted out and the infantry were waiting in their concentration areas on time. The 151st Brigade with the 28th New Zealand Battalion of Maoris attached

Map 27 *Supercharge*, November 1st–2nd

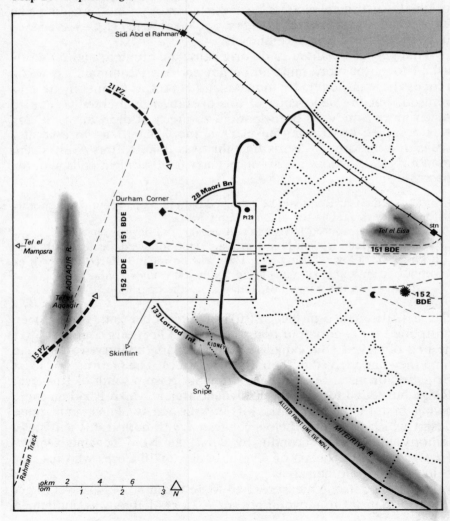

(they were to hold the first section of the northern flank of the advance), the minefield task force behind and following them the 44 Valentines of 8th R.T.R. were all grouped just south of Tel el Eisa, while to their south at the roots of the Two-bar and Square tracks were the Scots of 152nd Brigade, with 5th Seaforths on the brigade right, 5th Camerons on the left and 2nd Seaforths following to cover the south-western corner of the salient. The Royal Sussex Battalions of 133rd Lorried Infantry Brigade would follow to fulfil the same duties in the south as the Maoris in the north, and 38 Valentines of 50th R.T.R. would provide immediate armoured support.

In the plan of attack there was some similarity between *Supercharge* and the Australian section of *Lightfoot*, in that the shape of the advance was a rectangle some 4,000 yards wide and nearly 6,000 yards long which would take the assault from a line running south from just east of Point 29 along the line of the present defences towards Kidney, westwards to a line of similar length with its northern end almost on the Rahman Track. As with *Lightfoot* the advance would be covered by a powerful artillery barrage, this time from 296 field guns and 48 medium guns firing altogether some 54,000 rounds including, in specific places and at specific times, smoke rounds as direction indicators and tracer shells to demarcate brigade boundaries.

The minefield task forces were not so large as those for *Lightfoot*, as it was believed that this advance would not face such wide and concentrated mine-marshes, but what was expected was a scattering of those random, isolated patches of mines which had proved so troublesome before, so Scorpions were taking part in the advance.

Behind the infantry would follow first the 72 Shermans and Grants and 49 Crusaders of John Currie's 9th Armoured Brigade – still regarded by Freyberg as the only trustworthy armour in Eighth Army – then the 150 Shermans and Grants and 110 Crusaders of the two brigades – 2nd and 8th – of the 1st Armoured Division, still under General Briggs. When the armour had broken out through the advanced infantry positions, crossed the Rahman Track and reached the ridge north of Tel el Aqqaqir, it would all come under command of X Corps now concentrated on 'ground of its own choosing', and there General Lumsden would direct the armoured battle in which all that remained of 15th and 21st Panzer Divisions and of Ariete and Littorio would be destroyed.

In the meantime, armoured cars of the Royal Dragoons, the 12th Lancers and the 4th/6th South African Armoured Car Regiment would endeavour to break out through the northern or southern flanks of the advance, circle around well to the west of Tel el Aqqaqir and cause as much chaos and confusion in the Axis rear areas as possible.

As throughout the entire battle so far, the Royal Air Force and the South African Air Force opened the action and gave their unstinted support to their earthbound colleagues. During the evening of November 1st, Wellingtons with Albacores from the Fleet Air Arm bombed all known targets from Tel el Aqqaqir up to Sidi Abd el Rahman and westwards as far as El Daba, setting fire to several ammunition and supply dumps and thoroughly wrecking the Afrika Korps communications system.

On the ground, the infantry moved up to the line of cairns which marked the start line (General Wimberley was making sure that his Jocks at least would not suffer the confusion regarding position that had marred *Lightfoot*, and the 151st Brigade followed suit), Durhams shivering in their khaki drill but liberally coated with the fine pale dust through which they had marched, the Scots warmer in battle-dress and again wearing the St Andrew's Cross in white flannelette across their small-packs. Behind them the gunners waited, while as a safety precaution the two battalions of the 6th New Zealand Brigade who had been holding the line through which the attack would be launched, came quietly back; the opening barrage would fall very close to their recent positions.

At 0055 the infantry stepped over their tapes and walked forward, at 0105 the guns opened with yet another shattering bombardment with one shell bursting every twelve yards along the 4,000-yard line; dust and smoke plumed up in the now-familiar choking clouds, and as the men moved into them the guns lifted forward another hundred yards and from along the southern half of the assault came the high, piercing-sweet notes of the bag-pipes.

The Maoris on the extreme right flank met opposition almost from the start, the strongpoint just in front of Point 29 which was their prime objective proving strong indeed. One Maori company was practically wiped out in the initial assault, but the company on its left flank reached their objectives on time and dug in to form a base from which the survivors of the first company could be supported. This was as well, for the line of the Maori objectives had been slightly north of the path of the barrage and there were several enemy posts to be subdued by bayonet and bomb before the root of the northern flank of *Supercharge* would be securely linked to the Australians to the north.

South of the Maoris, the two assault companies of the 8th Durham Light Infantry broke quickly through a line of enemy posts to overrun a German tank recovery park and a medical dressing station, both occupied by men shocked almost to the edge of hysteria by the shelling. The first objective was reached on time but with the loss of about a hundred men and several of their officers, so the reserve company went through to reach the final objective (the corner near the Rahman Track) at about 0400, having collected nearly fifty prisoners en route. For the moment, however, they were out of contact with everyone as their wireless link had been destroyed, but the survivors of the other companies gradually came up, then the battalion heavy weapons, then New Zealand anti-tank and machine-gun platoons, and by dawn the 8th Durhams, though low in strength, were well established on their objectives.

On their right the 6th Durham Light Infantry, who had followed some 500 yards behind the 8th, met little opposition until they had passed the area in which the Maoris were fighting so hard, then came under heavy machine-gun fire from the north which it took a whole company to quell. But the other companies swung right to form a battalion front facing north between the corner of the salient and the intended positions of the Maoris though with a gap still between them, and again, anti-tank guns and heavy machine-guns quickly arrived. By dawn the Durham corner of the salient was secure.

On the left of the Durham Brigade sector, the 9th Durhams had met only a line of dug-in tanks and gun positions during the second half of their advance, and even these were not defended with great resolution as the barrage had been as effective here as on the right. They were on their final objective by 0400 and in touch with their brothers of the 8th, their heavy weapons and support anti-tank guns with them well before dawn. The Durham Brigade had therefore reached all their objectives on time at a cost to themselves of some 350 killed, wounded and missing, having taken the same number of prisoners who upon examination proved to be mostly from the Littorio and Trento Divisions, with a sprinkling from the 115th Panzergrenadier Regiment.

On the Durhams' left, the advance of the Scotsmen of 152nd Brigade had gone so like a drill that a fair picture of the night's proceedings can be gained from the signals sent by the brigade commander, George Murray, to General Freyberg:

0148   We are in touch with both battalions and everything appears to be going smoothly.

0218   There is light shelling and moderate machine-gun fire on our front. We have taken some prisoners, a mixture of Italians and Germans. Everything appears to be going according to plan.

0235   Newly laid minefield discovered.

0359   On our left flank our tanks are engaging enemy tanks.

0417   Both battalions have reached objective and are again in action with enemy tanks. Artillery concentration 'Roxbrough' called for and fired.

0525   Enemy tanks are melting away and battalions are getting supporting arms up. One Italian tank captured intact.

0535   Reorganisation of final objective is proceeding and battalions are linking up. Right gap is through and left will be open as soon as small minefield is cleared. Our casualties will not exceed 40 per battalion.[10]

Most of the Scots casualties had been suffered during assaults on dug-in tanks, but even from these little real resistance had been experienced while the few infantry posts they had encountered – Italian or German – had been surrendered by men totally shattered by the storm of fire which had passed over them. Whatever the co-ordination between other arms, that between infantry and gunners had now reached a state of near-perfection.

Between infantry and its immediate supporting armour co-ordination was good, too. The Valentines had in places been held up by uncleared minefields, and one troop of the 8th R.T.R. had missed a marked route and was badly delayed as a result, but the tank crews were determined to get through to their friends' support and by dawn most of them had done so. On the Jocks' left flank, enemy tanks had been reported holding up the formation of the south-facing front by the 2nd Seaforths, but they seemed to 'melt away' when both guns and Valentines came quickly into action, and well on time the Seaforths had made contact with the 2nd Royal Sussex on their left, whose line in turn was continued by the 5th Royal Sussex back to the original Oxalic Line where it was now held by the 5th/7th Gordons.

XXX Corps infantry had undoubtedly completed all its primary tasks in *Supercharge* well on time, and now it was up to the armour. As the first assault armour (as opposed to the support Valentines) due to come through was that of John Currie's 9th Armoured Brigade, no one doubted that it would be with them as quickly as determination, devotion and inspiring leadership could arrange.

It was going to need all of those qualities. Although orders had made it plain that 9th Armoured Brigade were to have priority in all tank replacements, it seems that as a result of the haste and strain of battle conditions more effort had gone into providing quantity than quality. Of the 123 tanks of various marks mustered that night, few were new, and the Crusaders issued to the Royal Wiltshire Yeomanry to replace their losses of that first night on Miteiriya Ridge were 'in a deplorable state. Nothing fitted. Nothing worked. Guns, compasses and radios were all faulty.'[11]

John Currie's brigade was therefore not in such a state as would fill their commander's breast with pride and hope – except perhaps with regard to the morale of his men, and here he faced an even more 'fearful mandate' than that accepted by Colonel Weir north of Thompson's Post. At the briefing conference held by General Freyberg on November 1st, the task for 9th Armoured Brigade – to advance past the infantry objective, break through the enemy defences before and immediately beyond the Rahman Track and then hold open the gap against enemy counter-attacks until the heavy brigades of the 1st Armoured Division had gone through – was so obviously one of difficulty and danger that when Currie's time came to make comment, he rather diffidently suggested that by the end of the day his brigade might well have suffered 50 per cent casualties.

To this Freyberg had replied with studied nonchalance, 'Perhaps more than that. The Army Commander says that he is prepared to accept a hundred per cent.'[12]

And in the dead silence which followed this pronouncement, those who were not thanking God they were not standing in Currie's shoes wondered how far down his command he would allow the fiat to percolate.

In the event he told his regimental commanders and these passed it on to most of their squadron commanders, but it would seem that the rest of the brigade as they waited in their assembly area were accepting the action to come as just another in which they would undoubtedly be the 'sharp end' of the assault, and suffer accordingly; but they had been there before, and not very long ago.

The problem for the moment was to get there, for in addition to the general dilapidation of their tanks and armament, the darkness of the night was immeasurably increased by the clouds of dust churned up by every movement, far worse in their estimation than ever before. Traffic and exploding shells, to say nothing of the thousands of marching feet, had by now pulverised the surface of the desert all the way from Alamein Station where by 1900 on November 1st they were forming up, to the proposed new infantry line nearly fifteen miles to the west; dust at least a foot thick carpeted the route the whole way, and that night there was a head wind.

Except for the leading vehicles in each column, therefore, the three regimental groups were condemned to a long journey in choking fog with very limited visibility. The leading group consisting of the 3rd Hussars with 33 tanks (but whose column including support infantry, anti-tank gunners and supply trucks totalled nearly 300 vehicles) made their way along the Sun track between the road and the railway as far as the Diamond track, which they joined to pass south of Tel el Eisa and into the main approaches to the battle zone. They were followed along Sun by the 44 tanks of the Royal Wiltshire Yeomanry together with the Brigade Tactical Headquarters and the head-quarters of the support group and the New Zealand Divisional Cavalry, and these in due course turned off along the Boomerang track, while to the south the Warwickshire Yeomanry column of about 120 vehicles including 46 tanks travelled on their own along the Moon track.

Extensions to all these main (and now battered) tracks were being hurriedly cleared by the engineers in the new *Supercharge* salient, but long before they reached them the 9th Armoured Brigade were in trouble. Collisions in the dark between tanks and lorries usually led to the soft-skinned vehicle being damaged even if both had been crawling along at snail-pace, and however clean the filters were when the vehicles started out, the dust was so thick that it soon choked them and throttled the engines. By the time the regimental groups were moving into the battle area quite a number of their support vehicles were already trailing far behind.

Across the infantry start line and into the salient, matters, of course, worsened. By now the Axis gunners had recovered from the first shock of attack and when necessary resited their guns, and their harassing fire was dropping into the rear areas through which 9th Armoured were making their way – adding to the deafening effect of the British barrage, still roaring over their heads to drop in front of the advancing infantry. The leading tanks of all three regimental groups were passing their first objective by 0330 (at which time both infantry brigades had still about 1,000 yards to go to their final objective) but behind them they were already leaving the wrecks of some of their tanks and many of their support guns or trucks. The Hussars had lost six of their tanks, and their anti-tank support had become so disorganised by the shelling that they had had to pull off the route and thus drop well behind.

The Wiltshires ran into scattered mines which blew the tracks off two of their Crusaders and delayed them until a Scorpion was brought up by the engineers to ease their progress, and A Squadron of the Warwickshires missed their way as a result of the destruction of guiding lamps, found themselves in a blind end entirely closed by mines and obviously moving in the wrong direction, so they had carefully to turn around and make their way back to the main stream, followed in turn by the other squadrons, whose members became increasingly sarcastic as time went by.

But nothing was allowed to halt the main advance, and by 0515 the 3rd Hussars had reached the forward infantry positions on the right, having lost twelve of their tanks, all of their anti-tank guns – at least for the time being – and with their infantry support so crippled by casualties that there was obviously no point in taking them forward on the next, crucial stage of the battle. Within a quarter of an hour the Royal Wiltshires were up on the left less eleven of their tanks, but there was for the moment no sign of the Warwickshires who should by now have reached the Scottish positions – and the covering barrage for the 9th Armoured Brigade was due to start at 0545.

The commanding officers of both the 3rd Hussars and the Royal Wiltshire Yeomanry urged Currie to allow the programme to continue as scheduled and not to wait for the Warwickshires, but Currie was worried about the narrowness of the gap which would be opened if he attempted to break through with only two-thirds of his brigade, so he persuaded Freyberg to postpone their main assault for half an hour by which time, in fact, the Warwickshires had arrived. So as the moment for the second barrage of the night crept nearer, the bulk of the 9th Armoured Brigade were on their start line, ready to follow their covering curtain of fire as it jumped forward 100 yards every three minutes until it had taken them across the Rahman Track and on towards the low ridge with its identifying Tel el Aqqaqir hump towards the southern end.

It was a tense, indeed crucial moment, both for the tank crews and for the whole of Eighth Army. Shells still hurtled overhead but in nothing like a concentrated barrage for the moment, the tanks lined up as directed, the commanding officers walked between the tanks and talked to the crews, to the surprise of many John Currie's command tank edged up into the front rank, and as zero hour approached the crews waited, the engines idled. So must have waited the Light Brigade at Balaclava.

Then at 0615 the barrage roared out again and crashed in front, drivers revved their engines and the whole line moved forward. Crusaders led the advance of all three groups with the heavy Grant and Sherman squadrons just behind, and at first everything seemed to go well although the 3rd Hussars' commanding officer's tank went up on a mine shortly after starting, and the wireless in the one he promptly commandeered was useless. But apart from that mishap, the line of tanks moved forward behind their artillery cover, flushing shell-shocked German and Italian infantrymen from their posts, machine-gunning them if they showed signs of further aggression, directing them to the rear with a jerk of the thumb if they wished to surrender; occasionally, in the speed and confusion of the night, running them down and crushing them beneath the steel tracks.

Both Hussars and Wiltshires made out and passed the line of telegraph poles which marked the Rahman Track running diagonally across their path, and one of the tank commanders noticed with a pang of concern that the top third of the one nearest to him was silvered with the light of dawn. But then they were past and suddenly amid enemy anti-tank guns, some of which had already been wrecked by the barrage, others now close and spitting fire. On the right, the Hussars' Crusaders had no option but to charge, and in the resulting mêlée lost almost immediately the squadron commander's tank and with it all contact with the heavy squadrons behind.

On their left, the Crusaders of the Wiltshires met at first with astonishing success, crashing into the German 50mm. and the Italian 47mm. guns and knocking them over, at one moment the triumphant drivers crushing a whole line of enemy gun trails under their tracks in one triumphant charge. It seemed briefly as though they could do nothing wrong – like a winning football team – and when four German officers tried make a bolt for it in a scurrying staff car, the Crusader squadron commander took a pot-shot at them with his revolver and was astonished to see the petrol-tank explode and the car go up in flames.

But all the time, the silver was creeping down the telegraph poles and eventually the light touched the top of Aqqaqir Ridge. At this, as later described by one of the survivors, 'The whole world seemed to blow up,' for on and just behind the ridge had lain in wait the main enemy defences – 88mm. and 75mm. anti-tank guns against which the British tanks, silhouetted against the paling eastern sky, were as defenceless as had been the British infantry against the German machine-guns on July 1st, 1916, the first day of the Somme.

The comparison with that occasion and also with the charge of the Light Brigade at Balaclava now took a more tragic reality. The western horizon cracked with fire along its base, and first the Crusaders and then the Grants and Shermans glowed red hot where the heavy shells hit them, then slewed aside and brewed, their crews leaping for safety when they could, often turning back to try to rescue their trapped and agonised companions.

Then the Wiltshires, renewing their tradition of getting further forward than anyone else and with John Currie still among them and in the forefront of the battle, suddenly came under fire from the south – from tanks which they had thought to be the Warwickshires but which were in fact the 15th Panzer. The last of the Wiltshires' Crusaders brewed up, the heavy squadrons of both the Hussars and the Wiltshires fired smoke in order to cover escaping crews – as much in danger from the Durham infantry behind them as from the enemy machine-gunners in front – and John Currie strove to keep control of the battle by shouted word of command for by now all wireless sets were out of action through damage or injury to the operators.

On the left flank, the Warwickshires were out on their own owing to a navigational error which had taken them too far south, but their story was similar to those of the Wiltshires and the Hussars. At first in the dark they had won unexpected success against the lighter anti-tank guns, machine-gun posts and dug-in tanks, smashing the heavy weapons, herding the infantry away to the sides and rear, dropping grenades into gun-pits or open tank-turrets; but once the light grew they suffered the same fate as the others. First from the heavy anti-tank guns on the ridge, then from the panzers in the gap they had themselves left on their right flank came crippling fire which tore the Crusaders apart and brought both Grants and Shermans to a shuddering halt.

Thus, though they had bitten deeply into the enemy defences, were the tanks of the 9th Armoured Brigade brought to a halt – without having torn the hole through which 1st Armoured Division were to pass. They had, however, as one of them was to remark later, 'made a bloody big dent' and if 2nd Armoured Brigade came up now they should be able to deepen it and get through themselves.

This, at least, was John Currie's belief, and as Brigadier Lucas Phillips says in the most detailed account of this action written:

> All that he could see was a world of devastation – devastation of the enemy, indeed, their shattered guns sprawling at crazed angles, their detachments lying dead, but devastation of his own brigade also. As far as the eye could see lay the terrible record – tank after tank burning or wrecked, the smoke of their burning mingled with the cold mist, the crimson shafts from the eastern sky tincturing all objects with the hue of blood. Only here and there could he see a tank still defiantly shooting it out with the more distant guns and the tanks of the Afrika Korps. He was very angry, very bitter. In fulfilment of his orders, he was ready to sacrifice all if Fisher's brigade had been there to crash through whatever ragged breaches he had torn in the enemy's wall of guns.[13]

Of the 94 tanks which had followed him forward from the infantry defences, 75 had been wrecked, and of the 400-odd officers and men who had manned them, 230 were dead, wounded or missing – and the battle still raged, the enemy gun-line still existed and was doubtless being strengthened, and there was no sign of the two brigades who were surely supposed at this juncture of the battle to be sweeping through his ranks to complete the annihilation of the enemy defences, and so to justify the price his own brigade had paid so far.

In the circumstances, it is not surprising that the thought that should they attempt it they too might suffer the same fate as his own brigade hardly crossed his mind; or that possibly he had himself made a fatal misjudgment when he obtained that half-hour postponement of the advance.

Freyberg, of course, was almost as perturbed as Currie at the non-arrival of the leading formations of 1st Armoured Division in what they both considered the crucial area, and three times in fifteen minutes he had rung up Leese, to ask him to urge Lumsden, to order Briggs, to press Fisher, to get his tanks forward both farther and faster; the battle was still bedevilled by the problems of two corps, each with different structures, fighting on the same ground – two corps, moreover, between which existed some antagonism.

The other problems stemming from this anachronism still existed, too, and 2nd Armoured Brigade had spent the time since they had left their assembly area at 0230 grinding their way forward in choking clouds of dust through a confined area even more congested than the corridor through which they had tried to find a way on the opening night of the battle. Durham and Highlander supply parties were hurrying forward towards their comrades in action, engineers were still clearing minefields, gun-pits pocked the area at every turn, ambulances swayed and twisted towards and through their ranks, demanding precedence by the compassion of their task. And as before, the area was packed first with the tails of the two infantry brigades, then with the tail of the 9th Armoured Brigade – and through all this the tanks of three more regiments had now to make their way, followed closely by their own tails which added up to a total of over a thousand vehicles.

The wonder was not so much that 2nd Armoured Brigade were late, but that they got through at all – and in fact Fisher's tanks were in action very shortly after Freyberg's third call to Leese. On the right the Queen's Bays had passed the Durhams and were closing up to the Rahman Track, in the centre the 9th Lancers were also past the infantry front line; only the 10th Hussars on the left were still well behind, having been misdirected at one point and subsequently having been forced like the Warwickshires to back-track.

All three regiments as they came up through the half-light passed through heavy enemy shelling, streams of German and Italian prisoners sent back by Currie's tank crews and, as the light grew, the bursts of armour-piercing and H.E. shells which had missed the 9th Armoured. In front the ground was dotted with the flaming remains of Currie's tanks, and soon one of the regimental commanders saw Currie himself coming back so he went forward to meet him. He was bloody late, Currie told him, but 9th Armoured Brigade had made the gap and now it was up to him and his colleagues from 2nd Armoured Brigade to get forward through it as quickly as possible; and when, after looking at the scene of flame and chaos stretching out towards the ridge, the newcomer said, 'I have never seen anything, sir, that looks less like a gap!' Currie was very angry indeed.[14]

The fact remained that still along the line of the Aqqaqir Ridge lay a formidable enemy defence against which even the Shermans and Grants would dash themselves to pieces if they attacked it in daylight. Moreover, it seemed that there would very shortly be a perhaps even more important function for the newly arrived armour to perform than exploiting whatever success the 9th Armoured Brigade had won, for warnings were coming through from XXX Corps that intercepted signals indicated counter-attacks soon to be expected from 21st Panzer Division coming down from the north. With the presence of the 15th Panzer formations between the remnants of the Wiltshires and the Warwickshires, another could obviously be expected from the west – and at the very least, the Durhams and Highlanders would need protection.

There was another point to be considered, too. The ultimate task for 1st Armoured Division was to destroy the Axis armour 'on ground of their own choosing' – and if they chose now to do the job along the Rahman Track instead of across the Aqqaqir Ridge, they would have additional fire-power from the anti-tank guns of the infantry brigades close by, together, as it happened, with those which had been attached to the 3rd Hussars and which had just arrived.

It is still almost impossible to discover who made the decisions and how they were arrived at, and certainly one can have sympathy for all the commanders. Freyberg and Currie were both pleading for exploitation of the 9th Armoured Brigade's sacrifices, Montgomery's orders had been that 1st Armoured Division should follow through and fight on or beyond the ridge, Lumsden was certainly well aware of the unpopularity of both himself and his command in view of the failures of the past few days, even of the past few months. Yet at divisional and brigade level they faced the realities of the situation developing across the Rahman Track, and this would seem to have led to some dichotomy of thought.

As early as 0745 Freyberg had somewhat tartly suggested that 'a very senior officer' should be up front invigorating the armour, and perhaps as a result Lumsden himself arrived at 1st Armoured Division H.Q. just before 0800. He warned Briggs of possible counter-attack, but told him to push Fisher's 2nd Armoured Brigade forward to Currie's assistance – but by this time Fisher's observers had told him that both the Bays on the right and the 9th Lancers in the centre were already across the Rahman Track, despite the fact that the infantrymen could see quite clearly that they were not. Briggs, too, seems somehow to have been aware that Fisher was wrong and that the two regiments had, in fact, taken up hull-down positions in broken ground just forward of the Durham corner in which they were already engaged with panzers coming down from the north.

Not only could they not for the moment easily disengage to go further forward, but one suspects that General Briggs did not want them to despite the orders he was getting from above – and the resulting confusion probably explains a certain ambiguity which colours the logged record of a series of signals which passed between divisional and brigade commanders. At 0904, Fisher, increasingly worried by the differing pressures being exerted upon him, asked, 'Is it intended that I push on or stay?' to which Briggs replied, 'Your instructions are to destroy tanks and get into positions where you can' – which in the circumstances was hardly the clearest possible order.

Very shortly afterwards, Fisher replied, 'In accordance with orders, Brigade has taken up positions ready to take on attack from west or north. Being engaged by tanks and anti-tank guns.' And somewhat tetchily, Briggs then ordered, 'Destroy opposition and get on,' following it shortly afterwards with, 'We must have room. You must push on.'[15]

But by this time, not only were the Bays and the remnants of the 3rd Hussars together with some of the Valentines of 8th R.T.R. working themselves into sound defensive positions facing north, but 9th Lancers and the Wiltshires were together amid the Durham and Seaforths' forward positions facing west, and the Warwickshires, 10th Hussars and the 50th R.T.R. were exchanging shots with panzers away to the south-west on the Rahman Track. Moreover, all armour was now under command of X Corps as it had been decided to specify a time for this to happen – 0910 – instead of the perhaps long-drawn-out event of arrival on the 'chosen ground'.

It must be said that in their decision to fight what was to develop into one of the fiercest tank battles of the desert war where they did, the armoured commanders had the support of their subordinates. They all by now knew what would happen if they tried in daylight to assault a line of guns on or behind a ridge, and in case any of them had forgotten they could see what had happened to the 9th Armoured Brigade. Now they took hull-down positions wherever they could find ground broken enough to allow it, and waited for the enemy to come out and attack them; and as the sun rose higher in the sky, they could see to the north a new line of enemy anti-tank guns and a group of panzers already massing behind it.

The Bays and the remnants of the 3rd Hussars were very quickly to reap the benefits of their positions, for they had hardly taken them when a line of panzers and Italian tanks moved north on the far side of the Rahman Track, apparently to join the assembling force – and two panzers and three M13s were promptly put out of action.

But not all the counter-attacks were to be so easily dealt with, and soon afterwards some of the panzers taking part in what was probably an attempt to 'pinch out' the salient at its root, carefully probed forward until they found a gap between the Maoris and the 6th Durhams through which they might have penetrated into the salient itself. It is impossible now to be certain what first caused them to hesitate, but it may have been the sheer mass of vehicles, movement and apparent chaos with which they were faced, for by mid-morning the salient presented an astonishing sight.

Flat as a billiard table, it was packed with men, guns, ammunition and vehicles amid which German and Italian shells exploded constantly but with no perceptible pattern, raising more dust to add to the clouds already caused by the movement, and occasionally smoke when they hit and set vehicles alight. And some of the vehicles moving across the salient were now those of the 8th Armoured Brigade, still following their original *Supercharge* orders to make their way through to the support of 2nd Armoured Brigade in the

break-out across the Aqqaqir Ridge – though by now their commander, Brigadier Custance, was aware that there had been modifications.

On the right flank of their advance were the Crusaders of the
Staffordshire Yeomanry accompanied by their battery of R.H.A.
25-pounders – and it was someone amongst them who first became
aware of the panzer threat along the northern flank of the salient.
They immediately swung right and within a few minutes a small and
entirely separate battle was being fought across a sector of the salient
itself – while traffic still streamed forward under the two-way exchange of fire between the two protagonists, and eddied continually
around the Staffordshires.

But soon this was just a small part of a much bigger conflict – the
one, in fact, for which much of the planning of the battle had been
directed, between the massed armour of X Corps and that of the
Panzerarmee.

It raged from 1100 to 1300 on November 2nd, with the remaining
panzers of 15th and 21st Panzer Divisions and the lighter tanks of
Littorio (Ariete were all still down in the south) trying valiantly to
eliminate the new salient by destroying the Crusaders, Grants and
Shermans of the now concentrated 1st Armoured Division. At times
it would seem that over 120 mixed panzers and Italian tanks were
engaged in co-ordinated attacks on the northern, north-western and
western faces of the salient, their first onslaught being supported by
Stukas and all of them backed by as much artillery support as
Rommel could organise, including the twenty-four 88mm. guns he
still had in the vicinity.

But the British now were in the tactical position which they had so
often envied their opponents. They held a strong defensive line with
effective anti-tank fire to back up the already powerful Grant and
Sherman armament, not to speak of the massive field artillery which
'on call' could interfere and blanket Axis concentrations as soon as
they were identified. Above all, they had the constant support of the
Allied air forces – British, South African and American – whose
fighters made short work of the Stuka attacks and whose impeccable
eighteen-bomber formations seemed almost permanently stationed
over the battlefield. (They made seven appearances in those two
hours.)

The desert, quivering in the heat haze, became a scene that defies sober
description. It can be discerned only as a confused arena clouded by the
bursts of high explosive, darkened by the smoke of scores of burning tanks
and trucks, lit by the flashes of innumerable guns, shot through by red,
green and white tracers, shaken by heavy bombing from the air and
deafened by the artillery of both sides. Upon the British forces in the
funnel – tanks, infantry and supporting arms – a 'torrent of shell and shot'

was poured in from three sides. In the words recorded by the sober historian of the 9th Lancers, 'for hours the whack of armour-piercing shot on armour plate was unceasing'. Overhead, fierce conflicts were fought in the air as the Germans twice attempted to attack the British armour with Stukas, only to be fought off by the R.A.F.[16]

It was an unequal battle from every point of view, for not only did the British have complete domination of the air, but they could afford to lose tanks at a far higher rate than could their opponents; but above all, events had at last conspired to force the Afrika Korps to attack in daylight and across open ground, and as a result to suffer the kind of losses which they had so often in the past inflicted upon their opponents. By the end of the day, Afrika Korps was down to 35 panzers still in battle order and 20 Italian tanks, while the battered remains of over 100 still smoked on the battlefield from which it was quite evident that the exhausted recovery teams could rescue only a very small proportion.

Losses for that day among the British armour had by no means been small, of course, but 8th Armoured Brigade had not been heavily involved and were thus still strong, while Pip Roberts's 22nd Armoured Brigade had not been involved at all and now was ordered to assemble south of Tel el Eisa where, on orders issued by Montgomery early that morning, they would be joined by the 4th Light Armoured Brigade coming up rapidly from the south, thus to reconstitute under John Harding the whole 7th Armoured Division as it had begun the battle.

By evening all the British armour would be in the north, and its most experienced component poised for a crucial role. In addition, the early morning reports had revealed to General Montgomery one small but highly significant success away on the southern flank of the *Supercharge* salient, and this he was determined to exploit.

The approach march from the assembly areas to the start lines had not been comfortable for anyone, but it was probably less uncomfortable for the armoured car regiments than for anyone else. They were not marching through the thick dust, and on the other hand they were not choking in clouds flung up by huge wheeled or tracked formations clanking along in front. They were, however, conscious of the fact that they could not, like the infantry, individually fling themselves to the ground when shells burst nearby, nor find cover from shrapnel or splinter behind the flimsy sides of their vehicles. Ahead, the night was already full of the fire and sound of battle and for the men of A and C Squadrons of the Royal Dragoons it was something of a comfort that their path lay to the south where matters seemed quieter.

The leading car reached the end of the marked tracks and edged quietly ahead between anti-tank guns waiting to go forward, its commander making sure that the cars immediately behind were closing up and then directing the driver to lead off into the dark. The car promptly fell into a slit-trench and had to be abandoned.

Another car took the lead and quite soon the column of Daimlers and Humbers had passed through a line of infantry digging themselves in. The Dragoons were now in no-man's-land. The night was dark and in the immediate vicinity quiet, so they pressed ahead and were soon into enemy territory itself – a fact quickly made apparent to them when yet another leading car fell into a hole in the ground, this time the gun-pit of an 88mm. with its crew dead around it.

The column wound slowly on, a late moon now giving them a better chance to avoid trouble. At last they hit a track which seemed to lead in their desired direction, and after a short wait to allow the tail-enders to close up, they drove quickly forward:

> One or two more cars, including three petrol replenishing lorries, got stuck in slit trenches, but most of them pulled out when dawn broke and fought their way up to us. The enemy were too astounded to do anything as we came through, or else the Italian section thought we were Germans, and the German section thought we were Italians. They waved swastika flags at us with vigour and we replied with 'Achtung!' and anything else we could think of which, with an answering wave, would get us through their lines. As it grew lighter they stared and blinked at us. Although a warning artillery barrage had been going on all night they couldn't believe their eyes. They would goggle at us from short range, see our berets, bolt away a few yards, pause as if they didn't think it was true, and come back to take another look.[17]

The Dragoons sped through ammunition and stores dumps as dawn broke, and shortly afterwards found themselves amid the tents and dug-in trucks and lorries of a brigade or perhaps divisional headquarters. They shot up all standing vehicles, shot down any sign of opposition (there was very little, such was the element of surprise), collected a colonel and two majors as prisoners, and pushed on into the open spaces of the desert to set about their main task of raiding the Axis supply columns. They also sent off the essential coded signals to inform Eighth Army that at last one of their units had found a way through the enemy defences.

It was as yet just the first small trickle through the dam, but what could it portend?

Montgomery was determined that it should portend the final breakthrough and the destruction of the Panzerarmee – and following the military principle of reinforcing success, as soon as he had assimilated the morning situation reports for the entire front, he ordered Lumsden to shift as much as possible of the armoured weight to the south-west corner of the salient, as quickly as possible. Lumsden could not, of course, disengage 2nd Armoured Brigade or the remnants of the 9th from the ferocious battle now being fought in front of the Durhams, and the Staffordshires of the 8th Armoured Brigade must stay where they were until the northern face of the salient was secure – but the rest of 8th Armoured Brigade should skirt the southern edge of the main battle, leave 2nd Armoured Brigade to deal with 15th and 21st Panzer formations, and themselves endeavour to break through around or south of Tel el Aqqaqir.

But if a really large-scale breakthrough was to take place down there – say with the whole of 7th Armoured Division in addition to 8th Armoured Brigade – then more space would be required for deployment and manoeuvre, probably south of the salient itself, and infantry must secure it. Skinflint and Snipe both lay within striking distance of the battalions along the southern flank, and they should be taken as quickly as possible, certainly before the day – November 2nd – was out.

Neither of these moves, however, would solve the problem posed by the existence of that line of anti-tank guns on the Aqqaqir Ridge north of the Tel, and one way or another it must be destroyed. According to Fisher, his 2nd Armoured Brigade were on the Rahman Track and although they were fighting hard they did not seem to be suffering severe losses; when darkness fell their survivors should be able to advance under artillery cover and break that gun-line – and they could have infantry support for the operation from the rifle battalions of the 7th Motor Brigade who were now well forward in the salient. Lumsden should organise this for tonight.

As for the main Eighth Army long-term objectives, a breakthrough westward or southward was now imminent, so what was required immediately was the organisation of a balanced force both to make the final lunge and then to exploit it. The problem, of course, would again be posed by the shortage of infantry, though there were still a few reserves upon which Montgomery could draw.

Howard Kippenberger's 5th New Zealand Brigade had been waiting ever since it had been withdrawn from Miteiriya Ridge specifically to carry out an exploitation role, and they could be joined by 5th Indian Brigade from the 4th Indian Division which had hardly as yet been seriously engaged in the battle. In addition, the Durham Brigade was evidently in need of withdrawal from the salient for reorganisation, for Freyberg had reported that although their losses had not been unduly severe, their hold on the salient corner was not as firm as it might have been – not surprisingly in view of the armoured battle being fought all around them and of their own comparative inexperience. He had suggested that the two battalions of the 6th New Zealand Brigade at the base of the salient take over from them – and once this had happened, the Durhams could withdraw, reorganise, and quickly be ready for further employment.

A fourth brigade was also available and close at hand. The 154th Brigade of Argyll and Sutherland Highlanders, Black Watch and Gordons were already in position behind their brothers of 152nd Brigade holding the southern half of the salient, and could be launched through quite easily when the moment came.

But speed in everything was essential, and by noon – when the battle along the western edge of the salient was at its height – the staff officers were racing around the XXX Corps area with the orders, the commanders were barking at their adjutants and company commanders, the quartermasters were cursing their fate and shouting for more petrol, more trucks and where the hell had the ammunition column got to? And in view of the fact that the rush was causing such anomalies as XXX Corps issuing orders direct to Highland Division troops still supposedly under Freyberg's command, at Freyberg's suggestion a new and clear dividing line was agreed. He would still command all troops in the northern half of the salient, while the Scots in the southern half returned to their own divisional commander, Douglas Wimberley, who would assume responsibility for the immediate operations down there.

All this lightning change and replanning might easily have resulted in chaos, for the attack by the 2nd Seaforths and the Valentines of 50th R.T.R. on Skinflint was as a result first postponed from 1600 to 1800, then to 1830 and then back to 1815, which not unnaturally thoroughly confused the gunners. There were thus a couple of false starts which in normal circumstances could have spelt disaster – but in the event the men of the Trieste Division holding Skinflint showed no inclination to resist, over 100 giving themselves up immediately the Seaforths arrived. These thus took the post with no casualties at all, though four of the Valentines had been lost on mines or to shell-fire on the way up.

As for Snipe, the 5th Royal Sussex had planned for an advance supported by artillery at 1900, but long before then came signs that the Trieste formations there considered themselves already outflanked, so the Royal Sussex marched across (unfortunately losing seven men in a minefield on the way) and took at no cost the position for which the 2nd Rifle Brigade had fought so long and so valiantly.

Needless to say, not everything had gone as well elsewhere during that afternoon and evening (of November 2nd). Brigadier Custance had by midday managed to disengage the Staffordshire Yeomanry from the panzers on the northern flank and tried to drive south-westward through the positions held by the Camerons, but the German anti-tank guns were still lying in wait and although the 8th Armoured Brigade later claimed to have knocked out eleven enemy tanks, they lost six Crusaders themselves and made no progress.

There was thus, despite Brigadier Fisher's continued belief to the contrary, no live British armour west of the Rahman Track when darkness fell.

General Lumsden's plans for the attack that night on the enemy defences in front of and on the ridge were, to start off with, extremely ambitious. His original orders, given verbally at about 2000 on November 2nd, were to the effect that both brigades of the 1st Armoured Division were to advance due westwards under cover of the heaviest artillery barrage that could be arranged, while 7th Motor Brigade followed and then wheeled left to cover the armour's southern flank. But an hour later, under pressure either from his brigade commanders or perhaps Montgomery himself, he modified them to an advance at first by the motor brigade to a known area of resistance across the Rahman Track, followed by the 2nd Armoured Brigade who would pass through and on to high ground about a mile and a half further on, while 8th Armoured Brigade drove across on the left towards a similar area of high ground just south of Tel el Aqqaqir. If all went well, he suggested that 22nd Armoured Brigade which would have been brought down from Tel el Eisa would then swing even wider south and, perhaps with the other 7th Armoured Division brigade, drive up to the coast with Ghazal Station (see rear endpaper) as their objective.

Far too little time, however, had been allowed for reconnaissance or even proper briefing, and the Motor Brigade battalions – 2nd and 7th Rifle Brigade and 2nd King's Royal Rifle Corps – had already spent a very uncomfortable day being sporadically shelled in the salient, and generally hanging about awaiting orders and employment. The two Rifle Brigade battalions eventually assembled behind the Durham positions (now being taken over by the 6th New Zealanders) short of both men and vehicles and even somewhat uncertain of their exact objectives. Nevertheless, at 0115 on November 3rd the riflemen duly set out behind their hastily organised artillery cover, and the 2nd Rifle Brigade on the right (now commanded by Major Pearson) crossed the Rahman Track successfully after storming a couple of enemy posts, but then ran into fire from anti-tank guns which wrecked the carriers, and machine-gun fire from Italian tanks which drove the men to ground. There was obviously little chance of their own anti-tank guns coming up, and after the punishment the battalion had taken six days earlier on Snipe, plus the realisation that 7th Rifle Brigade had not caught them up on the left, it is not surprising that Pearson soon asked for, and received, permission to withdraw.

The 7th Rifle Brigade had met with even less success. They had been late at the start line and thus lost whatever advantage the singularly ragged artillery cover might have given them, ran into totally unexpected opposition before they reached the track which resulted in companies losing touch and finally, as control went, the men scattering. By daybreak on November 3rd, small groups of survivors of both battalions, some on foot and some in the remaining carriers, filtered back through the New Zealand line with all the stain of dismal failure visible in their faces and in their bearing.

The third battalion, the 2nd K.R.R.C., had attacked through the 5th Camerons on the south-western corner of the salient, their objective the area where the Rahman Track crossed over the Aqqaqir Ridge, just to the south of the Tel itself. Congestion behind the Camerons had delayed their arrival on the start line, which they crossed about an hour after their opening artillery cover had been fired, and as a result they found themselves up against solid opposition almost 1,000 yards short of the ridge. Here, too, there was some misunderstanding about the true objective so the riflemen, perhaps with the admirable intention of matching the deeds of their fellow Green Jackets a week before, dug themselves in and positioned their anti-tank guns as they came up for all round defence.

Dawn revealed their position more similar to that of the Pioneers in the Saucer than that of the 2nd Rifle Brigade at Snipe, for they were overlooked from the ridge (where they were supposed to be) and there were several enemy posts much nearer, one within a stone's throw. However, their wireless was still in operation and they managed to report their progress, though owing to some misinterpretation along the line, General Lumsden gained the impression that they had, in fact, reached their objective and were firmly in control of it.

As it was now obviously too late for the armoured brigades to advance to the ridge, and as he was at least aware that the objectives in the north had not been taken, Lumsden therefore instructed the 8th Armoured Brigade to try to 'feel their way' forward and around the south of the supposed K.R.R.C. positions, and he sent out the 4th/6th South African Armoured Car Regiment in a pre-dawn dash to attempt to swing around on the same course and join the Royal Dragoons. They were back some two hours later with accounts of minefields and strong opposition from all along the ridge – which was confirmed by infantry observers, but not believed by 7th Motor Brigade, 1st Armoured Division or X Corps.

The attempts by 8th Armoured Brigade, aided later by the 2nd, to obey Lumsden's orders to get forward came to little during November 3rd except the destruction of some enemy anti-tank guns between the track and the ridge at the expense of a great deal of ammunition, and the loss of three tanks in a well-intentioned attempt to rush the ridge and take the pressure off the unfortunate K.R.R.C. These remained where they were all day, unknowingly basking in high level approbation, for no doubts at all existed throughout the armoured command that they were actually on the ridge, and also by the afternoon that 8th Armoured Brigade formations were at least halfway towards them and well across the Rahman Track.

Though the report which went to the Army Commander outlining this situation was thus over-optimistic, there were other promising reports during the day which were quite true. From the XIII Corps sector came reports of fires and explosions behind the lines opposite which seemed to have no relation to any specific action, and the hopes they aroused were confirmed by air reconnaissance which told of long columns of marching men and convoys of vehicles moving north-westwards. Moreover, early in the morning the signal intercept service had reported that 90th Light Division headquarters had ordered one of its forward infantry battalions to send vehicles to help bring out the heavy weapons still held by 125th Regiment around Thompson's Post, and when Morshead ordered patrols out to hinder the movement, they reached Barrel Hill without opposition and found no enemy positions between there and the coast. Further south, the Australians along the western face of the Point 29 salient found that they could move about quite freely, and some of them even walked across to the nearest known German positions which they promptly ransacked for souvenirs.

There was no doubt, therefore, that the Panzerarmee was drawing back – but Montgomery wanted them held for a little longer where they were, so that he could slip the armour out and around from the south to cut off their withdrawal. Lumsden must therefore urge his armoured brigades to keep up the pressure all day – which they were certainly doing – and also to be ready to move quickly when darkness fell. Infantry from Wimberley's Highland Division would move forward in the late afternoon and take position just south of the valiant K.R.R.C. on Aqqaqir Ridge, thus gaining control of the Rahman Track to the south, and through that area the whole 1st Armoured Division would drive south-west and west, then swing north to pen the enemy against the coast.

The 7th Armoured Division would follow and swing out wider towards Ghazal Station, while the New Zealand Division with the 4th Light Armoured Brigade under command (it was still coming up from the south) would follow behind with Sidi Ibeid as their first objective, then Fuka or even Matruh should opportunity favour them.

November 3rd was obviously another day when speed of decision and action would be the keynote, a condition heightened as the morning passed and reports came in from Coningham's H.Q. that every aircraft which came in brought tales not only of enemy withdrawal in the south, but of dense traffic on the coast road and all tracks leading off it to known enemy centres. Needless to say, every fighter and fighter-bomber that could climb into the air was out attacking these routes, especially the main road from Daba back as far as Matruh – but, significantly, they were up against far more opposition than they had met of late, for Me 109s and 110s were out guarding the traffic in unexpected strength.

So the orders went out, the plans were laid for the night's operations which, it was confidently expected, would result in the long-awaited break-out, the freeing of the entire Eighth Army from the morass of minefields and close enemy defences in which they had been confined for so long, the release into the open desert and the thrills of a triumphant chase.

Such was the atmosphere of excitement and euphoria that no notice was taken in the higher echelons of command of the increasingly worried pronouncements of the men at the front, especially the forward artillery observers, that the whole of the length of the Aqqaqir Ridge and especially the ground around the Tel was still occupied by German anti-tank formations, and that neither the K.R.R.C. nor any of the 8th Armoured Brigade tanks were even across the Rahman Track.

General Wimberley, like all the other divisional commanders that day, had a very busy time indeed. He now had three attacks to launch in the course of twelve hours, two of them each by one of his own beloved Scots battalions and one by the 5th Indian Brigade, and whatever he and his staff could do to ensure that they all succeeded at the smallest possible cost would be done. He checked that start lines were agreed and marked out as clearly as possible, that battalion commanders were adequately briefed and were given time to pass necessary information on to their men – and above all that adequate artillery cover was laid on for each advance, properly organised and accurately planned.

He was thus astonished, then bewildered and finally infuriated when he was rung up by XXX Corps's commander, General Leese himself with whom Wimberley was on close and friendly terms, to be told that General Briggs had heard of his detailed plans and was protesting vigorously. The proposed barrage to protect the first of Wimberley's attacks – that by the 5th/7th Gordons from the Skinflint area to just south of Tel el Aqqaqir – would, claimed General Briggs, fall far too close if not actually upon the positions held by the K.R.R.C.s, having on its way caused untold losses among the advanced formations of 8th Armoured Brigade!

Nothing that Wimberley said, no other authority which he quoted could change the instruction that the artillery cover must be cancelled, for General Briggs persisted in his claim and in it he was supported by General Lumsden. Wimberley was moreover ordered that the Gordons and the Valentine crews of 8th R.T.R. who would be accompanying them should be told of the reasons for their lack of cover, and that their task was simply that of advancing through areas already taken by the armour to a location already held by British infantry.

The only alleviation of the order which Wimberley could extract was that the guns could put down smoke to guide the Gordons towards their objective – and late in the afternoon, the force set out with the Jocks riding on the leading Valentines. For the first twenty minutes progress was excellent, then the Valentines passed through the last smoke-screen to drive forward into a setting sun which effectively blinded the drivers and tank commanders, and a storm of vicious anti-tank and machine-gun fire which swept down from the ridge upon them, putting 20 tanks immediately out of action with 27 of their crew members including seven officers; and by the time they had pulled back, 98 of the Gordons were killed, wounded or missing.

What rubbed salt into an already grievous wound was that even while the men and the tanks were undergoing their ordeal, 1st Armoured Division rang up the Highland Division H.Q. to say that the artillery cover should be allowed to proceed after all, as information had just come in from which they concluded that their infantry and tanks were perhaps not quite so far forward as had been believed.

Later that night Wimberley spoke again to General Leese on the subject of another of the attacks, and sounded so despondent over the loss of his Gordons that Leese himself was worried. 'Surely now you, Douglas, of all people are not going to lose heart!' he said, at which Wimberley rallied – and at least had no trouble in ensuring that the other two attacks were properly covered by artillery.

That by the 11th Indian Brigade took a great deal of organisation, for the 1st/4th Essex on the right were only given their orders at 1915, and then had to find and cross the start line which was a long way away at the far end of the crowded and congested salient. The 3rd/10th Baluchs were supposed to take the left flank but could not be found so the reserve battalion, the 6th Rajputana Rifles, took their place and – despite all this – the attack went in on time at 0230 on November 4th and was completely successful. The Essex took 100 exhausted Panzergrenadiers prisoner, found another eighty on their objective on the Rahman Track some three miles south of Tel el Aqqaqir, and was joined there quite quickly by both the Rajputanas and the Baluchs who followed through without opposition.

As for the third attack by the 7th Argyll and Sutherland Highlanders on Tel el Aqqaqir itself, by dawn they were on their objective with no casualties at all, to find it and indeed the length of the ridge abandoned. The Afrika Korps, indeed the whole Panzerarmee, had withdrawn during the night, leaving behind in the Alamein defences just a few stragglers, some wrecked artillery, random areas of unexploded mines and a considerable number of ingenious booby-traps.

The Battle of El Alamein was over, and all that remained was for Eighth Army to organise its effective exploitation.

12 · Break-out and Pursuit

However grimly and realistically Rommel and his staff may have regarded the progress of the battle before November 2nd, the impact of *Supercharge* and the immediate consequences shook them severely.

They had foreseen the size and timing of the attack but been deceived as to its location, for they had, of course, no means of knowing of Montgomery's last-minute change of mind. They had therefore expected it in the north, driving out of the Australian salient south of Hill 28 towards Sidi Abd el Rahman, and no reports which might have corrected the misconception arrived for some time, as R.A.F. aircraft fitted with radio-jamming equipment had been operating in the area and the pre-assault bombing had wrecked several vital communication centres.

Rommel's staff had even contributed to their own mystification, for in an attempt to distract British attention from the main task they had arranged for an artillery programme to be fired to the south of the expected danger area. This fell into the *Supercharge* area but was so meagre by British standards that it was hardly noticed by Freyberg and his troops who assumed it was nothing but Axis reaction to their own barrage – but it helped to mask what was really happening down there.

Rommel, therefore, had made no immediate alterations to his plans to deal with the expected British assault when the *Supercharge* barrage opened, merely ensuring that 21st Panzer and 90th Light were properly deployed to seal off the attack if and when it broke through towards Sidi Abd el Rahman, and it was not until nearly dawn, when some of the communications had been restored, that the true location of the new battle was realised. Even with German efficiency some confusion thus resulted and the first attacks on the salient by 21st Panzer from the north and 15th Panzer with tanks from Littorio and Trieste from the west were both uncoordinated and hastily mounted.

Several of the panzer commanders, moreover, especially from 21st Panzer Division, now came up against the Sherman for the first time and were dismayed to find themselves outgunned – and by a tank apparently impervious even to the fire from their previously infallible 88mm. anti-tank shield. They also found themselves for the first time in an action in which their orders gave them no latitude to draw back behind that anti-tank shield but insisted that they stay in front and hammer out a victory against the enemy by themselves, without infantry of their own to consolidate their advances, without – so far as they could see – an enemy infantry position for them to assault; just that line of huge, invulnerable tanks supported by massive artillery fed from inexhaustible ammunition dumps, while enemy bombers cruised implacably overhead, unloading steel and high explosive upon them with devastating impartiality.

It was a shattering experience for the morale of the men, and for the structure of the formations themselves. Nearly 120 German panzers and Italian tanks were drawn into the battle fought out on the afternoon of November 2nd along the western and northern faces of the *Supercharge* salient – and at the end of it only 35 panzers and 20 Italian tanks were still runners; and all present were well aware that the British still had vast reserves of both tanks and guns to draw upon.

That evening Rommel decided he must withdraw the Panzerarmee from the battle to new lines from which he could fight delaying actions until either his own forces were strengthened or Montgomery's forces tired – or ran out of supplies. From his staff he therefore obtained details of the artillery and anti-tank defences still in position behind which he could manoeuvre, from von Thoma he gathered the sobering truth about the remaining strength of Afrika Korps – and from his own experience he drew the conclusion that if he acted quickly and with resolution, a major part of his army could still be saved to fight again.

The first problem was that of immediate disengagement. Ariete must come north to add their armour to what was left of the Afrika Korps and thus form a screen behind which the infantry could get away – accepting the fact that the Italian tanks could not return to the south, whatever the developments down there; and he ordered the infantry of X Corps – Pavia and Brescia – to pull back to their pre-Alam Halfa positions. Bologna and Trento infantry in the centre would draw back to the line of the Telegraph Track, leaving rearguards of course, and he would organise transport to begin lifting them further back during the night of November 3rd. Priority was to be given to Italian troops 'as their fighting value is smaller' – but 'not a single German soldier is to be left behind', especially not from the Ramcke Brigade who with the Folgores would have been holding the line in the south.

Thompson's Post and the whole Tel el Eisa salient would also now be completely evacuated, the troops there drawing back first to the line of the Telegraph Track and thus helping 90th Light to hold the northern extremity of the Panzerarmee defences.

Much of this could be put in hand immediately, so that by the evening of the next day (November 3rd) the mass of the Italian infantry of Panzerarmee would be poised ready for deployment or further retreat as circumstances dictated, while the mobile formations of the Afrika Korps, plus the Ariete and 90th Light Divisions, formed in the north a protective screen which could – indeed must – hold the enemy east of a line running south through Ghazal Station while the rest of the army got away. In the meantime, no British armour must be allowed to cross the track, and those armoured cars which had reputedly broken through must be found and destroyed – or at least driven away from the supply routes.

Having drawn up the orders and seen that they were despatched and understood, Rommel then reported his intentions to Rome and Berlin, and spent the next few hours listening anxiously for sounds of a repeat of the previous night's violent bombardment.

But there was little except local action, and by morning the mass of Italian infantry were moving back out of close contact with the enemy, some reports even indicating that troops from Littorio and Trieste once they had left their front-line positions were streaming away out of control. In the centre, too, positions previously held by the Bologna Division had been totally evacuated, so Ariete were ordered to wait just north of the Deir el Qatani area in case they should be needed to plug vital gaps.

Otherwise, all moves seemed to be proceeding smoothly, and shortly after 0900 on November 3rd Rommel drove along the coast through dense traffic, mostly belonging to Italian supply and administration formations which he had ordered back to Fuka. For the moment there was an unaccountable absence of enemy aircraft, but he did not doubt that they would soon be overhead – although perhaps they were even now attacking the Italian infantry movements down in the south. At about 1000 he received reports from General von Thoma and Oberst Bayerlein; the British armour were still deployed around the north-western and western faces of their new salient, facing the line of anti-tank guns behind which waited the thirty-odd panzers which still remained to the Afrika Korps. It seemed for the moment that the enemy intended no aggressive moves; presumably Montgomery was reorganising his artillery for yet another massive bombardment, preceding yet another step forward by his infantry and armour.

Perhaps, then, *now* was the moment to begin the main withdrawal from the battle, first to whatever defensive positions the Fuka Line could provide, then to whatever defensive positions the rest of the

North African desert might provide for a weakened and poorly supplied army battling against a Juggernaut. Unless he was prepared to throw away the lives of his men in a pointless sacrifice, this was a course which he would have to take sooner or later – and the moment seemed propitious.

Shortly after 1030 Rommel made the decision. The disengaged Italian infantry should continue their march to the rear towards Fuka, after their supply services, and as much transport as possible must be sent down to them. Ariete must come further north, instructions must be given to 15th and 21st Panzer Divisions to be ready to move back to the area south of Ghazal as soon as darkness fell, for the 90th Light to move back along the coast towards El Daba, and for the anti-tank formations of 164th Division around the salient to be ready to slip away immediately they received the order to do so, some time after midnight. Down in the south, Ramcke Brigade must be warned to be ready to move out during the night, and Folgore told to do so during the first quiet period after sunset.

To protect these moves, every aircraft the Luftwaffe could get into the sky must be made available, in fact they should be there now as it surely would not be long before the R.A.F. arrived over these dense streams of traffic, of which Rommel was himself at that moment a vulnerable member.

At which reflection yet another of the 'Party Rally' formations arrived overhead and it was only by some frantic driving that he and his escorts arrived back at his headquarters just after midday. His staff immediately began issuing the detailed orders for the night's withdrawal, and it was after the bulk of them had been sent off that he was handed the Führer's reply to his report of the night before:

To FIELD MARSHAL ROMMEL

It is with trusting confidence in your leadership and the courage of the German–Italian troops under your command that the German people and I are following your heroic struggle in Egypt. In the situation in which you find yourself there can be no other thought but to stand fast, yield not a yard of ground and throw every gun and every man into the battle. Considerable air force reinforcements are being sent to C.-in-C. South. The Duce and the Comando Supremo are also making the utmost efforts to send you the means to continue the fight. Your enemy, despite his superiority, must also be at the end of his strength. It would not be the first time in history that a strong will has triumphed over the big battalions. As to your troops, you can show them no other road than that to victory or death.

ADOLF HITLER[1]

The Führer had spoken. And issued a death warrant.

It was a bitter blow to Rommel, not only in that the order if obeyed would mean the end of the Panzerarmee and especially of his beloved Afrika Korps, but also that his military judgment was being overruled at the level from which he had always in the past received support. For the first time in the African Campaign he did not know what to do, for unlike his fellow generals on the Russian Front, he had not yet learned the occasional necessity of disobeying the Führer, or the techniques of doing so without placing his own life and those of his family in jeopardy.

The Führer's directive could hardly have arrived at a more inopportune moment, too, for although the orders for the retreat had gone out, there was undoubtedly time for Rommel to cancel them – and in doing so to condemn his army to destruction. He rang von Thoma who reported tersely that Afrika Korps had now only 24 panzers left and that they must withdraw to regroup, and when he had heard the message from Hitler, suggested temporising along the lines that 'minor withdrawals for tactical adjustments' would surely not constitute disobedience of a direction at strategic level.

But Rommel knew that this would be neither practicable nor acceptable and having always in the past insisted upon unconditional and meticulous obedience from his own subordinates, saw the dangers in not applying the same principles to himself. Whatever his own feelings upon the matter, he must issue orders implementing the Führer's directive, commanding every formation to stand firm and be prepared 'on instructions from the highest level' to fight to the last man and the last round of ammunition; and if it proved difficult as a result of orders which had already gone out to persuade men who had already glimpsed their release from intolerable conditions to return to face them again, then the sternest measures would have to be used.

Some time was spent drafting a reply to Hitler's edict, accepting that all formations would be ordered to stand firm where they were, but pointing out that losses in German infantry to date approximated to 50 per cent, in artillery 40 per cent, that only 24 panzers were now left to Afrika Korps and that the Littorio and Trieste Divisions had been to all intents and purposes wiped out; and Rommel's A.D.C., Leutnant Berndt – a long-term Nazi Party member – was despatched to the Führer's H.Q. to attempt to point out to him that unless he changed his directive Panzerarmee Afrika would quickly be destroyed, and that great harm had befallen it already.

But in the meantime, the orders went out: 'I demand all possible efforts to be made to retain possession of the present battlefield, so that operations now in progress may be brought to a victorious conclusion.' Although there were undoubtedly several formations, especially among the Italians, who might choose to take little notice of the order, there would still be many staunch and patriotic Germans who would feel it their duty to obey, whatever the consequences.

The problem, however, would be getting the orders to them while it was still practicable for them to be obeyed, for 'order-counterorder' was quickly producing its inevitable chaos. Some of the administrative and supply services had long foreseen the ultimate necessity of a retreat, and lorries had been loaded and dumps prepared for destruction even before Rommel's first set of orders had gone out – and by the time he set about trying to reverse them, the road convoys were already on the move and the dumps were burning. Communications were still poor, enemy aircraft still ranged the battlefield shooting up every unit, static or mobile, they could find, messages failed to get through, wireless was still being jammed.

By the time darkness fell on the evening of November 3rd, Panzerarmee was unbalanced, the German element uncertain of their roles, the majority of the Italian infantry, one suspects, determined to get away from the scene of their recent ordeals before the next phase brought them even more suffering. Along the southern portion of the Aqqaqir Ridge and the Rahman Track stretching down from it, the 164th Division formations found that the Italians whom they had been 'corseting' had gone, that the gaps left were far too wide for them to cover without reinforcement and that all transport had disappeared; and as apparently their commander did not receive the later 'standstill' order, they marched out that night having repulsed the attack by the Gordons, and before either the 5th Indian Brigade or the Argyll and Sutherlands had arrived.

To the north, too, 90th Light were by dawn back as far as Ghazal, while 15th Panzer were back about six miles west of the Aqqaqir Ridge, their left flank on a twelve-foot-high rise called Tel el Mampsra adjoining the right flank of 21st Panzer Division, which in turn curved north-east as far as the railway line. Somewhere to the south of 15th Panzer lay the Ariete with what was left of the Trieste Motorised Division, mustering between them almost a hundred tanks – but at the best only M13s, all of them in need of service and maintenance.

As has been suggested before, military affairs occasionally acquire an impetus of their own, and little or nothing can be done to check it, even the direct interference of one of the most powerful men in history.

Dawn on November 4th brought Eighth Army the news of victory in the long hard-fought battle, heavy early morning mist, and a traffic jam in the salient which surpassed all previous experience.

With the concentration in the north of all Eighth Army armour (in fact of the major part of Eighth Army's fighting strength) the armoured formations themselves had reverted with one exception to their original divisions – the 1st Armoured Division consisting of Fisher's 2nd Armoured Brigade and the 7th Motor Brigade, the 10th Armoured Division (under Gatehouse) consisting of Custance's 8th Armoured Brigade and the 133rd Lorried Infantry Brigade, and John Harding's 7th Armoured Division consisting of Roberts's 22nd Armoured Brigade and the 131st Lorried Infantry Brigade newly formed from the Queen's battalions; and all of them, plus the 4th Light Armoured Brigade now attached to Freyberg's New Zealanders in place of the annihilated 9th Armoured, were trying to get through and out into the desert by the exit most likely to be mine-free, the *Supercharge* salient:

> Little if any attempt seems to have been made at a higher level to co-ordinate the confusion that was bound to arise from so many divisions struggling to push out through the bottle-neck of the salient area. It would have been hard enough if all had been under the command of the same corps; with two different corps, who were not on the best of terms anyway, both trying to carry out the same task in the same area, it was chaotic. There is no other word to describe the incredible confusion of that dark night in a sea of dust. Vehicles of every formation were travelling in every direction on every conceivable track, looming up in front of each other from unexpected directions out of the thick, stifling pall of dust.[2]

Obviously, the first tanks likely to get away from such confusion would be the ones who had fought along the western face, and Fisher's 2nd Armoured Brigade with the divisional commander General Briggs and the surviving riflemen of the 7th Motor Brigade were ready to move at dawn – if only they could see where they were going and what stood against them. It was nearly 0800 before the mist disappeared, and shortly afterwards the armoured cars of the 12th Lancers moved carefully forward, followed by the Shermans and Grants of the Bays, the 9th Lancers and the 10th Hussars, across the Rahman Track at last, up and over the northern end of the Aqqaqir Ridge – to see in front of them and barring their route to El Daba the remaining Afrika Korps panzers and anti-tank guns, grouped on each side of the rise of Tel el Mampsra.

There was never any great doubt as to what the end of the ensuing battle would be, but neither was there any doubt that the Afrika Korps rearguards would resist to the last. One of their first shells wrecked the tank in which General Briggs was travelling and quite soon after several more tanks were ablaze – and with an appreciation that every vehicle which could move would be required during the next few days, Briggs ordered the armour back while artillery came up over the ridge behind them to deal with the Afrika Korps anti-tank fire. Slowly but inexorably, the line of panzers and guns was smashed, and towards noon it was seen that some of the panzers were drawing back and a few of the guns were being towed away – and as

30-1 After Alamein Montgomery wrote, 'We could not have won the battle in twelve days without that magnificent Australian Division'

32 Hollow triumph: Rommel about to receive his baton from the Führer,
September 30th, 1942

33 Manifest defeat: General von Thoma reports to General Montgomery after his
capture, November 4th, 1942

the British tanks and trucks drove cautiously towards the Tel, they saw amid the wreckage of the battle and the groups of German infantrymen and gunners rising reluctantly with their hands in the air from hastily dug trenches, the tall, weatherbeaten figure of a German general, dressed in a correct field uniform with epaulettes and decorations, standing beside a burning tank, impervious to the heat, the sand, the bullets which still whistled close.

General der Panzertruppe Wilhelm Ritter von Thoma had decided that he would soldier no more under a regime of 'unparalleled madness' and that if his men were to be expected to stand firm and fight against obviously overwhelming odds, then he should be there with them. He had taken his *Kampfstaffel* into the forefront of the battle and seen it destroyed around him.

By this time, a much bigger battle was also being fought some seven miles to the south.

The 'Desert Rats' – John Harding's 7th Armoured Division – had spent the night in the salient itself and at 0630, their planned advance having been twice delayed, the Crusaders and Grants of the 22nd Armoured Brigade felt their way out of the south-west corner into and through the positions taken by the 5th Indian Brigade a few hours before. They drove further down the Rahman Track and just after 0800, as their leading troops were turning west into the desert, they came under fire from 88mm. guns, well sited to cover the track, which obviously had to be destroyed or chased away.

As Pip Roberts deployed his tanks and brought up his artillery, however, orders arrived from General Harding that he should 'push aside' the enemy force and get past it, but when Roberts sent forward his armoured cars – two troops of the 11th Hussars – to find a way around and start cutting enemy communications up towards El Daba, they found no open space but instead a lot more enemy tanks and guns.

Roberts had, in fact, bumped into the Ariete Division with its hundred-odd Italian tanks together with most of the remaining Italian XX Corps artillery, and some random tank and infantry units from Littorio and Trieste, who on their northern flank were in touch with the 15th Panzer Division. Quantitatively it was undoubtedly a formidable force, and qualitatively in many ways as well, for if its tanks were mostly of the type which justified their pejorative title of 'mobile coffins', the Italian troops themselves were the best of Rommel's allies and their artillery was as good as any in the Panzerarmee.

It therefore very soon became evident to Harding that Roberts would be unable to leap-frog his brigade away to the left to get around this enemy block, and that the whole of 7th Armoured

Division would be engaged. The Queen's battalions of the Lorried Infantry Brigade (44th Division had at last been liquidated) had by now cleared the salient to come down in support of the armour, gun batteries wheeled into position and all preparations for a set-piece battle began.

It raged throughout the whole of the morning, on through the noonday haze and well into the afternoon – and neither side made any appreciable troop or armoured movements during the entire time, both apparently prepared to leave the battle to the gunners; but as at last the light began to fade, the Italian and German forces fell back and Roberts's tanks drove forward to take the field upon which they counted the shells of but 29 Italian tanks, a few guns and some 450 prisoners. What had happened to the rest of Ariete remained for a short time something of a mystery.

Meanwhile, however, the 8th Armoured Brigade and 133rd Lorried Infantry of Gatehouse's 10th Armoured Division, originally ordered to drive westwards between the 1st Armoured to the north and the 7th to the south, had by midday extricated themselves from the confusion of the salient, and were about to drive across to Tel el Aqqaqir when new orders arrived from Lumsden: instead they were to drive south, circle around the battle being fought there, and attempt to cut off the remnants of the Panzerarmee with a drive up to the coast at Galal, thirty miles to the west. As they were adjusting their line of march to this new direction, they were caught by one of the few successful Stuka attacks of the whole battle and thoroughly dispersed – and by the time they had reassembled to move off it was late afternoon. The leading squadrons drove down the Rahman Track towards the area of the dying battle fought by Harding's troops, whereat Brigadier Custance decided to pull off to the east and leaguer for the night, his men being, in his opinion, untrained for movement during the dark hours.

Thus by the end of the first day of the break-out after Alamein, the 1st Armoured Division under General Briggs had only advanced some five miles to Tel el Mampsra (for after the surrender of von Thoma they hardly moved at all), 10th Armoured Division under General Gatehouse was still east of the Rahman Track, and 7th Armoured Division under General Harding, although it had destroyed or at least dispersed Rommel's last major armoured force, was still in the area of the battle only two or three miles west of the track. Lumsden's X Corps had not, therefore, achieved much success if their object had been to cut off the remnants of the Panzerarmee.

On the other hand, they had held in place a significant part of the remaining enemy strength, and if circumstances allowed them to continue to hold it there was every reason to believe that it would be destroyed.

But if a 'cutting off' operation was intended, there was now another Allied force well positioned to carry it out.

Bernard Freyberg had been convinced that the enemy were cracking as early as the afternoon of November 3rd, and as soon as news of the Argyll and Sutherlands' occupation of Tel el Aqqaqir had reached him, he was off on a personal reconnaissance of the country to the south of the Tel to find a way through for his two brigades and the remnants of the 9th Armoured Brigade, plus the 4th Light Armoured Brigade which he had prised out of Montgomery as replacement for John Currie's force after their sacrifice in front of Aqqaqir Ridge.

Satisfied as to its practicability, Freyberg had then to contain his soul in patience while his own 6th Infantry under Brigadier Gentry with Currie's remaining tanks disengaged themselves from the north-west corner of the salient, Howard Kippenberger's 5th Brigade came across from the base of the salient, and 4th Light Armoured Division, whom he wanted to lead his force at last out into the open (he intended to drive straight to Fuka, fifty-five miles to the west), arrived from their latest reported position close to Alamein Station!

It is astonishing what men can do when motivated with enthusiasm. The Royal Scots Greys and the armoured cars of the 2nd Derbyshire Yeomanry managed to thread their way through the confusion of the salient by shortly after 0800, and although the rest of the 4th Light Armoured still tailed back past Tel el Eisa they were determined to get into the battle, for down in XIII Corps's area they had seen very little action.

The brigade were with Freyberg by 1000, and at 1030 he sent their armoured cars away down the Rahman Track to discover and report on the action being fought there by his old friend John Harding and his Desert Rats. Soon afterwards he sent the Stuarts and Grants of the Greys to support the cars, and by midday both his infantry brigades were up and he was holding a conference with the brigade commanders – during which reports came in that the Greys were themselves in action, away to the south and west of the main battle which they had by-passed.

It was time to move – and to move fast, for Freyberg wanted to be clear by nightfall not only of the entire Alamein battlefield, but also of the interfering and often confining restrictions which proximity to other divisions – especially armoured ones – so frequently brought about. He set out with his Tactical Headquarters early in the afternoon, assured that the rest of his force would follow as soon as they had collected and stowed away water and rations for eight days, 360 rounds for each field gun and petrol for 200 miles – and em-bedded in his thoughts was the declaration by Brigadier Gentry of the 6th Brigade that every man in the force had been waiting for three years for such a victory and such an advance as now stretched before them, and would willingly travel all night without sleep – and the next day if necessary – in order to consolidate it.

In his diary, Freyberg wrote late that night:

> We began to pass through enemy positions and tanks of the Panzer Divisions that would fight no more, burning transport, and large calibre guns. It was a change much appreciated to speed across open desert away from the dust heap of the Alamein front. As the Div. swept south-westwards the guns of the tanks and arty were in action to the north where the British armour were fighting the Panzer rearguard. 4 Lt Armd Bde were ahead. Behind them marching apparently quite cheerfully were columns of PWs with a solitary armoured car or truck as an escort, carrying a few wounded and a single guard armed with a Tommy gun. We passed an infantry (or artillery) position almost intact with guns in position and ammunition boxes empty . . . [3]

They passed through Sidi Ibeid and hit the old Barrel Track, but when he judged they were south of El Daba Freyberg halted the head of the column to allow the rest of his force to catch up – especially in view of the fact that a signal had just come in reporting indications that Rommel's remaining armour were also making for Fuka, and he felt that he would need more strength than he had at present should he come across them there.

It was midnight before Kippenberger's brigade came up, and they had hardly reported when a small battle broke out at the tail of the column where an enemy force of about seventy men, most probably from the Ramcke Parachute Brigade, attacked presumably in the hope of capturing transport with which to make their escape to the north. Mortars and heavy automatic machine-guns played their parts in this brief but violent encounter, and at the end of it the raiders got away with some vehicles and eight prisoners, leaving behind them seventeen of their own men killed. They had killed eight of the New Zealanders and wounded twenty-six, and set light to an ammunition truck which then acted as a beacon for the 6th Brigade and the rest of Freyberg's force as it came up – but the incident confirmed Freyberg's opinion that he must keep his force concentrated in this open, unmapped, unknown and featureless waste, dotted with wrecked vehicles, sewn with old and now-forgotten minefields – and populated again, as it had been during those far-off days of the June retreat, by random bodies of troops who might or might not prove to be hostile when contact was made.

He would wait to see what daylight brought before continuing his drive to Fuka.

Daylight brought confusion to the whole desert area, chiefly because late in the previous afternoon (November 4th) either common sense or loyalty to his men had overridden Rommel's sense of duty to the Führer. Until then the orders to stand firm had been holding fast the 90th Light Division, what little remained of the two panzer divisions and the Ariete conglomerate, in a position where at least two-thirds of them were being systematically annihilated by the British artillery – but after a conversation with Bayerlein who had yet again been put in command of the Afrika Korps, Rommel decided that further sacrifice was pointless.

The staff were told to pack and move the headquarters back to Fuka as quickly as possible, and it seems that Rommel and Bayerlein themselves raced around the battlefield releasing the formations from their ordeals – and in no uncertain terms, for Rommel accepted that this was to be an affair of *sauve qui peut* in which those who could climb aboard vehicles might get away, those left without transport almost certainly would not.

The result had been the sudden disappearance of organised resistance in front of the British armoured divisions who were, not unnaturally, relieved, and as darkness was near only too glad to retire into leaguer until dawn. But plans for the next day were being drawn up at Eighth Army and X Corps headquarters on the assumption that Panzerarmee would still be present to give battle on November 5th, and the first orders which went out were based on that assumption. Briggs and Harding were to continue their battles, Custance to drive for Galal, and Freyberg for Fuka.

But then reports came in from both the R.A.F. and the armoured car and raiding units (for both the L.R.D.G. and the S.A.S. were out now watching and occasionally attacking the coast road) of Axis traffic streaming westward in even greater density, and realisation that Rommel had ordered a general retreat dawned upon the headquarter staffs. Now everything must be directed towards cutting off as large a portion of the Panzerarmee as possible, and speed would be the keynote.

Briggs and Harding were now to drive their respective divisions west-north-west to the coast, Briggs aiming for El Daba and Harding on his left to hit the road a few miles to the west; Gatehouse was to take his headquarters and his lorried infantry along the top of the Escarpment to where the road climbed it just west of Fuka, and Custance was to follow as quickly as his tanks would roll to support him there; and Freyberg, who would now be transferred from XXX Corps to X Corps and thus come under Lumsden's command (so much for his hopes for independence) would drive parallel to Gatehouse and then curve around to the north towards Maaten Baggush and capture for the R.A.F. the string of landing-grounds near Sidi Haneish.

All armoured car units – and now in addition to the Royals both

the 3rd and 4th South African Armoured Car Regiments were
out – would concentrate near Fuka and attempt to block the road up
the Escarpment.

The headquarters of the armoured divisions received their emended
orders in good time and by 0700 Briggs's armoured brigade (2nd,
under Fisher) were on their way to El Daba with the riflemen of 7th
Motor Brigade on their heels. They met no opposition until they were
on the outskirts of the village when an 88mm. opened fire and killed
the officer who had taken von Thoma prisoner the day before, and the
armoured brigade then swung around to cut the road west of the village
while the riflemen mounted an attack along the road from the east; by
1230 El Daba had been taken with about 150 stragglers and the 88mm.

On the 1st Armoured Division's left flank, Pip Roberts's 22nd
Armoured Brigade had kept pace, quickly realised that El Daba had
been evacuated and then learned from their 11th Hussar reconnaissance troop in front that the road where they were aiming for it was
almost deserted, and that to catch a sizeable bag they would have to
sweep much further west. Without waiting for orders, Harding
therefore pulled back into the desert and drove slightly south of west
on a course which would take the 7th across the Barrel Track and –
though he did not know it then – the path of the New Zealanders.

It was left to the 8th Armoured Brigade under Brigadier Custance to
reap whatever profits were to be earned that day, oddly enough
because it would seem that Gatehouse had failed to pass on the
'emended' order. B Squadron of the 11th Hussars had led them off at
0600, and after a brush with an enemy column more intent on getting
away than staying and fighting – and twice crossing the route of the 7th
Armoured Division without, apparently, noticing any sign of them –
they arrived at Galal, their original objective, and ensconced themselves across both road and railway by about 1100. A small enemy
column arrived soon afterwards and was collected and shepherded
away by the 3rd R.T.R., and then just after midday the head of quite a
large force was seen driving unconcernedly towards them from El
Daba, which they had obviously vacated just before Fisher's troops
had arrived.

Not unlike the Support Group of the 7th Armoured Division at
Beda Fomm twenty-one months before, the 8th Armoured waited in
their hull-down positions and, at exactly the right moment, opened fire
with every gun they had. The result was spectacular and rewarding, for
after less than an hour's hectic confusion the whole enemy column had
been captured or destroyed, 14 panzers and 29 Italian tanks having
been accounted for, four guns, over 100 vehicles in running order and
nearly 1,000 prisoners; and shortly afterwards 11 more tanks and
several more vehicles were found abandoned to the south. All that
Brigadier Custance now required was petrol for the captured vehicles

and some organisation to deal with his prisoners; it was a problem which would grow.

Freyberg's column had in the meantime continued on their way towards Fuka, but very shortly after starting out they caught up with what later proved to be the remains of 15th Panzer Division, and the Grants of the Greys fought a brisk and successful battle with them. By the time the Germans managed to disentangle themselves and draw away, the Greys had put five panzers out of action and captured two intact – and at about the same time, the 1st K.R.R.C. riflemen with the column rounded up several hundred German and Italian infantrymen, including the commander of the Trento Division and most of his staff, who had been blundering about the desert for the last two days.

Successes such as these, however, bred their own problems and by noon Freyberg's force was strung out over many miles of the Barrel Track, and some at least of his manpower had to be diverted to guard duties. By this time, too, his new orders had reached him (though not, apparently news of his transfer to Lumsden's command) and shortly afterwards the head of his column arrived at the fencing around a marked minefield which ran south from the Fuka Escarpment – and when they felt their way up it they found that the only obvious gap was covered by the guns of at least two highly efficient German rearguards. By 1500 some of the leading tanks were through, but it was quite obvious that it would be a long time before the rest of Freyberg's force were west of the minefield, and until then Fuka was open for the survivors of Panzerarmee to use as refuge or channel.

They were arriving often four vehicles abreast on and alongside the narrow ribbon of the road, every truck, tank, gun-limber and lorry full or covered with troops of whom very few were still in cohesive formations. As a general rule discipline held firm, perhaps because stern measures had been taken during the first hours of the retreat – and were known to have been taken. Rommel himself had arrived at Fuka during the early hours of November 5th and watched with anger and sorrow in his heart as the troops flooded in, knowing as he did by now that there were no prepared defences here, no 'Fuka Line', no rest for his exhausted men. The enemy aircraft were bombing and machine-gunning the packed roads, and during that afternoon they found Rommel's H.Q. by wireless intercept and bombed it twice, driving Rommel and Westphal into slit-trenches nearby; and still the traffic came in, though for the moment the rearguards held the nearest enemy force back from the top of the pass.

Then came news of yet another outflanking force further out in the desert and Rommel knew that he must go further back, to Mersa Matruh for the moment – but then where? And how far?

He and his headquarters moved out after dark:

It was a wild helterskelter drive through another pitch-black night. Occasional Arab villages loomed up and dropped behind us in the darkness, and several vehicles lost contact with the head of the column. Finally, we halted in a small valley to wait for daylight. At that time it was still a matter of doubt as to whether we would be able to get even the remnants of the army away to the west. Our fighting power was very low. The bulk of the Italian infantry had been lost. Of the XXI Corps, part had been destroyed after a stiff resistance against the overwhelmingly superior British, and part of it had been overtaken in its retreat and taken prisoner; the vehicles which we had repeatedly demanded for them from the Italian Supply H.Q. had not arrived. The X Italian Corps was on the march south-east of Fuka, short of water and ammunition and, to be quite frank, with no hope of escaping to the west . . .

As for the XX Italian Motorised Corps, it had been practically wiped out on the 4th November – no more than a few companies and detachments remained in the hands of the Corps' staff . . .

The only forces which retained any fighting strength were the remnants of the 90th Light Division, the Afrika Korps' two divisions – now reduced to the strength of small combat groups, the Panzer Grenadier Regiment Afrika and a few quickly scratched-together German units, the remains of the 164th Light Division. Tanks, heavy A.A. guns, heavy and light artillery, all had sustained such frightful losses at El Alamein that there was nothing but a few remnants left.[4]

They still had one or two factors on their side, however, such as that adrenalin tends to flow faster into the veins of men escaping from a trap than into those closing it, and that they now constituted a tightly knit mass imbued with one single aim. They were also travelling along the only road in the locality; and their luck was about to change.

The outflanking force which had precipitated Rommel's retirement from Fuka was Pip Roberts's 22nd Armoured Brigade which Harding had sent off on his own responsibility on a 'long hook' aimed past Fuka. They had been delayed for a short time by the passage in front of them of the tail of Freyberg's force, and then again when they, too, ran into the minefield which was holding up the New Zealanders away to the north. For well over an hour the 11th Hussars hunted for a way through or around – and then some of the attached engineers discovered that the minefield was a dummy – one, moreover, which had been laid by the British during the June retreat.

By this time Roberts had received clear orders – he was to help Freyberg take the Sidi Haneish airstrips – but it was nearly 1800 before his brigade were across the dummy minefield, the lorried infantry brigade (131st) which should have been with him were still some fifteen miles behind, and he was very short of petrol. Sending out the Hussars to reconnoitre the immediate surroundings, he ordered his brigade into leaguer and hoped that both his infantry and his petrol lorries would be up soon.

To the north of Roberts's brigade, Freyberg was still unaware that the minefield which had been holding his force up was a dummy and so was still trying to get the last units of 4th Light Armoured Brigade and his two infantry brigades through a gap under enemy fire. The presence of the hostile guns and all the reports he had received during the afternoon convinced him that strong enemy forces were occupying Fuka and he had no wish to expose his men to another such action as they had experienced at Minqar Qaim, now only a short way away. The bulk of his armour had got through the gap in full daylight, so just before dusk under cover of an attack towards the guns by the armour and smoke fired by the main artillery, 5th Brigade rushed through (the fences had been widened but no suspicions aroused by the fact that nothing else had been found in the vicinity) – but he held 6th Brigade back in reserve. They would all, he decided, now dig in and wait to see what tomorrow would produce.

During that morning (of November 5th) General Lumsden had realised that Rommel's forces were slipping away, and that the comparatively short hooks being made by three of the divisions under his command were unlikely to prove profitable – but there was still another at his disposal, for after their capture of El Daba the 1st Armoured Division had gone into leaguer to the west of the village, where they were counting their prisoners and trying to organise their despatch to the rear. At 1430 they received from X Corps orders that 2nd Armoured Brigade should move off 'at once' on a long, seventy-mile dash to Bir Khalda where they should be by dawn, poised and ready to drive up and capture Mersa Matruh, thirty-five miles away to the north – and with the base, perhaps a major part of whatever was left of Panzerarmee Afrika.

Brigadier Fisher was by this time feeling the effects of the strain of battle and perhaps this explains the delay, for nearly six hours were to pass before the 12th Lancers led the armoured formations off, and when darkness fell two hours later they found themselves still amongst the coastal maze of slit-trenches, old gun-pits, minefields and criss-crossing tracks, all still carrying traffic from every conceivable formation travelling in every direction. Nevertheless, the brigade struggled on and by dawn the leaders had travelled fifty-five miles in twelve hours – which in the circumstances was a thoroughly commendable performance – but they were fifteen miles short of Bir Khalda and the tail of the division was still twenty-three miles behind; and shortly after 0900 (November 6th) the whole division came to a halt through lack of fuel, its leading tanks still short of their dawn objective.

It was 1100 before their B echelon support arrived with petrol for two of the armoured regiments (that for the Bays had gone astray and was stuck in soft sand) and 1330 before those which had been refuelled could start out again, which they did under the brigade second-in-command, as Brigadier Fisher had finally succumbed and gone back to base with the empty petrol trucks.

By this time, Freyberg's force were all through the dummy minefield and driving for the top of the Escarpment overlooking Sidi Haneish and Maaten Baggush. They had run into an enemy column on the way, and after a brisk running fight cut off its tail and collected about five hundred prisoners including one hundred Germans from the 90th Light Division – and to their left, 22nd Armoured Brigade had refuelled about midday and were aiming for the landing grounds along the top of the Escarpment to the west of Sidi Haneish, below which, according to their reconnaissance troops of the 11th Hussars, was a considerable body of enemy troops, probably the last of the 21st Panzer Division.

Back to the east, Gatehouse's 10th Armoured Division with the 8th Armoured Brigade contentedly counting its profits, had been visited by Montgomery during the morning (he had come up to 'apply some ginger') and curtly told to close up along the coast road, clear all the rear area of enemy stragglers – and send every drop of petrol they could spare across the desert to Briggs's 1st Armoured Division; but at about this time, another factor began to complicate the problems facing the Eighth Army in its pursuit of the beaten enemy.

Quite early in the morning pilots returning from flights along the coast had given warning of low cloud moving in from the sea, and by 1000 heavy rain was falling along the coastal strip and moving inexorably inland. By noon the recently captured landing-grounds at El Daba were unusable and fighters could only operate from the all-weather strips back behind Alamein, wheeled vehicles except on the road were sinking to their hub-caps and tracked vehicles were emptying their petrol tanks even more rapidly than usual, at one time Shermans needing three gallons to travel one mile. By afternoon the rain had developed into a steady downpour and every formation not on the road was bogging down. The experience of the New Zealanders was typical of all:

> On the escarpment plateau widening pools filled the hollows where the sand lay deep, turning them into morasses impassable to most vehicles and then overfilling, gouged channels down to lower levels. Only on the rocky ridges was travel possible, but many of these soon stood isolated like islands in the sea of rain. From the escarpment, miniature water-falls cascaded down to the coastal plain to form streams which swept across the

road and railway towards outlets through the sand dunes on the beach.

As the New Zealand brigades drove north towards the road, first the trucks with only rear-wheel drive, then those with four-wheel drive, fell behind. As each truck sank to its axles in the wet sand, the men aboard dismounted from the shelter of cabs and canopied trays and, in the cold persistent rain, dug channels for each wheel. With camel thorn, sand trays, discarded enemy tents, or anything that would help the wheels to grip placed in the channels, the men hauled and heaved their trucks to firmer ground. At first the tracked tanks and carriers were able to tow some of the wheeled vehicles, but soon too many trucks were immobilised and even the tracked vehicles were finding the going treacherous. The rearmost vehicles, driving over ground whose crust had been churned up by those in front, were the first to succumb, so that before long the brigade columns were stretched out over many miles of desert. By late afternoon the men in charge of most of the heavy trucks carrying troops and stores had given up the struggle and the advance slowly ground to a standstill.[5]

Yet another complication was that the weather also seriously affected wireless communication. A large number of the vehicles in Eighth Army were now equipped with sound, reliable transmitter/ receivers, but present conditions caused gross over-use of the facility as everyone tried to inform their commanders of their individual plight and request assistance, and then as even heavier storms swept in from the north, severe atmospheric interference brought about a complete signals black-out. Command from Army down to company level became powerless to effect the onward movement of troops, as it had only the roughest idea of where they were, lacked all means of communication with them – and could have given nothing but empty exhortations to 'get on', if they had. So the command fumed, and the troops cursed the weather and the conduct of the war with sardonic impartiality.

Ironically, though November 6th was the day when the last possibility of cutting off Rommel's forces slipped from Eighth Army's grasp, it was also for Panzerarmee a day of dejection and, at some levels, of near-panic. The weather, of course, contributed to the former, for a condition of sodden misery does not make for the clarity of vision which could see extra possibilities of escape through the pouring rain – but the latter was caused by the realisation that their next backstop was Mersa Matruh, that it was filled with workshops and stores which had been built up over the weeks and, as the port was quite evidently indefensible, as much of this as possible must be destroyed in the extremely short time before evacuation further west.

And how much further west, how soon, and what was awaiting them there? One narrow road as far as Sollum which they knew to be so heavily and systematically mined on each side that it would be dangerous if not impossible to move even a metre off it, routes to the south threading their ways through uncharted minefields on sand already pulverised by months of traffic and now turned by the rain into quagmires, and most ominous of all for those who stayed on the road, two winding passes up the steep escarpment at Halfaya and Sollum where they would almost certainly be bombed – and could be blocked and destroyed by any sizeable enemy force which reached the tops before them.

Yet Rommel himself was by no means despondent, and from his writing one gathers the impression that he was assuaging the pain of defeat and retreat by concentrating on the technical problems of getting his army back into some form of safety – and arguing with his superiors. Hitler's reluctant agreement that Panzerarmee should be allowed to pull back as far as Fuka had arrived the morning after Rommel had issued the relevant orders, as had a similarly grudging missive from Mussolini which ended with the order, 'You must, however, make certain that the non-motorised units are withdrawn too . . . ' without, of course, indicating where either the transport or the petrol for the operation was to be found.

November 6th gave Rommel a short respite from direct command problems and even a little good news, for he was told that 5,000 tons of petrol had arrived at Benghasi – though as he had so often pointed out Benghasi was a long way away; and less than a hour later came news that half the petrol had been destroyed in an air attack. But 2,500 tons gave him some ground for confidence and the loss of the other 2,500 an extra edge to his tongue when in the afternoon an emissary from Maresciallo Cavallero, Generale Gandin, arrived to inquire about plans for the future.

'This,' wrote Rommel later, with some relish, 'suited me very well.'[6]

With fewer than twenty tanks, fewer than twenty anti-tank guns, fewer than fifty field guns, fewer than five thousand men, far less than adequate transport for them all and practically no petrol – Rommel informed the Generale – there was no point in making plans for anything except a retreat as far and as fast as possible, endeavouring occasionally to hinder the enemy but not attempting anywhere to give battle. There was nothing, he insisted, except their own logistic difficulties to stop the British driving straight through into Tripolitania if they wished to, and only British hesitation had allowed Panzerarmee remnants to escape this far or might now allow them to slip away deep into Libya where they might, if they were lucky, be given opportunity to reorganise. In respect of which, he hoped to have them there within the week, and Il Duce's message brought by Gandin that he expected the Italo-German forces to stand on the frontier and deny so much as a metre of the Italian Empire in North Africa to the foe, was a waste of breath. Empty, bombastic breath, true, but nevertheless a waste.

Generale Gandin departed as shaken as Barbasetti had been a few days previously, and Rommel, having released a great deal of his nervous tension, resumed the task of organising the retreat. To the south-west with their backs to the Charing Cross minefields, 15th Panzer were watching with some apprehension the movements through the murk of a body of 'about a hundred tanks' which in the event remained away to the south in soaking isolation all night, while to the south-east the remnants of 21st Panzer, brought to a halt through lack of petrol near Qasaba but with the Voss rearguard group out just beyond it, reported that British tanks from the famous 7th Armoured Division were groping their way towards them.

In the circumstances there was nothing the 21st could do but rely upon their own expertise and luck – and neither deserted them. They drained the petrol from all bogged and damaged vehicles, fought off the approaches (by Roberts's 22nd Armoured Brigade) by prodigal use of their remaining ammunition, pulled back after dark having demolished every vehicle and gun they could not take with them, and made their way westwards through that pitch-black and torrential night, arriving at Charing Cross shortly after dawn – having met and been replenished by a supply column en route! How it happened only the Gods of War might explain.

November 7th brought more surprises, not all as welcome. The stores at Matruh proved disappointing, the bulk having been plundered by earlier arrivals most of whom had pressed on west-wards, or destroyed during the previous day's panic; what was left – for instance a warehouse full of Italian boots – though useful was rarely able to meet the most pressing requirements. On the other hand, it was late in the day before conditions improved sufficiently for the mass of the enemy armour to make any really threatening moves, though 90th Light rearguards at Gerawla were forced back a short distance after probing attacks had been made on them during the late afternoon; otherwise the British seemed for the moment to be indulging in one of their 'pauses for regrouping'.

What had been most welcome to Rommel was the arrival of Generalleutnant Karl Buelowius as Chief Engineer to the Panzer-armee, for the little man was a positive genius at demolitions and booby-traps, at any device, in fact, which would prove a nuisance to and so delay a pursuer. He seemed totally undeterred by the tactical situation into which he was being plunged, positively relishing the intricacies of the tasks which would face him.

Welcome too – though for reasons of personality not so welcome as Buelowius – was the unexpected arrival of Generalmajor Hermann

Ramcke with six hundred of his men, after an epic crossing of the desert from their battle positions south of Ruweisat Ridge. They had ambushed and captured a British supply column and its lorries, and the Generalmajor greeted Rommel with a peculiarly metallic and sardonic smile, metallic as his false teeth were of stainless steel, sardonic because his Fallschirmjäger Brigade was really a Luftwaffe unit and had made themselves highly unpopular with their airs and demands among the soldiers; and Ramcke made few bones about his suspicion that the army had deliberately deserted them as a result.

But their valour was unquestioned and an addition of six hundred such fighting men would come in especially useful at that moment, for Rommel had made another decision. The weather was holding the enemy back now, but they would presumably start moving again as soon as the desert surface dried out; so he would whip his forces out of Matruh that very night on a seventy-mile dash along the road which would take them to Sidi Barrani and within striking distance of those vital passes at Sollum and Halfaya.

They began moving even before dusk with the fighting formation vehicles, partly by accident and partly by design, mixed in with the flood of more expendable traffic and so suffering less concentrated attack from enemy air forces – which in any case seemed now to be more interested in the congestion building up through and below the passes; and when daylight came on the morning of November 8th there was a 25-mile queue along the coast road, solidly jammed up against Halfaya and Sollum by the sheer rapidity and efficiency of the retreat. Fortunately, although there was still some disorder among the administrative and non-combatant formations on the run, cold discipline was now ruling at the tail of the column, strengthened by rising hopes of escape.

Then at midday two further aspects of the war in North Africa assumed significance, one strategic and the other tactical. There had been rumours of great events at the other end of the Mediterranean since early morning, and shortly after 1100 came confirmation; huge invasion fleets had entered the western end of the Mediterranean and landed Anglo-American forces in vast numbers at Oran and Algiers (and others further west at Casablanca) – which raised the possibility, however remote, that any rebuilt Panzerarmee might be caught and crushed between two Colossi. More immediately and much closer to home, Rommel's trusted quartermaster, Major Otto, informed him that the press of traffic below the Escarpment would require two days to clear through the passes if the enemy air attacks were to continue on such a scale, even if none of their ground forces intervened.

Obviously, this latter problem concerned Rommel most for the moment, and that evening he drove across to assess the situation for himself – and was forced to agree with Otto. The traffic was in fact moving with admirable efficiency with control points manned by picked officers who kept the vehicles moving, ruthlessly jettisoned damaged or broken-down trucks, guns or even tanks, and dealt effectively with drivers whose nerve broke under the bombing.

But it was obvious that more risks would have to be taken if the combat units at the end of the queue were to be saved for the trials to come. Whatever remained of the Italian XX Corps, therefore, escorted by the 3rd Reconnaissance Battalion, must immediately break away to the south, skirt the eastern end of the Escarpment and drive for Habata – and from there watch the British and do everything possible to keep them from the tops of the passes; even the staunch remains of the Afrika Korps might have to go the same way to reduce the pressure along the road – though they were now reduced to four panzers, all badly in need of service and maintenance. Down on the plain the 90th Light would continue to provide the rearguard.

And now Rommel had another minor but irritating problem to deal with. Il Duce was still clamouring for defence of the Italian Empire, and Cavallero had ordered the Pistoia Division and a few other random battalions to the Egyptian–Libyan frontier, including even the Giovani Fascisti (Young Fascist) Division of virtually untrained youngsters from Siwa – and asked that Rommel should take them under command. His reply was curt and dismissive; he had neither transport nor administration to spare for such an addition to his forces as the Pistoia, and as for the Giovani Fascisti, if they managed to escape from Siwa he suggested that they go straight to Mersa Brega where they could be employed refurbishing the defences from which the Afrika Korps had emerged eleven months before, on their victorious advance first to Gazala and then to Alamein. For there was no doubt in Rommel's mind that that was the nearest position in which Axis forces might offer some resistance to the Eighth Army – and perhaps not even there.

By the morning of November 9th there were still a thousand vehicles waiting on the plain below the Halfaya and Sollum Passes, despite the night's operations which had been surprisingly successful – and now the plan must be to get them and everyone else in the area up and over the top, then back into Cyrenaica. Motor-cyclists raced away from his headquarters whipping in every unit and straggler they could find as far back as Sidi Barrani, 15th and 21st Panzer Division units after all drew back and started up the narrow hair-pin bends, 90th Light pulled their rearguards further in as enemy armour probed along towards them – and all day long the Kittyhawks machine-gunned between the cliff-tops and Spitfires attacked along the plain. That night Wellingtons and Halifaxes bombed the top of the Escarpment and on towards the frontier around Capuzzo.

In the meantime, Rommel had had an opportunity to assess the strength of the army left to him:

> For manning the Sollum front we had 2,000 Italian and 2,000 German fighting troops with 15 German anti-tank and 40 German field guns, and a few Italian anti-tank guns and several Italian field guns.
>
> For the mobile reserve we had 3,000 German and 500 Italian fighting troops with 11 German and 10 Italian tanks, 20 German anti-tank guns, 24 anti-aircraft guns and 25 field guns.[7]

The most important thing was to get them all out – and that morning British armour and New Zealand infantry were reported assembling in force south of Buq Buq, obviously about to launch a concerted drive along the coast. The orders were issued, 90th Light efficiently and almost invisibly drew in their outer rearguards and by midday they were driving up the Sollum Pass, their passage marked by explosions as Generalleutnant Buelowius's engineers blew the road to pieces, or tumbled the bordering cliffs where they existed across it. By late afternoon the division, once again the rearguard of Panzerarmee, were watching with some curiosity from the top of the Escarpment as the leading Stuarts (of the 4th Light Armoured Brigade) felt their way through the mined approaches to the bottom of Halfaya. Three of them blew up.

To the west, the remainder of Panzerarmee were flooding back into Cyrenaica, few units bothering with interim halts at such places as Sidi Azeiz or Bardia but driving straight for Tobruk; and by this time, Rommel had no plans for remaining there for anything but the briefest pause.

He had now had time to draw some conclusions with regard to the Anglo-American invasion of North Africa and the obviously imminent arrival of their forces in Tunisia, and he wished to make them known to higher authority or at least to discuss the ramifications of the development with them. To his mind, there was now no chance whatsoever of holding General Montgomery's forces back anywhere in Libya or Tripolitania longer than it would take them to bring up artillery and supplies, and organise a holding frontal attack combined with a hook by armour around to the south. Admittedly, the British general seemed to be showing exceptional caution in the advance so far, and there seemed still to be a characteristically British slowness of thought and deliberation about every move the Eighth Army made; but with American industrial power and American armies behind them, they could afford to take their time.

Nowhere east of Tunisia itself was there a single position in which a defence line could not be outflanked from the south by armoured or even motorised formations (with which it was quite evident that Rommel himself was not going to be supplied) and moreover, even the Tunisian frontier would have to be abandoned. Not until the Gabes–Wadi Akarit position was reached ninety miles inside Tunisia, in Rommel's opinion, could a defence line be formed which could not be turned. But there Montgomery could be held at bay and, providing troops and supplies arrived from Germany in sufficient quantities to keep the Anglo-American forces back in Algeria, *and providing his own forces too were properly supplied and reinforced*, then a real blow could be prepared and launched against the British which would throw them back to the east.

Nowhere short of Gabes could such a plan come to fruition, nowhere short of Gabes could the implacable progress of the Eighth Army be halted – and if the High Command were not prepared to allow what was left of the Panzerarmee to retreat there, and then to provide him with the human and industrial material with which to rebuild it, then the best and quickest solution to the problems which faced them all – in Berlin and Rome as much as in Tunis or Tobruk – would be to organise an evacuation along Dunkirk lines for his own force and also for any in Tunisia, and abandon the North African theatre once and for all.

This, in fact, was what the Axis Powers would have to do in the long run anyway, for with Anglo-American naval power controlling the Atlantic, Anglo-American industrial potential growing at a rate which Germany and an Occupied Europe could never match, and American manpower now available to swell the hostile armies and air forces, North Africa was already a dwindling asset and would soon become a bleeding and costly burden.

But to his requests that Maresciallo Cavallero and Generalfeld-marschall Kesselring come out to Africa to discuss these matters with him he received reply that they were both too busy, and to his requests for directions as to the immediate future he was told that as he apparently lacked the means to obey Il Duce's instructions to hold the enemy back in the Halfaya region, then he must so delay them that preparations now being made for a defensive line at Mersa Brega would be completed. There he would find awaiting him not only the Giovani Fascisti Division, but also the La Spezia infantry division and the Centauro armoured division, both of which were at that moment being organised for despatch to the front.

The fact that the rate of retreat might depend upon the military prowess of the enemy far more than on any other factor did not seem to have entered the minds of Comando Supremo, though the events of the next few hours might cause them to wonder. On the night of November 10th/11th New Zealand infantry stormed Halfaya Pass and by the morning leading units of the 4th Light Armoured Brigade were up at the top, taking prisoner three batteries of German artillery and a large detachment of the Pistoia Division who had shown little desire to live up to their regimental motto 'Valiant unto Death'.

British forces were then suddenly reported south of the Gambut airfields, and when they were identified as leading units of the 7th Armoured Division Rommel ordered all rearguards in the frontier area back as quickly as possible. By noon on the 11th they were at El Adem and turning into Tobruk where they hoped to stop for a while – both to rest and reorganise and also to get away the thousands of tons of supplies still there – and to Rommel's fury he found that the transport planes which had flown in had brought him not petrol, but an extra 1,100 men for whom he had neither transport nor ammunition, even for the rifles and light machine-guns which was all they brought with them.

That night reports came back of serious traffic jams ahead through the uncleared minefields and defensive positions around Gazala (although the first of the refugees from Alamein had already passed through Benghasi) but during the following morning (November 12th) British armoured cars and light tanks were seen at Acroma, and the possibility of heavier tanks sweeping around and cutting the Via Balbia to the west was too great. With no further hesitation Rommel ordered everybody out and into the Jebel country as quickly as they could get there.

Tmimi, Martuba, Derna – the names recalled the two advances and the one retreat of the last twenty-one months – and by the evening of the 14th both the panzer divisions and the 90th Light were past them and on their way to Barce. There had been bombings and breakdowns, accidents and narrow escapes (though Buelowius's demolitions and booby-traps held off the closest pursuit) and as ever the nagging worry of petrol shortage. Cavallero had sent forward the German Air Attaché Ritter von Pohl with instructions that Cyrenaica must be held for at least a week longer (he knew better than to come up with such a message himself) and Rommel took the opportunity to point out that sixty tons per day would not save an army whose most miserly quartermaster agreed that they needed two hundred and fifty. This at least brought them a further sixty tons that day which allowed them to move off the following morning – but November 15th very nearly proved to be the day of final disaster for the original formations of the Afrika Korps.

Early in the morning as they were just clearing Giovanni Berta, 90th Light suddenly found themselves under attack from Stuarts and armoured cars, so with the fear that heavier tanks would soon be along they raced off down the coast road – but another Mediterranean storm swept in from the sea, the battered roads cracked and churned under the weight of traffic, and attempts to move off them floundered into mud. By the evening they had only the smallest margin of petrol left – and 15th and 21st Panzer Divisions on the

Maraua road were stranded, still short of Barce, with none at all.

What made the position even more infuriating was that panic somewhere had gripped the staff, and they had turned several petrol ships back from Benghasi in case their precious cargo fell into enemy hands, in addition to ordering one tanker already in port to leave with still a hundred tons aboard; and they then compounded their sins by ordering the demolition of the ammunition dump at Barce just as the troops who could put it to good use were about to enter.

Fortunately the rains (and Buelowius) delayed the pursuers even more than the pursued, and by November 18th, 90th Light were in Benghasi at last with a reaguard back at Benina, 21st Panzer were down at Ghemines, 15th further south at El Magrun with the 33rd Reconnaissance Battalion forward at Sceleidima, while Rommel and his headquarters had reached Zuetina by the coast and the first formation of Centauro to arrive were forward at Antelat. The Ramcke Brigade were already working on the defences on the coast at Mersa Brega, while La Spezia and Pistoia formations extended the line inland.

Rommel, however, was still both worried and angry. The British were at Msus, their armoured cars attacking his scanty rearguards – and ever present in his mind was the possibility of outflanking forces cutting off his own still to the north by a thrust down the Trig el Abd, similar to the one which had destroyed Bergonzoli's army in the very first desert offensive. A British convoy with a strong naval escort had also been reported off Derna, and in the supposition that it was en route for Benghasi yet more Italian shipping laden with petrol – this time naval destroyers – had been turned back, some of the stores there had been burnt, more loaded on to barges which were sunk as soon as they put to sea – and the harbour and dock installations destroyed or severely damaged even while 90th Light were still holding the port. As no further purpose would be served by them remaining there, he ordered them south the following day and watched with sorrow and anguish as they and the other units to the north filtered back, hundreds of their vehicles on tow and all in a condition of battered disrepair. By the night of November 23rd/24th, all the Axis troops were back in the Mersa Brega positions, close to where they had started out so adventurously ten months before.

But ten months before he had had at his disposal two excellent and well-equipped panzer divisions and an adequate stock of both fuel and ammunition; now there was nothing but the tattered remains of those divisions plus the totally inexperienced Centauro armour, to provide a flank guard to a static position into which equally in-experienced Italian infantry were being fed, easy prey to enemy armoured and motorised columns who could cut them off by a simple swing around the south.

It was essential for them to be stationed further back, so in an attempt to get the demand for a stand between Brega and El Agheila cancelled he sent off one of the more intelligent Italian officers, Generale de Stefanis, commander of the XX Corps, to Rome to try to explain the realities of the situation there. In the meantime, Kesselring and Cavallero were at last available to see him, and they and Maresciallo Bastico arrived at Arco dei Fileni (Marble Arch, some fifty miles west of El Agheila) for what Rommel hoped would be a reasoned discussion.

Both the meeting and de Stefanis's trip to Rome were a waste of time. Even while de Stefanis was away a directive arrived from Hitler confirming Il Duce's order that the Mersa Brega line was to be held at all costs, and promising massive reinforcements of men, guns and tanks to ensure that it was; and it was quite obvious at the Marble Arch meeting that the generals all knew of the instruction and would not countermand it, even though they also knew that the promises which accompanied it would not be kept – if only because everything which came across the Mediterranean now would go via Tunis and there be requisitioned for the battle against the new invaders. And as an added twist of the knife in Rommel's soul, he was informed that he and his force would once again revert to Maresciallo Bastico's command!

Having made the position clear, the visitors then attempted to assauge the bitterness with flattery, assuring Rommel of their admiration for his feat in bringing his army back eight hundred miles along a single roadway without major loss. It was surely a feat unique in the annals of warfare – but when Rommel asked pointedly what Bastico advised him to do if the 7th Armoured Division chose to ignore the Brega and Agheila positions and just drive past to the south on their way to Tripoli, his question was met with sullen silence.

Then followed a minor but intensely irritating episode which deeply affected Rommel, revealing in stark relief the scale of the reverses he had suffered. The night after the meeting at Marble Arch, in order to obtain some relief from worry and tension he attended a cinema show put on for the headquarter staff and troops; the films were light and trashy but there was also a newsreel, weeks old, which, as a vengeful fate would have it, showed Rommel at the Berlin press reception making that ill-fated assertion, 'We have the door to all Egypt in our hands. What we have, we hold!' Even Rommel's presence and the deep loyalty the majority of the audience felt for him could not restrain the sardonic laughter which greeted the declaration.

Much worse was to follow. The next day came the decisions made over his head after the Marble Arch meeting. Il Duce demanded not only that the Mersa Brega line be held but that Rommel should launch an attack against the British as soon as possible – supported, he announced, by a strongly reinforced Luftwaffe which even Kesselring admitted would not be available. Moreover, in the event of a British attack coming before Rommel's, then Bastico alone was empowered to give an order to retreat – an order, Comando Supremo directed, that he was only to give in the direst emergency.

Enough was enough; not only had Rommel's pride been deeply hurt, but he was tired and the illness from which he had not fully recovered when he returned to Egypt was plaguing him again. He would return to Europe, hoping that a brief respite there would do him good, and also that he could secure an interview with the Führer and explain to him the realities of the situation in Africa.

He was quite confident that General Montgomery would not attempt any serious challenge to the Mersa Brega positions in the short time he would be away.

In this Rommel was quite justified; General Montgomery had not the slightest intention of attacking the Mersa Brega–El Agheila positions until he had amassed enough strength in the area to be assured of victory, and indeed, enough to take his forces well on their way to Tripoli. There was to be no repeat in 1943 of the riposte of January 1942 or of Rommel's first lightning success of April 1941 – and in taking every possible measure to ensure against such reverses the Army Commander had the support of every man under his command, especially those who had taken part in either or both of the previous débâcles. The magic of Rommel's name, his reputation for rebounding with unexpected strength and brilliant exploitation from every reverse, had contributed greatly to the caution with which the X Corps divisions had pursued him, and the wariness with which even now the armoured cars and light tanks of 7th Armoured Division watched and approached the Mersa Brega positions.

That caution had not, of course, been the sole reason for Eighth Army's failure to 'put the whole Panzerarmee in the bag' – the expressed intention of General Montgomery at and before the time of the break-out. Lack of training, lack of trust, and logistical problems had all contributed, especially the first two at the beginning.

Montgomery had trained the infantry of Eighth Army specifically for the 'break-in' battle and they had succeeded admirably. His instructions for the training of the armour had resulted in their concentration on what Gatehouse had called 'a static role', more as mobile artillery than as a rapidly moving striking force, and the experiences of both 1st and 10th Armoured Division during the battle had not led them to believe that the Army Commander would allow them a great deal of individual responsibility afterwards. In this they

were quite right, for it was Montgomery's nature to try to keep a tight
personal control on every battle – and even with the break-out
achieved the relationship between himself and General Lumsden was
neither happy nor relaxed. As a result the original X Corps divisions
made short hooks to the coast – one of which it should be remembered was the most successful of all – and only the column under the
trusted Freyberg and the 7th Armoured Division from XIII Corps
under the equally trusted John Harding made thrusts likely to prove
really effective.

These two were defeated first by the accident of the dummy
minefield and then by logistics, the rain dealing a final blow to their
hopes.

As far as logistics were concerned, one of the problems facing the
supply columns was that for those first crucial days everything had
to be channelled out through that narrow *Supercharge* salient, feet
deep in dust and getting deeper every hour, pocked with trenches and
gun-pits, dotted with wrecked vehicles and guns, still treacherous by
reason of the random undiscovered mine, and choked with traffic
coming back the other way. The conditions were not helped by bad
traffic control as the best men were up forward, and bad driving
discipline because the battle had been won now, and euphoria ruled.

And very soon one of the iron rules of war made itself felt – the
further a victorious army advances, the longer its lines of communication and supply; all Eighth Army's problems would indeed
have been eased had they caught Rommel's forces before they had
reached Fuka.

Once they – and the leading British formations – were over the
frontier, Montgomery had then to cope with yet another perennial
problem, shortage of infantry, exacerbated now by the demand from
the Australian Government that as the battle had been won, General
Morshead and his division should return home in order to play their
part in the defence against the new danger in the Pacific. The men
who had 'crumbled' the enemy and held the northern salient, who
had isolated Thompson's Post and won time for the launching of
Supercharge, would not be available for the pursuit. It was a heavy
loss, but it had been expected; at least the New Zealanders would
remain, as would the 4th Indian and, of course, General Wimberley's
Highlanders.

Nevertheless, Montgomery had felt it necessary to call a pause at
the frontier because of the difficulties of supply and also for reorganisation – only armoured cars, some light tanks and some artillery
units would immediately go on into Cyrenaica, in formations not
dissimilar to those of the Jock Columns of the first desert campaign.
Freyberg's force must rest and reorganise, 7th Armoured Division
replace its more battered and worn tanks and vehicles with fresh ones

with a view to carrying on the pursuit, 1st and 10th Armoured Divisions concentrate on clearing up the whole of the area east of the Wire. After all, between them they had contributed largely to victory in a hard-fought battle lasting twelve days, and in a further six days had chased the remnants of the famous Panzerarmee two hundred and fifty miles; it was not surprising that organisationally they were somewhat out of breath, and anyway there were prisoners to be marshalled back, and thousands of weapons, vehicles and dumps littering the Western Desert of Egypt which must be quickly checked and when possible put to good use.

But contact with Rommel's forces had to be kept, of course, and on November 14th four columns were sent out under command of 7th Armoured Division. Each had detachments of field, anti-tank and anti-aircraft guns and engineers, and the first was grouped around the armoured cars of the 12th Lancers. Their task was to drive for Martuba and capture the landing-ground there, and when the R.A.F. had taken over to drive on to Derna for the same purpose.

The second column was detached from the 4th Light Armoured Brigade and contained a troop of Grant tanks, and their task was to follow the first column to Martuba but then to proceed along the main road through the Jebel Akhdar to Benghasi. The other two columns were to drive hard for El Adem, then on November 15th to take the southern route through Tengeder, capture the landing-ground at Msus and then probe down towards Antelat. Every column contained men who had been over the ground before, and every column commander was instructed that his main task was to report every action fought and every contact made with the enemy, as quickly as possible.

These had been the forces, backed by remarkably little else on the ground, which had chivvied Rommel's Panzerarmee remnants out of Tobruk, the Afrika Korps through the Jebel, and finally the combined Italo-German forces back into the Mersa Brega positions. They had, however, been fully supported by the R.A.F. who had sent in parties to clear landing-strips as soon as they were captured, driven the German fighters out of the sky and guarded the army formations from Stuka attacks. And every night the bombers were out (including the American heavy bombers) over Tobruk at first, then Benghasi and Tripoli, sinking Rommel's supply ships, and robbing him in one week of nearly 10,000 tons of fuel.

As soon as it had become obvious to General Montgomery that Rommel and what remained of his forces were going to get away, he reasoned that they would not stop to give battle before the El Agheila positions. With this in mind, as soon as he had attended to organisational plans to ensure that some pressure at least was kept up on the retreating enemy, he turned his mind to the problems of defeating them there.

The first was to get the forces and the men he wished to command them assembled in the forward area. With the success of XXX Corps in the recent battle to recommend him, General Leese was the obvious choice of commander for the next one, which would, equally obviously, be a corps, not an Army, battle. Leese must therefore move up as soon as possible into the forward area, and his new XXX Corps divisions would be the 7th Armoured, the 51st Highland and the New Zealanders. X Corps was nominally already in the Jebel, although only formations of the 7th Armoured Division – to be transferred anyway – were there with the command; which was to change. After the difficulties between Army and X Corps commands during Alamein, not even McCreery would press for General Lumsden's retention within Eighth Army.

General Horrocks therefore would take over X Corps, now composed of 1st Armoured and the 4th Indian Divisions, and as soon as XXX Corps were in place, Horrocks would establish his command in and around Benghasi as an insurance against another of Rommel's explosive counter-attacks should the enemy forces somehow gather sufficient strength to mount one. If they did not, then X Corps would be available for exploitation of XXX Corps's breakthrough.

By November 29th, Montgomery's plans for the battle were complete. Two brigades of the Highland Division would drive frontally against the Mersa Brega position down the coast road, 7th Armoured Division plus the third Highland brigade would attack the enemy line some ten miles to the south at Bir es Suera and drive for the Via Balbia between El Agheila and El Mugtaa, and the New Zealand Division, still with the 4th Light Armoured Brigade under command, would make a huge left hook to the south, cut through between Sidi Tabet and Marada and drive for Marble Arch or even Nofilia. The main operation would begin on the night of December 16th/17th, but the New Zealanders with so much farther to go – probably over very difficult country – would leave their assembly point at El Haseiat two or three days before.

There were thus at most eighteen days for 7th Armoured and the Highlanders – and only fourteen for the New Zealanders – to organise themselves again for battle, and for the Army Q Branch to solve all the problems of supplying them with whatever they would need to defeat Rommel again and drive him back perhaps another hundred miles. No time must be wasted.

The Gods of War now favoured the Eighth Army. The harbour facilities at Benghasi were not so badly damaged as had been feared, traffic control was improved and strictly enforced to keep the convoys moving, and although petrol supplies presented a problem, ammunition dumps abandoned during the retreat through the Jebel eleven months before were found virtually undisturbed. Supplies poured in through the harbours of Tobruk and Benghasi, were brought up further every day by rail from the Delta as the line was repaired (it was in use as far as Matruh – 130 miles from Alamein – by November 14th) and trucked on from there. General Montgomery had no doubt that all would be well on time.

So far as General Leese was concerned, matters were proceeding quite well for him too. The line his forces had to breach swept from Mersa Brega on the coast around to Maaten Giofer some forty miles away on the Agheila–Marada track, then down along it for ten miles to Sidi Tabet. Salt marshes, broken ground and soft sand would undoubtedly make it difficult for tanks or wheeled vehicles to manoeuvre, and minefields would certainly cover the gaps between them – though by no means as thick or as wide as those his infantry and engineers had recently conquered.

In any case, the crucial movement would be that by General Freyberg's force around the flank, and there luck was favouring them. The armoured cars of the King's Dragoon Guards and the specialists of the Long Range Desert Group had provided the answers to the most pressing problems, and the latter would also furnish guides for the New Zealanders, leading them over the first hundred miles of comparatively good going to Chrystal's Rift (named after the K.D.G. captain who discovered and reconnoitred it). The K.D.G. would then take them through the rift, with the L.R.D.G. taking over again afterwards and leading them on as far as Fortune would allow. The men were rested and keen (the Highlanders had even held a review with the officers in kilts), more Shermans were arriving, and there would again be no shortage of ammunition.

Then on the evening of December 9th, reports from Highlander patrols told of movements behind the enemy lines which looked remarkably like withdrawals; by the evening of the 12th it was quite evident that Rommel and his forces were getting out.

Rommel's visit to Europe had not been a success. He had left Libya on the morning of November 28th and was at the Führer's head-quarters at Rastenburg by 1600, having called in briefly at Wiener-Neustadt to speak to his wife on the way. His reception first by Keitel and Jodl was wary and cool, and then at 1700 by Hitler chilly in the extreme, even when Hitler had recovered from his astonishment that Rommel should have left Africa without receiving his permission to do so.

But at first he had at least received attention while he recounted the course of the battle at Alamein and events since and, at the end, praise. His conduct of all operations, Hitler announced and the surrounding court nodded in agreement, had been faultless and indeed unique.

But when Rommel went on to suggest that although delaying actions might be fought in the desert or in Tunisia for a while, it should be accepted that in the end Africa would have to be abandoned, the storm broke. Retreat and evacuation was all that his generals ever suggested, the Führer screamed; he had had exactly the same trouble last year with the generals on the Russian Front and had had to insist the armies stayed where they were – and now they were suggesting the same thing about Stalingrad. But they would stay where they were and consolidate the victories he had already given them in the east – and so would Rommel in Africa.

There would be no retreat from Mersa Brega, there would be no more throwing away or abandoning of valuable weapons – which in view of the fact that Rommel claimed that 10,000 of his 15,000 men were unarmed was the only possible explanation – and most important of all, there would be no more thought of leaving Africa. Such an abandonment would weaken Mussolini's position to such an extent that he could be overthrown and Italy might then break the Pact of Steel; or even switch to the other side.

Germany's attention and indeed her destiny were now directed to the east. Here battles were being fought which reduced the affairs in North Africa to the level of skirmishes, and the Führer had no time and little patience for them; it was the duty of the men he sent there to execute their responsibilities properly, to vanquish the Reich's enemies and to do so without distracting his mind with unnecessary trifles.

Yes – all right! Rommel needed more weapons, more supplies and more men. But the person most responsible for the North African theatre and everything that happened in the Mediterranean was Il Duce, and Rommel should return to Rome immediately accompanied by Reichsmarschall Goering who would argue Rommel's case, bring the whole of his persuasive personality to bear on the problem and see that Rommel was properly supported.

With which Rommel was dismissed – to spend the next two days in Goering's specially furnished train, listening to the fat fool's pluming self-approbation, to his boasting, to his bland dismissal of all Rommel's troubles as caused by his own exhaustion and weakness which had, according to the Reichsmarschall, induced in him a spirit of debilitating pessimism. Even the fact that Frau Rommel joined the train on November 29th served only as temporary relief, and by the time they had arrived in Rome, Rommel was even more depressed than when he had left Africa.

In Rome, his suggestion that his forces should retire to Tunis and join the newly strengthened forces there to form a powerful striking force with which to administer a spectacular defeat upon the Anglo-Americans – which had for a time in the train received Goering's approval – was curtly rejected by Kesselring on the grounds that enemy air forces based at Tripoli, Algiers and Malta would make Tunisia uninhabitable. But somewhat to his surprise, Mussolini and the Italian generals were at last sufficiently realistic to see that if Rommel's forces remained too long in the Mersa Brega positions, they would be lost; and by now the majority were Italians.

He should, they agreed, make all necessary plans for a retreat to Buerat where, they assured him, some fortifications already existed, others would now be built as soon as materials and labour could be sent there, and the non-motorised infantry at Mersa Brega should go as quickly as possible. The Afrika Korps, with their panzer strength now up to fifty-four, the reconstituted Ariete and the Centauro should stay in the Mersa Brega–El Agheila positions until the enemy attacked, then retreat to the Buerat Line as slowly as possible using every conceivable device and tactic to inflict damage and loss upon their pursuers. Ample petrol stocks would be built up and there would be no further shortages.

This slightly more realistic attitude in Rome was at least a partial relief though Rommel arrived back in Africa a profoundly depressed man. The Buerat Line might be a step in the right direction but it was a very short step, and would in any case be dependent not only upon the authorities in Rome keeping their promises about sending petrol, but the Royal Navy and the Royal Air Force allowing it to arrive.

There was, as it happened, enough fuel immediately available for the operation of withdrawal to commence, and on the night of November 6th the first of the Italian infantry pulled out. Orders had been issued that this was to be done as quietly and unostentatiously as possible, so Rommel was infuriated and then very worried when he learned that the lorries transporting them had driven off with headlights blazing, their cargoes cheering and singing, presumably with relief. But no immediate reactions were forthcoming from the enemy side of the line, and on the next night the Giovani Fascisti went back, followed on the 8th by the Pistoia; and the Ariete and the armoured divisions would have followed immediately had there been any petrol left.

Enough did arrive during the following days to lift the armour at least back to El Mugtaa, and as on November 11th it became apparent that the Highland Division opposite the Mersa Brega front were about to attack, the orders went out, the rearguards were posted, the main formations drew away and by midnight the Via Balbia was again filled with panzers and guns driving westwards.

In fact, on the evening of November 11th the Highland Division were merely mounting a heavy raid, that being all which could be managed in the time.

When the reports had reached General Montgomery that Rommel seemed to be about to withdraw, he had advanced the date of the main attack by forty-eight hours to the night of the 14th/15th, thereby screwing even tighter an already tight schedule. Nevertheless, the artillery cover was fired on time – falling for the main part on vacated positions – and both the Highland Division and the 7th Armoured drove in along their allotted paths.

They met little direct resistance from enemy strongpoints or even artillery, but they quickly ran into minefields sewn now with anti-personnel mines, and along roads or tracks infested with the most ingenious booby-traps that Generalmajor Buelowius could devise. At one point in the pursuit which followed, C Squadron of the 11th Hussars were feeling their way through the wadis and ditches to the south of the Via Balbia:

> Here, in extremely difficult country, a minefield had been laid with such skill and care that its mines were practically impossible to see, and 'C' ran into it without the slightest warning. The car in which Lieutenant J. French was leading No 3 Troop fell a victim first, when the explosion which wrecked the car killed outright Trooper C. F. Blakey, and wounded both French and Trooper Whittard. Only then was it discovered that both the two remaining cars were already right in the middle of the mines, with the result that the whole Troop was immobilised for the remainder of the day.[8]

It took engineers with special equipment four hours to clear a way out for the first car, for every mine was found to have been booby-trapped and there were some detonating mechanisms which had been buried so deep that the detectors were unavailing. Eventually, the first car was driven out with both the commander and gunner tip-toeing in front of each wheel searching for signs of further ground disturbance – and when a second car tried to creep out along the first's tyre-tracks it promptly blew up on a mine which had been hidden deep under those which had been removed:

> Daybreak on December 16th showed that the enemy had fallen back, and 'A' Squadron reached Marble Arch at noon, despite the fact that both the road and its verges were so heavily mined that the armoured cars were forced to pick their way cross-country over broken ground and bogs.[9]

But infantry-carriers, gun-limbers or tanks needed roads or hard desert surfaces and now the war was moving into very different country. There were flower-decked meadows to rejoice the artistic heart, but the flowers grew in soft soil and what hard ground there was usually lined the sides of ravines. As a result the Highland Division's progress had been reduced – along and abreast of the road but almost without active enemy resistance – at times to one mile an hour, by the combination of booby-traps and broken ground.

The New Zealanders had completed their hook successfully – though without all their armour as the soft going used so much petrol that they outran their supplies – but they ran into the 15th Panzer Division cannily positioned to hold the road open for the 21st Panzer, still defending the defile at El Mugtaa against the Highlanders. There was a brisk engagement, broken off when Rommel issued orders for a full retreat to Nofilia, just enough petrol having arrived for this to take place.

Again the Italo-German forces escaped, and the New Zealand historian admirably summed up:

> The high hopes of cutting off even some of the retreating enemy had come to nothing, partly because greater speed was possible along the road than across the desert, partly because the enemy was well-seasoned and adopted the orthodox safeguards of flank and rearguards, and partly because of the difficulties of deploying by night in unknown country at the end of a long and tiring move . . . [10]

This was to be the story all the way, and there is no doubt that Buelowius thoroughly deserved the promotion and tributes which Rommel later awarded him. He turned the advance of Eighth Army in the closing days of 1942 into a snail-paced nightmare, and saved Rommel's forces from the dire straits into which petrol shortages – for none of Comando Supremo's promises were kept – threatened to plunge them. They were back in Nofilia by December 16th, out two days later and into Sirte where they were left in peace until Christmas Day when 15th Panzer, who were serving there as rearguards, had suddenly to abandon their festivities and move out fast in the face of a movement towards them by tanks of 7th Armoured Division. They, and indeed all of Rommel's forces, were back in the Buerat defences by the last day of the year.

They were to be left there, occasionally bombed by the R.A.F. or the American heavy bombers but undisturbed by ground forces other than raiders against their lines of communication, until the middle of January – for Montgomery had been caught in a logistic trap.

Tobruk was now 800 miles to the rear and, in addition to the thousand or more tons of supplies a day the Army needed, the air forces wanted forward all-weather fighter strips as quickly as possible and even more solidly constructed strips for bombers; and Montgomery was as keen as they were that they should have them. Very quickly Benghasi was open and supplies were pouring through – but even Benghasi was 300 miles from Nofilia and nearly 450 from

Buerat – and who knew what Buelowius would have done to the roads as he had passed over them?

But 230 miles beyond Buerat lay Tripoli, an even bigger port than Benghasi, and if it could be taken quickly then the demolitions might be as quickly dealt with, and the logistic problems which had so beset Eighth Army since they had crossed the Egyptian frontier would be solved.

But how to get there?

At least four divisions would be needed to be certain of breaking the Buerat Line – or even successfully outflanking it in this new kind of country – and in order to ensure full support in case of accident, at least two more divisions would be needed close at hand. XXX Corps would therefore consist of 50th and 51st (Highland) Divisions, 7th Armoured and, of course, the New Zealanders; Horrocks could bring his 1st Armoured Division and the 4th Indian up into the El Agheila area while Leese assembled his divisions between there and Nofilia and only armoured cars and Stuarts with light artillery would operate further forward.

But the tonnage of stores needed to sustain six divisions would strain transport to the limit, and when the advance began the problems would increase – and could not long be borne. Montgomery's calculations made it quite clear that once his forces began to move forward against Buerat, they would have only ten days in which to reach and secure a new source of large-scale supply.

Tripoli in ten days . . . or he would be forced to bring his army back in a withdrawal which would reawaken memories of past misfortunes, would damage the victorious image of the Eighth Army and might even affect morale within it. He and they must therefore take their time now and thus be invincible when the moment for battle arrived.

So through the last days of 1942, the divisions moved into their assembly areas, the ships unloaded at Tobruk and Benghasi, and the long columns of trucks and lorries roared continuously along the narrow roads which the engineers were labouring all the time to keep passable; while up front even more engineers still risked their lives every minute dismantling Buelowius's masterpieces, and losing 170 of their number while so doing.

And further up in front, the armoured cars of 11th Hussars, the King's Dragoon Guards and the Royal Dragoons, and the Stuarts and R.H.A. Batteries attached to them, moved carefully along the roads and winding tracks leading up to and across the Buerat positions, exchanging shots with their opposite numbers of Rommel's reconnaissance battalions, sometimes losing cars, sometimes lives. And waiting for the next onslaught to begin.

There was no *feu de joie* among the Germans as 1942 died, and if the few British present who had witnessed the fireworks twelve months before could at least reflect that they were now some three hundred miles forward of where they had been then, they had arrived by a peculiarly circuitous route.

And in human terms, a costly one. At Alamein alone Eighth Army had lost 13,500 in killed and wounded and the enemy must have lost at least half that number in their defensive battle. Heaven alone knew how many on both sides had been lost on the way there – or since.

There were so many gone – some to graves, some to hospitals, some to prison-camps, some to other theatres of war; a tiny fraction even back to civilian life. Of those who were gone for ever, some had been fools, some incompetent, some just unlucky; but amongst them, on both sides, had been the bravest and the best.

Appendix I:
Forces Engaged at the Battle of Gazala, May 26th, 1942

Allied Forces

Commander-in-Chief, Middle East   General Sir Claude Auchinleck

EIGHTH ARMY
Lieutenant-General Neil M. Ritchie

XIII Corps – Lieutenant-General W. H. E. 'Strafer' Gott

1st South African Division – Major-General D. H. Pienaar
    1st South African Infantry Brigade
    2nd South African Infantry Brigade
    3rd South African Infantry Brigade

2nd South African Division (in Tobruk) – Major-General H. B. Klopper
    4th South African Infantry Brigade
    6th South African Infantry Brigade
    9th Indian Infantry Brigade

50th (Tyne and Tees) Infantry Division – Major-General W. H. C. Ramsden
    69th Infantry Brigade
    150th Infantry Brigade
    151st Infantry Brigade

1st Army Tank Brigade – Brigadier W. O. L. O'Carroll

32nd Army Tank Brigade – Brigadier A. C. Willison

XXX Corps – Lieutenant-General Willoughby Norrie

1st Armoured Division – Major-General H. Lumsden
    2nd Armoured Brigade
    22nd Armoured Brigade
    201st Guards Brigade Group

7th Armoured Division – Major-General F. Messervy
    4th Armoured Brigade
    7th Motor Brigade
    3rd Indian Motor Brigade
    29th Indian Infantry Brigade Group
    1st Fighting French Brigade Group

German and Italian Forces

Comandante Superiore   Generale d'Armata Ettore Bastico

PANZERARMEE AFRIKA
Generaloberst Erwin Rommel

Deutsches Afrika Korps – Generalleutnant Walther K. Nehring

15th Panzer Division – Generalleutnant Gustav von Vaerst (until May 27th)   Oberst Eduard Crasemann (from May 27th)
    Panzer Regiment 8
    Infantry Regiment 115
    Panzerjäger Abteilung 33
    Reconnaissance Battalion 33
    Artillery Regiment 33

21st Panzer Division – Generalmajor Georg von Bismarck
    Panzer Regiment 5
    Infantry Regiment 104
    Panzerjäger Abteilung 39
    Reconnaissance Battalion 3
    Artillery Regiment 155

90th Light Division – Generalmajor Ulrich Kleeman
    Infantry Regiment 155
    Infantry Regiment 200
    Sonderverband 288
    Panzerjäger Abteilung 190
    Reconnaissance Battalion 580
    Artillery Regiment 190

Corpo d'Armata di Manovra XX – Generale di Corpo d'Armata Ettore Baldassarre

Ariete Armoured Division – Generale di Divisione Giuseppe de Stefanis
    132nd Armoured Regiment
    132nd Artillery Regiment
    8th Bersaglieri Regiment

Trieste Motorised Division – Generale di Divisione Azzi
    65th Infantry Regiment
    66th Infantry Regiment
    9th Bersaglieri Regiment

Gruppe Cruewell – Generalleutnant Ludwig Cruewell

Corpo d'Armata X – Generale di Corpo d'Armata Benvenuto Gioda
  Brescia Division – Generale di Divisione Giacomo Lombardi
  Pavia Division – Generale di Divisione Antonio Franceschini

Corpo d'Armata XXI – Generale di Corpo d'Armata Enea Navarini
  Trento Division – Generale di Divisione Getti
  Sabratha Division – Generale di Divisione Mario Soldarelli

Appendix II:
Forces Engaged at the Battle of Alamein, October 23rd – November 6th, 1942

Allied Forces

Commander-in-Chief, Middle East   General the Hon. Harold Alexander

EIGHTH ARMY
Lieutenant-General Sir Bernard L. Montgomery

X Corps – Lieutenant-General Herbert Lumsden

1st Armoured Division – Major-General R. Briggs
   2nd Armoured Brigade
   7th Motor Brigade

10th Armoured Division – Major-General A. H. Gatehouse
   8th Armoured Brigade
   24th Armoured Brigade
   133rd Lorried Infantry Brigade

XIII Corps – Lieutenant-General Brian G. Horrocks

7th Armoured Division – Major-General A. F. Harding
   4th Light Armoured Brigade
   22nd Armoured Brigade
   131st Infantry Brigade (after November 1st)

50th Infantry Division – Major-General J. S. Nichols
   69th Infantry Brigade
   151st Infantry Brigade
   1st Greek Infantry Brigade

44th Infantry Division – Major-General I. T. P. Hughes
   131st Infantry Brigade (until October 30th)
   132nd Infantry Brigade

Fighting French Brigade – Brigadier-General P. Koenig

XXX Corps – Lieutenant-General Oliver Leese

4th Indian Division – Major-General F. I. S. Tuker
   5th Indian Infantry Brigade
   7th Indian Infantry Brigade
   161st Indian Infantry Brigade

51st (Highland) Division – Major-General D. N. Wimberley
   152nd Infantry Brigade
   153rd Infantry Brigade
   154th Infantry Brigade

9th Australian Division – Major-General L. J. Morshead
   20th Australian Infantry Brigade
   24th Australian Infantry Brigade
   26th Australian Infantry Brigade

2nd New Zealand Division – Major-General B. C. Freyberg, V.C.
   5th New Zealand Brigade
   6th New Zealand Brigade
   9th Armoured Brigade

1st South African Division – Major-General D. H. Pienaar
   1st South African Infantry Brigade
   2nd South African Infantry Brigade
   3rd South African Infantry Brigade

23rd Armoured Brigade Group – Brigadier G. W. Richards

German and Italian Forces

PANZERARMEE AFRIKA
General der Kavallerie Georg Stumme (until October 24th)
Generalleutnant Wilhelm Ritter von Thoma (until October 25th)
Generalfeldmarschall Erwin Rommel

Deutsches Afrika Korps – Generalleutnant Wilhelm Ritter von Thoma

15th Panzer Division – Generalleutnant Gustav von Vaerst
   Panzer Regiment 8
   Panzergrenadier Regiment 115
   Panzerjäger Abteilung 33
   Machine-gun Battalion 8
   Reconnaissance Battalion 33
   Artillery Regiment 33

21st Panzer Division – Generalmajor Heinz von Randow
   Panzer Regiment 5
   Panzergrenadier Regiment 104
   Panzerjäger Abteilung 39
   Reconnaissance Battalion 3
   Artillery Regiment 155

90th Light Division – Generalleutnant Theodor Graf von Sponek
  Infantry Regiment 155
  Infantry Regiment 200
  Infantry Regiment Afrika 361
  Panzergrenadier Regiment Afrika
  Panzerjäger Abteilung 190
  Reconnaissance Battalion 580
  Artillery Regiment 190

164th Infantry Division – Generalmajor Carl-Hans Lungershausen
  Panzergrenadier Regiment 125
  Panzergrenadier Regiment 382
  Panzergrenadier Regiment 433
  Reconnaissance Battalion 220
  Artillery Regiment 220

22nd Parachute Brigade – Generalmajor Hermann Ramcke

Corpo d'Armata X – Generale di Corpo d'Armata Edoardo Nebba

Brescia Division – Generale di Divisione Brunetto Brunetti
Pavia Division – Generale di Brigata N. Scattaglia

Corpo d'Armata XX – Generale di Corpo d'Armata Giuseppe de Stefanis

Ariete Armoured Division – Generale di Brigata Francesco Arena
Littorio Armoured Division – Generale di Divisione Gervasio Bitossi
Trieste Motorised Division – Generale di Brigata Francesco La Ferla
Folgore Parachute Division – Generale di Divisione Enrico Frattini

Corpo d'Armata XXI – Generale di Corpo d'Armata Enea Navarini

Trento Division – Generale di Brigata Giorgio Masina
Bologna Division – Generale di Divisione Alessandro Gloria

Notes

Crown copyright material throughout this book is reproduced by permission of the Controller of Her Majesty's Stationery Office.

Prologue

1 Winston S. Churchill, *The Second World War, Vol. III*, Cassell 1950, p. 356.

1 *Embattled Spring*

1 Crown copyright, quoted in John Connell, *Auchinleck*, Cassell 1959, pp. 420–1.
2 Crown copyright, ibid., pp. 423–4.
3 Major-General F. W. von Mellenthin, *Panzer Battles: A Study of the Employment of Armor in the Second World War*, Ballantine (New York) 1971, copyright by the University of Oklahoma Press, pp. 104–5.
4 Quoted in Major-General I. S. O. Playfair *et al.*, *History of the Second World War* (hereafter referred to as the *Official History*), *The Mediterranean and Middle East, Vol. III*, H.M.S.O. 1960, p. 154.
5 Vladimir Peniakoff, *Popski's Private Army*, Pan 1957, p. 127. This and all subsequent extracts from this title are reprinted by permission of the Estate of Vladimir Peniakoff.
6 Quoted in Philip Warner, *The Special Air Service*, William Kimber 1971, p. 50, reprinted by permission of the S.A.S. Regimental Association.

2 *No Drums, No Trumpets*
(with acknowledgment to T. S. Eliot)

1 *The Rommel Papers*, ed. B. H. Liddell Hart, Collins 1953, p. 194.
2 Ibid., p. 195.
3 Crown copyright, quoted in John Connell, *Auchinleck*, Cassell 1959, pp. 506–7.
4 Crown copyright, quoted, ibid., p. 515.
5 *Rommel Papers*, ed. Liddell Hart, p. 206.

6 Ibid.

7 Ibid., p. 208.

8 Major-General G. P. B. Roberts, personal account of May 27th, 1942, unpublished.

9 Quoted in *Crisis in the Desert*, ed. J. A. I. Agar-Hamilton and L. C. F. Turner, Oxford University Press (Cape Town) 1952, p. 32. This and all subsequent extracts from this title are reprinted by permission of the Government Printer, Pretoria, South Africa.

10 J. A. Pitt-Rivers, *The Story of the Royal Dragoons, 1938–1945*, William Clowes n.d., p. 44.

11 Birkby, Carel, ed., *The Saga of the Transvaal Scottish Regiment 1932–1950*, Howard Timmins (Pty) Ltd (Cape Town) for Hodder and Stoughton 1950, pp. 464–5, quoted in *Crisis in the Desert*, ed. Agar-Hamilton and Turner, p. 34.

12 Quoted in Desmond Young, *Rommel*, Collins 1950, p. 124.

13 Quoted in *Crisis in the Desert*, ed. Agar-Hamilton and Turner, p. 38.

14 Quoted in Correlli Barnett, *The Desert Generals*, Pan 1962, p. 154.

15 Crown copyright, quoted in *Crisis in the Desert*, ed. Agar-Hamilton and Turner, p. 39.

16 Quoted in Antony Brett-James, *Ball of Fire: The Fifth Indian Division in the Second World War*, Gale and Polden (Aldershot) 1951, p. 177.

17 Major-General I. S. O. Playfair *et al.*, *Official History, The Mediterranean and Middle East, Vol. III*, H.M.S.O. 1960, p. 233.

18 Ibid., pp. 234–5.

19 Roy Farran, *Winged Dagger*, Fontana 1954, p. 144.

20 *Rommel Papers*, ed. Liddell Hart, p. 217.

21 Ibid., p. 218.

22 Crown copyright, quoted in Connell, op. cit., p. 540.

23 Playfair, op. cit., pp. 238–9.

24 Crown copyright, quoted in *Crisis in the Desert*, ed. Agar-Hamilton and Turner, p. 68.

25 *Royal Artillery Journal*, April 1948, quoted, ibid., p. 69.

26 *Rommel Papers*, ed. Liddell Hart, p. 222.

27 Crown copyright, quoted in Connell, op. cit., p. 430.

28 Winston S. Churchill, *The Second World War, Vol. IV*, Cassell 1951, p. 331.

29 Crown copyright, quoted in Playfair, op. cit., pp. 246–7.

30 Crown copyright, quoted, ibid., p. 247.

3 'A progression of avoidable disasters'
(General W. G. F. Jackson)

1 *The Sidi Rezeg Battles 1941*, ed. J. A. I. Agar-Hamilton and L. C. F. Turner, Oxford University Press (Cape Town) 1957, p. 225. This extract is reprinted by permission of the Government Printer, Pretoria, South Africa.

2 Draft history of the Rand Light Infantry, quoted in *Crisis in the Desert*,

ed. J. A. I. Agar-Hamilton and L. C. F. Turner, Oxford University Press (Cape Town) 1952, p. 81.

3 Birkby, Carel, ed., *The Saga of the Transvaal Scottish Regiment 1932–1950*, Howard Timmins (Pty) Ltd (Cape Town) for Hodder and Stoughton 1950, p. 487, quoted in *Crisis in the Desert*, ed. Agar-Hamilton and Turner, p. 82.

4 *Crisis in the Desert*, ed. Agar-Hamilton and Turner, p. 91.

5 Ibid., p. 115, footnote.

6 *The Rommel Papers*, ed B. H. Liddell Hart, Collins 1953, p. 225.

7 Quoted in *Crisis in the Desert*, ed. Agar-Hamilton and Turner, pp. 122–3.

8 Heinz W. Schmidt, *With Rommel in the Desert*, Harrap 1951, p. 144.

9 Major-General F. W. von Mellenthin, *Panzer Battles: A Study of the Employment of Armor in the Second World War*, Ballantine (New York) 1971, copyright 1956 by the University of Oklahoma Press, p. 144.

10 Field Marshal Lord Carver, *Tobruk*, Batsford 1964, p. 212.

11 *Crisis in the Desert*, ed. Agar-Hamilton and Turner, p. 150.

12 Quoted, ibid., p. 194.

13 Crown copyright, quoted, ibid., pp. 194–5.

14 Crown copyright, quoted, ibid., p. 209.

15 Ibid., p. 210.

16 Quoted, ibid., pp. 210–11.

17 Crown copyright, quoted, ibid., p. 214.

18 Crown copyright, quoted, ibid., p. 217.

19 P. Caccia-Dominioni, *Alamein*, Allen and Unwin 1966, p. 137.

20 M. W. Brown, 'For You the War is Finish', in *History of the Second World War*, *Vol. III*, ed. Barrie Pitt, Purnell 1967, p. 1003.

21 Quoted in *Crisis in the Desert*, ed. Agar-Hamilton and Turner, p. 237.

22 Francis Tuker, *Patterns of War*, Cassell 1948, p. 89.

23 Crown copyright, quoted in Major-General I. S. O. Playfair *et al.*, *Official History, The Mediterranean and Middle East, Vol. III*, H.M.S.O. 1960, p. 286.

24 *Crisis in the Desert*, ed. Agar-Hamilton and Turner, p. 248.

25 Quoted, ibid., p. 255.

26 Major-General Sir Howard Kippenberger, *Infantry Brigadier*, Oxford University Press 1949, pp. 132–3.

27 Ibid., p. 135.

28 Lieutenant-Colonel G. R. Armstrong, in *R.A. Commemoration Book*, pp. 220–1, quoted in *Crisis in the Desert*, ed. Agar-Hamilton and Turner, p. 261.

29 General W. G. F. Jackson, *The North African Campaign 1940–43*, Batsford 1975, p. 243.

30 *Rommel Papers*, ed. Liddell Hart, p. 238.

31 Armstrong, op. cit., p. 222, quoted in *Crisis in the Desert*, ed. Agar-Hamilton and Turner, p. 263.

32 *Crisis in the Desert*, ed. Agar-Hamilton and Turner, p. 266.

33 See Barrie Pitt, *The Crucible of War: Western Desert 1941*, Cape 1980, pp. 458–9.

34 *Rommel Papers*, ed. Liddell Hart, p. 239.

35 *Crisis in the Desert*, ed. Agar-Hamilton and Turner, p. 291.

36 *Rommel Papers*, ed. Liddell Hart, p. 246.
37 Quoted in *Crisis in the Desert*, ed. Agar-Hamilton and Turner, p. 296.
38 Quoted, ibid., p. 300.
39 Quoted, ibid., p. 310.
40 Quoted, ibid., p. 314.

4 *First Alamein*

1 John Connell, *Auchinleck*, Cassell 1959, p. 626.
2 *The Rommel Papers*, ed. B. H. Liddell Hart, Collins 1953, p. 253.
3 Major-General Sir Howard Kippenberger, *Infantry Brigadier*, Oxford University Press 1949, p. 169.
4 *Rommel Papers*, ed. Liddell Hart, p. 257.
5 Ibid.
6 Kippenberger, op. cit., p. 139.
7 Crown copyright, quoted in Connell, op. cit., p. 618.
8 Kippenberger, op. cit., p. 183.
9 Ibid., p. 184.
10 Ibid., p. 188.
11 Ibid., p. 189.
12 Ibid., p. 190.

5 *Churchill Intervenes*

1 Quoted in Winston S. Churchill, *The Second World War, Vol. IV*, Cassell 1951, p. 352.
2 Quoted, ibid., p. 400.
3 Quoted in Lord Moran, *Churchill, The Struggle for Survival 1940–65*, Constable 1966, p. 46.
4 Churchill, op. cit., p. 277.
5 Crown copyright, quoted in John Connell, *Auchinleck*, Cassell 1959, p. 500.
6 Moran, op. cit., p. 50.
7 Ibid.
8 Lord Tedder, *With Prejudice*, Cassell 1966, p. 313.
9 See Churchill, op. cit., p. 414.
10 Quoted in Alun Chalfont, *Montgomery of Alamein*, Weidenfeld and Nicolson 1976, p. 5.
11 Field Marshal the Viscount Montgomery of Alamein, *Memoirs*, Collins 1958, p. 32. This and all subsequent extracts from this title are reproduced by permission of Viscount Montgomery of Alamein.
12 Chalfont, op. cit., p. 113.
13 Montgomery, op. cit., p. 35.
14 Ibid., p. 36.
15 By permission of Sir Denis Hamilton on behalf of the Montgomery Archive.
16 Montgomery, op. cit., p. 83.

17 By permission of Sir Denis Hamilton on behalf of the Montgomery Archive.
18 By permission of Sir Denis Hamilton on behalf of the Montgomery Archive.
19 Quoted in Alan Moorehead, *Montgomery*, Four Square 1958, p. 79.
20 Quoted, ibid.
21 Quoted, ibid.
22 Quoted, ibid., p. 80.
23 By permission of Sir Denis Hamilton on behalf of the Montgomery Archive.
24 Crown copyright, quoted in Chalfont, op. cit., p. 95.
25 Crown copyright, quoted, ibid.
26 Crown copyright, quoted, ibid., p. 99.
27 Quoted in Ronald Lewin, *Montgomery as Military Commander*, Batsford 1971, p. 11.

6 'A cool and refreshing breeze'

1 Quoted in Major-General I. S. O. Playfair *et al.*, *Official History, The Mediterranean and Middle East, Vol. III*, H.M.S.O. 1960, p. 319.
2 Winston S. Churchill, *The Second World War, Vol. IV*, Cassell 1951, pp. 421–2.
3 Quoted in Nigel Nicolson, *Alex, The Life of Field Marshal Earl Alexander of Tunis*, Weidenfeld and Nicolson 1973, p. 157.
4 Major-General Sir Francis de Guingand, *Operation Victory*, Hodder and Stoughton 1947, pp. 136–7.
5 Field Marshal the Viscount Montgomery of Alamein, *Memoirs*, Collins 1958, p. 103.
6 De Guingand, op. cit., p. 139.
7 Vladimir Peniakoff, *Popski's Private Army*, Pan 1957, p. 211.
8 Quoted in Alun Chalfont, *Montgomery of Alamein*, Weidenfeld and Nicolson 1976, p. 156.
9 *The Rommel Papers*, ed. B. H. Liddell Hart, Collins 1953, p. 268.
10 Ibid., p. 247.
11 Quoted in Fritz Bayerlein, 'The Battle of Alam Halfa', in *History of the Second World War, Vol. III*, ed. Barrie Pitt, Purnell 1967, p. 1152.
12 *Rommel Papers*, ed. Liddell Hart, p. 285.
13 Quoted in Correlli Barnett, *The Desert Generals*, Pan 1962, p. 321.
14 By permission of Sir Denis Hamilton on behalf of the Montgomery Archive.

7 Daffodil, Hyacinth, Snowdrop and Tulip

1 Vladimir Peniakoff, *Popski's Private Army*, Pan 1957, p. 174.
2 General Sir John Hackett, letter to author, July 18th, 1978.
3 Gordon Landsborough, *Tobruk Commando*, Cassell 1956, p. 95.
4 Fitzroy Maclean, *Eastern Approaches*, Pan 1956, p. 201.
5 Peniakoff, op. cit., p. 198.

8 *Prelude to Battle*

1 By permission of Sir Denis Hamilton on behalf of the Montgomery Archive.
2 By permission of Sir Denis Hamilton on behalf of the Montgomery Archive.
3 Fritz Bayerlein, 'El Alamein', in *The Fatal Decisions*, ed. Seymour Freidin and William Richardson, Michael Joseph 1956, p. 90.
4 Ibid., p. 91.
5 Ibid.
6 David Irving, *The Trail of the Fox*, Weidenfeld and Nicolson 1977, p. 198.

9 *El Alamein: The Onslaught*

1 Major-General D. N. Wimberley, 'Scottish Soldier', Vol. II, p. 41, unpublished.
2 Quoted in Field Marshal Lord Carver, *El Alamein*, Batsford 1962, p. 109.
3 Ibid., p. 123.
4 George Greenfield, 'The Fighting at Alamein', in *History of the Second World War, Vol. III*, ed. Barrie Pitt, Purnell 1967, p. 1173.
5 Wimberley, op. cit., p. 43.
6 Quoted in Nigel Hamilton, *Monty, The Making of a General, 1887–1942*, Hamish Hamilton 1981, p. 790.
7 Quoted in Ronald Walker, *Alam Halfa and Alamein, Official History of New Zealand in the Second World War 1939–45*, Historical Publications Branch, Department of Internal Affairs (Wellington) 1967, p. 304.
8 By permission of Sir Denis Hamilton on behalf of the Montgomery Archive.
9 By permission of Sir Denis Hamilton on behalf of the Montgomery Archive.
10 Quoted in Walker, op. cit., p. 312.

10 *Pause for Reflection*

1 *The Rommel Papers*, ed. B. H. Liddell Hart, Collins 1953, p. 304.
2 Ibid., p. 306.
3 Ibid., pp. 309–10.
4 Ibid., p. 310.
5 George Greenfield, 'The Fighting at Alamein', in *History of the Second World War, Vol. III*, ed. Barrie Pitt, Purnell 1967, p. 1173.
6 *Rommel Papers*, ed. Liddell Hart, p. 306.
7 Brigadier C. E. Lucas Phillips, *Alamein*, Pan 1965, p. 224.
8 Major R. H. W. S. Hastings, *The Rifle Brigade in the Second World War*, Gale and Polden (Aldershot) 1950, pp. 175–6.
9 *Rommel Papers*, ed. Liddell Hart, p. 310.

11 *The Crumbling Process*

1 By permission of Sir Denis Hamilton on behalf of the Montgomery Archive.
2 *The Rommel Papers*, ed. B. H. Liddell Hart, Collins 1953, pp. 311–12.
3 Barton Maughan, *Tobruk and El Alamein*, Australian War Memorial (Canberra), p. 709.
4 Brigadier C. E. Lucas Phillips, *Alamein*, Pan 1965, p. 249.
5 Barton Maughan, op. cit., p. 715.
6 *Rommel Papers*, ed. Liddell Hart, p. 315.
7 Ibid., p. 316.
8 Quoted by Arthur Bryant, *The Alanbrooke War Diaries 1939–43: The Turn of the Tide*, Fontana 1957, p. 423.
9 By permission of Sir Denis Hamilton on behalf of the Montgomery Archive.
10 Quoted in Lucas Phillips, op. cit., p. 273.
11 Ibid., p. 278.
12 Ibid., p. 270.
13 Ibid., p. 287.
14 Ibid., p. 292.
15 Quoted, ibid., p. 294.
16 Ibid., p. 298.
17 Quoted in Field Marshal Lord Carver, *El Alamein*, Batsford 1962, p. 168.

12 *Break-out and Pursuit*

1 Quoted in *The Rommel Papers*, ed. B. H. Liddell Hart, Collins 1953, p. 321, footnote.
2 Field Marshal Lord Carver, *El Alamein*, Batsford 1962, p. 184.
3 Quoted in Ronald Walker, *Alam Halfa and Alamein, Official History of New Zealand in the Second World War 1939–45*, Historical Publications Branch, Department of Internal Affairs (Wellington) 1967, pp. 445–6.
4 *Rommel Papers*, ed. Liddell Hart, pp. 339–40.
5 Walker, op. cit., pp. 445–6.
6 *Rommel Papers*, ed. Liddell Hart, p. 341.
7 Ibid., p. 347.
8 Brigadier Dudley Clarke, *The Eleventh at War*, Michael Joseph 1952, p. 270.
9 Ibid., p. 271.
10 Major-General W. G. Stevens, *Bardia to Enfidaville, Official History of New Zealand in the Second World War 1939–45*, Historical Publications Branch, Department of Internal Affairs (Wellington) 1962, p. 57.

Index

Map 28 Breakout and Pursuit, November 4th-6th

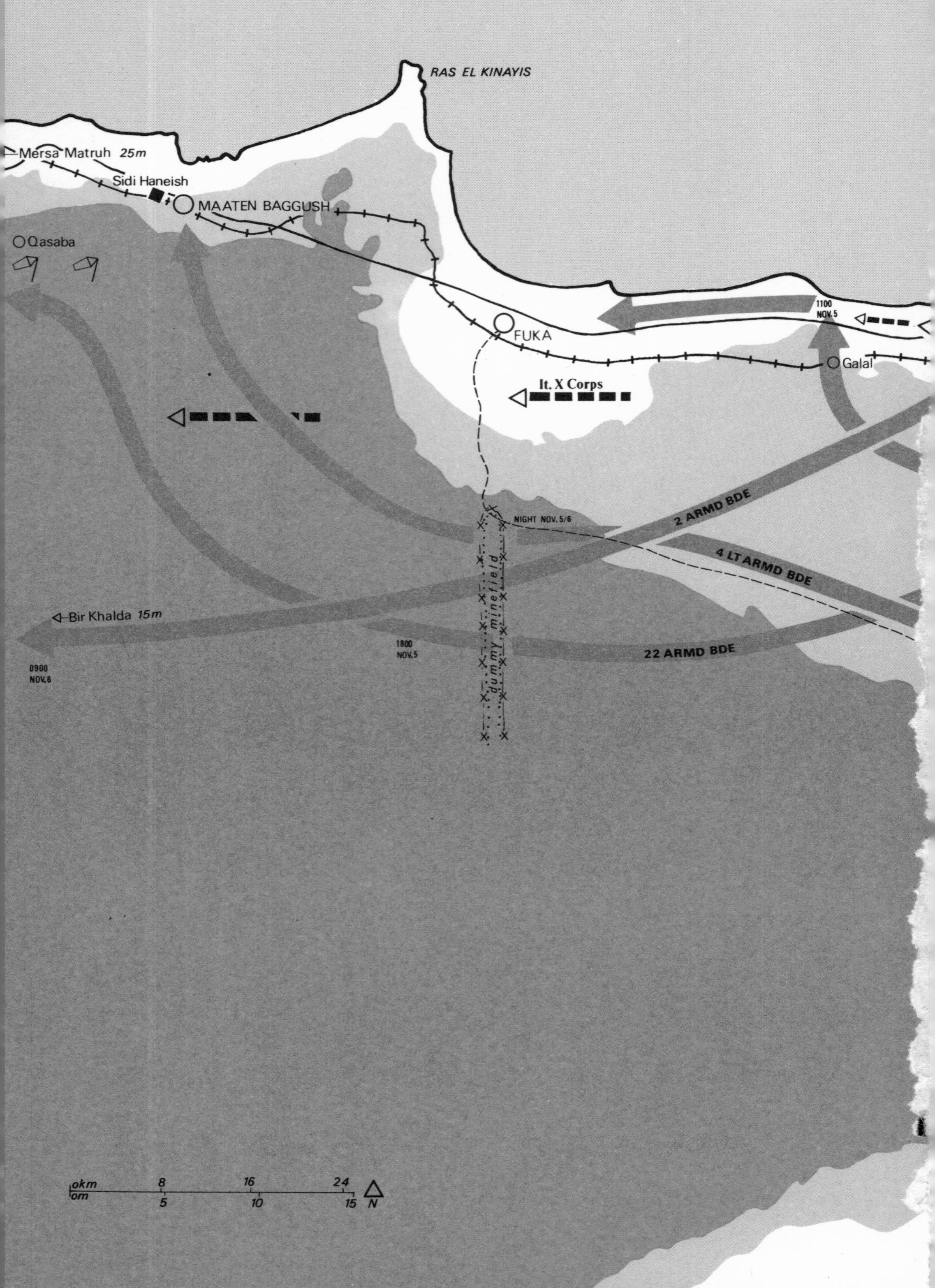

RAS EL KINAYIS

Mersa Matruh *25m*

Sidi Haneish

MAATEN BAGGUSH

Qasaba

FUKA

It. X Corps

Galal

1100
NOV.5

2 ARMD BDE

4 LT ARMD BDE

NIGHT NOV. 5/6

Bir Khalda *15m*

1800
NOV.5

22 ARMD BDE

dummy minefield

0900
NOV.6

0km		8		16		24	△
0m		5		10		15	N